Problem Solving and The Computer: A Structured Concept with PL/I (PL/C)

Problem Solving and The Computer: A Structured Concept with PL/I (PL/C)

Second Edition

JOSEPH SHORTT
THOMAS C. WILSON
University of Guelph
Ontario

ADDISON-WESLEY PUBLISHING COMPANY
Reading, Massachusetts
Menlo Park, California · London · Amsterdam · Don Mills, Ontario · Sydney

This book is in the
ADDISON-WESLEY SERIES IN COMPUTER SCIENCE

Michael A. Harrison
Consulting Editor

Reproduced by Addison-Wesley from camera-ready copy prepared by the authors.

 Printed in the United States of America. Published simultaneously in Canada.
Library of Congress Catalog Card No. 78-74692.

ISBN 0-201-06916-4
FGHIJKLM-HA-898765432

To Anne and Moira

Preface to the Second Edition

This second edition differs in two important ways from its predecessor. First, the original material has been considerably extended with the inclusion of two new chapters on file processing. In fact, we feel that there is now sufficient material for a full year course. Second, the first edition has been updated to reflect the increased scope and power of the PL/C compiler since the first edition was written.

All examples in Chapters 2 through 12 have been modified (where necessary) to reflect Release 7.6 of the PL/C compiler, which is the most recent version at the time of writing. Fortunately most of these changes are editorial in nature and do not have any impact on the results or implementation of the examples. One crucial change in implementation, though, is in the SKIP option for stream input. PL/C has been modified subsequent to Release 6.6 to conform to the implementation of the PL/I-F compiler. (The SKIP on the first GET statement is no longer ignored.) Appendices A and C have also been changed to conform to Release 7.6.

The two new chapters have been added to illustrate the fundamentals of files, especially disk files. They make no explicit reference to PL/C; instead all examples are done using the PL/I-F compiler. However, we have been careful not to use options which are unsupported by PL/C Release 7.6.

The new chapters include discussions of the uses of secondary storage and motivation for files, many applicable file processing algorithms and applications (both sequential and nonsequential), plus specific techniques: STREAM and RECORD files, PICTURE data, sequential and indexed-sequential organization, and DIRECT accessing.

In addition, we also introduce the role of the operating system and the basics of its job control language. Rather than a rigorous presentation of JCL, we show what it is for, what it can achieve, and some examples of its use. We attempt to be compatible with our earlier philosophy that concepts are more important than details. As a result, we have indicated that JCL may be required if the student is using PL/I and have left it up to the instructor to give the pertinent details for the local installation. On the other hand, if the student is using PL/C, the file definition can be built into the PL/C procedure and the details hidden. The following files are included in the PL/C procedure at the University of Guelph:

```
//INFO    DD UNIT=3330,SPACE=(TRK,(1,3)),DCB=LRECL=80
//MASTER  DD UNIT=3330,SPACE=(TRK,(5,2))
//TEMP1   DD UNIT=3330,SPACE=TRK,(5,3)),
//   DCB=(RECFM=FB,LRECL=80,BLKSIZE=400)
//TEMP2   DD UNIT=3330,SPACE=(TRK,(5,2)),
//   DCB=(RECFM=FB,LRECL=80,BLKSIZE=400)
//TEMP3   DD UNIT=3330,SPACE=(TRK,(5,2)),
//   DCB=(RECFM=FB,LRECL=80,BLKSIZE=400)
```

We have used these files for five years to illustrate auxiliary STREAM files while concealing the actual JCL.

We are pleased to acknowledge the assistance of Debbie Robinson in typing the draft manuscript for Chapters 13 and 14. We also acknowledge the help of various faculty and students whose suggestions were included in the revisions to the first twelve chapters.

Guelph, Ontario
January 1979

J. Shortt
T. C. Wilson

Preface to the First Edition

With the expanding use of the computer in the problem-solving process, increasing numbers of people in all disciplines are finding it desirable or necessary to learn computer programming. Nevertheless, until quite recently there were almost as many programming styles as there are programming languages; there was no one really good way to program a computer. However, the concept of structured programming, formulated by E. W. Dijkstra and successfully demonstrated in the development of a large system for the New York Times by IBM, has revamped the points of view of many people in the industry. Structured programming has now been recognized as an effective programming style and is being adopted as the prescribed technique in many computing applications.

Structured programming begins with an overall problem which is broken down into a series of simpler problems; these may, in turn, be further refined. The goal is to develop solution procedures which have simple, easily understandable structures, rather than compact but complex forms. When a solution procedure developed according to the rules of structured programming is expressed in a programming language, the result is usually a clear and correct program.

There is a need for a good basic textbook which introduces beginning programmers to the techniques of structured programming from day one; it is much easier to teach good habits than to correct bad ones. This text, we feel, fills this need. The text is based on a course in introductory programming which we give at the University of Guelph. It is aimed at readers who have little or no familiarity with the art of using a computer to solve problems. There are no prerequisites other than common sense. In particular, unlike many introductory texts, there is no mathematical bias although mathematics is not neglected.

There are three major points of emphasis. First, we stress some basic techniques in general problem solving and algorithm design quite apart from any computer implementation. We emphasize that an orderly approach to solving problems is more crucial to good programming than is mastery of language details. Second, our approach to solving general problems and ultimately to writing programs is consistent with structured programming practice. Finally, the programming language used is PL/I as implemented in the PL/C compiler. We attempt to put it in perspective as merely one notation in which algorithms may be written.

Structured programming is taught by example rather than mere lip service. Our problem-solving guidelines just happen to lead to the appropriate "top-down" approach. Internal PROCEDURES are introduced earlier than in most textbooks so that the only control mechanisms required are (i) sequential flow, (ii) IF_THEN_ELSE, (iii) DO WHILE and (iv) CALL. To assist in the production of readable programs we use no abbreviations, employ meaningful variable names, supply comments in programs, indent each level of code, supply (and label) all END statements, and balance IF with ELSE when the logic becomes complex. To further emphasize the need for "clean" code, the GOTO statement is not introduced until the last chapter. This is not done because we equate structured programming with "GOTOless programming"; rather it is to discourage indiscriminate use of the GOTO.

Our method of presentation usually involves first solving some problem without concern for the computer. Then essential language features are introduced as they are needed to convert this solution into a PL/I program. This approach, applied to a wide variety of problems throughout the book, attempts:

1. to show by example that language-independent problem solving should precede "programming";
2. to convey something of the "art" of problem solving by showing our guidelines in action in many different contexts;
3. to present language features in a motivating and typical context;
4. to introduce a number of important algorithms, such as searching, file updating, sorting, text editing, numerical integration, and basic matrix manipulation.

We attempt to make the examples as accessible as possible. They are not preponderantly mathematical and in many cases are phrased in an amusing way. (They also show actual computer printouts run under release 6.6000 of PL/C.) We feel that this text is more "painless" than others in the area because of its pedagogical approach and its introduction of concepts and language features in contexts which "cry out" for them and display their value.

Most chapters include three "standard" sections:

1. The precise rules for using the language features introduced in that chapter (collected at the end for easy reference);
2. a special problem, solved in detail, whose solution incorporates as many preceding language elements as possible and discusses several practical considerations in their use;
3. exercises for student solution.

The first eight chapters contain the basic material, which could constitute a course on programming fundamentals if time does not permit covering the entire book. If an instructor so desires, external procedures and built-in functions could be treated much earlier in a course than their placement in Chapter 11 would indicate.

There are also special sections in Chapters 3, 4, 5, and 6 which, together with the CHECK prefix in Chapter 12, constitute a guide to the testing, diagnosis, and repair of programs.

Since full PL/I is a vast language, we have chosen to explain the features of PL/I which are implemented in the PL/C compiler. However, these are the most important and frequently used facilities of PL/I, so we believe the text could be used in either a PL/I or PL/C context. The important differences between PL/I and PL/C are noted as they occur, as well as in Appendix A. Our examples were run under PL/C release 6.6000. The options in effect were PAGES=007, TIME=(000,003), ERRORS=(050,050), SORMGIN=(002,072,001), LINECNT=060, NOBOUNDRY, FLAGW, XREF, ATR, NOLIST, UDEF, SOURCE, DUMP, NODUMPARRAY, NOM91, NOCOMMENTS, CHECK.

During the preparation of this book we have depended heavily on the good graces of many people. Our wives, children, and (former) friends have endured much. We are grateful to Anne Stocco who suffered with us through the first six chapters, preparing a legible first draft from our handwritten versions. Thanks are due to the reviewers whose suggestions we found extremely helpful. Our special thanks go to Carol Pratt who completed the draft and with heroic dedication prepared the final copy which you are now reading. However, we claim sole credit for any errors which may remain.

Guelph, Ontario
October, 1975

J. Shortt
T.C. Wilson

Contents

CHAPTER 11
MORE ON PROCEDURES

CHAPTER 12
OTHER TOPICS

CHAPTER 13
DISK FILE FUNDAMENTALS AND STREAM I/O

Chapter 1 Problem Solving and Algorithms

1.1 INTRODUCTION

Computers have emerged as an important tool for helping man to cope with large masses of information and the elaborate calculations required for many modern problems. Their role in our society as well as their possible usefulness to us make it appropriate that we learn how computers can be used.

By the same token, we should know their limitations. There is a popular myth that a computer is some sort of contemporary oracle, which can provide quick solutions to a whole host of problems, merely for the asking. On the contrary, a computer does not decide for us how to approach or solve particular problems. Rather, it merely performs the mechanics of a procedure which some human being has already proposed and formulated. The dazzling speed at which computers accomplish their work unfortunately blinds us to the fact that their calculations are the culmination of hours, weeks, or even years of human problem solving effort.

Therefore, if you wish to use a computer, by far the most important thing to know is how to analyze problems and organize solutions yourself! Thus, the first skill to acquire is the ability to confront and reduce any problem to manageable proportions, regardless of whether use of a computer is contemplated or even appropriate. (In fact, most problems are not amenable to computer solution.)

The essence of good problem solving ability is a careful, systematic approach rather than an impetuous attack. The ability to approach problems calmly and rationally need not be an hereditary accident. It is a skill which can be practiced and learned with the aid of a few simple guidelines. A primary purpose of this book is to explain what these guidelines are and to show how they are applied -- not necessarily in the context of computers.

If your problem happens to be appropriate for using a computer, then the solution must be phrased in a special language, called a "programming language," for communication to the computer. The other major aim of this book is to show how your proposed solution can be expressed in the PL/I programming language. An important byproduct of this should be some appreciation of what computers can and cannot do.

1.2 BASIC TECHNIQUES FOR PROBLEM SOLVING

Before focusing on computers we should consider some guidelines for approaching any problem. One especially useful and succinct statement of such guidelines was given by Rene Descartes, a founder of modern philosophy, in his *Discourse on Method*:

1. Never accept anything as true unless it is certainly and evidently such: carefully avoid all precipitation and prejudgement.
2. Divide each of the difficulties into as many parts as possible.
3. Think in an orderly fashion, beginning with the things which are the simplest and easiest to understand, and gradually reach toward the more complex.
4. Make enumerations so complete and reviews so general that it is certain nothing is omitted.

Although these guidelines were written over three hundred years before the first electronic computer was built, they remain so applicable that we shall adopt them as rules. On the whole, these rules constitute a plea to be more systematic and less impulsive. We will continue to echo this plea. Especially when dealing with computers, a careful, thorough approach to the original problem is an essential ingredient for a successful outcome.

The individual rules, which focus on different aspects of problem solving, may appear so simple that you may be tempted to dismiss them. However they are practiced with dismaying infrequency, and their mastery is by far the major requisite for using computers. In the remainder of this section, we will recast these rules in more modern terms and give examples of how they might be applied.

1.2.1 Understanding a Problem

Problems very often seem more complex than they really are because they are not clearly understood. A hazily grasped problem leads to a fuzzy solution, which is often no solution at all to the real problem. One interpretation of Descartes' first rule is to be sure of what you want. Don't make rash assumptions and jump to conclusions. Instead, try the following:

> Rule I
> Analyze your problem carefully, attempting to understand its specific aspects and the requirements of an acceptable solution.

Suppose you are an architect and builder who has just won a contract to design and construct a housing development for 100 families. Surely you won't begin by gathering some construction workers and saying, "O.K. Let's put up some houses." Instead you first put on your architect's hat to design the houses and organize the project. Though your basic problem -- to plan 100 housing units -- seems simple, a great many constraints and special considerations surround the project. For example, you might be able to satisfy the immediate objective by constructing one large high-rise apartment building. But stipulations in your contract, the city zoning laws or good taste may preclude this course and suggest another: 100 individual houses. Then you must consider such basic constraints as how much land is available per house and whether certain building materials are required by severe weather or by local fire regulations. Any builder who ordered his materials without first weighing such issues would soon be facing a more critical problem: how to feed a hungry family without any income.

By this stage, you should have a more precise understanding of what your problem really is, e.g., to construct 100 brick houses on half-acre lots. Once you can state your problem more accurately, a direction of solution will sometimes become apparent. However, further considerations may be appropriate before plunging ahead with the details of design. For the builder, another important factor is money. How much can you invest and at what price should each house sell? If the houses are built too cheaply, you may not be able to cope with all the resulting law suits. If you invest too much time and money, you may owe the bank for 100 examples of architectural splendor which no one can afford to buy. Neither extreme is really a "solution" to your original problem. The only acceptable solution may be some middle course, such as three bedroom, split-level houses with car ports.

Understanding what constitutes an acceptable solution may tell you two things: whether there is any feasible solution; and if so, how far to proceed with it. If your banker will only extend you enough credit to build tar paper shacks, now is the time to withdraw from the project. On the other hand, if you are capable of building the required kinds of houses, market and financial considerations may dictate how many frills to include or for how many months the construction may go on.

Assessing what level of result you want is a frequently neglected consideration but should occur at an early stage. Unless your goals appear feasible within your means, they are not worth pursuing. This point is especially important if use of a computer is contemplated. A computer's calculating speed is so impressive that it may seem capable of performing any well defined computation. For example, a computer is sometimes used to play games, like checkers. It has been estimated that the game of checkers comprises some 10^{20} possible move sequences. Theoretically, the computer could examine all possible moves and pick a sequence which would assure its victory. However, even if a computer could check one million moves per second (which is somewhat faster than present machines), it could only check about 10^{13} moves in one year (10^6 moves/sec × $3{\times}10^7$ sec/year). Thus it might not make its move for some 10^6 (one million) years! Unrealistic expectations can make an otherwise simple problem insurmountable. If you will settle for competent play rather than perfect play, then checkers is a feasible game for a computer.

This discussion could well be summarized by the old adage: "Understanding a problem is half of the solution." The more complete and precise the understanding, the more apparent may be the course of action.

1.2.2 Decomposing a Problem

As your understanding of a problem becomes more refined, your statement of the problem becomes correspondingly more detailed. However, as a problem becomes more detailed and constrained, it also becomes more difficult to deal with all at one time. This is where Descartes' second rule comes into play, which we rephrase as follows:

> Rule II
> Attempt to break your problem into simpler, relatively independent parts, and then focus on the separate parts.

There are various approaches to realizing this procedure of problem decomposition. The most useful is probably:

> Rule II(a)
> Attempt to break a problem into a sequence of smaller problems, so that the solution of one subproblem followed by the solution of the next, and so on, will provide a solution to the original problem.

For example, when building a house, a multitude of steps are involved, ranging from digging the foundation to putting knobs on the kitchen cabinets. Rather than losing his way in a forest of often unrelated details, a sensible builder would identify the major phases in his construction project. These might be, (i) the foundation; (ii) the frame and walls; (iii) services, such as wiring and plumbing; (iv) roofing; and (v) finishing. These steps are relatively independent. They may well employ different people to carry them out -- carpenters, roofers, plumbers, plasterers -- and in some cases cannot overlap in time. For instance, nothing else can begin until the foundation is completed. This independence is what allows the designer to concentrate on each major phase separately.

Of course, each such phase is a problem in itself which may be broken down similarly into a sequence of even smaller steps. Thus, building the foundation might involve: (i) clearing the land; (ii) digging the basement; (iii) building wooden molds; and (iv) pouring the concrete. By the time each major phase has been decomposed into smaller steps, the entire project can be described as a sequence of perhaps 40 or 50 specific operations.

The purpose of decomposing problems is to spare you from the details of how other solution steps perform their function when developing any one step. However, you must never lose sight of what the other parts of the solution are supposed to do, for they are seldom completely independent. There are usually certain steps which must precede others because other steps rely on their results. The frame of a house must precede the roof, and the roof will invariably follow the same outline as the frame. You must not design a frame which will cause too many problems with the roof. Therefore, when focusing on individual steps of your solution, don't completely ignore their context and common goal.

The preceding discussion has been concerned only with the construction plans of a single house. Yet the original problem was to construct 100 houses. However, since most developments consist of nearly identical houses, the design and construction plans for one house apply to all the others as well. All one has to do is repeat the basic construction process 100 times, with perhaps some minor variations.

Ignoring the need for 100 houses until now was an instinctive application of the second problem simplification rule:

> Rule II(b)
> If your problem involves performing some repeated process, attempt to isolate the action which is required in one instance from the repetitive aspect.

A great many problems involve dealing with several very similar things (houses, customers, financial transactions, experimental data items). When such a problem occurs, it is best to first concentrate on how to handle an individual case. If your solution for one case is sufficiently general, it becomes an easy matter to repeat that solution procedure for all the cases.

In case you just don't know where to begin, perhaps it is because special cases make the problem appear too confusing. It might help to <u>temporarily</u> ignore special and unusual cases. Don't worry initially about the relatively few houses on corner lots or the custom designed house that your mother will eventually occupy. This allows you to concentrate on the "standard" or "routine" cases. Once this is done, most exceptional cases can then be handled by minor modifications to your "standard" solution. This technique, which is suggested by Descartes' third rule, is summarized in the following tip:

> Tip
> First attempt to solve the problem for the simplest case or the most likely set of circumstances. When you reach a satisfactory solution for this, then extend your solution to cover special cases or less likely contingencies.

The initial design should make provision for eventual inclusion of special cases, but should not become entangled in their details. After all, if your solution procedure won't work for the standard situations, it does not matter how well it handles exceptional cases.

1.2.3 The Problem Solving Process

The rules for refining a problem into more manageable parts can be applied in an endless variety of combinations. However, to be effective, they should be applied slowly and carefully. Our rule (suggested by Descartes' third rule) for carrying out the decomposition of problems is:

> Rule III
> When breaking a problem into simpler parts, perform the decomposition gradually in several stages. Make use of more general criteria in the early stages and more specific criteria later.

What this means can be seen from the house building example. Although Descartes also suggested dividing a problem "into as many parts as possible," we did not do this all in one step. Rather, we isolated the problem of building one house from the problem of constructing a development. Then the construction of one house was divided into five major phases. Then these phases were individually analyzed and further subdivided. In other words the decomposition of the problem occurred in several stages. Furthermore, the early stages involved the more global, general considerations, while later stages focused on more and more detail. Our first steps in decomposition hinged on such major issues as building walls and a foundation. Not until much later should we worry about whether to put shutters on the south windows or a cupola on top. This movement from general to specific considerations gives this style of solving problems the name "top-down."

We suggest that each step in the decomposition produce no more than five simpler problems. As far as how many steps are needed, the only rule of thumb is to keep analyzing and decomposing until you have isolated subproblems which are simple enough to solve easily. The ability to do this is a skill which requires intuition and experience, but it is a skill well worth developing -- particularly if you intend to use a computer!

Nevertheless, no matter how thorough the analysis, some feature or special circumstance is almost invariably overlooked when designing the first (second, third and fourth) version of the solution procedure. You should never try to save time by ignoring

Rule IV
Review and reconsider your proposed solution to ensure that it is complete and correct.

The day of the open house is not the time to suddenly realize that you forgot to include bathroom plumbing. We regret to say that one review is seldom sufficient. Rule IV should be applied at every step in the solution. As you "solve" one subproblem, reconsider your proposal to make sure it does precisely what is required by that subproblem. Whenever you combine separate subsolutions, make sure they are compatible. Check that you have covered all the special cases. Never hesitate to review a proposed solution procedure in the faith that you will (almost) always find something to add, modify or delete.

An admonition to proceed carefully and reconsider all proposals is also provided from our culture in the form of several proverbs, such as "a stitch in time saves nine," and "an ounce of prevention is worth a pound of cure."

1.3 ALGORITHMS

When you visit your doctor, all you may know is that you have an ache. He engages in dialogue with you and tries a few tests until he has found the exact location and nature of the problem. You then expect him to provide the solution.

Such is not the case if you turn to a computer for assistance with a problem Your relationship to the computer is more analogous to the architect's relationship to the construction crew. The workers do not help him decide how the houses should be built. Rather, they carry out the specifications on his blueprint. A computer does not directly assist you in organizing your thoughts or inventing a solution procedure. You must have your procedure in hand, and the computer merely manipulates numbers or information according to your prescription. If your solution procedure is wrong, the computer's output will be wrong. This is why you must master the art of problem solving if you hope to use the computer effectively.

However, the analogy between the architect and the computer user is not complete. The architect can revise parts of the plan to allow for changing or unanticipated circumstances once construction has begun. If he has omitted anything or left some specifications unclear, the construction crew can tell him about it or ask for clarification.

On the other hand, the procedure which you would have the computer try out must specify precisely what to do in all cases. There is no room for sloppiness. The computer is a machine, devoid of compassion or insight, which does exactly what is commanded. Your proposed solution must be expressed with a level of detail and precision far in excess of that required for normal human communication.

The sort of solution procedure required by a computer is called an "algorithm." An algorithm is defined as a procedure for solving a specific problem, expressed as a finite number of rules, which is complete, unambiguous and guaranteed to terminate in a finite number of applications of these rules. The word "algorithm," incidentally, derives from the name of a ninth-century Persian mathematician al-Khowarizimi, who wrote a famous book on Rules for Restoration and Reduction.

However, before seeing some examples of algorithms, it might be helpful to see a non-algorithmic procedure. The reason is that most human communication is far less precise than a blueprint or construction schedule. We take for granted how much meaning we convey, with gestures, inflections and the context of our words. Some procedure may be "correct" in the sense that it could be successfully tried by a human of reasonable intelligence. But it may not yet be an algorithm. It is not sufficiently refined for presentation to a computer.

For example, consider the following solution to the problem of how to prepare Oeufs Sautes (fried eggs):

> A little melted butter or oil lining a moderately hot pan will eliminate sticking. Break eggs in directly from shell, or pour from cup. Pan should be hot enough so white sets speedily, but not so hot that white burns or sticks. Choose a flexible spatula for turning; tip the pan slightly toward the spatula so that the egg almost slides onto it.

This sort of solution, known as a "recipe," is correct in the human sense. Julia Child could follow its instructions and have perfect fried eggs every time. However she, being a chef, understands the terminology and has enough background to make the correct assumption whenever something is left unspecified in the original recipe.

Most of us, on the other hand, are not chefs. We have no idea what type of pan to use, what temperature to set the stove, or when to turn the eggs. The recipe says nothing about the type of pan and is imprecise regarding temperature: "Pan should be hot enough ...

but not so hot ...." Not only does the recipe fail to say when to turn the eggs, but it never explicitly says to turn them at all. It only hints at turning by recommending a flexible spatula for that purpose. Someone who takes things too literally might even go on frying the eggs forever, because the recipe says nothing about when to stop!

Thus at lower levels of "understanding" the original recipe fails to communicate how to fry eggs. It is imprecise, incomplete and ambiguous. A computer would not be able to make fried eggs from such a recipe.

In contrast to the vagueness of the fried eggs recipe, we now present an example of an algorithm. We don't bother to develop this algorithm here, since Euclid has already done the work for us.

Although it was not originally presented in algorithmic form, Euclid's method for finding the greatest common divisor (GCD) of two positive integers is perhaps the most famous algorithm in mathematics. The GCD of two integers is the largest positive integer which exactly divides both numbers. For example the GCD of 2 and 4 is 2; the GCD of 24 and 30 is 6.

One form of the Euclidean algorithm for finding the GCD of the positive integers, i and j, is given in Fig. 1.1.

1. Write down the numbers, say i and j, in that order, on a line. Proceed to step 2.
2. Compare the two numbers. If the numbers are equal, then each of them is the required result. If not, then proceed to step 3.
3. If the first number is smaller than the second, interchange them. Proceed to step 4.
4. Subtract the second number from the first and replace the two numbers under consideration by the subtrahend (the former second number) and the difference, respectively. Proceed to step 2.

Fig. 1.1 Euclidean Algorithm to Find GCD of Two Integers.

For algebraic reasons, the values of i and j will eventually become equal. Consequently this procedure is guaranteed to halt at step 2 with the correct result, provided i and j start out as positive integers.

Fig. 1.2 shows how this algorithm would be used to actually find the GCD of 2 and 4. We suggest that you try out this algorithm on other pairs of integers.

Step No.	Action	Resulting Values of First Number (i)	Second Number (j)
1.	Record values	2	4
2.	Since $i \neq j$, proceed		
3.	Since $i<j$ exchange:	4	2
4.	Replace i by j and j by i-j:	2	2
2.	Since $i=j$, stop	(GCD is 2)	

Fig. 1.2 Application of Euclidean Algorithm to Find GCD of 2 and 4

Notice that most steps in the original algorithm are followed by the step listed on the line below (except for step 4 and the last time through step 2). This successive progression through consecutive steps is so common, it will always be assumed in every algorithm, unless there are explicit instructions to the contrary. Thus the phrase "proceed to the following step" can always be omitted, being implied by convention.

Besides announcing the result, at the end, the role of step 2 in Fig. 1.1 is to determine whether an additional application of steps 3 and 4 is necessary. This role becomes clearer when Euclid's GCD algorithm is expressed in the form shown in Fig. 1.3. In this figure the convention of going to the next step is observed. Here step 2.2 does not procede to step 3 since its completion does not imply that all of step 2 is completed. However, when step 2 determines that enough applications of steps 2.1 and 2.2 have occurred, the convention says to apply step 3 next. Though stated differently, this version of the algorithm does exactly the same operations as the version shown in Fig. 1.1.

1. Write down the numbers, i and j, in that order on a line.

2. Repeat the remainder of level 2 (steps 2.1 and 2.2) as long as the two numbers are not equal:

   2.1 If the first number is smaller than the second, then interchange them.

   2.2 Subtract the second number from the first. Replace the first number by the subtrahend (the second), and replace the second by the difference.

3. The result is the value of either i or j.

4. Stop.

Fig. 1.3 The Euclidean Algorithm Restated

One feature of the Euclidean algorithm worth noting is the use of names, such as "first number"and "second number" as well as i and j, to refer to actual but unspecified positive integers. These names are simply algebraic variables, whose particular values may differ from one application of the algorithm to the next and which may change during the course of carrying out the algorithm. Since computers are designed to process information, algorithms appropriate for computers make heavy use of variable names to denote whatever information is to be processed. In fact, these algorithms usually revolve around a few variables whose values they keep changing and examining. For example, every step in the Euclidean algorithm either alters or compares the values of i and j. Thus, variables are the common thread connecting one step of an algorithm with the others. Identifying what values to denote by variables is therefore a crucial decision. If you decide just which values are to be processed before you design your solution procedure, then the steps of your eventual algorithm will be more compatible, since they will be dealing with the same data. Because of this unifying role of data, we propose the following special rule for problem solving:

Special Rule
For problems which primarily manipulate information, decide at the beginning what data are necessary for the solution and develop every stage of the solution procedure with this decision in mind.

1.4 AN EXAMPLE OF ALGORITHM DEVELOPMENT

Now that we have explained both the techniques of problem solving and their desired result, an algorithm, we should attempt to combine these ideas and actually derive an algorithm.

Suppose you must automate a scheme to count the votes in an election between two candidates for one office. Each ballot contains two boxes, and each voter is supposed to mark an X in the box for the one candidate of his choice. Since the process must be automated, your first task is to develop an algorithm. Begin by applying the rules of general problem solving.

Rule I says to understand the problem and the required result before doing anything else. The desired result is simply a pair of numbers -- the total vote for each of the candidates. The natural way to obtain these numbers would be to inspect each ballot and maintain running totals of validly marked preferences. When all the ballots have been inspected, the two running totals would represent the desired result.

The special rule says to decide what data are required for the solution. Of course we need two variables with which to maintain the two running totals. We shall refer to these as "first total" and "second total." In addition, as each ballot is encountered, we must also note the contents of both boxes. We will let "box 1" and "box 2" refer to the contents of the boxes on the ballot currently being examined. Thus four variables are required.

A variable like "first total" which is used to keep a running total, is called a counter. A counter is repeatedly incremented like the odometer on a car which counts the total mileage. But the first time the variable is incremented (added to), it must already contain some value for the increment to legitimately be "added" to the variable's current contents. In most cases, this initial value should be 0, as is the case with the mileage on a new car. Whatever it is, you must explicitly set every counter variable to some initial value. In our example, 0 is chosen since no votes have been recorded before seeing the first ballot (in a fair election).

With this in mind, we follow Rule II(a) and decompose our solution into a sequence of basic steps:

1. set both counters to 0;
2. tally the votes;
3. display the results (the two counters);
4. end.

Step 2 obviously needs elaboration, and so we apply Rule II in an attempt to decompose it. Since tallying votes involves repeatedly inspecting very similar ballots, Rule II(b) suggests isolating the action taken on each ballot from the repetitive aspect. Thus step 2 becomes:

```
2.     repeat while any unprocessed ballots remain;
2.1       process the next ballot;
```

What gets repeated, of course, is the remainder of level 2, i.e., step 2.1.

Processing one ballot, step 2.1, involves two things (applying Rule II(a) again): inspecting the ballot; and adding 1 to the appropriate counter. Now we have:

```
2.     repeat (level 2) while any unprocessed ballots remain;
2.1       inspect the next ballot;
2.2       increment the appropriate counter;
```

Upon more careful examination of how to increment the appropriate counter, we realize the need to ignore invalid ballots. However, our special Tip suggests bypassing this complication for the moment and dealing with the standard (valid ballot) case first. Hence, step 2.2 becomes:

```
2.2.1        if box 1 is X then increment first total;
2.2.2        if box 2 is X then increment second total;
```

Now we can extend these steps to handle invalid ballots. Suppose you recognize two types of invalid ballot : (i) a ballot on which no marks are made; and (ii) a ballot on which both boxes are marked with an X.[1] Case (i) will cause no difficulty, for our solution only alters a total when it sees an X. However, case (ii) would cause both totals to be incremented. Hence, we must refine the solution so that totals are changed only when one box is marked:

```
2.2.1        if box 1 is X and box 2 is not X then
                increment first total;
2.2.2        if box 2 is X and box 1 is not X then
                increment second total;
```

---

[1]There are other invalid cases which will be considered shortly. Can you think of them?

However Rule IV suggests a review of our solution at every stage of its development. If the review is made here, we may notice a third type of invalid ballot: (iii) a ballot on which either box contains any mark other than an X. This case is not covered by our solution. A ballot with an X in one box and a check mark in the other would incorrectly be presumed valid. Thus the box which does not contain the X must specifically be blank -- not simply "not X." So now we have:

```
2.2.1       if box 1 is X and box 2 is blank then
               increment first total;
2.2.2       if box 2 is X and box 1 is blank then
               increment second total;
```

Satisfied that every possibility has been covered, we now collect all these components of the solution into one algorithm:

```
1.     set both counters to 0;
2.     repeat (level 2) while any unprocessed ballots remain;
2.1       inspect the next ballot;
2.2.1     if box 1 is X and box 2 is blank
             then increment first total;
2.2.2     if box 2 is X and box 1 is blank
             then increment second total;
3.     display results (first total and second total);
4.     end.
```

One more review (Rule IV) does not reveal any other omissions, and so we are ready to try out the algorithm.

1.5 ANOTHER EXAMPLE OF ALGORITHM DEVELOPMENT

As a second example of algorithm development, consider the problem of making mortgage payments on the house of your dreams. Suppose your banker has suggested two or three alternative payment plans, involving different monthly amounts, different down payments, etc. You would like to know the true implications of each payment plan, but your banker hasn't the heart to reveal their ultimate financial consequences. Therefore you must figure them out for yourself.

Rule I says to analyze your problem and decide what sort of solution you want. What you really wish to know is the length of time and total amount of money which each plan entails. The length of time is given by the number of monthly payments involved. The number of payments and total amount could be computed by keeping track of both values while carrying out a payment plan to completion. Of course, making actual monetary payments over several years is an infeasible way to compute two numbers. However, the same bookkeeping could be duplicated by following an algorithm which imitates the process of making house payments. This algorithm could then be tried out using each set of figures suggested by your banker. The outcomes would then help you choose one of the plans.

An algorithm of this sort, which imitates on paper or on a computer some process which could occur in the real world, is called a "simulation." The basic steps of a procedure to imitate one of the suggested payment plans would be:

1. do the initial bookkeeping;
2. make a down payment;
3. keep making monthly payments until debt is paid;
4. report the number of monthly payments and total amount;
5. end.

One conspicuous feature of this procedure is the repetitive nature of making monthly payments (step 3). Rule II(b) suggests breaking step 3 into two parts:

3. repeat (level 3) while any unpaid balance remains;
3.1 make one monthly payment;

The Special Rule also recommends identifying what data values are required. First of all, the result consists of two values: (1) the number of payments; and (2) the total amount paid. Initially both of these values are 0, and each value will be increased as payments are made. In addition, we must keep track of the values which constitute a particular payment plan. These are the values which your banker is willing to quote: (3) the principal (the price of the house); (4) the down payment; (5) the amount of the regular monthly payment; and (6) the interest rate charged on the unpaid balance. During the application of your algorithm, you must also keep track of (7) the unpaid balance, so that you can decide at step 3 whether enough payments have been made. Initially the unpaid balance is equal to the principal.

Keeping these values in mind, each basic step of the procedure can now be independently refined into smaller steps, applying Rule II(a). The initial bookkeeping becomes:

1.1 initialize the number of payments and total amount to 0;
1.2 obtain values for the principal, down payment, monthly payment and interest rate;
1.3 set the unpaid balance equal to the principal;

Steps 2 and 3 are devoted to inspecting and altering these initial values. In particular, when a down payment is made in step 2, two values are affected:

2.1 deduct the down payment from the unpaid balance;
2.2 add the down payment to the total amount paid;

The bookkeeping required for each monthly payment (step 3.1) is somewhat more involved. Since interest is charged on the unpaid balance, this balance will have increased since the time of the previous monthly payment. The first step would be to compute the unpaid balance for the current month. Then after making the payment, the values required for the result should be updated:

3.1 compute the current unpaid balance (previous unpaid balance + interest on previous unpaid balance);
3.2 deduct monthly payment from the current unpaid balance (make the payment);
3.3 add the monthly payment to the total amount paid;
3.4 add 1 to the number of monthly payments;

If we reconsider these steps, as suggested by Rule IV, we may notice an oversight. The very last monthly payment may be less than the regular monthly amount; it need only cover the unpaid balance. Hence, our procedure should include another step to determine the appropriate current payment. Consequently, steps 3.2 and 3.3 which now refer to "monthly payment," should be rephrased to refer to "current payment." The result is:

```
3.1     compute the current unpaid balance;
3.2.1   if monthly payment < unpaid balance then (normal case)
            current payment is the regular monthly payment;
3.2.2   otherwise (last payment) current payment is equal
            to unpaid balance;
3.3     deduct current payment from current unpaid balance;
3.4     add current payment to total amount paid;
3.5     add 1 to the number of monthly payments;
```

Further review (Rule IV) does not reveal any problems with the individual steps. Therefore, we assemble the pieces of our procedure into the algorithm of Fig. 1.4.

Inspection of the overall algorithm (Rule IV again) does not disclose any inconsistencies among the parts or any omissions -- provided each payment plan which it is to evaluate is a "reasonable" plan and will eventually pay for the house. However, the proposed payments may conceivably be so low or the interest rate so high that the debt increases forever and the procedure never stops. It is important to recognize the limitations of your algorithms, e.g., what types of data they can and cannot handle. Whether or not to have your algorithm screen out inappropriate data depends on how it will be employed. We will assume that your banker proposes only feasible payment plans and therefore will accept the algorithm of Fig. 1.4.

```
1.1   initialize the number of payments and total amount to 0;
1.2   obtain values for the principal, down payment, monthly
          payment and interest rate;
1.3   set the unpaid balance equal to the principal;
2.1   deduct the down payment from the unpaid balance;
2.2   add the down payment to the total amount paid;
3.    repeat (level 3) while any unpaid balance remains;
3.1     compute the current unpaid balance (previous unpaid
            balance + interest on previous unpaid balance);
3.2.1   if monthly payment < unpaid balance then
            current payment is regular monthly payment;
3.2.2   otherwise (last payment)
            current payment equals unpaid balance;
3.3     deduct current payment from unpaid blanace;
3.4     add current payment to total amount paid;
3.5     add 1 to the number of monthly payments;
4.    report the number of monthly payments and total
          amount paid;
4.    end.
```

Fig. 1.4 Algorithm to Evaluate One Proposed Payment Plan

1.6 REVIEW

Of the skills required to solve a problem using a computer, the ability to develop an algorithmic solution procedure is the most important and, unfortunately, the least mechanical. This skill is largely a matter of experience and human insight. Hopefully, the rules given in this chapter will guide your experience in the right direction, and the examples throughout the book will contribute to your insight. With practice, the application of these problem solving rules will become second nature.

1. Analyze your problem carefully, attempting to understand its specific aspects and the requirements of an acceptable solution.

2. Attempt to break your problem into simpler, relatively independent parts, and then focus on the separate parts.

   (a) Attempt to break a problem into a sequence of smaller problems, so that the solution of one subproblem followed by the solution of the next, and so on, will provide a solution to the original problem.

   (b) If your problem involves performing some repeated process, attempt to isolate the action which is required in one instance from the repetitive aspect.

   In case of trouble, just attempt to solve the problem for the simplest cases or most likely set of circumstances. This may suggest the structure of a more general solution procedure.

3. When breaking a problem into simpler parts, perform the decomposition gradually in several stages. Make use of more general criteria in the early stages and more specific criteria later.

4. Review and reconsider your proposed solution to make sure it is complete and correct.

1.7 EXERCISES

1.1 The process of multiplication is a short form for doing repetitive addition. Thus

$$2 \times 6 = 2+2+2+2+2+2$$
$$\text{or} \quad 6 \times 2 = 6+6$$

Describe an algorithm to obtain the product of any two positive integers (the multiplicand and the multiplier) using only the process of addition.

1.2 When any positive integer (the dividend) is divided by another positive integer (the divisor), the result is a quotient and a remainder; the remainder is greater than or equal to zero and less than the dividend. Division can be done by repeated subtractions.

Describe an algorithm to determine the quotient and remainder when any positive integer is divided by any other positive integer.

1.3 One method of multiplying two positive integers requires only the ability to multiply and divide by 2 and to add. The division yields an integer result by rounding down if necessary. Thus 9 divided by 2 will yield 4. The technique, known as the Russian Peasant Algorithm, can be illustrated by the following example.

To multiply 9 by 3:

write them side by side	9	3
divide the first and multiply the second by 2	4	6
until the left-hand	2	12
number is 1	1	24

Now add up all the right-hand numbers which appear opposite odd left-hand numbers, i.e., 24+3 = 27 = 9×3

Describe an algorithm to multiply i by j using the Russian Peasant Algorithm. You may assume i ≥ j.

1.4 The Euclidean algorithm described in this chapter works only for positive integers, i.e., integers ≥ 0. Write a more general version of the Euclidean algorithm so it works for any pair of integers.

1.5 The vote counting algorithm described in this chapter does not account for spoiled ballots. Devise an algorithm to count the votes for each candidate and to provide a count of the spoiled ballots as well.

1.6(a) Write an algorithm for evaluating a more realistic mortgage payment plan where each payment plan has the following characteristics:

(i) you are quoted amounts for the principal, down payment, regular monthly payment, and annual interest rate;

(ii) after making the down payment, you make twelve monthly payments before interest is computed on the remaining debt (amount still to be paid);

(iii) thereafter the interest is compounded annually, at the end of every twelve monthly payments. Of course, payments continue until the house is paid off.

At the end of every year (twelve payments) display the number of monthly payments so far and the remaining debt including interest. When the payments finally end, display the number of monthly payments and total amount paid (including the down payment).

(b) Your algorithm will be even better if it includes the following features:

(i) your algorithm does not pay more than the remaining debt when making the final payment;

(ii) your algorithm should detect payment plans which will never terminate. In this case, your algorithm should print an appropriate message and stop.

(iii) your algorithm should be able to evaluate several plans rather than just one.

1.7 One method for finding a path through a maze is to walk through it, always keeping your right hand on a wall. Stated another way this becomes: "turn right when you can and turn left only when you must."

Consider a mechanical man with the following limitations:

(i) he can move forward (only), one pace at a time;

(ii) he can turn right (90°);

(iii) he can turn left (90°);

(iv) he can determine whether or not there is a wall immediately ahead of him;

(v) he can determine when he has left the maze;

(vi) he can only perform <u>one</u> of the above functions at any one time;

If the mechanical man is placed facing into any maze, describe an algorithm which will help him enter the maze and find his way to an exit.

(As an aside, Theseus had to enter a labyrinth to slay the Minotaur. His girl-friend helped him get back out. What was her name?)

1.8 The numerals in the ancient Roman system of notation are still used for certain limited purposes. The common basic symbols and their decimal equivalents are I=1, V=5, X=10, L=50, C=100, D=500, and M=1000.

Roman integers are written according to the following rules:

1. If a letter is immediately followed by one of equal or lesser value, its value is added to a cumulative total. Thus, XX=20, XV=15, VI=6.

2. If a letter is immediately followed by one of greater value, its value is subtracted from a cumulative total. Thus IV=4, XL=40, CM=900.

Design an algorithm to translate any string of Roman numerals into its decimal equivalent.

Chapter 2 Introduction to Programming

2.1 USING A COMPUTER TO SOLVE PROBLEMS

If you plan to solve a problem with the aid of a computer, your first task is to devise a solution procedure and refine this procedure into an algorithm. When you are satisfied with the algorithm, it must then be rewritten in a language which the computer is able to interpret. English is too imprecise; the meanings of its words depend too much on nuance, context, and human experience. Instead, algorithms must be expressed in a "programming language," having only a limited vocabulary and extremely precise grammatical rules for building unambiguous instructions from the basic vocabulary. Thus, learning to use a computer also requires learning some "foreign" programming language. This chapter provides an introduction to one of the major programming languages, called PL/I ("programming language one"). PL/C is a somewhat simpler dialect of PL/I, which consists of PL/I's most important features without some of its more exotic ones. Throughout this book we will use the features of PL/I which are common to PL/C, so that both languages are being discussed simultaneously. Any differences will be noted at the appropriate places as well as in Appendix A.

When your algorithm is expressed in a programming language, such as PL/I, it is usually called a <u>program</u>. However, before it can be submitted to the computer, your program must still be transcribed from paper onto some suitable medium, usually punched cards. Only then can the computer "try out" your algorithm.

This attempt to carry out your algorithm is called the <u>execution</u> of your program. The preparation of a program should be carefully distinguished from its execution. Program preparation is an activity requiring human skills, while the execution is only possible after the preparation steps and is the one step involving a computer. Once a program is prepared correctly, it can be executed over and over, applying the same program to different data each time.

Program execution is not the final step. It is always necessary to review the results of execution. If the results are not acceptable, then some part of the problem solving process must have contained an error, which needs to be corrected. This process of correcting errors is called "program debugging" and is easily the most gruesome and frustrating of these steps. Unfortunately, far too many programmers spend the major portion of their time debugging their proposed "solution." If more time and attention were devoted to initial program preparation -- and to general problem solving in particular -- there would be fewer (ideally zero) errors to eliminate. Once again the wisdom of the culture: "an ounce of prevention is worth a pound of cure."

All these steps are summarized below, as well as in Fig. 2.1.

A. Program Preparation

1. Devise a solution procedure for the problem by applying the guidelines of Chapter 1;
2. Refine this procedure into an algorithm by specifying every detail concerning how to perform this sequence of actions;
3. Express this algorithm in a programming language;
4. Record the resulting program on punched cards;

B. Program Execution

5. Try out your program on the computer;

C. Review of Results

6. Inspect the results of program execution. If they are not satisfactory, you must, depending on the severity of the difficulty, revise your approach (return to step 1), modify your algorithm (return to step 2), correct language errors (return to step 3) or keypunching mistakes (return to step 4); then try again.

2.2 A FIRST PROGRAM

To see what a PL/I program looks like, we will consider a program to solve the very simple problem of summing the integers 3 and 4. An algorithm for this problem is shown in Fig. 2.2(a). In Fig. 2.2(b) the algorithm is rewritten as a PL/I program. The close correspondence should be obvious. After this program is punched on cards and executed, the output from the computer is shown in Fig. 2.2(c). The program itself appears near the top and the result of the computation near the bottom. The following sections will explain the details of each statement in Fig. 2.2(b), as well as how to prepare the program for execution.

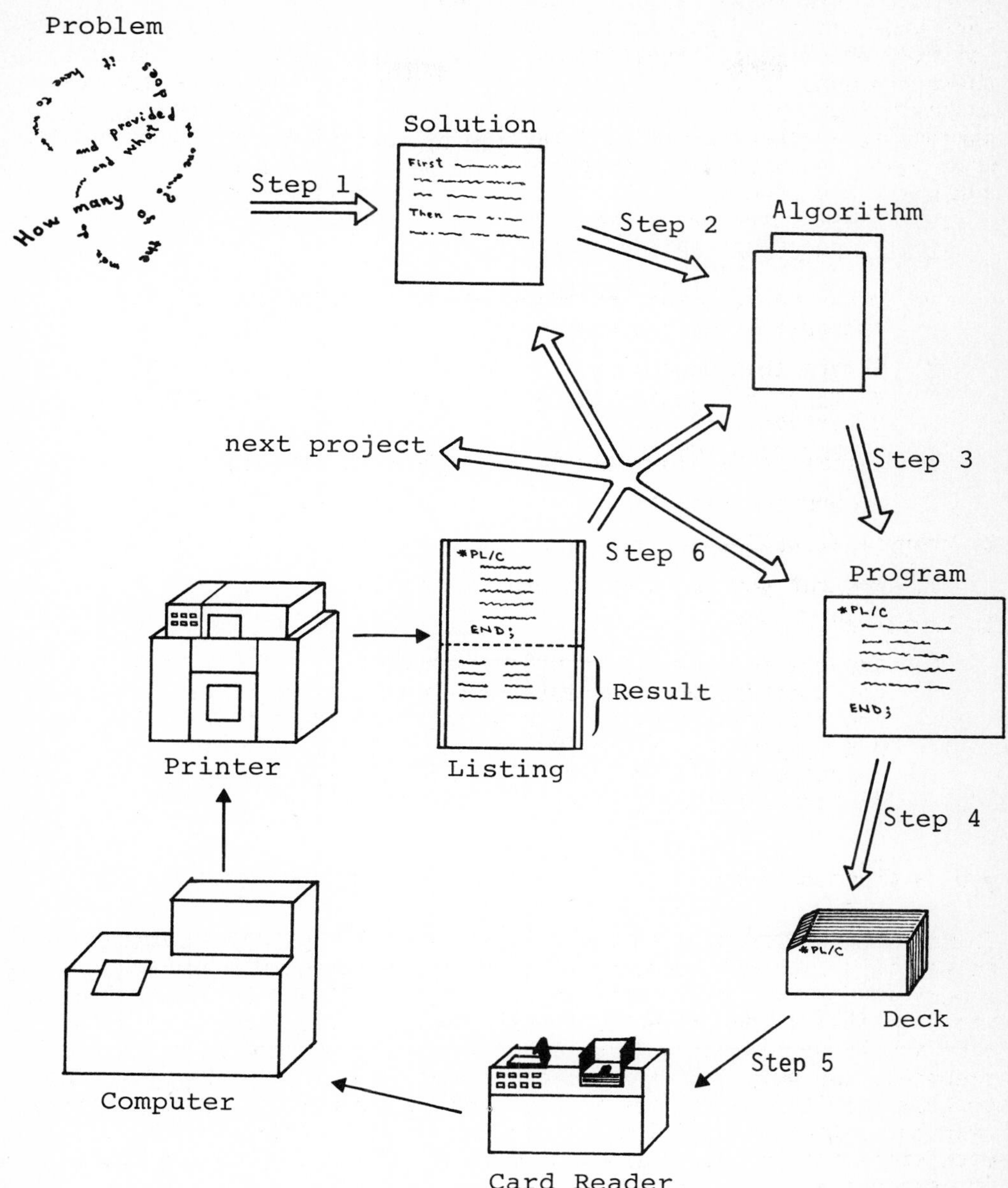

Figure 2.1 The Problem Solving Process.

1. let first number be 3;
2. let second number be 4;
3. set the total to the first number plus the second number;
4. display the total;
5. end.

Fig. 2.2(a) Algorithm to find the sum of two integers

```
FIRST:  PROCEDURE OPTIONS (MAIN);
        DECLARE (FIRST_NUMBER,SECOND_NUMBER,TOTAL) FIXED(5,0);
        FIRST_NUMBER = 3;
        SECOND_NUMBER = 4;
        TOTAL = FIRST_NUMBER + SECOND_NUMBER;
        PUT DATA (TOTAL);
        END FIRST;
```

Fig. 2.2.(b) Program to find the sum of two integers

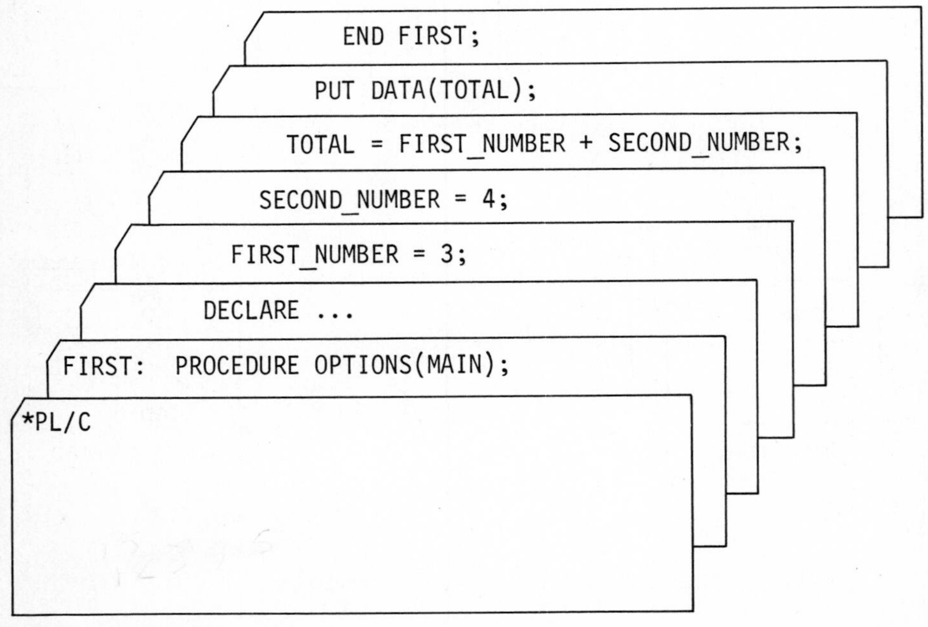

```
$PL/C MONITOR=(U,S,A),A,X,CMPRS,NOHDRPG

*OPTIONS IN EFFECT*     TIME=(0,15,00),PAGES=30,LINES=2000,ATR,XREF,FLAGW,NOCMNTS,SORMGIN=(2,72,1),ERRORS=(50,50),TABSIZE=6528,
*OPTIONS IN EFFECT*     SOURCE,OPLIST,CMPRS,NOHDRPG,AUXIO=10000,LINECT=60,NOALIST,MONITOR=(UDEF,NOBNDRY,SUBRG,AUTO),MCALL,NOMTEXT,
*OPTIONS IN EFFECT*     DUMP=(S,F,L,E,U,R),DUMPE=(S,F,L,E,U,R),DUMPT=(S,F,L,E,U,R)

0FIRST:  PROCEDURE OPTIONS (MAIN);                                    PL/C-R7.6-000 06/28/78 21:01 PAGE   1

  STMT LEVEL NEST BLOCK MLVL  SOURCE TEXT

      1                         FIRST:  PROCEDURE OPTIONS (MAIN);
      2    1         1                  DECLARE (FIRST_NUMBER,SECOND_NUMBER,TOTAL) FIXED (5,0);
      3    1         1                  FIRST_NUMBER = 3;
      4    1         1                  SECOND_NUMBER = 4;
      5    1         1                  TOTAL = FIRST_NUMBER + SECOND_NUMBER;
 *    6    1         1                  PUT DATA (TOTAL);
      7    1         1                  END FIRST;
```

PL/C Program

```
DCL NO.        IDENTIFIER                    ATTRIBUTES AND REFERENCES

    1          FIRST                         ENTRY,DECIMAL,FLOAT(6)

    2          FIRST_NUMBER                  AUTOMATIC,ALIGNED,DECIMAL,FIXED(5,0)
                                             3,5

    2          SECOND_NUMBER                 AUTOMATIC,ALIGNED,DECIMAL,FIXED(5,0)
                                             4,5

    2          TOTAL                         AUTOMATIC,ALIGNED,DECIMAL,FIXED(5,0)
                                             5,6
```

To be explained in Chapter 3

```
ERRORS/WARNINGS DETECTED DURING CODE GENERATION:

     WARNING: NO FILE SPECIFIED. SYSIN/SYSPRINT ASSUMED. (CG0C)
```

Ignore

```
TOTAL=        7;
```

Result of program

```
IN STMT     7  PROGRAM RETURNS FROM MAIN PROCEDURE.

IN STMT     7  DYNAMIC FLOW TRACE:
                0000->0001         0007->0000

IN STMT     7  SCALARS AND BLOCK-TRACE:

***** MAIN PROCEDURE FIRST

TOTAL=        7          SECOND_NUMBER=        4  FIRST_NUMBER=        3


NON-0 PROCEDURE EXECUTION COUNTS:
NAME         STMT COUNT  NAME        STMT COUNT  NAME        STMT COUNT  NAME        STMT COUNT  NAME        STMT COUNT
FIRST        0001 00001


         COMPILATION STATISTICS  (0007 STATEMENTS)       |                  EXECUTION STATISTICS
SECONDS  ERRORS  WARNINGS  PAGES  LINES  CARDS  INCL'S | SECONDS  ERRORS  WARNINGS  PAGES  LINES  CARDS  INCL'S  AUX I/O
   .05       0        1       1     40      9       0 |    .01       0         0      1      5      0       0        0
-------------------------------------------------------+---------------------------------------------------------------
BYTES   SYMBOL TABLE   INTERMEDIATE CODE   OBJECT CODE |  STATIC CORE   AUTOMATIC CORE   DYNAMIC CORE   TOTAL STORAGE
USED       519(   1K)        168(   1K)      134(   1K) |    340(   1K)      465(   1K)       0(   0K)     1457(   2K)
UNUSED   25593(  24K)      25574(  24K)    51744(  50K) |  50995(  49K)    50995(  49K)   25574(  24K)    50995(  49K)

THIS PROGRAM MAY BE RERUN WITHOUT CHANGE IN A REGION  49K BYTES SMALLER USING TABLESIZE=   130
```

Remainder to be explained in Chapter 3

Figure 2.2(c)

2.3 THE PROCEDURE AND END STATEMENTS (plus Entry Names)

A PL/I program consists of major sections called procedures, which are sequences of statements having

PROCEDURE

and

END

as the first and last statements, respectively. In order to distinguish different procedures, PL/I requires that each procedure have a name, called an entry name. Also, every statement in PL/I must end with a semicolon (;). Thus a procedure always resembles the following prototype:

```
CLYDE:  PROCEDURE  ;
        -  }
        -  }  other statements describing
        -  }  the procedure
        END CLYDE  ;
```

The entry name in this case is CLYDE, but it can be almost any reasonable name you desire.[1] Note that the entry name (CLYDE) is separated from the remainder of the statement it names (PROCEDURE) by a colon (:). The same entry name is also placed after the END statement in order to identify exactly what (procedure) is being "ended" at that point.

PL/I also requires that one of the procedures in a program be designated as the main procedure, which means the first one to be executed. This main procedure designation is made by the statement:

<entry name>: PROCEDURE OPTIONS (MAIN);

Here we introduce a special notation, < >. This notation designates a class of objects, such as all legitimate entry names, from which you are to select any specific member, such as CLYDE. Another example is <digit> which refers to any of the ten symbols 0,1,...,9.

Until Chapter 8, the programs we encounter will consist of a single (main) procedure. Consequently, these programs have a form resembling the following example, where the entry name ONLY was chosen in this instance:

```
ONLY:  PROCEDURE OPTIONS (MAIN);
       ___  }
       ___  }  other PL/I program statements
       ___  }
       END ONLY;
```

2.4 VARIABLES AND THE DECLARE STATEMENT

Computer programs are usually written to solve a class of problems rather than one specific problem. Thus one might write a program to find the area of a triangle whose sides have lengths denoted by a, b,

[1]The precise rules for valid entry names are given in section 2.11.

and c, rather than one whose sides have specific lengths 3, 4, and 5. To this end, PL/I uses symbolic names, or variables, to represent data. Since computers primarily manipulate data, the programs governing them make heavy use of variables in order to designate data. Note the central role played by variables FIRST_NUMBER, SECOND_NUMBER, and TOTAL in the program of Fig. 2.2(b).

A PL/I variable can be thought of as a "place" in the computer where we can store data and from which we can retrieve (or "access") data; we can also change the data in the variable by storing something else there. However, a variable can hold only one piece of information at a time. Thus once a change has been made, the previous data is lost forever; only the most recent data is available for accessing.

In some ways, using a variable to store data is analogous to writing information on a blackboard. When a number (or any piece of information) has been written on a blackboard, we can inspect that number as many times as we like without changing the number itself. But if we wish to change the number on the board, we first erase the old number and then write down the new one.

Depending on the type of computer, there are many thousands of these "places" available for storing data. They are called memory locations. They can be designated by almost any reasonable variable names you care to invent.[2] For each distinct variable name employed in your program, a distinct memory location is set aside and is identified by that name. Every occurrence of the same name in your program refers to the same memory location. You need not be concerned about the details of this assignment of variable names to memory locations. You have (for now) as many locations at your disposal as required, and you are assigned only as many as your program requests.

For example, in Fig. 2.2(b) FIRST_NUMBER, SECOND_NUMBER, and TOTAL are distinct variable names and consequently are assigned to three separate memory locations, represented by rectangles below:

FIRST_NUMBER	
SECOND_NUMBER	
TOTAL	

PL/I uses an equal sign (=) to store data in a memory location. The location is identified by the variable name on the left of the = sign, and the value to be stored is described on the right. Thus the two statements

```
FIRST_NUMBER = 3;
SECOND_NUMBER = 4;
```

produce the following effect when the program is executed:

[2]The rules for constructing valid variable names are given later in this section.

FIRST_NUMBER	3
SECOND_NUMBER	4
TOTAL	

This use of an = sign to store data is called an assignment statement. In the assignment statement

```
TOTAL = FIRST_NUMBER + SECOND_NUMBER;
```

the variables FIRST_NUMBER and SECOND_NUMBER refer to the same two memory locations as before. When this statement is executed, the current values (3 and 4) are retrieved from these locations, added together, and the result is stored in TOTAL. After executing all three assignment statements, the outcome is:

FIRST_NUMBER	3
SECOND_NUMBER	4
TOTAL	7

Note that the contents of FIRST_NUMBER and SECOND_NUMBER remain unaffected by the assignment of their sum to TOTAL. An assignment statement alters only the variable on the left of the = sign.

A final observation is that subsequent execution of a statement such as:

```
SECOND_NUMBER = TOTAL;
```

would have produced the following situation:

FIRST_NUMBER	3
SECOND_NUMBER	7
TOTAL	7

Notice that the previous value of SECOND_NUMBER would have been lost by storing a new number in that memory location.

2.4.1 Variable Names

The rules for constructing valid variable names are:

i) Each variable name must begin with a letter of the alphabet or one of the special symbols @, # or $.

ii) A variable name may be up to 31 characters in length.

iii) After the first character, the variable name may include any of the 26 letters of the alphabet (A through Z), any of the

10 digits (0 through 9), the underscore character "_" (this is an upper case W on the IBM 029 keypunch) or the special characters @, # or $.

Some examples of valid variable names are:

i) X

ii) NUMBER1

iii) #SEVEN

iv) THIS_IS_A_VERY_LONG_IDENTIFIER

Some invalid variable names are:

i) 1WORD - does not begin with a letter or special character.

ii) IS_IT? - "?" is an invalid character for a variable name.

iii) ONE.TWO - "." is an invalid character for a variable name.

iv) THIS ONE - no blanks allowed in a variable name.

Since PL/I permits long variable names, there is no excuse for using variable names which are not meaningful. Notice that in Fig. 2.2(b) the variable names used are FIRST_NUMBER, SECOND_NUMBER, and TOTAL. Without affecting the outcome of the program, I, J, and K could have been selected as variable names instead, but these names shed no light on their own role or the purpose of the statements in which they occur. Unfortunately, people are prone to use short, uninformative names. The extra time spent to select illuminating variable names is insignificant compared to the time which can be squandered later trying to decipher an unreadable program!

A word of caution is due here. Unlike PL/I, PL/C has a list of reserved words which, even though "valid" variable names in terms of the above rules, may not be used as variables. A complete list of these words is given in Appendix B.

2.4.2 The DECLARE Statement

The variable names which you choose to use are announced by the DECLARE statement. This statement, which normally follows the PROCEDURE statement, as in Fig. 2.2(b), has another important function. The computer can store information of many different types (e.g., numbers or characters) and in many forms (e.g., as integers or as numbers with decimal digits). It is the responsibility of you, the programmer, to state what basic kind of information you want to record in each variable and how you wish to have this information represented inside the computer. Such characteristics of a variable are called its attributes. The DECLARE statement is your means of ascribing attributes to variables.

Don't panic. You do not require a knowledge of the internal workings of a computer to carry out this responsibility. In fact, certain assumptions will be made automatically on your behalf if you fail to declare all the attributes of all your variables. However, we do not recommend that you rely on the "default" conventions of PL/I. If you DECLARE exactly what you want, you will encounter fewer problems.

The DECLARE statement in line 2 of Fig. 2.2(b), for example, gives all three variables, FIRST_NUMBER, SECOND_NUMBER, and TOTAL, the attribute FIXED (5,0). The attribute FIXED indicates, among other things, that only numeric information can be stored in the corresponding memory locations. The first number, 5, indicates how many digits can be stored in each location, and the second, 0, says how many of these digits are to the right of the decimal point. This means that each of these variables is to be used for storing whole numbers (integers) and that at most a five-digit number can be stored. Each of these variables can therefore store only integers in the range -99,999 to +99,999, inclusive.

Of course there are many other possible attributes, but for the time being 5-digit integers will serve our purposes. Thus, until more attribute possibilities are disclosed (Chapters 5 and 6), we will declare most variables as

```
FIXED(5,0)
```

At any rate, the general form of the DECLARE statement is:

```
DECLARE <variable>  <attributes>;
```

However, other forms of this statement are permissible. If several variables are being declared with <u>identical</u> attributes, you may put the variables in a list, enclosed by parentheses:

```
DECLARE (<list of variables>) <attributes>;
```

The variables in this list, as in every other list we will encounter, must be separated by commas. It is also permissible to use multiple DECLARE statements. Thus

```
DECLARE (ONE,TWO,THREE)  FIXED(5,0);
```

is equivalent to the following <u>three</u> statements:

```
DECLARE ONE FIXED(5,0);
DECLARE TWO FIXED(5,0);
DECLARE THREE FIXED (5,0);
```

One more equivalent form has individual variables paired with their associated attributes and these pairs arranged in a list, as shown in the following statement:

```
DECLARE
   ONE FIXED(5,0),
   TWO FIXED(5,0),
   THREE FIXED(5,0);
```

2.5 THE ASSIGNMENT STATEMENT

The general form of the assignment statement is:

```
<variable> = <arithmetic expression>;
```

The assignment statement is by far the most widely used statement in PL/I, since it is the major means of moving data among memory locations, of performing calculations, and of changing the values of variables. Fig. 2.2(b) provides three examples in lines 3, 4, and 5. The effect of such assignment statements as:

```
TOTAL = FIRST_NUMBER + SECOND_NUMBER;
```

has already been discussed (in Section 2.4). This particular assignment statement is actually quite typical. Any assignment statement causes the following to occur:

1. The expression on the right hand side of the = sign is evaluated;

2. This value is then placed in the memory location named by the variable on the left hand side of the = sign.

Note that every assignment statement causes some variable to receive (i.e., be "assigned") a new value (Step 2), thereby obliterating whatever value that variable may have contained previously. The resulting movement of a value into a memory location gives the = operator in PL/I an "active" role, which is quite different from its use in mathematics to express a static relationship.

The way this new value is obtained (Step 1) may be quite trivial. For example,

```
FIRST_NUMBER = 3;
```

merely places the number 3 in memory location FIRST_NUMBER. The statement

```
MARVIN = JOE;
```

would merely place a copy of the current value of JOE into location MARVIN. The value could also be derived from some simple combination of other values, such as the sum of FIRST_NUMBER and SECOND_NUMBER. On the other hand, the value to be placed in the left hand variable may be the result of an enormously complex arithmetic expression. The rules for constructing these expressions are given in the next section.

First, though, a warning: if you attempt to assign a value with fractional parts, such as 2.75, to an integer type variable, <u>only</u> the integer part of the value (i.e., 2) will be stored! Fractional parts will be thrown away without rounding. Therefore, if X is DECLAREd as

```
FIXED(5,0)
```

the following statement gives X the value 6:

```
X = 6.95;
```

However, if X had been DECLAREd as

```
FIXED(7,2)
```

then X would have been able to hold decimal digits, and therefore would have received the value 6.95.

2.5.1 Arithmetic Expressions in PL/I

Arithmetic expressions in PL/I resemble ordinary algebraic expressions and are evaluated according to the normal rules of algebra, for example if you were asked to give the answer to the following "skill testing question"

$$6 + 3 \times 2$$

you would hopefully arrive at the answer 12. There is no ambiguity as to whether you perform the addition or the multiplication first, because you recall (from extensive primary schooling) that multiplication occurs before addition or, as we say, multiplication has <u>higher priority</u> than addition. The comparable expression in PL/I would be

```
6 + 3 * 2
```

the value of which is also 12. In PL/I, the symbol * is the multiplication operator, and here too multiplication is performed before addition.

However, you may also recall that the order of operations may be changed by the introduction of parentheses into the expression. Thus (6+3)×2 gives an answer of 18, not 12, because the parentheses force us to do the addition first. The same is true in PL/I. The statement

```
NUMBER = (6+3)*2;
```

would store the value 18 in location NUMBER.

If n is an algebraic variable, then 5n would represent 5 times the value of n. However, in PL/I, multiplication must be explicitly denoted by the * operator. Thus 5*N would be the comparable expression, and

```
A*(B+C)
```

would correspond in PL/I to a(b+c) in algebra.

Besides addition and multiplication, PL/I has three other arithmetic operators for combining pairs of numbers, namely subtraction, division, and exponentiation (raising to a power). These so-called "binary" operators are shown in Fig. 2.3.

PL/I also has two "unary" operators which are merely the positive and negative versions of a number, i.e., the "signed" versions. Thus +A is the same thing as A, while -A is the negative of A.

Operation	PL/I Symbol	Algebraic Expression	PL/I Equivalent	Relative Priority
exponentiation	**	a^n	A**N	3
multiplication	*	ab or a×b	A*B	2
division	/	a÷b or a/b	A/B	2
addition	+	a+b	A+B	1
subtraction	-	a-b	A-B	1

Fig. 2.3 Basic Binary Arithmetic Operators in PL/I

Fig. 2.3 also gives the relative priorities of the operators. In the absence of parentheses, operations with higher priority (larger priority number) are performed first. Notice that these priorities apply only to binary operators. Unary operators must be treated as a separate case. When an expression in PL/I is preceded by a unary plus or minus, the effect is the same as if a zero were written before the unary operator. Thus

```
-A     is equivalent to 0-A
+B*C   is equivalent to 0+B*C
-A**B  is equivalent to 0-A**B
```

Arithmetic expressions are constructed in PL/I much like they are constructed in algebra. The ultimate constituents are numbers -- either fixed constants or else variables (current contents of memory locations). If more than one number is involved, then the constants and/or variables are alternated with arithmetic operators, with parentheses possibly being included for clarity or to override the conventional evaluation rules.

For example, the following are all valid arithmetic expressions in PL/I:

```
28          I+J-K
+6          A*B/C-E+3.25
X           (C-D)*(F+G)
-P          -(P)
```

The _rules for constructing valid arithmetic expressions_ are:

A "basic element" is either:

(a) a constant (an expressly written number),
(b) a single variable,
or (c) an arithmetic expression enclosed in parentheses.

An arithmetic expression consists of either:

(a) a basic element,
(b) a basic element preceded by a + or - sign (i.e., an explicitly written positive or negative quantity),
or (c) a sequence of basic elements, separated by single arithmetic operators.

The _rules for evaluating expressions_ merely reflect the different priorities of operators and the ability to override these priorities with parentheses.

1. First, evaluate all subexpressions enclosed in parentheses, beginning with the innermost ones,
2. Perform all exponentiations (from right to left),
3. Perform all multiplications and/or divisions (from left to right),
4. Finally, perform all additions and/or subtractions (from left to right).

Example If X=2, Y=4, and Z=5, evaluate Y/X*Z.

Using Rule No.	Evaluate	Result	Reduced Expression
3	Y/X	2	2*Z
3	2*Z	10	answer is 10

Example If A=2, B=3, C=4, and D=5, evaluate D+(A+B)*C.

Using Rule No.	Evaluate	Result	Reduced Expression
1	(A+B)	5	D+5*C
3	5*C	20	D+20
4	D+20	25	answer is 25

Example If A=2, B=3, C=4, D=5, evaluate (C*D/(A*D))+B+C*D/A.

Using Rule No.	Evaluate	Result	Reduced Expression
1	(A*D)	10	(C*D/10)+B+C*D/A
1&3	C*D	20	(20/10)+B+C*D/A
1	(20/10)	2	2+B+C*D/A
3	C*D	20	2+B+20/A
3	20/A	10	2+B+10
4	2+B	5	5+10
4	5+10	15	answer is 15

A complicated expression, such as this one, should be generously parenthesized for the sake of clarity. It is much easier to understand the following equivalent expression:

((C*D)/(A*D))+B+((C*D)/A)

Of course, some parentheses may be essential to the correct evaluation of an expression. This is particularly true when division is one of the operators. The following example resembles the preceding one, except for the complete absence of parentheses. Notice the difference this makes in the outcome.

Example If A=2, B=3, C=4, and D=5, evaluate C*D/A*D+B+C*D/A.

Using Rule No.	Evaluate	Result	Reduced Expression
3	C*D	20	20/A*D+B+C*D/A
3	20/A	10	10*D+B+C*D/A
3	10*D	50	50+B+C*D/A
3	C*D	20	50+B+20/A
3	20/A	10	50+B+10
4	50+B	53	53+10
4	53+10	63	answer is 63

Example If X=3 and Y=2 then evaluate -X**Y. Since this expression contains a unary minus, let us first rewrite the expression as 0-X**Y.

Using Rule No.	Evaluate	Result	Reduced Expression
2	X**Y	9	0-9
4	0-9	-9	answer is -9

The same result would not have been obtained from (-X)**Y since this is equivalent to (0-X)**Y whose value is 9.

Too many parentheses are better than too few. Whenever you are in doubt as to the order of evaluation, use parentheses to enforce the order you desire. A lack of parentheses in complicated expressions only makes the expressions harder to understand.

A final warning concerns the division of one integer by another. You should never write expressions in which one constant is divided by another constant. That is, never include terms like 1/3. The reasons for this are beyond the scope of this book and have to do with the way PL/I handles the precision of intermediate results. To be safe, assume that at least one of the operands in a division must be a variable, and preferably both should be.

Before leaving the subject of division, let us consider the following section of code:

```
DECLARE (X,Y,Z) FIXED (5,0);
X=13;
Y=5;
Z=X/Y;
```

The value assigned to Z will be 2 and not 2.6. The reason for this is quite straightforward. The variable Z can only store integer values (because its attributes are FIXED (5,0)), and so it receives only the integer portion of the result. The fractional part is discarded without rounding!

We could preserve this fractional part as in the following code:

```
DECLARE (X,Y) FIXED (5,0),
        Z FIXED (7,2);
X=13;
Y=5;
Z=X/Y;
```

Now, because we can have up to two decimal places precision, Z will receive the value 2.60.

2.6 THE PUT DATA STATEMENT

It would be a shame if, after toiling for hours to develop a program which produces long-awaited results, you never get to see those results. This is exactly what will happen if you do not explicitly request to see some values from some of the memory locations.

All you need do is include the statement:

```
PUT DATA (<list of variables>);
```

and this causes the computer to print out the current values of all variables appearing in the list. Thus, line 6 of Fig. 2.2(b) would cause the computer to print out the current value of the variable TOTAL. Had we wished to print out the values of all variables in the program, that statement might have read:

```
PUT DATA (FIRST_NUMBER, SECOND_NUMBER, TOTAL);
```

The PUT DATA statement does more than print out the current values of the variables -- it also supplies their names as can be seen from Fig. 2.2(c). These values are printed in the same order in which the variables are listed in the PUT DATA statement.

2.7 FLOW OF CONTROL

The previous sections have discussed the rules for writing various PL/I statements correctly, with an eye toward their eventual effect at the time of program execution. In this section we focus only on program execution, and in particular on the order in which PL/I statements are executed.

Recall that the statements in algorithms did not need to say "proceed to the next statement." At execution time, the person following the algorithm was assumed to move through the list of instructions in order, one at a time, unless explicitly directed to skip or repeat some.

Similarly, when the program in Fig. 2.2(b) is being executed, each statement is executed in the order in which the computer encounters it. The concept of a computer completely executing one statement of a program before "moving" on to execute some other statement is extremely important. The sequence in which the statements get executed is known as the <u>flow of control</u>.

If we ignore, for the moment, statements 1 and 2 in Fig. 2.2(c), which supply special "getting started" information, the computer begins execution with statement 3 and continues sequentially through the rest of the statements until it encounters the END of the program at statement 7. Programs like this one which begin at the top of a procedure and flow sequentially to the bottom are easy to understand, making this program structure highly desirable. However, most programs do not have such simple flow of control. Most programs, like most algorithms, contain statements which may be repeated or bypassed in some situations. Nevertheless, every execution of a program has some particular flow of control, since statements must be executed in some order.

Clearly, the order in which the program statements are placed is vital to the correct execution of the program. For example, if we had mistakenly interchanged statements 5 and 6 in Fig. 2.2(b), then the program would not execute properly, since this would have caused the computer to encounter the PUT DATA statement before any value had been stored in the variable TOTAL. Then we would be asking the computer to print out a value (TOTAL) when none has been calculated and stored there.

2.8 RUNNING PROGRAMS AND PL/C CONTROL CARDS

Once your algorithm has been rewritten in a programming language, your program must still be prepared for presentation to a computer. This is by far the simplest and most mechanical of the steps in program preparation. Unfortunately, a computer cannot read your program, such as the program shown in Fig. 2.2(b), from a sheet of paper. The program must be presented to the computer via the medium of punched cards.[3] The first step in the process then is to transcribe your program from paper to cards, using a keypunch machine to produce a separate card for each line of the program. In producing

---

[3]There are exceptions, e.g., mark sense cards or interactive terminals, which need not concern us here.

these cards you do not use column 1 nor columns 73-80 for PL/I statements. No more than one statement should appear on any one card. However, a single statement may occupy as many cards as required.

Since there are other programming languages besides PL/I, you must announce what language you are using. For PL/C programs this information is conveyed by the very first card, which must contain the symbols *PL/C in columns 1-5.[4] (Note that column 1 is used on this card.) The *PL/C card may also contain other identifying information if you wish. This information, which is usually your name, may consist of up to 20 characters placed within quotes and following the characters ID=, as shown in Fig. 2.2(c). The *PL/C card and the *DATA card (to be described in Section 2.10) are known as control cards and are not properly part of the PL/C language since their role is other than to describe algorithms. Information about control cards required to execute PL/I programs (which are not run under PL/C) can be obtained from your own computer installation.

Although "running" a program on a computer involves a simple mechanical process (the exact details of which may vary among installations), the jargon is standard. Any collection of cards is called a deck. When a deck is to be run or executed on the computer, it is placed on a device called a card reader (either by you or, more often, by an operator) and the cards are read in to the computer. This introduces a unit of work, called a job, for the computer. When your job has executed, a printer prints the results on paper, called a listing or printout, which is what you should review. Fig. 2.2(c) is a copy of such a printout. We suggest another look at Fig. 2.1 where these things are shown within the entire process of solving problems with a computer.

2.9 COMMENTS

So far, all the statements we have seen have either conveyed information to the computer, or caused the computer to perform some useful function. There is another type of statement which does neither. In fact, it is not aimed at the computer at all -- it is intended solely to help human beings read a computer program. This statement is called a comment and consists of any message whatsoever enclosed between the special symbols /* and */ . The following is an example of a comment:

```
/* THIS IS A #1_$X@ COMMENT */
```

As programs become more complicated, it is not always possible to tell from the PL/I (or any other language) code just what the program is supposed to do. Comments supplement the limited powers of expression of computer languages and explain the underlying algorithm, assumptions, limitations, and motivations of a program. Comments comprise part of the program documentation. Especially as programs become large and complex (some contain thousands of statements), comments are an indispensible aid to revealing what a

---

[4]There are also exceptions here. This depends on your local computer installation.

program is supposed to do. But they are suprisingly helpful even with "simple" programs.

Two of the special ways in which comments should be used in every program are as follows: (i) the porpose of each program should be stated at the beginning; and (ii) the use of each variable in a program should be explained by a separate comment -- this set of comments is often referred to as the "variable dictionary." Fig. 2.4 shows both types of comments incorporated into a program. The simplicity of this program does not allow the full value of the variable dictionary to be revealed. However, with larger programs one of the major causes of errors and frustration is failure to have a clear, consistent role for each variable. Creating a variable dictionary forces you to decide the exact purpose of every variable and serves as a record of your decision, so that each variable will be used consistently throughout program development.

```
SECOND:  PROCEDURE OPTIONS(MAIN);
         /*PROGRAM TO COMPUTE SUM OF 2 INTEGERS*/
         DECLARE FIRST_NUMBER FIXED(5,0)/*1ST NUMBER FROM DATA*/,
            SECOND_NUMBER FIXED(5,0)/*2ND NUMBER FROM DATA*/,
            TOTAL FIXED(5,0)/*SUM OF 2 NUMBERS*/;
         GET LIST (FIRST_NUMBER,SECOND_NUMBER);
         TOTAL = FIRST_NUMBER + SECOND_NUMBER;
         PUT DATA (FIRST_NUMBER,SECOND_NUMBER,TOTAL);
         END SECOND;
```

Fig. 2.4 Program Containing Comments and a GET LIST Statement

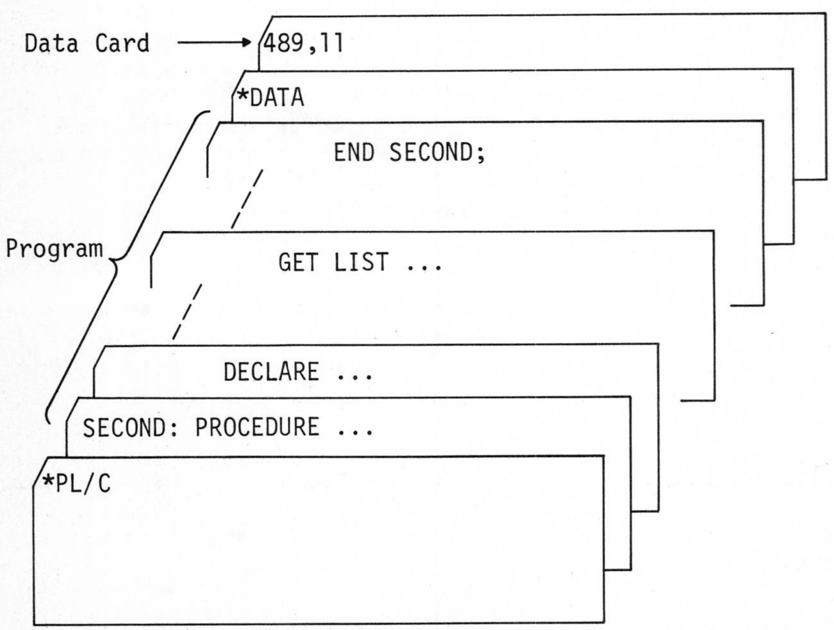

Fig. 2.5 A Card Deck Containing a Data Card

2.10 THE GET LIST STATEMENT

The problem solved by the program in Fig. 2.2(b) is much too restrictive[5] -- it will only find the sum of 3 and 4. Should we wish to use it to find the sum of 489 and 11 we would have to change two of its statements (3 and 4). A slightly more useful program would be one which could find the sum of <u>any</u> two integers.

The program shown in Fig. 2.4 solves this more general problem. <u>Each</u> time such a program is executed, it must be informed which two numbers are to be added during this particular execution. This communication of values involves some action on the parts of both (i) the program and (ii) the user who submits the program for execution.

The program must explicitly request values to be entered from the outside world by executing a GET statement. The GET LIST statement in line 6 of Fig. 2.4 for example, requests that two values be "read in" and stored in variables FIRST_NUMBER and SECOND_NUMBER, respectively.

On the other hand, the user must specify which values are to be entered when the GET LIST statement is executed. Such values, supplied from "outside" the program, are called <u>data</u> and are usually recorded (keypunched) on <u>data cards</u>. The control card *DATA in Fig. 2.5 indicates that the cards which follow are not properly part of the PL/I program, but rather contain data for use during the current execution of the program.[6] The values themselves are recorded on subsequent cards (last card of Fig. 2.5). In this example, locations FIRST_NUMBER and SECOND_NUMBER would receive the values 489 and 11, respectively, when the GET LIST statement is executed.

In general, great quantities of data may be supplied. One or more values, separated by blanks and/or commas, are punched on a card. All 80 columns of a data card may be used, and there may be as many data cards as required to hold all the values. The numbers on data cards are considered to be arranged in one continuous <u>stream</u>, with the first value on any card considered to follow the last (rightmost) value on the preceding card (if any).

The general form of the GET LIST statement is:

```
GET LIST (<single variable>);
```

or

```
GET LIST (<list of variables>);
```

There may be several GET LIST statements executed in a program. Each time a GET LIST is executed, enough consecutive values are extracted from the stream of data to supply a new value for every member of the variable list. Every execution of a GET LIST statement begins taking

---

[5]In fact it is too simple to bother doing on a computer. An amazing number of problems are better solved by hand. However, since this program does serve some pedagogical purpose, we will continue to discuss it.

[6]As promised in section 2.1, the other <u>control card</u> *DATA is now revealed. Like *PL/C it is punched in columns 1-5 of a separate card and is not considered part of the PL/C language.

values from the place in the data stream where the previous GET LIST (if any) left off. That is, the data values are obtained consecutively according to their order in the stream, and no data value is ever "read in" a second time. The GET LIST statement stores the values it obtains from data cards into the variables in the order in which the variables appear in its variable list.

Consider the following example to GET values for the variables I, J, K, and L from two data cards.

```
GET LIST (I,J);
GET LIST (K,L);
     .
     .
     .
6,11,48          1st data card
38               2nd data card
```

After execution of both GET LIST statements the variables will have these values:

I	6	J	11	K	48	L	38

Exactly the same result occurs from either of the following configurations:

```
GET LIST (I,J,K,L);
 .
 .
 .
6                    1st data card
11  48               2nd data card
38                   3rd data card
```

or

```
GET LIST (K,L);
GET LIST (J,I);
 .
 .
 .
48,38                1st data card
11  6                2nd data card
```

2.11 REVIEW OF RULES

1. The process of solving problems with a computer involves the following steps:

   i) devise a solution procedure,

   ii) refine this procedure into an algorithm,

   iii) express this algorithm in a programming language,

   iv) transcribe this program onto punched cards, as well as producing the required control cards and data cards,

   v) submit this deck for execution on the computer,

vi) examine the results of execution, and if unsatisfactory, return to an early step in an attempt to remedy the difficulty.

2. Every PL/C job submitted to the computer must have a *PL/C control card. If the job requires data cards, these must be placed after the *DATA card. In general a PL/C job is organized as:

```
*PL/C
        ⎫ PL/C
        ⎬ program
        ⎭ statements
*DATA
        ⎫ data
        ⎭ cards          (optional)
```

3. Every PL/I program must begin with a PROCEDURE statement and end with an END statement. The general form of the main PROCEDURE statement is

   <entry-name>: PROCEDURE OPTIONS (MAIN);

   The END statement has the form

   END <entry-name>;

4. Variable names

   i) must begin with a letter of the alphabet or one of the special characters $, # or @;

   ii) may be up to 31 characters in length; and

   iii) may only be made up of any combination of the letters of the alphabet, the digits 0 to 9, and $, #, @ or _.

5. The entry-name of a main procedure may be constructed according to the rules for variable names except that it may not exceed <u>seven</u> characters. An entry-name is always followed by a colon (:).

6. All variables in a program should be DECLAREd, namely,

   DECLARE (<list of variables>) <attributes>;

   or

   DECLARE <single variable> <attribute>;

   or

   DECLARE <list of variable-attribute pairs>;

7. The assignment statement has the form:

   <variable> = <arithmetic expression>;

   The arithmetic expression is first evaluated, and then this value replaces the previous contents of the indicated variable.

8. The input statement has the form:

   GET LIST (<list of variables>);

   or

   GET LIST (<single variable>);

9. The output statement has the form:

```
PUT DATA (<list of variables>);
PUT DATA (<single variable>);
```

10. All PL/I statements must end with a semi-colon (;).

11. PL/I statements may be recorded on cards only from column 2 to column 72 inclusive. There should be at most one statement per card; however, a statement may extend over several cards.

12. Data may be recorded anywhere on a data card. Individual data items must be separated by blanks or commas or both.

These rules are a skeleton on which we shall build. Some of them will be enhanced as we progress, but none of them will be fundamentally changed. They should be thoroughly understood before proceeding.

2.12 REVIEW PROBLEM

Suppose your friend Max has conjectured that two squares with sides of length a and b, respectively, have a combined (total) area equal to the area of one square with sides of length (a + b), as shown in Fig. 2.6.

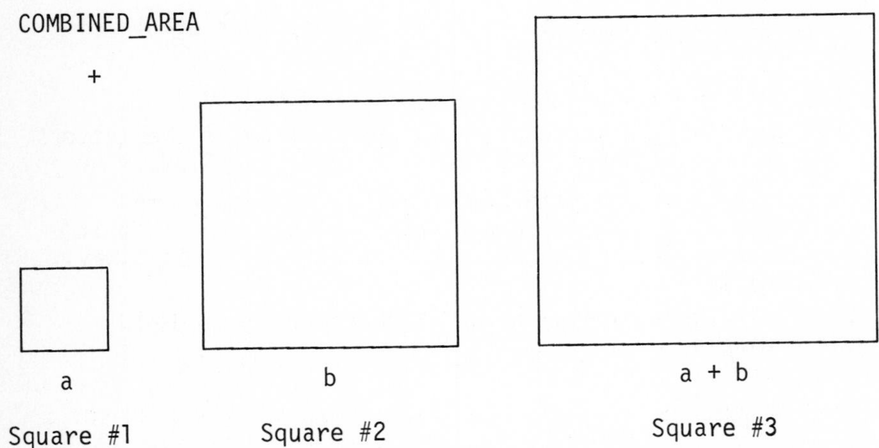

Fig. 2.6 The Three Squares of Max.

Your intuition (developed during one or more years of grade 10 geometry) convinces you that Max is wrong. Since you have forgotten how to manage mathematical proofs, you offer a counter example (an instance where his conjecture does not work). Unfortunately, Max mistrusts your calculations and even more foolishly will believe only the output of a computer. Poor Max does not realize that the computer is ever obedient to the human programmer, and its output is no better than the human's solution to a problem. However, rather than lecturing him on the dangers of computer deification and the evils of computer tyranny, you decide to humor him just this once by writing a program to provide a counterexample.

As always, begin by analyzing your problem. In order to persuade Max, your program should yield two numbers: (i) the combined areas of two squares, square #1 and square #2, having sides a and b, respectively; and (ii) the area of a square #3 with sides (a+b). Since both of these numbers are ultimately derived from the values of a and b, the solution may be structured as follows:

```
1.    obtain values for a and b;
2.    compute and display the "combined area" of squares
         #1 and #2;
3.    compute and display the area of square #3;
4.    end.
```

Step 2 needs elaboration. Even the wording of step 2 suggests the next level of decomposition:

```
2.1   compute the combined area of squares #1 and #2;
2.2   display the combined area of squares #1 and #2;
```

The computation (step 2.1) involves finding the areas of two other squares and adding these areas. Hence:

```
2.1.1 compute area of square #1;
2.1.2 compute area of square #2;
2.1.3 add these areas;
```

Turning to step 3 we have:

```
3.1   find area of square #3;
3.2   display the area of square #3;
```

Combining these steps, the overall solution is then:

```
1.     obtain values for a and b;
2.1.1  find area of square #1  (side a);
2.1.2  find area of square #2  (side b);
2.1.3  find combined area;
2.2    display combined area;
3.1    find area of square #3  (side a+b);
3.2    display area of square #3;
4.     end.
```

After reviewing this solution, we can see no loopholes which could hinder us from convincing Max, and so we write down the algorithm in PL/I. In order to write the program we must choose names, remember to declare variables, and follow the rules of PL/I for constructing statements. We must also select values for a and b. However, just in case the set of values we choose fails to disprove Max's conjecture, we would like to execute the program another time using different values for a and b. Thus we do not assign particular values to a and b within the program. Instead we will use the GET statement to obtain values from a data card, so that if a second try is necessary we need only supply a different data card without altering the program. The program corresponding to our algorithm is then:

```
UNDOMAX: PROCEDURE OPTIONS (MAIN);
       /*GIVEN TWO SQUARES WITH SIDES OF LENGTH A AND B, DOES
       THEIR COMBINED AREA EQUAL THE AREA OF A SQUARE WITH SIDE
       A+B?*/
       DECLARE
          A FIXED(5,0), /*SIDE OF SQUARE #1*/
          AREA#1 FIXED(5,0), /*AREA OF SQUARE #1 */
          B FIXED(5,0), /*SIDE OF SQUARE #2 */
          AREA#2 FIXED(5,0), /*AREA OF SQUARE #2*/
          COMBINED_AREA FIXED(5,0), /*AREA OF SQUARES #1 AND #2 */
          AREA#3 FIXED(5,0); /*AREA OF SQUARE WITH SIDE A+B */
       GET LIST(A,B);
       AREA#1=A**2;
       AREA#2=B*B;
       COMBINED_AREA=AREA#1+AREA#2;
       PUT DATA(COMBINED_AREA);
       AREA#3=(A+B)**2;
       PUT DATA(AREA#3);
       END UNDOMAX;
```

Note how B was multiplied by itself in the computation of AREA#2. Of course this is algebraically equivalent to B**2. Also note that parentheses are required in the statement which computes AREA#3. However, this could also have been written

```
AREA#3=(A+B)*(A+B);
```

All that remains now is to keypunch the procedure, supply control cards and a data card, execute the job, and gloat at Max. Try 11 and 24 as values for a and b:

```
*PL/C
 UNDOMAX:  PROCEDURE
                    } remainder
                    } of program
           END UNDOMAX;
*DATA
11,24
```

Incidentally, the algebraic solution of this problem is preferable to using a computer. If a and b are the sides of the two small squares, then their combined area is $a^2 + b^2$. Max claims that this number always equal $(a+b)^2 = a^2+2ab+b^2$. However, asserting that $a^2+b^2 = a^2+2ab+b^2$ implies that $0 = 2ab$, which means that either $a=0$ or $b=0$.

2.13 EXERCISES

Assume all variables in this section have been DECLAREd as FIXED(5,0).

2.1 What values will be printed by each of the sections of code?

```
(i)   N = 1;
      N = 2;
      N = N+1;
      PUT DATA (N);
```

```
(ii)  K = 12;
      L = 4;
      M = 3;
      N = K/L/M;
      PUT DATA (N);
```

```
(iii) K = 5;
      L = 2;
      M = K/L;
      PUT DATA (M);
```

```
(iv)  K = 5;
      L = 2;
      M = K/L*L;
      PUT DATA (M);
      M = (K/L)*L;
      PUT DATA (M);
```

```
(v)   J = 10;
      K = 12;
      L = 2;
      M = 8;
      N = (J+(K*L)-M+J)*M/(K-J)-M**L;
      PUT DATA (N);
```

2.2 What values will be stored in the variables if the statement

```
GET LIST (FIRST,SECOND,SECOND, FIRST);
```

reads data from the data card:

```
13,14,15,16,17
```

2.3 If the statement

```
GET LIST (SECOND,FIRST,THIRD);
```

caused the following values to be stored

FIRST	19
SECOND	38
THIRD	24

(a) in what order did these values appear on the data card?

(b) Display the results of executing PUT DATA (THIRD,FIRST,SECOND);

2.4 Which of the following statements contains an error? Explain the error.

```
(i)    A = A+1;
(ii)   B = (C) + (N/Q);
(iii)  B+C = D;
(iv)   GET LIST (A,(B+C),D);
(v)    PUT DATA X;
(vi)   X = Y,Z;
(vii)  GET LIST (Y,Z);
(viii) N = (M+N);
```

2.5 The following program is supposed to compute and print the squares of the first three natural numbers. Why does it fail to do so? How would you correct it so that it works properly?

```
SQUARES:  PROCEDURE OPTIONS (MAIN);
          DECLARE (NUM,NUM_SQ) FIXED(5,0);
          NUM = 1;
          NUM_SQ = NUM*NUM;
          NUM = NUM+1;
          NUM_SQ = NUM*NUM;
          NUM = NUM+1;
          NUM_SQ = NUM**2;
          PUT DATA (NUM_SQ);
          END SQUARES;
```

2.6 Design an algorithm and write a program to separate a three-digit number into its component digits and compute their sum. For example, if the number is 456, then the sum of the digits is 4+5+6 = 15.

2.7 Design an algorithm and write a program to inspect a three-digit number and print out the number together with the number formed by reversing its digits. For example, if the number is 456 you should produce 456 and 654.

<u>Hint</u>: avoid numbers ending in zero or double zero.

Chapter 3 Repetitive and Alternative Execution

While it would not be worth the effort to write a program for adding one pair of integers, you might consider writing one to find the sum of ten thousand pairs of integers. This problem lies more in the realm of the computer than do the problems of Chapter 2, since one of the computer's great strengths is its ability to repeat a set of instructions over and over again.

It is probably fair to say that most programs perform relatively simple calculations but repeat these calculations again and again on volumes of data which are too large for human processors to cope with effectively. Recall how the algorithms of Chapter 1 also involved repeating some basic process, such as making a mortgage payment or inspecting a ballot in order to update a vote total. This chapter introduces some of the features in PL/I which enable you to program algorithms of this type. In particular, you can request that certain sequences of PL/I statements be repeated until a sufficient number of repetitions has occurred. However, the need to know when to stop the repetitions means that you must be able to ask whether all the ballots have been counted or whether your debt to the bank has been paid. Therefore the first topic to consider is how one asks such questions in PL/I.

3.1 RELATIONAL OPERATORS

One way to "phrase a question" in PL/I involves comparing two numeric values. For example, you could keep asking whether your current debt to the bank is greater than 0. The phrase "is greater than" is an example of a <u>relational operator</u> and describes the way in which two numbers are being compared. Here the two numbers are current debt and 0. There are several other relational operators. You could have asked whether your current debt "is equal to" 0, or perhaps whether it "is less than or equal to" 500 dollars. PL/I uses special symbols to represent its relational operators, as shown in Fig. 3.1. For example, if your current debt is recorded in a variable named DEBT, then your program could determine whether your debt is greater than 0, by using the expression:

DEBT > 0

in the proper context.

PL/I SYMBOL	MATHEMATICAL SYMBOL	MEANING	
=	=	is equal to	
¬=	≠	is not equal to	
<	<	is less than	
>	>	is greater than	
<=	≤	is less than or equal to	equivalent
¬>	≯	is not greater than	
>=	≥	is greater than or equal to	equi- valent
¬<	≮	is not less than	

Fig. 3.1 Relational Operators in PL/I

Note the similarity between the symbols used by PL/I and those used in mathematics. The only "unfamiliar" symbol may be ¬ which represents "not." Also note that this use of an = sign as a relational operator causes no value to be assigned to a variable and is much different than the "active" role of = in an assignment statement. The intended use will be clear from the context.

Any particular comparison of two values, such as

DEBT > 0

is called a <u>logical expression</u> and has only one of two possible outcomes: true or false. At any one time, either your current debt is greater than 0 or else it isn't. The statement that 35 is less than 27, written 35 < 27, is either true or false. (This logical expression happens to be permanently false.) There is no third alternative, no "maybe true."

Thus, every logical expression itself has a value of either true or false, which is quite different from the two arithmetic values being compared. You should verify that the logical expressions shown in Fig. 3.2 indeed have the values shown.

VARIABLE	VALUE
I	3
J	4
K	5

LOGICAL EXPRESSION	VALUE
I ¬= J	true
I <= K	true
J > 6	false
K >= 5	true
9 < J	false
I = J-2	false
(2*J) = (I+K)	true

Fig. 3.2 Values for Some Logical Expressions

What makes logical expressions useful in PL/I is their ability to compare the current values of variables or arithmetic expressions during execution. The result of any particular comparison is, of course, either true or false, and this outcome can be used to select alternate courses of action within a program. As long as your debt really is greater than 0, you must keep making payments. Once your debt no longer is greater than 0, you may cease paying. In other words, payments should continue being made as long as the logical expression

DEBT > 0

remains true. Once the value of variable DEBT has been reduced to 0 or less, the logical expression becomes false.

Since logical expressions often determine the conditions under which some process may occur or be repeated, logical expressions will often be called conditions.

3.2 REPETITIVE EXECUTION AND THE DO WHILE STATEMENT

Since repeating a group of instructions is such a common feature of algorithms and therefore of programs, one of the most important statements in PL/I is DO WHILE, which governs such repetitive actions. This is the first PL/I statement encountered so far, which can divert the flow of control at execution time from its conventional sequential course and cause control to flow through some other group of instructions.

The DO WHILE statement tells the computer to repeatedly execute a subsequent group of statements while some condition remains true. An END statement is used to indicate the end of this group, i.e., how many statements are subject to repetition. The general form of this construction is:

```
<label>:  DO WHILE (<condition>);
             ( statements to   )
             ( be executed     )
             ( while the       )  range
             ( condition is    )
             ( true            )
          END <label>;
```

A *label* is simply a name of your own invention which is used to identify a statement and is separated by a colon (:) from the statement it identifies. The label on the DO WHILE and an identical label following the corresponding END serve the same purpose as did entry names on a pair of matching PROCEDURE and END statements. The major difference is that a label is not limited to seven characters. The label after the END indicates just what is being "ended." The following is a more concrete example, using a specific label, which might appear within the program to simulate mortgage payments:

```
                 .
                 .
                 .
PAYMENT:  DO WHILE (DEBT > 0);
             ( statements to do
             ( bookkeeping for
             ( a single
             ( mortgage payment
          END PAYMENT;
                 .
                 .
                 .
```

On encountering the DO WHILE statement during execution, the logical expression within the parentheses is first evaluated. If its value is true, then all statements between the DO WHILE and its corresponding END statement are executed. Then *control transfers back up to the DO WHILE statement*! The entire process, including testing of the condition is then repeated and will continue to be repeated as long as the condition remains true. Presumably, some execution of these statements will eventually make the condition false. On the next execution of the DO WHILE, its false value will be detected, and control will skip to the first statement following the matching END. All statements following DO WHILE and preceding its corresponding END are said to be within the *range* of the DO WHILE, and the transfer of control back to the DO WHILE statement forms a *loop*. The execution of the DO WHILE loop is shown pictorially in Fig. 3.3.

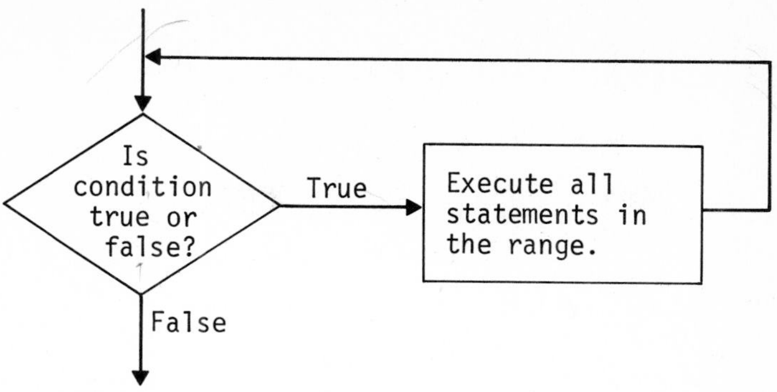

Fig. 3.3 Execution of the DO WHILE Loop

Three points about the DO WHILE loop must be emphasized. First, it requires an END statement to indicate the extent of the range of the loop. (We will eventually encounter even more uses for the END statement.) A more important point concerns the logical expression attached to the DO WHILE. Flow of control can only enter the loop if the expression is true, but, as can be seen from Fig. 3.3, <u>it will remain in this loop as long as the condition remains true.</u>[1] It follows then that you must do something <u>inside</u> the range to modify the value of the condition if you ever hope to stop the repetitions. The situation is analogous to a spacecraft in orbit. The ship will remain in orbit unless someone fires an engine to alter its trajectory and get it out. The third point is that there is only one way in and one way out of the loop.[1] In fact, the DO WHILE statement itself serves as both entry point and exit point. The condition is tested before and after every execution of the range (including the last).

Though other means exist to control repetitive execution, by using DO WHILE you will minimize your difficulties in understanding the flow of control in programs. More importantly, you will be able to write programs which will be clear and less susceptible to errors.

3.2.1 An Example Using DO WHILE

Suppose you make fifty stock transactions every day. The net dollar profit or loss on each transaction is recorded by a signed integer on a data card (a positive integer for profit, negative for loss). We want a program which will compute the total profit for one day, i.e., add together the fifty signed integers from data cards.

---

[1]At least this is true as long as our guidelines are observed, and your programs remain "structured."

As a first stab, we might try the following (correct) algorithm:

1. obtain 50 values from data cards;
2. add these 50 values together;
3. display the result;
4. end.

Unfortunately this algorithm will require all 50 values to be in memory locations simultaneously. The corresponding program will therefore require at least 50 different variable names, not to mention having long, unwieldy statements.

A much neater approach is to recognize that the same process is being repeated 50 times. A single application of this process involves two things:

1. obtain a value for one transaction;
2. add this value to a running total;

This suggests the need for only two variables: one to hold the value for the current transaction; and one to represent the total. Furthermore, since a total must have some initial value in order to add the <u>first</u> transaction value to it, the total must be explicitly initialized to 0. The following algorithm results from these considerations:

```
1.    initialize the total to 0;
2.    repeat (the remainder of level 2) 50 times;
2.1      obtain a value for one transaction;
2.2      add this value to the total;
3.    display total;
4.    end.
```

This algorithm still requires some refinement to explain just how one goes about implementing step 2. One method would be to maintain a count of how many values had been processed so far, i.e., after processing each value, increase the count by one. The processing would then continue as long as the count was less than 50 (the eventual number of values to be processed). Of course this count should also be initialized to 0, to reflect the fact that no values have been obtained when the processing begins. Application of this technique yields the algorithm shown in Fig. 3.4(a) and the program shown in Fig. 3.4(b).

3.2.2 Use of Counters

Notice in Fig. 3.4 that the value of the DO WHILE condition depends on the value of the variable COUNT. As long as COUNT is less than 50, the condition is true and the program will continue in the loop The only way out of the loop is to make the value of COUNT at least 50, and this is being done by adding 1 to the value of COUNT <u>every</u> time through the loop. If this line had been left out, then the program might continue in the loop forever, were it not for other problems this phenomenon would cause.

```
1.1   initialize total to 0;
1.2   initialize count to 0;
2.    repeat (remainder of level 2) while count <50;
2.1      obtain value for one transaction;
2.2      add this value to total;
2.3      increase count by 1;
3.    display total;
4.    end.
```

Fig. 3.4(a) Algorithm to Add Fifty Values

```
             /* FIGURE 3.4(B) */
FIFTY:   PROCEDURE OPTIONS (MAIN);

         /* A PROGRAM TO READ AND ADD FIFTY VALUES */

         DECLARE
            TOTAL FIXED (5,0), /* TOTAL OF FIFTY VALUES */
            COUNT FIXED (5,0), /*NO. VALUES SUMMED SO FAR*/
            VALUE FIXED (5,0); /* CURRENT VALUE */

         /* INITIALIZE TOTAL AND COUNT */

         TOTAL = 0;
         COUNT = 0;

         /* LOOP TO PROCESS FIFTY VALUES */

LOOP:    DO WHILE (COUNT < 50);
            GET LIST (VALUE); /* OBTAIN A VALUE */
            TOTAL = TOTAL + VALUE; /* ADD TO TOTAL */
            COUNT = COUNT + 1; /* INCREMENT COUNTER */
         END LOOP;

         PUT DATA (TOTAL); /* DISPLAY TOTAL */

         END FIFTY;
```

Fig. 3.4(b) Program to Implement the Algorithm in Fig. 3.4(a)

The variable COUNT in this example is known as a counter (because of its role, not because of its name which was chosen to reflect its role). Its value at any point in time is equal to the number of times that some action has been performed. In this case, the "current" value of COUNT is the number of values which have been incorporated into the total.

Recalling Section 1.4, all counters in a program must be set to some initial value, usually 0 or 1. The decision to initialize the counter to 0 or to 1 often depends on the answer to one question: "Do you wish to count the things you have done or the things you are going to do?" If you wish to count the things you have done, then in the beginning you have done nothing, and the counter must be set to 0, as was done in Fig. 3.4.

On the other hand, if you prefer to let COUNT indicate which pair of variables is <u>about to be processed</u>, then COUNT should be initialized to 1, since you presumably start with transaction number 1. Since you still want to include the fiftieth value, you do not want to stop the repetitions when COUNT reaches 50. Rather you want to continue repetitions for every value of COUNT less than 51 (or equivalently for values less than <u>or equal to</u> 50). To further dramatize this, we show three equivalent control structures in Fig. 3.5. With so many possible alternatives, it is extremely important to have a clear and consistent role for each variable in your program. This is a good place to emphasize the importance of the variable dictionary for recording what you do intend each variable to represent.

```
         COUNT=0;/*THE NUMBER OF VALUES PROCESSED*/
LOOP_1:  DO WHILE (COUNT <50);
                   }
                 range
                   }
            COUNT=COUNT+1;
         END LOOP_1;


         COUNT=1;/*THE NUMBER OF THE VALUE ABOUT TO BE PROCESSED*/
LOOP_2:  DO WHILE (COUNT <51);
                   }
                 range
                   }
            COUNT=COUNT+1;
         END LOOP_2;


         COUNT=1;/*THE NUMBER OF THE VALUE ABOUT TO BE PROCESSED*/
LOOP_3:  DO WHILE (COUNT <=50);
                   }
                 range
                   }
            COUNT=COUNT+1;
         END LOOP_3;
```

Fig. 3.5 Logically Equivalent Control Structures

3.3 ALTERNATIVE EXECUTION WITH IF-THEN-ELSE

Suppose that you want more information about your 50 daily stock transactions than simply the net profit. You also want to know the total amount earned by your profitable stocks and the total amount lost by your unprofitable transactions. We shall call these quantities "total gain" and "total loss," respectively. Total gain is the sum of all the positive integers on the data cards, and total loss is the sum of all the negative integers. Consequently, the algorithm for computing these numbers must maintain two running totals: gain and loss. It will repeatedly obtain an individual value, decide whether it is positive or negative, and add this value to the appropriate total. Since net profit is merely the sum of these two totals (total loss is negative), it may therefore be computed after these first two totals have been established. The resulting algorithm is shown in Fig. 3.6.

```
1.1    initialize total gain and total loss to 0;
1.2    initialize count to 0;
2.     repeat (remainder of level 2) while count <50;
2.1       obtain value for one transaction;
2.2       if value is positive then
             add value to total gain;
2.3       otherwise
             add value to total loss;
2.4       increment count by 1;
3.     net profit is total gain + total loss;
4.     display total gain, total loss, and net profit;
5.     end.
```

Fig. 3.6 Algorithm I to Find Total Gain, Total Loss, and Net Profit from 50 Transactions

The most striking difference between this algorithm and the algorithm to find only net profit (Fig. 3.4(a)) is the choice between two alternative actions in steps 2.2 and 2.3. Considering 0 to be positive, we rewrite these steps below:

```
2.2   if value ≥ 0 then
         add value to total gain;
2.3   otherwise
         add value to total loss;
```

Notice that each possible value for a transaction is added to one total or the other -- but never to both. The decision about which total to update depends on the comparison between the current value and 0, which, of course, can be depicted by the PL/I logical expression:

```
VALUE >= 0
```

If the value of this logical expression is true, then the first alternative (updating the total gain) should be taken. Otherwise the expression is false, and the second alternative should be taken.

A construction called IF-THEN-ELSE in PL/I provides the ability to make just such decisions by executing one of two alternative statements, based on the truth or falsehood of a logical expression. Its general form is shown in Fig. 3.7.

General Form of IF-THEN-ELSE

```
IF <logical expression> THEN
        <statement #1>;
ELSE
        <statement #2>;
```

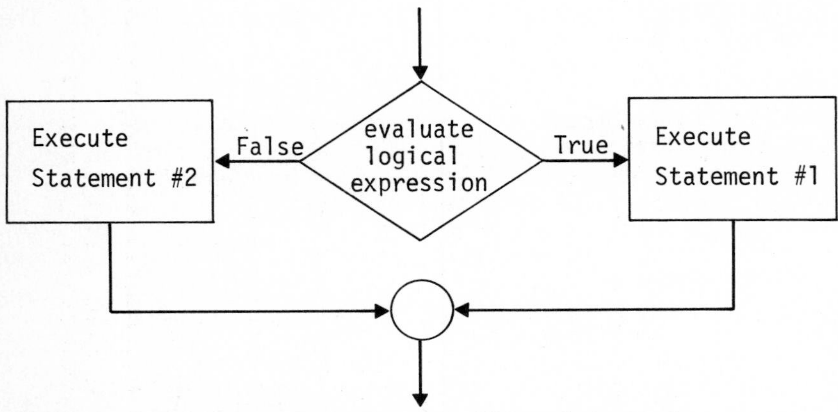

Fig. 3.7 How IF-THEN-ELSE Influences Flow of Control

Using this construction, steps 2.2 and 2.3 of our algorithm could be expressed as follows:

```
IF VALUE >= 0 THEN
   TOTAL_GAIN = TOTAL_GAIN + VALUE;
ELSE
   TOTAL_LOSS = TOTAL_LOSS + VALUE;
```

Note how closely this code resembles the original steps in the algorithm. ELSE in PL/I corresponds to the English word "otherwise." Fig. 3.8 shows the complete PL/I program for the algorithm of Fig. 3.6.

3.3.1 Using IF Without ELSE

IF and ELSE are actually two distinct statements in PL/I. The ELSE statement is always used in conjunction with a preceding IF statement to specify the alternative action to be taken in the case where the condition is not true. The IF statement, however, may occur without any subsequent ELSE. This form, called the IF-THEN construction, is a special case of IF-THEN-ELSE and is shown in Fig. 3.9.

```
                                    /* FIGURE 3.8 */
 1                         STOCK1: PROCEDURE OPTIONS(MAIN);

                                   /*DETERMINE TOTAL GAIN, TOTAL LOSS, AND NET PROFIT
                                     PROFIT FROM 50 STOCK TRANSACTIONS */

                                   DECLARE
 2    1        1                      GAIN FIXED(5,0), /*RUNNING TOTAL OF PROFITABLE SALES*/
                                      LOSS FIXED(5,0), /*RUNNING TOTAL OF UNPROFITABLE SALES*/
                                      NET_PROFIT FIXED(5,0), /*SUM OF GAIN AND LOSS*/
                                      VALUE FIXED(5,0), /*AMOUNT OF CURRENT TRANSACTION*/
                                      COUNT FIXED(5,0); /* NUMBER OF TRANSACTIONS PROCESSED*/

                                   /* INITIALIZE VARIABLES */

 3    1        1                   GAIN = 0;
 4    1        1                   LOSS = 0;
 5    1        1                   COUNT = 0;

                                   /* PROCESS FIFTY TRANSACTIONS */

 6    1        1           TRANSACTION:
                                   DO WHILE(COUNT < 50);
 7    1   1    1                      GET LIST (VALUE);

                                      /* CHECK FOR GAIN OR LOSS */

 8    1   1    1                      IF VALUE >= 0 THEN
 9    1   1    1                         GAIN = GAIN + VALUE;
                                      ELSE
10    1   1    1                         LOSS = LOSS + VALUE;
11    1   1    1                      COUNT = COUNT + 1;
12    1   1    1                   END TRANSACTION;

                                   /* COMPUTE NET PROFIT AND DISPLAY RESULTS */

13    1        1                   NET_PROFIT = GAIN + LOSS;
14    1        1                   PUT DATA(GAIN,LOSS,NET_PROFIT);

15    1        1                   END STOCK1;
```

General Form of IF-THEN

```
IF <logical expression> THEN
        <statement>;
```

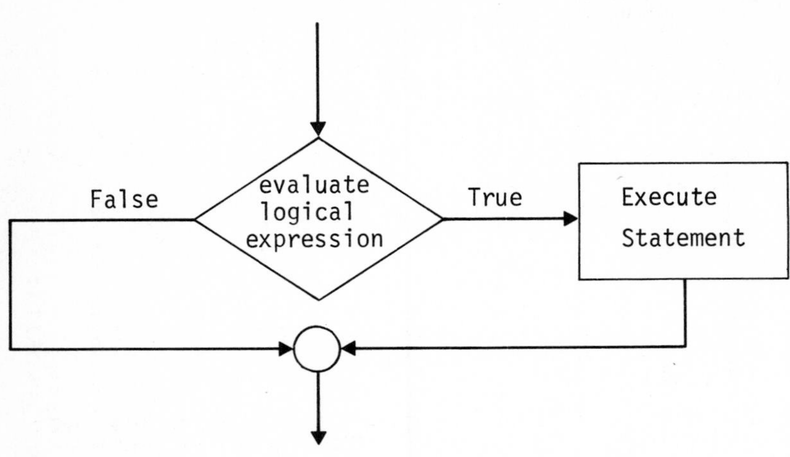

Fig. 3.9 How IF-THEN Influences Flow of Control

The IF-THEN construction is appropriate when one of the "alternatives" is to take no action at all. In other words, you may want to perform some action under certain conditions and simply bypass that action otherwise. In such cases the ELSE is superfluous.

As an example of its use, consider another approach to the calculation of total gain, total loss, and net profit. You may have noticed that any one of these quantities is merely the sum or difference of the other two. We can therefore derive net profit and total gain first (by maintaining two running totals), then later take their difference to find total loss. This approach yields the algorithm of Fig. 3.10.

In step 2.2, each value gets added to net profit, regardless of its sign. Step 2.3 also adds the value to total gain, provided the value is positive. However, if the value is negative, it has no further effect within the loop. Thus step 2.3 can be expressed as an IF statement with no associated ELSE. Fig. 3.11 shows the program corresponding to the algorithm of Fig. 3.10.

3.3.2 An Example Using DO WHILE and IF-THEN-ELSE

The algorithm derived in Section 1.5, for computing the number and total amount of mortgage payments, can be directly rewritten in PL/I using the DO WHILE, IF, and ELSE statements. We suggest a careful comparison between the algorithm as presented in Section 1.5 and the PL/I version shown in Fig. 3.12. The only extra feature in the

```
1.1   initialize total gain and net profit to 0;
1.2   initialize count to 0;
2.    repeat (remainder of level 2) while count <50;
2.1      obtain value for one transaction;
2.2      add this value to net profit;
2.3      if value ≥ 0 then
            add this value to total gain;
2.4      increase count by 1;
3.    total loss is net profit - total gain;
4.    display total gain, total loss, and net profit;
5.    end.
```

Fig. 3.10 Algorithm II to Find Total Gain, Total Loss, and Net Profit

```
         /* FIGURE 3.11 */
STOCK2: PROCEDURE OPTIONS(MAIN);

        /*DETERMINE TOTAL GAIN, TOTAL LOSS, AND NET
          PROFIT FROM 50 STOCK TRANSACTIONS */

        DECLARE
           GAIN FIXED(5,0), /* TOTAL PROFITABLE SALES */
           LOSS FIXED(5,0), /*TOTAL UNPROFITABLE SALES*/
           NET_PROFIT FIXED(5,0), /* GAIN PLUS LOSS */
           VALUE FIXED(5,0), /* CURRENT TRANSACTION */
           COUNT FIXED(5,0); /*NO. TRANSACTIONS PROCESSED*/

        /* INITIALIZE VARIABLES */

        GAIN = 0;
        NET_PROFIT = 0;
        COUNT = 0;

        /* PROCESS FIFTY TRANSACTIONS */

TRANSACTION:
        DO WHILE(COUNT < 50);
           GET LIST (VALUE);
           NET_PROFIT = NET_PROFIT + VALUE;

           /* CHECK IF THIS IS A GAIN */

           IF VALUE >= 0 THEN
              GAIN = GAIN + VALUE;
           COUNT = COUNT + 1;
        END TRANSACTION;

        /* COMPUTE LOSS AND DISPLAY RESULTS */

        LOSS = NET_PROFIT - GAIN;
        PUT DATA(GAIN,LOSS,NET_PROFIT);

        END STOCK2;
```

Fig. 3.11 Program to Implement Algorithm II of Fig. 3.10

```
        /* FIGURE 3.12 */
PAYMENT:
    PROCEDURE OPTIONS (MAIN);

    /* A SIMPLIFIED MORTGAGE REPAYMENT CALCULATION.
       THIS PROGRAM IS NOT FINANCIALLY VIABLE BECAUSE
       INTEREST IS CALCULATED ON A MONTHLY AND NOT
       ON A DAILY BASIS. */

    DECLARE
       #PAYMENTS FIXED (5,0), /* NO. OF PAYMENTS */
       TOTAL FIXED (7,2), /* TOTAL PAID */
       PRINCIPAL FIXED(7,2), /* COST OF HOUSE */
       DOWN_PAYMENT FIXED (7,2), /* DEPOSIT */
       MONTHLY FIXED (7,2), /*REG. MONTHLY PAYMENT*/
       CURRENT_PAYMENT FIXED (7,2), /*CURRENT PAYMENT*/
       INTEREST FIXED (7,2), /* ANNUAL INTEREST RATE */
       BALANCE FIXED (7,2); /* UNPAID BALANCE */

    /* INITIALIZE VARIABLES */

    #PAYMENTS = 0;
    TOTAL = 0.0;

    /* READ COST,MONTHLY PAYMENT,ANNUAL INTEREST RATE,
       DEPOSIT AND SET UP INITIAL BOOK-KEEPING */

    GET LIST (PRINCIPAL,DOWN_PAYMENT,MONTHLY,INTEREST);
    PUT DATA (PRINCIPAL,DOWN_PAYMENT,MONTHLY,INTEREST);
    BALANCE = PRINCIPAL;
    BALANCE = BALANCE - DOWN_PAYMENT;
    TOTAL = TOTAL + DOWN_PAYMENT;

    /* PROCESS ALL PAYMENTS UNTIL PAID OFF */

SINGLE_PAYMENT:
    DO WHILE (BALANCE > 0);

       /* INTEREST FOR ONE MONTH CALCULATED AS
          1/12TH ANNUAL INTEREST */

       BALANCE = BALANCE + (INTEREST * BALANCE) / 12;

       /* CHECK FOR CASE WHERE LAST PAYMENT
          IS MORE THAN UNPAID BALANCE */

       IF MONTHLY < BALANCE THEN
          CURRENT_PAYMENT = MONTHLY;
       ELSE
          CURRENT_PAYMENT = BALANCE;

       /* REDUCE UNPAID BALANCE AND INCREASE
          PAYMENTS TO DATE. */

       BALANCE = BALANCE - CURRENT_PAYMENT;
       TOTAL = TOTAL + CURRENT_PAYMENT;
       #PAYMENTS = #PAYMENTS + 1;
    END SINGLE_PAYMENT;

    /* DISPLAY RESULTS */

    PUT DATA (#PAYMENTS,TOTAL);

    END PAYMENT;
```

Fig. 3.12 Program to Find Total Number of Mortgage Payments by Algorithm of Section 1.5

program is the PUT statement immediately following the GET statement. This displays the input values for the particular mortgage payment plan under investigation. When developing any program, it is a good idea to print all input values as soon as they have been obtained. This will help you decide whether errors are due to program logic problems or to improper data. In many applications, such as this one, these extra PUT statements are retained after the program is working correctly, since it is desirable to have information about input values anyway.

3.4 USE OF FLAGS

The DO WHILE condition can be compared to a traffic light which is either green or red. When the light is green the computer drives through the range, executes its statements, and returns to the DO WHILE. If the light is still green, the computer circles the block (range) again, but if red, then execution continues beyond the range.

A <u>flag</u> is a variable which takes on only two values, usually 0 and 1, and which may be used to simulate the traffic light. For example, consider a "flag" variable named FLAG, and let us associate the value 0 with green and 1 with red. Then the basic structure for repeating the loop while the light is green (FLAG is 0) might look like this:

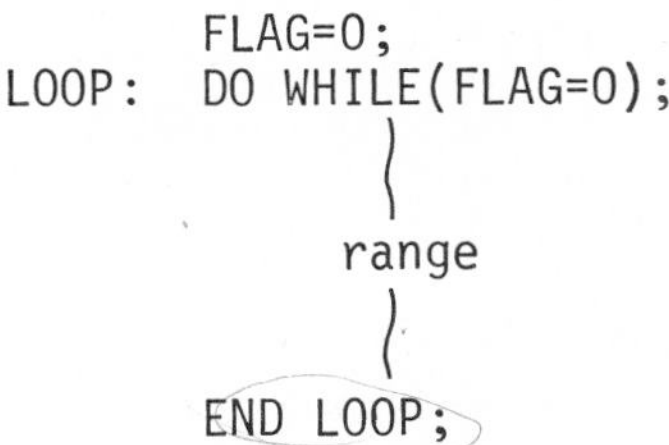

```
        FLAG=0;
LOOP:   DO WHILE(FLAG=0);
                 |
               range
                 |
        END LOOP;
```

Note that flags, like counters, should be initialized. Since a flag should contain either 0 or 1 whenever it is inspected, one of these values must be assigned before the first inspection. Again notice that some statement within the range must eventually cause the flag to become 1, so that the loop will not repeat forever. An example will be given shortly.

Returning to the problem of tabulating profits from stock transactions, we note that the solutions proposed so far had a serious limitation. They permitted only a predetermined number (e.g., 50) of transactions to be processed. These programs would be unusable if we had 5 or 10,000 or an unknown number of transactions to process.

One rather crude way of generalizing our program is to have it recognize the <u>last</u> number. If this could be done, then an arbitrary number of values could be processed and a counter would no longer be needed (at least for control purposes). After processing each value, we simply ask if that was the final one, and if so set a flag (i.e., turn on the red light) to stop subsequent looping.

Unfortunately, there is no sacred way of recognizing the final number. There is often nothing unique about your last data entry. However, it may be possible to include one extra value at the end, simply in order that it may be recognized. Whether this is even feasible depends on the particular application. For example, if you are certain that the value 99999 never occurs within your normal data, you might place an "extra" data card at the end of your deck, containing this special value. You could then watch for this card and set the flag using the statement:

```
IF VALUE = 99999
```

Fig. 3.13 shows part of a program which uses this idea in an (unsuccessful) attempt to find the gain, loss, and net profit for an arbitrary number of stock transactions.

```
              .
              .
              .
          FLAG = 0;
LOOP:     DO WHILE(FLAG = 0);
             GET LIST (VALUE);
             IF VALUE >= 0 THEN
                GAIN = GAIN + VALUE;
             ELSE
                LOSS = LOSS + VALUE;
             IF VALUE = 99999 THEN
                FLAG = 1;
          END LOOP;
              .
              .
              .
```

Fig. 3.13 Program Fragment Which Uses Special Last Card but Incorrectly Includes this Card as Valid Data

This approach has two major drawbacks. First, it cannot be used if your "normal" data could possibly include the value which you hope can uniquely identify the last card. Worse yet, your results will be <u>wrong</u>, since 99999, the artificial final value, will have been processed as if it represented a legitimate stock transaction.

Fortunately, this second drawback can be remedied by restructuring the algorithm to avoid processing the last value. (The first drawback will be dealt with in Section 3.5.) We proceed slowly here, since it is essential to understand how the algorithm is restructured.

Since we want to avoid processing the special "end of data" card, we should attempt to recognize it and set the flag (if appropriate) immediately after reading any data from the cards. As soon as this flag is set, we also wish to exit from the loop immediately. This implies that the <u>final</u> steps in the range of the DO WHILE are to read some data and set the flag if appropriate. Then, because the DO WHILE is the next statement executed, the flag will immediately be tested and subsequent execution of the loop abandoned if the flag is set.

Of course we still wish to "process" one transaction value each time through the loop. Also, we must read only one value on each execution of the loop, in order to keep input in step with the processing. These observations, combined with the argument in the previous paragraph, imply that the loop should be:

```
       repeat the following while flag is 0;
    1.       process a value;
    2.       obtain a value;
    3.       if this value is 99999 then set flag to 1;
```

Obviously, steps 1 and 2 cannot refer to the _same_ pair of numbers! It is impossible to process values which have not yet been read from data cards. Hence, these statements must be interpreted as follows:

```
       repeat the following while flag is 0;
    1.       process a previously obtained value;
    2.       obtain a new value;
    3.       if this value is 99999 then
                set flag to 1;
```

In other words, the value read at the end of one execution of the loop is the value to be processed on the _next_ execution of the loop (unless it sets the flag and causes the looping to stop).

The only problem remaining involves the _first_ execution of the loop, since a value must be available in order to be processed. The solution is to read this first value _before entering the loop_ for the first time, i.e., before the first execution of the DO WHILE. One final safeguard is to test even the "first" value obtained to see whether there was _any_ valid data and whether the loop should be entered at all. This makes the algorithm just a bit more foolproof and therefore general. The algorithm and corresponding program are shown in Fig. 3.14.

3.5 THE ENDFILE CONDITION

The introduction of a special card to mark the end of data was an artificial contrivance which is not always feasible. One reason may be the inability to guarantee that the chosen special value does not occur among the legitimate data. Another problem is sometimes the physical inability to append an artificial value to a collection of data. The most common problem, though, is simply forgetting to include the special card in the deck.

Fortunately there is a better way to realize when the end of data has been reached. The idea is simple: if you attempt to obtain another data value and fail to find one, then the end of data has been reached. Fig. 3.15 shows an algorithm to process an arbitrary quantity of data, incorporating this idea.

To code such an algorithm in PL/I, we must be able to test whether an attempted read (a GET statement) was unsuccessful. Facilities to do this will be presented later in this section.

First, however, consider what happens to a program which simply runs out of data without making any provision for this eventuality. Fig. 3.16 shows what happens to the program from Fig. 3.14(b) when no special termination card (9999 in this case) is supplied. After processing the final data card (the flag is still 0), the computer attempts to execute a GET statement to obtain more data even though there is no more data left! This inability to complete the GET

```
1.    initialize values;
2.    set flag to 0;
3.    read first value;
4.    if this value is 99999 then
         set flag to 1;
5.    repeat the following while flag is 0;
5.1      process the previous value;
5.2      obtain a new value;
5.3      if this value is 99999 then
            set flag to 1;
6.    display results;
7.    end.
```

Fig. 3.14(a) Algorithm to Process Arbitrary Number of Values, Using "Extra" Value of 99999 to Recognize End of Data

```
          /* FIGURE 3.14(B) */
STOCK3: PROCEDURE OPTIONS(MAIN);

        /* DETERMINE TOTAL GAIN, TOTAL LOSS AND NET PROFIT
           FROM AN ARBITRARY NUMBER OF STOCK TRANSACTIONS*/

        DECLARE
           GAIN FIXED(5,0), /* TOTAL PROFITABLE SALES */
           LOSS FIXED(5,0), /*TOTAL UNPROFITABLE SALES*/
           NET_PROFIT FIXED(5,0), /*SUM OF GAIN AND LOSS*/
           VALUE FIXED(5,0), /* CURRENT TRANSACTION */
           FLAG FIXED(5,0); /* USED TO STOP LOOPING*/

        /* INITIALIZE VARIABLES */

        GAIN = 0;
        LOSS = 0;
        FLAG = 0;

        /* READ FIRST TRANSACTION AND CHECK IF IT IS THE
           "SPECIAL" VALUE */

        GET LIST(VALUE);
        IF VALUE = 99999 THEN
           FLAG = 1;

        /* PROCESS UNTIL "SPECIAL" VALUE ENCOUNTERED */

TRANSACTION:
        DO WHILE(FLAG = 0);
           /* CHECK FOR GAIN OR LOSS */
           IF VALUE > 0 THEN
              GAIN = GAIN + VALUE;
           ELSE
              LOSS = LOSS + VALUE;
           GET LIST(VALUE); /* READ NEXT VALUE */
           IF VALUE = 99999 THEN /*IS IT "SPECIAL" VALUE?*/
              FLAG = 1;
        END TRANSACTION;

        /* COMPUTE NET PROFIT AND PRINT RESULTS */
        NET_PROFIT = GAIN + LOSS;
        PUT DATA(GAIN,LOSS,NET_PROFIT);

        END STOCK3;
```

Figure 3.14(b)

```
1.    set flag to 0;
2.    obtain first value;
3.    if attempt to find value was unsuccessful then
         set flag to 1;
4.    repeat while flag is 0;
4.1      process the previous value;
4.2      obtain a new value;
4.3      if attempt to find value was unsuccessful then
            set flag to 1;
5.    display results;
6.    end.
```

Fig. 3.15 Algorithm to Process an Arbitrary Number of Values, Using "Unsuccessful Read Attempt" to Recognize End of Data

```
STMT LEVEL NEST BLOCK MLVL  SOURCE TEXT

                                          /* FIGURE 3.16 */
  1                            STOCK4: PROCEDURE OPTIONS(MAIN);

                                       /* DETERMINE TOTAL GAIN, TOTAL LOSS AND NET PROFIT
                                          FROM AN ARBITRARY NUMBER OF STOCK TRANSACTIONS*/

  2    1          1                    DECLARE
                                          GAIN FIXED(5,0), /* TOTAL PROFITABLE SALES */
                                          LOSS FIXED(5,0), /*TOTAL UNPROFITABLE SALES*/
                                          NET_PROFIT FIXED(5,0), /*SUM OF GAIN AND LOSS*/
                                          VALUE FIXED(5,0), /* CURRENT TRANSACTION */
                                          FLAG FIXED(5,0); /* USED TO STOP LOOPING*/

                                       /* INITIALIZE VARIABLES */

  3    1          1                    GAIN = 0;
  4    1          1                    LOSS = 0;
  5    1          1                    FLAG = 0;

                                       /* READ FIRST TRANSACTION AND CHECK IF IT IS THE
                                          "SPECIAL" VALUE */

  6    1          1                    GET LIST(VALUE);
  7    1          1                    IF VALUE = 99999 THEN
  8    1          1                       FLAG = 1;

                                       /* PROCESS UNTIL "SPECIAL" VALUE ENCOUNTERED */

  9    1          1            TRANSACTION:
                                       DO WHILE(FLAG = 0);

                                          /* CHECK FOR GAIN OR LOSS */

 10    1    1     1                       IF VALUE > 0 THEN
 11    1    1     1                          GAIN = GAIN + VALUE;
 12    1    1     1                       ELSE
                                             LOSS = LOSS + VALUE;
 13    1    1     1                       GET LIST(VALUE); /* READ NEXT VALUE */
 14    1    1     1                       IF VALUE = 99999 THEN /*IS IT "SPECIAL" VALUE?*/
 15    1    1     1                          FLAG = 1;
 16    1    1     1                    END TRANSACTION;

                                       /* COMPUTE NET PROFIT AND PRINT RESULTS */

 17    1          1                    NET_PROFIT = GAIN + LOSS;
 18    1          1                    PUT DATA(GAIN,LOSS,NET_PROFIT);
 19    1          1                    END STOCK4;

***** ERROR IN STMT   13  END OF FILE REACHED. (EX02)
ABOVE ERROR IS FATAL.  PROGRAM IS STOPPED.
```

Fig. 3.16 Attempt to Implement Algorithm of Fig. 3.15 - Termination Card Missing

causes an error. Consequently, the following error message is printed:

ERROR IN STMT 13 END OF FILE REACHED. (EX02)

END OF FILE in this case means "end of data cards," since collections of data in a computer system are known as "files." Not knowing what else to do in this case, the system terminates your program as indicated by the message PROGRAM IS STOPPED.

You can prevent execution from stopping when data runs out simply by providing some alternative in that case. This is done by the statement:

ON ENDFILE (SYSIN) <statement specifying action to be taken>;

In our case, since the desired action is to set variable FLAG to 1 _as if_ a special end-of-data card had just been read, we would write:

ON ENDFILE (SYSIN) FLAG=1;

The statement, FLAG=1, is called an "ON-unit" and its absence in Fig. 3.16 gave rise to the second message:

ABOVE ERROR IS FATAL

ON-units say what to do whenever some exceptional condition occurs. In this case, the condition called ENDFILE is running out of data in the file (collection of data) called SYSIN. SYSIN happens to be the name of the file comprised by your data cards and stands for SYStem INput. Since exhausting input data is the only such condition considered until Chapter 12, you can take

ON ENDFILE (SYSIN) <statement>;

as a standard formula for now.

Armed with this statement, we can rewrite the general algorithm from Fig. 3.15 in PL/I. The result is shown in Fig. 3.17, and this can be taken as our standard form for any PL/I program which uses ON ENDFILE to halt a repetitive input process.

```
            .
            .
            .
        ON ENDFILE (SYSIN) FLAG=1;
        FLAG=0;
        GET first value;
  loop: DO WHILE(FLAG=0);
             ) code to process
             ) previously read value
           GET  next value;
        END loop;
            .
            .
            .
```

Fig. 3.17 General Form of an Input Process Which Halts When an Attempted GET is Unsuccessful

Note that the ON statement specifies what to do whenever any GET statement is unsuccessful anywhere in the program. Consequently the single ON statement in Fig. 3.17 implements both steps 3 and 4.3 from Fig. 3.15.

A program for tallying stock transactions, which also uses ON ENDFILE to set the flag, is shown in Fig. 3.18. The statement numbers in Fig. 3.18 show that this line is counted as two separate statements; statement 7 is not really missing after all.

The most important feature of ON statements is that their execution establishes a specific action to be taken at any time in the future when the condition happens to occur. Our particular ON statement says, in effect: "Whenever any future execution of any GET statement in this program fails because no more data values remain to be read, then set variable FLAG to 1 at that time (not now) and continue executing at the statement following the unsuccessful GET." Once an ON statement is executed, the alternative it provides to halting the program remains in effect for the duration of the program. It need not be reexecuted.

Contrast this with the action of IF and most other statements. The IF statement says to take some action (specified after THEN) at this point in time, provided some condition is currently true. However, once executed, a particular IF statement has no direct influence unless it is later reexecuted.

3.5.1 Finding Largest and Smallest Values

In order to demonstrate another application of flags and ON ENDFILE, we will attempt to find the largest value in a set of integers. Without knowing any special properties of the set, one has to inspect every value in the set before knowing which is the largest. The problem in a computer environment is that we often inspect the values in the set one at a time, and we do not wish to, or cannot, look back over all previously encountered values.

The strategy is to keep track of the largest value seen so far as we progress through the set. Each new value encountered is compared with the largest value seen prior to this one. If the current value is greater than this "largest" value, we now have a new candidate for largest value; we can forget the old one and need only remember the new one for future comparisons. On the other hand, if the current value is not greater, then the already recorded value still stands as the largest seen so far. When this comparison has been made for the final value, then the "largest value seen so far" will in fact be the largest value in the entire set. Finding the smallest value in a set is similar.

However, in order to get this algorithm started, there must be some initial candidate for largest value with which to make the first comparison. A suitable choice for an initial value would be the first member of the set to be inspected. After all, this is the largest value seen after looking at only one value. The comparisons then would begin with the second value in the set.

One resulting algorithm is shown in Fig. 3.19(a). However, step 3 requires knowledge of whether uninspected values remain in the set, in order to determine whether to obtain and compare another value. This is only possible if the size of the set is known in

```
STMT   SOURCE STATEMENT

                      /* FIGURE 3.18 */
   1  STOCK5: PROCEDURE OPTIONS(MAIN);

              /* DETERMINE TOTAL GAIN, LOSS
                 AND NET PROFIT FROM AN
                 ARBITRARY NUMBER OF STOCK
                 TRANSACTIONS */

              DECLARE
   2             GAIN FIXED(5,0),
                 LOSS FIXED(5,0),
                 NET_PROFIT FIXED(5,0),
                 VALUE FIXED(5,0),
                 FLAG FIXED(5,0);

              /* GAIN : TOTAL PROFITABLE SALES
                 LOSS : TOTAL LOSING SALES
                 NET_PROFIT : SUM OF GAIN AND LOSS
                 VALUE : CURRENT TRANSACTION
                 FLAG : END OF DATA FLAG */
              /* INITIALIZE VARIABLES */

   3          GAIN = 0;
   4          LOSS = 0;
   5          FLAG = 0;
   6          ON ENDFILE (SYSIN) FLAG = 1;

              /* READ FIRST VALUE */

   8          GET LIST(VALUE);

              /* PROCESS UNTIL NO MORE DATA LEFT */

   9  TRANSACTION:
              DO WHILE(FLAG = 0);

                 /* CHECK FOR GAIN OR LOSS */

  10             IF VALUE > 0 THEN
  11                GAIN = GAIN + VALUE;
                 ELSE
  12                LOSS = LOSS + VALUE;

                 /* TRY TO READ NEXT VALUE */

  13             GET LIST(VALUE);
  14          END TRANSACTION;

              /* COMPUTE NET PROFIT AND
                 PRINT RESULTS */

  15          NET_PROFIT = GAIN + LOSS;
  16          PUT DATA(GAIN,LOSS,NET_PROFIT);

  17          END STOCK5;
```

Fig. 3.18 Program Using ON ENDFILE to Implement Algorithm of Fig. 3.15

advance! If the algorithm is to inspect sets whose size is unknown, you must first attempt to obtain another value in order to find out if there remains another value. This consideration leads to the algorithm in Fig. 3.19(b). This algorithm is in the correct form for implementation with a flag variable and the ON ENDFILE statement. The corresponding program is shown in Fig. 3.20

3.6 PROGRAM STYLE AND DOCUMENTATION

Too many programmers ignore the fact that their programs must be intelligible to people as well as executable by machines. As a result, many programs, which may even be logically correct, remain undecipherable and therefore useless. Every program must be understandable to its author and to anyone wishing to use or modify it later. No matter how well a program may be understood today, by tomorrow some of its conventions and idiosyncracies will be forgotten. Consequently, you will save yourself and others hours of frustration if your program's "secrets" are clearly revealed. It is well worth the effort to arrange the statements in ways which reflect their logical relationships and to supplement them with ample documentation. Although program appearance and documentation have no effect on any particular execution, they have great influence on human readers and hence on the successful development and future use of your programs.

For example, consider the very simple program:

```
X:  PROCEDURE OPTIONS (MAIN);
    DECLARE (A,B,C)FIXED(5,0);
    C=1;
Y:  DO WHILE (C<=10);
    GET LIST (A);
    B=A*3;
    PUT DATA (A,B);
    C=C+1;
    END Y;
    END X;
```

The only thing we can tell (by poring through all the code) is that this program repeatedly multiplies some numbers by 3 and prints some results. It has no concrete meaning. Its purpose is hidden. We cannot even deduce anything from the name of the procedure. Contrast that program with the structurally identical version which was written with a human reader in mind, shown in Fig. 3.21.

This version uses the following clarifying devices:

(1) comments to explain the purpose of the procedure and the role of each variable (a "variable dictionary");

(2) self-explanatory variable names and labels;

(3) indentation of the range of the DO WHILE and of the parts of the DECLARE statement;

(4) blank lines (cards) to separate logically distinct sections of the program, which would otherwise have been visually congested.

```
1.    obtain 1st value from set;
2.    set largest equal to this first value;
3.    repeat while values remain to be obtained;
3.1      obtain next value from set;
3.2      if current value > largest (seen so far) then
            set largest equal to current value;
4.    display largest;
5.    end.
```

Fig. 3.19(a) Algorithm to Find Largest Value in a Set Whose Size is Known in Advance

```
1.    obtain 1st value from set;
2.    set largest equal to this first value;
3.    obtain next value from set;
4.    repeat while values remain to be compared;
4.1      if current value > largest (so far) then
            set largest equal to current value;
4.2      obtain next value from set;
5.    display largest;
6.    end.
```

Fig. 3.19(b) Algorithm to Find Largest Value in a Set Whose Size is not Known in Advance

```
            /* FIGURE 3.20 */
FINDMAX:PROCEDURE OPTIONS (MAIN);

        /* FIND AND DISPLAY THE LARGEST VALUE AMONG
        AN ARBITRARY NUMBER OF VALUES ON DATA CARDS*/

        DECLARE
           VALUE FIXED(5,0), /*MOST RECENT VALUE */
           MAX FIXED(5,0); /*LARGEST VALUE SO FAR */

        /* INITIALIZE FLAG AND SET ENDFILE CONDITION */

        FLAG = 0;
        ON ENDFILE(SYSIN) FLAG = 1;

        /* READ FIRST VALUE AND CONSIDER IT AS
           LARGEST SEEN SO FAR */

        GET LIST(VALUE);
        MAX = VALUE;

        /* CONTINUE READING AND PROCESSING VALUES */

        GET LIST(VALUE);

COMPARE:DO WHILE(FLAG = 0);
           IF VALUE > MAX THEN
              MAX = VALUE;
           GET LIST(VALUE);
        END COMPARE;

        /* DISPLAY LARGEST VALUE SEEN */

        PUT DATA(MAX);

        END FINDMAX;
```

Fig. 3.20 Program to Implement Algorithm of Fig. 3.19(b)

```
PAYROLL: PROCEDURE OPTIONS (MAIN);
         /* A PROGRAM TO COMPUTE GROSS WAGES AT
         THE RATE OF $3.00 PER HOUR WORKED FOR
         EACH OF 10 EMPLOYEES*/
         DECLARE HOURS FIXED(5,0),/*HOURS WORKED*/
            GROSS FIXED(5,0),/*GROSS PAY*/
            COUNT FIXED(5,0);/*WHICH OF THE 10
            EMPLOYEES IS UNDER CONSIDERATION*/

         COUNT=1;
COMPUTATION:
         DO WHILE (COUNT<=10);
            GET LIST (HOURS);
            GROSS=HOURS*3;
            PUT DATA (HOURS,GROSS);
            COUNT=COUNT+1;
         END COMPUTATION;

         END PAYROLL;
```

Figure 3.21

English text which is not broken down into chapters, sections, and paragraphs would be very difficult to read. Therefore rules for structuring prose were developed to make relationships between ideas more apparent to the reader and to highlight certain aspects of the writer's thoughts. Paragraphing conventions for program writing serve the same purpose. The conventions for indentation (3) and the separation of distinct sections of code with explanatory comments or blank lines (4) serve the same purpose. So that you may adopt them as your own, the stylistic conventions used throughout the book are summarized below:

1. All labels begin in column 2.
2. All statements which are not nested begin in column 10. If the label is too long to permit this, then the label should be placed on a separate card.
3. ALL DECLARE statements should be grouped at the beginning of the procedure in which they appear.
4. No more than one statement should be placed on one card. If a statement continues to more than one card, all continuation cards must be indented 3 columns from the original beginning column of the statement.

```
col. 2─┐       ┌─col. 10
       ↓       ↓
       LOOP:   DO WHILE(N < 20);
                  :
               END LOOP;
       LONGER_LABEL:
               DO WHILE(M < 40);
                  :
```

5. IF-THEN-ELSE statements should be coded as:

   i) THEN keyword on the same line as the IF and condition;
   ii) THEN clause begins on a new line indented 3 spaces;
   iii) ELSE keyword on a new line at the same level of indenting as the corresponding IF;
   iv) ELSE clause on a new line indented 3 spaces.

   e.g.
```
IF A>B THEN
   PUT LIST (A);
ELSE
   PUT LIST (B);
```

6. Each DO statement causes the current indenting level to be increased by 3, i.e., the range of each DO is indented 3 columns.

```
         ┌─col. 10
         ↓
LOOP:    DO WHILE(N < 20);
            PRODUCT = PRODUCT*N;
            N = N + 2;
         END LOOP;
```

7. END statements should be aligned under the DO, PROCEDURE, or BEGIN which they terminate, and they should bear the corresponding label or entry name.

3.7 PROGRAM DEVELOPMENT AND TESTING - I

When a program won't work, it is said to contain "bugs." Any attempt to repair an incorrect program is called <u>debugging</u>. The debugging techniques to be described here and in later chapters are all practical ways to carry out the final rule from Chapter 1: "Review and revise ...." Traditionally debugging has consumed the vast majority of program development time and has been the leading contributor to frustration, neurosis, and breakdown among programmers. However this need not be the case. As we preached in Chapter 1, careful, step-by-step, top-down solution of problems will usually lead to almost perfect programs. The best way to approach debugging is with "defensive programming" (as in defensive driving) so that any required repairs will be minor.

However, if you think your programs will never need debugging, you are mistaken (and you probably haven't tried programming yet). Mechanical errors and minor logical oversights are almost inevitable. Here, it is important to diagnose and repair errors in a sensible, careful way, just as it is advisable to write programs carefully in the first place.

3.7.1 Compile-Time Errors

Before undertaking a discussion of errors, it is necessary to understand just what PL/I does for you inside the computer. Surprisingly, the commands executed by the machine are actually not those of PL/I at all! Each type of computer has its own unique "machine language," and this is the only language which it can interpret. However machine language is so detailed and complicated that higher-level languages, such as PL/I, were developed to spare humans from this detail and to permit easier communication with the machines. To enable the computer to carry out the instructions of your program, special programs called compilers must first translate programs written in a high-level language into machine language.

Thus, when you submit a PL/I program to the computer, your job is processed in two stages:

(1) the PL/I compiler translates your PL/I program into an equivalent machine-language version; then

(2) this machine-language version of your program is executed by the computer.

These two stages are referred to as compile-time and run-time, (or execution time) respectively. As the compiler translates each PL/I statement, it also watches for superficial, mechanical errors. For example, it can tell when parentheses don't match, when an arithmetic expression is invalidly constructed, or (usually) when a "required" comma is missing. These are called "syntax errors," to distinguish them from the logic errors, such as dividing by 0, which will not be discovered until your program is executing. If the compiler detects an error, it then prints an error message on the listing immediately under the offending program statement. For example, if your program listing contains:

```
GET LIST (A BE);
ERROR SY06 MISSING COMMA
```

this indicates an invalidly constructed GET statement which you must correct. It probably also means that you forgot the comma between variables A and BE. However, the real problem may be an unintentional blank within the single variable ABE. Only you know which is really correct! Even for such simple problems you must use your head and not put all your trust in the compiler. Whatever the source of error though, these minor so-called compile-time errors should be your first concern. They will be indicated by messages within your listing, and they should all be readily repairable.

Obviously in computer programs details are very important. If you are not sure of the correction or if you fail to make the right modification on the first try, consult the error messages in Appendix C or a PL/I language manual for precise rules. Some of the most common mechanical errors to guard against are:

i) forgetting the semicolon at the end of each statement;

ii) inserting blanks or commas where they don't belong;

iii) omitting blanks, commas, or parentheses where they are required (Omitting the parentheses around the condition on a DO WHILE is especially common.);

iv) misspelling or mispunching (e.g., PROCEEDURE is wrong);

v) extending a statement beyond column 72 (Even though characters from columns 73-80 appear on the listing, they are ignored by the compiler and are therefore not properly included in the program.)

Since comments may be quite lengthy, they are especially prone to extending beyond column 72. If the closing marker, */, happens to lie beyond column 72, then everything in your program up to the next */ (if any) which does lie to the left of column 72 is erroneously considered part of the comment. A quick check can be made for this by scanning the statement numbers along the left hand side of the listing. Make sure that all your intended statements have statement numbers and that none were incorporated into comments.

Unlike PL/I, PL/C is designed to keep going until the errors become insurmountable. This means that it not only points out compile-time errors but even makes a provisional repair in an attempt to avoid stopping. Fortunately it indicates each repair it makes, so that the previous example would have generated an additional message:

```
                GET LIST(A BE);
        ERROR  SY06 MISSING COMMA
        PL/C USES  GET LIST(A,BE);
```

Once again, we caution that the repair made by PL/C might not be the appropriate modification. Do not be guided blindly by error messages. Use them primarily to determine where errors occur. Use your own judgement to make the correction. This is especially true when a long list (three or more) of error messages is printed beneath one statement. This indicates that PL/C had to make several assumptions -- with a higher chance of being wrong.

3.7.2 Other Compile-Time Diagnostic Services

PL/C also provides other diagnostic services. One is the attribute listing which appears immediately after the program listing as in Fig. 3.22. This list gives each variable and label appearing in the program in alphabetical order, together with their attributes. This list should be scanned to check for two things: (i) unexpected names, indicating misspellings or mispunchings; and (ii) unexpected attributes, indicating that a variable was not DECLAREd or was declared incorrectly.

In some installations a cross reference list also gives the statement numbers of all statements referring to each variable or label as in Fig. 3.22. This allows you to find the statements containing the misspellings. More important, it enables you to find every statement where a given variable may possibly be assigned a new value. This is useful in diagnosing "run-time errors," described in Section 3.7.3.

The program in Fig. 3.22 is an incorrect version of the "payroll" program from Section 3.6. Although no compile-time error messages appear, there are two mechanical errors in this program which can be found by perusing the attribute listing. First, note the "unexpected" variable name, GLOSS, which appears in statement 6. It is evidently a misspelling of GROSS. Also the attribute FLOAT(6) of variable

```
 STMT LEVEL NEST BLOCK MLVL  SOURCE TEXT

                                          /* FIGURE 3.22 */
    1                        PAYROLL:PROCEDURE OPTIONS(MAIN);

                                      /* DETERMINE GROSS PAY FOR 10 EMPLOYEES */

    2    1          1                 DECLARE
                                         GROSS FIXED(5,0) /*GROSS PAY*/,
                                         COUNT FIXED(5,0) /*NO. OF EMPLOYEE IN PROCESS*/;

    3    1          1                 COUNT = 1;
    4    1          1        LOOP:    DO WHILE (COUNT <= 10);
    5    1    1     1                    GET LIST(HOURS); /* READ HOURS WORKED */
    6    1    1     1                    GLOSS = HOURS * 3; /* HOURLY RATE IS $3.00 */
    7    1    1     1                    PUT DATA(HOURS,GROSS);
    8    1    1     1                    COUNT = COUNT + 1;
    9    1    1     1                 END LOOP;

   10    1          1                 END PAYROLL;
DCL NO.        IDENTIFIER                             ATTRIBUTES AND REFERENCES


    2           COUNT                                 AUTOMATIC,ALIGNED,DECIMAL,FIXED(5,0)
                                                      3,4,8,8

                GLOSS                                 AUTOMATIC,ALIGNED,DECIMAL,FLOAT(6)
                                                      6

    2           GROSS                                 AUTOMATIC,ALIGNED,DECIMAL,FIXED(5,0)
                                                      7

                HOURS                                 AUTOMATIC,ALIGNED,DECIMAL,FLOAT(6)
                                                      5,6,7

    4           LOOP                                  STATEMENT LABEL CONSTANT

    1           PAYROLL                               ENTRY,DECIMAL,FLOAT(6)

HOURS= 3.00000E+01     GROSS=        ?;       HOURS= 3.30000E+01     GROSS=        ?;       HOURS= 3.50000E+01
GROSS=        ?;       HOURS= 4.20000E+01     GROSS=        ?;       HOURS= 3.80000E+01     GROSS=        ?;
HOURS= 4.10000E+01     GROSS=        ?;       HOURS= 5.00000E+00     GROSS=        ?;       HOURS= 4.80000E+01
GROSS=        ?;       HOURS= 4.00000E+01     GROSS=        ?;       HOURS= 3.80000E+01     GROSS=        ?;


IN STMT    10  PRCGRAM RETURNS FROM MAIN PROCEDURE.

IN STMT    10  DYNAMIC FLOW TRACE:
            0000->0001     10*(0009->0004)        0004->0010         0010->0000

IN STMT    10  SCALARS AND BLOCK-TRACE:

***** MAIN PROCEDURE PAYROLL

GLOSS= 1.14000E+02     HOURS= 3.80000E+01     COUNT=       11        GROSS=        ?
```

Figure 3.22

HOURS suggests a problem with the DECLARE statement. In our case the variable HOURS was inadvertently omitted from the DECLARE. Whenever this happens, "default" attributes are assumed.

3.7.3 Run-Time Errors

The compiler can only check for syntax errors, i.e., invalid constructions. Far more subtle are the run-time errors, which are those which arise once your compiled program begins executing. For example, there is no way the compiler can know in advance whether your program will attempt to GET more data than is provided. Thus an END OF FILE error can occur only as a result of actually executing too many GET statements for the amount of data. Consequently, the messages reporting run-time errors are generated amongst the output at the end of the listing as the errors arise.

Not all run-time errors are indicated by ERROR messages. Furthermore, some run-time errors may be merely byproducts of uncorrected compile-time errors. For example, as the program in Fig. 3.22 is executed, the value printed out for the variable GROSS is a "?". This indicates that when the computer tried to find a value for GROSS, none was available -- the value of GROSS is said to be undefined. The reason is simply that GROSS was misspelled as GLOSS in the line immediately preceding the PUT statement. As a result, the erroneous variable GLOSS got the value which GROSS was supposed to get. Once the misspelling is corrected, the run-time error will vanish.

Notice also the funny looking output for the variable HOURS. This is a result of failing to DECLARE HOURS as FIXED(5,0). This strange output will be explained in Chapter 6.

It is important to observe that the statement cited in an error message is not necessarily the ultimate source of the error. It is merely the place where the effects of the error happen to show up. In the above case, statement 6 is at fault; although the problem surfaces only when statement 7 is executed.

Unfortunately many run-time errors are symptoms of problems with logic, perhaps even with the algorithm. If the program is a faithful representation of an erroneous algorithm, no error messages may be generated. The computer system cannot detect whether your program will behave as desired. It can only respond when some particular computation cannot be completed normally. Thus the only evidence of trouble might be unreasonable output. Hence, you should always inspect the results to insure that they conform to your expectations. If the results are wrong, first make sure your program accurately reflects your algorithm. If it does not, then repair your program, but if it does, then correcting your algorithm is in order.

Whether run-time error messages are generated or not, logic errors are often difficult to diagnose. At this point, you become a detective; and debugging changes from a science to an art. However, PL/C provides much information to help you.

(1) Run-time error messages may be interspersed with your output.

(2) There will be a message following your output which indicates the last executed statement. If there were no "fatal" errors, the message will state:

IN STMT xx PROGRAM RETURNS FROM MAIN PROCEDURE

Otherwise, it will indicate a catastrophic error by:

ABOVE ERROR IS FATAL. PROGRAM IS STOPPED.

(3) Many installations provide a post-mortem dump. This is a list of the values of all variables at the time the program terminated. Check this carefully for unexpected values or for the symbol "?", which indicates that no value was ever assigned. You should understand why each unassigned variable failed to receive a value. The two most common reasons are: (i) a misspelled or incorrect variable name was used; or (ii) control failed to reach a statement which would assign a value.

The next two types of PL/C diagnostic information help you trace the flow of control.

(4) The label/entry count indicates how many times the flow of control arrived sequentially[2] at each label in the program. The major use for this information is to determine whether control ever reached certain parts of your program.

(5) The dynamic flow trace provides more detailed information about the recent history of flow of control. For example in Fig. 3.22, the flow trace indicates that the program began executing at statement 1. After executing the intervening statements in the normal sequence (which is not shown in the flow trace), flow of control skipped from statement 9 to statement 4 ten times. Finally, control skipped from statement 4 to statement 10, at which point the program terminated (indicated by a branch to 0000). Although this particular program was short enough to show its entire history in the trace, in general only the eighteen most recent nonsequential jumps in flow of control are shown.

3.7.4 Debugging Example

As an example of how this information can be used, consider Fig. 3.23 No error messages were generated. The results look reasonable: a quick check shows that every second number is three times the preceding number, as desired. However, there are only 9 pairs of numbers, while ten were expected. Thus, something is wrong. There are several clues to help you diagnose the trouble:

(i) The post-mortem dump shows a final value of 10 for COUNT, which indicates the number of the "next" employee to be processed (consult the comment within the DECLARE statement if you need reminding). In a correct program, its final value should be 11, since the loop terminates instead of processing a nonexistent eleventh employee.

(ii) The flow trace shows by 0009*(0009 → 0004) that the loop was executed only nine times.

---

[2]Or as a result of executing GOTO, see Chapter 12.

```
STMT LEVEL NEST BLOCK MLVL  SOURCE TEXT

                                  /* FIGURE 3.23 */
  1                          PAYROLL:PROCEDURE OPTIONS(MAIN);

                                     /* DETERMINE GROSS PAY FOR 10 EMPLOYEES */

  2    1          1                  DECLARE
                                        HOURS FIXED(5,0) /*TOTAL HOURS WORKED*/,
                                        GROSS FIXED(5,0) /*GROSS PAY*/,
                                        COUNT FIXED(5,0) /*NO. OF EMPLOYEE IN PROCESS*/;

  3    1          1                  COUNT = 1;
  4    1          1          LOOP:   DO WHILE (COUNT < 10);
  5    1    1     1                     GET LIST(HOURS); /* READ HOURS WORKED */
  6    1    1     1                     GROSS = HOURS * 3; /* HOURLY RATE IS $3.00 */
  7    1    1     1                     PUT DATA(HOURS,GROSS);
  8    1    1     1                     COUNT = COUNT + 1;
  9    1    1     1                  END LOOP;

 10    1          1                  END PAYROLL;

HOURS=        30       GROSS=       90;      HOURS=       33       GROSS=       99;      HOURS=       35
GROSS=       105;      HOURS=       42       GROSS=      126;      HOURS=       38       GROSS=      114;
HOURS=        41       GROSS=      123;      HOURS=        5       GROSS=       15;      HOURS=       48
GROSS=       144;      HOURS=       40       GROSS=      120;

IN STMT    10  PROGRAM RETURNS FROM MAIN PROCEDURE.

IN STMT    10  DYNAMIC FLOW TRACE:
               0000->0001     9*(0009->0004)      0004->0010      0010->0000

IN STMT    10  SCALARS AND BLOCK-TRACE:

***** MAIN PROCEDURE PAYROLL

COUNT=        10       GROSS=      120       HOURS=       40
```

Figure 3.23

(iii) Since only nine sets of output appear, and since the only PUT statement is inside the loop, the loop was executed only nine times.

All of this information, of course, suggests the same thing: we must modify the program so that it executes the loop one additional time. There are two basic ways to accomplish this: (i) change the condition on the DO WHILE so that it also allows the loop to execute when COUNT equals 10; this may be done by making the condition either (COUNT<=10) or (COUNT<11) or (ii) since COUNT is used only to control the loop, it may be initialized to 0 instead of to 1, which changes its "meaning" but also allows it to be incremented one more time before halting the loop.

We choose the first method because it does not change variable meanings. It is therefore a correction rather than a redefinition of the algorithm. By changing statement 4 of Fig. 3.23 to

```
DO WHILE (COUNT<=10);
```

we obtain the program of Fig. 3.24.

Alas! Now we see the run-time error message that the ENDFILE condition occurred; there was insufficient data for the number of GET statements. It often happens that correcting one error brings another problem into view. However, by inspecting the evidence, we see that this time the loop successfully executed nine times, and was in the process of executing a tenth time, when termination occurred in statement 5. Since the only GET statement in the program occurred within the loop, it was executed exactly ten times. Therefore the problem must be in the data! The data as well as the program logic can be responsible for errors. By checking the data cards, we see that one of them was inadvertently omitted. After supplying this missing card, the program will execute properly.

3.7.5 General Tips

The following are widely practiced in programming. In order to avoid simple mechanical errors we suggest: (i) using coding forms for writing programs; these forms have every column marked to help you count blanks and avoid coding beyond column 72; (ii) put at most one PL/I statement on each card for ease of alteration; (iii) in the DECLARE statement, put each variable, or at least only variables with identical attributes, on separate lines for ease of alteration.

Insert a PUT statement with the same variable list immediately after every GET statement. This enables you to see what data were actually read in. Once the program is working well, these PUT statements may be removed if you wish.

When you are unable to diagnose run-time errors by straightforward deduction, try the following:

i) Carefully work through your program by hand, preferably for a simple case, such as one data card or no data cards; you might encounter the same problems as the computer did.

ii) Obtain more information about intermediate variable values and flow of control. If you wonder whether or how often some statement is executed, put a label on it and check the label count

```
STMT LEVEL NEST BLOCK MLVL  SOURCE TEXT

                                          /* FIGURE 3.24 */
   1                               PAYROLL:PROCEDURE OPTIONS(MAIN);

                                          /* DETERMINE GROSS PAY FOR 10 EMPLOYEES */

   2    1          1                      DECLARE
                                             HOURS FIXED(5,0) /*TOTAL HOURS WORKED*/,
                                             GROSS FIXED(5,0) /*GROSS PAY*/,
                                             COUNT FIXED(5,0) /*NO. OF EMPLOYEE IN PROCESS*/;

   3    1          1                      COUNT = 1;
   4    1          1               LOOP:  DO WHILE (COUNT <= 10);
   5    1     1    1                         GET LIST(HOURS); /* READ HOURS WORKED */
   6    1     1    1                         GROSS = HOURS * 3; /* HOURLY RATE IS $3.00 */
   7    1     1    1                         PUT DATA(HOURS,GROSS);
   8    1     1    1                         COUNT = COUNT + 1;
   9    1     1    1                      END LOOP;

  10    1          1                      END PAYROLL;

HOURS=       30        GROSS=       90;       HOURS=       33        GROSS=       99;       HOURS=       35
GROSS=      105;       HOURS=       42        GROSS=      126;       HOURS=       38        GROSS=      114;
HOURS=       41        GROSS=      123;       HOURS=        5        GROSS=       15;       HOURS=       48
GROSS=      144;       HOURS=       40        GROSS=      120;
***** ERROR IN STMT    5  END OF FILE REACHED. (EX02)
ABOVE ERROR IS FATAL.  PROGRAM IS STOPPED.

IN STMT     5  DYNAMIC FLOW TRACE:
            0000->0001      9*(0009->0004)

IN STMT     5  SCALARS AND BLOCK-TRACE:

***** MAIN PROCEDURE PAYROLL

COUNT=       10        GROSS=      120        HOURS=       40
```

Figure 3.24

after the next run. If you wish to see how the values of certain relevant variables are changing, don't be afraid to insert additional PUT statements at key locations in the program. If you don't even know which variables to focus on, you can display the (current) values of <u>all</u> variables in your program, by executing the statement:

```
PUT ALL;
```

This gives output similar to the post-mortem dump, but at any time you wish during execution.[3] However, because of the quantity of output, this statement is not recommended for large programs unless your situation is desperate.

Finally, if your installation does not automatically provide all of the debugging aids listed above, they can be yours merely by requesting them on the *PL/C card. Each has its special "keyword" in PL/C:

attribute listing	ATR
cross-reference list	XREF
label/entry count post-mortem dump dynamic flow trace	} DUMP=(S,F,L,E,U,R,)

Simply place the appropriate keywords in any order, separated by commas after the ID='xxxx' field on the *PL/C card. For example:

```
*PL/C ID='JOE',XREF,DUMP=(S,F,L,E,U,R),ATR
```

3.8 REVIEW OF RULES

1. A <u>simple</u> <u>condition</u> has the general form:

   <arithmetic expression><relational operator><arithmetic expression>

   It also has the value of either TRUE or FALSE.

2. The general form of the DO WHILE statement is:

```
<label>:   DO WHILE (<condition>);

               instructions to be    |  range
               executed while the    }  of the
                condition  is TRUE   |  DO WHILE

           END <label>;
```

3. The general form of the IF-THEN-ELSE construction is:

```
IF <condition> THEN
     <statement #1>;
ELSE
     <statement #2>;
```

   Statement #1 is executed if the condition is TRUE; otherwise statement #2 is executed.

---

[3]The PUT ALL; statement is available only in PL/C, not in PL/I.

4. The general form of the IF_THEN statement is:

```
IF <condition>  THEN
      <statement>;
```

When IF is used without ELSE, the <statement> is executed if the condition is TRUE and is bypassed otherwise.

5. The simplest form of the ENDFILE statement is:

```
ON ENDFILE (SYSIN)  <assignment statement>;
```

Once executed, it remains in effect for the duration of the program. The ENDFILE statement should normally precede the first GET statement in a program.

3.9 REVIEW PROBLEM

Suppose a biologist has discovered a new strain of microorganism which he named "splodges." Splodges were found to multiply quickly, doubling their number every three hours in the absence of an inhibiting chemical known as TBA. If k drops of TBA are put into a culture containing n splodges, then the growth rate is slowed depending on the size of the population n compared to the dose k, as shown in Fig. 3.25.

Original Population	Drops of TBA	Relative Amounts	Population 3 Hours Later
n	none	---	2n
n	k	$n < 2k$	$2n - k$
n	k	$n \geq 2k$	$2n - 2k$

Figure 3.25

One dose of TBA is effective for only three hours, but additional doses may be applied. The biologist would like a program to simulate the growth of some initial splodge population for any specified sequence of TBA treatments at three hour intervals. The simulation of growth should stop whenever the population dies out or the treatments of TBA cease.

The inputs to such a program will be the initial splodge population and the number of drops of TBA for each treatment in the series. The output should report the time, the population, and the previous dose of TBA for each three hour period of the simulation.

The variables to be maintained are the time, the current population, and the current amount of TBA.

The basic algorithm is as follows:

```
1.     initialize time, population and first dose for start of
          simulation;
2.     print the initial time (0) and population n;
3.     repeat the following while treatment with TBA continues
          and some splodges remain alive;
3.1       compute how many splodges will be alive after 3 more
             hours;
3.2       update the time (by 3 hours);
3.3       print the time, population and dose;
3.4       read the dose of TBA to be applied at that time;
4.     display the time and population;
5.     end.
```

The time should be initialized to 0, and the initial population and initial dose of TBA will be read from data cards (Step 1).

The computation of population growth is straightforward from the table of Fig. 3.25:

```
3.1.1   if population n < 2k then
           new population is 2n - k;
3.1.2   otherwise
           new population is 2n - 2k;
```

Deciding when to halt the simulation (Step 2) provides the only subtlety. One reason for stopping is reaching the end of the prescribed treatments. This is represented by running out of data, which can be handled in the usual way, by causing an indicator to be set. The other reason for stopping is running out of splodges. Once either of these conditions occurs, it is not necessary to distinguish whether the data or the splodges has run out. Consequently, reduction of the population to zero or below should set the same termination indicator as the end of file condition.

The complete algorithm may now be shown in Fig. 3.26, and the corresponding program is Fig. 3.27. Note how Steps 1.3 and 3.5.2 of the algorithm are both implemented by the (same) ON ENDFILE statement.

```
1.1     initialize time to 0 and termination indicator to off (0);
1.2     read the initial population n and initial dose k of TBA;
1.3     if no treatment specified then set termination indicator;
2.      print the time and population;
3.      repeat while treatments continue and splodges remain;
3.1.1      if population n < 2k then
              new population is 2n - k;
3.1.2      otherwise
              new population is 2n - 2k;
3.2        add 3 hours to time;
3.3        print the time, population, and dose;
3.4        if new population ≤ 0 then set termination indicator;
3.5        otherwise
3.5.1         read amount k of next dose of TBA;
3.5.2         if no more TBA then set termination indicator;
4.      display final population and time;
5.      end.
```

Fig. 3.26 Simulation of Growth of splodges

```
                  /* FIGURE 3.27 */
BIOLOGY:
        PROCEDURE OPTIONS (MAIN);

        /* A PROGRAM TO SIMULATE THE GROWTH OF SPLODGES IN
           THE PRESENCE OF THE INHIBITING CHEMICAL TBA */

        DECLARE
           TIME FIXED (5,0), /* UNITS OF TIME */
           SPLODGES FIXED (5,0), /* SPLODGE POPULATION */
           TBA FIXED (5,0), /* DOSAGE OF TBA */
           FLAG FIXED (5,0); /* TO TERMINATE EXPERIMENT */

        /* INITIALIZE VARIABLES */

        TIME = 0;
        FLAG = 0;
        ON ENDFILE (SYSIN) FLAG = 1;

        /* READ STARTING POPULATION AND FIRST TBA DOSAGE */

        GET LIST (SPLODGES,TBA);
        PUT DATA (TIME,SPLODGES);

CYCLE:  DO WHILE (FLAG = 0);/*PROCESS EXPERIMENTAL VALUES*/
           /* FIRST CATEGORY */
           IF SPLODGES < 2*TBA THEN
              SPLODGES = 2*SPLODGES - TBA;
           ELSE /* SECOND CATEGORY */
              SPLODGES = 2*SPLODGES - 2*TBA;
           TIME = TIME + 3; /* ADVANCE SIMULATION CLOCK */
           PUT DATA (TIME,SPLODGES,TBA);
           /* IS THE POPULATION EXTINCT? */
           IF SPLODGES <= 0 THEN
              FLAG = 1;
           ELSE /* IF NOT GET ANOTHER TBA DOSAGE */
              GET LIST (TBA);
        END CYCLE;

        /* PRINT RESULTS */

        PUT DATA (SPLODGES,TIME);

        END BIOLOGY;
```

Fig. 3.27 Program to Simulate Growth of Splodges by Algorithm of Fig. 3.26

3.10 EXERCISES

3.1 The roots of the quadratic equation

$$ax^2 + bx + c = 0$$

are given by

$$x = \frac{-b \pm \sqrt{b^2-4ac}}{2a}$$

i) If a=0 then the equation is said to be linear and not quadratic. Design an algorithm to examine one set of values for a, b, and c. The result of the algorithm should be the code 0 if a=0 and the code 1 if a≠0. In any event the values for a, b, and c should be displayed. Implement your algorithm by computer program.

ii) If b^2-4ac (called the discriminant) is ≥ 0 then the roots of the equation are real; otherwise they are complex. Assuming $a \neq 0$ design an algorithm to examine ten sets of values for a, b, and c and determine whether the roots are real or complex. The result of the algorithm should be the code 2 for real and the code 3 for complex. Again, all values for a, b and c should be displayed. Implement your algorithm by computer program.

iii) If the discriminant is zero then the roots are real and equal. Again assuming $a \neq 0$, design an algorithm to examine an arbitrary number of sets of values for a, b, and c, and determine whether the roots are real and unequal (code 21), real and equal (code 22) or complex (code 3). As usual, all values for a, b, and c should be displayed. Implement your algorithm by computer program.

3.2 If n is an integer, n factorial (written n!) is the product of all the integers from 1 through n, i.e., $n! = 1 \times 2 \times \ldots \times (n-1) \times n$. Write an algorithm to compute and print the factorial values of all the integers up to any specified integer M. Write a program to compute and print 1!,2!,3!,...,7!,8!(M=8).

3.3 The Fibonacci Series begins with the numbers 0 and 1 and generates each term by adding the two previous terms. Thus the first seven terms are 0,1,1,2,3,5,8. Devise an algorithm and write a program to produce the first twenty-five terms in this series.

3.4 The inventory of a small chain (five stores) of specialty shops (at most four different items per shop) is coded on data cards. The first number represents the stock number; the second is the amount of that item on hand at one store; the third is the unit price per item. For example,

87, 56, 3.29

means the store has 56 units of item 87 on hand and the cost price of each item is $3.29.

Describe an algorithm to calculate the total $ value of the inventory for each item and for the whole chain. Implement your algorithm by computer program. Your output should include the stock number as well as the dollar value.

3.5 The grades for a class of unknown size are recorded on data cards. Describe an algorithm to compute the class average to two decimal places and also count how many students fall into each of the following categories.

Category	Mark Range
1	$80 \leq$ mark
2	$70 \leq$ mark < 80
3	$60 \leq$ mark < 70
4	$50 \leq$ mark < 60
5	mark < 50

Implement your algorithm by computer program.

3.6 The formulae for converting between degrees Celsius and degrees Fahrenheit are:

$$F = (C \times 1.8) + 32$$
$$C = (F - 32) \times 5 \div 9$$

Describe an algorithm to convert Fahrenheit degrees from 0 to 212 in steps of 1 to degrees Celsius.

Describe an algorithm to convert Celsius degrees from 0 to 100 in steps of 1 to degrees Fahrenheit.

Implement each algorithm by a separate computer program. Note that there must be _no_ data cards for either program.

3.7 A palindrome is a string which reads the same from left to right as it does from right to left. The classic palindrome is "Able was I ere I saw Elba." An integer like 4884 is also a palindrome because it yields itself when its digits are reversed.

Design an algorithm to inspect an arbitrary quantity of integers and print out those which are palindromes. Although your familiarity with PL/I limits your programming power to 5-digit integers, your algorithm should work for any positive integer.

Implement your algorithm by computer program.

3.8 Consider an urn filled with green, white and orange balls. Nine players indulge in a game in which every player takes two balls each from the urn and score the results on the following basis.

If the first ball is green score 6 points.
If the first ball is white score 3 points.
If the first ball is orange score no points.
If the second ball is the same color as the first then the player gets a bonus of 2 points.

Notice that the second ball adds to the score only if it is the same color as the first; otherwise it does not count. To automate the game, the colors are coded as 1 for green, 2 for white, and 3 for orange. Each player, after drawing two balls from the urn, codes his colors on a data card. Describe an algorithm to score this game and implement your algorithm by computer program using all possible combinations as data to the program. Your output should show each ball drawn and the score for each player.

Chapter 4 Complex Flow of Control

So far we have seen three models of control: (i) *sequential*, (ii) *alternative*, as requested by IF, and (iii) *repetitive*, governed by DO WHILE. This chapter will introduce some additional language features to influence flow of control and will demonstrate how combinations of these facilities may be used to program algorithms of greater complexity.

4.1 DO GROUPS

With the constructions currently available to us we can only execute *one* statement based on the truth or falsity of a condition. Thus it is awkward to conditionally perform some action involving more than one statement. For example, to add 1 to a positive-number-count *and* to print out the number, whenever some number A is positive, we might write:

```
IF A >= 0 THEN
   POS_COUNT = POS_COUNT + 1;
IF A >= 0 THEN
   PUT DATA (A);
```

Though this code would work quite well, it suffers from the drawbacks of being lengthy, repetitious, unclear, and error prone. If we wanted to execute 15, 50, or 500 statements based on some condition, this technique would prove to be outrageously tedious and cumbersome.

Therefore PL/I provides an easy way of designating a *set* of statements to be executed as a group -- in this case as a result of an IF test. We delineate such a set by enclosing the statement between a DO and an END statement to form a *DO group*, whose general

form is

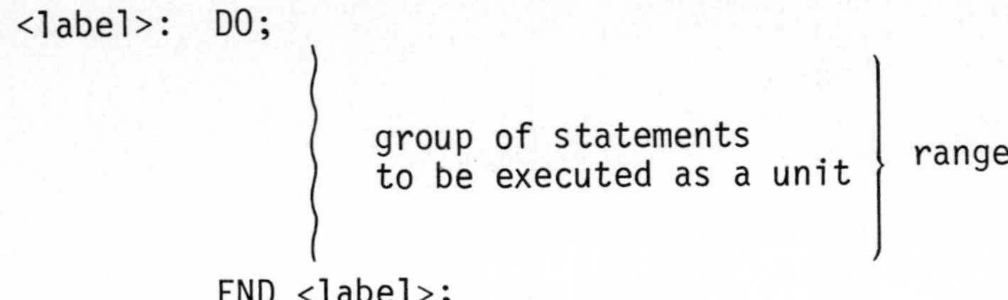
<label>: DO;
group of statements
to be executed as a unit
range
END <label>;

This form of the DO statement executes every statement in its range <u>once</u>, and then continues on to the next statement in the program. Unlike the DO WHILE statement, there is no repetition of the statements in the range.

DO groups are usually encountered as the result of IF_THEN or IF_THEN_ELSE statements and are used when we wish to do more than one thing as the result of a test. The original example in this section could be coded as:

```
                IF A >= 0 THEN
      POSITIVE:   DO;
                     POS_COUNT = POS_COUNT + 1;
                     PUT DATA(A);
                  END POSITIVE;
```

Notice how the <u>entire</u> DO group is the object of the THEN and either gets executed as a package when A is positive or else gets bypassed when A is negative. From the viewpoint of the surrounding program, a DO group behaves like a single statement, though possibly a very complex one.

Consider the problem of summing and counting both the positive and the negative values read from data cards. This entails maintaining two totals and two counts, as depicted by the algorithm of Fig. 4.1.

```
1.    initialize both totals and both counts to 0;
2.    obtain first value;
3.    repeat while values remain to be processed;
3.1      update the appropriate total and count;
3.2      obtain next value;
4.    display both totals and both counts;
5.    end.
```

Fig. 4.1 Summing and Counting Positive and Negative Values Separately

Of course the crux of the problem is updating the correct total and counter (Step 3.1). This could be done by the algorithm of Fig. 4.2.

It is certainly permissible to use DO groups in conjunction with the ELSE clause of an IF_THEN_ELSE. Consequently, the algorithm of Fig. 4.2 (plus obtaining the next value) might be programmed as shown in Fig. 4.3.

```
3.1.1     if value is positive then
3.1.1.1      add value to positive total;
3.1.1.2      add 1 to positive count;
3.1.2     otherwise
3.1.2.1      add value to negative total;
3.1.2.2      add 1 to negative count;
```

Figure 4.2

```
1              IF VALU >= 0 THEN
2    POS:         DO;
3                    PTOTAL = PTOTAL + VALU;
4                    PCOUNT = PCOUNT + 1;
5                 END POS;
6              ELSE
7    NEG:         DO;
8                    NTOTAL = NTOTAL + VALU;
9                    NCOUNT = NCOUNT +1;
10                END NEG;
11             GET LIST(VALU);/*NEXT VALUE*/
```

Figure 4.3

Since this code may appear complex, it might be useful to trace its execution. If the variable VALU has a positive or 0 value, then the program will flow from line 1 through lines 2, 3, 4, and 5. Where does it go from there? It can*not* go to line 6 because this is the ELSE clause covering the case where VALU is negative. Lines 7 through 10 constitute the DO group, which is the continuation of the ELSE clause begun in line 6. Hence after executing line 5, control passes directly to line 11. On the other hand, if VALU is negative then control will pass from line 1 to the balancing ELSE in line 6, then execute the associated DO group (lines 7, 8, 9, 10), and finally execute line 11, which is the next statement following the IF_THEN_ELSE construction.

We have already noted that any valid PL/I statement can be included in the range of a DO WHILE or DO group. It follows that we may include a DO statement itself in the range of any other DO; such DO's are said to be *nested*. An example of nested DO's is the program to implement the algorithm of Fig. 4.1, for maintaining totals and counts of positive and negative values. The code in Fig. 4.3, of course, updates a total and a counter for only one value. Just as the algorithm of Fig. 4.1 repeats Step 3.1 for each value to be processed, so the code for processing one value should be applied repeatedly by appearing within a DO WHILE loop. This is shown in Fig. 4.4. The next section will develop another algorithm and program which uses nested DO statements.

```
          /* FIGURE 4.4 */
NESTS:  PROCEDURE OPTIONS (MAIN);

        /* A PROGRAM TO SUM AND COUNT THE POSITIVE AND
           NEGATIVE INTEGERS IN AN ARBITRARY NUMBER OF
           DATA CARDS */

        DECLARE
           VALU FIXED (5,0), /*VALUE JUST READ FROM DATA*/
           PTOTAL FIXED (5,0), /* SUM OF POSITIVE VALUES*/
           PCOUNT FIXED (5,0), /* NO. OF POSITIVE VALUES*/
           NTOTAL FIXED (5,0), /* SUM NEGATIVE VALUES */
           NCOUNT FIXED (5,0), /* NO. NEGATIVE VALUES */
           FLAG FIXED (5,0); /* END OF DATA FLAG */

        /* INITIALIZE VARIABLES */
        NTOTAL = 0;
        NCOUNT = 0;
        PTOTAL = 0;
        PCOUNT = 0;
        FLAG = 0;
        ON ENDFILE (SYSIN) FLAG = 1;
        GET LIST (VALU);

PROCESS:DO WHILE (FLAG = 0);
           IF VALU >= 0 THEN
POS:          DO; /* PROCESS POSITIVE VALUES */
                 PTOTAL = PTOTAL + VALU;
                 PCOUNT = PCOUNT + 1;
              END POS;
           ELSE
NEG:          DO; /* PROCESS NEGATIVE VALUES */
                 NTOTAL = NTOTAL + VALU;
                 NCOUNT = NCOUNT + 1;
              END NEG;
           GET LIST (VALU); /* READ NEXT VALUE */
        END PROCESS;

        PUT DATA (PTOTAL,PCOUNT,NTOTAL,NCOUNT);

        END NESTS;
```

Fig. 4.4 Program to Implement Algorithm of Fig. 4.1 and 4.2

4.2 AN EXAMPLE USING DO

Problem Statement

A data deck contains an unknown number of integers. Write a program to determine the number of even integers and the number of odd integers in the data. Also determine the largest even integer and the largest odd integer in the data.

Solution

This problem requires two types of computations -- counting and determining largest values -- both of which can be done as the data are being read in. Hence, the solution to this problem fits a "standard" form:

```
1.     initialize variables;
2.     read first data item;
3.     repeat as long as data remain to be processed;
3.1       process current data;
3.2       read next data item;
4.     display results;
5.     end.
```

Step 3 virtually says "solve the problem," and so we must decompose it further. First isolate the processing of one integer from the repetitive aspect of processing all integers. Processing each integer, however, must be taken one step at a time. First determine if the integer is odd or even -- then do the processing appropriate to either odd or even integers:

```
3.1.1   if the integer is even then
           process an even integer;
3.1.2   otherwise
           process an odd integer;
```

We still have to further decompose Steps 3.1.1 and 3.1.2. Once we have found an even integer, we must do two things: add 1 to the even-integer counter and decide if this is the largest even integer. Two comparable actions are required in case the integer is odd. Hence, "processing" the next integer amounts to this:

```
3.1.1     if the integer is even then
3.1.1.1      increment even-integer count;
3.1.1.2      note whether this is largest even integer (so far);
3.1.2     otherwise (integer must be odd)
3.1.2.1      increment odd-integer count;
3.1.2.2      note whether this is largest odd integer (so far);
```

Recall from Section 3.5.1 that finding a largest integer may be done by remembering only the largest previously encountered integer. Each new candidate is compared to this value, and if larger, becomes the new "largest" integer seen so far. Hence Step 3.1.1.2 is more accurately written:

```
3.1.1.2   if integer is larger than previous largest even
             integer then it becomes new largest even integer;
```

Similarly for Step 3.1.2.2.

Recall that in Section 3.5.1 the first value encountered was used as the initial value for the maximum. We now introduce an alternative way of initializing the maximum. Because our variables have the FIXED (5,0) attributes, we know that the largest and smallest values which can be stored are 99,999 and -99,999 respectively. Hence if we initialized the "largest" integers seen so far to -99,999 we are guaranteed that any value read from data will be no less than this and so ensure its replacement by a valid data item. This method of initialization is preferable in this case, since the "first" even or odd integer may not appear among the data for some time. Hence, the overall algorithm is shown in Fig. 4.5.

```
1.1      initialize counters to 0;
1.2      initialize "largest" even and odd integers to -99999;
2.       read first integer;
3.       repeat as long as data remain to be processed;
3.1.1       if integer is even then
3.1.1.1        increment even counter by 1;
3.1.1.2        if integer > "largest" even integer seen so far then
                  this integer becomes "largest" even integer;
3.1.2       otherwise
3.1.2.1        increment odd counter by 1;
3.1.2.2        if integer > "largest" odd integer seen so far then
                  this integer becomes "largest" odd integer;
3.2         read next integer;
4.       display both counters and both largest values;
5.       end.
```

Figure 4.5

4.2.1 <u>Determining Whether an Integer is Even or Odd</u>

The algorithm of Fig. 4.5 appears correct and straightforward. However, the seemingly innocuous step (3.1.1) of deciding whether an integer is even is not so simple for a computer. We know that all even numbers are evenly divisible by 2. The computer, on the other hand, must be instructed how to determine if a number is evenly divisible by 2.

You will recall that if you divide 7 by 2 then the answer is 3 and you have 1 left over; mathematically speaking 7÷2 yields a quotient of 3 and a remainder of 1. If you now multiply the <u>quotient</u> by 2, you get a product of 6 -- <u>not</u> the original number 7. This is because 7 is not evenly divisible by 2, i.e., 7 is "odd". On the other hand, when an even integer is divided by 2, the remainder is 0, and the quotient is exactly half the original value. Thus when the quotient is multiplied by 2, the result is the original number. This suggests the following algorithm to determine whether an integer is even or odd:

```
1.     let q be the quotient of n÷2;
2.1    if n = 2 × q then
          n is even;
2.2    otherwise
          n is odd;
```

When you deal with numbers stored in FIXED(5,0) variables, you are dealing solely with integers. If you divide a number by 2 and store the result in a FIXED(5,0) variable, you will get <u>only</u> the integer portion of the answer (i.e., the quotient), because there is no room to store the fractional portion, if any. This suggests implementing Step 1 of this algorithm by the PL/I statement:

```
QUOTIENT = NUMBER/2;
```

where QUOTIENT is a FIXED(5,0) variable.

Armed with this technique and the algorithm of Fig. 4.5, we can formulate our PL/I program to solve the original problem. The code for this program is given in Fig. 4.6.

```
            /* FIGURE 4.6 */
ODDEVEN:
        PROCEDURE OPTIONS (MAIN);

        /* A PROGRAM TO COUNT THE NUMBER OF EVEN AND ODD
           INTEGERS IN A DATA DECK. IT ALSO FINDS THE
           LARGEST INTEGER IN EACH CATEGORY. */

        DECLARE
           EVEN_COUNT FIXED (5,0), /* COUNT OF EVEN #'S */
           ODD_COUNT FIXED (5,0), /* COUNT OF ODD #'S */
           LARGE_EVEN FIXED (5,0), /* LARGEST EVEN # */
           LARGE_ODD FIXED (5,0), /* LARGEST ODD # */
           QUOTIENT FIXED (5,0), /* ODD OR EVEN CHECK */
           NUMBER FIXED (5,0), /* NO. READ FROM  DATA */
           FLAG FIXED (5,0); /* END OF DATA FLAG */

        /* INITIALIZE VARIABLES */

        EVEN_COUNT = 0;
        ODD_COUNT = 0;
        LARGE_EVEN = -99999;
        LARGE_ODD = -99999;
        FLAG = 0;
        ON ENDFILE (SYSIN) FLAG = 1;
        PUT LIST ('COMPARE EVEN AND ODD INTEGERS');
        GET LIST (NUMBER);

LOOP:   DO WHILE (FLAG = 0);
           PUT SKIP DATA (NUMBER);
           /* IS NUMBER ODD OR EVEN? */
           QUOTIENT = NUMBER / 2;
           /* NUMBER IS EVEN IF NUMBER = QUOTIENT*2 */
           IF NUMBER = QUOTIENT * 2 THEN
EVEN:         DO; /* PROCESS EVEN NUMBERS */
                 EVEN_COUNT = EVEN_COUNT + 1;
                 IF NUMBER > LARGE_EVEN THEN
                    LARGE_EVEN = NUMBER;
              END EVEN;
           ELSE
ODD:          DO; /* PROCESS ODD NUMBERS */
                 ODD_COUNT = ODD_COUNT + 1;
                 IF NUMBER > LARGE_ODD THEN
                    LARGE_ODD = NUMBER;
              END ODD;
           GET LIST (NUMBER);
        END LOOP;
        /* CHECK FOR NUMBERS BEFORE PRINTING */
        IF EVEN_COUNT > 0 THEN
        PUT SKIP DATA (EVEN_COUNT,LARGE_EVEN);
        IF ODD_COUNT > 0 THEN
           PUT SKIP DATA (ODD_COUNT,LARGE_ODD);
        END ODDEVEN;

COMPARE EVEN AND ODD INTEGERS
NUMBER=       76;
NUMBER=       95;
NUMBER=       38;
NUMBER=      -29;
NUMBER=      264;
NUMBER=       57;
NUMBER=      398;
NUMBER=       -2;
NUMBER=       56;
NUMBER=      329;
EVEN_COUNT=          6       LARGE_EVEN=      398;
ODD_COUNT=          4        LARGE_ODD=      329;
```

Figure 4.6

Note the output produced by this program. The initial line is the result of executing the statement:

```
PUT LIST('COMPARE EVEN AND ODD INTEGERS');
```

The PUT LIST statement will print any message enclosed in quotes. This statement will be treated more fully in Chapter 5. The results appear on separate lines because the statement

```
PUT SKIP DATA(<variable list>);
```

was used. The SKIP causes the computer to stop printing on the current line and skip to a new line before printing the values in the variable list.

4.3 NESTING IF STATEMENTS

Suppose you must compare the scores of two teams and print a message to either identify the winning team or announce a tie. Your solution might be:

```
1.    if team A's score > team B's score then
         proclaim team A triumphant;
2.    otherwise
         decide whether team B wins or whether there was a tie;
```

This is clearly an IF_THEN_ELSE situation. However, if A is not victorious, a subsequent decision must be made and appropriate actions taken. This step (2) may be broken down as follows:

```
2.1   if team A's score < team B's score then
         proclaim team B victorious;
2.2   otherwise
         announce a tie;
```

This is obviously another IF_THEN_ELSE situation, which just happens to be one of the alternatives in an earlier IF_THEN_ELSE (Step 1). Whenever this happens, the IF statements are said to be nested. The combined algorithm is shown in Fig. 4.7.

```
1.    if team A's score > team B's score then
         proclaim A the winner;
2.    otherwise
2.1      if team A's score < team B's score then
            proclaim B the winner;
2.2      otherwise
            announce a tie;
```

Figure 4.7

To sort out complex logic, it is often helpful to draw a diagram of the possible decision sequences as shown in Fig. 4.8. Fig. 4.9 shows how this diagram relates to the PL/I version of the same decision sequence.

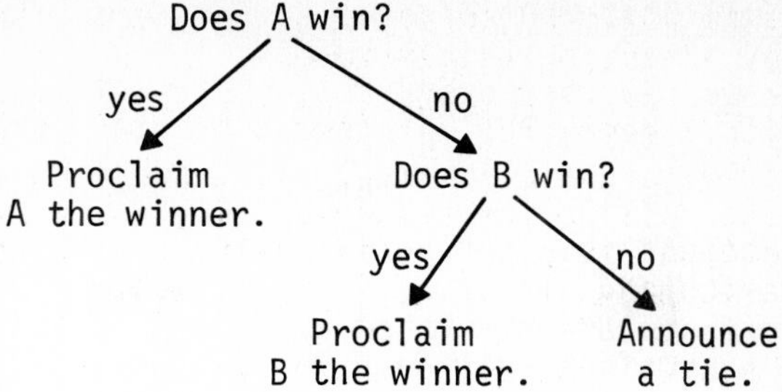

Figure 4.8

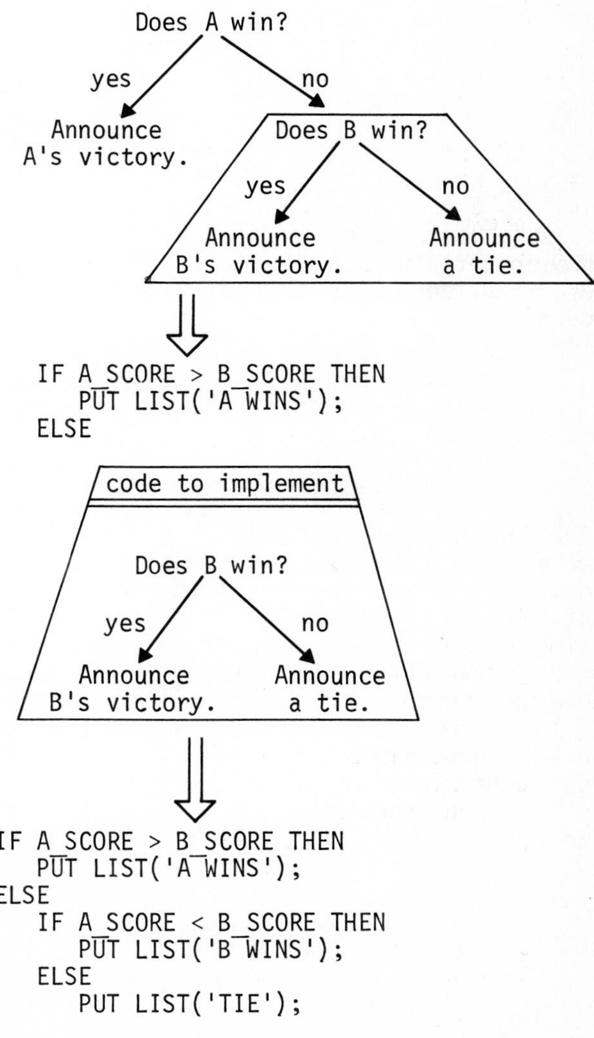

Figure 4.9

4.3.1 The Null Statement

In Chapter 2 we saw that every PL/I statement must end with a semicolon (;); i.e., every PL/I statement has the form:

```
statement;
```

The null statement is a perfectly valid PL/I statement consisting only of a semicolon. It says, in effect, to do nothing but continue on to the next statement. As an example, both of the following sets of code are equivalent, although the second contains a null statement.

```
IF A = B THEN
   PUT DATA (A);
PUT DATA (B);
```

```
IF A = B THEN
   PUT DATA (A);
ELSE;
PUT DATA (B);
```

The utility of the null statement is shown below.

4.3.2 Interpreting Nested IF's

Since making decisions conditioned on the outcome of earlier decisions is a very common situation, nested IF statements will arise frequently. As a rule, whenever IF's are nested, every IF should be balanced with a corresponding ELSE, even though no special action may be required in certain cases!

Failure to balance IF statements with ELSE statements can often lead to confusion.

Consider the following code:

```
IF A > 0 THEN                line 1
IF A < 10 THEN               line 2
PUT SKIP DATA (A);           line 3
ELSE GET LIST (B);           line 4
GET LIST (A);                line 5
```

What action does the computer take if (i) A=-1; (ii) A=20; (iii) A=8? We recommend that you attempt to answer these questions before proceeding.... Now that you have pondered the problem it should be clear that the crux of the matter is in deciding to which IF the ELSE in line 4 relates. In PL/I any ELSE balances the nearest preceding unbalanced IF in the same logical section of code.[1] Thus in the code shown above, the ELSE in line 4 balances the IF in line 2, i.e., the last unbalanced IF. Hence when A=-1, control will pass from line 1 to line 5; when A=20 control will pass from line 1 to line 2 to line 4 to line 5; when A=8 control will pass from line 1 to line 2 to line 3 to line 5.

We can rewrite this code in a much clearer manner:

```
IF A > 0 THEN
   IF A < 10 THEN
      PUT SKIP DATA (A);
   ELSE
      GET LIST (B);
ELSE;
GET LIST (A);
```

[1]In the same DO group, BEGIN block, or PROCEDURE.

This version accomplishes two things. First, each IF is balanced by an ELSE; and, since we recall that every ELSE balances the last unbalanced IF, there is no ambiguity as to their pairing. Second, by indenting the code we have made the flow of control much more understandable to a human reader.

This technique becomes even more valuable when more than two IF's are to be nested. Consider the following code:

```
IF A > 10 THEN                   line 1
IF A > 20 THEN                   line 2
IF A > 30 THEN I=I+1;            line 3
ELSE J=J+1;                      line 4
ELSE K=K+L;                      line 5
```

According to our rules the ELSE clauses in lines 4 and 5 balance the IF's in lines 3 and 2 respectively. Still, the code is much more legible in the following form:

```
IF A > 10 THEN
   IF A > 20 THEN
      IF A > 30 THEN
         I = I + 1;
      ELSE
         J = J + 1;
   ELSE
      K = K + 1;
ELSE;
```

In this form one can see at a glance which ELSE balances which IF without having to count backwards and that nothing special is to be done when A is not greater than 10.

Finally consider this example:

```
         IF A > B THEN                      line 1
BIG:        DO;                             line 2
               IF A > C THEN                line 3
                  PUT SKIP DATA (A);        line 4
               GET LIST ( A);               line 5
            END BIG;                        line 6
         ELSE PUT DATA (B);                 line 7
```

The ELSE in line 7 balances the IF in line 1, not the IF in line 3, because every ELSE balances the last unbalanced IF in the same logical section of code. Since the IF in line 3 is enclosed in the DO group labeled BIG, it is in a different logical section of code from line 1.

4.3.3 An Example Using Nested IF's

Suppose you wish to determine the proportion of males and the proportion of females who are over 30 years of age in a group of people who have just filled out data cards indicating their sex and age. The first number on each card is either 0 for a male or 1 for a female. The second number is the age.

This can be done for males by counting the number of males who are over 30 and the number who are under 30. Then at the end, the proportion over 30 is the first count (over 30 males) divided by the sum of both counters (all males). The proportion of over-30 females can be determined in a similar manner with two other counters. The general approach, which should now be familiar, is shown in Fig. 4.10.

1. initialize all four counters to 0;
2. read the first data card;
3. repeat while cards remain to be processed;
   3.1 increment the appropriate counter by 1;
   3.2 read another data card;
4. determine proportion of males over 30;
5. determine proportion of females over 30;
6. display results;
7. end.

Figure 4.10

The real problem is how to increment the correct counter for any one subject. This can be done by first determining the sex and then the age of the subject. The answers to these two questions should lead to the appropriate counter. This is summarized in Fig. 4.11 and can be implemented using nested IF statements, as shown in Fig. 4.12. The complete program for this problem is shown in Fig. 4.13. Note that the proportion variables are declared with attributes FIXED(5,2), so that decimal fractions can be represented. If integer variables had been used, the calculation of the proportions would have yielded only the integer portion, i.e., 0.

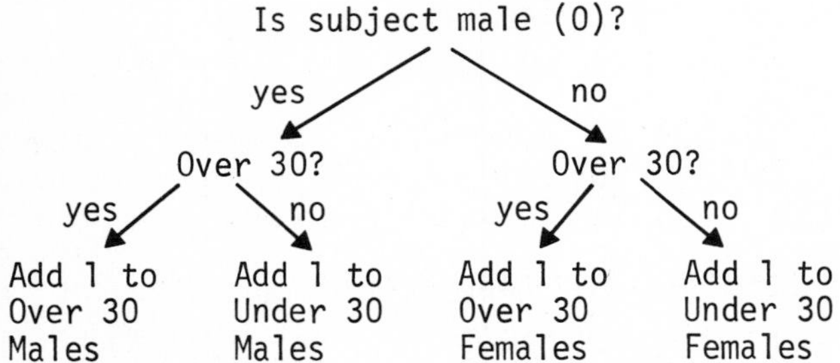

Fig. 4.11 Sequence of Decisions

```
IF SEX = 0 THEN
   IF AGE > 30 THEN
      OLDM = OLDM + 1;
   ELSE
      YOUNGM = YOUNGM + 1;
ELSE
   IF AGE > 30 THEN
      OLDF = OLDF + 1;
   ELSE
      YOUNGF = YOUNGF + 1;
```

Figure 4.12 Statements to Implement Fig. 4.11

```
             /* FIGURE 4.13 */
PROP:     PROCEDURE OPTIONS (MAIN);

          /* A PROGRAM TO COMPUTE THE PROPORTIONS OF MALES
             AND FEMALES OVER 30 IN A SAMPLE POPULATION */

          DECLARE
             OLDM FIXED (5,0), /* NO. MALES OVER 30 */
             YOUNGM FIXED (5,0), /* NO. MALES UNDER 30 */
             OLDF FIXED (5,0), /* NO. FEMALES OVER 30 */
             YOUNGF FIXED (5,0), /* NO. FEMALES UNDER 30 */
             MPROP FIXED (5,2), /* PROPORTION MALES OVER 30*/
             FPROP FIXED (5,2), /* PROP. FEMALES OVER 30 */
             SEX FIXED (5,0), /* 0=MALE; 1=FEMALE */
             AGE FIXED (5,0), /* AGE FROM DATA CARD */
             FLAG FIXED (5,0); /* END OF DATA FLAG */

          /* INITIALIZE VARIABLES */

          OLDM = 0;
          YOUNGM = 0;
          OLDF = 0;
          YOUNGF = 0;
          FLAG = 0;
          ON ENDFILE (SYSIN) FLAG = 1;
          GET LIST (SEX,AGE); /* READ FIRST DATA CARD */
LOOP:     DO WHILE (FLAG = 0);

             /* IS THIS A MALE? */

             IF SEX = 0 THEN

                /* AND IF SO IS HE OVER 30? */

                IF AGE > 30 THEN
                   OLDM = OLDM + 1; /* 1 MORE MALE OVER 30 */
                ELSE
                   YOUNGM = YOUNGM + 1;
             ELSE /* MUST BE FEMALE */

                /* IS SHE OVER 30? */

                IF AGE > 30 THEN
                   OLDF = OLDF + 1; /*1 MORE FEMALE OVER 30*/
                ELSE
                   YOUNGF = YOUNGF + 1;
             GET LIST (SEX,AGE); /* READ NEXT CARD */
          END LOOP;

          /* COMPUTE PROPORTIONS AND PRINT RESULTS */

          MPROP = OLDM / (OLDM + YOUNGM);
          FPROP = OLDF / (OLDF + YOUNGF);
          PUT DATA (MPROP,FPROP);

          END PROP;
```

Fig. 4.13 Program to Implement Algorithm of Fig. 4.10

4.4 COMPOUND CONDITIONS

The problem of the preceding Section (4.3.3) is to increment the appropriate one of four counters, depending on the sex and age of the current subject. The correct counter is determined by making a sequence of two-way decisions, which means using nested IF statements in the program. If the subject is male then ... if he also happens to be over 30, the count of over-30 males is increased by 1. This can be expressed another way: if the subject is both male and over 30, then the count of over-30 males is increased by 1. Note that this form of expression suggests making just one decision but basing it on a more complex condition: being both male and over 30. This can be expressed directly in PL/I by using the "Boolean operator" & which corresponds to the English word "and":

```
IF (SEX = 0) & (AGE > 30) THEN
   OLDM = OLDM + 1;
```

The & operator is one way of combining two simple conditions into a single, compound condition. In this case the compound condition is true only if both of the simple conditions are simultaneously true. If the value of SEX is not 0 (male), or if the value of AGE is less than or equal to 30, then the compound condition is false, and the counter is not incremented.

The other way of combining two simple conditions into a compound condition is to use the operator | , which corresponds to the English word "or." This operator requires only one (not necessarily both) of the simple conditions to be true in order to make the compound condition true. For example, to maintain a counter of all those who are not males over 30 years of age, you could write:

```
IF (SEX = 1) | (AGE <= 30) THEN
   OTHERS = OTHERS + 1;
```

If the subject is female (1), regardless of age, or if the subject is 30 or under, regardless of sex, then the counter OTHERS will be incremented. If the subject happens to be both female and not over 30 the counter will still get incremented. The only case in which it won't is when neither simple condition is true.

Perhaps a more direct way to count subjects who are not males over 30 is to use the operator ¬ , which means "not".

```
IF  ¬((SEX = 0) & (AGE > 30)) THEN
   OTHERS = OTHERS + 1;
```

The condition within the parentheses is true only when SEX is 0 (male) and AGE is over 30. The not operator (¬) reverses this and makes the compound condition true in every other case but that one. The not operator may be used to reverse the truth or falsehood of any other condition. Thus

```
DO WHILE (¬(FLAG = 1));
```

will continue the loop as long as FLAG does not become 1. The statement

```
DO WHILE (FLAG ¬= 1);
```

has exactly the same effect.

In summary, there are three Boolean operators, whose meanings are given in Fig. 4.14. They may be used to form compound conditions from simple conditions or other compound conditions. Compound conditions may be used by either the IF statement or the DO WHILE statement to control flow of control. Fig. 1.14 also contains several examples of compound conditions.

<table>
<tr><th>PL/C Symbol</th><th>English Name</th><th>Example</th><th>Meaning</th></tr>
<tr><td>&</td><td>"and"</td><td>(I=J) & (P=Q)</td><td>The condition is true only if I=J is true and P=Q is also true.</td></tr>
<tr><td>|</td><td>"or"</td><td>(I=J) | (P=Q)</td><td>The condition is true if (i) I=J is true or (ii) P=Q is true or (iii) both simple conditions are true.</td></tr>
<tr><td>¬</td><td>"not" or "it is not the case that"</td><td>¬(I=J)</td><td>The condition is true only if I = J is false, i.e., if I≠J.</td></tr>
</table>

(a)

<table>
<tr><th>Variable</th><th>Value</th><th>Condition</th><th>Value</th></tr>
<tr><td>I</td><td>3</td><td>(I=J) & (J=K)</td><td>false</td></tr>
<tr><td>J</td><td>4</td><td>(I¬=J) & (J<K)</td><td>true</td></tr>
<tr><td>K</td><td>5</td><td>(I>J) | (J<(K+1))</td><td>true</td></tr>
<tr><td></td><td></td><td>(I>J) | (K<J)</td><td>false</td></tr>
<tr><td></td><td></td><td>¬(I=J)</td><td>true</td></tr>
<tr><td></td><td></td><td>¬((I=J) & (J=K))</td><td>true</td></tr>
</table>

(b)

Fig. 4.14 Compound Conditions; (a) Boolean Operators, (b) Examples.

In the first four examples of Fig. 4.14, the parentheses are not strictly necessary but are present for the sake of clarity. When parentheses are not present or are used sparingly, priority rules dictate the order in which the operators are evaluated:

1. First evaluate parenthesized expressions, beginning with the innermost in case the parentheses are nested.

2. Next evaluate arithmetic expressions.

3. Then evaluate basic relational operators (e.g., <, >=, ¬<, etc.); this is the point at which true-false values emerge.

4. Finally, evaluate the Boolean operators in the following order:

   i) ¬ operators, left-to-right;

   ii) & operators, left-to-right;

   iii) | operators, left-to-right.

Rules 2, 3, and 4 may be expressed more succinctly by exhibiting the priorities of each operator, where higher priority operators are evaluated before operators with lower priority. PL/I operator priorities are given in Fig. 4.15.

Operator	Priority
**	7
*,/	6
+,-	5
=,¬=,<,<=,>,>=,¬<,¬>	4
¬	3
&	2
|	1

Fig. 4.15 Priority of Operators in PL/I

However, since these rules may be difficult to remember, and since complex conditions may be quite hard to read, we recommend liberal use of parentheses to clarify conditions. Thus

```
A + B <= C/D | A < M & C ¬> N
```

should never be written. Instead use

```
((A + B) <= (C/D)) | ((A < M) & (C ¬> N))
```

4.4.1 An Example Using Compound Conditions

We consider the vote-counting problem of Chapter 1, Section 1.4, modified to permit computer processing.

Problem Statement

The problem is to count the votes in an election between two candidates for one office, where the ballots have been transcribed onto data cards. Each card contains two numbers, each of which is either a 0, 1, or 2. If the first number is a 1, this indicates a vote for the first candidate; if the second number is a 1, this indicates a vote for the second candidate. Thus an X on the ballot produces a 1 on the card. If a box is left blank on the ballot, a corresponding 0 is placed on the card. Any other mark on the ballot produces a 2 on the card.

Problem Solution

The solution process has already been discussed in Chapter 1, and so it only remains to modify the final version of the algorithm in terms of the new problem statement. Besides using 0 and 1 to replace X and blank, the algorithm of Section 1.4 repeatedly read a ballot and processed it. To prepare for using the ENDFILE condition to recognize when no more ballots remain, we simply read the first ballot before entering the loop, and within the loop we process it and then read the next ballot. The resulting algorithm is shown in Fig. 4.16. The corresponding program is Fig. 4.17.

```
1.     set both counters to 0;
2.     inspect first ballot;
3.     repeat while any unprocessed ballots remain;
3.1       if box 1 is 1 and box 2 is 0 then
             increment first total;
3.2       if box 2 is 1 and box 1 is 0 then
             increment second total;
3.3       inspect next ballot;
4.     display both totals;
5.     end.
```

Fig. 4.16 Algorithm for Vote Counting Problem

4.5 PROGRAM DEVELOPMENT AND TESTING II

Errors arising from incorrect flow of control are among the most subtle and difficult types of errors to cure. Therefore every effort should be made to prevent such control errors. Shortcuts should be avoided here!

4.5.1 Algorithm Development and Testing

The first place to exercise care is in the design of the algorithm. When the logic is complex, we suggest the supplemental technique of drawing a diagram to chart the flow of control through sequences of decisions and actions. Such a diagram should be developed in conjunction with parts of the algorithm. The advantage of the diagram is the overall view it provides of the logic, while the strength of the algorithm is in systematically decomposing your problem into simpler parts. If these two representations of the same proposed solution both seem reasonable and correct, you can proceed to the coding process with more confidence. However, there is nothing sacred about that type of diagram. What matters is that your algorithm is correct. Whatever techniques help you organize or

```
            /* FIGURE 4.17 */
VOTES:   PROCEDURE OPTIONS (MAIN);

         /* A PROGRAM TO COUNT THE VOTES FOR A TWO MAN
            ELECTION, DISCARDING INVALID BALLOTS. */

         DECLARE
            BOX1 FIXED (5,0), /* BALLOT FOR 1ST CANDIDATE */
            BOX2 FIXED (5,0), /* BALLOT FOR 2ND CANDIDATE */
            TOTAL1 FIXED (5,0), /*1ST CANDIDATE'S TOTAL */
            TOTAL2 FIXED (5,0), /*2ND CANDIDATE'S TOTAL */
            FLAG FIXED (5,0); /* END OF DATA FLAG */

         /* INITIALIZE TOTALS TO ZERO AND SET FLAG */

         TOTAL1 = 0;
         TOTAL2 = 0;
         FLAG = 0;
         ON ENDFILE (SYSIN) FLAG = 1;
         GET LIST (BOX1,BOX2); /* READ FIRST BALLOT */

TALLY_VOTES:
         DO WHILE (FLAG = 0); /* PROCESS ALL BALLOTS */
            IF BOX1 = 1 & BOX2 = 0 THEN
               TOTAL1 = TOTAL1 + 1;
            IF BOX2 = 1 & BOX1 = 0 THEN
               TOTAL2 = TOTAL2 + 1;
            GET LIST (BOX1,BOX2); /* READ NEXT BALLOT */
         END TALLY_VOTES;

         PUT DATA (TOTAL1,TOTAL2);

         END VOTES;
```

Fig. 4.17 Program to Implement Algorithm of Fig. 4.16

Relative Risk* for Males Over 40

		Smoker	
		yes	no
Overweight	yes	4	2
	no	3	1

*Deduct 1 for regular exercise

Fig. 4.18 Heart-Attack Risk-Factor Table

Algorithm

```
1.      if age > 40 then compute and display risk;
```

First Refinement

```
1.      if age > 40 then
1.1        compute risk;
1.2        if exercising then
              reduce risk by 1;
1.3        display risk;
```

Second Refinement

```
1.      if age > 40 then
1.1        if smoker then
              compute risk for smoker;
1.2        otherwise (non-smoker)
              compute risk for non-smoker;
1.3        if exercising then
              reduce risk by 1;
1.4        display risk;
```

Last Refinement

```
1.      if age > 40 then
1.1        if smoker then
1.1.1         if overweight then
                 risk is 4;
1.1.2         otherwise
                 risk is 3;
1.2        otherwise (non-smoker)
1.2.1         if overweight then
                 risk is 2;
1.2.2         otherwise
                 risk is 1;
1.3        if exercising then
              reduce risk by 1;
1.4        display results;
```

Fig. 4.19 Algorithm Development to Implement Fig. 4.18

verify your solution should be used. For an example of complex logic, consider that step in an algorithm which determines a heart-attack risk-factor for males over 40 according to Fig. 4.18. The heart of the problem is determining the risk of a single subject. The step-by-step refinement of the solution for one man is shown in the development of the algorithm in Fig. 4.19.

No matter how carefully you expand your original algorithm, oversights and errors are possible. It is better to catch them now than after wasting time coding an incorrect solution. Therefore you should *try out your solution by hand* for a few simple cases at this stage.

For example, consider a thin, 46 year old who smokes and jogs. Follow the path through the diagram for this case and see what risk would be computed for him. If the answer (2) agrees with the table, try some other cases. If not, reconsider your algorithm.

Only when you are satisfied with your logic should coding begin. When the logic is complex you should observe the following guidelines.

1. Every DO statement should have its own matching END statement; and

2. Every IF statement should have its own matching ELSE statement, even if no special action is required in the ELSE case.

The code, of course, looks much like the algorithm. A quick check at this stage is to draw lines between matching IF-ELSE and DO-END pairs (Fig. 4.20). If none of the lines cross, then the nesting is at least structurally reasonable.

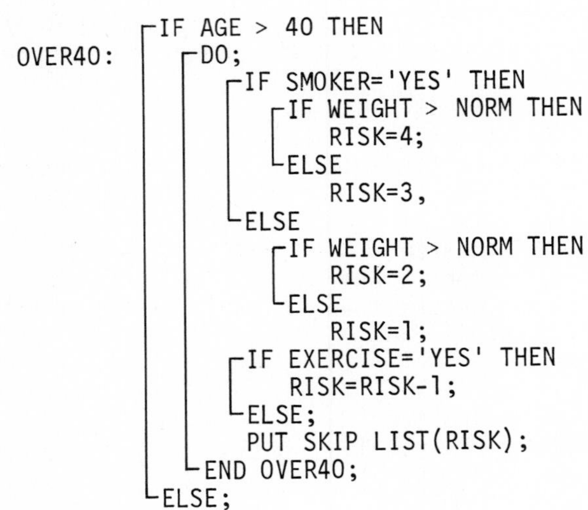

```
         IF AGE > 40 THEN
OVER40:     DO;
               IF SMOKER='YES' THEN
                  IF WEIGHT > NORM THEN
                     RISK=4;
                  ELSE
                     RISK=3,
               ELSE
                  IF WEIGHT > NORM THEN
                     RISK=2;
                  ELSE
                     RISK=1;
               IF EXERCISE='YES' THEN
                  RISK=RISK-1;
               ELSE;
               PUT SKIP LIST(RISK);
            END OVER40;
         ELSE;
```

FIG. 4.20 PL/I Code to Implement Figure 4.19

4.5.2 Program Testing and Debugging

Once a program is written, it must be tested before turning it loose on the world. It is much easier to test a program with only a few carefully selected data items than with the full complement of data your program may eventually handle. The data should be chosen to "try out" enough different paths through the logic to convince you that the program works. In fact the initial testing of a program should be "by hand" to verify that no serious mistakes have been made. When one or two examples have failed to disclose an error, then try your program on the computer with these same data values plus a few more well chosen data samples.

Use a small amount of data, so that you can work out the expected results by hand. If you don't know what to expect, you won't know if the program is, in fact, producing correct output. Also, if the results are not correct, you should be able to trace through the program execution by hand in order to discover what went wrong. This would be quite difficult if large quantities of data were involved.

For example, when testing the code of Fig. 4.20, use only one or two data items representing perhaps a thin, jogging, 46-year-old smoker and some contrasting individual, such as an old, overweight, sedentary non-smoker. You can determine from the table (Fig. 4.18) that their risks should both be 2.

When a program fails to work and any obvious errors have been corrected, the first thing to try is a very careful re-execution of the program by hand, as though you were a computer. If you don't discover where the error arose, then recheck your algorithm to see what result your "solution" should produce for this data. If you still cannot locate the error, then run your program again with only one instance of data which appears to be causing problems. By isolating the data which instigates an error, at least that error can usually be diagnosed and corrected.

When using PL/C, don't forget to utilize the flow history and label count produced at the end of your listing. However, as a last resort, you may obtain more information about the program by executing the statement

```
PUT FLOW;
```

at any suitable point in the program. Its execution produces a recent flow history similar to the one produced at the end of the listing.

If you cannot diagnose a problem even with all this information, we suspect you did not follow our suggestions about careful, modular design and testing of the algorithm as well as the program.

4.6 REVIEW OF RULES

1. The general form of a DO group is

```
<label>: DO;
           {  range of the DO
         END <label>;
```

   In this form, the statements in the range are not necessarily repeated. To the surrounding program a DO group behaves like a single statement. It may therefore be used as the THEN clause or ELSE clause in an IF statement.

2. The ELSE clause is used only in conjunction with the IF statement. In general, it balances the last unbalanced IF in the same logical section of code.

3. The null statement (;) may be used to make explicit that no special action is to be taken.

4.7 REVIEW PROBLEM

Blackjack is a gambling game played with a deck of playing cards. The rules for a simplified game played between two people, the dealer and you, are as follows:

i) All face cards have the value 10; all other cards have face value. (In actual fact, the ace can have the values 1 or 11 but that would make this example too difficult.)

ii) A game consists of several hands. The purpose of each hand is to accumulate cards whose values total as close to 21 as possible without exceeding 21.

iii) Each player gets one card each, you first, then the dealer.

iv) After the first cards have been dealt, you may call for as many cards as you need to get close to 21.

v) When you have sufficient cards, the dealer takes as many cards as he needs. However, when the dealer gets to 17 or more he cannot take any more. Your strategy will be to refuse cards once you get to 16 or more.

vi) The winner of each hand is the person closest to 21 without going over. In the event of ties, the dealer wins the hand.

Problem Statement

Write a computer program to play this simplified version of blackjack. The program should count the number of hands you win versus the number of hands the dealer wins. The input to the program will be 52 data cards with the one number (1 through 10) punched on each to represent the deck of playing cards. The data cards should be shuffled prior to running the program. The game continues until all 52 cards have been used. The hand in progress at that time is not counted.

Solution

As always we begin by analyzing the data requirements of the problem. Each player requires variables to record a card as dealt, a score for each hand and a counter to record the number of wins. The variables to tally the hands won by each player must be initialized to 0, so we can make an initial attempt at solving the problem.

```
1.    initialize variables as required;
2.    play successive hands until cards run out;
3.    print results;
4.    end.
```

Once again, as in so many problems, we have to eliminate the repetitive aspect. This time we must repeatedly deal hands, and so we modify Step 2.

```
2.      repeat until all cards dealt;
2.1        deal one hand to each player;
2.2        determine the winner of that hand;
```

Again we recognize that dealing one hand is not a one-shot action -- not if you plan to stay alive in a card game! Hands are dealt one card at a time from the top of the deck. Hence a further refinement:

```
2.      repeat until all cards dealt;
2.1        deal one card to player;
2.2        deal one card to dealer;
2.3        repeat until player has enough cards;
2.3.1         deal one card to player;
2.4        repeat until dealer has enough cards;
2.4.1         deal one card to dealer;
2.5        determine the winner;
```

Notice that we now have two loops within one loop. If we now sit back and look at this new development, we will find it is rather vague. The algorithm talks about the player and the dealer having "enough cards." How much is enough? In describing the game we said the player's strategy should be to refuse additional cards if his total count was 16 or more. This will be our criterion for "enough." Similarly, the dealer's strategy is to refuse cards if his total is 17 or more. Further, if the player has exceeded 21 already, the dealer wins automatically and so has "enough cards."

To build these conditions in we must also start keeping track of the score for each hand. Initially the score for both players is given by the first card they are dealt. The score then increases by the value of each additional card as it is dealt. So, the algorithm to play one hand is:

```
2.      repeat until all cards dealt;
2.1        get first card for player and make his score=its value;
2.2        get first card for dealer and make his score=its value;
2.3        repeat while player's score < 16;
2.3.1         get a card for player;
2.3.2         add its value to player's score;
2.4        repeat while player's score ≤ 21 and dealer's score < 17;
2.4.1         get a card for dealer;
2.4.2         add its value to dealer's score;
2.5        determine the winner of this hand;
```

Now we need only determine the winner (Step 2.5). The winner of each hand is the player with the highest score -- right? Wrong! The winner is the player whose score comes closest to 21 without going over 21. The scores at the end of each hand will fall into one of three categories:

a) the player exceeds 21,

b) the dealer exceeds 21,

or c) neither the player nor the dealer exceeds 21.

In case (a) the dealer wins, and in case (b) the player wins. Note that, because of the condition in Step 2.4, cases (a) and (b) can never occur simultaneously. In case (c) the player wins only if his score is higher than the dealer's; otherwise the dealer wins. Fig. 4.21 expresses this in algorithmic form.

```
1.      if player's score > 21 then
           add 1 to dealer's wins;
2.      else
2.1        if dealer's score > 21 then
              add 1 to player's wins;
2.2        else
2.2.1         if player's score > dealer's score then
                 add 1 to player's wins;
2.2.2         else
                 add 1 to dealer's wins;
```

Fig. 4.21 Determining Winner of One hand

Before wrapping up the final version of the algorithm, we must consider what to do when we run out of cards. In real life, the discarded cards will be picked up, shuffled and the deal will continue. That would unnecessarily complicate our problem. When we run out of cards, that is, reach end of file, we will simply ignore the hand on which we are currently working and finish off the program. So, if there are no cards remaining to be dealt, we should bypass the instructions to determine the winner of the hand. The complete algorithm is given as Fig. 4.22, and the corresponding PL/I program is shown in Fig. 4.23.

Note the number of times the algorithm asks whether cards have run out (Steps 2, 2.3, 2.4 and 2.5). The program correspondingly tests whether FLAG still has the value of 0 at the beginning of each major section of code (GAME, PLAYER, DEALER and SCORE). These tests may appear redundant, since three of them appear within a larger loop (Step 2 or GAME), which makes the same test itself. However, these tests are necessary. Their purpose is to ensure that we only count those hands which have a full complement of cards. We will most likely run out of cards somewhere inside the loop! Recall that the only action taken in this case is to set FLAG equal to 1. The program will then continue with the rest of the statements inside the loop. However, by testing for an exhausted deck at the beginning of each major section of the loop, these sections will be bypassed when the cards run out, and no further processing will be done.

As with any correct computer program, this one will give the same results each time it is run with the same input data. To enable you to verify the results shown in Fig. 4.23, the input to this particular run was in the following order (by rows):

```
5   7   9   5   9   5   7   8   8   6   3   6   6
9  10   7  10   7  10   3  10   4   4   8   1   4
1  10  10  10  10  10   5   3   8  10  10  10   2
2   6  10   2   3   1   1  10   2   9   4  10  10
```

```
1.         initialize player's wins and dealer's wins to 0;
2.         repeat until all cards dealt;
2.1           get first card for player and make his score=its value;
2.2           get first card for dealer and make his score=its value;
2.3           repeat while player's score < 16 and cards remain;
2.3.1            get a card for player;
2.3.2            add its value to player's score;
2.4           repeat while player's score ≤ 21 and dealer's score < 17
                 and cards remain;
2.4.1            get a card for dealer;
2.4.2            add its value to dealer's score;
2.5           if hand was not terminated because cards ran out then
2.5.1            if player's score > 21 then
                    add 1 to dealer's wins;
2.5.2            else
2.5.2.1             if dealer's score > 21 then
                       add 1 to player's wins;
2.5.2.2             else
2.5.2.2.1              if player's score > dealer's score then
                          add 1 to player's wins;
2.5.2.2.2              else
                          add 1 to dealer's wins;
3.         display number of wins for dealer and player;
4.         end.
```

Fig. 4.22 Algorithm for Blackjack

To get different results it will be necessary to shuffle the input deck. For now, you will have to do this manually, although it is possible to simulate physically shuffling the cards. We have also refrained from biasing this game in favor of the dealer -- it is absolutely fair within the strategies set. Since the dealer (the program) could inspect its opponent's hand, it would be a trivial matter to rig the program in the dealer's favor. Take our advice and never bet on games played against the computer unless you really understand the program (that is, unless you wrote it yourself).

```
            /* FIGURE 4.23 */
BLKJACK:PROCEDURE OPTIONS (MAIN);

        /* A PROGRAM TO PLAY A SIMPLIFIED TWO MAN BLACKJACK
           GAME. THE "CARDS" ARE THE VALUES 1 THRU 10 PUNCHED ON
           DATA CARDS TO MAKE UP THE VALUES IN A 52 CARD DECK. */

        DECLARE
           CARD1 FIXED (5,0), /* CARD DEALT TO PLAYER */
           CARD2 FIXED (5,0), /* CARD DEALT TO DEALER */
           SCORE1 FIXED (5,0), /* HAND SCORE OF PLAYER */
           SCORE2 FIXED (5,0), /* HAND SCORE OF DEALER */
           WINS1 FIXED (5,0), /* HANDS WON BY PLAYER */
           WINS2 FIXED (5,0), /* HANDS WON BY DEALER */
           FLAG FIXED (5,0);

        /* INITIALIZE VARIABLES */

        WINS1 = 0;
        WINS2 = 0;
        FLAG = 0;
        ON ENDFILE (SYSIN) FLAG = 1;

GAME:   DO WHILE (FLAG = 0);
           /* DEAL FIRST CARD */
           GET LIST (CARD1,CARD2);
           /* INITIALIZE SCORES FOR HAND */
           SCORE1 = CARD1;
           SCORE2 = CARD2;
           /* PLAYER WILL TAKE CARDS AS LONG AS HIS SCORE
              IS LESS THAN 16 */
PLAYER:    DO WHILE (SCORE1 < 16 & FLAG = 0);
              GET LIST (CARD1);
              SCORE1 = SCORE1 + CARD1;
           END PLAYER;
           /* DEALER WILL TAKE CARDS AS LONG AS HIS SCORE
              IS LESS THAN 17 AND THE PLAYER HAS NOT EXCEEDED 21 */
DEALER:    DO WHILE ( (SCORE2 < 17) & (SCORE1 < 22) & (FLAG = 0));
              GET LIST (CARD2);
              SCORE2 = SCORE2 + CARD2;
           END DEALER;
           /* DETERMINE THE WINNER FOR ONE HAND ONLY IF
              THERE ARE STILL CARDS IN THE DECK. */
           IF FLAG = 0 THEN
SCORE:        DO;
                 PUT SKIP DATA (SCORE1,SCORE2);
                 IF SCORE1 > 21 THEN
                    WINS2 = WINS2 + 1;
                 ELSE
                    IF SCORE2 > 21 THEN
                       WINS1 = WINS1 + 1;
                    ELSE
                       IF SCORE1 > SCORE2 THEN
                          WINS1 = WINS1 + 1;
                       ELSE
                          WINS2 = WINS2 + 1;
              END SCORE;
        END GAME;

        PUT SKIP DATA (WINS1,WINS2);

        END BLKJACK;


SCORE1=      19            SCORE2=      21;
SCORE1=      21            SCORE2=      17;
SCORE1=      16            SCORE2=      26;
SCORE1=      20            SCORE2=      18;
SCORE1=      23            SCORE2=       1;
SCORE1=      20            SCORE2=      20;
SCORE1=      23            SCORE2=       3;
SCORE1=      20            SCORE2=      20;
SCORE1=      16            SCORE2=      26;
WINS1=       4             WINS2=       5;
```

Fig. 4.23 Program to Implement Blackjack Algorithm of Fig. 4.22

4.8 EXERCISES

4.1 Triangles come in several different flavors: scalene, isosceles, equilateral and right angled. An isosceles triangle is one with any two sides equal; an equilateral triangle has three equal sides; a right angled triangle is one where the square of one side is equal to the sum of the squares of the other two; a scalene triangle is a triangle with none of the above properties.

Describe an algorithm to examine an arbitrary number of triplets representing sides of a triangle and decide whether they, in fact, could form a triangle and if so, which one of the four classes described above.

Implement your algorithm by a computer program which should produce as output the three sides considered and one of the messages: 'SCALENE', 'ISOSCELES', 'EQUILATERAL', 'RIGHT ANGLED', or 'NOT A TRIANGLE'.

4.2 A data deck contains an unspecified quantity of integers in the range [100,999]. Describe an algorithm to do the following:

i) read each number
ii) print the number
iii) if the sum of the digits in the number is even then print the number again
iv) otherwise print the individual digits.

Implement your algorithm by computer program.

4.3 Write a program which generates an interest table, showing the interest on $1000 after 1,2,...,9,10 years at the following annual interest rates: 8%, 8 1/4%, 8 1/2%, 8 3/4%, 9%.

4.4 A prime number is an integer whose only integer divisors are 1 and the number itself. Thus 1,2,3,5,7,11,13 are the first seven prime numbers.

(a) Write a program to determine whether a given number is a prime number.

(b) Write a program to generate the first twenty five prime numbers.

(c) Write a program to generate all the prime numbers between 100 and 200.

4.5 A "perfect number" is one, all of whose divisors (except itself) sum to the number. Thus 6 is a perfect number because its divisors, 3, 2, and 1, add up to 6. On the other hand 8 is not a perfect number because its divisors are 4, 2, and 1 which only sum to 7.

Describe an algorithm to find all perfect numbers less than or equal to some number, N. Implement your algorithm by computer program.

4.6 A pair of numbers, m and n, are called "amicable" if they have the following relationship:

the factors of m add up to n, and
the factors of n add up to m, and
m and n are not equal.

Find the smallest integer m such that m and n are an amicable pair. As with "perfect numbers" (Exercise 4.5), 1 is considered a divisor of m, but m is not considered one of its own divisors.

4.7 Two men go to a casino where they each pay $100.00 to participate in a game. They each have $100.00 left to play the game whose rules are:

1. Each man writes down a sum of money, called a bid, on a piece of paper.
2. Each bid must be greater than zero.
3. The bids are compared and the high bidder receives $20.00 from the casino and must pay the amount of his bid to the low bidder.
4. In the case of a tie, each bidder receives $10.00 from the casino.
5. Provided both players have money left, they must each make five bids.

Describe an algorithm to play this game and implement your algorithm by a PL/I program. The data for your program will consist of five cards each with two values representing the bids by each player. Your program output should have the form:

BID #	A_BID	B_BID	A_TOTAL	B_TOTAL
1	13.00	6.00	107.00	113.00
2	20.00	20.00	117.00	123.00
		.		
		.		
		.		

<u>Aside</u>: What <u>one</u> bid would you always make if you were playing this game?

4.8 A five lane bridge runs north and south. At fixed time intervals a traffic counter at each end supplies traffic densities for northbound or southbound traffic. Based on these densities, the number of lanes in each direction is dynamically changed. The traffic densities are given as 0 for no traffic, 1 for light, 2 for medium, and 3 for heavy. A density factor is computed at each time interval as the absolute value of the difference of the densities in each direction. The lane allocation is then made as follows:

i) If the density factor is zero, the lane allocation is 3 northbound and 2 southbound lanes.

ii) If the density factor is 1, the lane allocation will be 3-2 in favor of the current heavy traffic direction.

iii) If the density factor is 2 or 3, the lane allocation will be 4-1 in favor of the current heavy traffic direction.

Design an algorithm to show how to decide new lane allocations based on the traffic densities.

Suppose the traffic densities are given as two digits on a data card representing northbound and southbound traffic densities, respectively. Write a PL/I program to show the resulting lane allocation for each of the following data cards which represent every possible combination of traffic densities:

```
0 0
0 1
0 2
0 3
1 0
1 1
1 2
1 3
2 0
2 1
2 2
2 3
3 0
3 1
3 2
3 3
```

Chapter 5 Character Handling

Computers have achieved a sometimes exaggerated reputation for their ability to calculate with numbers. At the same time their capacity for text manipulation is seldom appreciated, even though nearly as much computer time is spent each year processing textual data as is spent in scientific numerical calculations.

One reason is historical. Computers had their initial impact in the world of numbers. Another reason is probably that text processing (reading, writing, and looking up telephone numbers) is so familiar to us as compared to algebra, that we don't regard the underlying operations as anything special.

In any case, computers are adept at handling text. Many modern businesses depend on this ability as do many of the most important computer applications, such as library and hospital systems, computer-assisted instructions, and many research endeavors. In fact, the PL/I compiler itself is a program which converts the text of your PL/I program into a form which the computer can execute. Thus your own program undergoes extensive manipulation as text in the hands of the compiler.

This chapter describes how computers process text, which will hereafter be called "character data." The term "character data" is significant, since text constitutes a separate category of data with its own appropriate operators, just as numbers constitute another category of data with its own operators. For example, it makes no sense to multiply your name by the body of a form letter, but it may make sense to append your name to a form letter, or to insert it in the right places.

5.1 CHARACTER STRINGS

The basic pieces of data in the world of characters are called *character strings*, and consist of any sequence of characters enclosed in single quotes. For example, the following are character strings:

i) 'HARVEY'
ii) '3*/$X@4B'
iii) 'HAVE A NICE DAY'
iv) '10'
v) ''

As example (ii) indicates, you may have any characters whatsoever within the string, including blanks which are also valid characters (iii). We will sometimes denote a blank by a "slashed b," b̸. Example (iv) shows the character 1 followed by the character 0, which looks to the eye deceptively like the number 10 -- but it isn't! It is merely a vertical line followed by an oval and has no numerical interpretation because the surrounding quotes give it a different interpretation. Example (v) shows a special string, called the *null string*, consisting of no characters. In the world of characters, it has a role similar to that of zero in the numeric world.

The quotes are essential, because some character strings could be mistaken for other things (e.g., variable names) without them. Because some character strings contain quote marks, as in IT'S OKAY, the quote mark itself is denoted by *two* consecutive quotes to eliminate ambiguity. This string would have to be written

'IT''S OKAY'

Be careful to distinguish such embedded quotes from the null string itself.

5.2 THE PUT LIST STATEMENT

In case you are growing weary of seeing every output value preceded by the variable name from which it came, there are other types of PUT statement besides PUT DATA. The statement

```
PUT SKIP LIST (<value1>,<value2>,...,<value n>);
```

will print the specified values from left to right without printing out any variable names. For example, if variables MAX and WELL contain the integers 25 and 64, respectively, then compare the following:

statement	output	
PUT SKIP DATA(MAX,WELL);	MAX=25	WELL=64
PUT SKIP LIST(MAX,WELL);	25	64
PUT SKIP LIST(25,64);	25	64

Note that the items displayed by PUT LIST need not originate in variables. You may therefore display a character string by putting it in a PUT LIST statement. For example, to print a title or other message on your output, use the following scheme:

```
PUT SKIP LIST('RESULTS FOR PROBLEM #6');
```

The same PUT statement may contain a mixture of character and numeric data for more interesting output, as follows:

```
PUT SKIP LIST('MAX CONTAINS',MAX,'IN PART',1);
```

which produces the line:

```
MAX CONTAINS        25        IN PART        1
```

Note that the 25 came from variable MAX, which could be recognized as a variable by the absence of quotes.

In PL/C, the maximum number of characters which may normally[1] be printed on one line is 120. Each line of print is subdivided into 5 fields of 24 characters each. When the first PUT LIST in a program is encountered, the values for the variables in the output list are printed, one to a field, beginning with the first field of the first line. Subsequent execution of a PUT LIST will cause the values to be printed in the field next to where the previous PUT statement left off. When all five fields on a line have been used, the printer moves to the first field of the next line. Thus the code:

```
DECLARE (I,J,K) FIXED(5,0);
I=10;
J=11;
K=12;
PUT LIST (I,J);
PUT LIST (K);
PUT LIST (I,J,K);
```

will produce the output in the following arrangement:

```
10        11        12        10        11
12
```

This is exactly the same output as would have been produced by:

```
PUT LIST (I,J,K,I,J,K);
```

Since character strings often extend to more than 24 characters, PL/C has some special rules to handle this situation. If such a string is exactly 24 characters long, then the next field on the printed line will be skipped for spacing purposes. If the string is more than 24 characters long, PL/C will continue printing into the next field without any break. However if printing of such a character string was begun in the last field of a line then it will be continued on the first field of the next line. To control the spacing across the line, a more powerful form of PUT will be described in Chapter 6.

However, it is possible to control the spacing between lines using either PUT DATA or PUT LIST. To skip n lines before printing, use SKIP(n), rather than SKIP. Thus SKIP(1) is equivalent to SKIP, SKIP(3) leaves two blank lines and prints on the third line, and SKIP(0) prints over the top of the current line. SKIP(0) is useful for such tricks as underlining other text. One can also use PAGE rather than SKIP to begin printing at the top of a new page. Thus the statements:

---

[1]This may be modified at different installations up to a maximum of 132.

```
PUT PAGE LIST('PREPARE THYSELF');
PUT SKIP(0) LIST('_______________  _ _ _ _ _ _');
PUT SKIP(1) LIST('IN THE BEGINNING ...');
```

produce the following output at the top of a new page:

```
PREPARE THYSELF
IN THE BEGINNING ...
```

It is possible to execute PUT statements which only control line spacing without mentioning any values, e.g., PUT SKIP(5); or PUT PAGE;. By executing PUT PAGE just before program termination, the PL/C diagnostic information will appear on a separate page from your last printed results. This trick makes for much cleaner output. However, to avoid wasting precious paper, we recommend that PUT PAGE not be used until the program is executing correctly.

5.3 CHARACTER VARIABLES AND MOVING CHARACTER DATA

Just as numbers may be stored in memory locations, so too may character strings. However, since character strings have properties quite different than those of numbers, they must be stored in the appropriate CHARACTER variables, quite distinct from numeric variables. As usual, your choice of variable names and attributes is announced by the DECLARE statement, as follows:

```
DECLARE (REMARK, MESSAGE) CHARACTER(80) VARYING;
```

This statement requests two memory locations, named REMARK and MESSAGE, to be used for holding CHARACTER strings. Since you don't know exactly how many characters will comprise the strings to be stored in these locations, you declare that their lengths will be VARYING but have a maximum of 80 characters per string. If you did happen to know in advance that only strings with 35 characters would reside there, you could have declared these locations as CHARACTER(35) without including the VARYING. However, we will retain the flexibility of VARYING for now.[2] Incidentally, the maximum length may be any number between 0 and 256.[3]

As with other data types, values may be stored in CHARACTER variables by using the assignment statement or by reading values from data cards with a GET statement.

The assignment statement,

```
<character variable> = <character expression>;
```

simply stores some character string in the character variable mentioned on the left of the = sign. A character expression is any character string or any variable or function which represents a character string.

---

[2]See Section 5.11.2 for a discussion of CHARACTER strings which are not VARYING.

[3]This restriction applies only in PL/C, not in PL/I.

For example,

```
REMARK = '@$*-/¢';
```

produces the following result in memory:

```
REMARK [@$*-/¢]
```

However, if A and B are <u>numeric</u> variables, the following two statements are improper -- they attempt to store numeric values into character variables, contrary to the desired separation of these two types of data![4]

```
REMARK = 6;
MESSAGE = A + B;
```

However, the statements

```
REMARK = '6';
MESSAGE = 'A + B';
```

produce the results:

```
REMARK [6]     MESSAGE [Ab+bB]
```

Character strings enclosed in quotes may be read from data cards into memory locations by executing a GET LIST statement. Conversely, if a character variable appears in a PUT statement, its value (i.e., the character string stored there) will be printed on the listing. For example, the statements

```
GET LIST(REMARK);
PUT SKIP LIST(REMARK);
PUT SKIP DATA(REMARK);
```

might copy the following data card onto the listing as follows:

data card	output
'I LOVE PL/C'	I LOVE PL/C REMARK = 'I LOVE PL/C'

5.4 STRING COMPARISON

Character strings can be compared to one another in order to make decisions. For example, to decide whether the string value just read into the variable REMARK happened to be the character string 'WOE IS ME', your program could ask

```
IF REMARK = 'WOE IS ME' THEN ...
```

Though strings do not have numeric magnitudes, they do all fall somewhere in what is called lexicographic ordering. This is the same alphabetic-type ordering used to search the library catalog or the telephone directory. In terms of this ordering you might say that 'TWELVE' comes before, or is lexicographically less than, 'TWO'; similarly 'MURPHY' is greater than (comes after) 'JONES'. Such

---

[4]In PL/C only, an attempt to store numeric data in a character variable results in an error message.

relationships can be posed by using the usual relational operators <, <=, =, >=, >, ¬=, ¬<, ¬>. For example you can ask whether the character string stored in REMARK precedes 'LAUGH' by

IF REMARK < 'LAUGH' THEN ...

Each character has a fixed place in the ordering just as each letter has a fixed place in the alphabet. Two strings are compared character by character, from left to right until (i) they differ in some corresponding position; (ii) they are found to be identical or (iii) the end of one string is reached before the end of the other. In case (i) the first differing characters are compared, and the ordering of these two characters determines the ordering of the strings. Thus 'TWELVE' < 'TWO' is true, because 'E' precedes 'O'. In case (iii) the shorter string is considered "less than" the longer, so that 'TWO' < 'TWOSOME' is also true. The blank is the first (smallest) character in the ordering, followed by the punctuation symbols, the alphabetic characters and the decimal digits 0,1,...,9 in that order. A special case is that a string of blanks is considered equal to the null string.

5.5 LENGTH BUILT-IN FUNCTION

PL/I provides many *built-in functions* which augment the basic operators in the language. A complete list of these is given in Appendix D. In the course of this chapter we introduce three of these functions.

One of the properties which a character string has is its length, i.e., the *number* of characters in the string. To determine this number for *any* string, use the built-in function LENGTH which has the general form:

LENGTH (<character expression>)

Use of this function will generate an integer number, which is the number of characters currently comprising the <character expression>. For example, to determine if the character variable MESSAGE has more than three characters currently stored in it, you might ask

IF LENGTH (MESSAGE) > 3 THEN ...

Since LENGTH generates a *number* it can be used in any context where you can legally use an *integer*. Thus you can print out the value by

PUT SKIP LIST (LENGTH (MESSAGE));

or save it for future use by

N = LENGTH (MESSAGE);

or even save a modified value by

N = LENGTH (MESSAGE) +1;

The LENGTH function is most useful for testing variables which have the VARYING attribute, since those character variables which do not have the varying attribute *never* change in length.

5.5.1 A Problem Using LENGTH

Suppose someone gives you a box of data cards containing an unspecified number of randomly selected words (within quotes) from the dictionary. You are to produce a list of those words from the first half of the alphabet (A-M inclusive) and compute the total word length of those same words.

The first step in deriving a solution is to recognize that you must maintain a variable for total word length and that as the words which meet the requirement are encountered, you can update this total and print those words. Note that "dictionary" words between A and M are those which come before N. An algorithm is shown in Fig. 5.1 and the corresponding program in Fig. 5.2.

5.6 BASIC STRING OPERATORS

5.6.1 Concatenation

When writing a letter, you append one word at a time to what you have already written until the letter is finished. At the end you can sign just your first name or attach your last name immediately after it for more complete identification. This operation of joining strings end to end is called concatenation and is as basic an operation on strings as addition is for numbers. Consequently, PL/I has a string concatenation operator, written as a pair of vertical lines (requiring two keypunch strokes):

```
MESSAGE = 'E' || 'AR';
```

This statement would produce the string 'EAR' and store it in variable MESSAGE. The following statement could use this result to construct the string 'DEAR JOHN', which might be a suitable beginning for your letter:

```
REMARK = 'D' ||MESSAGE||'ȸJOHN';
```

Now that REMARK contains 'DEAR JOHN', LENGTH(REMARK) is 9, assuming the variable is VARYING. If you were to concatenate more characters onto this string by executing:

```
REMARK = REMARK ||', GOODBYE.';
```

LENGTH(REMARK) would then become 19, since REMARK would now contain 'DEAR JOHN, GOODBYE.' as illustrated below.

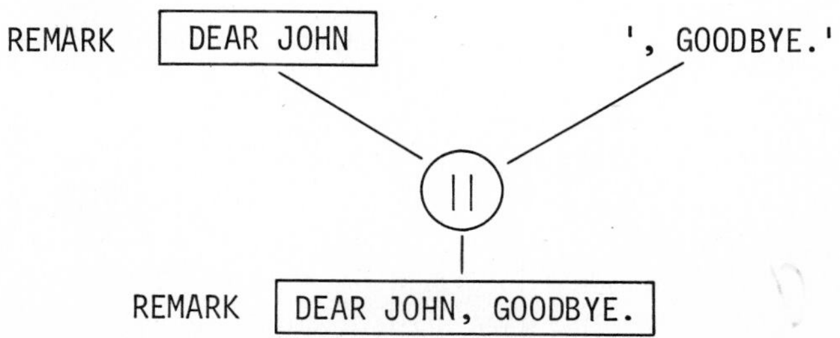

1. start with total length of 0;
2. read first word;
3. repeat as long as unprocessed words remain;
3.1 if the current word is < N, then;
3.1.1 print out the word; and
3.1.2 add its length to the total;
3.2 read the next word;
4. print out total length;
5. end.

Fig. 5.1 Algorithm to Find Total Length of Words Beginning with Letters A - M

```
          /* FIGURE 5.2 */
ALPHA:  PROCEDURE OPTIONS (MAIN);

        /* THIS PROGRAM READS AN INDEFINITE NUMBER OF
           WORDS ON DATA CARDS. IT PRINTS A LIST AND
           COMPUTES THE TOTAL LENGTH OF THOSE WORDS WHICH
           BEGIN WITH THE LETTERS A THRU M INCLUSIVE.
           WE ASSUME ALL WORDS START WITH SOME LETTER. */

        DECLARE
           WORD CHARACTER (80) VARYING,
           (TOTAL,NOMORE) FIXED (5,0);
        /* WORD = CURRENT WORD READ FROM DATA CARD
           TOTAL = TOTAL LENGTH OF ALL WORDS BEGINNING
                  WITH THE LETTERS A THRU M
           NOMORE = FLAG TO CONTROL END OF DATA */

        /* INITIALIZE VARIABLES AND PRINT HEADING */

        NOMORE = 0;
        TOTAL = 0;
        ON ENDFILE (SYSIN) NOMORE = 1;
        GET LIST (WORD);

LOOP:   DO WHILE (NOMORE = 0);

           /* DO WE PROCESS CURRENT WORD? */

           IF WORD < 'N' THEN

OUTCOME:       DO; /* PRINT WORD AND ADD ITS LENGTH */
                  PUT SKIP LIST (WORD);
                  TOTAL = TOTAL + LENGTH(WORD);
               END OUTCOME;

           GET LIST (WORD);
        END LOOP;

        PUT SKIP DATA (TOTAL);

        END ALPHA;
```

Fig. 5.2 Program to Implement Algorithm of Fig. 5.1

5.6.2 INDEX Built-in Function

Another basic operation is to scan text in order to find a particular word or phrase. For example, you might look through a telephone book (a rather large piece of text) for a particular name. Or you may receive a letter from Aunt Agatha which you expect will mostly describe her real and imagined ills. However, she always includes some scuttlebut about Aunt Sophy which you don't want to miss. What you do is quickly scan the letter to find the word "Sophy," so you will know where to begin reading.

This "finding" function is provided by PL/I through the built-in function INDEX whose form is

INDEX (<subject string>,<pattern string>)

Here, <pattern string> is the precise group of characters for which you are searching in the <subject string>. Thus if Aunt Agatha's letter was stored in the character variable LETTER, you might look for the <u>first</u> occurrence of SOPHY by using

```
INDEX (LETTER,'SOPHY')
```

Like LENGTH, INDEX generates an integer number. If the <pattern string> was <u>not</u> contained in the <subject string>, then this number is zero. However, if this number is not zero, then it represents the starting location of the <u>first</u> occurrence of the pattern in the subject.

Assuming that REMARK contains:

```
                 123456789
REMARK          |DEAR JOHN|
```

then the statement

```
M = INDEX ('DEAR PENELOPE', REMARK);
```

will cause the number zero to be stored in M, because the pattern did not occur in the subject. However, when searching for the name 'JOHN',

```
N = INDEX (REMARK, 'JOHN');
```

will store the number 6 in N since the string JOHN begins at position 6. The statement

```
L = INDEX ('DEAR PENELOPE', 'E');
```

will store the number 2 in L even though the letter 'E' appears four times in the subject. INDEX finds only the <u>first</u> occurrence of the pattern in the subject.

Note that INDEX, like LENGTH, can never be used on the left-hand side of an assignment statement nor in a GET statement, since neither function represents a memory location.

You might ask <u>whether</u> the string 'SOPHY' appeared in LETTER by writing

```
IF INDEX(LETTER,'SOPHY') ¬= 0 THEN ...
```

If 'SOPHY' appears, then INDEX will <u>not</u> be 0 and you can do whatever follows THEN. But be careful! IF LETTER should be something like

```
          123456789
LETTER  | MY PHILOSOPHY IS ... |
```

the value of INDEX(LETTER,'SOPHY') will be 9, whether a later reference was made to Aunt Sophy or not. You might have more success by including a blank in the pattern:

INDEX(LETTER,' SOPHY')

5.6.3 A Problem Using || and INDEX

Suppose you are given a list of words (each surrounded by quotes on a data card). From this list you are to select the words containing the character string 'TO' and join them together into a "sentence." Whether this sentence has any "meaning" or not, its words should be separated by a blank.

For example, given the input data

```
'SINCE' 'TOBY' 'TOOK' 'THE' 'OPENER' 'TOM' 'RUSHED' 'INTO' 'TOWN'
'FOR' 'ANOTHER'
```

your output should be

'TOBY TOOK TOM INTO TOWN'

Note that the output string can be built up word by word (just like a letter) from those words containing 'TO'. However, just as a variable which maintains a total must have an initial value of 0, the character variable where the eventual output string will be built must also have an initial value. This initial value should be "nothing at all," or the null string, since no words belong to the sentence initially. The algorithm is straightforward and is shown in Fig. 5.3. The corresponding program is Fig. 5.4.

```
1.    initially the sentence is empty;
2.    read the first word;
3.    repeat the following as long as there remain words to
         process;
3.1      if the current word contains 'TO' then
            append this word  followed by a blank
            to the end of the sentence;
3.2      read the next word;
4.    display the sentence;
5.    end.
```

Fig. 5.3 Algorithm to Concatenate Words Containing TO

```
           /* FIGURE 5.4 */
UNTO:     PROCEDURE OPTIONS (MAIN);

          /* THIS PROGRAM READS WORDS FROM DATA CARDS AND
             FORMS A SENTENCE FROM THOSE WORDS WHICH
             CONTAIN THE SUBSTRING "TO". SUCH AS TORONTO
             OR BOSTON. EACH WORD IN THE FORMED SENTENCE
             IS FOLLOWED BY A BLANK. */

          DECLARE
             WORD CHARACTER (20) VARYING,
             SENTENCE CHARACTER (250) VARYING,
             RUNOUT FIXED (5,0);

          /* WORD = CURRENT WORD READ FROM DATA CARD
             SENTENCE = SENTENCE FORMED FROM WORDS WITH THE
                        SUBSTRING "TO"
             RUNOUT = FLAG TO NOTE END OF DATA. */

          /*INITIALIZE VARIABLES AND SET ENDFILE CONDITION*/

          SENTENCE = '';
          RUNOUT = 0;
          ON ENDFILE (SYSIN) RUNOUT = 1;
          GET LIST (WORD);

BUILD:    DO WHILE (RUNOUT = 0);
             IF INDEX(WORD,'TO') ¬= 0 THEN
                SENTENCE = SENTENCE || WORD || ' ';
             GET LIST (WORD);
          END BUILD;

          PUT DATA (SENTENCE);

          END UNTO;
```

Fig. 5.4 Program to Implement Algorithm of Fig. 5.3

5.7 SUBSTR BUILT-IN FUNCTION

INDEX told you where the most interesting part of Aunt Agatha's letter began, but you must still focus your attention at that spot and read what she has to say about Aunt Sophy. In other words you must extract the juicy tidbits in order to savor them.

The ability to extract or isolate a substring (i.e., a portion) of another string is provided in PL/I by the SUBSTRing function whose general form is:

SUBSTR(<subject string>,<position where substring begins>,<length of substring>)

The second and third "arguments", position and length, are integer numbers or integer valued expressions, which describe the location and extent of the substring in the <subject string>. SUBSTR, unlike INDEX and LENGTH, actually produces a character string. Thus the value of SUBSTR('OPPOSITE',5,3) is the string 'SIT', and the value of SUBSTR('OPPOSITE',3,5) is the string 'POSIT'. Of course, this function must be used within an appropriate context. For example

```
DECLARE (PART,WHOLE) CHARACTER(20) VARYING;
        .
        .
        .
WHOLE = 'SENTENCE';
PART = SUBSTR(WHOLE,4,3);
```

would place the string 'TEN' in variable PART.

A very common sequence of actions is to first find a pattern using INDEX and then extract a substring which depends on where this pattern was found. Returning to Aunt Agatha's letter, if she always packs the meat of her message into the first seventeen characters of her first sentence about Sophy, you could extract and store this highlight by writing:

```
POSITION = INDEX(LETTER,'SOPHY');
MESSAGE  = SUBSTR(LETTER,POSITION,17);
```

The result is shown below:

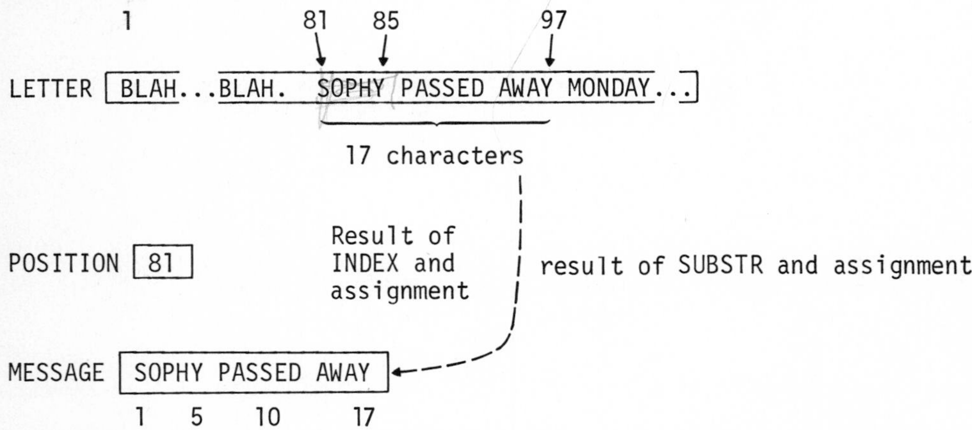

Having stored the starting position in the numeric-type variable POSITION, SUBSTR removed 17 characters, starting with the one currently stored in POSITION (i.e., the 81st). To extract simply the highlight, without the initial 'SOPHY', the second assignment statement could be:

```
MESSAGE = SUBSTR(LETTER,POSITION+6,11);
```

In this case, SUBSTR would yield an 11-character string, beginning with (POSITION+6), which in this case begins at position 87 and is the substring 'PASSED AWAY'.

A common special case is to inspect a single character. For example to ask if the third character of the string stored in REMARK happens to be an 'E', you could write:

```
IF SUBSTR(REMARK,3,1) = 'E' THEN ...
```

In reality you cannot rely on Aunt Agatha to confine her remarks about Aunt Sophy to 17 characters. In fact, once she gets on the subject, she is likely to continue on to the end of the letter about Aunt Sophy. By omitting the third "argument," the length specification, SUBSTR will provide the remainder of the original string beginning at the specified position. Thus

SUBSTR(LETTER,POSITION)

would yield everything from the position specified in POSITION to the end of the string in LETTER. The utility of this feature will be shown below.

The position argument must be some integer number between 1 and the length of the subject string. Further, if the length parameter has value N and the position parameter has value M, then M+N-1 must not exceed the length of the subject string.

For example, if the variable REMARK has contents:

```
                    1 2 3 4 5 6 7 8 9 1011
REMARK             |F E B R U A R Y ƀ 2 1|
```

it would be illegal to reference

SUBSTR (REMARK,12,2)

because there is no 12th position in REMARK. Similarly a reference such as

SUBSTR (REMARK,9,4)

would generate an error because there is no substring of length 4 beginning in position 9. The largest available substring has length 3.

5.8 BASIC STRING EDITING

To <u>delete the initial character</u> of the string in MESSAGE, extract all but the first character from (old) MESSAGE and make this substring the new value of MESSAGE:

```
MESSAGE = SUBSTR(MESSAGE,2);
           12345
MESSAGE   |ABCDE|
(before)

MESSAGE   |BCDE|
(after)
```

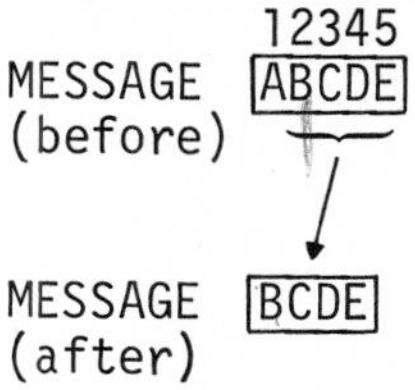

To <u>break up</u> a string into parts, SUBSTR can be used to extract each part. This is the reverse of concatenation.

```
NAME = 'SOMETIMES';
FIRST = SUBSTR(NAME,1,4);
LAST = SUBSTR(NAME,5);
  NAME  |SOMETIMES|

  FIRST |SOME|      LAST |TIMES|
```

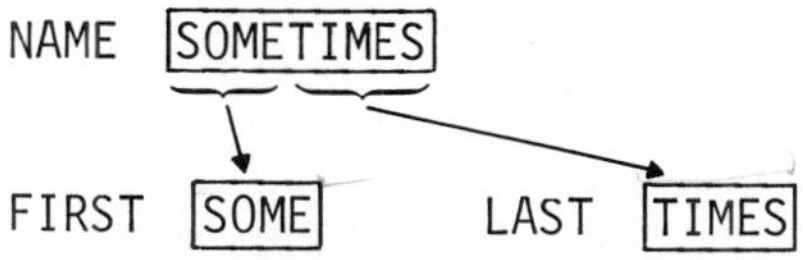

To <u>delete</u> characters from the interior of a string, simply obtain the substrings surrounding the portion of the string to be deleted and reassemble (i.e., concatenate) these substrings without the intervening characters.

For example, to find and delete the first blank, in NAME, where NAME currently contains 'JOHN DOE', first find the blank and then concatenate the preceding and succeeding substrings:

```
N = INDEX(NAME,' ');
NAME = SUBSTR(NAME,1,N-1)||SUBSTR(NAME,N+1);
```

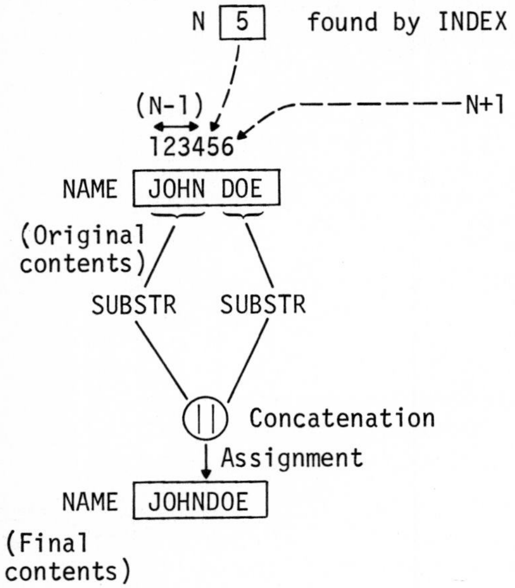

N [5] found by INDEX

(N-1) N+1

123456

NAME [JOHN DOE]

(Original contents)

SUBSTR SUBSTR

(||) Concatenation

Assignment

NAME [JOHNDOE]

(Final contents)

Inserting characters is comparable. To insert John's middle initial, Q, between the blank and John's last name, simply redefine NAME to contain its original initial substring, followed by 'Q.b̸', followed by its original final substring (his last name):

```
N = INDEX(NAME,' ');
NAME = SUBSTR(NAME,1,N)||'Q. '||SUBSTR(NAME,N+1);
```

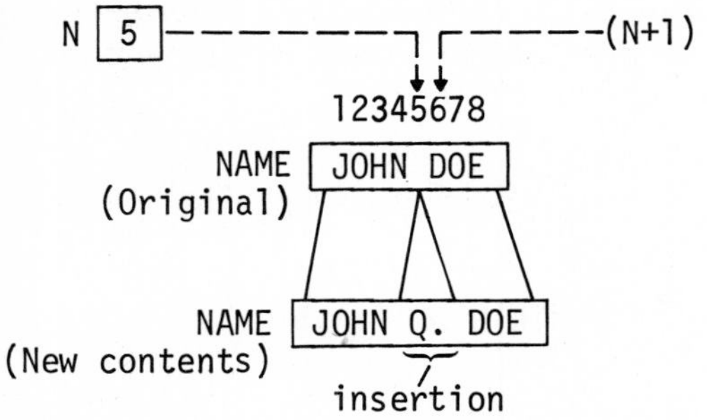

N [5] (N+1)

12345678

NAME (Original) [JOHN DOE]

NAME (New contents) [JOHN Q. DOE]

insertion

Replacing one substring (or character) by another could be done by first deleting the old substring and then inserting the new substring in the same place. However, a better way is to construct a new value by concatenating the substrings to be retained with the new replacement string. Thus to replace the Q in 'JOHN Q. DOE' by an X, you could write:

```
NAME = SUBSTR(NAME,1,5) || 'X' || SUBSTR(NAME,7);
```

If an old substring is being replaced by a new string of exactly the same size (e.g., single characters), SUBSTR can be used in a very special way, as a pseudo variable. This means that it may appear on the lefthand side of an assignment statement to indicate which portion of a character string is to have its value altered. For example, to replace the letter 'Q' by the letter 'X' in the string 'JOHN Q. DOE', which is residing in NAME, write:

```
SUBSTR(NAME,6,1) = 'X';
```

to produce the result:

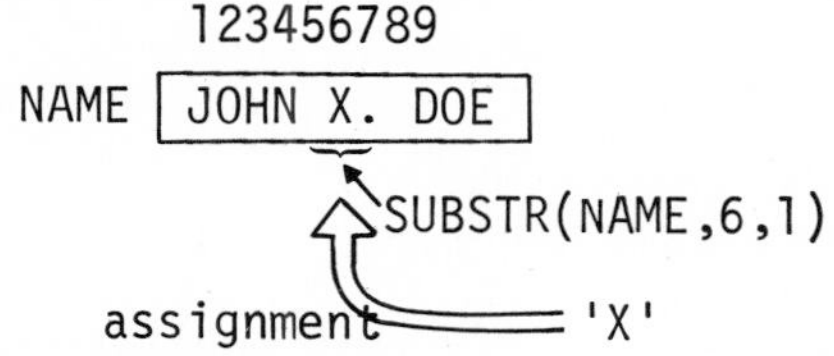

To replace 'JOHN' by 'BILL', write:

```
SUBSTR(NAME,1,4) = 'BILL';
```

5.8.1 An Example of String Editing

Suppose you are given several data cards, each containing someone's first name, last name, and ID number, separated by single blanks and all enclosed by one pair of quotes:

'JOHN DOE 68472'

You are to produce a list of names without ID numbers, giving the last name first and first name last, separated by a comma. This card should yield:

DOE,JOHN

Since each line of output is a simple transformation of a different card, the cards can be processed one at a time within the familiar repetitive control structure:

```
1.    read first card;
2.    repeat as long as unprocessed cards remain;
2.1      process (i.e., edit) the card;
2.2      print out the edited version;
2.3      read the next card;
3.    end.
```

The problem now is how to "process" one card. Scanning the data from left to right, we might

```
2.1.1   obtain the first name;
2.1.2   obtain the last name;
2.1.3   construct a string by concatenating the last
           name, a comma, and the first name;
```

Focusing on step 2.1.1, we know that the first name extends from the beginning up to the first blank. Thus

```
2.1.1.1  find the first blank;
2.1.1.2  extract the substring up to but not including this
            first blank to obtain the first name;
```

Obtaining the last name (2.1.2) is a bit more subtle. The second name extends from the first to the second blank. However, if you search the original data for a blank using INDEX, you will merely rediscover the first blank. You will find the second blank only if you begin the search past the first blank. Thus since you have already extracted the first name, delete the first name and first blank from the data. What remains will begin with the last name, followed by a blank.

```
2.1.2.1  delete the first name and first blank from the
            input string;
2.1.2.2  find the first blank within this modified string
            (it will correspond to the second blank in the
            original data);
2.1.2.3  extract the substring up to but not including
            this blank, to obtain the last name;
```

Assembling all these steps to "process" one card, you will see the basic string operations required:

	steps	suggested operation
2.1.1.1	find blank;	INDEX
2.1.1.2	extract first name;	SUBSTR
2.1.2.1	delete first name and blank;	SUBSTR
2.1.2.2	find next blank;	INDEX
2.1.2.3	extract last name;	SUBSTR
2.1.3	construct string for output;	||

The complete program is shown in Fig. 5.5.

5.9 REVIEW OF RULES

1. All character variables must be declared by either

   a) DECLARE (<list of variables>) CHARACTER(n);

   or

   b) DECLARE (<list of variables>) CHARACTER(n) VARYING;

   where n is the maximum number of characters to be stored in the variables ($0 \le n \le 256$ in PL/C).

2. Concatenation of strings is accomplished by

   $<string_1>||<string_2>||\ldots||<string_n>$

3. The general form of the LENGTH built-in function is

   LENGTH(P_1)

   where P_1 is any character string or character expression.

```
           /* FIGURE 5.5 */
NAMES:   PROCEDURE OPTIONS (MAIN);

         /* THIS PROGRAM PROCESSES DATA CARDS CONTAINING
            A PERSON'S FIRST NAME, LAST NAME, AND OTHER
            INFORMATION, ALL SEPARATED BY SINGLE BLANKS.
            FOR EACH CARD, THE PROGRAM PRINTS THE LAST NAME
            FOLLOWED BY A COMMA FOLLOWED BY THE FIRST
            NAME. */

         DECLARE (
            INPUT, /* MOST RECENTLY READ CARD */
            REMAINDER, /*EVERYTHING AFTER 1ST BLANK ON CARD*/
            FIRST, /* THE FIRST NAME */
            LAST, /* THE LAST NAME */
            NAME) /* THE OUTPUT NAME */
                  CHARACTER (80) VARYING,
            (NOMORE, /* FLAG TO INDICATE END OF DATA */
            BLANK1, /* POSITION OF FIRST BLANK ON CARD */
            BLANK2) /* POSITION OF 2ND BLANK ON CARD */
                    FIXED (5,0);

         NOMORE = 0;
         ON ENDFILE (SYSIN) NOMORE = 1;
         GET LIST (INPUT);

CHANGE:  DO WHILE (NOMORE = 0);

            /* FIND POSITION OF FIRST BLANK ON DATA CARD */

            BLANK1 = INDEX(INPUT,' ');

            /* COPY OUT FIRST NAME */

            FIRST = SUBSTR(INPUT,1,BLANK1 - 1);

            /* ISOLATE REMAINDER AFTER FIRST NAME */

            REMAINDER = SUBSTR(INPUT,BLANK1 + 1);

            /* FIND POSITION OF FIRST BLANK IN REMAINDER */

            BLANK2 = INDEX(REMAINDER,' ');

            /* COPY OUT LAST NAME */

            LAST = SUBSTR(REMAINDER,1,BLANK2 - 1);

            /* NOW FORM NEW NAME FOR OUTPUT */

            NAME = LAST || ',' || FIRST;
            PUT SKIP LIST (NAME);
            GET LIST (INPUT);
         END CHANGE;

         END NAMES;
```

Figure 5.5

LENGTH generates an integer number representing the number of characters currently stored in P_1.

4. The general form of the INDEX built-in function is

$$INDEX(P_1,P_2)$$

where P_1 and P_2 are any character strings or character expressions. INDEX generates an integer number which specifies the starting position in P_1 of the first occurrence of P_2. If this number is zero then P_2 does not exist within P_1.

5. The general form of the SUBSTR built-in function is

$$SUBSTR(P_1,P_2,P_3)$$

where P_1 is any character string or character expression and P_2 and P_3 are any unsigned integers or integer-valued arithmetic expressions. ($P_2>0$, $P_3\geq0$). SUBSTR generates a character substring from P_1, beginning at position P_2 and extending for length P_3. If P_3 is omitted then it is assumed to have value

$$LENGTH(P_1) - P_2+1.$$

In other words, the remainder of P_1 is selected. If P_2 is omitted then it is assumed to have value 1.

<u>Note</u> $0 < P_2 \leq LENGTH(P_1)$

$0 \leq P_3 \leq LENGTH(P_1)-P_2+1$

6. The <u>collating sequence</u> or <u>lexicographic ordering</u> in PL/I is

b̸ . < (+ | & $ *) ; ¬ - / , % _ > ? : # @ ' = A B C D E F G H

I J K L M N O P Q R S T U V W X Y Z 0 1 2 3 4 5 6 7 8 9

5.10 REVIEW PROBLEM (SCANNING STRINGS)

The example of Section 5.8.1 suggests a very important text-processing technique -- scanning a string from left to right to pick out several substrings. This scan relied on the presence of special characters (the blanks between words) to identify the substrings it sought (the first and last names). It also discarded the portion of the input string which had already been scanned to avoid rediscovering an already processed substring. The next subsection (5.10.1) solves a problem with a scan which uses these same ideas. However, the scan presented is more general, since the number of substrings to be extracted is not known in advance. Section 5.10.3 offers a completely different style of scan for contrast.

5.10.1 <u>A String-Scanning Problem</u>

Suppose you are given a data card containing a single sentence, enclosed in quotes. Blanks or commas separate each word, and the last word is followed immediately by a period. You are to find the total word lengths of all words in the sentence.

For this problem, you can scan the sentence to isolate successive words. As you find them, add their lengths to the current total.

Thus the solution is:

1. start with a total of 0;
2. read the sentence;
3. find each word and add its length to the total;
4. print the total;
5. end.

Finding individual words (Step 3) would seem to be much simpler if the sentence has exactly one blank between each word. Any sentence containing blanks and commas can be converted to this "ideal" form by some preliminary editing. For now we will assume that such editing has been done, so that our sentence contains only single blanks between words.

Step 3 can be accomplished via the following scan: The first word is everything before the first blank. Once you have reached a particular blank in the string, the "next" word is everything from the next character up to the next blank -- except the last word, which is followed by a period rather than a blank. Thus each word, except the last, can be identified by looking for the blank following it. If already discovered words and blanks are discarded, the "next" word will always be the substring preceding the "first" blank in whatever remains of the original sentence.

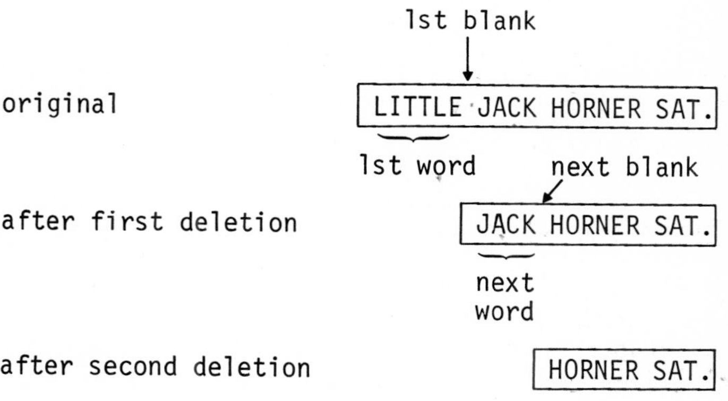

Fig. 5.6 Illustration of One String Scanning Technique

When the remaining string contains no more blanks, you will have reached the last word, which extends up to the final period. Thus Step 3 is:

3.1 repeat until the last word is reached;
  3.1.1 find and delete the next word and the following blank;
  3.1.2 add the length of this word to total;
3.2 add the length of the last word to total;

Note that the length of the last word is one less (discounting the period) than the length of the remaining sentence.

Step 3.1.1 can be further refined:

```
3.1.1.1   find next blank in sentence;
3.1.1.2   extract the next word, i.e., the substring
             preceding this blank;
3.1.1.3   delete this word and blank from sentence;
```

Collecting these steps together yields the complete algorithm:

```
1.        start with a total of 0;
2.        read the sentence;
3.1       repeat while sentence still contains a blank;
3.1.1.1      find next blank;
3.1.1.2      extract next word (preceding blank);
3.1.1.3      delete the word and the blank;
3.1.2        add word length to total;
3.2       add length of final word to total;
4.        print total;
5.        end.
```

The resulting program is shown in Fig. 5.7.

5.10.2 Augmenting the Above Algorithm by Preliminary Editing

In order to find the total word length of sentences containing commas and strings of blanks, we must first convert "wayward" sentences into the correct form. In other words, we wish to "edit" each sentence read in until it achieves the form suitable for "processing" it with the algorithm of Section 5.10.1.

We can first dispense with commas by replacing them with blanks. Since there may be several commas requiring replacement, the following process is suggested:

```
1.     repeat while sentence still contains a comma;
1.1       find first comma;
1.2       replace this comma by a blank;
```

The resulting sentences will contain one period, no other punctuation, and arbitrary numbers of blanks before or after each word (including the last). For these sentences what we must do is:

```
2.     replace sequences of consecutive blanks by a
          single blank;
3.     delete any blank preceding the final period.
```

Since any sequence of consecutive blanks before the period will already have been shrunk to one by Step 2, Step 3 may be rephrased:

3.   replace 'b̸.' by '.'

To collapse sequences of blanks (Step 2), one might look for pairs of blanks, then for sequences of length 3, of length 4, etc. However, you have to call a halt somewhere, e.g., with sequences of length 10, but you cannot be sure that no sentence will appear having 11 or more blanks in a row. Besides, you may have to write a great many statements to carry out this plan.

Consider the fact that every sequence of three or more consecutive blanks consists in fact of substrings of pairs of blanks. If you find the first pair of blanks in a longer sequence and replace

```
             /* FIGURE 5.7 */
WORDLG1:
         PROCEDURE OPTIONS (MAIN);

         /* THIS PROGRAM READS ONE SENTENCE WHOSE WORDS
            ARE SEPARATED BY A SINGLE BLANK. THE SENTENCE
            IS FOLLOWED BY A PERIOD AND NO OTHER
            PUNCTUATION IS ALLOWED. THE PROGRAM IS TO
            COMPUTE THE TOTAL WORD LENGTH OF ALL WORDS
            COMPRISING THE SENTENCE. */

         DECLARE
            (WORD,SENTENCE) CHARACTER (200) VARYING,
            (TOTAL,BLANK) FIXED (5,0);

         /* SENTENCE = WHATEVER REMAINS TO BE SCANNED IN
                       THE ORIGINAL SENTENCE. THIS
                       INITIALLY CONTAINS THE ORIGINAL
                       SENTENCE BUT WORDS ARE
                       REMOVED AS THEY ARE DISCOVERED.
            WORD = WORD MOST RECENTLY FOUND IN SENTENCE.
            TOTAL = TOTAL LENGTH OF WORDS FOUND SO FAR.
            BLANK = POSITION OF NEXT BLANK IN SENTENCE. */

         TOTAL = 0;
         GET LIST (SENTENCE);
         PUT SKIP DATA (SENTENCE);

         /* WE SCAN SENTENCE AS LONG AS IT HAS A BLANK */

SCAN:    DO WHILE (INDEX(SENTENCE,' ') ¬= 0);

            /* FIND POSITION OF BLANK */

            BLANK = INDEX(SENTENCE,' ');

            /* COPY THIS WORD */

            WORD = SUBSTR(SENTENCE,1,BLANK - 1);

            /* STRIP THE WORD FROM THE SENTENCE */

            SENTENCE = SUBSTR(SENTENCE,BLANK + 1);

            /* ADD THE LENGTH OF THE WORD TO TOTAL */

            TOTAL = TOTAL + LENGTH(WORD);
         END SCAN;

         /* ADD IN THE REMAINING WORD IN SENTENCE BUT
            DEDUCT 1 FOR THE PERIOD */

         TOTAL = TOTAL + LENGTH(SENTENCE) - 1;
         PUT SKIP DATA (TOTAL);

         END WORDLG1;
```

Figure 5.7

the pair by a single blank, then the remaining sequence of blanks contains one less than the original. Repeatedly replacing pairs by single blanks keeps shrinking the size of the sequence until the remainder contains only two and finally only one blank. The algorithm is therefore:

```
2.    repeat while sentence still contains a pair of blanks;
2.1      find first pair of blanks;
2.2      replace this pair of blanks by one;
```

Combining these steps yields the algorithm for editing:

```
1.    repeat while sentence still contains a comma;
1.1      find first comma;
1.2      replace this comma by blank;
2.    repeat while sentence still contains a pair of blanks;
2.1      find first pair of blanks;
2.2      replace this pair of blanks by one blank;
3.    replace 'b̸.' by a period;
```

The code for this is shown in Fig. 5.8, and has been incorporated into the program from Section 5.10.1 (see Fig. 5.7) exactly where it belongs -- following the input of the sentence and before the "processing."

Note that it is not really necessary to physically delete initial substrings. The INDEX function could have searched for the first blank within the SUBSTRing consisting of the unscanned portion of the string.

5.10.3 An Alternative Approach

The problem of determining total word length may be solved in a much different way by observing that the total word length is equal to the length of the sentence minus the number of blanks and punctuation characters. This observation applies to <u>any</u> sentence, not necessarily a specially structured one. However, we <u>will</u> restrict our attention to sentences containing only one period, no other punctuation, and any number of blanks.

The above observation suggests this approach:

```
1.    read the sentence;
2.    determine the number of blanks in the sentence;
3.    total word length = length of sentence - (number of
         blanks and period);
4.    print the total word length;
5.    end.
```

The only complex step is determining the number of blanks (Step 2). For this we will devise a different sort of scan -- one which inspects each individual character of the sentence and does not discard previously scanned material. To do this, we maintain a memory location indicating the current scan position in the sentence, and we methodically advance this number to move through the string:

```
2.1   the initial number of blanks is 0;
2.2   the initial position of the scan is character 1;
2.3   for each character in the sentence;
2.3.1    if the character is a blank, add 1 to number of blanks;
```

```
              /* FIGURE 5.8 */
WORDLG1:
        PROCEDURE OPTIONS (MAIN);

        /*  THIS PROGRAM IS AN EXTENSION OF FIG. 5.7. IT
            FINDS THE TOTAL WORD LENGTHS OF WORDS IN A
            SENTENCE WHICH ARE SEPARATED BY AN ARBITRARY
            NUMBER OF BLANKS. TO DO THIS IT USES AN
            "EDITING" MODULE TO REDUCE SEQUENCES OF BLANKS
            TO A SINGLE BLANK AND TO REMOVE ANY BLANKS
            IMMEDIATELY BEFORE A PERIOD. */

        DECLARE
            (WORD,SENTENCE) CHARACTER (200) VARYING,
            (TOTAL,BLANK,PAIR) FIXED (5,0);

        /* PAIR = THE ONLY NEW VARIABLE, INDICATES THE
            POSITION OF THE NEXT PAIR OF BLANKS TO BE
            COMPRESSED TO 1 */

        TOTAL = 0;
        GET LIST (SENTENCE);
        PUT SKIP DATA (SENTENCE);

        /* THE FOLLOWING IS THE EDITING MODULE USED TO PUT
            SENTENCE INTO A FORM THAT THE PROGRAM OF FIG.
            5.4 CAN HANDLE. IT IS APPLIED AS LONG AS THERE
            ARE AT LEAST TWO CONSECUTIVE BLANKS IN SENTENCE
            AND  A BLANK PRECEDES A PERIOD. */

COMMAS: DO WHILE (INDEX(SENTENCE,',') ¬= 0);
            /* REPLACE EACH COMMA WITH A BLANK */
            PAIR = INDEX(SENTENCE,',');
            SUBSTR(SENTENCE,PAIR,1) = ' ';
        END COMMAS;

EXPUNGE:DO WHILE (INDEX(SENTENCE,'  ') ¬= 0);
            /* FIND STARTING POSITION OF A PAIR BLANKS */
            PAIR = INDEX(SENTENCE,'  ');
            /* REMOVE ONE OF THE BLANKS */
            SENTENCE = SUBSTR(SENTENCE,1,PAIR - 1) ||
                SUBSTR(SENTENCE,PAIR + 1);
        END EXPUNGE;

        /* NOW FOR THE BLANK BEFORE THE PERIOD */
        PAIR = INDEX(SENTENCE,' .');
        IF PAIR ¬= 0 THEN
            SENTENCE = SUBSTR(SENTENCE,1,PAIR - 1) || '.';

        /* NOW WE CAN APPLY THE COUNTING PROGRAM FIG. 5.4*/

SCAN:   DO WHILE (INDEX(SENTENCE,' ') ¬= 0);
            BLANK = INDEX(SENTENCE,' ');
            WORD = SUBSTR(SENTENCE,1,BLANK - 1);
            SENTENCE = SUBSTR(SENTENCE,BLANK + 1);
            TOTAL = TOTAL + LENGTH(WORD);
        END SCAN;

        TOTAL = TOTAL + LENGTH(SENTENCE) - 1;
        PUT SKIP DATA (TOTAL);

        END WORDLG1;
```

Figure 5.8

Step 2.3 still needs elaboration:

```
2.3     repeat while position on the scan is ≤ end of sentence;
2.3.1      if the current position contains a blank,
              add 1 to number of blanks;
2.3.2      move scan to next character position;
```

Hence, the complete algorithm is:

```
1.      read the sentence;
2.1     the initial number of blanks is 0;
2.2     the initial position of the scan is at character 1;
2.3     repeat while position of the scan is ≤ length of sentence;
2.3.1      if current position contains a blank, add 1 to
              number of characters;
2.3.2      move scan to next position (i.e., add 1 to position);
3.      total word length = (length of sentence - (total number
           of blanks +1 for the final period));
4.      print total word length;
5.      end.
```

See Fig. 5.9 for the program.

```
             /* FIGURE 5.9 */
WORDLG2:
         PROCEDURE OPTIONS (MAIN);

         /* THIS PROGRAM READS ONE SENTENCE WHOSE WORDS
            ARE SEPARATED BY AN ARBITRARY NUMBER OF BLANKS.
            THE ONLY PUNCTUATION IS A PERIOD AT THE END.
            ITS PURPOSE IS TO COMPUTE THE TOTAL WORD LENGTH
            OF ALL WORDS IN THE SENTENCE. */

         DECLARE
            (WORD,SENTENCE) CHARACTER (200) VARYING,
            (BLANKS,POSITION,TOTAL) FIXED (5,0);

         /* SENTENCE = ORIGINAL SENTENCE FROM DATA CARD
            BLANKS = TOTAL NO. BLANKS FOUND SO FAR.
            POSITION = CURRENT POSITION IN SENTENCE.
            TOTAL = TOTAL WORD LENGTH. FINAL RESULT */

         GET LIST (SENTENCE);
         PUT DATA (SENTENCE);
         BLANKS = 0;
         POSITION = 1;

         /* EXAMINE EACH CHARACTER IN SENTENCE */

SCAN:    DO WHILE (POSITION <= LENGTH(SENTENCE));

            /* IS THIS CHARACTER A BLANK? */

            IF SUBSTR(SENTENCE,POSITION,1) = ' ' THEN
               BLANKS = BLANKS + 1;
            POSITION = POSITION + 1;
         END SCAN;

         /* WORD LENGTH = TOTAL LENGTH MINUS ALL BLANKS
            MINUS 1 FOR THE CLOSING PERIOD. */

         TOTAL = LENGTH(SENTENCE) - (BLANKS + 1);
         PUT SKIP DATA (TOTAL);

         END WORDLG2;
```

Figure 5.9

5.11 PROGRAM DEVELOPMENT AND TESTING -- III

The editing algorithm (Section 5.10.2) and the first character-counting algorithm (Section 5.10.1), though used in conjunction to solve one problem, were developed quite separately. In fact the counting algorithm was developed, coded, and tested before the editing algorithm was even begun. This separation was not just for pedagogical reasons. We recommend developing and testing each significant part of your program independently, and combining the parts into a larger program only when you are satisfied that each part works correctly by itself. The reason is similar to the reason for developing the original algorithm one step at a time: small problems are easier to solve and debug than large ones. Once each module or part is checked out, the only remaining source of error is their interconnection, i.e., the output of the first may not quite match the input requirements of the second. However, this is much easier to check than the overall performance of the entire program.

The implication is that it might be advisable to code and test the editing algorithm all by itself. To do this, it must be imbedded in a special "test program," which declares the necessary variables, reads in some data, and prints the results as shown in Fig. 5.10. Once the test program works, combine the edit and counting modules and try the complete program, as was shown in Fig. 5.8.

Suppose the original problem had requested the calculation of total word lengths for each of an arbitrary number of sentences. It makes sense to write and test a program to process one sentence before tackling the larger problem. However, once the code for handling one sentence (editing + character counting) is working, it is a simple matter to imbed this in the necessary control structure (ENDFILE, DO WHILE) and test the composite.

Note that during the test (Fig. 5.10), the edited sentence was displayed with PUT DATA rather than PUT LIST, so that its exact extent would be disclosed by the surrounding quotes. Without these quotes it would be difficult to check that no initial or trailing blanks were present. The same applies to displaying the input data, which should always be printed when a module is being tested.

Note, too, that it is neither necessary nor profitable to test such a program with a 70-word, 250-character sentence. A three or four word sentence will do just as well. As a rule, when testing programs you do not need as much data as would be processed by a typical run of the final version. One reason is to avoid unnecessary computation.

A better reason is that a small amount of test data will allow you to find the source of errors more easily. Large volumes of data may cause a flood of output which either overwhelms you with the profusion of errors or else conceals an error from conspicuous view. A small data sample will help you notice and focus on the errors; and then, if necessary, it is feasible to work through the program steps by hand until you reproduce the error and can identify its source.

Working through an algorithm step-by-step for some typical data is also a good way to check its validity before translating it into code. In fact, attempting to "process" some specific data item by hand is often a good source of ideas for devising the original algorithm! Whether you are just planning an approach or correcting faulty code, you must carefully keep track of how sample data would look at each step. For this purpose "a picture is worth a thousand words." Draw a box for each important string or variable, label the box by the variable name, and at each step of the algorithm examine or alter the contents of each box exactly as prescribed by the algorithm or program. Reread this paragraph and put it into practice. It may contain the most valuable tip in the entire book!

```
           /* FIGURE 5.10 */
TESTMOD:
        PROCEDURE OPTIONS (MAIN);

        /* TEST PROGRAM TO VERIFY THE CORRECTNESS OF THE
           EDIT MODULE OF FIG. 5.8 */

        DECLARE
           SENTENCE CHARACTER (200) VARYING,
           PAIR FIXED (5,0);

        GET LIST (SENTENCE);
        PUT SKIP DATA (SENTENCE);

        /* NOW THAT THE INPUT HAS BEEN READ AND
           DISPLAYED, THE FOLLOWING CODE IS TO BE TESTED */

COMMAS: DO WHILE (INDEX(SENTENCE,',') ¬= 0);
           /* REPLACE EACH COMMA WITH A BLANK */
           PAIR = INDEX(SENTENCE,',');
           SUBSTR(SENTENCE,PAIR,1) = ' ';
        END COMMAS;

EXPUNGE:DO WHILE (INDEX(SENTENCE,'  ') ¬= 0);
           /* FIND STARTING POSITION OF A PAIR BLANKS */
           PAIR = INDEX(SENTENCE,'  ');
           /* REMOVE ONE OF THE BLANKS */
           SENTENCE = SUBSTR(SENTENCE,1,PAIR - 1) ||
              SUBSTR(SENTENCE,PAIR + 1);
        END EXPUNGE;

        /* NOW FOR THE BLANK BEFORE THE PERIOD */
        PAIR = INDEX(SENTENCE,' .');
        IF PAIR ¬= 0 THEN
           SENTENCE = SUBSTR(SENTENCE,1,PAIR - 1) || '.';

        /* DISPLAY THE RESULT OF THE EDIT CODE */

        PUT SKIP DATA (SENTENCE);

        END TESTMOD;
```

Fig. 5.10 Program to Test Edit Module Used in Fig. 5.8

Though the test data need not be voluminous, it must be carefully selected to test the program under a variety of possible conditions. Besides trying one or two "typical" input strings, try extreme data as well. For example, you might submit an "already edited" sentence to the editing module to ensure that the editor does not alter it. Trying a 1-word sentence containing <u>no</u> blanks might also be informative.

5.11.1 Debugging Example (Problem with SUBSTR)

Let us augment the program from Fig. 5.8 so that it also counts the number of words in the sentence. This would seem to be a trivial modification, requiring only a minor insertion of new code. This modified program is shown in Fig. 5.11. It initializes a counter named WRDS to 0 and adds 1 to WRDS immediately after processing each word. On one test of this program, the output was

SENTENCE = ' ALL RIGHT.'

TOTAL = 8   WRDS = 3

```
                  /* FIGURE 5.11 */
 1 WORDLG1:
          PROCEDURE OPTIONS (MAIN);

          /* USE ALGORITHM #1 TO COMPUTE TOTAL WORD
             LENGTH IN SPECIALLY STRUCTURED
             SENTENCE. ALSO TRY TO COMPUTE THE NO.
             OF WORDS IN THE SENTENCE */

          DECLARE
 2           (WORD,SENTENCE) CHARACTER (200) VARYING,
             (TOTAL,BLANK,WRDS) FIXED (5,0);

          /* SENTENCE = WHAT REMAINS TO BE SCANNED
                        IN THE ORIGINAL SENTENCE.
             WORD = WORD MOST RECENTLY FOUND.
             TOTAL = TOTAL LENGTH OF WORDS FOUND.
             BLANK = POSITION OF NEXT BLANK.
             WRDS = NO. WORDS IN SENTENCE */

 3        TOTAL = 0;
 4        WRDS = 0;
 5        GET LIST (SENTENCE);
 6        PUT SKIP DATA (SENTENCE);

          /* SCAN SENTENCE WHILE IT HAS A BLANK */

 7 SCAN:  DO WHILE (INDEX(SENTENCE,' ') ¬= 0);
 8           BLANK = INDEX(SENTENCE,' ');
 9           WORD = SUBSTR(SENTENCE,1,BLANK - 1);
10           SENTENCE = SUBSTR(SENTENCE,BLANK + 1);
11           TOTAL = TOTAL + LENGTH(WORD);
12           WRDS = WRDS + 1;
13        END SCAN;

          /* ADD IN THE REMAINING WORD IN SENTENCE
             BUT DEDUCT 1 FOR THE PERIOD */

14        TOTAL = TOTAL + LENGTH(SENTENCE) - 1;
15        WRDS = WRDS + 1;
16        PUT SKIP DATA (TOTAL,WRDS);

17        END WORDLG1;
```

Fig. 5.11 Unsuccessful Modification of Program in Fig. 5.8

Fortunately, the sample sentence was short enough to let you notice that the word count, WRDS, is incorrect. A check indicates that your program logic is all right; so you draw some pictures and begin to trace the program execution. By the time you reach Statement 8 (Fig. 5.11), the pertinent variables contain the following values:

```
         123456789
SENTENCE | ALL RIGHT.|

   BLANK |    1|        WRDS |    0|

                       TOTAL |    0|
```

Note that SENTENCE has not yet been altered and that INDEX found a blank in position 1. Then when you execute Statement 9 and extract a substring of length BLANK-1, you will be extracting a string of length 0, i.e., the null string. Since its LENGTH is 0, Statement 11 does not affect TOTAL, but it does erroneously add 1 to WRDS in Statement 12. The initial blank thus caused the problem.

Since your algorithm was designed assuming that each blank terminates a word, it obviously cannot handle sentences with initial blanks. The edit program, as it stands, will not provide a remedy since it only reduces sequences of blanks to one.

This example illustrates how important it is to understand exactly what assumptions your program makes and what type of input it can handle. This is especially true with text handling. In this case your options are to either (i) explicitly outlaw input sentences with initial blanks or (ii) modify the editing program to remove all initial blanks.

The example also illustrates how much care and knowledge may be required in certain programming and debugging situations. In particular, it was necessary to know that SUBSTR returns the null string whenever its parameters are not reasonable, i.e., if the initial position and length parameters would not indicate a proper substring. Unfortunately you do not always get warnings or error messages when such things happen.

5.11.2 Problems with Strings of Different, Fixed Lengths

Another common problem occurs when using strings of different, fixed lengths. The symptoms are that blanks mysteriously appear, and other characters are inexplicably lost. Omitting the VARYING attribute in a declaration, for example, causes the character variables to receive a permanent, fixed length -- regardless of what strings are eventually stored there! For example,

```
DECLARE (A,B) CHARACTER(4);
```

creates two variables which will always have LENGTH of 4. The following statements show what happens when strings of different length are stored there:

statements	effect
A = 'XY';	A | X Y ƀ ƀ |
B = 'LMNOPQ';	B | L M N O |

This illustrates a general rule:

(1) if a string is too short for a fixed-length variable (or field), <u>blanks are added on the right</u> to make it the correct length;

(2) if a string is too long for a fixed-length variable (or field), the excess characters <u>on the right</u> are <u>truncated</u>, i.e., lost.

To avoid such considerations, we recommend use of VARYING until more sophistication is acquired. However, there are other causes for fixed-length fields, such as the SUBSTR pseudo-variable which replaces a fixed number of characters in a string. Thus, using B above,

SUBSTR(B,1,2) = 'X';

produces B | X ƀ N O |

For a more dramatic example, suppose the edit program (from Section 5.10.2) failed to declare SENTENCE as VARYING. (This version of the program is shown in Fig. 5.12). Every time an interior blank is deleted (within EXPUNGE loop), another blank is added on the right in order to make the result equal in length to 200, the permanent length of SENTENCE. Eventually the "edited" input will be assembled in the initial portion of SENTENCE. However, this will be followed by a long sequence of blanks. The program will repeatedly find an adjacent pair of blanks in this sequence, delete the first and inconspicuously add another on the right. Therefore the program will keep finding pairs of blanks forever -- at least until it has executed for the maximum allowable time, at which point it will terminate with an error message.

Note the diagnostics at the end of Fig. 5.12. They show the correctly edited input in the initial portion of SENTENCE, with the sequence of blanks beginning at position 19. The loop also executed over 12,000 times!

Exceeding the time limit is also always a symptom of a logic error on your part. It most often results from your failure to set a flag or increase a counter within a loop which was intended to eventually terminate the loop. However, if this is not the case, then the problem may be more subtle, as it was in this example.

```
                /* FIGURE 5.12 */
TESTMOD:
        PROCEDURE OPTIONS (MAIN);

        /* THIS PROGRAM IS AN ERRONEOUS VERSION OF
           FIG. 5.10. THERE IS ONLY ONE WORD OF DIFFERENCE
           IN THE TWO PROGRAMS. */

        DECLARE
           SENTENCE CHARACTER (200),
           PAIR FIXED (5,0);

        GET LIST (SENTENCE);
        PUT SKIP DATA (SENTENCE);

        /* NOW THAT THE INPUT HAS BEEN READ AND
           DISPLAYED, THE FOLLOWING CODE IS TO BE TESTED */

COMMAS: DO WHILE (INDEX(SENTENCE,',') ¬= 0);
           /* REPLACE EACH COMMA WITH A BLANK */
           PAIR = INDEX(SENTENCE,',');
           SUBSTR(SENTENCE,PAIR,1) = ' ';
        END COMMAS;

EXPUNGE:DO WHILE (INDEX(SENTENCE,'  ') ¬= 0);

           /* FIND STARTING POSITION OF A PAIR BLANKS */
           PAIR = INDEX(SENTENCE,'  ');

           /* REMOVE ONE OF THE BLANKS */
           SENTENCE = SUBSTR(SENTENCE,1,PAIR - 1) ||
              SUBSTR(SENTENCE,PAIR + 1);
        END EXPUNGE;

        /* NOW FOR THE BLANK BEFORE THE PERIOD */

        PAIR = INDEX(SENTENCE,' .');
        IF PAIR ¬= 0 THEN
           SENTENCE = SUBSTR(SENTENCE,1,PAIR - 1) || '.';

        /* DISPLAY THE RESULT OF THE EDIT CODE */

        PUT SKIP DATA (SENTENCE);

        END TESTMOD;

SENTENCE='TEST,   THIS  MODULE  .

***** ERROR IN STMT    12  TIME LIMIT EXCEEDED (EXE5)

IN STMT    12  DYNAMIC FLOW TRACE:
             0000->0001          0008->0005          0005->0009  9999*(0012->0009)
       2472*(0012->0009)

IN STMT    12  SCALARS AND BLOCK-TRACE:

***** MAIN PROCEDURE TESTMOD

PAIR=       19            SENTENCE='TEST THIS MODULE .
```

Fig. 5.12 The Program of Fig. 5.10 With SENTENCE Declared as Fixed-Length (by mistakenly omitting VARYING)

5.12 EXERCISES

5.1 Devise an algorithm and develop a program which can read a sentence with no punctuation except for a period at the end and which prints out the sentence containing the same words but in reverse order (with a period at the end). For instance, the sentence

MY DOG HAS FLEAS.

would become:

FLEAS HAS DOG MY.

5.2 Devise an algorithm and develop a program which can read a sentence with no punctuation except for a period at the end and print out a sentence consisting of the same words in the same relative positions but with the letters of each word reversed. Thus the sentence

I AM FINE.

would become

I MA ENIF.

5.3 Write a program which can determine whether the non-blank characters on a data card constitute a palindrome. See exercise 3.2 for a discussion of palindromes.

5.4 Suppose you are employed by a mad literary reformer who is determined to rid the English language of all words containing what he considers unnecessary vowels. He wants you to assist in his mission by writing a program to replace the character sequences EE and EA with an E in any word containing these sequences. You should also delete final Y's and final E's, even those resulting from a previous replacement. For instance, the phrase

CREEPY FLEA

would become

CREP FL

For this problem, quotes may be used to surround individual words for ease of input.

5.5 Design an algorithm and write a program to read an arbitrary number of words of text and discover the following:

a) the total number of words;
b) the number of words containing 1, 2, 3, and 4 letters;
c) the number of words containing the letter S;
d) the number of words which begin with a letter between B and G, inclusive;

For this problem, quotes may be used to surround individual words for ease of input.

5.6 Design an algorithm and write a program to read an arbitrary number of words of text and discover

a) how many of these words have vowels (A,E,I,O,U) for at least half of their constituent characters, such as the words I,PLEASE,OH,TAKE,PIE.

b) what percentage of the alphabetic characters in the text are vowels.

For this problem, quotes may be used to surround individual words for ease of input.

5.7 As chief censor of the State of ADANAC (1984) it is your job to implement the latest government decree. This decree is to the effect that henceforth red will be called white and white will be called red. Describe an algorithm to scan an arbitrary piece of text and replace every original instance of the words RED and WHITE with WHITE and RED, respectively. Be careful that you do not keep changing the same word over and over.

Implement your algorithm by computer program and test it on the text of this exercise, i.e., the previous paragraph

5.8 Suppose you have just received the following coded message:

```
Y3MLD2MLVW2M3REMX2NBMLDVJMJ2UX2LMW2JJNA2TM
3REXM4XRAXNWMHV66M6VC263MY2MHRXCVQAKM
H2MDR42M3REMB2JVAQ2BMLD2MN6ARXVLDWMHVLDMM
UNX2MNQBM4NLV2QU2TMJVQU2MNMARRBMN6ARXVLDWM
UNQMWNC2MURBVQAM2NJ3K
```

You are to decode this message (of under 256 characters) with the aid of a computer. The message was coded by replacing each character of the original alphabet with a character from the code alphabet:

regular alphabet

A	B	C	D	E	F	G	H	I	J	K	L	M	N	O	P	Q	R	S	T	U	V	W	X	Y	Z	,	ƀ	.
N	Y	U	B	2	P	A	D	V	Z	C	6	W	Q	R	4	F	X	J	L	E	S	H	5	3	G	T	M	K

code alphabet

You will <u>de</u>code your message by replacing code characters with corresponding characters from the regular alphabet. Thus

ARRBM6EUC

would be decoded as:

GOOD LUCK

You may not use the TRANSLATE function to solve this problem.

5.9 One function of a compiler is to check for syntax (grammatical) errors in your program statements. In this exercise you are to write a program to implement a few of these syntax checking tasks. Suppose your input data consists of several, possibly incorrect PL/I assignment statements. Make sure that each prospective assignment statement has the following properties:

i) the statement must contain exactly one = sign;
ii) only a single variable precedes the = sign;
iii) a variable or constant must follow immediately after the = sign;
iv) the final symbol must be a semicolon, and this must be preceded by a variable or constant.
v) no two variables or constants may appear without an intervening operator (=, +, -, *, /);
vi) no two consecutive operators may appear without an intervening variable or constant. (This item and item (iii) are more restrictive than the actual PL/I syntax rules.

When your program examines a statement, it should print the statement and say whether it is valid according to these rules. You may assume that the variables are single alphabetic characters and that the constants are one-digit integers. You may also ignore parentheses, unary operators, and exponentiation. You may find the VERIFY function useful (Section 11.1.2).

Try your program on the following data:

```
A = *B*C
D+E = F;
A = B*C-2/D+7*E;
G = Q R-3;
X = Y/Z = 1;
S = T-/V;
U = 1;
W = 6+;
```

5.10 Expand exercise 5.9 to also test for correctly nested parentheses, such as

( ), (( ))( ), ( )((( ))( ))

Parentheses are not considered "operators" in terms of the rules in exercise 5.9. A left parenthesis "(" can only occur where a variable or constant is expected, and a right parenthesis ")" can only occur where an operator is expected.

Chapter 6
Data Presentation and Representation

Until now we have dealt primarily with only two types of data (character strings and integers with at most five digits), and we have left it to the computer to "find" the input items on data cards and to place the results wherever it wished on the listing. If you have ever received a computer-generated bill, you realize that it can handle other types of data, such as numbers with digits after the decimal point, and can exercise greater control over its output so that the amounts appear in the correct boxes on the bills. One purpose of this chapter is to describe some of these other data types, in particular numbers with decimal digits and large integers. The other purpose is to introduce facilities which permit you greater flexibility and control over input and output. The more exotic data types and input-output techniques will be left till later chapters.

6.1 FIXED DECIMAL AND FLOAT DECIMAL ATTRIBUTES

Most of the numerical examples so far have used integer-valued variables which were declared as FIXED(5,0). The number 5 indicates that up to 5 digits can be stored in such a variable. However this number can be as large as 15. For example we can create variables for 10-digit integers with the attribute FIXED(10,0).

We can also create variables for numbers with fractional parts, i.e., digits to the right of a decimal point, by generalizing the FIXED attribute to FIXED(m,d). In this form m specifies the maximum number of (significant) digits which can be stored in the variable. The maximum value for m is 15. d is the number of these digits which lie to the <u>right</u> of the decimal point. Thus if we had

```
DECLARE X FIXED(7,2);
```

we could store any of the following numbers in X:

(i) 12345.67 (ii) -99999.99 (iii) 139.45 (iv) 39

(v) 39.00 (vi) 938.7

Notice that in (ii) the sign of the number does not count as one of the digits.

The following examples give some attributes and the corresponding storage representation where d represents a decimal digit.

FIXED(7,0)	ddddddd
FIXED(7,2)	ddddd.dd
FIXED(5,5)	.ddddd

By using the full capability of the FIXED attribute, a wide range of decimal numbers as well as integers can be stored in memory.

However, very large and very small numbers, such as 250000000000000 and .0000000000006, are difficult to read and write in this form. Such numbers frequently arise in arithmetic, e.g., as a result of dividing two numbers which differ greatly. To accommodate such a wide range of possible results, the decimal point should be more flexible in terms of its placement or, in other words, be allowed to "float" rather than remain in a fixed position. Consequently there is a conventional "scientific" or exponential notation to represent such extreme values and the wide range in between. For example, 250000000000000 may be written more compactly as:

$$2.5 \times 10^{14} \text{ or as } 250 \times 10^{12}$$

To see how this works, consider several alternative ways of writing 123.45, all of which represent this same value:

$$123450 \times 10^{-3}$$
$$12345 \times 10^{-2}$$
$$1234.5 \times 10^{-1}$$
$$123.45 \times 10^{0}$$
$$12.345 \times 10^{1}$$
$$1.2345 \times 10^{2}$$
$$.12345 \times 10^{3}$$

Clearly the value of such a number depends on the power of 10 by which it is multiplied. This power of 10 is called the exponent. If it is positive, it indicates how many positions the decimal point should be moved to the right in order to restore the "natural looking" form. If the exponent is negative, it indicates how far to move the decimal point to the left.

If you want to write a number in PL/I using exponential notation, it is not possible to use a "×" sign or to write a tiny exponent to the upper right of a 10. Instead, PL/I uses a comparable but slightly different notation. For example, the way of writing 1.2345×10^2 is:

1.2345E2

Here the 2 following "E" is the exponent. You might write the constant 1234.5 x 10^{-1} as:

1234.5E-1

To create variables in PL/I which contain their values in exponential notation, use the declaration:

DECLARE (<list of variables>) FLOAT(n);

This declaration provides variables in which to store the n most significant digits of the number together with the appropriate modifying exponent (n can be any integer between 0 and 16). Such variables will then be able to hold the n most significant digits of numbers, ranging from extremely small to extremely large. Fig. 6.1 shows a simplified version of how some numbers would be stored in a variable declared with the FLOAT(6) attribute. In actual fact the internal representation is much more complex and beyond the scope of this text.

Decimal Number	FLOAT(6) Representation
63.7	.637000 x 10^2
806	.806000 x 10^3
-1043.7	-.104370 x 10^4
.0036	.360000 x 10^{-2}
0	.000000 x 10^0

Fig. 6.1 "FLOATing-Point" Number Representation in Memory

Notice that the digit immediately to the right of the decimal point is always greater than zero (except in the special case of the number zero itself). The approximate largest and smallest absolute values which can be stored with the FLOAT(6) attribute are 10^{75} and 10^{-78} respectively. Here again zero is a special case. These strange values are due to the nature of the IBM/360 and /370 hardware.

Floating point variables should be used whenever the arithmetic is extensive or a wide range of possible values could be involved. They should always be used in division! Consider variable X, which is declared as FIXED(5,2). This variable can hold only three significant digits to the left of the decimal point and two to the right. Therefore X could not store the result of either of the following divisions:

800 ÷ .20 = 4000
.20 ÷ 800 = .00025

Yet both results have fewer than six significant digits, so either could be accurately stored in a variable declared as FLOAT(6). The internal representations would be as follows:

4000 = .400000 x 10^4

.00025 = .250000 x 10^{-3}

Constants in exponential notation should be used instead of integers when doing division. Thus

```
ANS = X/2.0E0;
```

is preferable to

```
ANS = X/2;
```

If the value of a FIXED variable must be used in division, its floating point (exponential) form can be obtained by using the built-in function FLOAT. For example, if X is declared as FIXED, the following statement employs the floating point equivalent of X:

```
ANS = FLOAT(X)/2.0E0;
```

When FLOATing point numbers are printed by PUT LIST, they are printed in exponential notation. Thus

```
DECLARE A FLOAT(6),B FIXED(5,2);
A=29.62;
B=29.62;
PUT SKIP LIST (A,B);
```

will produce the output:

```
2.96200E+01     29.62
```

This value for A is to be interpreted as 2.96200 times 10 raised to the power of +01, i.e., 2.96200 x 10^1=29.62. Similarly if A had been assigned the value -0.0036 then PUT LIST (A) would have produced -3.60000E-03. We will see in the next section how you may avoid this exponential notation when printing FLOAT numbers.

6.2 INPUT OF NUMBERS

In Chapter 2 we stated that a GET LIST statement causes the input of values from the data stream, beginning at the point where the last GET LIST left off.

6.2.1 The GET SKIP LIST Statement

It is possible to modify the manner in which values are read and force the computer to begin reading from the start of a new data card each time a GET is executed. In the same way that PUT SKIP DATA or PUT SKIP LIST causes the computer to begin a new line of print, we can introduce SKIP into the GET LIST statement:

```
GET SKIP LIST (<list of variables>);
```

This form of the GET reads values for the variables in the list and begins reading from the next data card which has never been read before. For example, consider the following:

```
GET LIST (I,J);              GET SKIP LIST (I,J);
GET LIST (K);                GET SKIP LIST (K);

9                            9
8,7,5  data cards            8,7,5
6                            6
```

When executed in conjunction with the data shown, these sets of code will result in the following values being stored:

I	9	I	8
J	8	J	7
K	7	K	6

The left-hand set of values are those we would normally expect. On the right-hand side the number 7 has been ignored in the input stream because GET SKIP LIST (K) causes the reading to begin on a new data card. Notice that the first GET SKIP LIST really causes the computer to pass over the first data card -- even though the first data card has yet to be read, it will be passed over by the SKIP option.[1]

The motive for using the GET SKIP form is to read only the initial portion of several similar cards. For example, each card may pertain to a different customer, experiment, or transaction but contains more information than is required by your application. Having extracted the data of interest, the remainder of the card is bypassed by the next GET SKIP. This is especially useful when the remainder of the card is blank but you are doing input under EDIT, as described below.

6.2.2 Input under EDIT Control

In the world of commercial data processing, numbers which are being input to a computer program are not always separated by blanks or commas, because blanks and commas take up valuable space. The common practice is to conceptually divide the data card into groups of columns called fields and interpret the contents of each field as a different number or character string. For example, if a card represents an employee for a payroll program, the card might be laid out with the employee number in columns 1 to 4, the hourly rate in columns 5 to 8 (decimal point in col. 6) and the hours worked in columns 9 to 13 (decimal point in col. 11). A typical data card for such an application is shown in Fig. 6.2.

Since data cards are used for many applications, we cannot rigidly specify that every data card be divided into the same predetermined set of fields. Each application may require a different set of fields, and so we have to be able to specify the fields to be used for the current application. For example, we must specify that there are three numbers on the card in Fig. 6.2, located in columns 1-4, 5-8, and 9-13, respectively.

We accomplish this by the GET EDIT statement whose general form is:

```
GET EDIT (<list of variables>) (<format list>);
```

or

```
GET SKIP EDIT (<list of variables>) (<format list>);
```

---

[1] The reader is advised to check this at his/her own installation. Some versions of PL/I and PL/C may not skip the first card.

The statement to read the card in Fig. 6.2 might be:

```
GET EDIT(EMPLOYEE,RATE,HOURS) (F(4),F(4,2),F(5,2));
```

As with the GET SKIP LIST statement, the SKIP is optional and serves only to begin reading from column 1 of a new card. However, this is almost always desired when using GET EDIT, and so GET SKIP EDIT is the usual form. This statement reads values for the variables in the input list from fields on the data card specified by the format list. Thus it is the format list which describes how the data card is subdivided into fields, as well as how to interpret the contents of each field (e.g., as an integer, real number, or character string). On the other hand, the variable list specifies where to store the data after reading it from the card. It indicates which variables are to receive values, exactly like the variable list in the GET LIST statement. Be careful never to confuse the roles of these two lists! They are summarized in Fig. 6.3.

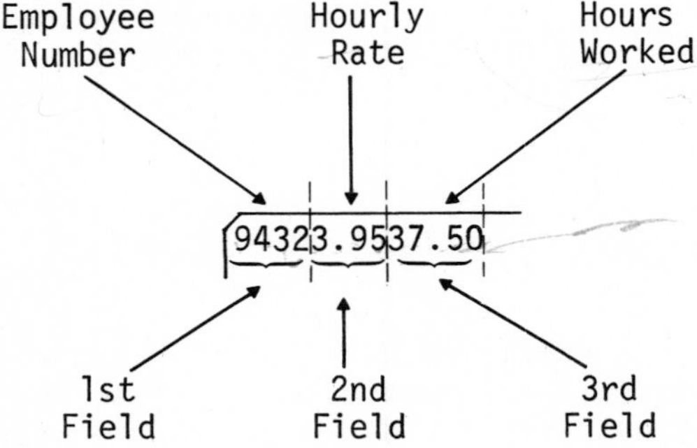

Fig. 6.2 Data Card for a Simple Payroll

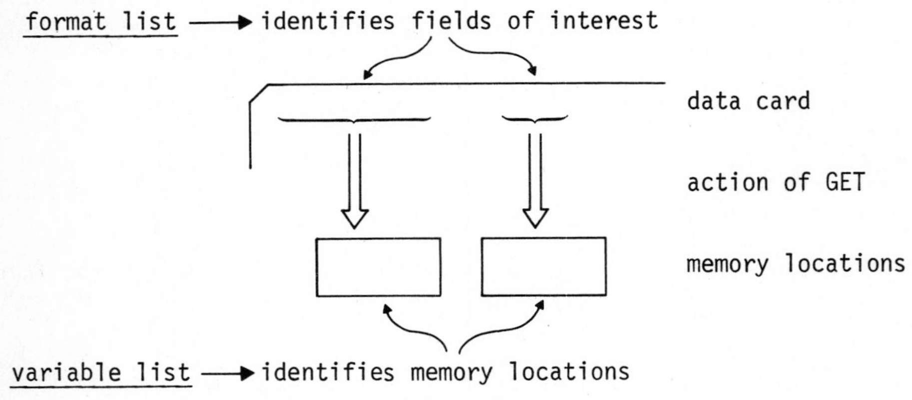

Fig. 6.3 The roles of the Format List and Variable List

6.3 FORMAT LISTS

Each single field is described by a special code called a format item. The format item specifies the number of columns which comprise the field and the type of data to be expected there. A format list consists of one or more format items, depending on how many fields need to be described. The format items in this list are separated by commas and always describe consecutive, adjacent fields from left-to-right. The construction of format lists will be described throughout the remainder of this chapter.

6.3.1 Integer Input

To read integer numbers from a data card we use the format item F(w) which indicates that a field w columns wide is to be treated as a single integer number. Notice that it does not tell where this field begins. All fields begin immediately to the right of the previous field. For the first format item in a list, the field begins in column 1. Thus, to read only the employee number from the data card in Fig. 6.2 we might use

```
GET SKIP EDIT (NUMBER) (F(4));
```

Fig. 6.4 shows some examples of input under EDIT control. Example (a) shows how the first format item is associated with the first variable and the second item with the second variable. Example (b) shows that a blank in a field of length 1 is interpreted as a zero. In general, if a numeric field of length N contains only N blanks then that field is treated as zero. Example (c) shows that trailing blanks in a field are ignored. In this case 43ƀ is read for the variable J and the trailing blank is ignored to produce the value 43. In the same example we see that leading zeros are discarded as in everyday use, i.e., 014 becomes 14. Example (d) shows that leading blanks, as well as leading zeros are ignored. Example (e) has an imbedded blank in the first field (between 3 and 0) and causes only that portion of the field preceding the imbedded blank to be read. Example (f) emphasizes that the field width (the w in F(w)) refers to physical columns on the card -- not to the number of digits in the integer. If a + or - sign may appear on the card, the position it occupies must also be included.

6.3.2 Floating Point and Fixed Point Input

Numbers containing decimal points can be read from data cards by using the F(w,d) format item where w is the width of the field and d is the number of digits to the right of the decimal point. For example,

```
GET SKIP EDIT(X,Y) (F(6,2),F(6,3));
```

```
123.5946.482
```

will cause the following values to be stored:

X [123.59]   Y [46.482]

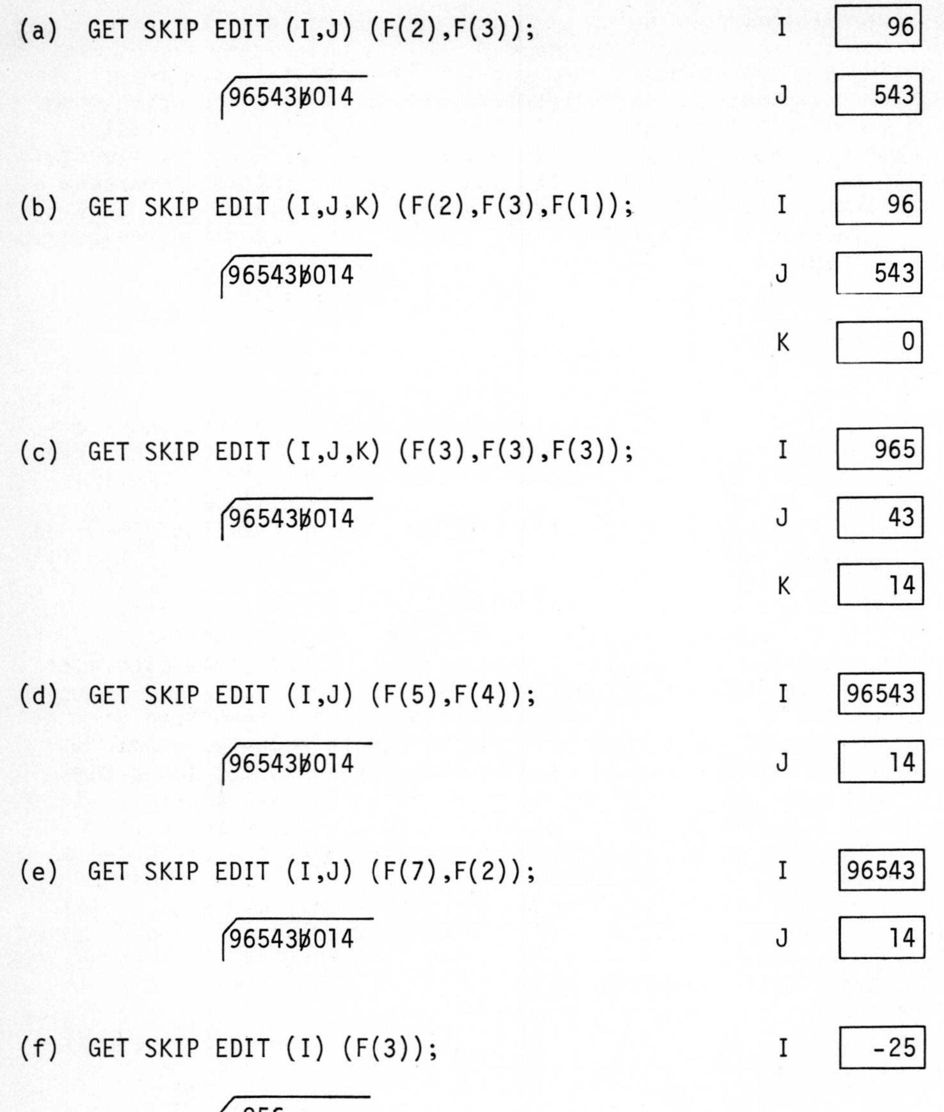

Fig. 6.4 Some Examples of GET EDIT

Note that if a decimal point appears on the card, the space it occupies must be included in the field width. The same applies for an explicit + or - sign. The numbers in format items refer to physical positions and not necessarily to significant digits (as do the numbers in DECLARE statements).

Sometimes you will know which columns a number occupies but not the exact location of the decimal point. Fortunately PL/I permits the use of F(w,0) when the field actually contains an explicit decimal point. Using this format item, the decimal point will be placed in the same position as it appears on the data card. Thus

```
GET SKIP EDIT (X,Y) (F(6,0),F(6,0));
```

```
123.5946.482
```

will produce the same effect as the previous example:

X [123.59] Y [46.482]

We recommend that you make life easier by always reading decimal numbers using F(w,0) on input <u>provided the data card field contains an explicit decimal point</u>.

The above is the most useful special case of the following general rule: Whenever a data card and a format item both specify a decimal point but disagree on its position, the data card overrides the format item and determines the position.

On the other hand, if a field contains a known number of decimal digits (and is the same on every card), the decimal point need <u>not</u> appear on the card. In this case, the format item describing that field <u>must</u> indicate where the decimal point belongs.

For example:

```
GET SKIP EDIT(X,Y) (F(4,2),F(3,1));
```

```
12345678
```

stores the following values in X and Y:

X [12.34] Y [56.7]

The first format item F(4,2) defines a field of width 4 and indicates that 2 of the four digits read should appear after a decimal point. Consequently the decimal point is inserted, causing 12.34 to be stored.

6.3.3 Two Other Format Items

There is a special format item, X(w), which says to <u>ignore</u> a field of width w. This format item is used to skip over an interior field whose contents are not needed by your program. Since no data is transferred from this field, there should be <u>no</u> corresponding variable in the variable list. For example, if you want only the employee number and the hours worked from the data card from Fig. 6.2,

```
94323.9537.50
```

the statement:

```
GET SKIP EDIT(NUMBER,HOURS) (F(4),X(4),F(5,0));
```

would store the values:

NUMBER [9432]   HOURS [37.50]

This example also shows that different kinds of format items may be freely intermixed in the format list.

It is also possible (but seldom necessary) to read numbers which are expressed in scientific or "exponential" notation. This is done using the format item E(w,d), where w is, again, the total field width and d the number of digits after the decimal (not counting those in the exponent). Thus, the number 4.756E-18 could be input using E(9,3).

6.4 OUTPUT OF NUMBERS UNDER EDIT

The placement of output values by the printer can be controlled by the PUT EDIT statement whose general form is:

```
PUT EDIT(<variable-list>) (<format-list>);
```

or

```
PUT SKIP EDIT(<variable-list>) (<format-list>);
```

The roles of the variable list and format list must be carefully distinguished, as they were for the GET EDIT statement. Here the variable list specifies where to obtain values from main memory, while the format list describes how these values should appear on the paper. The format list consists of format items which describe consecutive fields from left-to-right across a line of printer paper. For the present we will limit each PUT statement to exactly one line of output and will therefore use the PUT SKIP EDIT form. PUT SKIP(n) EDIT or PUT PAGE EDIT are also permissible for skipping n lines or for skipping to a new page, respectively, before printing begins.

The PUT EDIT statement closely resembles the GET EDIT statement. However, EDITed output is more commonly needed than EDITed input, and the format statements for output tend to require more care and to become more complex than for input.

Some examples of PUT EDIT are shown in Fig. 6.5. In these examples K, Y, and Z have the values indicated at the top of the page (1289, 489.654 and 12.9384 respectively). The result of each PUT EDIT is shown immediately below the PUT and a blank is denoted by "b̸". The line at the left represents the page margin.

Example (a) shows a four digit number printed in a five position integer-type field. The format item in a PUT EDIT statement reserves the specified number of positions for the value to be printed. This, like all numeric values, is then printed, right justified in the reserved field, i.e., preceded by blanks if the number does not consume the entire field width.

Example (b) shows two values which appear on the printer as one number: 1289489.654. We cannot distinguish that two numbers were supposed to appear. Unlike PUT LIST, each field under PUT EDIT begins where the last one left off. Example (c) corrects this situation by increasing the field width for y and hence introducing some space between the values. Note that the format item F(w,d) reserves w spaces, including a decimal point and d digits to the right of the decimal point.

In main memory: K [1289] Y [489.654] Z [12.9384]

(a) PUT SKIP EDIT (K) (F(5)):

```
|ɓ1289
 F(5)
```

(b) PUT SKIP EDIT (K,Y) (F(4),F(7,3));

```
|1289489.654
 F(4) F(7,3)
```

(c) PUT SKIP EDIT (K,Y)(F(4),F(10,3));

```
|1289ɓɓɓ489.654
 F(4)  F(10,3)
```

(d) PUT SKIP EDIT (Y,Z) (F(6,2),F(6,2));

```
|489.65ɓ12.93
 F(6,2) F(6,2)
```

(e) PUT SKIP EDIT (Y) (F(6,3));

```
|89.654
 F(6,3)
```

(f) PUT SKIP EDIT (Y,Z) (F(5,0),F(5));

```
|ɓ489.ɓɓɓ12
 F(5,0) F(5)
```

Fig. 6.5 Some Examples of PUT EDIT

Example (d) shows that when the stored number has more digits to the right of the decimal point than you provide space for on the printer, the least significant digits are truncated (chopped off) without warning.

Example (e) is a common error for beginning programmers. To print the number 489.624 requires seven print positions in total (count them). The format item in example (e) only specifies 6 print positions, three of which are to the right of the decimal point, leaving only two positions to print the three most significant digits in Y. Fortunately in such cases PL/C issues the error message:

IN STMT xx ERROR EXAB SIZE ERROR. DIGITS LOST = nn

where nn are the actual digits which were not printed -- in this case the message would contain DIGITS LOST = 4. If the number is negative, space must also be provided for printing the sign.

Example (f) points out that when F(w,0) is used to print a fixed or floating point number, the decimal point is included in the output. However when F(w) is used only the integer portion of the number is printed.

Values can also be displayed in scientific notation by using the format item E(w,d), where w is the total field width and d is the number of digits to the right of the decimal point. One digit will appear to the left of the decimal point. Thus if -24.68 were printed under E(12,5), the result would be -2.46800E+01. The value 0.0003687 under E(12,2) would appear as ƀƀƀƀ3.68E-04.

6.4.1 Format Items for Output Spacing

There are several format items which allow you to control the precise position on the page where the next field of data will begin. These "positioning" format items transmit no data themselves and consequently have no corresponding variable in the variable list. Their functions can be compared to the various mechanisms for positioning the paper or the carriage in a typewriter. However, the printer differs from a typewriter in one important respect -- the paper can never back up. Once a printer has passed any line, it can never return to that line for additional printing.

These format items fall into two basic categories, depending on whether they control spacing within one line or between lines. Since we recommend for beginners that each PUT statement handle only one line at a time, this first category is of most interest.

There are two basic means of spacing within a line. The first is the format item X(w), which says to leave a blank field of width w (between the previous field and the next one). This is comparable to hitting the space bar on a typewriter w times. The other way is to say COLUMN(n), which specifies that the next field is to begin at column n, i.e., n spaces from the left hand margin. This is like pressing the tabulator key on a typewriter where position n has been preset with a tab. Fig. 6.6 illustrates their use in four different PUT EDIT statements, which produce identical lines of output.

The format items which control spacing between lines follow two general rules: (1) they can never move the paper backwards to an earlier line; and (2) they always position the printer at the beginning of a line. There are three such format items.

```
NUM   | 9432|
HRS   |37.50|
```

In each case the actual output looks like the following:

```
 ,margin
/
|      9432     37.50
```

(a) PUT SKIP EDIT(NUM,HRS) (F(10),F(10,2));

```
|ƀƀƀƀƀƀ9432ƀƀƀƀƀ37.50
  F(10)     F(10,2)
```

(b) PUT SKIP EDIT(NUM,HRS) (X(6),F(4),X(5),F(5,2));

```
|ƀƀƀƀƀƀ9432ƀƀƀƀƀ37.50
 X(6) F(4) X(5) F(5,2)
```

(c) PUT SKIP EDIT(NUM,HRS) (COLUMN(7),F(4),COLUMN(16),F(5,2));

```
COLUMN(7)      ┌COLUMN(16)
      ↓        ↓
|ƀƀƀƀƀƀ9432ƀƀƀƀƀ37.50
       F(4)     F(5,2)
```

(d) PUT SKIP EDIT(NUM,HRS) (X(4),F(6),COLUMN(14),F(7,2));

```
             ┌COLUMN(14)
             ↓
|ƀƀƀƀƀƀ9432ƀƀƀƀƀ37.50
X(4) F(6)    F(7,2)
```

Fig. 6.6 Alternative Ways of Spacing Within Line

SKIP(n) moves the printer n lines beyond the current line. If printing then occurs on this new line, there will be n-1 blank lines between this new line and the previous printed line. Thus, to leave one blank line, use SKIP(2). SKIP(n) corresponds to hitting the carriage return bar on a typewriter n times (with single line spacing). SKIP is equivalent to SKIP(1). The special case SKIP(0) returns to the beginning of the current line, and is useful for such things as underlining. SKIP(n) as a format item is therefore similar to SKIP (n) used outside the format list, as in PUT SKIP(n) EDIT. The difference is that the SKIP format item permits lines to be skipped between the printing of some of the values in the variable list. For example, for the values NUM=9432 and HRS=37.50, the statement:

```
PUT SKIP EDIT(NUM,HRS) (F(4),SKIP(2),F(5,2));
```

would produce this output:

```
margin
     └───→|9432                    (line 1)
          |                        (line 2)
          |37.50                   (line 3)
```

Another printer positioning item is LINE(n), which moves to the nth line from the top of the current page -- provided this would not cause the paper to back up. The other positioning item is PAGE, which moves to the first line of a new page. Because of its potential for wasting paper, the PAGE feature should not be included unless a program is already running correctly. PAGE and LINE(n) may also be placed outside the format list.

6.5 CHARACTER INPUT-OUTPUT

The input or output of characters is accomplished by using the format item A(w) which specifies a character field of width w.

6.5.1 Character Input

When a field of a card is designated as a character string by an A format item, it is not necessary to enclose the character input in quotes. Thus if a data card contains:

```
JOYEUX NOEL. BONNE ANNEE.
```

this can be read into the variable GREETING by

```
GET SKIP EDIT (GREETING) (A(25));
```

Since we have dispensed with the quote marks around the input string, quote marks which do appear on the card are read as part of the string. Thus it is no longer necessary to code apostrophes by two quote marks on data cards.

```
GET SKIP EDIT (REMARK) (A(10));
```

```
IT'S OKAY.
```

will result in

REMARK | IT'S OKAY. |

Of course blanks are also valid characters. In all future examples character input will be performed under EDIT, and no quotation marks will be used to enclose the data.

6.5.2 Character Output

Consider the variable GREETING which still has contents:

GREETING | JOYEUXbNOEL.bBONNEbANNEE. |

The statement

```
PUT SKIP EDIT (GREETING) (A(25));
```

will produce the following output (with no surrounding quotes):

page margin ——→ |JOYEUX NOEL. BONNE ANNEE.

However

```
PUT SKIP EDIT (SUBSTR(GREETING,1,12)) (A(25));
```

will produce

|JOYEUXbNOEL.bbbbbbbbbbbbb
A(25)

When a string is smaller (here length 12) than the field in which it will be printed (here length 25), it is left justified in their output field, unlike numbers which are right justified. In other words a short string is "padded" with blanks to the right to make it the size of the field. Similarly,

```
PUT SKIP EDIT (GREETING) (A(3));
```

will produce

|JOY

Here the character string (of length 25) is much too long to fit in a field of width 3. Again the character string is left justified in the field and so the right most characters are "truncated" (i.e., lost) without warning.

When the format item A is used without an accompanying field width, PL/I will provide the exact field width for the string to be printed.

One can often avoid truncation and padding problems by simply using the format item, A. Thus if we say:

```
PUT SKIP EDIT (SUBSTR(GREETING,20)) (A);
```

we will get:

page margin ——→ |ANNEE.| ←— end of field

This format item is often used for printing literal character strings as:

```
PUT PAGE EDIT ('TITLE') (A);
```

The use of an A format item without a field width is most appropriate with VARYING length variables and with explicit strings of characters. For example, in Fig. 6.7(a) non-VARYING variables are printed, and the field widths are the same as their permanently declared lengths. The result in Fig. 6.7(b) is usually preferred.

(a)
```
DECLARE (FIRST,LAST) CHARACTER(10);
FIRST = 'JOE';
LAST = 'SCHMOE';
PUT SKIP EDIT(LAST,',',FIRST) (A,A,A);
```

```
|SCHMOEbbbb,JOEbbbbbbb
 \_______/ ↑ \_______/
     A     A     A
```

(b)
```
DECLARE (FIRST,LAST) CHARACTER(10) VARYING;
FIRST = 'JOE';
LAST = 'SCHMOE';
PUT SKIP EDIT(LAST,',',FIRST) (A,A,A);
```

```
|SCHMOE,JOE
 \____/↑\_/
   A   A A
```

Fig. 6.7 Use of Format Item, A. (a) With Fixed Length Variables; (b) With VARYING Length Variables.

Note that using the general A format item to print VARYING length variables produces field widths which depend on the data. If other values are to be printed on the same line, they should be aligned in the correct columns by using COLUMN(n) rather than X(w).

6.6 ABBREVIATIONS IN FORMAT LISTS

Printing a large number of similar values on a line often requires a long sequence of identical format items in the format list. Rather than writing each one in the format list, you may write the format item once, preceded by a <u>repetition factor</u> (and a blank), which tells how many times to repeat the format item. For example, the two PUT statements below are completely equivalent:

```
PUT SKIP EDIT(A,B,C,M,N) (F(6,1),F(6,1),F(6,1),F(5),F(5));

          PUT SKIP EDIT(A,B,C,M,N) (3 F(6,1),2 F(5));
```

You may even request repetition of <u>sequences</u> of format items by enclosing one such sequence in parentheses and preceding this by a repetition factor and a blank. For example, the following PUT statements are completely equivalent:

```
PUT SKIP EDIT(K1,A,B,K2,C,D,K3,E,F)
    (F(5),F(7,1),F(7,1),F(5),F(7,1),F(7,1),F(5),F(7,1),F(7,1));

PUT SKIP EDIT(K1,A,B,K2,C,D,K3,E,F) (3 (F(5),F(7,1),F(7,1)));

PUT SKIP EDIT(K1,A,B,K2,C,D,K3,E,F) (3 (F(5),2 F(7,1)));
```

We recommend that these shorthand forms not be used until you have acquired considerable experience in basic formatting.

6.7 PROGRAM DEVELOPMENT AND TESTING -- IV

Format errors can be among the most difficult kind of problem to detect and diagnose. By far the best way to handle these problems is to try and avoid them. The following paragraphs provide some specific suggestions which can save you literally hours of frustration. Their basic message is that simplicity is the best policy. Unfortunately, formatting is both so powerful and potentially complex that many beginning programmers feel tempted to try out the challenges of its most elegant features. This temptation must be avoided until you have mastered basic formatting. Even then you will be flirting with danger.

The first suggestion is not to use EDIT input-output at all, until you have perfected the working portion of your program. Formatted data is the frosting on the cake and can usually be left until the end. It involves details which should not affect your algorithm. Premature attention to such details diverts your attention from the central issue of algorithm development. If your answers are incorrect, it doesn't matter how handsomely they are displayed! Simply use GET LIST and PUT DATA or PUT LIST until your basic program is working properly.

Another suggestion is to have each PUT statement print exactly one line at a time, i.e., one line per execution. Also avoid shorthand forms, even if more writing and keypunching may be required. In other words, write simple, straightforward PUT statements. The two PUT statements below each print two values on a separate line. This effect is obvious from their form.

```
PUT SKIP EDIT(A,B) (F(10,2),F(10,2));
PUT SKIP EDIT(C,D) (F(10,2),F(10,2));
```

The following statement does exactly the same thing:

```
PUT EDIT(A,B,C,D) (2 (SKIP,2 F(10,2)));
```

but you will probably just take our word for it, since the format list is too complicated to unravel. It is much better to write simple statements that are easy to understand and correct than to write elegant statements which remain unfathomable.

Another suggestion is to be generous with spacing. Don't use an F(4) or F(5) field to print a variable just because you know (or think) that the variable will contain no more than four digits. Even if all your values are sufficiently small to fit in the field, your output may look cramped along the left hand margin of the page. If some value turns out to be too large, some digits will be truncated, and the visible remaining digits will be wrong. By using wide output fields some nasty truncation problems may be avoided, and other problems may stand out more visibly. Don't be stingy with field widths; most installations permit 120 characters per print line.

In a sense, designing format lists is a type of programming which uses a somewhat awkward, restricted language. Like any type of programming, the coding should not begin until you have decided exactly what you want. Format lists should be planned in advance for the same reason that algorithms should precede programming -- to avoid errors. However, formats reflect the layout of data on a card or line rather than being "algorithmic." Consequently their design does not employ an algorithm. Instead it should involve actually writing down on paper a few typical cards or output lines exactly as you want them to appear on the listing. Then by underlining or using some other notation, the fields can be identified and appropriate format items written to describe each field.

For example, suppose you plan to generate a report of the general form shown in Fig. 6.8.

```
             WORK REPORT

NAME          HOURS          RATE
***************************
SMITH          32.0          4.85
JONES          37.5          4.25
SCHMOE          8.5          1.75
  .              .             .
  .              .             .
  .              .             .
***************************
```

Figure 6.8

As indicated in this rough version, your report should have three aligned columns, with headings positioned above each one. Since the heart of the report consists of names and amounts, let us first draw one typical line of this type. At this stage consider what the longest name and largest amounts might be, and provide more than enough space for these. For example, write:

SCHLEIERMACHERȸȸȸȸȸ99.9ȸȸȸ9.99

Now decide on how the fields should be defined. Since numeric quantities are right justified in fields and character strings are left justified, the following fields were chosen:

SCHLEIERMACHERȸȸȸȸȸ99.9ȸȸȸ9.99

A(16)   F(7,1) F(7,2)

The numeric fields were chosen to allow three more spaces than the size of the largest number, in order to keep adjacent columns of numbers from running together. The A(16) format item was used, since there was no advantage here in using an unspecified field width.

From this it is an easy step to writing the appropriate PUT statement. However, before casting this decision in cardboard, we should make sure that this layout is compatible with the rest of the report. Since this layout will happen to work, the corresponding PUT statement is:

```
PUT SKIP EDIT(NAME,HRS,RATE) (A(16),F(7,1),F(7,2));
```

There are <u>three</u> other basic line formats to be considered. The first is a line with a single character string in the center, namely the title line containing the phrase WORK REPORT. In order to get it centered, note that this phase contains 11 characters (counting the blank) and that our typical line contains 30 characters. Thus the middle (6th) character of WORK REPORT should be about 15 positions from the margin. That is, the first character, W, should appear in column 10. This suggests several possible PUT statements:

```
  i) PUT PAGE LIST('ƀƀƀƀƀƀƀƀƀWORKƀREPORT');
 ii) PUT PAGE EDIT('WORK REPORT') (COLUMN(10),A(11));
iii) PUT PAGE EDIT('WORK REPORT') (X(9),A(11));
```

The PUT PAGE form was chosen, since a report may look neater if it begins at the top of a new page.

To determine the layout of line 2 containing the headings, begin by writing those headings above the three fields of your "typical" line.

```
X(4)        A(14)       A(8)    A(4)
ƀƀƀƀNAME              HOURS   RATE
SCHLEIERMACHERƀƀƀƀƀ99.9ƀƀƀ9.99
```

In this case NAME was written slightly to the left of the center of SCHLEIERMACHER, since that name is atypically long. The choice of fields was suggested by the fact that character strings must be left justified in their fields. The corresponding PUT statement is now obvious:

```
PUT SKIP(3) EDIT('NAME','HOURS','RATE')(X(4),A(14),A(8),A(4));
```

Here SKIP(3) was used to provide 2 blank lines under the title.

The last remaining type of line consists of 30 asterisks, since the "typical" line is 30 characters long. There is a convenient built-in function, REPEAT, for concatenating a character string with itself a specified number of times to produce a string which consists of many duplicates of the original. For instance, REPEAT('ABC',2) will generate the string 'ABCABCABC', and REPEAT('*',29) will generate a string of thirty asterisks. Thus to print a string of thirty asterisks, you could use:

```
  i) PUT SKIP LIST(REPEAT('*',29));
 ii) PUT SKIP EDIT(REPEAT('*',29))(A(30));
iii) PUT SKIP EDIT(REPEAT('*',29))(A);
```

Now that the PUT statements for each of the <u>four different types</u> of line have been designed, by placing them at the correct points in the program, a neat, balanced report will be generated by the printer. Their positions in the program will likely be something like Fig. 6.9.

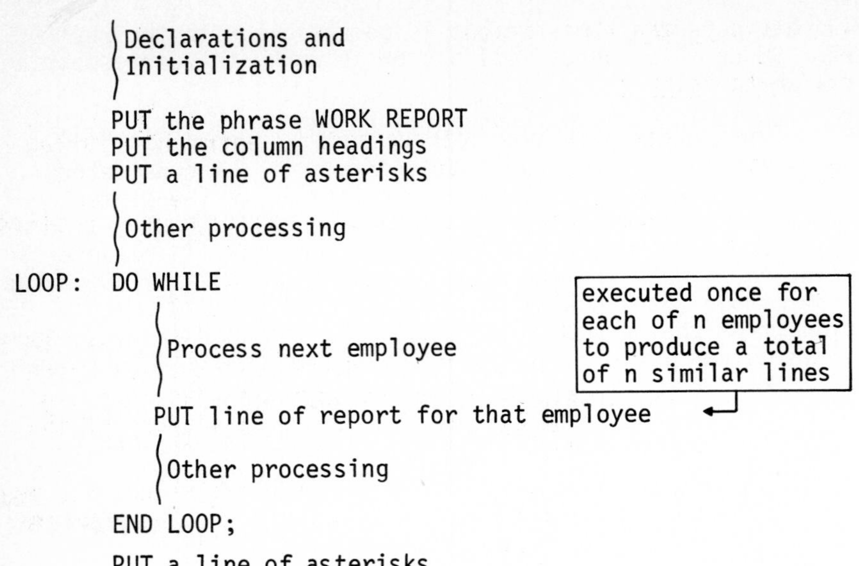

```
         Declarations and
         Initialization

         PUT the phrase WORK REPORT
         PUT the column headings
         PUT a line of asterisks

         Other processing

   LOOP: DO WHILE
                                              executed once for
            Process next employee             each of n employees
                                              to produce a total
                                              of n similar lines
            PUT line of report for that employee

            Other processing

         END LOOP;
         PUT a line of asterisks
```

Fig. 6.9 One Way of Organizing a Report Generating Program to Produce the Report of Fig. 6.8

6.8 REVIEW OF RULES

1. The general forms for EDIT statements are:

   GET EDIT (<list of variables>) (<format list>);

   PUT EDIT (<list of variables>) (<format list>);

   where a format list is a collection of format items, separated by commas. The roles of the variable list and format list are summarized in Fig. 6.10.

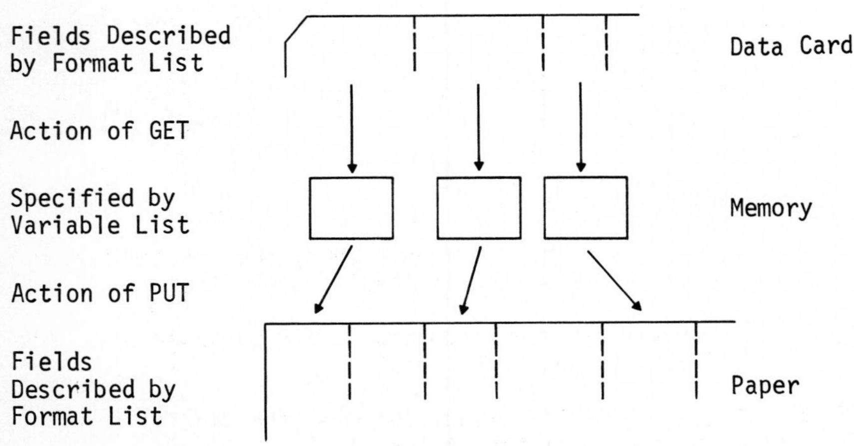

Figure 6.10

2. The basic format items are:

2.1 Data-Related

These items must have a corresponding entry in a variable list.

F(w) on output prints an integer right-justified in a field of width w.

on input reads w card columns as one integer.

F(w,d) on output prints a decimal number right-justified in a field of width w. The width w must provide space for the decimal point and any possible minus sign. The number will have d digits to the right of the decimal point.

on input reads a numeric field of width w and interprets the number read as having d digits to the right of the decimal point.

For input use F(w,0) when there is an explicit decimal point in the data.

A(w) on output prints a character string left-justified in a field of width w.

on input reads a field of width w and interprets the result as a character string of length w.

A on output prints any character string.

on input this form is not permitted.

E(w,d) read or print (right-justified) a number in exponential notation in a field of width w with d digits to the right of the decimal point. On output one digit will be written to the left of the decimal (for a total of d+1 significant digits). This may be adjusted by using the form E(w,d,s), where s represents the number of significant digits. On output, at least six extra spaces should be provided in w for ± signs, the decimal point, the letter E, and a 2-digit exponent.

2.2 Spacing-Related

These items are only for positioning the printer and do not have corresponding items in the variable list.

X(w) skips a field of size w on input or generates a blank field of size w on output.

COLUMN(n) moves (right) to position n on the card or print line,
COL(n) for the beginning of next field.

SKIP(n)   skip to beginning of nth line beyond current line (or n cards beyond current card).

LINE(n)   advance printer to beginning of line n.

PAGE   advance printer to beginning (line 1) of new page.

3. When there are fewer format items than variables, PL/I returns to the start of the format list to satisfy the requirements of the remaining variables.

4. When there are more format items than variables, the superfluous format items are ignored.

6.9 EXERCISES

6.1 Suppose a company keeps its customer records on data cards which are formatted as follows:

cols. 1-7	ID Number
cols. 8-20	Last Name
cols. 21-22	Initials (no periods)
cols. 23-28	Balance (decimal in col. 26)
cols. 29-34	Other numeric data

You are to produce from this list of cards a report of the following form:

CUSTOMER	BALANCE
A.B. CHADWICK	294.23
D.E. FERGUSON	15.62
etc.	etc.

Use the following data as input:

```
9326417CHADWICKƀƀƀƀƀAB294.23111111
9651124FERGUSON     DE 15.62222222
9834186MARTIN       XQ147.32333333
9692883MAIN         DM  1.05444555
9355561NOXIOUS      OB879.21666777
9472185PRATT        CC650.00888999
9641727SPRATT       JJ 84.07112233
9311462THROCKMORTONƀZA333.33445566
```

6.2 Since the ID numbers in the data of Exercise 6.1 all begin with 9, and since the fifth digit of the ID is used only for a currently discontinued administrative reason, the company has decided to use only the 2nd, 3rd, 4th, 6th, and 7th digits of the ID. Produce a list of compact identifiers from the data of Exercise 6.1, containing these shortened ID numbers, the first two initials and the first letter of the last name:

```
32617ABC
65124DEF
  etc.
```

You may not use the concatenation operation.

6.3 From the data of Exercise 6.1, generate (not on separate pages though) a series of form letters addressed to these customers. Each letter should resemble the following:

```
DEAR MR. CHADWICK,
   YOU OWE US $294.23.

DEAR MR. FERGUSON,
   YOU OWE US $15.62.
```

6.4 The accounts receivable records for a department store contain customer name, balance at start of month and transactions during the month. The record for each customer is recorded on a data card as:

col. 1-15 customer name
col. 16-21 opening balance (decimal point in col. 19)

Then up to eight transactions are coded in fields of 7 columns. The first column in a field contains a blank if the transaction is a charge or a zero if the transaction is a payment; the remaining six columns contain the amount of the transaction, right justified with the decimal point in the 5th column of the field. For example the card

```
WILLIAMSONb̸R.J.238.750b̸76.94b̸152.00
```

is the record for R.J. Williamson whose opening balance was 238.75. During the period he made a payment of 76.94 and incurred a charge of 152.00.

You have to write a program to update these accounts monthly and produce a recap report in the form:

```
                 ACCOUNTS RECEIVABLE RECAP

         OPENING      TOTAL       TOTAL        CLOSING
 NAME    BALANCE      CHARGES     PAYMENTS     BALANCE
```

Of course, the report must include totals for each column except NAME. In addition the closing balance should be marked with an * if no payment was made during the period.

Design an algorithm for this project and then implement it in PL/I. All I/O must be EDIT directed. Test your program on the following data:

```
WILLIAMSONb̸R.J.238.750b̸76.94b̸152.00
JONESb̸C.b̸b̸b̸b̸b̸b̸b̸b̸62.50b̸b̸10.00b̸b̸39.52b̸b̸18.75
STEVENSONb̸T.C.b̸584.38b̸146.730225.000112.50b̸b̸58.49
BATHURSTb̸A.b̸b̸b̸b̸140.61
CONNELLYb̸A.A.b̸b̸b̸19.53b̸b̸28.43
```

6.5 Product numbers are frequently designed so that they can be checked for validity by computer. One such scheme for a five-digit number is as follows:

(i) add the first, fourth and fifth digits,

(ii) subtract the sum of the second and third digits from the result of (i),

(iii) if the result of (ii) is 5 then the number is a valid product number.

Write a PL/I program to inspect an arbitrary amount of product numbers, each punched in columns 1 to 5 of a data card. The program should print each number and the message VALID or INVALID as necessary.

6.6(a) Write a program to read some text and count the number of occurrences of the words AND, GOOD, FOR, EVER, and words of four or fewer characters. Your input data should consist of continuous text with no quotation marks. The input text should also be printed out. Your program should produce a histogram of the number of occurrences of each special word. Your histogram should have the following general form, where each * represents one occurrence of the word, and the number in parentheses is the number of occurrences:

```
OCCURRENCE OF WORDS IN TEXT CONTAINING xx WORDS:
        AND   *****                       (5)
        GOOD  **                          (2)
        FOR   ****                        (4)
        EVER  **                          (2)
yy WORDS WERE UNDER 5 CHARACTERS
```

The following data should be used:

Stones and clay not mud and hay will last for ever and a day. If you ever had such a good time that you felt sick for ever and good for nothing then you won't forget to be ever vigilant and ever so good the next time you go for a good time and are tempted to overdo it.

Hint: REPEAT(<string>, n) will generate a character string consisting of n+1 occurrences of <string>.

(b) Generalize this program so it can count the occurrences of any specified list of words. This list of special words should appear on the first data card and use a single blank as a separator between words. Don't forget to include these words in the histogram.

6.7(a) Write a program to examine an arbitrary number of words of text and present a histogram (as in Exercise 6.6) showing the frequencies of the word lengths, i.e., the number of words in each of the following categories of word lengths:

word length

- 1-2 characters (short)
- 3-4 characters (medium-short)
- 5-6 characters (medium-long)
- 7-8 characters (long)
- 9 or more characters (very long)

(b) In addition to the histogram of frequencies, produce another histogram of "cumulative frequencies," i.e., the number of words in each of the following categories:

1 or 2 characters
4 or fewer characters
6 or fewer characters
8 or fewer characters
1 or more characters (total number of words)

6.8(a) Write a program to generate the following coordinate system:

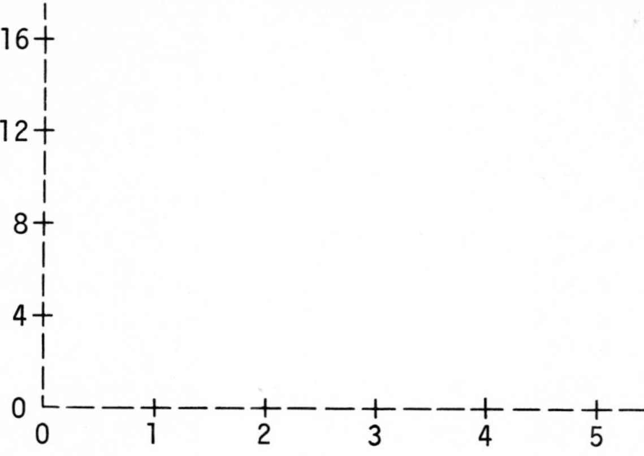

(b) In addition to the coordinate system, plot the points of the function

$$4x + y = 16$$

for x values of .5,1,1.5,2,2.5,3,3.5.

<u>Hint</u>: It is possible to put variables within a format item, such as COLUMN(N), to represent a different column, N, each time the PUT EDIT statement is executed.

Chapter 7 One-dimensional Arrays

7.1 THE CASE FOR ARRAYS

The programs considered up to this point have required only a few variables. When large amounts of data were involved, our usual approach was to read or generate one "unit" of data, process it, and then either print the result or incorporate it in some total or in other summary information. Since each such "unit" of data could be discarded after being processed, the same memory locations and code were reused to handle a long succession of similar items.

Not all applications are of this type. Often the data must either be retained after initial processing or be assembled in memory before processing can begin.

Suppose we must find the average of three numbers and then print every number greater than the average. In this case, we cannot determine the average until all three numbers have been read. Then all the numbers must be inspected again to find out which ones are greater than the average. The simplest approach is to retain all the numbers in memory. An algorithm for such a problem might be:

```
1.    get values for a, b, and c;
2.    compute average of a, b, and c;
3.    if a > average then print a;
4.    if b > average then print b;
5.    if c > average then print c;
6.    end.
```

While this algorithm may not appear too formidable, consider the corresponding solution for 300, or 3,000, numbers. In this case, to invent and declare so many distinct names could easily tax both your imagination and your wrist. Worse yet, even though many data items receive similar processing, they cannot be handled by identical code, since the code must refer to different variable names in each case. Don't panic! You won't have to resort to writing innumerable declarations and just as many "almost identical" lines of code.

The ability to handle large numbers of similar data items economically is provided in PL/I by arrays. This chapter is devoted to describing the uses of this very important and common programming facility in its simplest form, "one-dimensional arrays."

7.2 DECLARING AND REFERENCING ONE-DIMENSIONAL ARRAYS

An array is simply a collection of memory locations of the same type. A one-dimensional array is a list of memory locations and bears a similar relation to a simple variable as a party invitation list does to the name of a single invited guest.

If you were making up an invitation list, you would not explicitly write before each person's name "first invited guest," "second invited guest," etc. Instead, you might write "invited guests" at the top of a sheet of paper and then assume each following line would identify a different guest. Similarly to request a list of 100 memory locations, you do not need to make 100 explicit declarations. Instead you declare a single array name and indicate how many locations are included in the list. For example:

```
DECLARE GUEST_LIST(100) CHARACTER(60);
```

would request a list of 100 variables, each capable of holding a 60-character string. The variables in the list may be of other types as well, and so the general form is:

```
DECLARE <array name>(size) <attributes>;
```

Whatever the attributes, however, all the variables in a single array must be of the same type. Thus each array is homogeneous.

When you make up an invitation list, you do not create an amorphous bunch of indistinguishable names. You presumably put each name on a different line. This permits you to refer to the fourth name on the list, even though you did not explicitly write "4th invited guest" before his name. Similarly the declaration of an array implicitly creates enough different names so that your program can reference individual locations in the array. For example, to reference the 4th variable in the array declared above, your program could use the name:

```
GUEST_LIST(4)
```

Of course, this would have to appear in a context where a variable name is appropriate, such as:

```
PUT SKIP EDIT(GUEST_LIST(4)) (A(60));
```

However, in the appropriate context a reference to an array element behaves just like a reference to a simple variable. Fig. 7.1(a) shows how declaring an array of four integer variables implicitly generates four different variable names. Fig. 7.1(b) shows how these variable names behave like any other variable name in PL/I statements.

Fig. 7.1(c) illustrates a most important point: the particular array element being referenced can itself be denoted by a variable. In fact, it can be denoted by an arithmetic expression, as shown in Fig. 7.1(d). This is the facility which allows the <u>same</u> code to refer to different items in the list merely by repeatedly executing the code with different values for the variable which indicates the current position in the array. Fig. 7.1(e) depicts how 9 could be added to every element of the array by executing the statement:

```
VALUE(PSN) = VALUE(PSN)+9;
```

four times with different values for PSN each time. PSN is the variable which indicates the position currently being accessed. As its value is systematically altered, so is the position being referred to in the array.

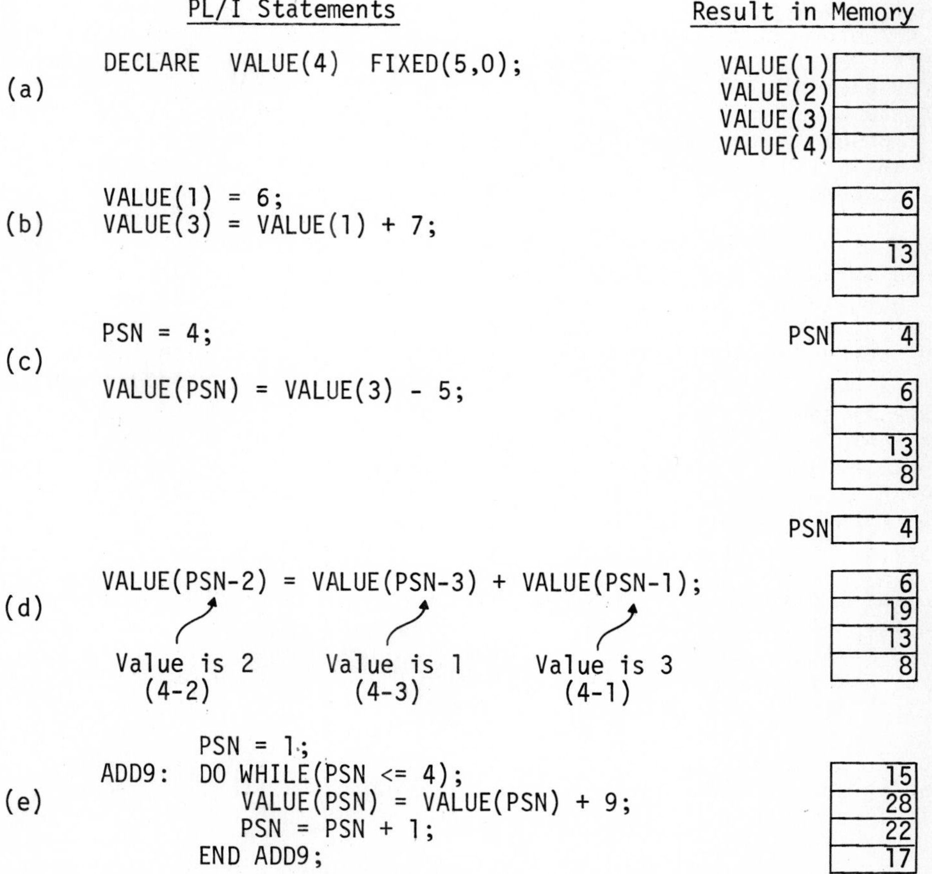

PL/I Statements
Result in Memory
(a)
DECLARE VALUE(4) FIXED(5,0);
VALUE(1)
VALUE(2)
VALUE(3)
VALUE(4)
(b)
VALUE(1) = 6;
VALUE(3) = VALUE(1) + 7;
6
13
(c)
PSN = 4;
VALUE(PSN) = VALUE(3) - 5;
PSN 4
6
13
8
PSN 4
(d)
VALUE(PSN-2) = VALUE(PSN-3) + VALUE(PSN-1);
Value is 2 (4-2)
Value is 1 (4-3)
Value is 3 (4-1)
6
19
13
8
(e)
PSN = 1;
ADD9: DO WHILE(PSN <= 4);
VALUE(PSN) = VALUE(PSN) + 9;
PSN = PSN + 1;
END ADD9;
15
28
22
17

Fig. 7.1 Declaring and Referencing one-Dimensional Arrays

7.3 PROCESSING ARRAY ELEMENTS

This last example, Fig. 7.1(e) is so important that we have displayed its step-by-step execution in Fig. 7.2. It is important because it typifies the most common way of using arrays, namely, "moving through" the array processing each element in the same way but processing only one element at a time.

The statements which govern the movement through an array are so common, they should become part of your standard programming repertoire. They are shown in Fig. 7.3. Of course the type of "processing" may range over a great many possibilities, such as updating values (Fig. 7.1e and 7.2), printing values (Fig. 7.4a), adding values onto a running total (Fig. 7.4b) and generating new values (Fig. 7.4c). Note how the same basic control structure (Fig. 7.3) appears in each of the examples of Fig. 7.4.

7.3.1 Reading Values into an Array

It is certainly possible to GET values from data cards for successive array elements. The code would look much like Fig. 7.4(a), with GET instead of PUT. In fact, just as in the case of simple variables, it is impossible to manipulate array elements before values have been stored in those locations (usually done by using either assignment or GET statements). Consequently, many programs involving arrays include a loop near the beginning to GET starting values from data cards.

However, it is not necessary to have values in those array locations which are never referenced. To put it differently, just because an array has been DECLAREd to consist of a certain number of memory locations does not mean that all these locations must be used. Your party invitation list may be on a sheet of paper with twenty lines, but if you have only seven friends, you will use only seven lines of the list.

What is important is that you start with a sheet of paper large enough to accommodate all the friends' names which might occur to you. Similarly, when dealing with unknown quantities of data to be read from cards into an array, you should DECLARE a sufficiently large array to hold all the data and not worry if there isn't enough data to fill the array.

The implication is that when filling an array with GET statements, you may not make it to the end of the array if you exhaust the data cards first. Your DO WHILE statement governing movement through the array should therefore test for no more data. It should also continue to test that your position is still within the array, since you may have more data than array elements. The resulting code, shown in Fig. 7.5, is a blend of movement through an array (Fig. 7.3) and reading an arbitrary number of values using ON ENDFILE. (Of course, this is unnecessary if you know in advance how much data will be read in.)

There is a further implication for subsequent processing of this data. Only those array elements containing values can be manipulated. Any subsequent processing must be prevented (by the DO WHILE) from venturing into undefined portions of the array. The effective "size" of the array becomes the number of values actually stored rather than the number of declared locations. Of course this number can be

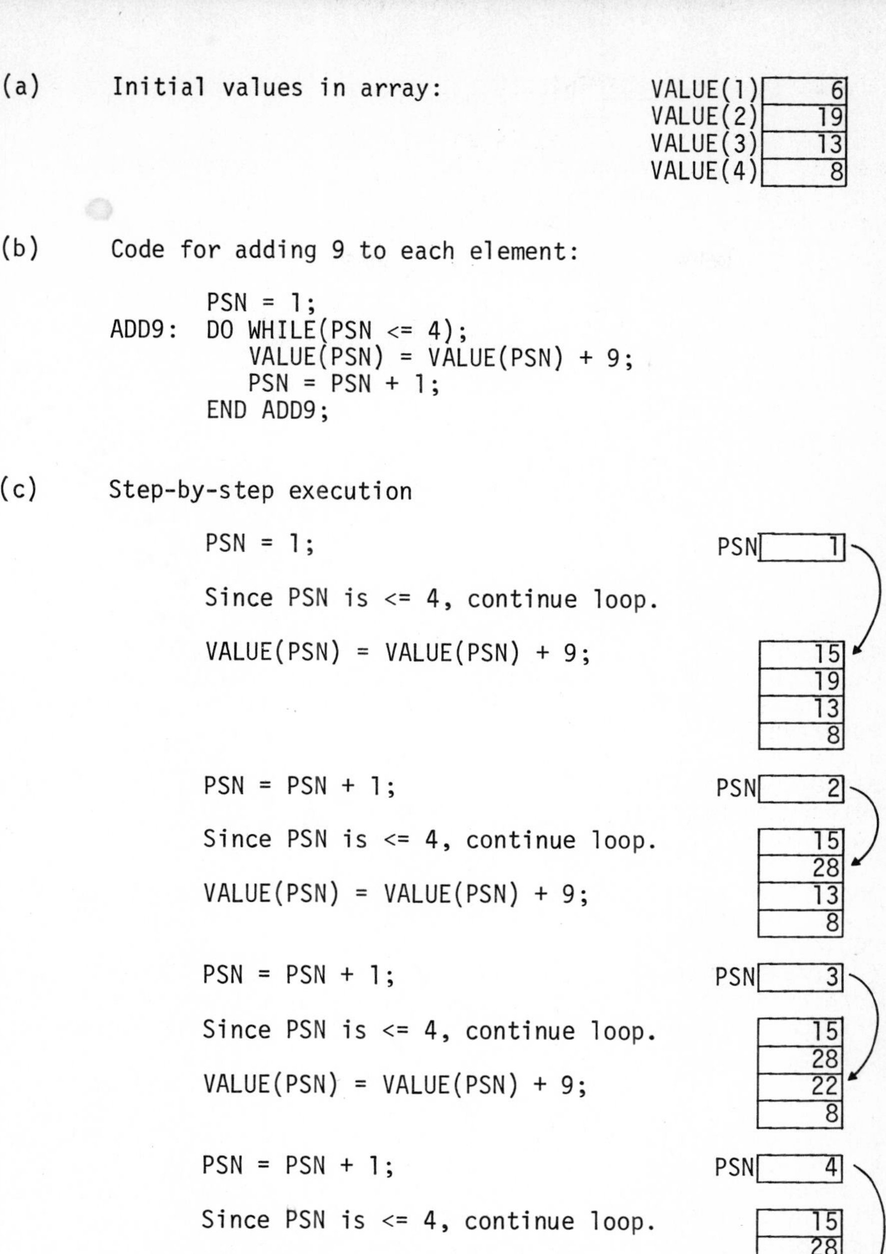

(a) Initial values in array:

(b) Code for adding 9 to each element:

```
       PSN = 1;
ADD9:  DO WHILE(PSN <= 4);
          VALUE(PSN) = VALUE(PSN) + 9;
          PSN = PSN + 1;
       END ADD9;
```

(c) Step-by-step execution

PSN = 1;

Since PSN is <= 4, continue loop.

VALUE(PSN) = VALUE(PSN) + 9;

PSN = PSN + 1;

Since PSN is <= 4, continue loop.

VALUE(PSN) = VALUE(PSN) + 9;

PSN = PSN + 1;

Since PSN is <= 4, continue loop.

VALUE(PSN) = VALUE(PSN) + 9;

PSN = PSN + 1;

Since PSN is <= 4, continue loop.

VALUE(PSN) = VALUE(PSN) + 9;

PSN = PSN + 1;

Since PSN is <u>not</u> <= 4, stop loop.

Fig. 7.2 Step-by-step processing of an array

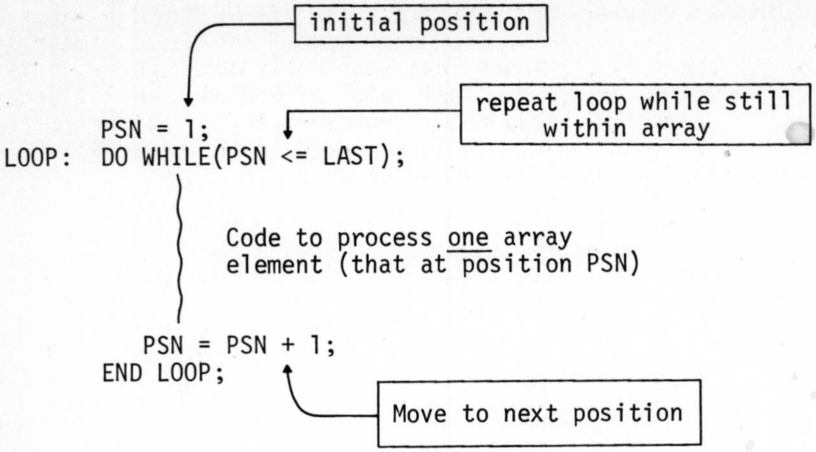

```
                                  ┌─────────────────┐
                  ┌───────────────│ initial position│
                  │               └─────────────────┘
                  ▼                          ┌─────────────────────────┐
         PSN = 1;              ┌─────────────│ repeat loop while still │
                               ▼             │      within array       │
  LOOP:  DO WHILE(PSN <= LAST);              └─────────────────────────┘
              )
              )     Code to process one array
              )     element (that at position PSN)
              )
            PSN = PSN + 1;
         END LOOP;
                  ▲
                  │              ┌───────────────────────┐
                  └──────────────│ Move to next position │
                                 └───────────────────────┘
```

Fig. 7.3 Control Structure for Moving Through an Array

```
DECLARE ARY(5) FIXED(5,0);
```

(a) Printing the values stored in an array, <u>assuming values have already been stored</u> in the array:

```
        PSN = 1;
OUTPUT: DO WHILE(PSN <= 5);
           PUT SKIP LIST(ARY(PSN));
           PSN = PSN + 1;
        END OUTPUT;
        .
        .
        .
```

(b) Adding the values of array elements into a total:

```
        TOTAL = 0;
        K = 1;
 ADDUP: DO WHILE(K <= 5);
           TOTAL = TOTAL + ARY(K);
           K = K + 1;
        END ADDUP;
        .
        .
        .
```

(c) Storing the first five even integers (2,4,6,8, and 10) in an array:

```
        N = 1;
  EVEN: DO WHILE(N <= 5);
           ARY(N) = 2*N;
           N = N + 1;
        END EVEN;
        .
        .
        .
```

Fig. 7.4 Examples of Array Processing

determined by noting the last array position filled by the input loop. In Fig. 7.5 PSN will indicate the next "empty" array location prior to executing GET. If the input loop stops only because the array is filled (FLAG is still 0), the final value of PSN will be 101, one more than the number of items read. However, if GET fails to obtain a value (FLAG is 1), PSN will be incremented again, making its final value greater by two than the number of array items.

```
          DECLARE ARY(100) FIXED(8,2);
              .
              .
          ON ENDFILE(SYSIN) FLAG = 1;
          FLAG = 0;
              .
              .
          PSN = 1
          /*TEST FOR SUFFICIENT LOCATIONS AND DATA*/
   INPT:  DO WHILE((PSN <= 100) & (FLAG = 0));
             GET LIST(ARY(PSN));
             PSN = PSN + 1;
          END INPT;
          IF FLAG=0 THEN
             #ITEMS = PSN - 1;
          ELSE
             #ITEMS = PSN - 2;
```

Fig. 7.5 Reading an Arbitrary Number of Values into an Array

7.3.2 Linear Searching

One of the common types of processing is searching, which entails inspecting the array values to find a particular value or to test for some property. There are many ways of searching, but the most straightforward is to start at the top of a list and examine its elements one-by-one to see which item (if any) happens to be what you are looking for. This method is called "linear searching" and clearly fits the pattern of "moving through an array" in Fig. 7.3.

There are many possible motives for searching, and these determine what happens when the item you seek is discovered. For example, when a desired item is found, you might print a message, set a flag, record the current position, increase a counter, discontinue the search, or some combination of these. Some possibilities are shown in Fig. 7.6, where the array being searched is the array ARY of Fig. 7.5. It presumably contains decimal numbers in positions 1 through #ITEMS. Fig. 7.6(a) answers the question: where does the value 25 occur? The position number is printed whenever 25 is encountered, possibly more than once. Fig. 7.6(b) answers the question: how many negative numbers are contained in the array? This question cannot be answered until all the values have been inspected, but each time a negative value is found, a counter is incremented.

Fig. 7.6(c) answers perhaps the most common question: does the value 25 occur in the list (not where or how often).

(a) Finding <u>where</u> the number 25 occurs:

```
         PSN = 1;
FIND25:  DO WHILE(PSN <= #ITEMS);
            IF ARY(PSN) = 25 THEN
               PUT SKIP LIST (PSN);
            PSN = PSN + 1;
         END FIND25;
```

(b) Finding <u>how many</u> negative values occur:

```
         COUNT = 0;
         PSN = 1;
NEGS:    DO WHILE(PSN <= #ITEMS);
            IF ARY(PSN) < 0 THEN
               COUNT = COUNT + 1;
            PSN = PSN + 1;
         END NEGS;
         PUT SKIP DATA (COUNT);
```

(c) Finding <u>whether</u> the number 25 occurs:

```
         FOUND = 0;
         PSN = 1;
ANY25:   DO WHILE(PSN <= #ITEMS);
            IF ARY(PSN) = 25 THEN
               FOUND = 1;
            PSN = PSN + 1;
         END ANY25;
         IF FOUND = 1 THEN PUT LIST ('25 FOUND');
            ELSE PUT LIST ('25 NOT FOUND');
```

Fig. 7.6 Examples of Linear Searching in an Array Which was Initialized in Fig. 7.5

The technique we have chosen is to initialize a flag (called FOUND) to 0 and to set this flag to 1 when and if 25 is encountered. Notice that upon completion of the search, FOUND will be 0 only if 25 never occurred. The first occurrence of 25 would have set FOUND to 1. Any later occurrences would merely have set it to 1 again. There is <u>no</u> way of ever resetting it to 0.

Determining <u>whether</u> some value is present in a list of numbers corresponds to checking a party invitation list to see whether Lance Sterling's name was included. You would probably answer this question by starting at the top of the list and reading each name until you reached either Lance's name or the last name on the list. The point is that upon finding him among the guests, you would discontinue the search since it would be pointless to read further. This decision to quit can be a real time-saver if the list is very long, and a similar decision can also save time on the computer. In other words, continue the search while you are still within the array <u>and</u> the desired value has not yet been found (the flag is still 0). The modification to the DO WHILE in Fig. 7.6(c) is obvious. (This modified search is also included later in part of Fig. 7.8.)

7.4 MULTIPLE AND DYNAMICALLY CHANGING ARRAYS

7.4.1 Searching as a Prelude to Updating

One common reason for searching an array is to select an array item to be updated, i.e., modified or replaced. For example, every time you visit the doctor, the receptionist will search the patient files and if yours is found, increase your bill and add any pertinent medical information to the file.

The same array (file drawer) may be searched many times, e.g., whenever a patient shows up. Some of these searches may even be for the same item. If you fall down the stairs after leaving the doctor's office, you may return for stitches and cause the receptionist to find your file again.

Even when a search fails to find the desired item, there may be an important consequence, namely that this item gets added to the array as a new value. Thus, if you are a new patient, the receptionist will not be able to find your file and will make out a new one. Any subsequent search for this same item will, of course, successfully discover this new occurrence. Within the limitation of the number of memory locations declared for an array, its effective size (i.e., the number of values currently stored) may change as the result of searches and updates.

Of course, values may be deleted as well, causing (the useful portion of) an array to "shrink" instead of "grow." However, deleting elements from an array is more difficult than appending new values, and the medical reasons for removing a patient's file are too gruesome to describe. Therefore we will defer this topic until Section 7.5.1.

7.4.2 Multiple Arrays

Let us focus on that most important aspect of any business: billing the customers. During the course of a month, various charges accumulate in each customer's account. At the end of the month, the data of interest consists of a large number of customer names and an equal number of bills to be sent. Since the names and amounts are different data types (character strings and decimal numbers), two separate arrays[1] would be required to hold this information in a computerized billing system. The simplest way to associate the correct name with the correct amount is to (conceptually) place the lists side by side and have corresponding names and amounts at corresponding positions in their respective arrays. Fig. 7.7 depicts this correspondence between arrays and also shows how they might be processed in tandem, in this case, how their values would be printed side-by-side.

---

[1]Structures, introduced in Chapter 10, offer an alternative way to store mixed data types.

```
DECLARE CUSTMR(100) CHARACTER(40);
DECLARE AMT(100) FIXED(7,2);
```

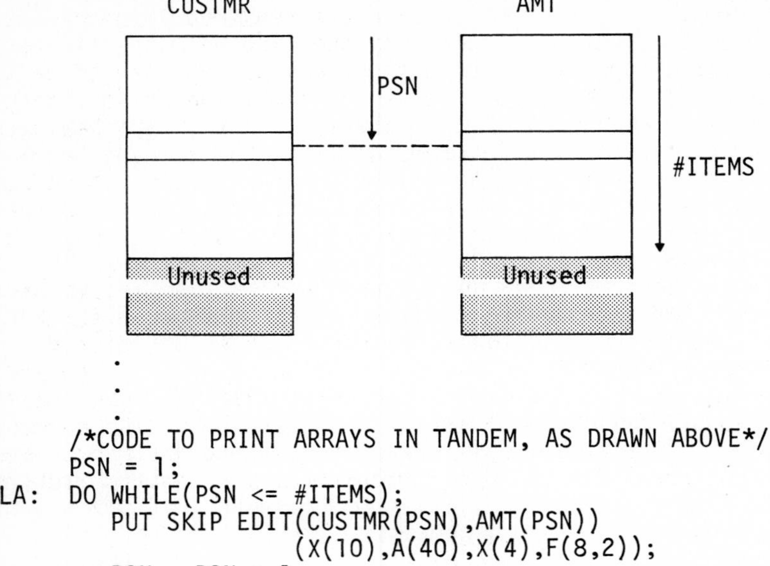


```
          .
          .
          .
        /*CODE TO PRINT ARRAYS IN TANDEM, AS DRAWN ABOVE*/
        PSN = 1;
DISPLA: DO WHILE(PSN <= #ITEMS);
           PUT SKIP EDIT(CUSTMR(PSN),AMT(PSN))
                        (X(10),A(40),X(4),F(8,2));
           PSN = PSN + 1;
        END DISPLA;
          .
          .
          .
```

Fig. 7.7 The Use of Arrays in Tandem

7.4.3 A Problem Involving Multiple Arrays

The previous sections have provided sufficient background to develop a complete solution to an end-of-month billing problem.

Problem Statement

Suppose a company records all its individual customer charges on data cards during the course of a month. Each card has the form:

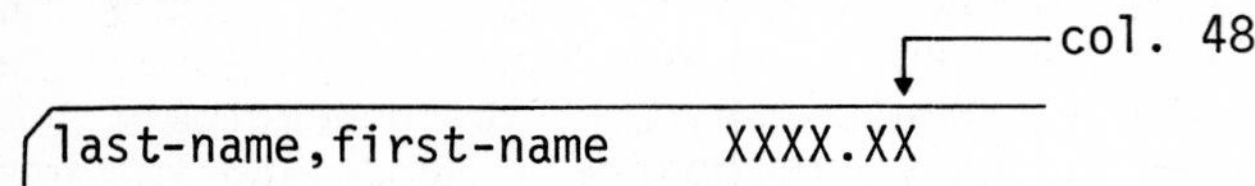

There are at most 100 different customers. However, each customer may have any number of cards (possibly none), depending on how many charges have been made to his account. We must write a program to produce a report in which the name of each customer owing money appears once followed by the total amount he owes.

Solution

When an array problem is suspected, there are two special steps which should precede the algorithm.

First, make sure that it really is an array problem, i.e., that large amounts of very similar data are required in memory at one time. Here this is the case. Since only one line of output is permitted per customer, and since one customer may be represented on several data cards, there must be some way of combining several cards for a customer into one result. This suggests that when a new card is considered, the program must decide if it has already begun collecting information on that customer. If so, the new information can be combined with that already on hand. This, however, requires retaining information in main memory concerning every customer seen so far, presumably in an array.

Second, decide on the size, type, number, and relationship of the array(s). Two arrays are required, since both names (CHARACTER information) and amounts (numeric information) must be recorded. Since there are at most 100 customers, and since only the name and total charges must be maintained for each one, arrays of 100 locations should be sufficient. As described in Section 7.4.2, corresponding positions in the two arrays represent the same customer. Here it would be a good idea to draw a diagram of the "data structure," like that in Fig. 7.7.

Algorithm

Note that the number and identity of customers owing money during any one month cannot be predicted. Therefore, we will let the arrays "grow" (Section 7.4.1) as new customer names are encountered. The basic algorithm is:

```
1.    initialize the number of current items to 0;
2.    read first data card;
3.    repeat while cards remain to be processed;
3.1      process most recent card;
3.2      read next card;
4.    print results;
5.    end.
```

Of course, the heart of the algorithm is Step 3.1, which may be expanded into:

```
3.1.1    search the array of customer names to see where the
            current name has occurred previously;
3.1.2    if found (i.e., not a new name) then update the amount
            he owes in the corresponding position of the other
            array;
3.1.3    otherwise make a new entry in both arrays for this
            newly encountered customer;
```

The search (3.1.1) is basically the search described at the end of Section 7.3.2, which is stopped as soon as the desired item is found. Because it stops upon success, the position of the desired item is available for use later.

Only Step 3.1.3 may need elaboration here:

3.1.3.1 increase number of current items by 1;
3.1.3.2 store the new name in this "last" position of the customer array;
3.1.3.3 store the amount owed in the corresponding position of the other array;

Note that printing the results amounts to printing two arrays in tandem, as in Fig. 7.7. Also note that the values from data cards are <u>not</u> read directly into the arrays, since it must still be determined by a search whether they will constitute new array items or merely be used to update a present array item! Thus the complete program can be written, as shown in Fig. 7.8.

7.5 SORTING AND EFFICIENT SEARCHING

As long as data is stored in arrays in the order of its arrival or in any other arbitrary fashion, finding specific items by linear searching is as (in)efficient as any other method. However, when dealing with large volumes of data, plunging in at the top of the list and inspecting each item in turn can be <u>very</u> time consuming for either a human or a computer.

What if names appeared in the telephone directory in whatever order customers paid their bills? You would have an extremely difficult time finding anyone's number (unless your friends all paid their bills in advance). When you <u>search</u> for a phone number, you make heavy use of the fact that the names have been <u>sorted</u> into alphabetical order. Thus you can quickly direct your search to the correct page, column, and name.

Sorting is the process of ordering data in some linear sequence, and its motive is to facilitate later searching. For example, if the report generated by the billing program of Fig. 7.8 were sorted, it would be much easier for a human to read. There are also computerized search algorithms which can take advantage of sorted, ordered data to work much more efficiently than linear searching. One such algorithm will be described in Section 7.5.3.

First, however, two quite different sorting algorithms will be described, the first because it is "natural" and the second because it is "efficient." It is interesting to see how two such entirely different approaches are both able to solve exactly the same problem. In fact there are many other algorithms for sorting which work equally well.

7.5.1 <u>Selection Sorting</u>

Suppose someone handed you a list of numbers on a sheet of paper and asked you to sort them in ascending order, i.e., with the smallest first and largest last. You would probably construct a new list in the following way: find the smallest number and write it at the top of the new list; find the next smallest number and write it in the next (second) position of the new list; and continue this until every original number had been copied into the new list. To help keep track of which numbers had already been copied, you would probably cross out each number as you copied it and from then on would ignore

```
            /* FIGURE 7.8 */
BILL:    PROCEDURE OPTIONS (MAIN);

         DECLARE
            CUSTMR(100) CHARACTER (40), /* CUSTOMER NAMES*/
            AMT(100) FIXED (7,2), /* AMOUNTS OWED */
            NEW_NAME CHARACTER (40), /* NAME FROM DATA*/
            NEW_AMT FIXED (7,2), /* AMOUNT FROM DATA */
            NO_MORE FIXED (5,0), /* END OF DATA FLAG */
            FOUND_FLAG FIXED (5,0), /* FOR SEARCHING ARRAY*/
            #NAMES FIXED (5,0), /* NO. NAMES IN ARRAY */
            PSN FIXED (5,0); /* POSITION IN ARRAY */

         /* INITIALIZE VARIABLES */

         #NAMES = 0;
         NO_MORE = 0;
         ON ENDFILE (SYSIN) NO_MORE = 1;
         GET LIST (NEW_NAME,NEW_AMT);

PROCESS:DO WHILE (NO_MORE = 0);
            /* INITIALIZE PSN AND FOUND_FLAG PRIOR TO
               SEARCHING FOR NEW_NAME */
            PSN = 1;
            FOUND_FLAG = 0;
            /* SEARCH ARRAY FOR NEW_NAME */

SEARCH:     DO WHILE (FOUND_FLAG = 0 & PSN <= #NAMES);
               IF CUSTMR(PSN) = NEW_NAME THEN
                  FOUND_FLAG = 1;
               ELSE
                  PSN = PSN + 1;
            END SEARCH;

            /* UPDATE OLD ENTRY OR MAKE NEW ONE */

            IF FOUND_FLAG = 1 THEN
               AMT(PSN) = AMT(PSN) + NEW_AMT;
            ELSE
NEW_ENTRY:     DO;
                  #NAMES = #NAMES + 1;
                  CUSTMR(#NAMES) = NEW_NAME;
                  AMT(#NAMES) = NEW_AMT;
               END NEW_ENTRY;
            GET LIST (NEW_NAME,NEW_AMT);
         END PROCESS;

         /* PRINT REPORT */

         PUT PAGE EDIT ('CUSTOMER NAME','BALANCE')
            (A(43),A(10));
         PSN = 1;

DISPLAY:DO WHILE (PSN <= #NAMES);
            PUT SKIP EDIT (CUSTMR(PSN),AMT(PSN))
               (X(2),A(40),F(8,2));
            PSN = PSN + 1;
         END DISPLAY;

         END BILL;
```

Figure 7.8

it in your search for the smallest. In other words, you would instinctively execute the following algorithm:

```
1.     repeat as many times as there are numbers in the original
          original list;
1.1       search the original list for the smallest remaining
             value;
1.2       copy that number into the next empty position of
             the new list;
1.3       delete (cross out) that number from the original
             list;
2.     end.
```

The new list will be sorted in ascending order. The same kind of algorithm could also sort character strings in alphabetical order. To sort in descending order, you would search for the largest remaining value each time. Any of these variations is called "selection sorting," since the basic step consists of searching remaining elements in order to "select" the next one for the new list.

A computer could obviously be programmed to imitate this natural, human method of sorting. Assuming the original list is an array, a second array of the same size would be needed for the new (sorted) list. Even if an entire selection sort is not to be programmed, the way such a program would use these arrays is worth discussing.

7.5.1.1 <u>Searching for the Smallest Value in an Array</u> Determining a smallest value (Step 1.1) is similar to finding a largest value -- a problem already discussed in Chapter 3. Recall that the strategy is to begin with a candidate which is certainly no smaller than the actual smallest value. As each new value is inspected, it is compared with the current "most promising candidate," and if smaller, then it becomes the new "smallest value seen so far."

Before now we only wished to know the <u>value</u> of the smallest item. However, since Step 1.3 of the current algorithm is going to delete the smallest item, the search algorithm (Step 1.1) should also note its <u>position</u>. Whenever a new "smallest" value is encountered, we thus record both its value and its position.

These modifications as well as the underlying array are reflected in this algorithm to search for a smallest value:

```
1.1.1      initialize min to value of first array element and
              record its location as 1;
1.1.2      initialize current (search) position to 2;
1.1.3      repeat while still within the array;
1.1.3.1       if item at current position < min then
1.1.3.1.1        set min = value at current position;
1.1.3.1.2        set location of min = current position;
1.1.3.2       add 1 to current position;
```

7.5.1.2 <u>Copying Values from One Array to Another</u> The copy step (1.2) is quite simple. Note that the overall program would be using some counter variable, say N, to keep track of how many times the basic search-copy-delete step is repeated. The value of this counter also happens to equal the next free position in the new array whenever it is time to perform a copy. That is, the first item copied goes into position 1, the second item into position 2, etc. Assuming the new array is named NEW and that the search has left the current "smallest" value in variable MIN, the copy step could be implemented by the statement:

```
NEW(N) = MIN;
```

An alternative solution would be to copy the value directly from the old array, OLD, into position N of NEW. This can be done since the search also has recorded the position in OLD where this "smallest" value was found. If variable MIN_LOC contains this position number, the following statement would work:

```
NEW(N) = OLD(MIN_LOC);
```

Note that this would _not_ work if the deletion had occurred _before_ the copy.

7.5.1.3 _Deleting Elements from an Array (and Insertion)_ Step 1.3 requires that an item be deleted from an array so that it will not be rediscovered by a subsequent search. Three basic approaches to this will be described.

The first approach is the simplest and is recommended in the current application. It consists of _replacing_ the item to be deleted by some very large value, which could not possibly be mistaken for the minimum value during a later search. This corresponds to drawing a line through a list item on a sheet of paper, so that your eye will ignore that item in the future. The "deleted" position in the list is still occupied, but not with an item of interest.

The other two approaches effectively shorten the list, so that every item which remains is still of interest. This may become an advantage when there are very few deletions in relation to the total number of searches. For example, the death of a patient should be a rare occurrence compared to the number of office visits requiring a search of all the doctor's files. Thus medical files may be physically removed when a patient dies so that subsequent searches do not have to waste time inspecting locations occupied by "artificial" values of no further interest. The choice between the two remaining approaches depends on whether the ordering of elements is important.

The second approach to deletion may be used when the order of elements does not matter. The element to be deleted is replaced by the last element in that list, and the effective length is reduced by one. In our example, if variable MIN_LOC contains the position in OLD of the item to be deleted, and #ITEMS contains the current number of meaningful entries, then the following statements would accomplish the deletion:

```
OLD(MIN_LOC) = OLD(#ITEMS);
#ITEMS = #ITEMS - 1;
```

The third approach is more drastic and corresponds to cutting out the deleted item with scissors and taping the two remaining parts of the list back together. However, this method does preserve ordering. In an array this is achieved by copying each array element lying beyond the deleted position into the immediately preceding position. The concept and the code to do the copying is shown in Fig. 7.9. Because of the obvious amount of processing involved, this method of deletion by physical movement should only be used when the effort is justified by the need for ordering.

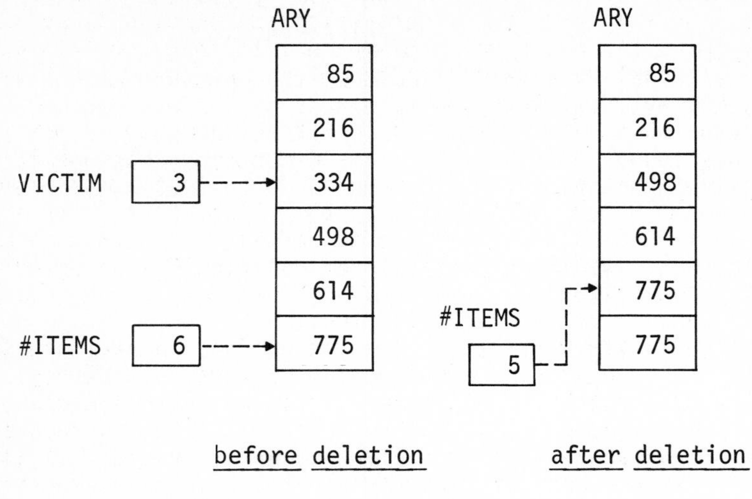


```
         /* VICTIM CONTAINS THE POSITION OF ITEM*/
         /*TO BE DELETED*/
         PSN = VICTIM + 1;
COPY:    DO WHILE(PSN <= #ITEMS);
            ARY(PSN - 1) = ARY(PSN);
            PSN = PSN + 1;
         END COPY;
         #ITEMS = #ITEMS - 1;
```

Fig. 7.9 Deletion by Physical Movement of Subsequent Items in an Ordered List

The counterpart of deletion is, of course, insertion of new elements. If it is not possible to merely append new items to the end of an array, as was done in Section 7.3, there are two other possibilities. If previous deletions of the first ("artificial replacement") type have occurred, it is possible to first search the array for one of these artificial values, and then store the new one in this effectively unoccupied location. However, if the list must remain ordered, then some array items will have to be moved out of the way, requiring a sequence of copies similar to that for physical deletion (Fig. 7.9). For insertion the copying must begin with the last item and proceed backwards! Note how this physical insertion and deletion resembles the corresponding operations on character strings (Section 5.7).

7.5.2 The Bubble Sort

While the selection sort may conform to the natural, human sorting method, it is not as efficient as some other methods. One obvious drawback to the sort, as we have presented it, is that it requires two arrays of the same size. (A modified selection sort can be performed on only one array -- see Exercise 7.1.) For very large lists, there may not be sufficient memory space available for both arrays. Another problem is that selection sorting takes no advantage of any (partial) ordering which may exist among some elements of the list. It resolutely performs N complete searches of all array locations, no matter what the data.

Another sort which requires only one array and is more sensitive to data is the bubble sort. (There are many variations to this sort method, and the one presented here is probably the most common.) The bubble sort is more efficient than the selection sort because it will "quit early" if it can get the data sorted in a hurry. We do not mean to imply that this is the "most efficient" sorting method; there are many more efficient sorting algorithms, and whole books have been written on the topic of sorting alone.

Though bubble sorting takes a much different approach than selection sorting, there are examples in human experience. For example, Aunt Agatha (remember her from Chapter 5?) keeps several potted plants on her window sill. She also likes to keep the shortest plants on the left and arrange them in order of increasing height (just another idiosyncracy). After housecleaning she puts the pots on the sill in an arbitrary order. Then if she notices a shorter plant immediately to the right of a tall plant, she interchanges them. Then if she notices another pair of pots next to each other but out of order, she interchanges these two. Eventually, after interchanging enough consecutive pairs, she will get all the pots in order. Having performed a bubble sort, she then clucks contentedly and sits down to watch a soap opera.

This technique of interchanging pairs of consecutive elements which are out of order (when applied more systematically) is the basic notion of bubble sorting. Although it sounds straightforward, the process of interchanging two values, say X and Y, is a bit subtle. The naive approach might be to:

1. set X equal to the value of Y;
2. set Y equal to the value of X;

However setting X equal to Y obliterates the former value of X and causes both variables to take on the original value of Y. The second step merely resets Y to its original value (which is the current value of X), i.e., it accomplishes nothing. Rather, consider the problem of interchanging the contents of two bottles, e.g., white and red wine. You must pour the contents of one bottle, say the white wine, into a third container. Having emptied this bottle, the red wine is poured into it. Finally the white wine from the third container can be poured into the bottle which formerly held red wine. The problem of interchanging the values of two variables is similar to this. It involves three steps (acts of pouring) and requires short-term use of a third variable, K (the third container). Such an interchange is accomplished by the following steps:

1. save the value of X in K;
2. set X equal to the value of Y;
3. copy the value of K into Y;

If the values being exchanged are in consecutive positions (I and I+1) of an array ARY, then the following code would exchange one pair:

```
TEMP = ARY(I);
ARY(I) = ARY(I+1);
ARY(I+1) = TEMP;
```

7.5.2.1 Performing One Pass Through an Array In order to build this interchanging operation into an effective sorting algorithm, the pairs of items must be inspected systematically. Let us assume that Aunt Agatha is myopic and can see only two adjacent pots at a time. To make sure she doesn't miss any pairs of pots, she always scans her window sill from left to right, all the way across. She calls such a scan "making a pass."[2]

Moving through an array once from top to bottom, inspecting every adjacent pair of locations for the possibility of an interchange, is also called one pass. To see what happens during a single pass, consider Fig. 7.10(a). The array ARY contains 5 numbers and therefore 4 adjacent pairs of locations (1&2, 2&3, 3&4, 4&5). Notice that consecutive pairs overlap. In general, if an array contains N items, there are N-1 different adjacent pairs and therefore N-1 comparisons and possible interchanges during one pass. In Fig. 7.10 the array is being sorted in ascending order, so a pair is interchanged only if it violates this order, i.e., if the first element is larger than the second.

The algorithm for one pass is as follows:

```
1.    begin with the first pair of elements;
2.    repeat N-1 times (once for each pair);
2.1      if current pair is out of order then
            interchange current pair;
2.2      move to the next pair of elements;
```

Although the result in Fig. 7.10(a) is "more ordered" than the original list, it is not completely ordered. One pass is evidently not enough.

7.5.2.2 The Complete Bubble Sort If enough complete passes are made through the array, the values eventually become sorted. The question is: how many passes are necessary?

The first answer is that a maximum of N-1 passes may be needed for an array of N elements. Notice in Fig. 7.10(a) how the largest value, 17, was moved to the last position by the first pass. The second pass, Fig. 7.10(b), moved the second-largest element, 13, to the second-last position. On the ith pass, the ith largest element gets moved to the ith position from the end. After N-1 passes the smallest element will be left in position 1.

The array for Fig. 7.10 turned out to be sorted by the end of the second pass, but for some arrangements of initial data, the maximum of 4 passes would be required. To be safe rather than sorry, a conservative algorithm for the bubble sort would be:

```
1.    repeat N-1 times;
1.1      perform one complete pass;
```

---

[2]That is not what Uncle Fred means by "making a pass."

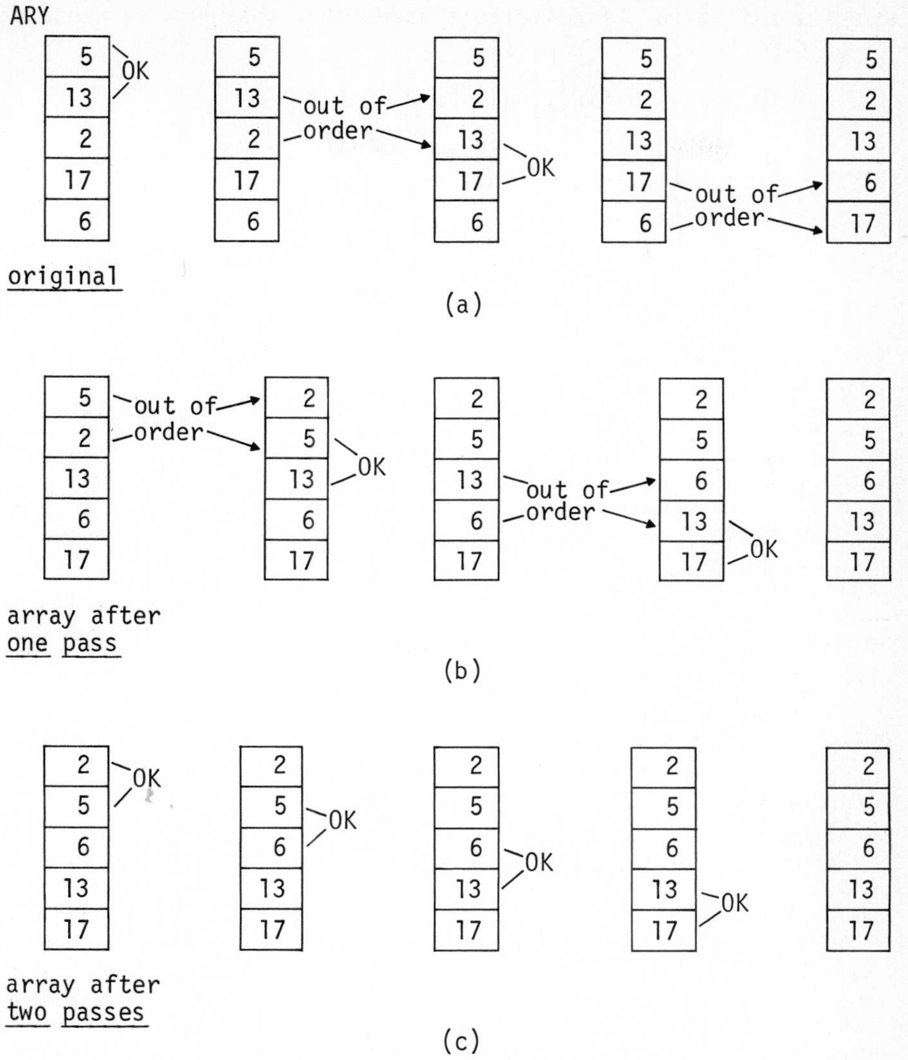

Fig. 7.10 The Bubble Sort. (a) A single pass through an array; (b) A second pass which happens to achieve complete ordering; (c) A final pass to confirm ordering.

However, in most cases the full maximum of N-1 passes will not be required (as in Fig. 7.10). Fortunately, there is an easy way to tell when the array is completely sorted. If a complete pass finds every consecutive pair in order and does not have to make any interchanges, then the values are already sorted and the algorithm may quit. This would be the case in Fig. 7.10(c). Simply set a flag to 0 before making each pass, and set it to 1 whenever an interchange is made. At the end of the pass, if the flag is still 0, the array is ordered. But if the flag is 1, then one or more interchanges occurred, and at least one more pass will be required. This more efficient algorithm is:

```
1.        set flag to 1 (indicates that another pass may be needed);
2.        repeat while flag is 1;
2.1          set flag to 0;
2.2          begin with first pair of elements;
2.3          repeat N-1 times;
2.3.1           if current pair is out of order then
2.3.1.1            interchange this pair;
2.3.1.2            set flag to 1;
2.3.2           move to next pair;
3.        end.
```

Fig. 7.11 Algorithm for Bubble Sort

7.5.3 <u>Searching Ordered Arrays</u>

Just as there are several different algorithms for sorting data, there are also several searching algorithms which exploit the fact that the data are ordered. One of these, called the "binary search," will be described in Chapter 11. Another, called the "quadratic search," is explained below.

Because the names in the telephone directory are ordered, you need not read <u>every</u> name until you find the one you want (i.e., do a linear search). Instead, you (i) instinctively turn to the approximate vicinity in the book; (ii) read the first name on each page (usually highlighted in bold type) until you determine the correct page; (iii) select a name from each column until you have narrowed the search to a particular column and part of a column; and, finally, (iv) do a linear search within that area. The basic approach of the quadratic search is to first take large steps to zero-in on the right area, followed by a linear search within that area. A more realistic analogy would be to search the phone book using only steps (ii) and (iv).

The search begins by sampling items at regular intervals from the beginning of the array. For best results these items should be $\sqrt{n}$ positions apart, where n is the total number of entries in the array.[3] If n is a perfect square, such as 36, then there are altogether $\sqrt{n}$ items at intervals of $\sqrt{n}$.

The only problem is that the correct area of the array cannot be known for certain, until the initial search has gone beyond that area to the next and inspected an item larger than the one desired. However, the solution is to then "back up" to the preceding area and perform the linear search from there. This is shown in Fig. 7.11 where the value 56 is being sought. Notice that a total of only six array elements have to be inspected, versus the 15 comparisons required by the linear search.

---

[3]This is the reason for calling this method a "quadratic" search. If n is not a perfect square, the algorithm must handle the final section of the array as a special case.

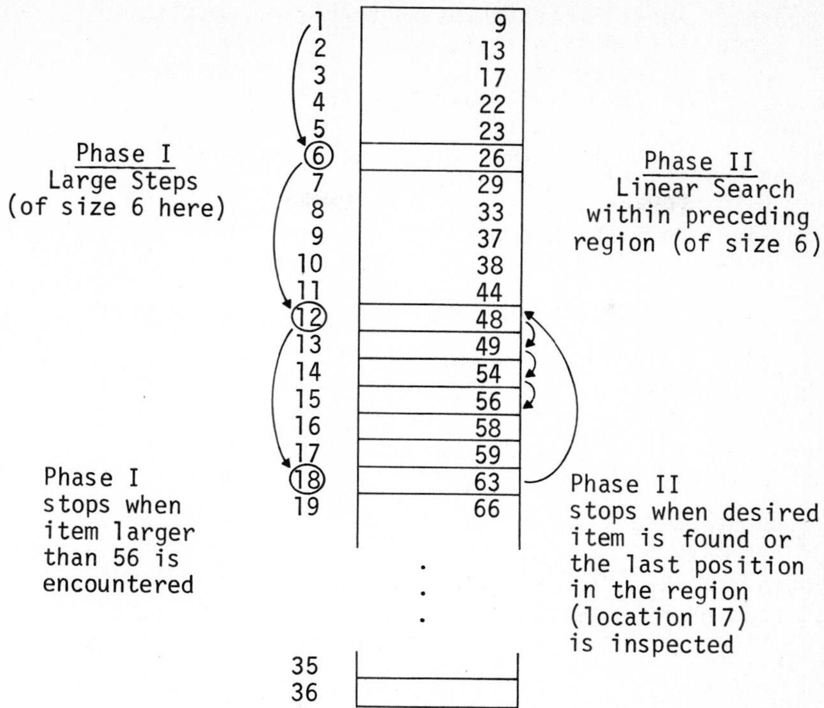

Fig. 7.11 A Quadratic Search for Value 56

7.5.4 Merging

In data processing we are frequently faced with the problem of producing one sorted list from two sorted arrays. We might, for example, have an alphabetical list of female students and an alphabetical list of male students from which we are to construct an alphabetical listing of all students. Such a listing can be produced by merging the two original lists.

Observe how we might merge the following arrays to print a report in alphabetical order:

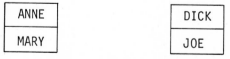

We begin by comparing "ANNE" with "DICK" and since "ANNE" is smaller we print it.

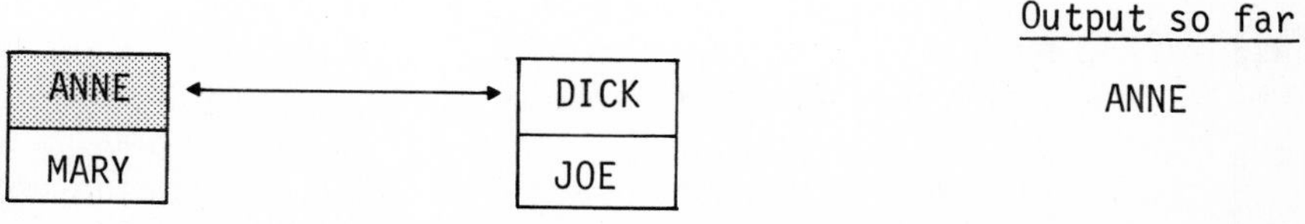

Now compare the next girl, "MARY," with "DICK," and print "DICK."

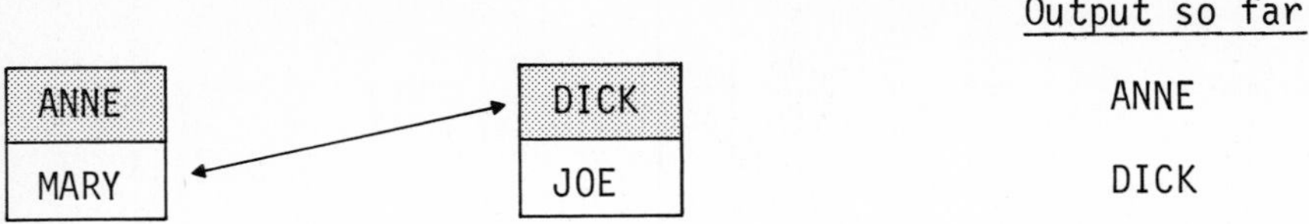

Since the last name was a boy's, we now compare the next boy's name, "JOE," to the current girl's name, "MARY," and print "JOE."

Output so far

ANNE	DICK	ANNE
MARY	JOE	DICK
		JOE

At this point we have exhausted all the names in one array. Since both arrays were originally in ascending order we need only print the remaining names in the remaining array and the output list will also be in ascending order. Of course, we could have been storing the selected names in a third array rather than printing them.

This process is known as a two-way merge (since 2 arrays were merged) and consists of two basic steps: (1) As long as both original arrays contain elements, we do comparisons and select the smallest one; (2) As soon as one array has been exhausted we simply select the remaining elements in the other array.

We now develop the algorithm to produce a sorted list from two sorted arrays A (of length n) and B (of length m). We assume A and B are in ascending order and so is the resulting list. Again this "list" may be either another array or directly output.

```
1.     begin at position 1 in both lists, A and B;
2.     repeat while elements remain in both A and B arrays;
2.1       move "top" element from A or B, whichever is
             smaller, to the output list;
3.     if B is empty then
          move remaining elements from A to the output list;
4.     otherwise
          move remaining elements from B to the output list;
5.     end.
```

The essence of Step 2.1 is to compare the ith element of A with the jth element of B and move just one of these elements to the output list. This is accomplished by:

```
2.     repeat while i ≤ n and j ≤ m;
2.1       if A(i) ≤ B(j)
             then move A(i) to output list;
2.2       else
             move B(j) to output list;
```

Since we moved an element from only one array, we must increase the index of that array to avoid reusing the same element. We do not touch the index of the "other" array, since the item from the "other" array is still a candidate for selection. Note that at most one of the conditions in Steps 3 and 4 of the algorithm shown below will be true.

```
1.      initialize i and j to 1;
2.      repeat while i ≤ n and j ≤ m;
2.1        if A(i) ≤ B(j) then
2.1.1         move A(i) to output list;
2.1.2         increase i by 1;
2.2        otherwise
2.2.1         move B(j) to output list;
2.2.2         increase j by 1;
3.      repeat while i ≤ n;
3.1        move A(i) to output list;
3.2        increase i by 1;
4.      repeat while j ≤ m;
4.1        move B(j) to output list;
4.2        increase j by 1;
5.      end.
```

7.6 SPECIAL FEATURES

7.6.1 Referencing an Entire Array

It is often necessary to perform an identical operation on every element of an array. When this is the case, it is not always necessary to explicitly indicate individual array elements. A common instance is the need to initialize every element of an array to 0. Three ways to do this are indicated in Fig. 7.12.

```
DECLARE A(100) FIXED(5,0);
```

(a)

```
A(1) = 0;
A(2) = 0;
A(3) = 0;
  .
  .
  .
A(98) = 0;
A(99) = 0;
A(100) = 0;
```

(b)

```
      PSN = 1;
INIT: DO WHILE(PSN <= 100);
         A(PSN) = 0;
         PSN = PSN + 1;
      END INIT;
```

(c)

```
A = 0;
```

Fig. 7.12 Initializing an Array to 0

As Fig. 7.12(c) shows, use of an array name without parentheses implies that every individual element is to be involved in the same operation. The statement A = 0; is really a shorthand notation of the code in Fig. 7.12(a).

This abbreviated form may be used in more complex statements as well, provided that every array is used in its entirety and that the arrays mentioned in an assignment statement are of the same size. Fig. 7.13 shows three examples of this. Note especially the GET statement, which is equivalent to:

```
GET LIST(A(1),A(2),...,A(99),A(100),B(1),B(2),...,B(100));
```

```
DECLARE(A(100),B(100)) FIXED(5,0);
/*READ 100 VALUES FOR A FOLLOWED BY 100 VALUES FOR B */
GET LIST(A,B);
/*ADD EACH ELEMENT OF B TO THE CORRESPONDING */
/*ELEMENT OF A--THE EQUIVALENT of 100 ASSIGNMENTS */
A = A + B;
/*INCREMENT EACH OF THE 100 ELEMENTS OF B BY 1 */
B = B + 1;
    .
    .
    .
```

Fig. 7.13 Manipulating Entire Arrays

7.6.2 The Iterated DO

"Moving through" an array is such a common process, that we identified a standard control structure to govern this movement in Fig. 7.3. That control structure is repeated in Fig. 7.14(a). However, there is an abbreviated control structure, shown in Fig. 7.14(b), which does exactly the same thing, i.e., it specifies a "position" or index variable, an initial value for that variable, an amount to be added at the end of each execution of the loop, and a final value to be used for terminating the repetitions. The termination rule is also the same: repeat the loop until the index variable's value exceeds the final value. This statement, called the iterated DO, has the general form:

```
<label>:  DO <index> = <initial value> TO <final value> BY
                                              <increment>;
```

Since the increment is usually 1, the phrase "BY 1" may be omitted, and an increment of 1 will be automatically supplied. This variation is shown in Figure 7.14(c). As with the full DO-WHILE form, the initial value, final value, and increment portions of the iterated DO may be constants, variables, or more complicated arithmetic expressions. (The increment may be an integer other than 1 or even be negative for moving backwards, provided the final value is less than the initial value.) To illustrate, consider the code in Fig. 7.15 which prints the last four elements of array ARY in both forward (Fig. 7.15a) and reverse (Fig. 7.15b) order.

If you wish to avoid some nasty debugging problems, you should never alter the values of the index value, initial value, final value, or increment value anywhere inside an iterated DO loop. Of course this statement and its matching END may be used in contexts other than array processing, but we suggest that its most "natural" application is to arrays.

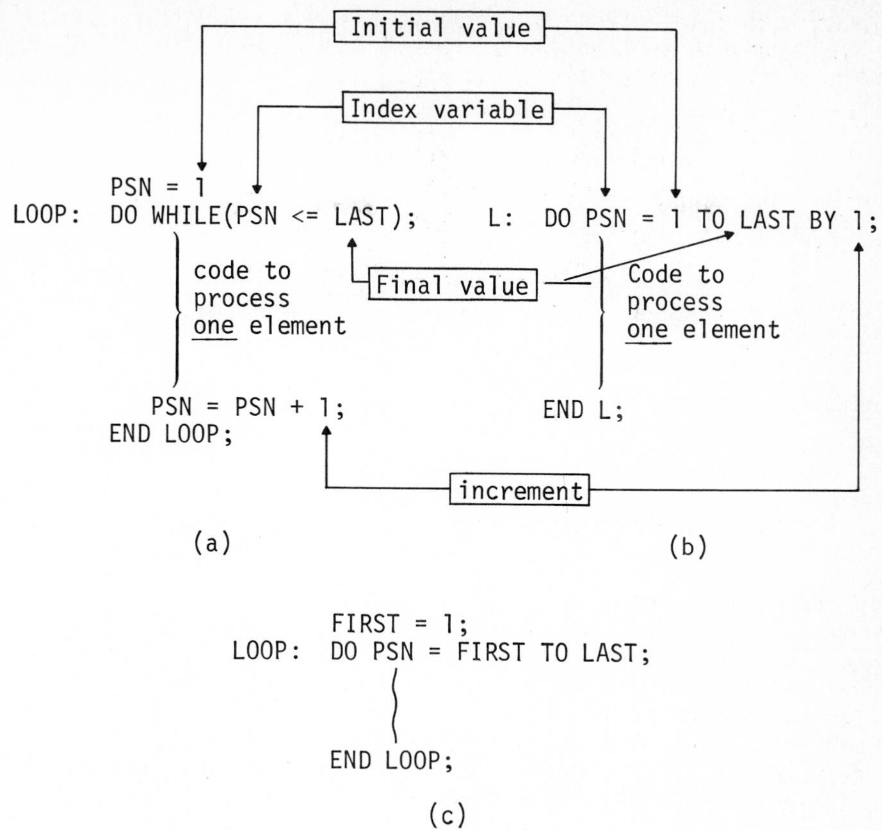

Fig. 7.14 The Iterated DO Statement

7.6.3 The Implied DO

For input-output lists -- <u>but in no other contexts</u> -- another abbreviation called the implied DO is allowed. If you are reading consecutive data values into consecutive positions of an <u>entire</u> array, you may simply write the array name in the variable list of the GET statement, as shown in Fig. 7.13. However, when only a <u>portion</u> of an array is to be filled or when the values are not destined for consecutive locations, you <u>must</u> indicate which elements are being filled at which times. For example, to read values for the first 50 elements of a 100-element array A, you could simply write out each element as indicated in Fig. 7.16(a). Alternatively, you could use a DO-loop as shown in Fig. 7.16(b) or (c). The new alternative, Fig. 7.16(d), identifies the particular array elements within the GET statement itself, using a form somewhat like the iterated DO statement. However, instead of being a true repetitive control structure, the implied DO is merely a shorter way of writing the form shown in Fig. 7.16(a). It is used in a similar way with PUT statements.

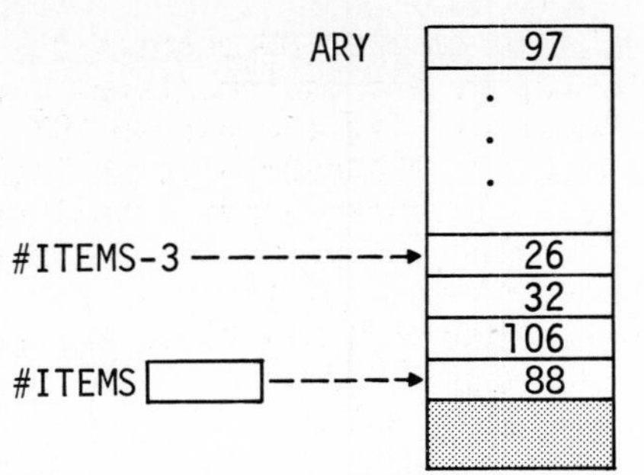


```
FORWRD:  DO PSN = (#ITEMS-3) TO #ITEMS;
            PUT LIST(ARY(PSN));
         END FORWRD;
```

output

26 32 106 88

(a)

```
REVERS:  DO PSN = #ITEMS TO (#ITEMS-3) BY -1;
            PUT LIST(ARY(PSN));
         END REVERS;
```

output

88 106 32 26

(b)

Fig. 7.15 Use of Iterated DO. (a) Moving Forward in Steps of 1; (b) Moving Backward in Steps of 1.

```
DECLARE A(100) FIXED(5,0);
```

(a)
```
GET LIST(A(1),A(2),A(3),...,A(48),A(49),A(50));
```

(b)
```
      PSN = 1;
LOOP: DO WHILE(PSN <= 50);
         GET LIST(A(PSN));
         PSN = PSN + 1;
      END LOOP;
```

(c)
```
LOOP: DO PSN = 1 TO 50 BY 1;
         GET LIST(A(PSN));
      END LOOP;
```

(d)
```
GET LIST ((A(PSN) DO PSN = 1 TO 50 BY 1));
```

Fig. 7.16 Reading Part of an Array (using the Implied DO in (d))

On the other hand, the implied DO permits the same sort of initial values, final values and increments as the iterated DO. It also assumes an increment of 1 if the phrase "BY 1" is missing. It also has an "influence over" whatever else is included within the same set of parentheses. In other words, the index variable is initialized, then everything preceding the DO is referenced once, then the index is incremented, and, if it is not greater than the final value, everything preceding the DO is referenced again, etc. This is illustrated in Fig. 7.17.

A
11
12
13
14
15

B
21
22
23
24
25

Two arrays, showing their current values

```
PUT LIST((A(I) DO I = 1 TO 3),(B(J) DO J = 1 TO 3));
```

equivalent to

```
PUT LIST(A(1),A(2),A(3),B(1),B(2),B(3));
```

produce output:

```
11  12  13  21  22  23
```

```
PUT LIST((A(I),B(I) DO I = 1 TO 3));
```

equivalent to

```
PUT LIST(A(1),B(1),A(2),B(2),A(3),B(3));
```

produce output:

```
11  21  12  22  13  23
```

Fig. 7.17 The implied DO on Output

Notice that the "DO-phrase" and all variables being repeated under its influence must be surrounded by their own set of parentheses.

7.6.4 Nonstandard Subscript Range

There are occasions when it would be more convenient to have array elements numbered from 0 to N-1, or between some other pair of numbers, rather than from 1 to N. For example, you might want to record the gross national product for the years 1950 through 1975 and be able to refer to a particular GNP in terms of the corresponding year. You can declare arrays with such nonstandard indices by giving both the lowest and highest locations, separated by a colon:

```
DECLARE GNP(1950:1975)  FIXED(12,0);
```

This creates an array of 26 elements named GNP(1950),GNP(1951),..., GNP(1974),GNP(1975).

7.7 REVIEW OF RULES

1. One-dimensional arrays must be <u>declared</u> in one of the two forms:

   ```
   DECLARE name(<# of elements>) <attributes>;
   ```

   or

   ```
   DECLARE name(<1st position>:<last position>) <attributes>;
   ```

   In the first (usual) form, the individual elements are numbered starting from 1. The second form is used to override this convention. All elements in any one array have identical attributes.

2. To <u>refer</u> to an individual element, use the term

   ```
   name(<arithmetic expression>)
   ```

   like an ordinary variable in the appropriate context. The arithmetic expression may be a constant, variable, or more elaborate expression whose value lies between the first and last positions of the array.

3. It is possible to refer to an <u>entire</u> array at one time, simply by using its name. However, this represents element-by-element referencing of the array and must be used in a context where this is appropriate, e.g., in a PUT or GET statement.

4. There are many methods of "processing" arrays, most of which involve the notion of "moving through" an array element-by-element. This movement is controlled by either of the following (equivalent) structures:

   ```
          PSN = initial;
   LOOP:  DO WHILE(PSN <= final);

              } "Process" element at
              }  position PSN

              PSN = PSN + increment;
          END LOOP;
   ```

   <u>or</u> (the iterated DO)

   ```
   LOOP:  DO PSN = initial TO final BY increment;

              } "Process" element at
              }  position PSN

          END LOOP;
   ```

If BY <increment> is omitted, the increment is assumed to be 1. In both cases PSN is an arbitrary variable.

5. The implied-DO form may be used <u>only</u> in the variable lists of GET and PUT statements. An example of the form is:

```
GET LIST((NAME(PSN) DO PSN = <initial> TO <final> BY <increment>));
```

The implied DO and its associated variable names must be enclosed in their own set of parentheses.

7.8 REVIEW PROBLEM

This problem will be an extension of the end-of-month billing problem from Section 7.4.3. The goal is to produce a report showing the balance of each customer account at the end of a month. This time, however, there are two basic categories of data cards:

The first category is a "master file" consisting of one card for each customer, with each such card containing his name and the balance of his account at the beginning of the month. The format of these cards is shown in Fig. 7.18(a).

The second category of data consists of several "transaction" cards, each representing an individual charge or payment which has occurred during the month. There may be many such cards for any one customer, but for the present we will assume that no new customers are encountered who were not already included in the master file. A "transaction" card has the form shown in Fig. 7.18(b).

Since each of these types of card has a different format, they must be read by different GET statements and cannot be freely intermixed. Therefore, we will put all the master file cards together, and all the individual transaction cards together. In order to signal the change from one type of data card to another, a special separator card is inserted between the two groups of cards (with the same format as the cards in the first group). The deck arrangement is indicated in Fig. 7.18(c).

The output requirement is that the end-of-month balance report is to have the names listed in alphabetical order and the amount owed by each customer.

In order to update an item in the master file to reflect a particular transaction, the master file will have to be searched to find the name of the customer involved. Since the names in the master file must be printed in order, and since an ordered file lends itself to more efficient searching, our first task would be to read and sort the master file if it were not already sorted. However, since most organizations keep their files in order, and since the master file for this month's billing is the (sorted) output from the previous month, we will assume that the master file cards are already sorted in alphabetical order!

With this assumption in mind, we can consider some alternative approaches to the problem. Our first impulse might be to read the master file into an array, read the transaction cards into another array, and for each transaction card, search and update the master file array. However, this approach has two drawbacks.

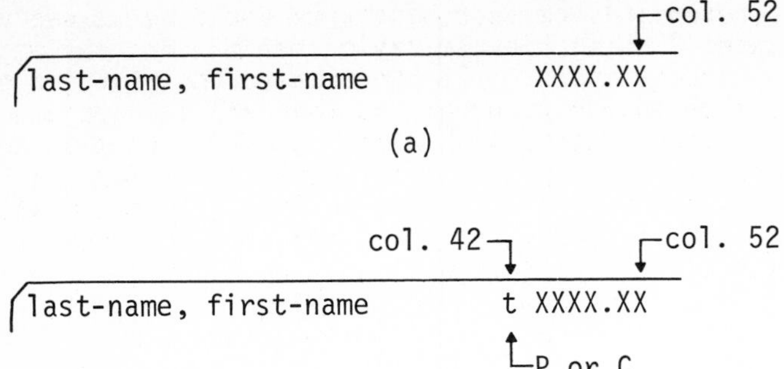

where "t" in column 42 indicates the type of transaction. It will be either the character 'P' for payment or 'C' for charge.

(b)

cards
of one type

separator (delimiter) card

cards
of other type

(c)

Fig. 7.18 Input for Review Problem. (a) Master File Card; (b) Individual Transaction Card; (c) Deck Arrangement.

The first drawback is that arrays are required for both the master file and the transactions. If there could be many items in either category, these arrays may be prohibitively large, since the arrays must have sufficient space to hold the maximum possible number of entries. A moment of reflection should reveal that the transactions need not all be in memory at the same time. As soon as a transaction has been incorporated into the master file, the transaction is no longer needed. Thus, a better strategy is to read only the master file into an array, and to search and update the master file immediately, as each transaction is read.

There remains a second drawback from which both the above approaches suffer. There may be a great many searches of the master file. Suppose m represents the number of entries in the master file. Then, on the average, a linear search will require m/2 comparisons, since, on the average, the desired name will be found half way through the file. If there are all together n transactions, there would be approximately $n \times (m/2)$ comparisons using linear searches. This may be quite a large number, representing lengthy, expensive processing time.

One way to decrease the searching time would be to use a more efficient method, such as the quadratic search. Another way is to first sort the transactions. All the transactions for the same customer will then appear together, so that all the updates for one customer can be done after a single search has found that customer's name in the master file. Better still, the search for a different customer's name need not start at the beginning of the master file. Since the transactions and master file are both in alphabetical order, the next customer's name will have to appear in the master file somewhere after the name of the previous customer. By the time a linear search has gone through the master file once, all the customers' names will have been found in the order in which they are required. This entails at most m comparisons.

Unfortunately, the need to sort transactions reintroduces the earlier problem of keeping so many arrays in memory at one time -- unless the master file is not stored in an array. In fact, the entire master file does not have to be in memory at once. If the transactions are sorted, then the entries to be updated in the master file will occur in the required order. The master file can be read one element at a time, updated if necessary, and then printed out. This approach avoids both the excessive array storage and the need for multiple linear searches. The algorithm appears in Fig. 7.19.

```
1.     initialize values;
2.     read all transaction cards;
3.     sort transaction cards;
4.     read first master file item;
5.     repeat while cards remain;
5.1       make all necessary updates to that master item;
5.2       print that master item;
5.3       read next master file item;
6.     end.
```

Figure 7.19

Note that this algorithm requires the transaction cards to be placed at the beginning of the data cards. Since each transaction card contains both character and numeric data, two arrays will be required for storage. Instead of storing the character P or C to indicate the type of transaction, it will be more efficient to simply store the negative amount of a payment. Then a payment and charge can be distinguished by their sign, and a customer's (negative) payments can simply be added to his charges when computing net amount owed. Therefore, each transaction card will first be read into separate variables before the name and (signed) amount are stored in the arrays. The program must also keep testing for the special separator card, which acts like an "artificial end-of-file." Since the separator card must have the same format as the transaction cards, we adopt the following:

```
                              col. 42┐        ┌col. 52
         _____________________________↓________↓______
        /ZZZZ                         X 9999.99
```

The separator card will not be stored in the arrays. Therefore, the input (Step 2) involves the following:

```
2.1    read first transaction card;
2.2    if it is separator card then
           set an indicator;
2.3    repeat while transaction cards remain;
2.3.1     if type of card is P (payment) then
              replace amount by its negative;
2.3.2     store the name and amount in next free position
              in arrays;
2.3.3     read next transaction card;
2.3.4     if it is separator card then set an indicator;
```

The bubble sort (Section 7.5.2) will be employed in Step 3 with the additional requirement that the customer and account arrays must be sorted together, so that related information remains in corresponding positions in both arrays. When a pair of elements is interchanged in one array, the corresponding pair in the other array must also be interchanged.

Step 5.1 can be elaborated as follows:

```
5.1    repeat while current transaction is for same customer
           as current master file item;
5.1.1     add transaction amount to amount owed in master
              file item;
5.1.2     move to next transaction;
```

Initially, blanks will be stored in the array of names, to avoid problems after all the transactions have been processed. The complete program corresponding to the algorithm of Fig. 7.19 is shown in Fig. 7.20. Your first glance at the code may give you the uncomfortable feeling that this program is too large for easy comprehension. In the next chapter we will recode the same algorithm in a more tractable way, which better reveals the algorithm's basic steps and shields the reader from so many details at one time.

7.9 EXERCISES

7.1(a) Write a complete program to implement the selection sort algorithm described in Section 7.5.1.

(b) Describe an algorithm to perform the selection sort using only one array (just large enough to hold the data to be sorted). Implement your algorithm by a PL/I program.

7.2 One of the measures used by cryptographers is the frequency with which different characters appear in a string of text (usually encoded). Describe an algorithm to examine a string of text and count the frequency of occurrence for each character in it. On completion of this, the characters and their frequency count should be printed in descending order of frequency. You may assume that only the 26 letters of the English alphabet are of interest. Punctuation is to be ignored.

Implement your algorithm by a PL/I program and test it using the text of this exercise.

```
          /* FIGURE 7.20 */
BILL2:   PROCEDURE OPTIONS (MAIN);

         /* A PROGRAM TO UPDATE CUSTOMER ACCOUNTS ACCORDING
            TO VARIOUS TRANSACTIONS DURING A PERIOD. */

         DECLARE
            CUSTMR(100) CHARACTER (40), /* ARRAY OF CUSTOMER NAMES */
            AMT(100) FIXED (7,2), /* ARRAY OF TRANSACTION AMOUNTS */
            NAME CHARACTER (40), /* CUSTOMER NAME */
            BALANCE FIXED (7,2), /* OWING BY CUSTOMER */
            DELIMITER_FLAG FIXED (5,0), /* END OF TRANSACTION FILE */
            PSN FIXED (5,0), /* CURRENT POSITION WITHIN ARRAYS */
            #NAMES FIXED (5,0), /* NO. DIFFERENT TRANSACTIONS */
            SORT_FLAG FIXED (5,0), /* SORTING FLAG */
            TEMP_NAME CHARACTER (40), /* TO SWAP NAMES IN SORT */
            TEMP_AMT FIXED (7,2), /* TO SWAP AMOUNTS IN SORT */
            NEW_AMT FIXED (7,2), /* AMOUNT OF TRANSACTION */
            TYPE CHARACTER (1), /* TYPE OF TRANS.; C = CHARGE; P = PMT*/
            NO_MORE FIXED (5,0); /* END OF DATA FLAG */

         /* INITIALIZE VARIABLES */

         CUSTMR = ' '; /* SET ALL CUSTOMER NAMES TO BLANK */
         AMT = 0.0; /* SET ALL CUSTOMER TRANSACTIONS TO ZERO */
         DELIMITER_FLAG = 0;
         PSN = 0;

         /* INPUT TRANSACTION FILE - END IS SIGNALLED
            BY CUSTOMER "ZZZZ". */
         GET SKIP EDIT (NAME,TYPE,NEW_AMT)
          (A(40),X(1),A(1),X(3),F(7,2));
         IF NAME = 'ZZZZ' THEN
            DELIMITER_FLAG = 1;

INPUT:   DO WHILE (DELIMITER_FLAG = 0);
            /* IF TRANS. IS A PAYMENT, CHANGE IT TO A MINUS
               QUANTITY SO ALL TRANS. CAN BE ADDED TO BALANCE */
            IF TYPE = 'P' THEN
               NEW_AMT = -NEW_AMT;
            PSN = PSN + 1;
            CUSTMR(PSN) = NAME;
            AMT(PSN) = NEW_AMT;
            GET SKIP EDIT (NAME,TYPE,NEW_AMT)
               (A(40),X(1),A(1),X(3),F(7,2));
            IF NAME = 'ZZZZ' THEN
               DELIMITER_FLAG = 1;
         END INPUT;

         #NAMES = PSN;

         /* SORT THE TRANSACTION FILE IN ALPHABETICAL ORDER */

         SORT_FLAG = 1;

SORT:    DO WHILE (SORT_FLAG = 1);
            SORT_FLAG = 0; /* ASSUME ARRAY IN ORDER */
            PSN = 1;

NEW_PASS:   DO WHILE (PSN <= #NAMES - 1);
               IF CUSTMR(PSN) > CUSTMR(PSN + 1) THEN
SWAP:             DO; /* SWAP NAMES AND AMOUNTS */
                     TEMP_NAME = CUSTMR(PSN);
                     CUSTMR(PSN) = CUSTMR(PSN + 1);
                     CUSTMR(PSN + 1) = TEMP_NAME;
                     TEMP_AMT = AMT(PSN);
                     AMT(PSN) = AMT(PSN + 1);
                     AMT(PSN + 1) = TEMP_AMT;
                     SORT_FLAG = 1;
                  END SWAP;
               PSN = PSN + 1;
            END NEW_PASS;

         END SORT;

         /* INITIALIZE PRIOR TO MASTER FILE */

         NO_MORE = 0;
         ON ENDFILE (SYSIN) NO_MORE = 1;

         /* FOR EACH CUSTOMER ON THE MASTER FILE, SEARCH THE
            TRANSACTION FILE AND UPDATE THE BALANCE IF REQUIRED. */

         GET SKIP EDIT (NAME,BALANCE) (A(40),X(1),F(7,2));
         PSN = 1;

PROCESS:DO WHILE (NO_MORE = 0);

UPDATE:     DO WHILE (CUSTMR(PSN) = NAME);
               BALANCE = BALANCE + AMT(PSN);
               PSN = PSN + 1;
            END UPDATE;

            PUT SKIP(2) EDIT (NAME,BALANCE) (X(10),A(40),F(10,2));
            GET SKIP EDIT (NAME,BALANCE) (A(40),X(1),F(7,2));
         END PROCESS;

         END BILL2;
```

Figure 7.20

7.3 The merge described in this chapter can be used to merge three sorted arrays into one sorted list. If the arrays to be merged are A, B, and C then we could merge A and B into a fourth array D. On completion of this phase, C and D could be merged to form the final sorted list.

Write a PL/I program to perform such a merge.

7.4 Consider an array, A, of length N with M entries in it. Let B be another array of length N. We can sort the entries in A as follows:

```
move A(1) to B(1);
consider A(2);
if A(2) ≥ B(1) then
   move A(2) to B(2);
otherwise
   move B(1) to B(2)
   move A(2) to B(1);
```

This effectively "inserts" A(2) in its proper position (so far) in B and maintains the elements of B in ascending order. In general, to move A(k) to its proper position in B, assuming j entries are currently stored in B, we do a linear search in B until we find the first B(i) such that A(k) > B(i). Then move all elements B(i) through B(j) down by 1 position and insert A(k) in position B(i). This technique is known as an <u>insertion sort</u>.

Describe an algorithm to sort N entries in an array using the insertion sort. Implement your algorithm by a PL/I program.

7.5 Recall the definition of a palindrome from Exercise 3.2 in Chapter 3. This problem requires you to print all numbers between 1 and N which are palindromes and also perfect squares.

We suggest that you begin by generating squares and then testing to see if they are also palindromes. Palindrome testing can be most easily done by decomposing the perfect square into its component integers and putting these integers into the elements of a one-dimensional array.

To help you get started, the first steps of the algorithm could be:

```
1.1    set j to 1;
1.2    get a value for n;
2.     repeat while j² ≤ n;
2.1       form the square of j;
2.2       if the square is a palindrome
             then display it;
2.3       add 1 to j;
3.     end.
```

7.6 The quadratic search was described in general form in Section 7.5.3. Formalize this description into an algorithm to find an item in an array which has precisely n^2 elements in it.

Implement your algorithm by computer program using 100 elements.

7.7 This problem is a modification of the review problem in this chapter. We again consider master file cards and transaction cards in the format described in the review problem. However, we now add two additional constraints:

i) no separator card may appear between the transaction and master cards

ii) new customers may appear in the transactions, i.e., those for whom there was no previous master record.

Using the selection sort of Exercise 7.1 process the data cards and produce a report similar to that of the review problem (Section 7.8).

7.8 Suppose in the previous exercise, the number of master file items is much smaller than the number of transactions, say 20 versus 200. The approach taken in the review problem would then be much too inefficient. Select a better algorithm and implement it. Note that you may, if you wish, rearrange the order of the data cards.

7.9 Recall the definition of the Fibonacci series from Exercise 3.3. When this series progresses, the number of digits in each number quickly exceeds 15, the maximum allowed for a FIXED number. Hence if you attempt to generate a number with 16 digits, a program error will result.

The problem can be overcome by decomposing numbers into their component digits and storing one digit in each element of an array. These arrays can then be added, element by element, ensuring that each element has exactly 1 digit stored in it.

Generate all numbers of the series until you reach the first one with 100 digits in it.

Chapter 8 Procedures — Part I

8.1 INTRODUCTION TO PROCEDURES

This chapter introduces a language construct called the "internal procedure," which enables you to write code at different levels of detail, just as your algorithms display different levels of detail at various stages of development. In addition, you may design your code in separate pieces, just as you refined certain parts of your algorithm separately. Designing and testing programs one block at a time is called "modular programming." In short, procedures permit code development to parallel algorithm development. This can make programs easier to write, easier to read, and easier to change, and also lets you write new programs which include previously written programs as constituent parts.

8.1.1 An Allegory About Procedures

We introduce the principles of internal procedures by way of a parable, in which the "recipe" will play the role of an internal procedure.

Suppose Melvin finally persuaded Gwendolyn to have dinner at his apartment. Having no experience with women, he was naturally very nervous. He therefore prepared a list of things to do that night so that he wouldn't bungle his potentially perfect evening. He decided on the following general plan:

1. fix drinks;
2. thaw and serve dinner;
3. fix drinks;
4. show her his stamp collection;
5. fix drinks;
6. accept the consequences;
7. end.

Luckily his friend Marcello suggested a sure-fire drink called a Tahitian Tidal Wave. He copied a recipe for the drink on a separate sheet of paper and stapled this to the back of his master plan.

At this point Melvin had completed his algorithm for a perfect evening. Since he has followed the top-down approach, his algorithm was developed in two stages (master plan and detailed recipe). However, he did not rewrite his master plan to physically include three copies of the same drink recipe. Instead he intended to follow the same, attached copy of the recipe whenever his master plan indicated drinks.

At last Gwendolyn arrived and Melvin began to execute his algorithm. Nervous though he was, whenever the master plan dictated drinks, he turned the page, made a perfect Tahitian Tidal Wave, and returned to the master plan. During the evening he did this successfully three separate times, with his only setback coming at Step 6.[1]

Undaunted, Melvin kept both the master plan and the drink recipe. He decided he could later try either the same general plan with a more potent drink recipe or else a different plan in conjunction with Tahitian Tidal Waves.

The fundamental concepts of procedures are revealed by this story. It is possible to develop your code in separate units (procedures) just as Melvin developed his master plan on one sheet of paper and copied the recipe on another. However, some procedures (like the master plan) may prescribe what to do but not all the details about how to do it. At these points your master procedure must refer to another procedure which supplies the missing details (like the recipe). If the "detailed" procedure is used more than once, your master procedure may contain several references to it, rather than requiring several separate copies of it.

The definitions of the procedures which constitute a program must be distinguished from the execution of the program. Melvin devised his plan prior to Gwendolyn's arrival. The execution involves following the master procedure until it references a more detailed procedure. This causes control (Melvin's attention) to switch to the indicated procedure, execute it step-by-step, and then resume the master procedure at the next step, i.e., following that particular reference to the recipe.

In addition, either procedure could be replaced or modified without having to alter the other procedure in any way. The ability to transfer a procedure from one context to another is referred to as "portability."

---

[1]Unfortunately, Gwendolyn disliked alcohol, chicken wings, stamps, and consequently Melvin.

8.1.2 Procedure Fundamentals

According to our methods until now, refinements of single steps in higher level algorithms were physically incorporated into the higher-level algorithm itself (see Fig. 8.1(a)). The result was one completely refined algorithm. The program was then written as a single (MAIN) procedure, resembling this algorithm.

On the other hand, as Melvin demonstrates, it is possible to leave some of the refinements of steps as separate algorithms and simply refer to these from the higher level algorithm. If some auxiliary algorithm is needed to implement more than one step, that same algorithm is referred to in more than one place. This is shown in Fig. 8.1(b). Among other things, this certainly avoids a lot of duplication of writing. But it is more than a labor-saving device.

The important point is that the code can be written as separate independent units (PROCEDUREs), just like the separate parts of an algorithm. The master plan is that PROCEDURE which is distinguished by OPTIONS(MAIN). The smaller parts, like the drink recipe, are set off by their own PROCEDURE and END statements, as shown below. Notice that it is very similar to the format of a main procedure with the "OPTIONS(MAIN)" omitted.[2]

```
<entry-name>:  PROCEDURE;
                  |
                  |  code to be
                  |  executed
                  |
               END <entry-name>;
```

Although the code for a procedure need only be written once, it may be used whenever its effect is needed in the master plan, simply by referring to it. Such references are made by the statement:

```
CALL <procedure entry-name>;
```

where the entry-name identifies which procedure should be applied. The effect is as if the procedure code appeared where its action was CALLed for.

The actual flow of control, however, is much like Melvin's turning to the recipe, doing what it says, and then returning to the next step in the master plan. When control reaches a CALL statement in the main procedure, it goes to the designated PROCEDURE, executes it and then returns to the following step in the main procedure. A procedure may be called any number of times and from any number of places.

There are two kinds of PROCEDURE called "internal" and "external." In this Chapter, we focus only on internal procedures. When assembling a deck, internal procedures are placed within the main procedure as shown in Fig. 8.2. While it is not necessary that procedures be grouped at the end of the main procedure, they should be placed there so as not to interfere with the reading of the main

---

[2] The entry name on an "internal" procedure is not restricted to a maximum of seven characters; any valid PL/I label may be used.

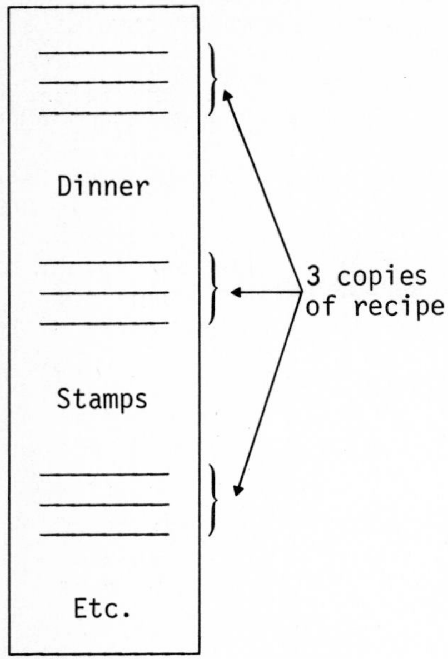

Fig. 8.1(a) The Single Procedure Concept

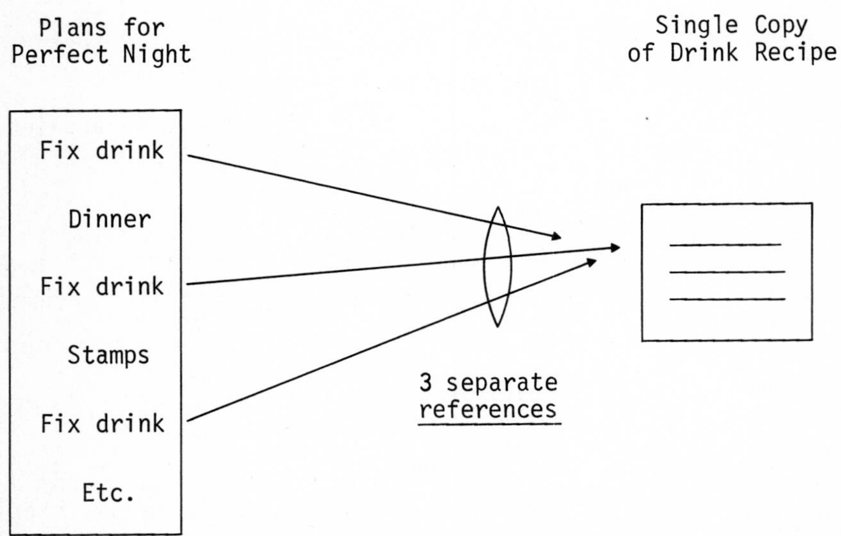

Fig. 8.1(b) The Procedure (separate recipe) Concept

procedure.[3] There is no danger of executing the internal procedures after completion of the main procedure code. They may be executed <u>only</u> by executing an explicit CALL statement. We also recommend placing a blank card before and after each internal procedure in order to help distinguish it from surrounding code.

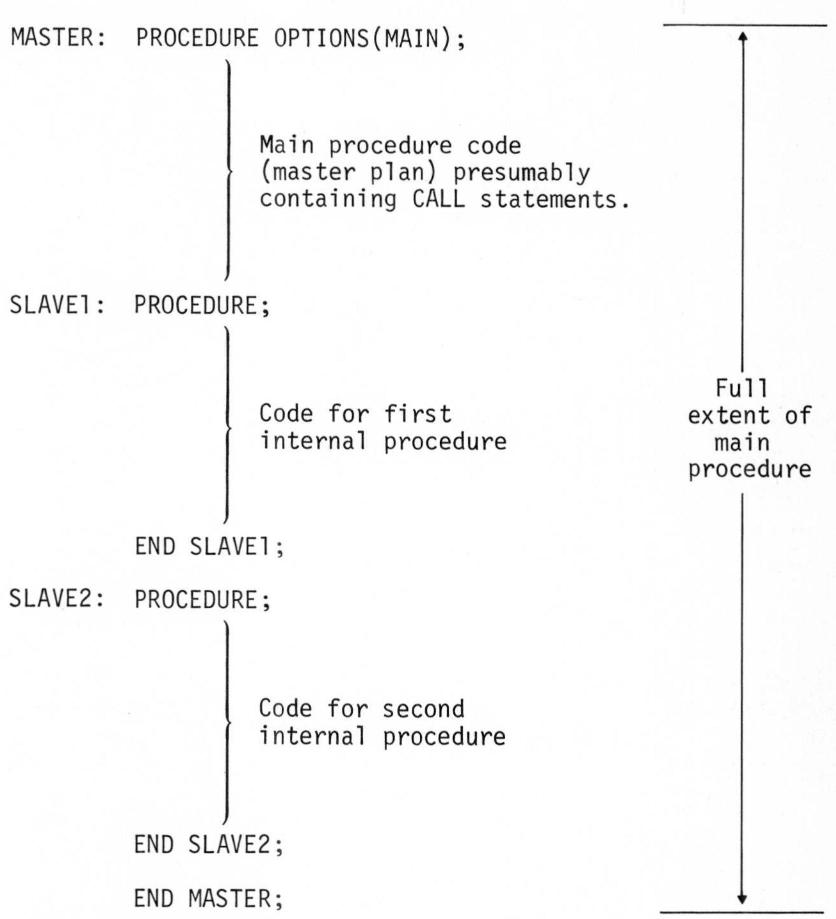

Fig. 8.2 Sample Deck Layout for Programs with Internal Procedures

[3]They are allowed to appear anywhere within the main procedure.

8.1.3 An Example

During the day Melvin works for the central weather bureau, which receives snowfall reports from two regional stations, each representing three cities. Each day both stations send in data cards containing three snowfall amounts, and Melvin is to compute the heaviest snowfall in each region. His algorithm is:

1. read the data for region #1;
2. compute the largest of 3 values;
3. print the result;
4. read the data for region #2;
5. compute the largest of 3 values;
6. print the result;
7. end.

When he took over the job, his friend Marcello had given him a program to compute the largest of three numbers, A, B, and C, and store the largest in MAXY:

```
MAXY = A;
IF B > MAXY THEN
   MAXY = B;
IF C > MAXY THEN
   MAXY = C;
```

Melvin simply made this program an internal procedure:

```
LARGE:  PROCEDURE;
        MAXY = A;
        IF B > MAXY THEN
           MAXY = B;
        IF C > MAXY THEN
           MAXY = C;
        END LARGE;
```

Armed with this new internal procedure, he wrote some code to implement his original algorithm:

```
SNOW:   PROCEDURE OPTIONS(MAIN);
        /*REPORT HEAVIEST SNOWFALLS*/
        DECLARE (A,B,C,MAXY) FIXED(5,2);
        /*FIRST REGION*/
        GET LIST(A,B,C);
        CALL LARGE;
        PUT SKIP DATA(MAXY);
        /*SECOND REGION*/
        GET LIST(A,B,C);
        CALL LARGE;
        PUT SKIP DATA(MAXY);
            }
            }  Where internal procedure
            }  will be placed
            }
        END SNOW;
```

He then placed the internal procedure inside his main procedure, executed the program and showed the results to his boss, Gwendolyn. The execution followed the path indicated in Fig. 8.3.

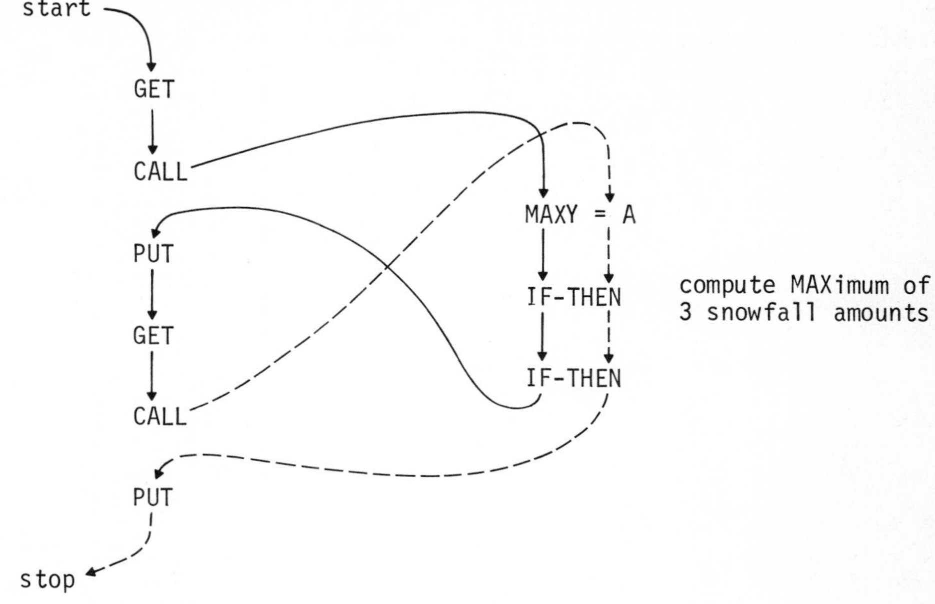

Fig. 8.3 Flow of Control with an Internal Procedure

Once again we see the three basic issues to keep in mind when using internal procedures:

1. Definition: A procedure is defined (once) by writing its constituent code enclosed between PROCEDURE and END statements;

2. Execution: At any point in another procedure where the effect of an internal procedure is needed, a CALL statement can divert control to the internal procedure. After its execution, control returns to the statement following the CALL statement in the CALLing procedure;

3. Placement: An internal procedure should be placed within the main procedure, i.e., before the END statement of the main procedure.

8.2 COMMUNICATION BETWEEN PROCEDURES

Another important issue is the exchange of values between two procedures. The main and internal procedures must be able to access some of the same memory locations. This is the only way the main procedure can supply particular values to the internal procedure or even be able to utilize the results of the procedure's computations.

The two basic methods of communicating are through (i) global variables and (ii) parameters.

8.2.1 Global Variables

As you will soon see, it is possible to declare variables inside procedures. However, when variables used in the main procedure are not declared within the internal procedure, they refer to the same memory locations in both procedures and are called "global variables."

Notice that there are no declaration statements in the procedure LARGE of Section 8.1.3. The variables A, B, C, and MAXY are therefore global variables. The procedure LARGE will find their locations from the main procedure, and any change made by LARGE will be available to the main procedure.

In general, any variable which exists in the main procedure is available to any other internal procedure unless that variable has been declared again in the internal procedure.

8.2.2 First Difficulty with Global Variables -- Inflexibility

Global variables restrict an otherwise general procedure to operating on a fixed set of variables. Suppose Melvin also wanted to print all six input values after printing the largest value for each region. His main procedure would probably do some awkward shuffling of data. Since LARGE can find the largest value only among locations called A, B, and C, he must save their original values elsewhere before CALLing LARGE the second time with new values in A, B, and C. For example, he might write:

```
          .
          .
          .
/*FIND MAXIMUM SNOWFALL IN FIRST REGION*/
GET LIST(A,B,C);
CALL LARGE;
PUT SKIP DATA(MAXY);
/*SAVE VALUES OF CITIES*/
FIRSTA = A;
FIRSTB = B;
FIRSTC = C;
/*FIND MAXIMUM SNOWFALL IN OTHER REGION*/
GET LIST(A,B,C);
CALL LARGE;
PUT SKIP DATA(MAXY);
PUT SKIP LIST(FIRSTA,FIRSTB,FIRSTC,A,B,C);
```

It would be much more useful to have a procedure which could find the largest value of any three variables. Besides adding flexibility to the internal procedure, there would be another important advantage. The two procedures could be written more independently if not bound to use identical variable names.

8.2.3 Parameters

It is possible to free a procedure from operating on specific variables by communicating with parameters rather than global variables. With this method each time the internal procedure is called, it is told which particular variables are to be used for communication during its current execution.

We write such procedures by adding a parameter list to the procedure statement thus:

```
&lt;entry-name&gt;: PROCEDURE (P1,P2, ...,Pn);
```

where P1,P2, ...,Pn must be simple variable names called parameters. They represent the names on which the procedure will operate, but they do not represent specific locations in memory. They merely serve as pseudonyms for such locations.

Let us illustrate by re-writing the procedure LARGE with parameters. The purpose of the procedure is to find the largest value of three variables and store this largest value in a fourth variable. Since these parameters can be any valid PL/I variable names, we choose arbitrarily the names X,Y,Z, and BIG. The PROCEDURE statement can now be written as:

```
LARGE:  PROCEDURE (X,Y,Z,BIG);
```

We must also DECLARE what kind of variables these parameters are intended to represent. Assuming they will represent FIXED-point numbers, we can write the procedure as:

```
LARGE:  PROCEDURE(X,Y,Z,BIG);
        DECLARE (X,Y,Z,BIG) FIXED(5,2);
        BIG = X;
        IF Y > BIG THEN
           BIG = Y;
        IF Z > BIG THEN
           BIG = Z;
        END LARGE;
```

This version of LARGE will find the maximum of any three variables whose attributes are FIXED(5,2) and store the maximum in a fourth variable of like attributes. LARGE will use the names X,Y,Z, and BIG to designate these variables, regardless of which actual variables may actually be involved.

Now that the procedure has been generalized to operate on any four suitable variables, each CALL to it must specify which particular values it should use during this execution. The CALL statement must supply a corresponding number of values or variables, called arguments. The CALL statement has the general form:

```
CALL <procedure entry-name> (A1,A2, ...,An);
```

where A1, A2, ..., An are the arguments on which the procedure is to operate this time. These arguments correspond to the parameters in three ways. First, they must correspond in number, i.e., if the procedure has four parameters then you must supply four arguments. Second, they must correspond in attributes, i.e., if the procedure has declared two parameters to be FIXED(5,0) and two to be FLOAT then you must supply two arguments of each type. Third, they correspond in position, i.e., the first argument corresponds to the first parameter, the second argument to the second parameter, etc.

For example, the CALL statement in Fig. 8.4 is a valid invocation of LARGE. In this case LARGE denotes the value of A (40.3) by X, the value of B (52.5) by Y, and the value of C (38.7) by Z. Since the location called BIG is actually MAXY, the result of LARGE is to store the largest value (52.5) in MAXY.

```
                 DECLARE (A,B,C,MAXY) FIXED(5,2);
                    .
                 A = 40.3;
                 B = 52.5;
                 C = 38.7;
                 CALL LARGE (A,B,C,MAXY);
                 PUT SKIP DATA (MAXY);
                    .
                    .
                    .
        LARGE:   PROCEDURE (X,Y,Z,BIG);
                 DECLARE (X,Y,Z,BIG) FIXED(5,2);
                 BIG = X;
                 IF Y > BIG THEN
                    BIG = Y;
                 IF Z > BIG THEN
                    BIG = Z;
                 END LARGE;
                    .
                    .
                    .
```

Fig. 8.4 A CALL to a Procedure with Parameters

On the other hand, the statement

```
CALL LARGE (A,B,C);
```

would be invalid because LARGE has four parameters and we have only supplied three arguments. Similarly code such as:

```
DECLARE (A,B,C,D) CHARACTER(10);
GET LIST (A,B,C);
CALL LARGE (A,B,C,D);
```

would cause an error because the arguments are CHARACTER variables and LARGE expects to operate only on FIXED decimal variables.

The only special point is that when a character string is being passed, the corresponding parameter in the procedure should be declared as CHARACTER(*). Figure 8.5 (Section 8.3) will show an example.

8.2.4 The Parameter Mechanism

To see how procedures with parameters work, examine the code in Fig. 8.4. When the first CALL is executed, control is transferred to LARGE and this procedure will establish a one-to-one correspondence between the parameters (X,Y,Z,BIG) and the arguments (A,B,C,MAXY). That is, it will use the storage location reserved for A in every reference to X, the storage location for B in every reference to Y, and so on.

Before the CALL is executed, the locations looked like:

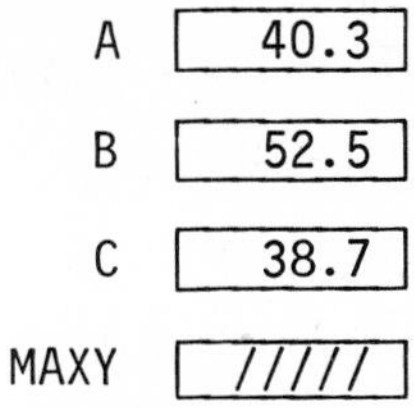

```
       A   [ 40.3  ]

       B   [ 52.5  ]

       C   [ 38.7  ]

    MAXY   [ ///// ]
```

where ///// indicates MAXY has no value. When control transfers to LARGE, the parameter names are appended to point to these locations with the result that they then look like:[4]

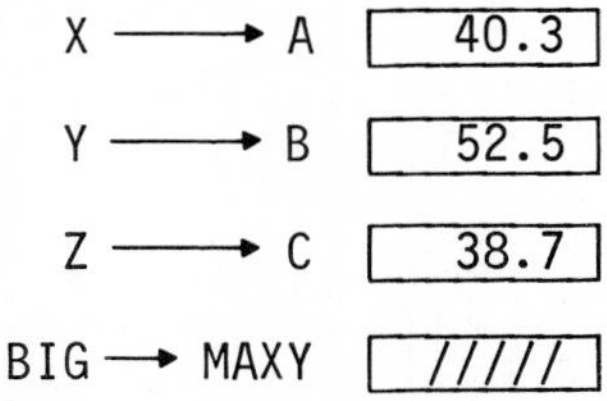

```
  X  ---->  A     [ 40.3  ]

  Y  ---->  B     [ 52.5  ]

  Z  ---->  C     [ 38.7  ]

BIG  ---->  MAXY  [ ///// ]
```

The procedure LARGE can now operate safely on variables X,Y,Z, and BIG without worrying about how they were named in the calling procedure. LARGE first executes BIG = X; which causes memory to change to:

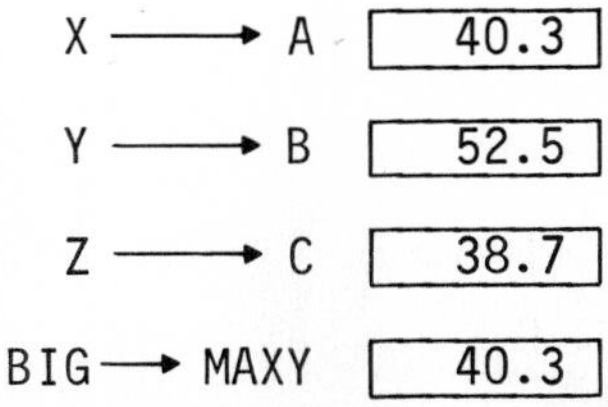

```
  X  ---->  A     [ 40.3  ]

  Y  ---->  B     [ 52.5  ]

  Z  ---->  C     [ 38.7  ]

BIG  ---->  MAXY  [ 40.3  ]
```

Notice that although the statement executed uses variables BIG and X, the actual contents of location MAXY have been changed. The variable BIG is merely a pseudonym for MAXY.

The procedure then proceeds to execute IF Y > BIG THEN BIG = Y; and storage again changes to:

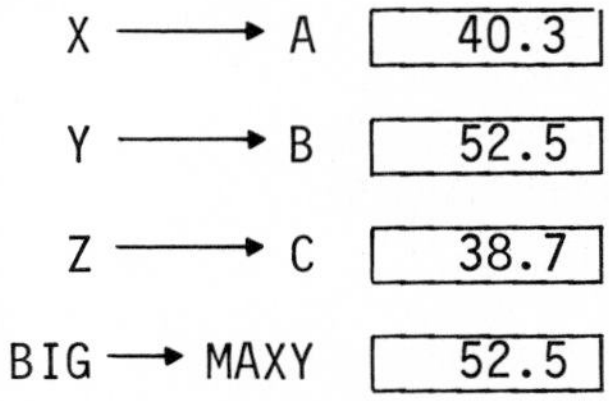

```
  X  ---->  A     [ 40.3  ]

  Y  ---->  B     [ 52.5  ]

  Z  ---->  C     [ 38.7  ]

BIG  ---->  MAXY  [ 52.5  ]
```

---

[4]The actual mechanism is more complex than our description indicates. Our intent is to convey the idea rather than provide a fully accurate explanation.

Execution of the next statement causes no change to storage and the procedure then terminates by returning control to the calling procedure. The main procedure can thus proceed to execute the statement PUT SKIP DATA (MAXY);. Although it did not explicitly assign any value to MAXY, the number 52.5 has been placed there by LARGE and can therefore be printed.

We stated previously that arguments and parameters must match in position. To explain more fully what is meant by this, suppose the CALL statement in Figure 8.4 is changed to:

```
CALL LARGE (MAXY,A,B,C);
```

Then on entry to the procedure, the following correspondence would be established:

```
  X ──→ MAXY  [ ///// ]
  Y ──→ A     [  40.3 ]
  Z ──→ B     [  50.5 ]
BIG ──→ C     [  38.7 ]
```

Now when the procedure comes to execute BIG = X; an error will occur because X now represents the undefined location MAXY. The correspondence between names occurs in their order of appearance.

It should now be apparent that, on a subsequent CALL, entirely different variable names could be supplied by the main procedure. For example, Melvin's procedure to compute and print the largest value for each region and then print all six input values (Section 8.2.2) could now be written:

```
     .
     .
     .
GET LIST(FIRSTA,FIRSTB,FIRSTC);
CALL LARGE(FIRSTA,FIRSTB,FIRSTC,FIRSTMAXY);
PUT SKIP DATA(FIRSTMAXY);
GET LIST(A,B,C);
CALL LARGE(A,B,C,MAXY);
PUT SKIP DATA(MAXY);
PUT SKIP DATA(FIRSTA,FIRSTB,FIRSTC,A,B,C);
     .
     .
     .
```

8.2.5 What Constitutes a Valid Argument

Here we examine in more detail what sorts of things can be placed in the argument list of a CALL statement. The overriding consideration is that <u>each argument should have the same attributes as the corresponding parameter</u> in the procedure.[5] If the procedure has

[5]Admittedly this rule can sometimes be broken in PL/I without causing disaster. However, violations often lead to greater difficulties if not outright error, and the exceptions are so complex that it is easier to simply follow our suggestion.

declared its second parameter as FIXED(10), then that is what should be supplied in the second argument of the CALL.

As a consequence, we suggest that you never supply a constant as an argument, i.e., do not say:

```
CALL LARGE (5,B,832,MAXY);
```

Constants almost never match in attributes with the corresponding parameter. If a constant must be used as an argument, first store it in a variable whose attributes will match and then pass the variable.

Since we have ruled out constants as arguments we can only pass five other things: (i) simple variables, (ii) individual array elements, (iii) structures, (iv) expressions, and (v) entire arrays.

Individual array elements are handled like simple variables. Thus, provided Q, Y, and array A are of the correct type, you can say:

```
CALL LARGE(A(3),Q,A(1),Y);
```

Structures, to be explained in Chapter 10, are also passed like simple variables, provided they are DECLAREd the same way in both procedures. The problem of passing entire arrays is deferred until Section 8.5.

This leaves only expressions to be discussed here. If the purpose of an argument is only to supply a value to the internal procedure, then it is permissible to have an expression for that argument. For example, if Q,R,S and T are DECLAREd with the correct attributes, then you could write:

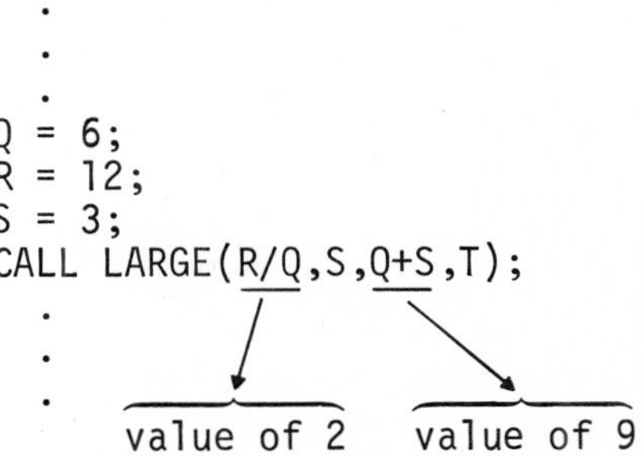

Any expression in an argument list is first evaluated. This value is then referred to by the corresponding parameter of the procedure. As a result, LARGE would place the value 9 in T, since 9 is the largest of 2, 3, and 9.

However, an expression cannot be used in any argument through which a result is returned! Thus the fourth argument of a CALL to LARGE cannot contain an expression. The reason is simple: an expression is not the name of any memory location and so does not designate a place in which the main procedure could find a result. For example, one could not write:

```
CALL LARGE(Q,R,S,R+Q);
```

In this case the initial argument-parameter correspondence would be as follows, and the main procedure would have no way to refer to the result:

```
X ——→ Q  [ 6]
Y ——→ R  [12]
Z ——→ S  [ 3]
BIG ——→  [18]
```

8.2.6 A Second Difficulty with Global Variables -- Side Effects

Suppose that Marcello had given Melvin a different recipe for finding the largest of A, B, or C, which had employed an extra variable, N. Melvin might have converted this into a procedure as follows:

```
LARGER:  PROCEDURE;
         N = A;
         IF B > N THEN
            N = B;
         IF C > N THEN
            MAXY = C;
         ELSE
            MAXY = N;
         END LARGER;
```

This procedure accomplishes the same function as LARGE (Section 8.2.1). Variable N merely contains the larger of A and B until it is compared with C within the procedure. However, because N is not declared in the procedure, it refers to the same memory location as any N which might have been used in the main procedure. That is, N is global in effect, even though its use should be purely internal to the procedure. Consequently, since N is assigned a value within the procedure, this new value replaces any previous value for N in the main procedure. If the main procedure, in fact, did employ an N, to have LARGER alter N would come as a complete "surprise." The main procedure certainly did not intend N for communication.

For example, suppose the main procedure uses N to count the number of times LARGER is called:

```
         N = 0;
            .
            .
            .
LOOP:    DO WHILE(N < 50);
            GET LIST(A,B,C);
            N = N + 1;
            CALL LARGER(A,B,C,MAXY);
         END LOOP;
```

No matter how often N is incremented, the final value of N will be the larger of the final values for A and B! Also, the loop will terminate whenever A or B has a value of 50 or more, and it will not terminate otherwise!

Such surprises are called "side effects" and result from inadvertently altering global variables within procedures, or, what is more common, altering variables which really should not be global. To have the main procedure avoid the use of such names is an undesirable bother. When an internal procedure needs such a variable, it is better to confine the effects of changing the variable to that particular procedure, i.e., to make such variables "nonglobal" or "local."

8.3 LOCAL VARIABLES

To restrict a variable to the context of an internal procedure, simply DECLARE it within that procedure. Such a variable is called a "local variable," and is not accessible outside that procedure. For example, the difficulty cited in Section 8.2.6 could be eliminated by rewriting LARGER to make N a local variable:

```
LARGEST:  PROCEDURE;
          /*N IS FOR PRIVATE USE OF THIS PROCEDURE*/
          DECLARE N FIXED(5,2);
          N = A;
          IF B > N THEN
             N = B;
          IF C > N THEN
             MAXY = C;
          ELSE
             MAXY = N;
          END LARGEST;
```

Even if the main procedure contains a variable N, the value of this variable is unaffected by changes to N within LARGEST.

The two names, though superficially the same, refer to two different memory locations! Whenever the internal procedure is CALLed, new memory locations are allocated to each of its local variables. Any reference inside the procedure to a local variable name is a reference to one of these "special" locations. However, they are allocated only for the duration of the procedure. So, when it terminates, their values and accessibility vanish.

As another example of where a local variable is required, consider the procedure in Fig. 8.5.

```
BLANKS:   PROCEDURE (S,N);
          /*  A PROCEDURE TO COUNT THE NUMBER OF
              BLANKS IN A STRING,S, AND RETURN
              THE NUMBER IN N */

          DECLARE  S  CHARACTER (*) VARYING,
                   N  FIXED (5,0);
          DECLARE  K  FIXED (5,0);

          N = 0;
COUNT:    DO  K = 1 TO LENGTH(S);
                 IF SUBSTR (S,K,1) = ' ' THEN N = N + 1;
          END COUNT;
          END BLANKS;
```

Fig. 8.5 Procedure to Count the Number of Blanks in a String

There are two special points to notice about this code. First there are two declare statements: One for the parameters and one for the index variable of the loop. In general we recommend separate DECLARE statements for parameters and local variables. The index variable, K, is being used only by the procedure to help examine each character of S in turn.

The second thing to notice about Fig. 8.5 is the declaration of the parameter S. There is no maximum length specified for S. Instead, the length is denoted by an asterisk (*). This notation is required by PL/C for any character string parameter and means that PL/C does not care about the length of the string. Whenever a specific argument is passed to BLANKS, the maximum length will be found from this argument.

The first point is the major point. By making K local, we have protected any other procedures from the effects of using this index. We have thus made BLANKS more independent.

There is, however, one side-effect problem which is so common and yet so subtle that it deserves a special word of warning.

By this point, you are probably aware that even if you do not DECLARE loop or array indices, such as I,J,K,L,M, or N, PL/I will still permit you to store integer values in such locations. A common reaction is to default these variables and save the time of key-punching the associated DECLARE statements. Of course, this also makes such variables global instead of local. This practice is often fatal when dealing with procedures.

An example is the program of Fig. 8.6, which could have utilized BLANKS (Fig. 8.5) to count and print the number of blanks in each of six character strings. Instead it uses the internal procedure SLOPPY, which does not DECLARE K. Suppose the first input string has more than 6 characters. The program will find the number of blanks in only that one string and then terminate with no error messages. The problem is that K was inadvertently global. When SLOPPY finished executing, it had made the value of K greater than 6. Consequently when the test of K is made in the main procedure, the loop is not repeated because K has apparently exceeded its upper limit of 6. The moral is not to take shortcuts -- declare all local variables.

In summary, there are three kinds of variables involved in internal procedures, as shown in Fig. 8.7 Any variable used in a procedure, which is not specifically intended for communication with other procedures, should be made a local variable by declaring it. Don't worry about whether the same name has been used elsewhere. That is just the point! By making such variables local, you ensure that they will not cause adverse side effects. Using local variables makes your procedures independent of the main program, so that duplicate names should not be a concern.

8.4 SCOPE OF VARIABLES AND NESTED PROCEDURES

Since the only restriction on local variable and parameter names is that they be valid PL/I names, the same name may occur in different procedures with different meanings by referring to different memory locations in each procedure. The scope of a variable refers to the extent of a program over which that variable name identifies the same memory location, i.e., has a consistent meaning. Stated differently,

```
         /* FIGURE 8.6 */
WRONG:   PROCEDURE OPTIONS (MAIN);

         /* A PROGRAM TO DEMONSTRATE THE SIDE EFFECTS OF
            GLOBAL VARIABLES. THE VARIABLE K IS GLOBAL WHEN
            IT SHOULD BE LOCAL TO THE TWO PROCEDURES WHICH
            MAKE UP THE PROGRAM. */

         DECLARE
            STRING CHARACTER (20) VARYING,
            NUMB FIXED (5,0); /* NO. BLANKS IN STRING */

LOOP:    DO K = 1 TO 6;
            GET LIST (STRING);
            PUT SKIP LIST (STRING);
            CALL SLOPPY (STRING,NUMB);
            PUT SKIP DATA (NUMB);
         END LOOP;

SLOPPY: PROCEDURE (S,N);

         /* THIS PROCEDURE IS TO COUNT THE NUMBER OF BLANKS
            (N) IN A CHARACTER STRING (S). IT FAILS TO
            DECLARE THE LOOP INDEX (K) THUS CAUSING SIDE
            EFFECTS IN THE CALLING PROCEDURE. */

         DECLARE
            S CHARACTER (*) VARYING,
            N FIXED (5,0);

         N = 0;

COUNT:   DO K = 1 TO LENGTH(S);
            IF SUBSTR(S,K,1) = ' ' THEN
               N = N + 1;
         END COUNT;

         END SLOPPY;

         END WRONG;
```

Figure 8.6

Variable	Declared in Internal Procedure	For Communication	Comments
Global	No	Yes	Known outside by same name
Parameter	Yes	Yes	Known outside, possibly by different name
Local	Yes	No	Not known outside

Fig. 8.7 Different Uses for Variables

knowing the scope of a variable tells you the region of code within which it can be used to convey the same information. If the same name is used in two different ways, then each "use" has its own scope, and these scopes may not overlap. At any one time, a name has at most one "meaning."

For example, if variable X appears in both a main procedure and an internal procedure, to which X will the computer refer when we use X in the internal procedure? The answer lies in the declaration statement(s) of the internal procedure. If X has been declared in the internal procedure, then the reference will be to the local X; otherwise it refers to the global X. Consider Fig. 8.8, in which both situations occur.

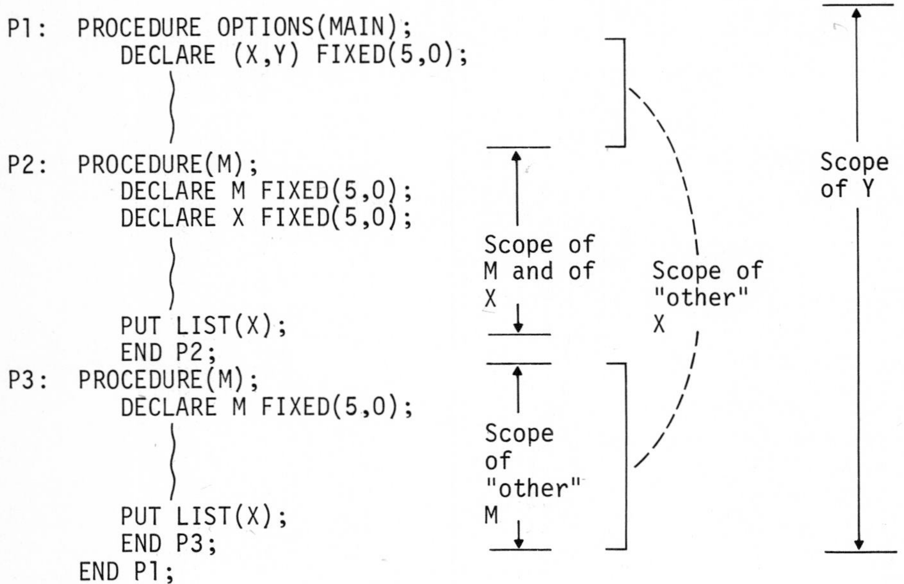

Fig. 8.8 Scope of Variables

In this figure, Y is a global variable known to every procedure. Since X is declared in P2, its use in P2 has nothing to do with its use elsewhere. However, the X in P3 refers to the same location as the X in P1 (P3 is internal to P1 and does not redeclare X). The M which occurs in P2 and again in P3 not only may refer to different locations in the two procedures, it may refer to different locations each time either procedure is called! This all depends on what was used as an argument. In any case P2 and P3 are mutually independent, and no variable declared in one (including parameters like M) may be accessed by the other.

8.4.1 Nested Procedures

Suppose Melvin had written his master plan for reporting snowfall as follows:

1. repeat 2 times;
1.1 produce a report for one region (3 cities);
2. end.

He then wrote an algorithm to produce a report for one region:

1.1.1 read 3 values;
1.1.2 use Marcello's method to find largest value;
1.1.3 print largest value;

If he makes this algorithm into a procedure, then his main procedure becomes basically two CALLs to this procedure. This internal procedure, in turn, consists of a GET statement, a CALL to LARGE, and a PUT statement. Since LARGE is used only by this (internal) procedure, it can be defined within the internal procedure (see Fig. 8.9). This is an example of "nesting" procedures, and it also illustrates how various levels of an algorithm may be directly converted into very readable code.

```
              /* FIGURE 8.9 */
WEATHER:PROCEDURE OPTIONS (MAIN);

        CALL REPORT;
        CALL REPORT;

REPORT: PROCEDURE;

        DECLARE (A,B,C,MAXY) FIXED (5,2);

        GET LIST (A,B,C);
        CALL LARGE;
        PUT SKIP DATA (MAXY);

LARGE:  PROCEDURE;

        MAXY = A;
        IF B > MAXY THEN
           MAXY = B;
        IF C > MAXY THEN
           MAXY = C;

        END LARGE;

        END REPORT;

        END WEATHER;
```

Fig. 8.9 Nested Procedures

The main procedure, of course, does not have access to the interior of its internal procedures; it may only call an entire procedure at a time. Consequently, it may not call more deeply imbedded procedures. Thus WEATHER cannot directly call LARGE, since REPORT is the only procedure immediately internal to WEATHER. However, there is nothing to prevent an internal procedure from defining its own internal procedures and calling them as needed.

8.4.2 Scope Rules for Nested Procedures

Nesting procedures naturally affects the scope of variables. However, any procedure containing internal procedures has the same relationship to them as the main procedure has to its internal procedures. Thus any procedure may CALL its own internal procedures, and any "local" variable this internal procedure declares is the version known to its own internal procedures (unless they, in turn, redeclare it).

For example, in Fig. 8.10(a), the procedure P3 is nested within P2; thus the X of P2 is the one accessible to P3. From P3's point of view, X is global, though its meaning does not extend beyond P2. In Fig. 8.10(b) X has been declared in P1 only. When P3 refers to X, it is the same X known in P2 and in P1. On the other hand, P3 has its own local Y, while P1 and P2 share another global variable known (to them) as Y.

Though scope rules may seem complex, a bit of terminology should help. We will call any procedure defined within another the "child"; the containing procedure will be called the "parent." Thus, in Fig. 8.10, P3 is the "child" of P2, while P2 is the "parent" of P3. An obvious extension makes P1 the "grandparent" of P3.

In these terms, there is only one scope rule:

> Whenever a name is used, it refers to the declaration of that name in the same procedure or in the nearest ancestor where a declaration occurred (parent, then grandparent, etc.).

8.4.3 Who Can Call Whom?

The name of a procedure (the entry-name on the PROCEDURE statement) is not known within the procedure itself. This means that no procedure may call itself.[6] Nor can any of its own internal procedures call it. For example, in Fig. 8.10, P3 cannot call any procedure.

Of course, the name is known to the procedure which contains its definition. Thus, in Fig. 8.10, P1 may call P2, and P2 may call P3. However, P1 may not call P3 directly, since the name of P3 is local to P2.

In familial terms, the name of any procedure is known to its own parent but to none of its earlier ancestors nor to itself or its offspring. Thus, in the direct ancestral nesting line, CALLs are limited to a procedure's own children.

However, since a procedure's name is known to its parent, it is also known to other internal procedures within the same parent. That is, it is known and may be CALLed by any of its own siblings and any of their offspring.

Looking the other direction, you (as a procedure) may CALL your own children, your own siblings, your parent's siblings, your grandparent's siblings, etc.

---

[6] Unless it is RECURSIVE as explained in Chapter 11.

```
P1:  PROCEDURE OPTIONS(MAIN);
     DECLARE X FIXED(5,0);
        ...
     CALL P2;
        ...
P2:  PROCEDURE;
     DECLARE X FIXED(5,0);
        ...
     CALL P3;
        ...
P3:  PROCEDURE;
        ...
     PUT LIST (X);   <-- X from procedure P2
     END P3;
     END P2;
     END P1;
```

(a)

```
P1:  PROCEDURE OPTIONS(MAIN);
     DECLARE(X,Y) FIXED;
        ...
     CALL P2;
        ...
P2:  PROCEDURE;
        ...
     CALL P3;
        ...
P3:  PROCEDURE;
     DECLARE Y FIXED;
        ...
     PUT LIST (X);   <-- X from procedure P1
     END P3;
     END P2;
     END P1;
```

(b)

Fig. 8.10 Scope of Variables

For example, if Melvin had wanted to calculate the largest snowfall for three 3-city regions and then calculate the largest overall snowfall, he could have written the procedure in Fig. 8.11. Here REPORT calls its sibling LARGE, and both of these procedures are called by their common parent, WEATHER. However if LARGE had been internal to REPORT, WEATHER would not have been able to call it. Also note the important use of parameters in this example.

```
            /* FIGURE 8.11 */
WEATHER:PROCEDURE OPTIONS (MAIN);

        /* A PROGRAM TO FIND THE LARGEST SNOWFALL
           FOR THREE 3-CITY REGIONS. */

        DECLARE
           REGION1 FIXED (5,2), /* MAX SNOW IN REGION 1 */
           REGION2 FIXED (5,2), /* MAX SNOW IN REGION 2 */
           REGION3 FIXED (5,2), /* MAX SNOW IN REGION 3 */
           BIG FIXED (5,2); /* OVERALL MAX SNOW */

        CALL REPORT (REGION1);
        CALL REPORT (REGION2);
        CALL REPORT (REGION3);
        CALL LARGE (REGION1,REGION2,REGION3,BIG);
        PUT SKIP DATA (BIG);

REPORT: PROCEDURE (ANSWER);
        /* A PROGRAM TO READ THREE VALUES AND RETURN
           THE MAXIMUM VALUE IN ANSWER. */
        DECLARE ANSWER FIXED (5,2);
        DECLARE (A,B,C) FIXED (5,2); /*VALUES TO BE READ*/

        GET LIST (A,B,C);
        CALL LARGE (A,B,C,ANSWER);
        PUT SKIP LIST (ANSWER);

        END REPORT;

LARGE:  PROCEDURE (X,Y,Z,MAX);
        /* A PROCEDURE TO FIND THE LARGEST VALUE OF THREE
           VALUES - X, Y, Z - AND RETURN IT IN MAX. */
        DECLARE (X,Y,Z,MAX) FIXED (5,2);

        MAX = X;
        IF Y > MAX THEN
           MAX = Y;
        IF Z > MAX THEN
           MAX = Z;

        END LARGE;

        END WEATHER;
```

Figure 8.11

8.5 ONE-DIMENSIONAL ARRAYS AS PARAMETERS

As indicated in Section 8.2.5, it is possible to pass arrays as arguments to a procedure. The CALL statement need only mention the array name as an argument. The called procedure must be told to expect an array as an argument by declaring the corresponding parameter as:

DECLARE <parameter-name> (*) <attributes>;

The * notation indicates that the parameter is a one-dimensional array whose length will be established when the procedure is called, since this depends on which array is passed by each CALL. Do not confuse this notation with that used for passing CHARACTER data.

However, unlike character strings, whose size can be determined by LENGTH, there is no direct way of determining how many elements have been stored in an array. This information must be explicitly conveyed. When passing an array, you must usually supply two pertinent parameters: the array name itself and also the current number of elements it contains. For example, a procedure to find and print the largest element in a one-dimensional array is shown in Fig. 8.12. This procedure could be called by writing

```
CALL MAXI(A,N);
```

where A is the name of some array, and N is the current number of meaningful values in it.

```
MAXI:  PROCEDURE(ARY,#ELTS);
       DECLARE ARY (*) FIXED(5,2),
               #ELTS   FIXED(5,0);
       DECLARE PSN     FIXED(5,0),
               MAXELMT FIXED(5,2);
       MAXELMT = ARY(1);
LOOP:  DO PSN = 2 TO #ELTS;
          IF ARY(PSN) > MAXELMT THEN
             MAXELMT = ARY(PSN);
       END LOOP;
       PUT SKIP LIST(MAXELMT);
       END MAXI;
```

Fig. 8.12 Procedure to Print Largest Element in a One-Dimensional Array

8.5.1 HBOUND and LBOUND

In the rare case where every array passed to a procedure is completely full, the number of elements need not be communicated as an argument. Since the number of (current) elements equals the declared size of such an array, the procedure may determine this size by using built-in functions. The function

HBOUND(<parameter array name>,1)

returns the largest (integer) number which can legitimately index the array.[7] This number is generally equal to its length, and so HBOUND for arrays would correspond to LENGTH for character strings.

However, if the array were originally declared with an initial index different from 1, then LBOUND (<parameter array name>,1) would return the smallest legitimate index. HBOUND and LBOUND together determine the length in this case.

[7]The 1 in the reference to HBOUND and LBOUND refers to the "first" dimension of the array. Other values might be appropriate in the context of Chapter 9.

For example, if every array passed to MAXI in Fig. 8.12 were full, then #ELTS could be eliminated, and the code for searching ARY could be rewritten:

```
              FIRST = LBOUND(ARY,1);
              LAST = HBOUND(ARY,1);
              MAXELT = ARY(FIRST);
       LOOP:  DO PSN = FIRST+1 TO LAST;
                 IF ARY(PSN) > MAXELT THEN
                    MAXELT = ARY(PSN);
              END LOOP;
```

8.5.2 A Procedure Example Using Array Parameters

A frequently encountered problem is to find the mean and standard deviation of a set of n values. The "mean" is another name for "average," and "standard deviation" indicates how widely the values tend to be spread. A "small" standard deviation indicates that most values are close to the mean. If the data values are stored in an array X, then the (sample) mean value $\overline{X}$ is given by:

$$\overline{X} = \frac{\sum_{i=1}^{n} x_i}{n}$$

The standard deviation, σ, is given by the following formula, where $\overline{x}$ is the mean as calculated above.

$$\sigma = \sqrt{\frac{\sum_{i=1}^{n} (x_i - \overline{x})^2}{n - 1}}$$

If we were asked to write a program to find the mean and standard deviation for, say, a set of class marks, the resulting algorithm might be:

1. read the marks;
2. calculate the mean value;
3. calculate the standard deviation;
4. print the mean and standard deviation;
5. end.

We shall write procedures to implement Steps 2 and 3. Notice that to calculate the standard deviation we require the mean value. Hence the code to calculate the mean will also be utilized in the calculation of the standard deviation. By making both procedures internal to (children of) the main procedure, the main procedure may call both, and the standard deviation procedure may also call MEAN.

A procedure to calculate the mean of a set of values stored in the array X is shown in Fig. 8.13. Note that this procedure deals with FLOATing-point numbers. This is a highly desirable attribute when doing any kind of scientific calculation. FIXED decimal numbers are notoriously unpredictable when division is involved, for reasons

```
        /* FIGURE 8.13 */
MEAN:   PROCEDURE (X,N,ANS);

        /* A PROCEDURE TO FIND THE MEAN VALUE OF THE FIRST
           N NUMBERS IN AN ARRAY, X. THE MEAN WILL BE
           RETURNED IN ANS. */

        DECLARE
           X(*) FLOAT (6), /* ARRAY OF NUMBERS */
           N FIXED (5,0), /* NO. ELEMENTS CONSIDERED */
           ANS FLOAT (6); /* MEAN VALUE SOUGHT */
        DECLARE
           K FIXED (5,0), /* INDEX FOR X */
           SUM FLOAT (6); /* SUM 1ST N ELEMENTS OF X */

        SUM = 0.0;

LOOP:   DO K = 1 TO N;
           SUM = SUM + X(K);
        END LOOP;

        ANS = SUM / N;

        END MEAN;
```

Fig. 8.13 A Procedure to Find the Mean Value of an Array of Numbers

```
        /* FIGURE 8.14 */
STD_DEV:PROCEDURE (X,N,ANS);

        /* A PROCEDURE TO FIND THE STANDARD DEVIATION
           FOR N NUMBERS IN AN ARRAY, X. */

        DECLARE
           X(*) FLOAT (6),
           N FIXED (5,0),
           ANS FLOAT (6); /* STANDARD DEVIATION */
        DECLARE
           K FIXED (5,0), /* INDEX FOR X */
           SUM FLOAT (6),
           VAR FLOAT (6), /* VARIANCE */
           XBAR FLOAT (6); /* MEAN */

        /* FIND MEAN VALUE */

        CALL MEAN (X,N,XBAR);

        /* FORM SUM OF SQUARES OF DIFFERENCES */

        SUM = 0.0;

LOOP:   DO K = 1 TO N;
           SUM = SUM + (X(K) - XBAR) ** 2;
        END LOOP;

        /* CALCULATE VARIANCE */

        VAR = SUM / (N - 1);

        /* CALCULATE STANDARD DEVIATION */

        ANS = SQRT(VAR);

        END STD_DEV;
```

Fig. 8.14 A Procedure to Calculate Standard Deviations

```
STMT LEVEL NEST BLOCK       SOURCE STATEMENT

                                          /* FIGURE 8.15 */
   1                              STATS:  PROCEDURE OPTIONS (MAIN);
                                          /* A PROGRAM TO CALCULATE THE MEAN AND
                                             STANDARD DEVIATION FOR UP TO 100 VALUES */
                                          DECLARE
   2      1            1                     VALUES(100) FLOAT (6),
                                             AVERAGE FLOAT (6), /* MEAN OF VALUES */
                                             SIGMA FLOAT (6), /* STD. DEV. OF VALUES */
                                             COUNT FIXED (5,0), /* # OF VALUES */
                                             FLAG FIXED (5,0);
   3      1            1                  FLAG = 0;
   4      1            1                  ON ENDFILE (SYSIN)
   5      2            2                     FLAG = 1;
   6      1            1                  COUNT = 1;
   7      1            1                  GET LIST (VALUES(COUNT));
   8      1            1          READIN: DO WHILE (FLAG = 0);
   9      1      1     1                     COUNT = COUNT + 1;
  10      1      1     1                     GET LIST (VALUES(COUNT));
  11      1      1     1                  END READIN;
  12      1            1                  COUNT = COUNT - 1;

  13      1            1                  CALL MEAN(VALUES,COUNT,AVERAGE);
  14      1            1                  PUT SKIP(2) EDIT ('THE MEAN VALUE IS',AVERAGE)
                                             (X(5),A(25),F(10,4));

  15      1            1                  CALL STD_DEV(VALUES,COUNT,SIGMA);
  16      1            1                  PUT SKIP(2) EDIT ('THE STANDARD DEVIATION IS',
                                             SIGMA) (X(5),A(25),F(10,4));

  17      1            1          MEAN:   PROCEDURE (X,N,ANS);
                                          /* A PROCEDURE TO FIND THE MEAN VALUE OF THE FIRST
                                             N NUMBERS IN AN ARRAY, X. THE MEAN WILL BE
                                             RETURNED IN ANS. */
                                          DECLARE
  18      2            3                     X(*) FLOAT (6), /* ARRAY OF NUMBERS */
                                             N FIXED (5,0), /* NO. ELEMENTS CONSIDERED */
                                             ANS FLOAT (6); /* MEAN VALUE SOUGHT */
                                          DECLARE
  19      2            3                     K FIXED (5,0), /* INDEX FOR X */
                                             SUM FLOAT (6); /* SUM 1ST N ELEMENTS OF X */
  20      2            3                  SUM = 0.0;
  21      2            3          LOOP:   DO K = 1 TO N;
  22      2      1     3                     SUM = SUM + X(K);
  23      2      1     3                  END LOOP;
  24      2            3                  ANS = SUM / N;
  25      2            3                  END MEAN;

  26      1            1          STD_DEV:PROCEDURE (X,N,ANS);
                                          /* A PROCEDURE TO FIND THE STANDARD DEVIATION
                                             FOR N NUMBERS IN AN ARRAY, X. */
                                          DECLARE
  27      2            4                     X(*) FLOAT (6),
                                             N FIXED (5,0),
                                             ANS FLOAT (6); /* STANDARD DEVIATION */
                                          DECLARE
  28      2            4                     K FIXED (5,0), /* INDEX FOR X */
                                             SUM FLOAT (6),
                                             VAR FLOAT (6), /* VARIANCE */
                                             XBAR FLOAT (6); /* MEAN */
                                          /* FIND MEAN VALUE */
  29      2            4                  CALL MEAN (X,N,XBAR);
                                          /* FORM SUM OF SQUARES OF DIFFERENCES */
  30      2            4                  SUM = 0.0;
  31      2            4          LOOP:   DO K = 1 TO N;
  32      2      1     4                     SUM = SUM + (X(K) - XBAR) ** 2;
  33      2      1     4                  END LOOP;
                                          /* CALCULATE VARIANCE */
  34      2            4                  VAR = SUM / (N - 1);
                                          /* CALCULATE STANDARD DEVIATION */
  35      2            4                  ANS = SQRT(VAR);
  36      2            4                  END STD_DEV;
  37      1            1                  END STATS;
```

Fig. 8.15(a) A Program to Find Mean and Standard Deviation

DCL NO.	IDENTIFIER	ATTRIBUTES AND REFERENCES
27	ANS	PARAMETER,ALIGNED,DECIMAL,FLOAT(6) 26,27,35
18	ANS	PARAMETER,ALIGNED,DECIMAL,FLOAT(6) 17,18,24
2	AVERAGE	AUTOMATIC,ALIGNED,DECIMAL,FLOAT(6) 2,13,14
2	COUNT	AUTOMATIC,ALIGNED,DECIMAL,FIXED(5,0) 2,6,7,9,9,10,12,12,13,15
2	FLAG	AUTOMATIC,ALIGNED,DECIMAL,FIXED(5,0) 2,3,5,8
28	K	AUTOMATIC,ALIGNED,DECIMAL,FIXED(5,0) 28,31,32
19	K	AUTOMATIC,ALIGNED,DECIMAL,FIXED(5,0) 19,21,22
31	LOOP	STATEMENT LABEL CONSTANT 31
21	LOOP	STATEMENT LABEL CONSTANT 21
17	MEAN	ENTRY,BINARY,FIXED(15,0) 13,17,29
27	N	PARAMETER,ALIGNED,DECIMAL,FIXED(5,0) 26,27,29,31,34
18	N	PARAMETER,ALIGNED,DECIMAL,FIXED(5,0) 17,18,21,24
8	READIN	STATEMENT LABEL CONSTANT 8
2	SIGMA	AUTOMATIC,ALIGNED,DECIMAL,FLOAT(6) 2,15,16
	SQRT	GENERIC,BUILT-IN FUNCTION 35
1	STATS	ENTRY,DECIMAL,FLOAT(6) 1
26	STD_DEV	ENTRY,DECIMAL,FLOAT(6) 15,26
28	SUM	AUTOMATIC,ALIGNED,DECIMAL,FLOAT(6) 28,30,32,32,34
19	SUM	AUTOMATIC,ALIGNED,DECIMAL,FLOAT(6) 19,20,22,22,24
	SYSIN	FILE,EXTERNAL 4
2	VALUES	(*)AUTOMATIC,ALIGNED,DECIMAL,FLOAT(6) 2,7,10,13,15
28	VAR	AUTOMATIC,ALIGNED,DECIMAL,FLOAT(6) 28,34,35
27	X	(*)PARAMETER,ALIGNED,DECIMAL,FLOAT(6) 26,27,29,32
18	X	(*)PARAMETER,ALIGNED,DECIMAL,FLOAT(6) 17,18,22
28	XBAR	AUTOMATIC,ALIGNED,DECIMAL,FLOAT(6) 28,29,32

Fig. 8.15(b) Cross Reference and Attribute Listing for Fig. 8.15(a)

scope of this text.[8]

calculate standard deviation requires the mean s in question, and rather than repeat all the code ,imply call MEAN in this new procedure, as shown in

STD_DEV calls MEAN to find the mean value and store .R. The loop, LOOP, then sums the squares of the een every element and this mean, as suggested by the npletion of this loop, the procedure then calculates ,ic (known as the sample variance) which is given by the fo

$$\sigma^2 = \frac{\sum_{i=1}^{n} (x - \overline{x})^2}{n - 1}$$

Finally STD_DEV calculates the standard deviation by computing the square root of this variance. To do this computation, STD_DEV calls on another built-in function, SQRT. This function requires a FLOATing point argument (greater than 0) and will return the square root of that argument as a FLOATing point number.

We can now put these two procedures together into a program to calculate the mean and standard deviation for up to 100 numbers as shown in Fig. 8.15. Fig. 8.15(a) shows the actual program listing while Fig. 8.15(b) shows the cross-reference and attribute listing. Note how the same names, such as ANS and K, often appear twice in Fig. 8.15(b). This reflects their uses in more than one procedure with different scopes.

Each procedure which goes to make up the program is allocated a <u>block</u> number as shown immediately to the left of the source statements in Fig. 8.15(a). The main procedure is block 1, the procedure MEAN is block 3 and the procedure STD_DEV is block 4. Note that the ON-unit of statement 5 also constitutes a block (2). These blocks are PL/I's way of organizing code into separate compartments of which procedures are only one type.

We now trace the execution of the program STATS assuming the input to be 10.0, 20.0, and 30.0, whose mean and standard deviation are easily calculated to be 20.0 and 10.0 respectively. On the call to MEAN at statement 13 the correspondence would be established as follows:

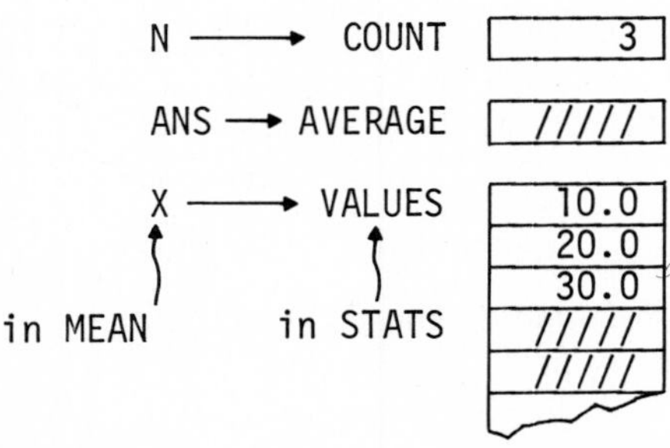

[8]Details can be found in IBM's PL/I (F) Language Reference Manual GC 28-8201-X, Section F.

Mean would then calculate the average as 20.0 and return this value through the parameter ANS to the argument AVERAGE. After printing this value, a call to STD_DEV in statement 15 will result in the following correspondence and local variables in STD_DEV:

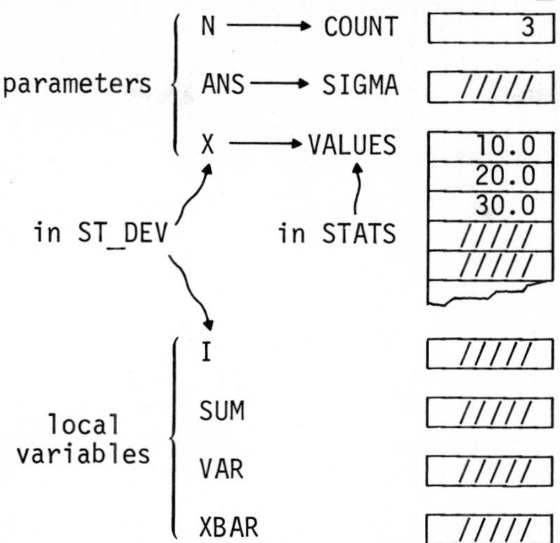

The procedure STD_DEV immediately calls MEAN again (statement 29) and will cause the following variable associations in MEAN:

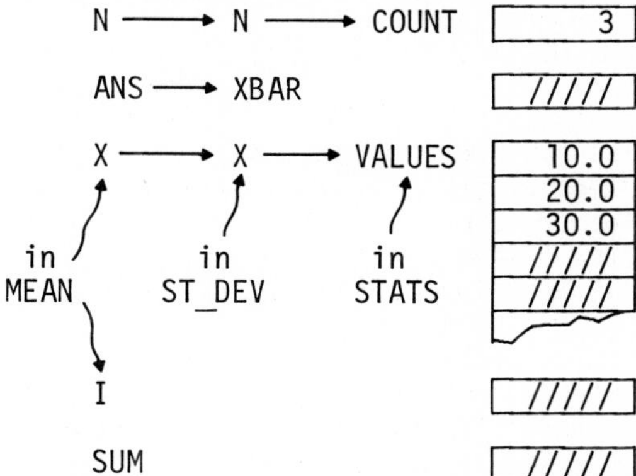

MEAN will again calculate the average and store it in its parameter ANS. There is no confusion as to which ANS will receive this value. Although there is a parameter called ANS in STD_DEV, the procedure MEAN has no way of knowing this. It only recognizes its own parameter. On return to STD_DEV, the storage for block 4 will look like the following:

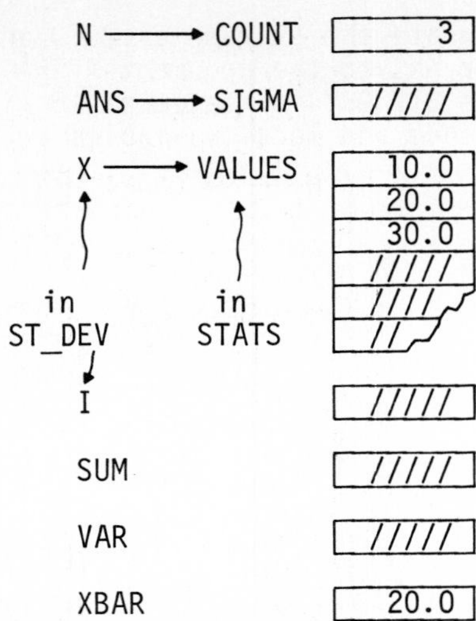

The procedure will then continue to execute and, just prior to returning to the main procedure (statement 36), storage will have the following values:

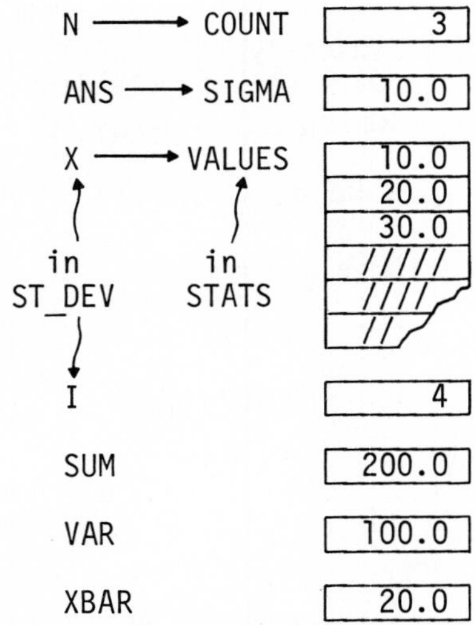

Thus on return to the main procedure, the variable SIGMA will have the required value of 10.0.

8.5.3 Final Reflections

Besides being a very natural and readable way to convert various levels of an algorithm into code, procedures serve several other useful purposes. They permit us to isolate repetitive sections of code into one location and in so doing are a great labor-saving device. Further, if they are general and independent, we can now remove these sections of code and transport them from program to program. Thus useful sections of code which we might use again and again should probably be written as procedures (mean, standard deviation, and sorting routines are examples).

The other big advantages to procedures is that they make for "clean" code in the main procedure. Fig. 8.15, for example, has all its main work done by two procedure calls. Someone reading such code is not distracted from the main procedure by the detailed code of MEAN and STD_DEV; yet it is there should he be interested.

Finally, let us recommend that as a beginning programmer you <u>draw</u> the argument-parameter correspondence and local variables as demonstrated earlier. Until you are thoroughly familiar with these conventions this is the best way to avert some nasty surprises.

8.6 REVIEW OF RULES

1. <u>General Form of Internal Procedures</u>

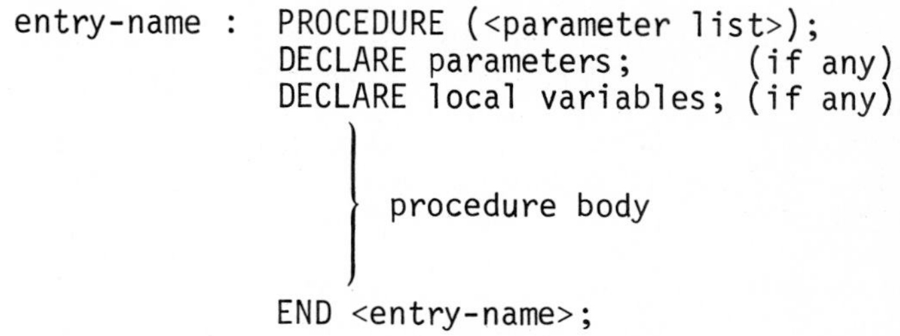
entry-name : PROCEDURE (<parameter list>);
DECLARE parameters; (if any)
DECLARE local variables; (if any)
procedure body
END <entry-name>;

2. <u>Deck Organization with Internal Procedures</u>

Every internal procedure must be completely within the main procedure, preferably before the END statement. Procedures may be nested within each other to a depth of 11.

3. <u>CALL Statement</u>

A procedure can only be invoked by the CALL statement whose general form is:

CALL <procedure entry-name> (<argument list>);

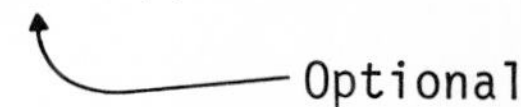
Optional

4. <u>Argument-Parameter Correspondence</u>

The arguments in a CALL statement must match the parameters in the corresponding procedure in (i) number, (ii) attributes, and (iii) position.

5. <u>Arrays as Parameter</u>

When a parameter represents a one-dimensional array it <u>must</u> be declared in the procedure as:

DECLARE <parameter> (*) <attributes>;

The CALL statement merely mentions the name of an array.

6. Character Variables as Parameters

When a parameter represents a character variable, the declaration of that parameter must be:

```
DECLARE <parameter> CHARACTER (*) VARYING;
                                  ↑
                                  └──── Optional
```

8.7 REVIEW PROBLEM

In this section we will recode the review problem for Chapter 7 (Section 7.8) using procedures. If you recall, the problem was to prepare an end-of-month billing of customers by updating a master account file to include all the previous month's transactions.

The algorithm was given in Fig. 7.19. The algorithm involves three major tasks: (1) input the individual transactions and store them in arrays; (2) sort the individual transactions; and (3) read, update, and print the master file. Since the most straightforward of these tasks, processing the master file (3), is also the ultimate purpose of solving this problem, the code to perform this processing constitutes most of the main procedure. However, the input (1) and sort (2) are both relegated to internal procedures. This considerably enhances the readability of the main procedure shown in Fig. 8.16. A comparison between this main procedure and the nonprocedurized program in Fig. 7.20 should persuade you of the improvement. The relatively brief main procedure in Fig. 8.16 is self-explanatory. If you desire more information about how the input and sort actually operate, the appropriate internal procedures can be examined. But this information is not needed to understand the basic steps of the solution.

In addition, the main procedure in Fig. 8.16 also corresponds to the original algorithm of Fig. 7.19. At the time this algorithm was written, we had formulated the overall strategy of the solution, but the details of the input process had not yet been specified. The precise mechanism of the input process, such as how to handle different types of transactions and how to recognize the separator card, were discussed and prescribed later. Similarly, the main procedure of Fig. 8.16 could have been written to implement the original algorithm, leaving the actual details of input for a subsequent internal procedure.

When the original algorithm was written, the sort (2) was not fully described, since any type of sort would suffice. The type of sort actually chosen was the bubble sort, which had already been developed in Section 7.5.2. Similarly, the main procedure merely calls a sort procedure without regard for what sorting method is employed.

The SORT procedure performs a bubble sort, but must reorder two arrays simultaneously. These arrays, called C and A, are passed as parameters. Note the use of asterisks in the DECLARE statement (Statement 40). Since the interchange of elements in two arrays requires three statements for each array, the code for swapping elements was placed in another procedure, SWAP, to avoid cluttering the SORT procedure with these details. SWAP is internal to SORT and has access to the values and arrays of the SORT procedure, since these are global from the point of view of SWAP. SWAP does declare the temporary locations required for the interchanges, since these are only for its own internal use. Note that setting the SORT_FLAG (Statement 50) could have been done within the SWAP procedure instead since it is only set when a swap occurs. However, placing it there would have been misleading, for the SORT procedure code would not have indicated why the SORT loop ever repeated.

```
STMT     SOURCE STATEMENT

                  /* FIGURE 8.16 */
   1   BILL3:   PROCEDURE OPTIONS (MAIN);

                /* A PROGRAM TO UPDATE CUSTOMER ACCOUNTS ACCORDING
                   TO VARIOUS TRANSACTIONS DURING A PERIOD. */

                DECLARE
   2               CUSTMR(100) CHARACTER (40), /* ARRAY OF CUSTOMER NAMES */
                   AMT(100) FIXED (7,2), /* ARRAY OF TRANSACTION AMOUNTS */
                   NAME CHARACTER (40), /* CUSTOMER NAME */
                   BALANCE FIXED (7,2), /* OWING BY CUSTOMER */
                   PSN FIXED (5,0), /* CURRENT POSITION WITHIN ARRAYS */
                   #NAMES FIXED (5,0), /* NO. DIFFERENT TRANSACTIONS */
                   NO_MORE FIXED (5,0); /* END OF DATA FLAG */

                /* INPUT TRANSACTION FILE */

   3            CALL INPUT (CUSTMR,AMT,#NAMES);

                /* SORT THE TRANSACTION FILE IN ALPHABETICAL ORDER */

   4            CALL SORT (CUSTMR,AMT,#NAMES);

                /* INITIALIZE PRIOR TO MASTER FILE */

   5            NO_MORE = 0;
   6            ON ENDFILE (SYSIN) NO_MORE = 1;

                /* FOR EACH CUSTOMER ON THE MASTER FILE, SEARCH THE
                   TRANSACTION FILE AND UPADTE THE BALANCE IF REQUIRED. */

   8            GET SKIP EDIT (NAME,BALANCE) (A(40),X(1),F(7,2));
   9            PSN = 1;

  10   PROCESS:DO WHILE (NO_MORE = 0);

  11   UPDATE:     DO WHILE (CUSTMR(PSN) = NAME);
  12                  BALANCE = BALANCE + AMT(PSN);
  13                  PSN = PSN + 1;
  14               END UPDATE;

  15               PUT SKIP(2) EDIT (NAME,BALANCE) (X(10),A(40),F(10,2));
  16               GET SKIP EDIT (NAME,BALANCE) (A(40),X(1),F(7,2));
  17            END PROCESS;
```

Fig. 8.16 Main Procedure of Account Updating and Billing Problem

```
18 INPUT:   PROCEDURE (NAMES,AMOUNTS,NUMB);

            /* A PROCEDURE TO READ NAMES AND AMOUNTS INTO TWO
               ARRAYS IN PARALLEL AND COUNT THE NUMBER OF ENTRIES */

            DECLARE
19             NAMES(*) CHARACTER (*),
               AMOUNTS(*) FIXED (7,2),
               NUMB FIXED (5,0); /* NO. OF ENTRIES IN ARRAYS */
            DECLARE
20             NAME CHARACTER (40), /* NAME FROM DATA CARD */
               AMT FIXED (7,2), /* AMOUNT FROM DATA CARDS */
               TYPE CHARACTER (1), /* TYPE OF TRANSACTION */
               FLAG FIXED (5,0); /* END OF TRANSACTIONS FLAG */

21          NAMES = ' ';
22          AMOUNTS = 0.0;
23          FLAG = 0;
24          NUMB = 0;
25          GET EDIT (NAME,TYPE,AMT) (A(40),X(1),A(1),X(3),F(7,2));
26          IF NAME = 'ZZZZ' THEN
27             FLAG = 1;

28 PUTIN:   DO WHILE (FLAG = 0);
29             IF TYPE = 'P' THEN
30                AMT = -AMT;
31             NUMB = NUMB + 1;
32             NAMES(NUMB) = NAME;
33             AMOUNTS(NUMB) = AMT;
34             GET SKIP EDIT (NAME,TYPE,AMT)
                  (A(40),X(1),A(1),X(3),F(7,2));
35             IF NAME = 'ZZZZ' THEN
36                FLAG = 1;
37          END PUTIN;

38          END INPUT;

39 SORT:    PROCEDURE (C,A,N);

            /* A PROCEDURE TO SORT TWO ARRAYS IN PARALLEL */

            DECLARE
40             C(*) CHARACTER(*),
               A(*) FIXED (7,2),
               N FIXED (5,0); /* NO. ELEMENTS IN C AND A */
            DECLARE
41             SORT_FLAG FIXED (5,0),
               K FIXED (5,0); /* POSITION IN ARRAY */

42          SORT_FLAG = 1; /* ASSUME ARRAY IS NOT IN ORDER */

43 SORT:    DO WHILE (SORT_FLAG = 1);
44             SORT_FLAG = 0; /* ASSUME ARRAY IN ORDER */
45             K = 1;
46 NEW_PASS:   DO WHILE (K <= N - 1);
47                IF C(K) > C(K+1) THEN
48 SWAP_THEM:            DO; /* SWAP ELEMENTS AND SET SORT FLAG */
49                          CALL SWAP;
50                          SORT_FLAG = 1;
51                       END SWAP_THEM;
52                K = K + 1;
53             END NEW_PASS;

54          END SORT;

55 SWAP:    PROCEDURE;
            DECLARE
56             TEMPC CHARACTER (40),
               TEMPA FIXED (7,2);
57          TEMPC = C(K);
58          C(K) = C(K+1);
59          C(K+1) = TEMPC;
60          TEMPA = A(K);
61          A(K) = A(K+1);
62          A(K+1) = TEMPA;

63          END SWAP;

64          END SORT;

65          END BILL3;
```

Fig. 8.16 (contd.) Internal Procedures of Account Updating and Billing Problem

8.8 EXERCISES

8.1 (a) Write a procedure with the heading

FACTOR: PROCEDURE (NUMB,SMALL);

The procedure will be given an integer value, NUMB, and will find its smallest prime factor, SMALL. On return NUMB will contain the original number divided by SMALL.

(b) Write a program which uses FACTOR to find all prime factors of any integer number.

8.2 Consider two lists containing names and ID numbers respectively. It is often useful to have these lists ordered by ID number as well as by name.

Assuming ID numbers are stored as character strings, write an internal procedure to do a parallel sort of two 1-D arrays of character strings, so that the first array is sorted in ascending order.

Write a PL/I program to:

i) read an arbitrary number of names and ID numbers (not over 100);
ii) sort them by name;
iii) print both lists;
iv) sort them by ID number;
v) print both lists.

8.3 When any sort is converted to a procedure, it is important that the procedure be able to sort in either ascending or descending order. Write a procedure with the heading

SORT: PROCEDURE (A,N,DIR);

which will bubble sort an array A of N elements which are character strings. The sort will be ascending if DIR = 'A' and descending otherwise.

Note that you must not have two copies of bubble sort code in the procedure -- one is sufficient.

Write a PL/I program to:

i) read an arbitrary number of names and ID numbers (as character strings);
ii) sort them in ascending order by name;
iii) print both lists;
iv) sort them in descending order by ID number;
v) print both lists.

8.4 In Chapter 7 we described the algorithm for a two-way merge. If this algorithm is coded as a procedure then it could be called repeatedly to produce one ordered array from N sorted arrays, by merging them two at a time.

Write a PL/I program which will produce one sorted list from 4 sorted arrays of maximum length 100 each. These arrays should, of course, have a different number of entries in each, and all should have more than 50 entries.

8.5 (a) Consider a character string representing a sentence. Words may be separated from each other by blanks, commas, colons, or semi-colons. The last word may be followed by a period, question mark or exclamation mark.

Write a procedure which will examine any sentence, in parameter SENTENCE, and return the first word, in parameter WORD, together with the remainder of the sentence (in SENTENCE).

(b) In analyzing text to determine the probable author, it is often useful to maintain frequency counts of the words used in the text.

Write a program which reads a sentence of up to 250 characters and then uses the procedure from part (a) to prepare a list of all words occurring in the text and the frequency count for each word.

8.6 (a) Write a procedure to find the location of any specified value in a one-dimensional array of character variables. If the desired value is not found, then this procedure should return location 0.

(b) If we are given two unsorted arrays A and B it is frequently desirable to produce a list of all things which are in A and not in B. For example if A contained W,X,Y,Z and B contained P,Q,X,Y then the list containing W,Z indicates which items are in A but not in B.

Write a procedure with the heading

```
DIFFERENCE: PROCEDURE (A1,N1,A2,N2,A3,N3);
```

which produces a list A3 of length N3 of all the items in A1 (length N1) which are not in A2 (length N2). If there are no items of A which satisfy this condition, N3 should be zero upon return. You may assume all arrays are CHARACTER and should use the procedure from part (a).

(c) Write a PL/I program to verify that all words in a given piece of text are taken from a fixed vocabulary. The program should accept as data the text in question followed by the words which are allowed in the vocabulary. For simplicity, each vocabulary word may be enclosed in quotes. The criterion for which your program is looking will be met if DIFFERENCE returns N3 = 0.

8.7 (a) Write a procedure with the following heading

```
INTERSECTION: PROCEDURE (A1,N1,A2,N2,A3,N3);
```

which produces in A3 (length N3) all the elements in A1 (length N1) which are also in A2 (length N2). If no elements meet this criterion then N3 should be zero upon return. You may employ the procedure of Exercise 8.6(a).

(b) A credit card operation maintains a list of fraudulent or stolen credit card numbers. Each hour it prepares a list of all credit card transactions (numbers and amounts) processed in the previous hour. Write a program which will use INTERSECTION to list and sum all illegal transactions.

(c) The INTERSECTION procedure can be implemented by calling the DIFFERENCE procedure of Exercise 8.6(b) twice. Try the program of part (b) again using this implementation of INTERSECTION. No changes to your main procedure should be required.

8.8 (a) Write a procedure with the heading

```
UNION: PROCEDURE (A1,N1,A2,N2,A3,N3);
```

which produces in A3 (length N3) a list of all the elements in A1 (length N1) or A2 (length N2). However each element may appear only once in A3. For example

A1	A2	A3
A	C	A
B	W	B
C	B	C
		W

You may employ the procedure from Exercise 8.6(a).

(b) Mailing lists are frequently formed by joining two other lists together. Write a PL/I program using UNION which creates one list of names from two separate lists. Of course you would not want the same name to appear twice on the new list.

8.9 Refer to the simple compiler rules given in Exercise 5.9. Now expand the problem to allow any length of variable name (up to 31 characters) and constants with fractional parts, i.e., containing a decimal point.

(a) Write a procedure to examine a character string and return the substring up to but excluding the operators ;, =, +, -, /, or *. It should also return the balance of the submitted character string.

(b) Write a second procedure to analyze the substring returned by the procedure in part (a). If this substring begins with an alphabetic character and all other characters are alphanumeric, then it should return the value 1. If the substring is all numeric except for possibly one period, it should return the value 2. If neither of these conditions is met it should return the value 0.

(c) Write a program using the procedures from (a) and (b) to analyze various PL/I assignment statements for syntactic validity as given by the rules of Exercise 5.9.

Chapter 9 Multi-dimensional Arrays

In Chapter 7, one-dimensional arrays were presented as a means of grouping many variables of the same type into a list. This gave the list a single name and allowed access to an individual item by specifying its position number. Multidimensional arrays are an extension of these ideas. The most useful is the two-dimensional array, which corresponds to the notion of a table.[1]

9.1 CONCEPTS AND FACILITIES

Suppose you owned a small chain of three stores which carried a rather diversified line of stock: shovels, hats, trucks, and statues. You might record your inventory as in the table of Fig. 9.1. This table contains a total of twelve values, arranged in three rows and four columns. Though it may seem silly now, failure to distinguish rows from columns is a common problem with two-dimensional arrays.

Anyway, to learn how many trucks you have in the Park Ave. store, you would look in the row labeled "Park Ave." and the column labeled "trucks" to find the number 24. Equivalently, you could have looked in the second row and third column. The crucial difference between a table and a list, is that you must specify two position numbers (row and column) to access an individual item in a table.

[1]Or equivalently, a "matrix" for the mathematically inclined.

Stock | | Items | | |
|---|---|---|---|---|---|
| | | Shovels | Hats | Trucks | Statues |
| Store Branch | Main St. | 50 | 645 | 19 | 3 |
| | Park Ave. | 30 | 132 | 24 | 1206 |
| | Suburban | 25 | 310 | 15 | 85 |

Fig. 9.1 Example of a Table Containing Values

A two-dimensional array corresponds to the data area of a table (the portion which contains the values, outlined in Fig. 9.1). To create a two-dimensional array named STOCK with three rows and four columns, holding integers, you would write:

```
DECLARE STOCK(3,4) FIXED(5,0);
```

In general, the declaration is:

```
DECLARE <array-name>(r,c) <attributes>;
```

where r is the number of rows and c is the number of columns. As with one-dimensional arrays, all elements of two-dimensional arrays must have identical attributes. For example, you cannot have an "extra" row containing labels, such as 'SHOVELS', 'HATS', etc.

Thus an array element must be referenced by specifying two numbers -- the particular row and particular column, in that order. To access the second row at the third column (to find how many trucks are at Park Ave.), use the subscripted variable name

```
STOCK(2,3)
```

in an appropriate context. For example, to find out if the Park Ave. store contains at least 15 trucks, you might write

```
IF STOCK(2,3) >= 15 THEN ...
```

As with one-dimensional arrays, the row and column numbers need not be explicit integers, but may also be the values of variables or arithmetic expressions. This allows successive uses of the same reference to refer to different elements of the array, by changing the row and/or column number each time. For example, one could add up the total number of hats by summing column 2 (assuming the array contains values):

```
           .
           .
           .
           SUM = 0;
    COL2:  DO ROW = 1 TO 3;
              SUM = SUM + STOCK(ROW,2);
           END COL2;
           .
           .
           .
```

Even this little example indicates the need to distinguish rows from columns. Even though there are four different columns, each one contains only three elements, because three is the number of rows each column traverses. Hence when moving down a column, the column number remains fixed while the row number is moved through its possible range of values.

Similarly, to set a FLAG to 1 if any item in the Main St. store has dropped to 10 or fewer, you would test each of the four items in row 1 as follows:

```
              .
              .
              .
       FLAG = 0;
ROW1:  DO COL = 1 TO 4;
          IF STOCK(1,COL) <= 10 THEN
             FLAG = 1;
       END ROW1;
              .
              .
              .
```

Note that in both the original declaration and all subsequent references, the first number (or 1st dimension) refers to rows while the second number (dimension) refers to columns. This order is so important to remember that we suggest repeating the phrase "row-column" fifty times and memorizing the word ROW1COL (pronounced "roll call").

9.2 ROW-BY-ROW OR COLUMN-BY-COLUMN PROCESSING

When all the elements of a 2-dimensional array are to be processed, you have the choice of organizing your task row-by-row or column-by-column. For example, in Fig. 9.2 we search a 2-dimensional array for the largest value. Suppose the array is created by

```
DECLARE ARY(5,10) FLOAT(6);
```

and that all 50 of its elements contain positive values. Scanning a <u>single row</u>, say row 4 for its largest value could be done as follows:

```
           MAX = 0;
           ROW = 4;
              .
              .
              .
ONE_ROW:   DO COL = 1 TO 10;
              IF ARY(ROW,COL) > MAX THEN
                 MAX = ARY(ROW,COL);
           END ONE_ROW;
              .
              .
              .
```

The complete search for a largest value involves repeating this type of scan <u>for every row</u>, as shown in Fig. 9.2(a). On the other hand, the code in Fig. 9.2(b) accomplishes the same thing by scanning every column. Here the inner loop scans a single column.

```
                  .
                  .
                  .
           MAX = 0;
ALL_ROWS:  DO ROW = 1 TO 5;
ONE_ROW:      DO COL = 1 TO 10;
                 IF ARY(ROW,COL) > MAX THEN
                    MAX = ARY(ROW,COL);
              END ONE_ROW;
           END ALL_ROWS;
                  .
                  .
                  .
```

(a)

```
                  .
                  .
                  .
           MAX = 0;
ALL_COLS:  DO COL = 1 TO 10;
ONE_COL:      DO ROW = 1 TO 5;
                 IF ARY(ROW,COL) > MAX THEN
                    MAX = ARY(ROW,COL);
              END ONE_COL;
           END ALL_COLS;
                  .
                  .
                  .
```

(b)

Fig. 9.2 Two Methods of Finding Largest Value in a Two-Dimensional Array. (a) Row-by-Row Search (b) Column-by-Column Search

Similar alternatives are available for input and output of 2-dimensional arrays as well. However, you must remember that the values come in a particular order from the data cards and that output must be produced line-by-line. The flexibility comes only from your ability to access the array either by rows or by columns.

Consider again the array STOCK but this time before any values have been stored in it (Fig. 9.3(a)). The input code shown in Fig. 9.3(b) stores the values by column. In Fig. 9.3(c) these values are output from STOCK by rows, and in Fig. 9.3(d) by columns.

data card: 11,12,13,14,15,16,17,18,19,20,21,22
array produced by:
DECLARE STOCK(3,4) FIXED(5,0);

STOCK

(a)

```
BYCOL:  DO J = 1 TO 4;
           GET LIST(STOCK(1,J),STOCK(2,J),STOCK(3,J));
        END BYCOL;
```

result:

STOCK

11	14	17	20
12	15	18	21
13	16	19	22

(b)

```
BYROW:  DO K = 1 TO 3;
           PUT SKIP LIST
              (STOCK(K,1),STOCK(K,2),STOCK(K,3),STOCK(K,4));
        END BYROW;
```

result:

```
11    14    17    20

12    15    18    21

13    16    19    22
```

(c)

```
OUTCOL:  DO J = 1 TO 4;
            PUT SKIP LIST(STOCK(1,J),STOCK(2,J),STOCK(3,J));
         END OUTCOL:
```

result:

```
11    12    13

14    15    16

17    18    19

20    21    22
```

(d)

Fig. 9.3 Input-Output of Two-Dimensional Arrays. (a) Data card and empty array; (b) Input by columns; (c) Output by rows; (d) Output by columns.

9.3 ABBREVIATIONS

Since arrays may grow very large, abbreviated forms are possible. The implied DO (Section 7.6.3) may also be used with two-dimensional arrays in input-output lists (and nowhere else). Figure 9.4(a) shows array STOCK being printed row by row with an implied DO used, instead of enumerating each element of row ROW, as was done in Fig. 9.3(c).

However, the implied DO, with its ability to specify only portions of a row (or column), is almost too powerful for this example. Since we are printing an <u>entire</u> row with each PUT statement, this complete row may be abbreviated as:

```
STOCK(ROW,*)
```

The asterisk (*) in the column dimension means "using each column traversed by this row." This form is shown in context in Fig. 9.4(b). This asterisk notation may appear in the first position to denote all rows within a column, and it may be used in other contexts as well. For example, to copy <u>column</u> 4 on top of column 1, you could write:

```
STOCK(*,1) = STOCK(*,4);
```

This is similar to using a one-dimensional-array name all by itself to denote the entire array. In fact, this is a one-dimensional array which comprises an entire column (in this case) of a two-dimensional array. It is also possible to use these and one-dimensional arrays of the same size in the same statement.

It is also possible to supply asterisks in <u>both</u> dimensions to represent the entire array. This may also be done by simply using the array name. In either case the interpretation is row-by-row. Thus either

```
PUT LIST(STOCK(*,*));
```

or

```
PUT LIST(STOCK);
```

would print all 12 values in the same row-by-row order as Fig. 9.4(a) and (b). However, these figures each involve three separate executions of their respective PUT statements and consequently generate three separate lines of code. On the other hand, the examples above generate the same 12 values using <u>one</u> execution of one PUT statement. In order to get the results printed on separate lines, some version of PUT EDIT must be used, as shown in Fig. 9.4(c) and (d).

Note that these abbreviated forms, with * used to denote an entire column, should only be employed when an <u>entire</u> row or column is to be processed. If these forms are used to print or modify a row or column which is only partially filled with values, then erroneous results will occur in the positions which do not contain values.

```
BYROW:  DO ROW = 1 TO 3;
           PUT SKIP LIST((STOCK(ROW,COL) DO COL = 1 TO 4));
        END BYROW;
```

(a) Use of Implied DO

```
BYROE:  DO ROW = 1 TO 3;
           PUT SKIP LIST(STOCK(ROW,*));
        END BYROE;
```

(b) Use of *-notation to mean "all columns" within the row (entire row)

```
PUT SKIP EDIT(STOCK(*,*)) (4 F(10),SKIP,4 F(10),
                           SKIP,4 F(10));
```

(c) Use of double*-notation to mean "entire array, row-by-row"

```
PUT EDIT(STOCK) (SKIP,4 F(10));
```

(d) Use of array name, to mean "entire array row-by-row"

Fig. 9.4 Some Abbreviated Forms for Printing Each Row of STOCK on Separate Line

9.4 A SAMPLE PROBLEM

Many of these features of two-dimensional arrays, plus some additional input-output considerations, will be illustrated in the solution of the following problem:

Problem: Given the names and four individual exam marks for several students in a class, compute the average mark for each student and the average achieved by the class on each exam. Then produce a report showing all this information.

Solution: One possible algorithm which parallels the problem statement is:

1. read the names and individual marks;
2. compute student averages;
3. compute exam averages;
4. print report;
5. end.

This algorithm requires all the data to remain in main memory from Step 1 until Step 4; but, this is possible if the class size is not "too large" and there are only 4 exams. We will assume that the class contains no more than 60 students which makes retaining all the marks in arrays quite feasible. Thus we will use this algorithm and some sort of array representation for the data.

Since computing averages is quite simple, the major considerations in this problem involve the input, storage, and output of this information. The most crucial decision is the appearance of the report.

The general organization shown in Fig. 9.5(a) seems reasonable.

Once this sample report has been sketched, an internal representation of the data is strongly suggested and is shown in Fig. 9.5(b). It consists of two arrays, since there are two types of information involved. The items in the array of NAMES correspond to entire rows of the array of MARKS. Note that MARKS contains an "extra" fifth column for the student averages and that both arrays must contain enough space (rows) for the maximum number of students.

This is not the only possible data organization, but it is appealing because of its resemblance to the desired report. Whatever organization you finally decide upon, we strongly encourage that you start by drawing a picture (like Fig. 9.5) whenever you have an array problem. If the picture seems correct and adequate, then stick to it and refer to it at every stage of code development.

NAME	EXAM1	EXAM2	EXAM3	EXAM4	AVG.
JOHN DOE	35	75	60	30	50.00
SUE SOO	45	48	52	59	51.00
--	--	--	--	--	--
--	--	--	--	--	--
GUY FINAL	85	80	70	65	75.00
AVERAGE	--	--	--	--	

(a)

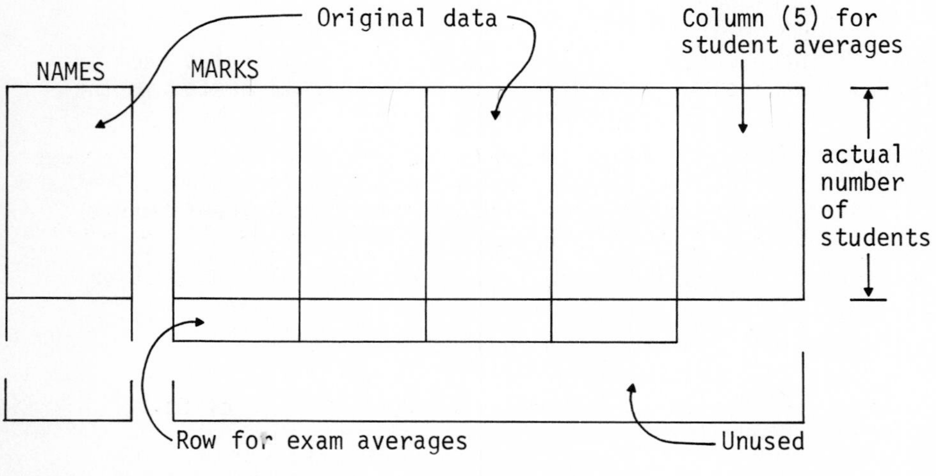

(b)

Fig. 9.5 Generation of Report from Two Arrays

In our case, the names can be limited to 20 characters, and since there are at most 60 students, we have the following declaration:

```
DECLARE NAMES(60) CHARACTER(20),
        MARKS(61,5) FLOAT(6);
```

We decided to use FLOAT because of the need for division when computing averages.

Having agreed on our array structure, we can now concentrate on individual steps of the algorithm. Suppose that data cards each have the following format:

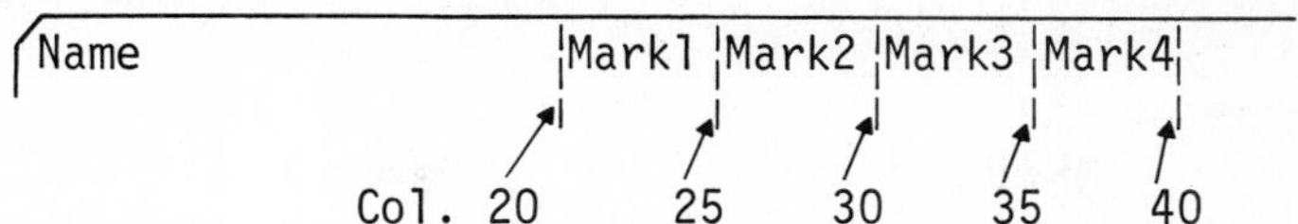

The input process (Step 1) also involves maintaining a count of the number of students, which leads to this refinement:

```
1.1     set count = 0;
1.2     get name and marks for 1st student;
1.3     repeat while data remains;
1.3.1      update count;
1.3.2      get name and marks for next student;
```

The count always equals the number of rows which have been filled or, equivalently, one less than the row number which is about to be filled. This observation leads to the code in Fig. 9.6 for reading the values into the arrays. The two GET EDIT statements are equivalent; except that SKIP is used in the second to ensure that it will begin with a new card. During the input process, the actual number of students, #STDNTS, is determined.

```
          /* FIGURE 9.6 */

        #STDNTS = 0;
        FLAG = 0;
        ON ENDFILE (SYSIN) FLAG = 1;
        NEW = #STDNTS + 1;
        GET EDIT (NAMES(NEW),(MARKS(NEW,XAM)
            DO XAM = 1 TO 4)) (A(20),4 F(5));

INPT:   DO WHILE (FLAG = 0);
            #STDNTS = #STDNTS + 1;
            NEW = #STDNTS + 1;
            GET SKIP EDIT (NAMES(NEW),MARKS(NEW,1),
                MARKS(NEW,2),MARKS(NEW,3),MARKS(NEW,4))
                (A(20),F(5),F(5),F(5),F(5));
        END INPT;
```

Figure 9.6

The computation of a <u>single</u> row average (part of Step 2) can be done as follows for row ROW:

```
                 SUM = 0;
        SUMROW:  DO XAM = 1 TO 4;
                    SUM = SUM + MARKS(ROW,XAM);
                 END SUMROW;
                 MARKS(ROW,5) = SUM / 4;
```

Of course, this same computation is repeated for each row by placing it inside another DO loop which varies the value of ROW from 1 to #STDNTS. Step 3, finding exam averages, is similar but involves averaging each of the four columns instead of rows. The complete program is shown in Fig. 9.7.

```
              /* FIGURE 9.7 */
GRADES:  PROCEDURE OPTIONS (MAIN);

         /* A PROGRAM TO COMPUTE THE INDIVIDUAL AND EXAM
            AVERAGES FOR UP TO 60 STUDENTS EACH WRITING
            FOUR EXAMS. */

         DECLARE
            NAMES(60) CHARACTER (20), /* STUDENT NAMES */
            MARKS(61,5) FLOAT (6), /* STUDENT MARKS */
            SUM FLOAT (6), /* MARK ACCUMULATOR */
            (#STDNTS,FLAG,NEW,XAM,ROW,COL) FIXED (5,0);

         /* INPUT STUDENT MARKS AND NAMES,
            MAINTAINING COUNT OF STUDENTS */

         #STDNTS = 0;
         FLAG = 0;
         ON ENDFILE (SYSIN) FLAG = 1;
         NEW = #STDNTS + 1;
         GET EDIT (NAMES(NEW),(MARKS(NEW,XAM)
            DO XAM = 1 TO 4)) (A(20),4 F(5));

INPT:    DO WHILE (FLAG = 0);
            #STDNTS = #STDNTS + 1;
            NEW = #STDNTS + 1;
            GET SKIP EDIT (NAMES(NEW),MARKS(NEW,1),
               MARKS(NEW,2),MARKS(NEW,3),MARKS(NEW,4))
               (A(20),F(5),F(5),F(5),F(5));
         END INPT;

         /* FOR EACH STUDENT COMPUTE (ROW) AVERAGE */

ROWAVG:  DO ROW = 1 TO #STDNTS;
            SUM = 0;

SUMROW:     DO XAM = 1 TO 4;
               SUM = SUM + MARKS(ROW,XAM);
            END SUMROW;

            MARKS(ROW,5) = SUM / 4;
         END ROWAVG;

         /* FOR EACH EXAM COMPUTE THE (COLUMN) AVERAGE */

COLAVG:  DO XAM = 1 TO 4;
            SUM = 0;

SUMCOL:     DO ROW = 1 TO #STDNTS;
               SUM = SUM + MARKS(ROW,XAM);
            END SUMCOL;

            MARKS(#STDNTS + 1,XAM) = SUM / #STDNTS;
         END COLAVG;

         /* PRINT OUT THE REPORT */

         PUT PAGE EDIT ('NAMES','EXAM1','EXAM2','EXAM3',
            'EXAM4','AVG') (X(7),A(13),4 A(7),A(3));
         PUT SKIP(2);

SHOWSTDNTS:
         DO ROW = 1 TO #STDNTS;
            PUT SKIP EDIT (NAMES(ROW),(MARKS(ROW,COL)
            DO COL = 1 TO 5)) (A(20),F(5),3 F(7),F(9,2));
         END SHOWSTDNTS;

         PUT SKIP(2) EDIT ('AVERAGE',(MARKS(#STDNTS+1,XAM)
            DO XAM = 1 TO 4)) (X(4),A(16),F(5),3 F(7));

         END GRADES;
```

Figure 9.7

9.4.1 Some Special Output Considerations

The only remaining aspect of Fig. 9.7 is the printing of the report. Although it would be possible to print the entire report using a single PUT EDIT statement with an intricate format list, a good general rule is to print no more than one line with any one PUT statement. Referring back to Fig. 9.5(b), we see that our report contains three different kinds of lines and thus should require three different PUT statements: (i) one for the column headings, (ii) another (repeated) for each student, and (iii) one for the exam averages.

The first line contains only column headings and could be generated by the statement:

```
PUT PAGE EDIT('NAMES','EXAM1','EXAM2','EXAM3','EXAM4','AVG')
            (X(7),A(13),5A(7));
```

Of more interest, however, is the PUT statement for a typical student (row). For row ROW, this might be either:

```
PUT SKIP EDIT(NAMES(ROW),(MARKS(ROW,COL) DO COL = 1 TO 5))
            (A(20),F(5),F(7),F(7),F(7),F(9,2));
```

or

```
PUT SKIP EDIT(NAMES(ROW),MARKS(ROW,*))
            (A(20),F(5),3 F(7),F(9,2));
```

In the second alternative, the * notation is possible since an <u>entire</u> row of MARKS is being printed. However, this still represents <u>five</u> different numeric variables and therefore requires five F format codes. Don't forget that this PUT statement is executed once for each value of ROW, running from 1 to #STDNTS.

The last type of PUT statement produces the last line of the report containing the character string 'AVERAGE' followed by four exam averages. Since the entire row of MARKS is not being printed, the * notation cannot be employed.

Just to illustrate another format mechanism, suppose that for a class of only a few students a second report was to look like this:

```
NAME          JOHN DOE          SUE SOO          . . . .
EXAM1            35               45
EXAM2            75               48
EXAM3            60               52
EXAM4            30               59
AVG              50               51
```

Using the same arrays as in Fig. 9.5(b), the PUT statement to print a typical line for <u>one</u> EXAM might be:

```
PUT SKIP EDIT('EXAM',COL,(MARKS(ROW,COL) DO ROW = 1 TO #STDNTS))
            (A(4),F(1),(#STDNTS) F(12));
```

Here each line of output corresponds to a particular <u>column</u> of MARKS. The variable COL contains the column number and supplies the integer appearing after the characters EXAM in each line of output. The variable #STDNTS contains the number of occupied rows in MARKS, or, in other words, the number of items stored in each column. Note that a variable enclosed in parentheses, #STDNTS in this case, may be used to indicate how many times to repeat a format item. Any parenthesized integer expression is permissible in this context.

9.5 ANOTHER ARRAY PROBLEM (USING PROCEDURES)

The following problem can be solved using a 2-dimensional array in a much different way than we have seen before. The emphasis here is on scanning and rearranging the array rather than on input/output. Each type of manipulation may be conveniently isolated as a procedure. This is usually the case with mathematical array processing.

The problem is to find a logically consistent sequence of activities which will culminate in leaving the house in the morning. The activities of interest are: getting dressed, actually leaving, getting out of bed, combing your hair (if any), brushing your teeth (if any), and showering. These events clearly should not take place in the order listed. Our task is to find some order which will "work."

What makes some orders "acceptable" is that certain events, like getting up, are supposed to precede others, like showering. Other pairs of events may occur in either order, such as showering and brushing teeth. The "input" to our algorithm will be the specification of certain pairs of events which have a necessary ordering. Sufficient pairs will be specified to imply all other orderings. For instance, the input may indicate that you must rise before you shower and that you must shower before you dress. These requirements imply that you also must rise before you dress. The "solution," if one exists, will be an overall ordering in which each individual pair observes a prescribed ordering if it has one.[2]

Just where arrays come in may be seen in Fig. 9.8(a). This figure shows a 2-dimensional array with one row and one corresponding column for each "event," i.e., the number of rows and columns are the same, and the kth row represents the same event as the kth column. This array depicts the specified necessary ordering among certain pairs of events. There is a 1 in the kth <u>row</u> and jth <u>column</u> to indicate that the kth event <u>must precede</u> the jth event. All other entries are 0.[3] Note the 1 in row 3 (rise) and column 6 (shower) to show that you must be out of bed before you shower. Conversely, row 6 and column 3 contains a 0, to indicate that you need not shower in order to get up. Of course you must get up before you can leave, but row 3 and column 2 need not be set to 1, since other intervening events must occur which will necessitate rising before leaving.

---

[2]In graph theory or operations research this problem is to order the vertices of a directed graph, so that all directed edges are oriented the same way. The ability to do this also demonstrates the absence of directed cycles in the graph.

[3]In graph theory, this array is called the "adjacency matrix."

	Dress	Leave	Rise	Hair	Teeth	Shower
Dress	0	1	0	0	0	0
Leave	0	0	0	0	0	0
Rise	0	0	0	1	1	1
Hair	0	1	0	0	0	0
Teeth	0	1	0	0	0	0
Shower	1	0	0	1	0	0

Fig. 9.8(a) Original Specification of a Sufficient Set of Necessary Orderings

If you scan the column for "rise" in Fig. 9.8(a), you will see that every entry is 0. This indicates that none of the other events has to precede getting out of bed. For this reason, getting up is called a source, since it may be the starting point of the remaining activities. Since it is the only "source" in our example, we select it as the first event.

Having done this, we have fulfilled an immediate prerequisite for three other events: hair, teeth, and shower, as can be seen from the three 1's in the row labeled "rise." In fact, you would now be free to either shower or brush your teeth, since these two events have only this one prerequisite (unlike combing hair). This can be seen in Fig. 9.8(b), in which the row and column representing "rise" have been interchanged with "dress" to become the first row and column (while "dress" has become the third). The "remaining" part of the array represents the remaining events and is outlined in Fig. 9.8(b). Within this part of the array, "teeth" and "shower" are both all-0 columns and therefore "sources" with respect to remaining events.

Selected as first event

	Rise	Leave	Dress	Hair	Teeth	Shower
Rise	0	0	0	1	1	1
Leave	0	0	0	0	0	0
Dress	0	1	0	0	0	0
Hair	0	1	0	0	0	0
Teeth	0	1	0	0	0	0
Shower	0	0	1	1	0	0

Remaining events

Fig. 9.8(b) First and Third Rows and Columns Interchanged After Selection of "Rise" as First Event

After choosing "teeth" as the second event, and moving its row and column into position, the array appears as in Fig. 9.8(c). Note that "leaving," which formerly occupied position 2, is now represented by the fifth row and column.

Selected as Second Event

	Rise	Teeth	Dress	Hair	Leave	Shower
Rise	0	1	0	1	0	1
Teeth	0	0	0	0	1	0
Dress	0	0	0	0	1	0
Hair	0	0	0	0	1	0
Leave	0	0	0	0	0	0
Shower	0	0	1	1	0	0

Remaining events

Fig. 9.8(c) Second and Fifth Rows and Columns Interchanged after Selection of "Teeth" as Second Event.

Another source (shower) would then be found among the remaining activities. This process of finding sources and interchanging rows and columns is repeated until only one activity remains (leaving). By this time the rows and columns have been moved around (with their labels) to look like Fig. 9.8(d). From this figure, we can read off the "logical" order of events as: rise, brush teeth, shower, comb hair, dress, and leave. Notice that all the 1's in this array are above the diagonal line. This can only happen if all 1 entries have smaller row numbers than column numbers. Of course, this means that every pair of events, where ordering matters, is in the prescribed order.

	Rise	Teeth	Shower	Hair	Dress	Leave
Rise	0	1	1	1	0	0
Teeth	0	0	0	0	0	1
Shower	0	0	0	1	1	0
Hair	0	0	0	0	0	1
Dress	0	0	0	0	0	1
Leave	0	0	0	0	0	0

Fig. 9.8(d) Final (Consistent) Ordering

Incidentally, failure to find a "consistent" ordering means that the original events contained some situation in which one event was waiting for another, which in turn was waiting for the first and would therefore never get done. A less artificial example of the same problem is to plan a large construction project in which possibly hundreds of interrelated processes must be sorted out and scheduled in a consistent way (e.g., so the foundation precedes the windows). The algorithm for this problem should now be clear:

```
1.      read the event names and determine number of events (n);
2.      read the array of necessary orderings among event pairs;
3.      repeat n-1 times while still successful;
3.1        find a source among the remaining events;
3.2        if successful then
3.2.1         make that source prior to the remaining events
                 and no longer a "remaining" event;
3.3        otherwise
              report failure;
4.      end.
```

Step 3.2.1 could be elaborated on to describe how an event becomes "prior" to others:

```
3.2.1.1   interchange this "source" with the first of the
             remaining events;
3.2.1.2   redefine "remaining" to now exclude this one;
```

Assuming the existence of procedures to (i) find a source and (ii) interchange the first row and column of a "subarray" with a selected row and column, respectively, it is already possible to code this main procedure (Fig. 9.9a).

Note the following about this procedure. The arrays are declared large enough to handle 10 events. However, in case the number of events is smaller than 10, as in our example, the event names are obtained one at a time in a loop which can determine their number, N. This value of N determines both the number of rows and number of columns of ARY which will be used. Hence N appears in both the iterated DO statement, which controls the row number, and in the implied DO, which controls column numbers in the GET statement.

The DO loop labeled SELECT combines the iteration feature and the WHILE clause. In order for repetitions of the loop to continue, both the value of the loop index and the WHILE condition must be acceptable. The index is adjusted and tested before the WHILE condition is tested.

Both internal procedures are given the same arguments: the array, its size, the FIRST of the remaining elements, and the variable SELECTED. FIND_SOURCE returns its result in SELECTED, which is either 0 if no source was found or else the row and column number of the newly found source. The procedure SWITCH is later told the position of this source, which is still recorded in SELECTED. SWITCH proceeds to interchange those rows and columns of ARY indicated by FIRST and SELECTED.

Both of the internal procedures are shown in the complete program of Fig. 9.9. Note that when multidimensional arrays are passed as parameters, the internal procedure declares the array with the number of the dimensions indicated by the number of asterisks.

```
              /* FIGURE 9.9 */
SCHEDUL:
        PROCEDURE OPTIONS (MAIN);

        /* A PROGRAM TO ORDER CERTAIN EVENTS ACCORDING TO
           A SET OF CONSTRAINTS. */

        DECLARE
           ARY(10,10) FIXED (5,0), /* ADJACENCY MATRIX */
           EVENTS(10) CHARACTER (10), /* EVENT NAMES */
           TEMP CHARACTER(10), /* NAME OF "SOURCE" */
           (FLAG,SUCCESS,FIRST,SELECTED,K,J,N) FIXED (5,0);

        /* READ THE NUMBER OF EVENTS, N */

        GET LIST (N);

        /* NOW READ THE N EVENT NAMES */

        GET LIST ((EVENTS(K) DO K = 1 TO N));

        /* READ N ROWS AND COLUMNS OF CONSTRAINTS,
           ROW MAJOR ORDER */

GETORDER:
        DO K = 1 TO N;
           GET LIST ((ARY(K,J) DO J = 1 TO N));
        END GETORDER;

        SUCCESS = 0;

        /* BEGIN SUCCESSIVE SEARCHES FOR SOURCES
           AND REORDER. */

SELECT: DO FIRST = 1 TO (N - 1) WHILE (SUCCESS = 0);
           CALL FIND_SOURCE(ARY,N,FIRST,SELECTED);
           IF SELECTED ¬= 0 THEN

EXCHANGE:     DO;
                 TEMP = EVENTS(FIRST);
                 EVENTS(FIRST) = EVENTS(SELECTED);
                 EVENTS(SELECTED) = TEMP;
                 CALL SWITCH(ARY,N,FIRST,SELECTED);
              END EXCHANGE;

           ELSE
              SUCCESS = 1;
        END SELECT;

LIST_ORDER:
        DO K = 1 TO N;
           PUT SKIP DATA (EVENTS(K));
        END LIST_ORDER;
```

Figure 9.9(a)

```
FIND_SOURCE:
        PROCEDURE (ARY,SIZE,FIRST,SELECTED);
        DECLARE
           ARY(*,*) FIXED (5,0),
           (FIRST,SIZE,SELECTED) FIXED (5,0);
        DECLARE (ROW,COL,COL_SUM) FIXED (5,0);
        SELECTED = 0;
        COL = FIRST;

NEXT_COL:
        DO WHILE (SELECTED = 0 & COL <= SIZE);
           COL_SUM = 0;

COL_SCAN:  DO ROW = FIRST TO SIZE;
              COL_SUM = COL_SUM + ARY(ROW,COL);
           END COL_SCAN;

           IF COL_SUM = 0 THEN
              SELECTED = COL;
           COL = COL + 1;
        END NEXT_COL;

        END FIND_SOURCE;



SWITCH: PROCEDURE (ARY,SIZE,FIRST,SELECTED);
        DECLARE
           ARY(*,*) FIXED (5,0),
           (FIRST,SIZE,SELECTED) FIXED (5,0);
        DECLARE (ROW,COL,TEMP) FIXED (5,0);

        /* INTERCHANGE ENTIRE COLUMNS NUMBERED
           FIRST AND SELECTED */

COLEXCH:
        DO ROW = 1 TO SIZE;
           TEMP = ARY(ROW,FIRST);
           ARY(ROW,FIRST) = ARY(ROW,SELECTED);
           ARY(ROW,SELECTED) = TEMP;
        END COLEXCH;

        /* NOW INTERCHANGE THE CORRESPONDING ROWS */

ROWEXCH:
        DO COL = 1 TO SIZE;
           TEMP = ARY(FIRST,COL);
           ARY(FIRST,COL) = ARY(SELECTED,COL);
           ARY(SELECTED,COL) = TEMP;
        END ROWEXCH;

        END SWITCH;

        END SCHEDUL;
```

Figure 9.9(b)

9.6 ARRAYS OF MORE THAN TWO DIMENSIONS

Arrays may be declared with as many as 31 dimensions. This means that references to their items may specify more than two position numbers or "subscripts." These arrays are obvious extensions of one- and two-dimensional arrays and behave similarly in all respects. For example, "cross-sections" of these arrays may be specified by using the * notation in one or more of the dimensions. When * notation or merely the array name is used, the (unspecified) indices on the right are assumed to cycle through their values fastest (corresponding to the row-by-row convention for 2-dimensional arrays).

9.7 REVIEW OF RULES

1. Declaration of Two-dimensional Arrays

   Every two-dimensional array must be declared by either

   i) DECLARE <array-name> (r,c) <attributes>;

      where r specified the number of rows
      and c specifies the number of columns
      r and c must be integer constants > 0.

or

   ii) DECLARE <array-name> (L_1:H_1,L_2:H_2) <attributes>;

      where L_i specifies the lower bound of dimension i
      and H_i specifies the upper bound of dimension i,

   e.g., the following declarations are equivalent:

```
DECLARE ARY(5,10) FLOAT(6);
DECLARE ARY(1:5,1:10) FLOAT(6);
```

2. Elements of a Two-dimensional Array are referenced by

   <array-name> (r,c)

   where r and c may be:

   i) integer constants

   ii) integer variables

   iii) integer valued expressions

3. Asterisk Notation

   Every element in a row may be referenced by

   <array-name> (r,*)

   for instance,

   X(1,*) = 0;

   sets every element in the first row of X to zero. Every element in a column may be referenced by:

   <array-name> (*,c)

for instance,

```
X(*,2) = X(*,2) + 1;
```

adds 1 to every element in the second column of x.
array may be referenced by

<array-name>

for instance,

```
GET LIST (X);
```

When an entire array is referenced by merely mentioning its name, the elements are accessed row-by-row.

4. Two-dimensional Arrays as Parameters

If a parameter of a procedure represents a two-dimensional array, then the parameter must be declared as

```
DECLARE <parameter-name> (*,*) <attributes>;
```

5. HBOUND and LBOUND

The upper and lower bounds of the kth dimension of a multi-dimensional array may be ascertained by HBOUND (<array-name>, K) and LBOUND (<array-name>,K), respectively.

9.8 EXERCISES

9.1 The set of marks for a certain course consisting of up to 50 data cards in the following format:

col.	1-15	surname
	19-20	initials
	25-39	five integer marks in fields of 3 columns each.

The marks represent scores on each of five tests and all tests are scored out of 100. To reduce these marks to a total of 100, the first card in the deck contains the weights for each exam. Thus if it read 0.2, 0.15, 0.1, 0.2, 0.35 then exam 1 would be worth 20%, exam 2 worth 15%, etc.

Design an algorithm to read these marks, weight them and print a report in alphabetical order in the following format:

```
           RAW SCORES        ACTUAL SCORES      TERM
NAME      1  2  3  4  5      1  2  3  4  5      MARK
```

where TERM MARK is the sum of the actual scores for each of the five exams.

9.2 When sorting two-dimensional arrays, it can become very expensive to move around entire rows of elements. One way to circumvent this problem is to store the indices of each row in a one-dimensional array. Then when a change is detected in the 2-D array, you merely swap the indices in the corresponding 1-D array. After the sort has been completed, the contents of the 1-D array will represent the sorted order of the row subscripts of the 2-D array.

Design an algorithm to perform the bubble sort on a 2-D array using this technique, and implement your algorithm by computer program. Be sure to print the sorted version of the 2-D array.

9.3 It is possible to place a knight on any square of a chess board and in 63 moves have him visit each of the remaining squares once and only once. This process is known as the Knight's Tour.

The design of an algorithm for such a process can be most efficiently done as follows.

> For any square x on the board let $P_i(x)$, i=1,2,... be the number of squares he can visit from x in i moves (excluding squares he has already visited). Then always move to the square x for which $P_1(x)$ is smallest. If more than one square has a "smallest" $P_1(x)$ then choose x for which $P_2(x)$ is smallest.

This technique has always been known to work for the standard 8×8 chess board. Implement your algorithm by a PL/I program.

9.4 It is possible to place eight queens on a standard chess board in such a way that they do not interfere with each other, i.e., no two are on the same column, row or diagonal.

Describe an algorithm which will accept as input one starting square for the first queen and will then place the seven others on the board. Note that if a square has co-ordinates (i,j) then the co-ordinates of all other squares on the right diagonal thru (i,j) sum to i+j. Similarly the absolute value of the difference of the co-ordinates for all squares on the left diagonal thru (i,j) is $|i-j|$.

Implement your algorithm by a PL/I program.

9.5 Recall from linear algebra that if matrix A is k×m and matrix B is m×n then the product AB is a k×n matrix where each element AB(i,j) is given by

$$AB(i,j) = \sum_{c=1}^{m} A(i,c)*B(c,j)$$

Design an algorithm to perform matrix multiplication and implement your algorithm by a PL/I program.

9.6 The operations of addition and multiplication in Boolean algebra are defined as:

a	b	a+b	a×b
0	0	0	0
0	1	1	0
1	0	1	0
1	1	1	1

In this system only the values 0 and 1 are used. Boolean multiplication is the same as ordinary multiplication. Boolean addition can be simulated by first doing ordinary additions and then changing any non-zero value to 1.

(a) Modify the algorithm of Exercise 9.5 so that it finds the product (in Boolean algebra) of two n×n matrices whose entries are 0's and 1's.

(b) The problem of ordering events described in Section 9.5 used only a sufficient number of necessary orderings to imply all the other ordering constraints. These orderings were represented by 1 entries in a Boolean matrix which we shall call P. We can derive explicit representations of <u>all</u> the implied orderings by computing (in Boolean algebra)

$$C = P+P^2+P^3+...+P^{n-1}$$

where n is the number of events. If event i must precede event j, then C(i,j) will be 1.

Write a program to compute C, given an initial matrix P of sufficient constraints.

Hints: i) $P^k = P \times P^{k-1}$

ii) If the 1 entries of P^k are all included among the 1 entries of $P+P^2+...+P^{k-1}$, then further calculations will add no new ordering relationships (1 entries).

9.7 The solution of a system of linear equations $A\underline{x}=\underline{b}$ can be done by a technique known as Gaussian elimination.

If A is an N×N matrix and $\underline{b}$ is a vector of length N then A and $\underline{b}$ can be stored in an $N\times(\overline{N}+1)$ array. The fundamental algorithm for Gaussian elimination is the following, where j is the row index, k the column index, and i is a "moving" column index:

```
1.        set k to 1;
2.        repeat while k < N;
2.1          set j to k+1;
2.2          repeat while j ≤ N;
2.2.1           set m to A(j,k) ÷ A(k,k);
2.2.2           set i to k;
2.2.3           repeat while i ≤ N+1;
2.2.3.1            set A(j,i) to A(j,i) - m×A(k,i);
2.2.3.2            add 1 to i;
2.2.4           add 1 to j;
2.3          add 1 to k;
3.        end.
```

Describe an algorithm to perform Gaussian elimination and then implement your algorithm by a PL/I program. The output should reveal that every array element below the main diagonal is zero.

9.8 The Gaussian elimination approach described in Exercise 9.7 can be enhanced by using "partial pivoting." This technique helps avoid some nasty arithmetic problems which are beyond the scope of this book. Simply stated, partial pivoting involves finding the row (j) which contains the largest absolute value in column k, and then exchanging row j and row k. In algorithmic form this is:

```
1.     set pos to k;
2.     set j to k+1;
3.     repeat while j ≤ N;
3.1       if |A(j,k)| > |A(pos,k)| then
             set pos to j;
3.2       add 1 to j;
4.     interchange row k and row pos;
```

This should be incorporated into the algorithm of Exercise 9 between Steps 2 and 2.1.

Implement Gaussian elimination with partial pivoting by a PL/I program.

9.9 On completion of Gaussian elimination we are in a position to find the values for $\underline{x}$ which satisfy $A\underline{x}=\underline{b}$. Since the matrix A is in upper triangular form, we can immediately find the value of x_n as A(n,n+1)/A(n,n). The other values of $\underline{x}$ can be found readily by back substitution:

$$x_j = [A(j,n+1) - \sum_{k=j+1}^{N} A(j,k)*x_k] \div A(j,j)$$

Note that if A(j,j) = 0 for any 1 ≤ j ≤ N then the system is singular.

Write a program to solve a system of linear equations using Gaussian elimination with partial pivoting and then finding the values for $\underline{x}$ by back substitution.

Chapter 10
Structures

In data processing one does not normally deal with data which is made up entirely of only numbers or only characters. In a payroll, for instance, one deals with a name, an identification number, a rate of pay, etc., and it is convenient to refer to this collection of related items by one name. However, these items cannot be stored in an array, because every item in an array must have the same attributes. Hence we need a new storage class for grouping together different types of data, which PL/I calls structures.

10.1 STRUCTURES AND THEIR DECLARATIONS

Considering a simple payroll we might need to use the following variables:

```
NAME    CHARACTER(20)
ID_NO   FIXED(7,0)
GROSS_PAY  FIXED(5,2)
NET_PAY    FIXED(5,2)
```

Internally each would be assigned a separate storage location. However, life would be much simpler if we could group these items together under one name, EMPLOYEE_RECORD, as shown in Fig. 10.1.

In this figure we have EMPLOYEE_RECORD at the outer level and the actual variables at the inner level, and it is only at this inner level that values can actually be stored. Fig. 10.2 gives an alternate representation of this hierarchical arrangement. Such diagrams are called "trees" because of their resemblance to trees in nature, except that the "root" is on top and the "leaves" are on the bottom.

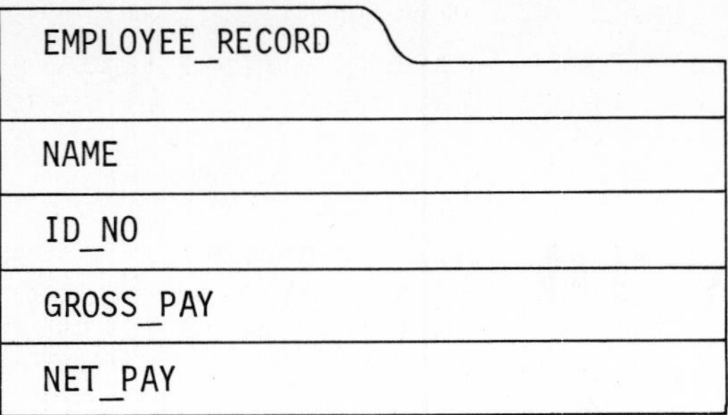

Fig. 10.1 Grouping Variables Together

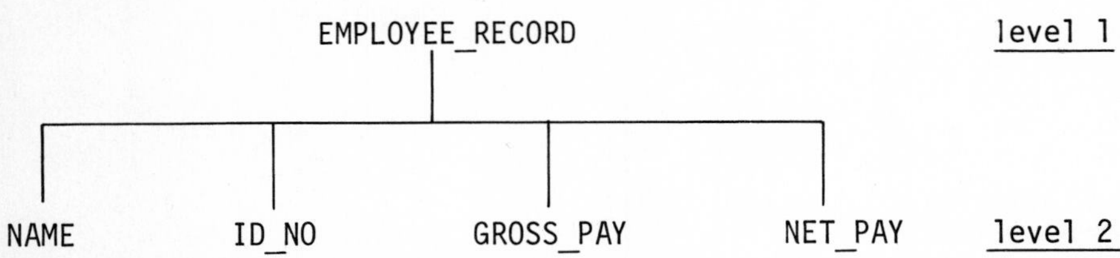

Fig. 10.2 Tree Structure of Fig. 10.1

The root (top) of such a tree is designated as level 1, and succeeding layers have higher level numbers. In Fig. 10.2, EMPLOYEE_RECORD is at level 1 and the actual variables are all at level 2.

This type of data organization in PL/I is described by the statement:

```
DECLARE 1 EMPLOYEE_RECORD,
          2 NAME CHARACTER(20),
          2 ID_NO FIXED(7,0),
          2 GROSS_PAY FIXED(5,2),
          2 NET_PAY FIXED(5,2);
```

This statement makes EMPLOYEE_RECORD the name of the entire structure as identified by the number 1 after DECLARE. Notice that a level 1 identifier does not have an attribute because it is not itself a variable but rather the name of a group of different kinds of variables. The level 2 identifiers (in this example) do have attributes because they are actual storage locations. The "leaves" of the tree (level 2 identifiers in this example) are called elementary items. In any structure, only the elementary items may contain values!

A reference to an elementary item should include the structure name[1] as well as the name of the item itself. These names are separated by periods. For example,

---

[1]The full referencing conventions are explained later in this section.

EMPLOYEE_RECORD.NAME

refers to the elementary item NAME within the structure EMPLOYEE_RECORD. Since an elementary item is a memory location, it can be used in any context where that type of variable is appropriate. For example,

```
EMPLOYEE_RECORD.NAME = 'WITHERSPOON,J.' ;
```

In a payroll system it is usually necessary to compute several deductions in order to arrive at the net pay. The structure of a typical set of deductions is shown in Fig. 10.3(b) and might be described by the PL/I structure:

```
DECLARE
   1 DEDUCTIONS,
      2 FED_TAX FIXED(5,2),
      2 STATE_TAX FIXED(5,2),
      2 SOC_SEC FIXED(5,2),
      2 OTHER FIXED(5,2),
      2 TOTAL FIXED(5,2);
```

Usually, however, the information of Fig. 10.3(a) and 10.3(b), pertaining to one employee, would be gathered together to form a single composite structure, such as that shown in Fig. 10.3(c). Notice that Fig. 10.3(a) has four elementary items, Fig. 10.3(b) has five elementary items, and Fig. 10.3(c), which combines them both, has nine elementary items. DEDUCTIONS is not an elementary item even though it appears at the second level, because there are items at the third level descending from it. Fig. 10.4 shows a possible structure declaration for Fig. 10.3(c).

When a structure, such as this EMPLOYEE_RECORD, contains subgroups of elementary items, such as DEDUCTIONS, the outermost (level 1) structure is called a <u>major structure</u> and all interior substructures are called <u>minor structures</u>.[2]

We can reference an elementary item by including every level name on the path between the root and the item, inclusive. For example to reference the item FED_TAX, we could write:

```
EMPLOYEE_RECORD.DEDUCTIONS.FED_TAX
```

When every level is mentioned, the reference is said to be <u>fully qualified</u>. We recommend that fully qualified names be used until you become very familiar with using structures.

However, as the above example shows, fully qualified references can become uncomfortably long. Consequently, any of the following abbreviated references <u>may</u> be valid:

(i) EMPLOYEE_RECORD.FED_TAX

(ii) DEDUCTIONS.FED_TAX

(iii) FED_TAX

---

[2]Since DEDUCTIONS is a minor structure, its level number (in this case 2) must be larger than the level number of EMPLOYEE_RECORD. Similarly any minor structure or elementary item contained within DEDUCTIONS must have a higher level number than that given DEDUCTIONS.

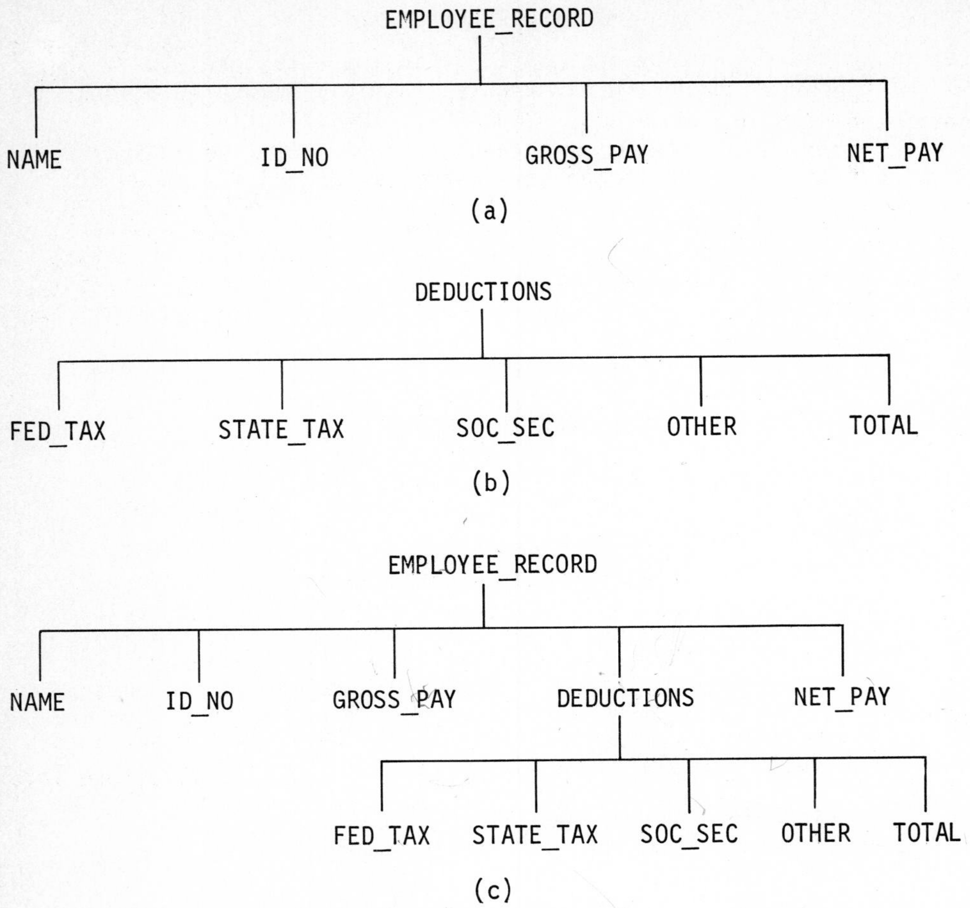

Fig. 10.3 Development of a Complete Payroll Record

```
DECLARE
   1 EMPLOYEE_RECORD,
      2 NAME CHARACTER(20),
      2 ID_NO FIXED(7,0),
      2 GROSS_PAY FIXED(5,2),
      2 DEDUCTIONS,
         3 FED_TAX FIXED(5,2),
         3 STATE_TAX FIXED(5,2),
         3 SOC_SEC FIXED(5,2),
         3 OTHER FIXED(5,2),
         3 TOTAL FIXED(5,2),
      2 NET_PAY FIXED(5,2);
```

Fig. 10.4 PL/I Structure Declaration to Implement Fig. 10.3(c)

These versions are obtained by omitting from the fully qualified name any major or minor structure names -- provided this does not produce an ambiguous reference, i.e., possible confusion with the name of some other variable in the program.

For example, if some other structure also contained a minor structure called DEDUCTIONS with an item called FED_TAX, then versions (ii) and (iii) could not be used. Or if EMPLOYEE_RECORD happened to contain the name FED_TAX within some other minor structure, then versions (i) and (iii) would be ambiguous. Simply using FED_TAX is like looking up the phone number of "Smith." This is not sufficient to identify which Smith, unless only one is listed in the directory.

10.2 ASSIGNMENT OF VALUES TO STRUCTURES

Values can be assigned to elementary items in the same way as to a simple variable. Thus for the structure in Fig. 10.4 we might calculate the federal tax as 22% of gross pay by

```
FED_TAX = GROSS_PAY * 0.22;
```

or

```
EMPLOYEE_RECORD.FED_TAX = GROSS_PAY * 0.22;
```

or

```
DEDUCTIONS.FED_TAX = EMPLOYEE_RECORD.GROSS_PAY * 0.22;
```

It is often necessary to copy one (major or minor) structure into another. For example, if we have structures A and W:

```
1 A,                        1 W,
   2 B FIXED(5,0),             2 X FIXED(5,0),
   2 C CHARACTER(2),           2 Y CHARACTER(2),
   2 D FLOAT(6);               2 Z FLOAT(6);
```

To copy the values of W into A, one could write either:

```
(i)  A.B = W.X;
     A.C = W.Y;
     A.D = W.Z;
```

or simply

```
(ii)  A = W;
```

Just as use of an array name without parentheses implies the use of all array elements (Section 7.6.1), the use of a structure (or minor structure) name, as in (ii), implies the use of every elementary item within that structure (or minor structure). For example, if structure H is defined as follows, with A rewritten alongside for reference,

```
1 H,
   2 J FIXED(5,0),
   2 K                          1 A,
      3 L FIXED(5,0),              2 B FIXED(5,0),
      3 M CHARACTER(2),            2 C CHARACTER(2),
      3 N FLOAT(6);                2 D FLOAT(6);
```

one could write:

```
A = H.K;
```

which is equivalent to:

```
A.B = H.K.L;
A.C = H.K.M;
A.D = H.K.N;
```

However, this can only be done if the (minor) structures involved have completely identical form (i.e., level structure) and attributes. Thus one could not write:

```
A = H;
```

because a different number of elementary items is represented by each side of the assignment statement. Consider the structure P, with A rewritten alongside for reference:

```
1 P,
   2 Q,                           1 A,
      3 R FIXED(5,0),                2 B FIXED(5,0),
      3 S FIXED(5,0),                2 C CHARACTER(20),
      3 T CHARACTER(20),             2 D FLOAT(6);
   2 U FLOAT(6);
```

One cannot say :

```
P.Q = A;
```

because only one of the three corresponding pairs of elementary items has the same attribute (A.B and P.Q.R are both FIXED). All three pairs of items must match for the assignment to be valid.

One cannot even say:

```
P = H;
```

because, even though the number of elementary items is the same and the attributes correspond, the form of each structure is different, as shown by the structure diagrams:

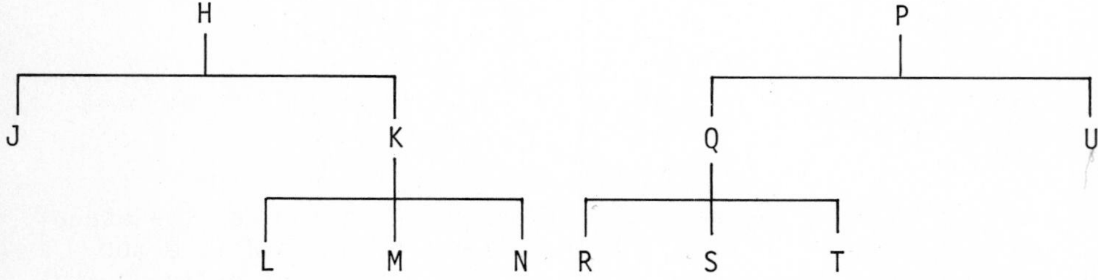

10.3 STRUCTURE INPUT-OUTPUT

Input-output probably provides the most common occasion for using a minor or major structure name to represent all of its constituent elementary items. For example, consider the structure defined by:

```
DECLARE 1 CUSTOMER,
          2 NAME,
             3 LAST CHARACTER(10),
             3 FIRST CHARACTER(5),
          2 AMOUNT FIXED(7,2);
```

and the following data card:

```
                 ┌─col. 10 ┌─col. 20
                 ↓         ↓
 ┌─────────────────────────────────
 │SMITH     HARRY  57.98
```

The statement

```
GET SKIP EDIT(CUSTOMER.NAME)(A(10),A(5));
```

would put 'SMITH' in LAST and 'HARRY' in FIRST.
The statement

```
GET SKIP EDIT(CUSTOMER)(A(10),A(5),F(7,2));
```

operating on the same data card would also put 57.98 into AMOUNT as well as initializing both parts of NAME.

The convenience of simply using structure names often encourages people to define structures in order to take advantage of this shortcut. For example, suppose the data cards for the payroll of Fig. 10.4 are coded as

```
col. 1 - 20   Name
col.25 - 31   ID Number
col.35 - 40   Gross pay (decimal point in col. 38).
```

Then we could read this data into the structure by:

```
GET SKIP EDIT (NAME,ID_NO,GROSS_PAY)
              (A(20),X(4),F(7),X(3),F(6,2));
```

After computing all the deductions and the net pay, we could output the values by:

```
PUT SKIP EDIT (NAME,ID_NO,GROSS_PAY,FED_TAX,STATE_TAX,
               SOC_SEC,OTHER,TOTAL,NET_PAY)
              (X(10),A(20),F(9),7 (X(3),F(6,2)));
```

Since every elementary item in the structure is to be printed in the same order as they were defined, we can immediately simplify the PUT statement by writing:

```
PUT SKIP EDIT(EMPLOYEE_RECORD)
             (X(10),A(20),F(9),7 (X(3),F(6,2)));
```

However, if you desire the elementary items to be output in some other order, then you must either: (i) specify individual elementary items in the output list in the desired order; or else (ii) declare the structure in the first place with its elementary items in the desired order for output.

The GET statement can be simplified if the input items are grouped into a new minor structure called INPUT, as shown in Fig. 10.5 and 10.6:

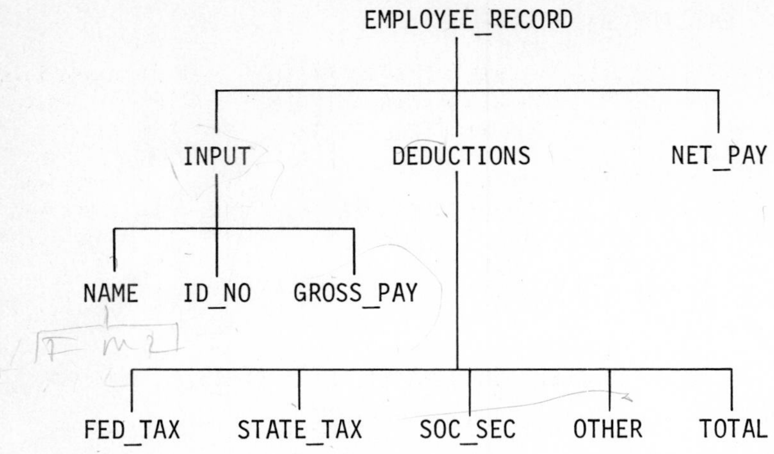

Fig. 10.5 A Restructuring of Fig. 10.3(c) to Group Input Items Together

```
DECLARE 1 EMPLOYEE_RECORD,
            2 INPUT,
                3 NAME CHARACTER(20),
                3 ID_NO FIXED(7,0),
                3 GROSS_PAY FIXED(5,2),
            2 DEDUCTIONS,
                3 FED_TAX FIXED(5,2),
                3 STATE_TAX FIXED(5,2),
                3 SOC_SEC FIXED(5,2),
                3 OTHER FIXED(5,2),
                3 TOTAL FIXED(5,2),
            2 NET_PAY FIXED(5,2);
```

Fig. 10.6 Declaration Corresponding to Fig. 10.5

Notice that we have not altered the storage locations in any way; all we have done is some internal grouping. We can now read into these variables by simply referring to the minor structure which contains them:

```
GET SKIP EDIT (INPUT) (A(20),X(4),F(7),X(3),F(6,2));
```

Once again, since the order of declaration is important, variables should be declared in an order compatible with I/O requirements insofar as possible.

Should we wish to suppress the DEDUCTIONS on output, then we can say:

```
PUT SKIP EDIT (INPUT,NET_PAY)
              (X(10),A(20),F(9),2 (X(3),F(6,2)));
```

10.4 ASSIGNMENT BY NAME

Suppose that only a portion of the EMPLOYEE_RECORD from Fig. 10.6 is to be printed, namely the NAME, GROSS_PAY, NET_PAY, STATE_TAX, and FED_TAX -- in that order! Since neither the major nor the minor structures are included in their entirety, no abbreviation of the output list seems possible. Even if all the DEDUCTIONS were to be printed, the STATE_TAX and FED_TAX are to be printed in a different order than they were declared; this would preclude merely mentioning DEDUCTIONS in the output list.

However, you might consider copying the relevant items from EMPLOYEE_RECORD into another structure which is specially designed for your output requirements:

```
DECLARE 1 OUTPUT_RECORD,
          2 INPUT,
             3 NAME CHARACTER(20),
             3 GROSS_PAY FIXED(5,2),
          2 NET_PAY FIXED(5,2),
          2 DEDUCTIONS,
             3 STATE_TAX FIXED(5,2),
             3 FED_TAX FIXED(5,2);
```

When the values have been copied from EMPLOYEE_RECORD to OUTPUT_RECORD, then they can be printed by executing:

```
PUT SKIP EDIT(OUTPUT_RECORD)(A(20),4 (F(8,2)));
```

Though tempting, it is not possible to perform the copying by:

```
OUTPUT_RECORD = EMPLOYEE_RECORD;
```

since both structures have different numbers of elementary items and different basic forms.

Copying one item at a time will work but is even more tedious than writing each item in the output list:

```
OUTPUT_RECORD.INPUT.NAME           =EMPLOYEE_RECORD.INPUT.NAME;
OUTPUT_RECORD.INPUT.GROSS_PAY      =EMPLOYEE_RECORD.INPUT.GROSS_PAY;
OUTPUT_RECORD.NET_PAY              =EMPLOYEE_RECORD.NET_PAY;
OUTPUT_RECORD.DEDUCTIONS.STATE_TAX=EMPLOYEE_RECORD.DEDUCTIONS.
                                             STATE_TAX;
OUTPUT_RECORD.DEDUCTIONS.FED_TAX  =EMPLOYEE_RECORD.DEDUCTIONS.
                                             FED_TAX;
```

Note, however, that the fully qualified name of each item being moved, is exactly the same in both structures except for the major structure names. Consequently, these selected items (those whose names are alike) can be moved by the statement:

```
OUTPUT_RECORD = EMPLOYEE_RECORD, BY NAME;
```

This BY NAME option affects all items whose names (and data types) are the same in every structure mentioned in the PL/I statement. For example, if OUTPUT_RECORD had also included the items PENSION and TOTAL as part of DEDUCTIONS, then TOTAL would also have been altered, but PENSION would have remained untouched.

10.5 ARRAYS AND STRUCTURES

Arrays and structures are both methods of handling groups of data. The essential difference is that arrays are for arranging similar items into lists or tables while structures are capable of grouping various kinds of things. Nevertheless, these two language facilities can often be used together to provide a very powerful method of organizing data.

For example, a book store might maintain a list of up to ten requests for any book which is currently not in stock. Associated with such a list might be the title and price of the book. The list of potential purchasers could be represented by an array, which would be part of a larger structure pertaining to the book:

```
1 BOOK,
   2 TITLE CHARACTER(100),
   2 PRICE FIXED(7,2),
   2 REQUEST (10) CHARACTER(40);
```

This structure would have the following sort of tree diagram:

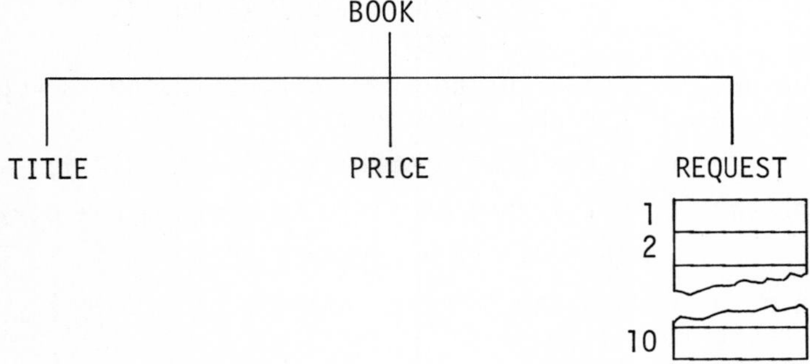

or, alternatively

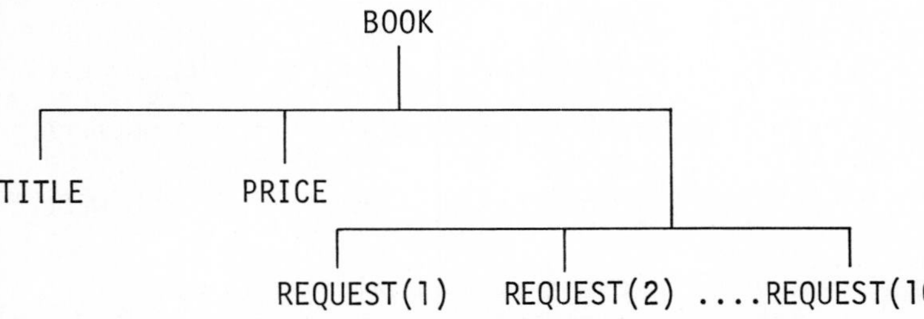

Multidimensional arrays may also be used within structures in order to group tables with other sorts of data:

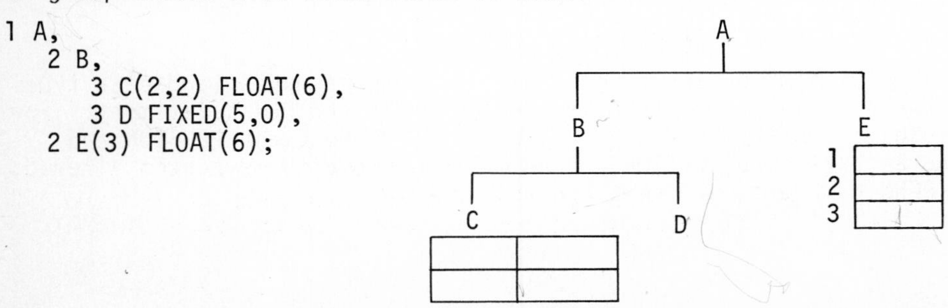

```
1 A,
   2 B,
      3 C(2,2) FLOAT(6),
      3 D FIXED(5,0),
   2 E(3) FLOAT(6);
```

Consider a farm whose current production in bushels and price per bushel are recorded as follows:

```
1 FARM,
   2 BARLEY,
      3 BUSHELS FIXED(5,0),
      3 PRICE FIXED(7,2),
   2 HOPS,
      3 BUSHELS FIXED(5,0),
      3 PRICE FIXED(7,2),
   2 CORN,
      3 BUSHELS FIXED(5,0),
      3 PRICE FIXED(7,2);
```

In this case, there are three minor structures which differ only in name. Exactly the same effect can be achieved by creating an array of three elements, where each element represents one crop and is one of these minor structures:

```
1 FARM,
   2 CROP(3),
      3 BUSHELS FIXED(5,0),
      3 PRICE FIXED(7,2);
```

By appending the subscript 3 to CROP, we have asked for three copies of the minor structure CROP:

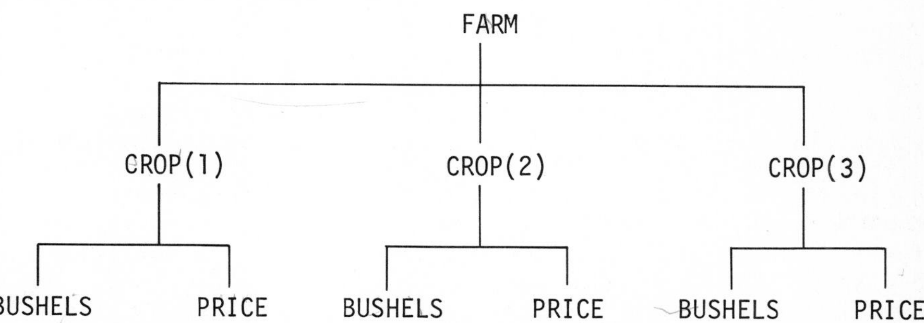

To reference item BUSHELS in substructure CROP(1), we use FARM.CROP(1).BUSHELS or perhaps CROP(1).BUSHELS. Notice now that a reference to FARM.CROP or to CROP is a reference to six storage locations, and a reference to FARM.BUSHELS is a reference to three storage locations

We can similarly set up arrays of major structures by adding a dimension to the level 1 name. For example, if we had two farms, we could make FARM an array of two elements to obtain two major structures:

```
1 FARM(2),
   2 CROP(3),
      3 BUSHELS FIXED(5,0),
      3 PRICE FIXED(7,2);
```

The resulting major structures are called FARM(1) and FARM(2), respectively, each of which contains 3 identical minor structures called CROP(1), CROP(2), and CROP(3), as shown by the tree diagram:

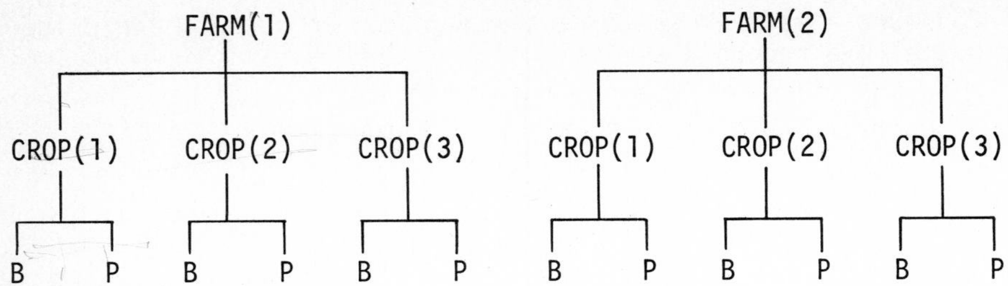

We note from the diagram that there are 12 storage locations associated with FARM. Clearly the use of arrays can considerably enhance the power of structures when the array elements are themselves structures.

10.6 THE DESIGN OF STRUCTURES

Structures are appropriate when related information of different types is to be associated. How various items should be associated depends on how the data is to be used. We have already noted (Section 10.3) that those items which are input and, if possible, those which are to be printed should be grouped within the same minor structures. With input-output, the order of declaration may also be important.

However, input-output is not the only consideration. When processing items, certain ones "naturally" belong together and certain groupings will emerge as most appropriate. Developing a structure should be done from the "top down," like developing an algorithm. In other words, make the fundamental distinctions among items first; then further refine each category.

Consider an antique car dealership which wants to automate its inventory records. The inventory consists of domestic and foreign cars for the period 1921 to 1926 inclusive. Within the domestic category we consider only cars made by GM, Chrysler, and Ford. The inventory is only to consist of the number of cars in each category, by year. Let us consider how we might arrange a PL/I structure to hold the required information. Since the inventory consists of two large groups of cars -- foreign and domestic -- the second level of the structure can reflect this:

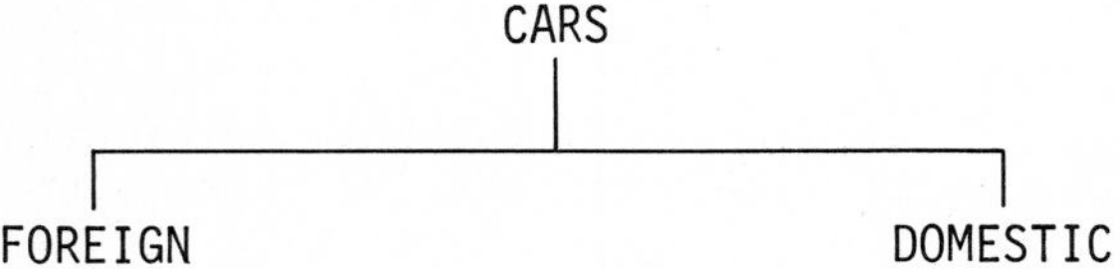

The foreign cars are not subdivided by manufacturer, but the domestic cars must be one of the "big three." Hence, the next elaboration is:

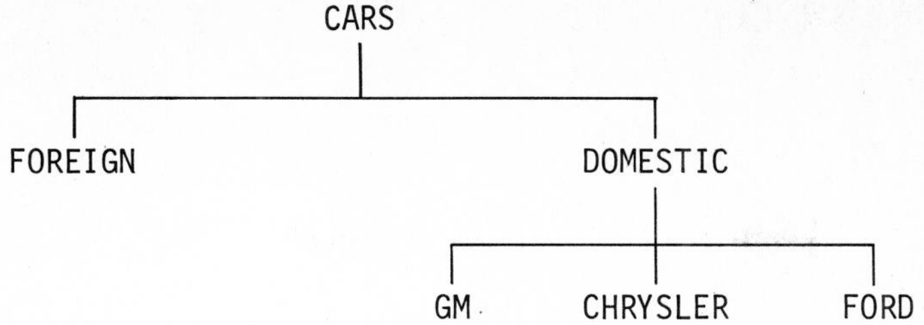

Finally we wish to maintain a count of each car in each category ranging over the period 1921-1926 inclusive. We thus need 6 storage locations for each of the categories and can accomplish this in either of the following ways:

```
DECLARE 1 CARS,
            2 FOREIGN(1921:1926) FIXED(5,0),
            2 DOMESTIC(1921:1926),
               3 GM FIXED(5,0),
               3 CHRYSLER FIXED(5,0),
               3 FORD FIXED(5,0);
```

or

```
DECLARE 1 CARS,
            2 FOREIGN(1921:1926) FIXED(5,0),
            2 DOMESTIC,
               3 GM(1921:1926) FIXED(5,0),
               3 CHRYSLER(1921:1926) FIXED(5,0),
               3 FORD(1921:1926) FIXED(5,0);
```

As another example consider recording temperatures for each day of each month of the year, where each day will have a morning and an afternoon temperature. Since there are twelve months to a year the skeleton structure will look like:

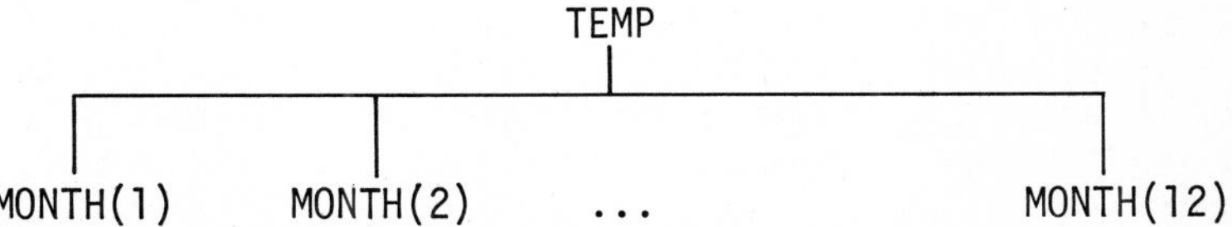

Within each month we require a maximum of 31 days which enlarges the structure to:

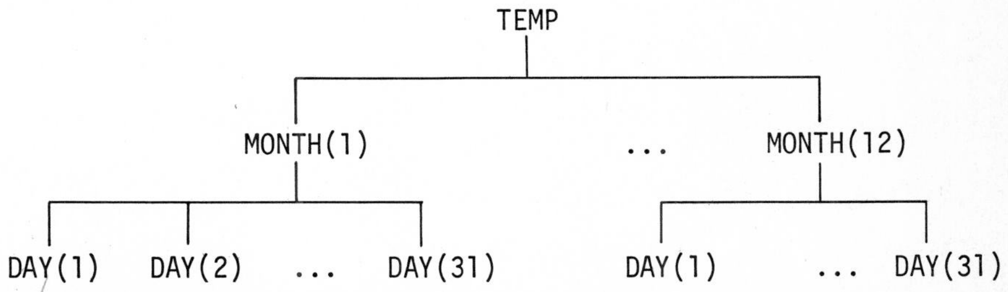

At the elementary levels, each day will hold a morning and afternoon temperature, and so the complete structure will be:

```
DECLARE 1 TEMP,
           2 MONTH(12),
             3 DAY(31),
               4 MORN FIXED(6,2),
               4 AFT FIXED(6,2);
```

We can now reference selected items of information either singly or in groups. To print the morning temperature for June 11th we can say:

```
PUT LIST (MONTH(6).DAY(11).MORN);
```

The afternoon temperatures for the eighth day of *every* month can be referenced by either MONTH.DAY(8).AFT or DAY(8).AFT. Similarly all the temperatures for January can be referenced by MONTH(1).DAY or by MONTH(1).

10.7 REVIEW OF RULES

1. A structure is a collection of variables, called "elementary items," which are not necessarily of the same data type. Selected items within a "major" structure may be grouped into "minor" structures, and these may be further grouped with other variables or other minor structures.

2. The grouping within a structure is specified by DECLAREing level numbers (followed by a blank) before each structure constituent. The (major) structure has level number 1, and all minor structures and elementary items have level numbers greater than 1.

3. Every minor structure must be completely declared before encountering the next minor structure not included within it. (Any item or minor structure is considered a part of its nearest predecessor which has a smaller level number.)

4. Use of a (minor) structure name implies a reference to *all* its constituent elementary items in the *same order* in which they were declared.

5. Only elementary items may have attributes, since only they denote storage locations.

6. Structure constituents at any level may be arrays.

7. The general form of the BY NAME assignment option is

   <structure> = <structure>, BY NAME;

10.8 REVIEW PROBLEM

Problem Statement

You are to generate a report of student averages from record cards which contain the following information:

col.		
col.	1 - 7	student ID number
	8	sex indicator -- 0 if male; 1 if female
	9 - 28	name
	29 - 38	numeric grades for each of 5 subjects -- two columns per grade.

The report is to consist of three lists: (i) all female students, (ii) all male students, and (iii) all students. Each list must be in ascending order according to average grade and must contain only student names, ID numbers, and average grade, in that order. You may assume that the total number of students does not exceed 100.

There are many ways of tackling this problem; however, we shall only present two. The first will illustrate the two-way merge and the use of procedures.[3] The second may turn out to be more efficient for most situations.

10.8.1 First Solution

An initial solution to the problem can be formulated as:

1. read the data, separating males and females;
2. compute the average grade for each student;
3. sort the male students;
4. sort the female students;
5. produce a sorted list of all students;
6. print the results;
7. end.

Notice that the list of all students (Step 5) is a blend of the lists of males (Step 3) and females (Step 4). This explains why Steps 3 and 4 precede Step 5 and also suggests using a merge (Section 7.5.4).

Before we can tackle the first step, we must decide on the type of storage to be used for our data. Since each student record consists of integers, characters and decimal numbers, this is clearly a situation where structures would be appropriate. However, the individual grades for each student need not be retained once the average is computed. Therefore, separate structures can be used for input and for subsequent retention of the data.

The layout of each input structure is straightforward, consisting only of eight elementary items in the same order as their values appear on a data card. Pictorially each record looks like:

DATA_CARD

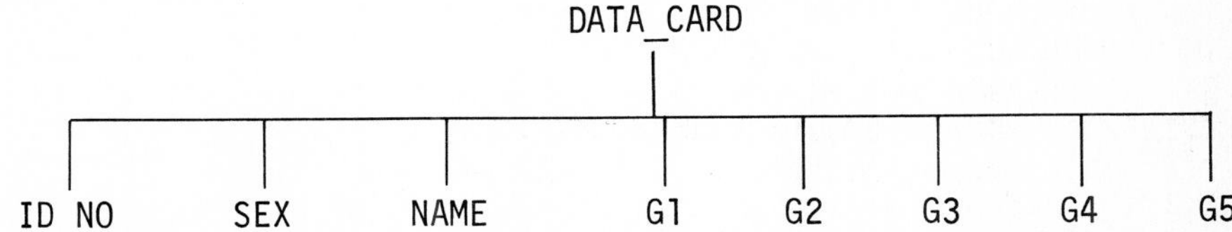

where G1 to G5 represent the grades for each of five subjects. If we look ahead to the output requirements we will see that it will be advantageous to do some regrouping:

---

[3] Admittedly we have a pedagogical motive for presenting this solution here.

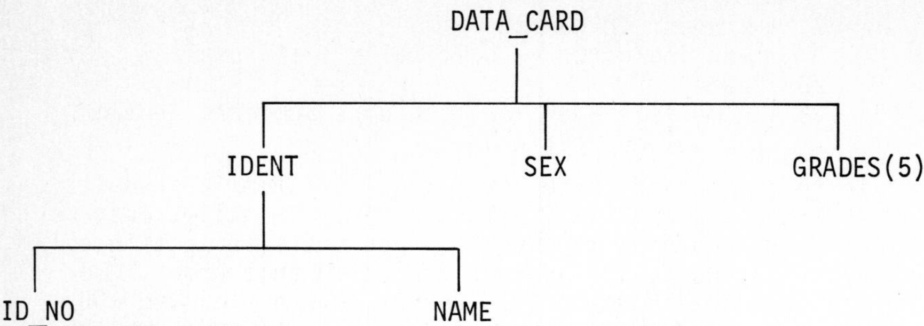

This grouping will facilitate the preparation of the output lists, since only the name and ID number will be shown on the reports.

To retain the records in storage we no longer need the grades -- only the grade average. After computing the average of the grades, the pertinent information about each student will then have the tree representation:

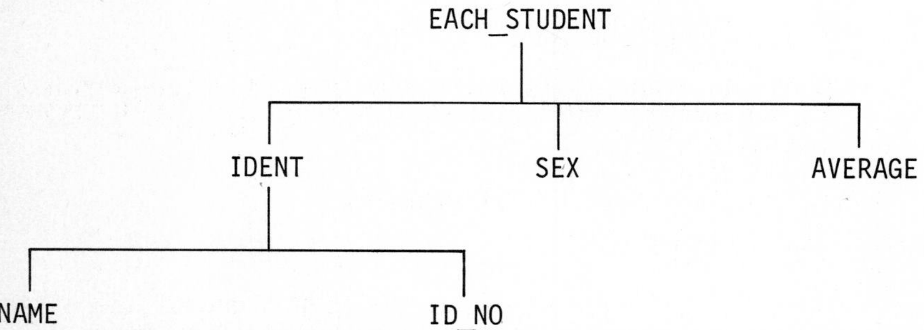

Note that the positions of NAME and ID_NO have been reversed from those on the input record, since this is the required order for output.

Since we do not know how many students fall into the male or female category, we must allow for as many as 100 records in each of the male and female categories. This means we need two 100-element arrays of EACH_STUDENT structures. With these data structures in mind we can elaborate the first step of our preliminary algorithm into:

```
1.      set male and female counters to zero;
2.      read first data card;
3.      repeat while data remain to be processed;
3.1        compute average grade;
3.2        if male record then
3.2.1         increase male counter by 1;
3.2.2         copy identity and sex data into male array;
3.2.3         copy average into male array;
3.3        otherwise
3.3.1         increase female counter by 1;
3.3.2         copy identity and sex data into female array;
3.3.3         copy average into female array;
3.4        read next data card;
```

Translating this into PL/I yields the program shown in Fig. 10.7. The assignment of values BY NAME in Statements 14 and 19 copies only

```
            /* FIGURE 10.7 */
STEP1:   PROCEDURE OPTIONS (MAIN);

         DECLARE
            1 DATA_CARD,
               2 IDENT,
                  3 ID_NO FIXED (7,0), /* ID. NO. */
                3 NAME CHARACTER (20),
               2 SEX FIXED (1,0), /* 0=MALE;1=FEMALE */
               2 GRADES(5) FLOAT (6), /* COURSE GRADES */
            1 MALES(100), /* RECORDS FOR MALES */
               2 IDENT,
                  3 NAME CHARACTER (20),
                  3 ID_NO FIXED (7,0),
               2 SEX FIXED (1,0),
            2 AVERAGE FLOAT (6), /* AVERAGE GRADE */
            1 FEMALES(100), /* RECORDS FOR FEMALES */
               2 IDENT,
                  3 NAME CHARACTER (20),
                  3 ID_NO FIXED (7,0),
               2 SEX FIXED (1,0),
               2 AVERAGE FLOAT (6),
            NO_MALES FIXED (5,0), /* NO. MALE STUDENTS */
            NO_FEMALES FIXED (5,0), /*NO. FEMALE STUDENTS*/
            AVE_GRADE FLOAT (6), /* AVERAGE GRADE */
            FLAG FIXED (5,0);

         /* INITIALIZE VARIABLES */

         NO_MALES = 0;
         NO_FEMALES = 0;
         FLAG = 0;
         ON ENDFILE (SYSIN) FLAG = 1;

         /* PROCESS INPUT DATA CARDS */

         GET EDIT(DATA_CARD.ID_NO,DATA_CARD.SEX,
            DATA_CARD.NAME,DATA_CARD.GRADES)
            (F(7),F(1),A(20),5 F(2,0));

SEPARATE:
         DO WHILE (FLAG = 0);
            /* COMPUTE AVERAGE GRADE */
            AVE_GRADE = SUM(DATA_CARD.GRADES)/5.0E0;
            /* DISCRIMINATE BY SEX */
            IF DATA_CARD.SEX = 0 THEN
MALE_STUDENTS:DO; /* PROCESS MALES */
                  NO_MALES = NO_MALES + 1;
                  MALES(NO_MALES) = DATA_CARD,BY NAME;
                  MALES(NO_MALES).AVERAGE = AVE_GRADE;
               END MALE_STUDENTS;
            ELSE
FEMALE_STUDENTS:
               DO; /* PROCESS FEMALE STUDENTS */
                  NO_FEMALES = NO_FEMALES + 1;
                  FEMALES(NO_FEMALES) = DATA_CARD,BY NAME;
                  FEMALES(NO_FEMALES).AVERAGE = AVE_GRADE;
               END FEMALE_STUDENTS;
            GET SKIP EDIT (DATA_CARD.ID_NO,DATA_CARD.SEX,
               DATA_CARD.NAME,DATA_CARD.GRADES)
               (F(7),F(1),A(20),5 F(2,0));
         END SEPARATE;

         END STEP1;
```

Figure 10.7

the name, ID number, and sex from one structure to the other. Also note the use of the built-in function SUM in Statement 10 to compute the average grade. This function will sum all the elements of an array, such as DATA_CARD.GRADES.

We are now in a position to sort the arrays of male and female student records. Since the sort has to be performed on more than one array, this is a natural place to use a procedure. The procedure can use the bubble sort (Section 7.5.2) to sort an array whose name and size are given as parameters. Since the array being sorted consists of structures, when two array elements are interchanged, the procedure must swap two structures. This requires that the procedure use a local structure to be used during the swap. Further, since the sort is by average grade, we only make comparisons on this item of the structure. The procedure to sort these arrays is included in the complete program of Fig. 10.8.

This figure also contains procedures to merge the sorted arrays and to print the reports. Although the merge and the output each occur only once, these tasks are performed by procedures in order to keep the details of their operation from cluttering the main procedure. This also allowed the program to be tested one procedure at a time. After the version shown in Fig. 10.7 was tested, the SORT procedure was added and tested. When this was working, the MERGE procedure was added and finally the REPORT procedure, to obtain the complete program of Fig. 10.8. Note that the MERGE procedure contains two of its own internal procedures. These procedures consolidate and conceal some rather gory code which would otherwise have to appear at various places in MERGE.

A minor time-saving modification was made to the original sort algorithm. Notice that after completing each pass through the array, we have reduced the number of elements to be sorted by one, via the statement J = J - 1;. Since each pass moves the largest remaining element in the array into its proper place, there is no reason to compare the larger elements which are already in their proper places.

Note also that we have enlarged the section of code which processes the input data cards. In Fig. 10.7, we assumed that any data cards which did not have a sex code of 0 must therefore be a 1. The version of Fig. 10.8 checks for erroneous sex codes and finds one, as shown on the output. It is good general practice to have your procedures (both main and internal) check the validity of input data, since errors in data invariably occur.

```
        /* FIGURE 10.8 */
MERGER: PROCEDURE OPTIONS (MAIN);

        DECLARE
            1 DATA_CARD,
               2 IDENT,
                  3 ID_NO FIXED (7,0), /* ID. NO. */
                 3 NAME CHARACTER (20),
               2 SEX FIXED (1,0), /* 0=MALE;1=FEMALE */
               2 GRADES(5) FLOAT (6), /* COURSE GRADES */
            1 MALES(100), /* RECORDS FOR MALES */
               2 IDENT,
                  3 NAME CHARACTER (20),
                  3 ID_NO FIXED (7,0),
               2 SEX FIXED (1,0),
            2 AVERAGE FLOAT (6), /* AVERAGE GRADE */
            1 FEMALES(100), /* RECORDS FOR FEMALES */
               2 IDENT,
                  3 NAME CHARACTER (20),
                  3 ID_NO FIXED (7,0),
               2 SEX FIXED (1,0),
               2 AVERAGE FLOAT (6),
            NO_MALES FIXED (5,0), /* NO. MALE STUDENTS */
            NO_FEMALES FIXED (5,0), /*NO. FEMALE STUDENTS*/
            AVE_GRADE FLOAT (6), /* AVERAGE GRADE */
            (FLAG,J,K) FIXED (5,0);

        /* INITIALIZE VARIABLES */

        NO_MALES = 0;
        NO_FEMALES = 0;
        FLAG = 0;
        ON ENDFILE (SYSIN) FLAG = 1;

        /* PROCESS INPUT DATA CARDS */

        GET EDIT(DATA_CARD.ID_NO,DATA_CARD.SEX,
            DATA_CARD.NAME,DATA_CARD.GRADES)
            (F(7),F(1),A(20),5 F(2,0));

SEPARATE:
        DO WHILE (FLAG = 0);
            /* COMPUTE AVERAGE GRADE */
            AVE_GRADE = SUM(DATA_CARD.GRADES)/5.0E0;
            /* DISCRIMINATE BY SEX */
            IF DATA_CARD.SEX = 0 THEN
MALE_STUDENTS:DO; /* PROCESS MALES */
                  NO_MALES = NO_MALES + 1;
                  MALES(NO_MALES) = DATA_CARD,BY NAME;
                  MALES(NO_MALES).AVERAGE = AVE_GRADE;
               END MALE_STUDENTS;
            ELSE IF DATA_CARD.SEX = 1 THEN
FEMALE_STUDENTS:
               DO; /* PROCESS FEMALE STUDENTS */
                  NO_FEMALES = NO_FEMALES + 1;
                  FEMALES(NO_FEMALES) = DATA_CARD,BY NAME;
                  FEMALES(NO_FEMALES).AVERAGE = AVE_GRADE;
               END FEMALE_STUDENTS;
               ELSE PUT SKIP(2) EDIT
                  ('***ERROR IN INPUT***',DATA_CARD)
                  (A(25),F(7),A(20),F(1),5 F(2));
            GET SKIP EDIT (DATA_CARD.ID_NO,DATA_CARD.SEX,
               DATA_CARD.NAME,DATA_CARD.GRADES)
               (F(7),F(1),A(20),5 F(2,0));
        END SEPARATE;

        /* NOW SORT MALE AND FEMALE RECORDS IN ASCENDING
            ORDER ACCORDING TO GRADE AVERAGE. */

        CALL SORT (MALES,NO_MALES);
        CALL SORT (FEMALES,NO_FEMALES);

        /* NOW PRINT THE SORTED RECORDS */

        CALL REPORT;

        /* NOW MERGE THE ARRAYS TO PRODUCE
            ONE SORTED LIST ON THE PRINTER. */
        PUT PAGE EDIT ('ALL STUDENTS SORTED BY AVERAGE')
            (X(10),A);
        CALL MERGE;
        PUT PAGE;
```

Fig. 10.8 Main Procedure of Grade Report Program

```
REPORT: PROCEDURE;
        DECLARE K FIXED (5,0);
        PUT SKIP(5) EDIT ('MALE STUDENTS SORTED BY AVERAGE')
                        (X(10),A);
        PUT EDIT ((MALES(K).IDENT,MALES(K).AVERAGE
            DO K = 1 TO NO_MALES))
            (SKIP(2),X(5),A(20),F(10),F(9,2));
        PUT SKIP(5) EDIT ('FEMALE STUDENTS SORTED'
            ,' BY AVERAGE') (X(10),A,A);
        PUT EDIT ((FEMALES(K).IDENT,FEMALES(K).AVERAGE
            DO K = 1 TO NO_FEMALES))
            (SKIP(2),X(5),A(20),F(10),F(9,2));
        END REPORT;

MERGE:  PROCEDURE;
        K = 1;
        J = 1;
        /* SELECT FROM EACH ARRAY UNTIL ONE EXHAUSTED */

BOTH:   DO WHILE (K<=NO_MALES & J<=NO_FEMALES);
            IF MALES(K).AVERAGE <= FEMALES(J).AVERAGE THEN
               CALL PRINT_MALE;
            ELSE
               CALL PRINT_FEMALE;
        END BOTH;
        /* IF NO MORE MALES PRINT BALANCE OF FEMALES */

PRT_FEM: DO WHILE (J <= NO_FEMALES);
            CALL PRINT_FEMALE;
        END PRT_FEM;
        /* IF NO MORE FEMALES PRINT BALANCE OF MALES */

PRT_MALE: DO WHILE (K <= NO_MALES);
            CALL PRINT_MALE;
        END PRT_MALE;
        END MERGE;

SORT:   PROCEDURE (A,N);
        DECLARE 1 A(*),
                  2 ID,
                       3 NA CHARACTER(*),
                       3 I FIXED(7,0),
                  2 S FIXED(1,0),
                  2 AV FLOAT(6),
                N FIXED(5,0);
        DECLARE 1 TEMP,
                  2 ID,
                       3 NA CHARACTER(20),
                       3 I FIXED(7,0),
                  2 S FIXED(1,0),
                  2 AV FLOAT(6),
                (FLAG,J,K) FIXED(5,0);

        /* BUBBLE SORT FOR AN ARRAY OF STRUCTURES, A,
           WITH N ENTRIES. SORT IS PERFORMED ON ELEMENT
           AV IN ASCENDING ORDER */

        J = N; /* J IS NO. OF ELEMENTS TO BE SORTED */
        FLAG = 1;
OUTER:  DO WHILE (FLAG = 1);
             FLAG = 0; /* ASSUME ARRAY IS SORTED */
PASS:        DO K = 1 TO J-1;
                  IF A(K).AV > A(K+1).AV THEN
SWAP:             DO; /* SWAP ELEMENTS AND SET FLAG */
                       TEMP = A(K);
                       A(K) = A(K+1);
                       A(K+1) = TEMP;
                       FLAG = 1;
                  END SWAP;
             END PASS;
             J = J - 1;
        END OUTER;
        END SORT;
PRINT_FEMALE: PROCEDURE;
        PUT EDIT   (FEMALES(J).IDENT,FEMALES(J).AVERAGE)
                  (SKIP(2),X(5),A(20),F(10),F(9,2));
        J = J + 1;
        END PRINT_FEMALE;
PRINT_MALE: PROCEDURE;
        PUT EDIT ( MALES(K).IDENT,MALES(K).AVERAGE)
                  (SKIP(2),X(5),A(20),F(10),F(9,2));
        K = K + 1;
        END PRINT_MALE;

        END MERGER;
```

Fig. 10.8 (contd.) Internal Procedures of Grade Report Program

```
***ERROR IN INPUT***      6900086WILLIAMS           TC36670697375


        MALE STUDENTS SORTED BY AVERAGE
MACDONALD            AF    7400909      49.80
FITZPATRICK          JP    7401561      55.60
LORD                 JB    7311891      65.80
NICKEL               B     6904537      66.40
PEARSON              DP    7303949      68.00
STEINER              JM    7235971      68.60
MONROE               FA    6901979      75.80
JONES                D     7203081      82.20
GILLESPIE            HD    7400860      82.20


        FEMALE STUDENTS SORTED BY AVERAGE
WELD                 T     7198232      61.20
CAMPBELL             SV    7236770      63.60
JENNINGS             GD    7304701      68.60
HARMAN               DG    7303577      80.80
THOMLINSON           RW    7317486      84.00


        ALL STUDENTS SORTED BY AVERAGE
MACDONALD            AF    7400909      49.80
FITZPATRICK          JP    7401561      55.60
WELD                 T     7198232      61.20
CAMPBELL             SV    7236770      63.60
LORD                 JB    7311891      65.80
NICKEL               B     6904537      66.40
PEARSON              DP    7303949      68.00
STEINER              JM    7235971      68.60
JENNINGS             GD    7304701      68.60
MONROE               FA    6901979      75.80
HARMAN               DG    7303577      80.80
JONES                D     7203081      82.20
GILLESPIE            HD    7400860      82.20
THOMLINSON           RW    7317486      84.00
```

Fig. 10.8 (contd.) Output from Grade Report Program

10.8.2 Second Solution

An alternative solution to this problem is now presented. The basis for this solution lies in the fact that we retain the sex identifier of each student throughout the entire program. Why then should we separate them into two arrays? Instead we can keep all the students in one array. Once we have sorted this array by average grade, we can then print all the males by going through it and checking the sex indicator. Similarly we can pick out the female students when the female list is being printed.

The savings in this method arise from the need for only one 100-element array instead of two, only one sort, and no merge.

The algorithm for this method is:

```
1.     set student counter to zero;
2.     read first data card;
3.     repeat while data remain to be processed;
3.1       compute average grade;
3.2       add 1 to student counter;
3.3       copy data and average into student array;
3.4       read next data card;
4.     sort all student records by average;
5.     print list of all male students;
6.     print list of all female students;
7.     print list of all students;
8.     end.
```

The complete program to implement this solution is shown in Fig. 10.9. In this program we have implemented the sort by calling the SORT procedure of Fig. 10.8. It is not possible to write one general procedure to sort an arbitrary array of structures, because each structure usually has a unique configuration.

The program of Fig. 10.9 should of course be developed in the same step-by-step manner as that of Fig. 10.8. We cannot emphasize too strongly that this kind of development applies to all computer programs. Writing and verifying each section of code is much more desirable than trying to code and solve the problem all at once. You may feel that we are belaboring this point, but, as you gain more and more proficiency in problem solving, there is an unfortunate tendency to forget about problem decomposition. Even though you may no longer need to break your problems into very small steps, they still must be subdivided into manageable steps. If these steps are then coded as separate procedures, required changes can usually be confined to an individual procedure. This makes modification of a program much more manageable as well.

```
          /* FIGURE 10.9 */
SECOND: PROCEDURE OPTIONS (MAIN);

        DECLARE
           1 DATA_CARD,
              2 IDENT,
                 3 ID_NO FIXED(7,0), /* ID. NUMBER */
                 3 NAME CHARACTER(20),
              2 SEX FIXED(1,0), /* 0=MALE;1=FEMALE */
              2 GRADES(5) FLOAT(6), /* COURSE GRADES */
           1 STUDENTS(100), /* RECORDS FOR ALL STUDENTS */
              2 IDENT,
                 3 NAME CHARACTER(20),
                 3 ID_NO FIXED(7,0),
              2 SEX FIXED(1,0),
              2 AVERAGE FLOAT(6), /* AVERAGE GRADE */
           NO_STUDENTS FIXED(5,0), /*NO. STUDENT RECORDS*/
           AVE_GRADE FLOAT(6), /*AVERAGE GRADE */
           (FLAG,K,J) FIXED (5,0);

        /* INITIALIZE VARIABLES */

        NO_STUDENTS = 0;
        FLAG = 0;
        ON ENDFILE (SYSIN) FLAG = 1;

        /* PROCESS INPUT DATA CARDS */

        GET EDIT(DATA_CARD.ID_NO,DATA_CARD.SEX,
           DATA_CARD.NAME,DATA_CARD.GRADES)
              (F(7),F(1),A(20),5 F(2,0));

PROCESS:
        DO WHILE (FLAG = 0);
             /* COMPUTE AVERAGE GRADE */
           AVE_GRADE = SUM(DATA_CARD.GRADES) / 5.0E0;
           /* CHECK FOR VALID SEX CODE */
           IF DATA_CARD.SEX = 0 | DATA_CARD.SEX = 1 THEN
INSERT:        DO; /* STORE RECORD */
                  NO_STUDENTS = NO_STUDENTS + 1;
                  STUDENTS(NO_STUDENTS) = DATA_CARD,BY NAME;
                  STUDENTS(NO_STUDENTS).AVERAGE = AVE_GRADE;
               END INSERT;
           ELSE
               PUT SKIP(2) EDIT ('***ERROR IN INPUT***',
                  DATA_CARD) (A(25),F(7),A(20),F(1),5 F(2));
           GET SKIP EDIT (DATA_CARD.ID_NO,DATA_CARD.SEX,
               DATA_CARD.NAME,DATA_CARD.GRADES)
                  (F(7),F(1),A(20),5 F(2,0));
        END PROCESS;

        /* NOW SORT BY AVE. GRADE, ASCENDING ORDER */

        CALL SORT(STUDENTS,NO_STUDENTS);

        /* NOW PRINT THE SORTED RECORDS */

        PUT SKIP(5) EDIT ('MALES SORTED BY AVERAGE')
           (X(10),A);

LISTM:  DO K = 1 TO NO_STUDENTS;
           IF STUDENTS(K).SEX = 0 THEN
               PUT SKIP(2) EDIT (STUDENTS(K).IDENT,
                  STUDENTS(K).AVERAGE)
                  (X(5),A(20),F(10),F(9,2));
        END LISTM;

        PUT SKIP(5) EDIT ('FEMALES SORTED BY AVERAGE')
           (X(10),A);

LISTF:  DO K = 1 TO NO_STUDENTS;
           IF STUDENTS(K).SEX = 1 THEN
               PUT SKIP(2) EDIT (STUDENTS(K).IDENT,
                  STUDENTS(K).AVERAGE)
                  (X(5),A(20),F(10),F(9,2));
        END LISTF;

        PUT PAGE EDIT ('ALL STUDENTS SORTED BY AVERAGE')
           (X(10),A);
        PUT SKIP(2) EDIT((STUDENTS(K).IDENT,
           STUDENTS(K).AVERAGE  DO K = 1 TO NO_STUDENTS))
           (SKIP(2),X(5),A(20),F(10),F(9,2));
        PUT PAGE;
        END SECOND;
```

Fig. 10.9 An Alternative Grade Report Program

10.9 EXERCISES

10.1 Consider the following structure:

```
DECLARE 1 DEALS(100),
          2 SALESMAN,
            3 REGION CHARACTER(5),
            3 OFFICE_NO FIXED(5,0),
            3 BADGE_NO FIXED(5,0),
            3 INDUSTRY CHARACTER(10),
        2 RECORD,
          3 YEAR_TO_DATE,
            4 QUOTA FLOAT(6),
            4 SALES FLOAT(6),
            4 COMMISSION FLOAT(6),
          3 THIS_MONTH,
            4 QUOTA FLOAT(6),
            4 SALES FLOAT(6),
            4 COMMISSION FLOAT(6);
```

i) How many storage locations are associated with it?

ii) Write <u>one</u> PUT statement to print out all the information available on the 37th salesman.

iii) Write <u>one</u> statement to compute and store the commission for all salesmen for the current month. The commission rate is 20% of monthly sales.

iv) How many values will be printed by

```
PUT LIST (RECORD);
```

if executed in conjunction with this structure?

10.2 A small liquor business keeps the following kinds of stock on hand at each of three locations:

75 brands of wine broken down as:

30 brands of white
35 brands of red
10 brands of sparkling

25 brands of whiskey broken down as:

9 brands of Scotch
10 brands of rye
4 brands of bourbon
2 brands of Irish

6 brands of gin

4 brands of vodka

5 brands of liqueurs

The owners wish to keep track of the number of bottles on hand in each category.

(a) Draw a tree structure to describe this collection of data.

(b) Write one DECLARE statement to set up the PL/I structure to store this information.

10.3 Suppose an instructor records the name and five equally-weighted test scores on a data card for each student in the class. The registrar also supplies data cards each containing a student's name, identification number and number of courses successfully completed prior to completing the above course. Write a program, using structures, which uses these two sources of data to produce:

(a) A report showing the name, identification number, final mark for this course, and number of courses successfully completed including this course. (If the final mark is below 50, then this course is not successfully completed.)

(b) The name and final mark of any student whose mark is below 50.

(c) The name of any student who is on the instructor's list but not the registrar's.

(d) The names of the top three students in the class in order of final marks.

(e) Provide more readable reports by generating the lists of parts (a), (b), and (c) in alphabetical order.

(f) Produce a table for the instructor showing the name, the five test scores, and the final mark for each student. The last row of this table should show the class average for each test score and the class average for the final mark.

10.4 The standings record for any team in a certain league consists of

i) team name (up to 10 characters)
ii) number of games played - P (integer)
iii) number of games won - W (integer)
iv) number of games lost - L (integer)
v) number of games tied - T (integer)
vi) percentage (floating point)

The percentage is obtained from the formula

$$PCT = \frac{(W+0.5\times T)*100}{P}$$

There are eight teams in the league (hence four games each week) and each week the scores of each game are reported to the league office. As league manager you have to automate the process of updating the league standings.

To simplify matters, you may assume the process begins at the start of the season. Your solution should include a procedure, UPDATE, which will examine each game result and update the records for both teams. Another procedure, SORT, should then sort the records into descending order by percentage. In case of a tie in percentage, the order of the teams should be left unchanged. Your program should handle several weeks' scores, printing out not only the scores but also the league standings each week. The standings report should be in the form: TEAM P W L T PCT

10.5 This program is an elaboration of Exercise 10.4. The record described in the previous exercise is enlarged to include points for and points against. This information is used to break ties in percentage. When two or more teams have the same percentage the higher standing is awarded to the team with the largest difference in points for and against.

Produce reports as described in the previous exercise but produce your standings in the form:

```
TEAM      P   W   L   T   F   A   PCT
```

where F is points for
A is points against.

Chapter 11
More on Procedures

The internal procedures explained in Chapter 8 introduced the fundamental notions of how a procedure is defined, invoked, and allowed to exchange information. In this chapter, the same basic principles remain, but three alternatives to standard internal procedures are described: (1) functions, which provide a different way to invoke procedures and return values; (2) external procedures, which are available for use to any other procedure; and (3) recursive procedures, which may even call themselves.

11.1 BUILT-IN FUNCTIONS

PL/I has some "basic" operators, such as + or ||, which use one or two values to produce a new value. Thus "6 + 3" really says to apply the + operator to 6 and 3, which yields the value 9. This expression cannot be used in isolation but rather must appear in a context where the resulting value is appropriate, for example, X = 6 + 3;.

Such operators as + are "basic" to the language because they correspond closely to the basic capabilities of the underlying computer. However, there are many other "operators" which are desirable to have which are not so directly related to machine operations although they may seem basic to you. For example, the square root or logarithm of a number are important algebraic functions with no direct realization on most computers. Fortunately, PL/I provides many of these functions as if they really were basic operations. These are the built-in functions, such as LENGTH, SUBSTR, INDEX, HBOUND, SQRT, to name a few which have appeared previously. (A complete list of available built-in functions is given in Appendix D.)

The only difference to the programmer between basic operators and built-in functions is the way they are written (invoked). You might write INDEX(STRING,CHAR) compared to STR1 || STR2, or perhaps SQRT(X) rather than -X. Such functions must, of course, appear in the proper context also.

However, these built-in functions are not actually machine operations. They are in fact procedures whose definitions are automatically provided in PL/I and which compute values by using more basic operations. Mentioning a function name with an argument list corresponds to a procedure call, and the arguments included within parentheses are passed as parameters to the function itself.

Besides being called by merely mentioning its name, a function differs from a procedure in another important way. Its result is not explicitly returned through a parameter; instead, it is implicitly returned to be used within some statement of the calling program. The value is returned as if it "replaced" the function reference in the statement where the call occurred. This is why function references (like basic operators) must be used in an appropriate context.

For example there is a built-in function named ABS, which returns the absolute value of a number. To find the absolute value of X, add this to Y, and store the result in Z, you would write:

```
Z = ABS(X) + Y;
```

The built-in function ABS returns the value to the very place in the assignment statement from which it is called. The execution of the assignment statement then proceeds using the returned value. For example, if X were -3 and Y were 8, then ABS(X) is 3, and the above statement adds 3 and 8 and stores 11 in Z.

On the other hand, you could have written your own internal procedure to compute absolute values as follows:

```
OWNABS:  PROCEDURE(ORIG,RESULT);
         /*FIND ABSOLUTE VALUE OF ORIG*/
         DECLARE (ORIG,RESULT) FLOAT(6);
         IF ORIG >= 0 THEN
            RESULT = ORIG;
         ELSE
            RESULT = -ORIG;
         END OWNABS;
```

Using this procedure to find the absolute value of X, add it to Y, and store the sum in Z, your code might be:

```
CALL OWNABS(X,XABS);
Z = XABS + Y;
```

In contrast to ABS, this method involves the return of the absolute value in an explicit variable, XABS, which you then employ in the subsequent assignment statement.

Thus a function may be regarded as a variant of a procedure which is called by mentioning its name and which returns a value to the interior of the statement where its name was mentioned. A consequence of this method of returning values, however, is that a function is "normally" used for producing only a single value. It would seldom "make sense" to compute two values and then insert these at the same place in a statement. An exception to this is a statement dealing with arrays, in which case it might "make sense" for a function to return an array of values. However, when more than one result is desired, it is more common to CALL a procedure.

11.1.1 Arrays as Arguments to Built-in Functions

Recall that it is possible to write statements in PL/I which manipulate entire arrays of the same size. For example, if X, and Y are arrays with identical declarations and X and Y are completely full, then you may write Y = X + Y; and cause elements of X to be added to corresponding locations in Y. Similarly, you could add the absolute value of each element of X to the corresponding element of Y by writing:

```
Y = ABS(X) + Y;
```

Unless expressly prohibited, an argument to a built-in function can be either an entire array or a single value (for simple variables, array elements, or expressions). When you use an array as an argument, however, the function will return an array, of exactly the same size, containing the result of applying that function to each individual element of the array argument. Of course, if more than one argument is required, all must be arrays of exactly the same size.

The choice between arrays or individual values for arguments is available only for built-in functions. Your own PL/I functions or procedures cannot duplicate this flexibility.[1]

11.1.2 Some Important Built-in Functions

Many of the built-in functions are standard mathematical functions such as exponential (EXP), logarithm (LOG), sine (SIN), cosine (COS), and other trigonometric functions. The meaning of such functions would presumably already be understood by anyone needing to use them.

However, in this section we examine three quite useful built-in functions which are probably not already familiar to the reader. Two of these, TRANSLATE and VERIFY, are available in both PL/I and PL/C while the third, RAND, is available only in PL/C.

One of the problems frequently encountered in the editing of data is that of verifying that a data field contains only certain allowed characters. For example, the registrar at your school may want to verify that student ID numbers contain only the digits 0 to 9. The code to verify that no illegal characters are included involves checking each character of the subject string against every legal character (in one version, eleven PL/I statements were required).

The function VERIFY can be used to obtain the same results. Its general form is:

```
VERIFY (<string1>, <string2>)
```

VERIFY returns an integer constant which indicates the position of the first character in <string1> which is not in <string2>. If all

---

[1]The GENERIC attribute, available in PL/I but not in PL/C, provides more of this sort of flexibility.

the characters in <string1> are also in <string2> then VERIFY will return zero. <string1> is then the subject string being tested, and <string2> is the string of valid characters. For example

```
VERIFY ('93A42','0123456789')
```

returns the value 3 to indicate that the third character, A, is not one of the decimal digits. However

```
VERIFY ('ABE','ABCDE')
```

will return the value zero because every letter in the first argument appears in the second one.

The second function, TRANSLATE, is useful for encoding or decoding information. Consider the trivial problem of changing each of the letters A, B, and C into the digits 1, 2, and 3, respectively. If the character string to be so encoded is stored in WORD, then the code to accomplish this might be:

```
        L = LENGTH(WORD);
LOOP:   DO PSN = 1 TO L;
           K = INDEX ('ABC',SUBSTR(WORD,PSN,1));
           IF K ¬= 0 THEN
              SUBSTR(WORD,PSN,1) = SUBSTR('123',K,1);
        END LOOP;
```

A similar result can be achieved using TRANSLATE whose general form is:

```
TRANSLATE (<string1>, <string2>, <string3>);
```

This function returns a character string which differs from <string1> only in that every character from <string1> which also appears in <string3> will be replaced by the corresponding character from <string2>. More precisely, if the jth character in <string1> appears in the kth position of <string3>, then the jth character from <string1> will be replaced by the kth character from <string2>. Thus <string1> is to be transformed, <string3> contains characters to be replaced (if they occur), and <string2> contains their corresponding replacements. For example, the code:

```
WORD = 'CAD';
NEW = TRANSLATE (WORD,'123','ABC');
```

will cause '31D' to be produced. The function does not alter the actual argument, WORD; it merely returns a string derived from WORD.

We recommend that <string2> and <string3> always be of equal length. If <string2> is shorter than <string3>, then <string2> will be padded on the right with blanks, but this situation can cause problems in trying to recover from the encoding.

The third function, RAND, of interest primarily in simulation, is a pseudo-random number generator and is <u>not</u> available in PL/I. The general form for RAND is

```
RAND (x)
```

where x is a floating point number, between 0 and 1 ($0 < x < 1$), having at least nine significant digits, with the rightmost digit being odd. RAND will produce pseudo-random numbers uniformly distributed over the interval (0.0, 1.0). Since its returned value is of the same form as its argument, RAND may be given its previous value as its next argument. Thus it is often invoked by repeated execution of the statement:

```
X = RAND (X);
```

For example, the following code will produce the sequence of random numbers shown:

```
                .
                .
                .
        X = 0.123456789;
LOOP:   DO K = 1 TO 6;
           X = RAND(X);
           PUT SKIP LIST(X);
        END LOOP;
                .
                .
```

Numbers Produced by RAND:

```
.670871540
.167474904
.986754145
.436417197
.007386065
.576714397
```

Instead of merely printing out such values, it would be possible to employ them in other ways. To simulate card shuffling, fifty two such numbers could be generated and stored in an array. Then this array of numbers could be sorted, and an array representing the cards could be sorted in parallel.

11.2 USER-DEFINED FUNCTIONS

It is possible for you to define your own functions which can be used much like the built-in functions. Thus you can, in effect, extend the PL/I language by adding your own operators. But this is what you do whenever you write any procedure! Like a function, a procedure may be CALLed upon as if it performed a single (though possibly complex) operation without regard for just how it accomplishes that operation.

User defined functions, though, are used like built-in functions. They are invoked by mentioning their names (with arguments) and return values to be used directly in the expressions where they are invoked, rather than through an explicit parameter.

Unlike built-in functions, however, user-defined functions in PL/I are only able to cope with either simple variables or arrays (not both) as arguments. They also differ, of course, in that your own functions must be defined much like procedures whereas built-in functions need not be defined by you.

For example, you can define your own function, say MYABS, to find the absolute value of a number, mimicking the built-in function ABS. It would be called in a similar way:

```
Y = MYABS(X) + Y;
```

and could be defined as follows:

```
MYABS:  PROCEDURE(ORIG) RETURNS(FLOAT(6));
        DECLARE ORIG FLOAT(6);
        IF ORIG >= 0 THEN
           RETURN(ORIG);
        ELSE
           RETURN(-ORIG);
        END MYABS;
```

In order to contrast function definitions with procedures invoked by a CALL, we repeat the code for OWNABS, an internal procedure for finding absolute value:

```
OWNABS:  PROCEDURE(ORIG,RESULT);
         DECLARE(ORIG,RESULT) FLOAT(6);
         IF ORIG >= 0 THEN
            RESULT = ORIG;
         ELSE
            RESULT = -ORIG;
         END OWNABS;
```

The comparison between the function procedure MYABS and the internal procedure OWNABS shows three differences, all resulting from the way a function returns a value. First, MYABS needs only one parameter, ORIG, since its result is returned implicitly and not through the parameter list. The second difference is the RETURNS clause in the PROCEDURE statement. This announces the form of the result as FLOAT(6). It is sort of like a declaration, except that the entire function (and not just a variable) is being declared as producing a FLOAT(6) type of value.

However, the function definition must also make clear exactly which value is to be returned. This, of course, depends on the outcome of a particular execution. When its argument is nonnegative, the function will return the original argument, ORIG, as its value; otherwise it will return the negative of this, i.e., -ORIG, as its value. Hence, the third difference is the presence of one or more RETURN statements within the body of the procedure, specifying the particular value to be returned.

The general form of a function definition is therefore:

```
<entry-name>:  PROCEDURE (<parameter list>) RETURNS (<attribute>);
                  )
                 {
                  )
               END <entry-name>;
```

where the RETURNS attribute announces the form in which you wish the answer to be returned to the calling procedure. The particular answer which the procedure calculates will be sent back by the statement:

```
RETURN (<variable>);
```

or

```
RETURN (<expression>);
```

Once the resulting value has been determined, there is no point in prolonging execution of the function. Therefore, execution of the

RETURN statement (i) causes the specified value to be supplied to some statement in the calling procedure, and (ii) causes control to return to this statement, thereby terminating execution of the function!

As another example, we shall write a function to find the greatest common divisor (GCD) of two integers by the Euclidean Algorithm (Chapter 1). (There is no built-in function for this purpose.)

The procedure will have two integers as arguments and will send back a positive integer as a result. Hence, the skeleton structure of the procedure will be:

```
GCD:  PROCEDURE (N,M) RETURNS (FIXED(5,0));
      DECLARE (N,M) FIXED(5,0);
          }
      END GCD;
```

The original algorithm in Chapter 1 modifies the values of those numbers whose GCD it is finding. However, procedures should never modify the values of parameters (unless the modification is to be expected by the calling routine). Otherwise, you run the risk of unexpected "side-effects." Accordingly, our procedure begins by copying the values of parameters N and M into local variables, I and J. After this the values of I and J can be manipulated without affecting the values of the parameters. The function definition is otherwise a direct restatement of the algorithm of Fig. 1.3:

```
GCD:  PROCEDURE (N,M) RETURNS (FIXED(15,0));
      DECLARE (N,M) FIXED(15,0);
      DECLARE (I,J,K) FIXED(15,0);
      I = N;
      J = M;

LOOP: DO WHILE(I ¬= J);
         IF I < J THEN
SWAP:       DO;/*INTERCHANGE I AND J */
               K = I;
               I = J;
               J = K;
            END SWAP;
         K = I - J;
         I = J;
         J = K;
      END LOOP;
      RETURN (I);
      END GCD;
```

The statement RETURN(I); is the equivalent of Step 3 in the algorithm (Fig. 1.3). The value of I at that point of the program is the GCD of N and M and RETURN(I) communicates this value to the calling procedure.

This GCD function is shown again in Fig. 11.1 in the context of a main procedure -- but with one modification. The original algorithm only applies to positive integers, but the function has been generalized to consider negative arguments as well. This was done by assigning the absolute values of the arguments to I and J, using the built-in function ABS. The cases N=0, M=0, N=M=0 are left to the reader as an exercise.

```
                    /* FIGURE 11.1 */
EUCLID: PROCEDURE OPTIONS (MAIN);

        DECLARE (A,B,K) FIXED (15,0);

LOOP:   DO K = 1 TO 3;
           GET LIST (A,B);
           PUT SKIP LIST (A,B,GCD(A,B));
        END LOOP;

GCD:    PROCEDURE (N,M) RETURNS (FIXED(15,0));
        DECLARE (N,M) FIXED (15,0);
        DECLARE (I,J,K) FIXED (15,0);
        I = ABS(N);
        J = ABS(M);

LOOP:   DO WHILE (I ¬= J);
           IF I < J THEN
SWAP:         DO;
                 K = I;
                 I = J;
                 J = K;
              END SWAP;
           K = I - J;
           I = J;
           J = K;
        END LOOP;

        RETURN(I);

        END GCD;

        END EUCLID;
```

Fig. 11.1 Program to Implement Euclidean Algorithm

A message beginning DEFAULT ATTRIBUTES FOR ENTRY GCD ... will result from Fig. 11.1. This is not an error! It arises from a convention within PL/C and PL/I whereby every variable beginning with the letters I through N will be given the default attribute FIXED BINARY (15) unless otherwise declared; all other variable names will be defaulted to FLOAT(6) unless otherwise declared. Even though GCD is the name of a procedure, it is subject to these conventions and we have over-ridden them by appending the attribute RETURNS (FIXED (15,0)) to the procedure. The message serves merely as a reminder of this fact; there is no error and the message can be safely ignored.

Regarding the attributes of the arguments, our rules required arguments and parameters to have identical attributes. A function like GCD would thus appear to work only for integers declared as FIXED(15,0). This would be an unfortunate limitation.

For trouble-free results, we still recommend that identical attributes be used. However, for the sake of flexibility you are allowed to pass arguments with slightly different attributes, e.g., those with different numbers of digits or characters. Thus the function GCD could also be used to operate on variables declared as FIXED(10,0). It can also work on other "integer" forms, such as FIXED BINARY(15). However, it cannot operate on variables which are declared with noninteger attributes, such as FLOAT(6) or FIXED(7,2). The reasons for this have to do with the representation of numbers inside the computer and are beyond the scope of this book.

11.3 THE TRAPEZOIDAL RULE AS A USER DEFINED FUNCTION

Function procedures are commonly used when programming mathematical applications. They allow formulae containing function references to be transcribed directly into PL/I statements. Consequently, we now present a mathematical example, which is derived from calculus and which people without exposure to calculus will have to take on faith.

The example we have chosen is to calculate the value of an integral by using the "trapezoidal rule." This rule is used to approximate the integral:

$$\int_a^b f(x)dx$$

and is given by the formula:

$$\int_a^b f(x)dx \simeq \frac{h}{2}[f(a) + f(b) + \sum_{k=1}^{n-1} 2f(a+kh)]$$

where $h = (b-a)/n$, and n is the number of trapezoids.

Our problem is to translate this formula (regardless of its origins) into a computer program. To do so we must repeatedly evaluate f(x) for various values of x, and this suggests using a function procedure to evaluate f(x). Also the procedure to calculate the value of the integral is sufficiently general to warrant being written as a function procedure as well. Fig. 11.2 shows the function procedure for approximating an integral by the trapezoidal rule.

```
TRAP:  PROCEDURE (A,B,N) RETURNS (FLOAT(6));
       DECLARE (A,B) FLOAT(6),
                  N FIXED(5,0);
       DECLARE (SUM,H) FLOAT(6),
                  K FIXED(5,0);
       H = (B - A)/N;
       SUM = F(A) + F(B);
LOOP:  DO K = 1 TO N - 1;
          SUM = SUM + 2.0E0 * F(A + K * H);
       END LOOP;
       SUM = SUM * H/2.0E0;
       RETURN (SUM);
       END TRAP;
```

Fig. 11.2 Function Procedure to Implement the Trapezoidal Rule

The function procedure TRAP depends on another function procedure F to supply values for the particular function f(x) being integrated. Regardless of what integral we are trying to evaluate, the definition of TRAP will never change since the method doesn't change. However, for each integral under consideration, the definition of the function procedure F will change, since it alone defines the particular function f(x) to be integrated. In PL/C this means that during an execution of the program only one function f can be integrated using TRAP. To integrate a different function, the definition of function procedure F would have to be changed and a subsequent run of the program would be required. This limitation does not apply to PL/I.[2]

Figure 11.3 shows TRAP when F is defined to represent $f(x) = x^2$. The integral being evaluated is

$$\int_0^2 x^2 dx$$

Some versions of PL/C may give the message:

WARNING CG09 CONVERSION REQUIRED TO MATCH
ARGUMENT X OF F

This message is due to the manner in which PL/C evaluates the expression F(A + K * H). The details of this calculation are beyond the scope of this book. However it is safe to say that the message can be ignored for most problems solved by beginning programmers.

The program in Fig. 11.3 also gives 2.67999 as the value of

$$\int_0^2 x^2 dx$$

whereas the exact analytic solution gives the answer as 8/3 or 2.66667. This difference is not due to any error on the part of the computer. Rather it is due to the fact that the trapezoidal rule is only an "approximation," and even at that, only 10 trapezoids were used. A larger number of trapezoids would have given a better approximation, since the area being calculated would have borne closer resemblance to the area under the curve of f(x).

11.4 EXTERNAL PROCEDURES

So far we have concentrated on breaking down a single problem into smaller subproblems and implementing some of these as procedures. You have probably noticed that certain subproblems keep recurring as parts of several larger problems. For example, the need to search or sort an array arises again and again, as do many mathematical functions. If you have already solved such a subproblem, why "reinvent the wheel"? One very important advantage of a procedure is that it can be reused in program after program to solve different

---

[2]In PL/I (but not in PL/C) it is possible to pass the entry-name of a procedure as an argument to another procedure using the ENTRY attribute. This would allow F to refer to different function procedures each time TRAP is invoked.

problems. This reusability is an important reason for making your procedures both general and "safe," e.g., by avoiding global variables and not altering parameters indiscriminately.

```
             /* FIGURE 11.3 */
QUAD:     PROCEDURE OPTIONS (MAIN);

          DECLARE
             (A,B) FLOAT(6),
             N FIXED (5,0);
          A = 0.0;
          B = 2.0;
          N = 10;
          PUT SKIP LIST
             (' THE INTEGRAL OF X**2 DX FROM 0 TO 2 IS');
          PUT SKIP LIST (TRAP(A,B,N));

TRAP:     PROCEDURE (A,B,N) RETURNS (FLOAT(6));
          DECLARE
             (A,B) FLOAT (6),
             N FIXED (5,0);
          DECLARE
             (SUM,H) FLOAT (6),
             K FIXED (5,0);
          H = (B - A)/N;
          SUM = F(A) + F(B);

LOOP:     DO K = 1 TO N-1;
             SUM = SUM + 2.0E0 * F(A + K*H);
          END LOOP;

          SUM = SUM * (H / 2.0E0);
          RETURN (SUM);

          END TRAP;

F:        PROCEDURE (X) RETURNS (FLOAT(6));
          DECLARE X FLOAT(6);
          DECLARE Y FLOAT(6);
          Y = X**2;
          RETURN (Y);

          END F;

          END QUAD;
```

Figure 11.3

Over the course of your "programming career," you will want to build a collection or so called <u>library</u> of commonly needed procedures. If they are documented and maintained in an orderly fashion, they can be inserted in various programs to be executed when they are needed.

In actual fact, there is no need to insert these procedures physically inside the main procedure. They can retain their separate identities by being placed "alongside" the main procedure. Such procedures are called <u>external</u>.

In this case we need only advise the system that other procedures following the main procedure are part of the same program. This is accomplished by placing a control card before each external procedure with *PROCESS punched in columns 1 through 8. A sample deck organization for such a program is shown in Fig. 11.4.

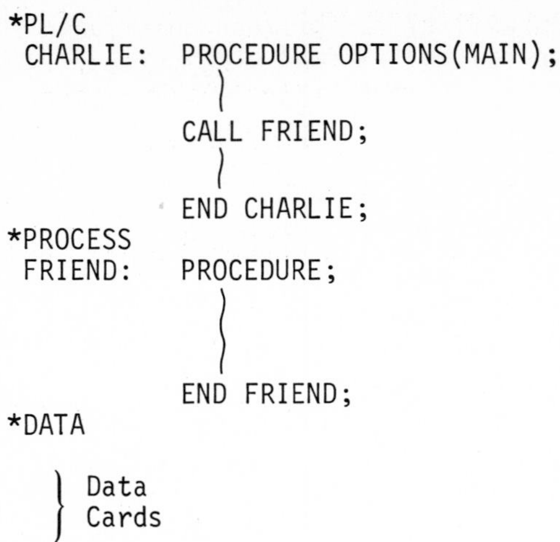

```
*PL/C
 CHARLIE:  PROCEDURE OPTIONS(MAIN);
              )
           CALL FRIEND;
              )
           END CHARLIE;
*PROCESS
 FRIEND:   PROCEDURE;
              )
           END FRIEND;
*DATA
    } Data
      Cards
```

Fig. 11.4 Deck Organization with External Procedures

Besides the fact that <u>each</u> external procedure is preceded by a *PROCESS card, the only other difference between internal and external procedures is that the name of an external procedure may not exceed seven characters in length.

A program must have one and only one MAIN procedure. The designation OPTIONS(MAIN) tells the system which of (possibly) several procedures to <u>begin</u> <u>executing</u>. From there it is up to your program to direct flow of control among its own procedures.

Incidentally, an external procedure may be called by any other procedure within the program (except, of course, by itself or one of its own internal procedures). In other words, an external procedure is "public."

Fig. 11.5 shows the result of placing the procedures from Fig. 11.3 external to the main procedure. Once again PL/C will object to the RETURNS attributes for TRAP and F, but as before we can safely ignore the messages.

11.4.1 <u>The EXTERNAL Storage Attribute</u>

Recall that there are three classes of variables within procedures: parameters, global variables, and local variables. Parameters and global variables are intended for interprocedure communication, while local variables serve the opposite purpose: to isolate the effects of changing a variable to the confines of the declaring procedure. Whenever a procedure declares (or uses) a variable, that variable is presumably global and therefore available to any internal procedure which does not use it as a parameter or explicitly redeclare it, making it local. However, such variables are global only with respect to the contained <u>internal</u> procedures. They are <u>not</u> available to external procedures.

```
STMT LEVEL NEST BLOCK MLVL  SOURCE TEXT

                                        /* FIGURE 11.5 */
  1                           QUAD:    PROCEDURE OPTIONS (MAIN);

  2    1          1                    DECLARE
                                          (A.B) FLOAT (6).
                                          N FIXED (5.0);
  3    1          1                    A = 0.0;
  4    1          1                    B = 2.0;
  5    1          1                    N = 10;
  6    1          1                    PUT SKIP LIST
                                          (' THE INTEGRAL OF X**2 DX FROM 0 TO 2 IS');
  7    1          1                    PUT SKIP LIST (TRAP(A.B.N));

  8    1          1                    END QUAD;

$PROCESS

  9                           TRAP:    PROCEDURE (A.B.N) RETURNS (FLOAT(6));
 10    1          2                    DECLARE
                                          (A.B) FLOAT (6).
                                          N FIXED (5.0);
 11    1          2                    DECLARE
                                          (SUM.H) FLOAT (6).
                                          K FIXED (5.0);
 12    1          2                    H = (B - A)/N;
 13    1          2                    SUM = F(A) + F(B);

 14    1          2           LOOP:    DO K = 1 TO N-1;
 15    1     1    2                       SUM = SUM + 2.0E0 * F(A + K*H);
 16    1     1    2                    END LOOP;

 17    1          2                    SUM = SUM * (H / 2.0E0);
 18    1          2                    RETURN (SUM);

 19    1          2                    END TRAP;

$PROCESS

 20                           F:       PROCEDURE (X) RETURNS (FLOAT(6));
 21    1          3                    DECLARE X FLOAT(6);
 22    1          3                    DECLARE Y FLOAT(6);
 23    1          3                    Y = X*X;
 24    1          3                    RETURN (Y);

 25    1          3                    END F;
```

Fig. 11.5 Use of External Procedure

Two procedures which are external to one another may also communicate via parameters or "global" variables. Transfer of values through parameters works as described before (Section 8.2.3). However, if two external procedures are to share a variable as if it were global, then <u>both</u> must explicitly declare it as EXTERNAL, as follows:

DECLARE <variable> <other attributes> EXTERNAL;

This EXTERNAL attribute indicates that the variable is not properly contained in the declaring procedure, but instead is "outside" this procedure and available to any other procedure declaring it EXTERNAL. Thus any name (which is not a parameter) appearing in two external procedures is assumed to represent two separate locations local to the respective procedures <u>unless</u> both procedures designate it EXTERNAL. This is just the opposite of the case for internal procedures.

The EXTERNAL attribute extends the scope of a variable. It can therefore be used to provide a data link between <u>any</u> two (or more) procedures, anywhere in a program. However, we recommend that its use be restricted to communicating between external procedures, and even then it should be employed only when there is some special reason for not using parameters. Fig. 11.6 illustrates some possible changes in scope due to EXTERNAL.

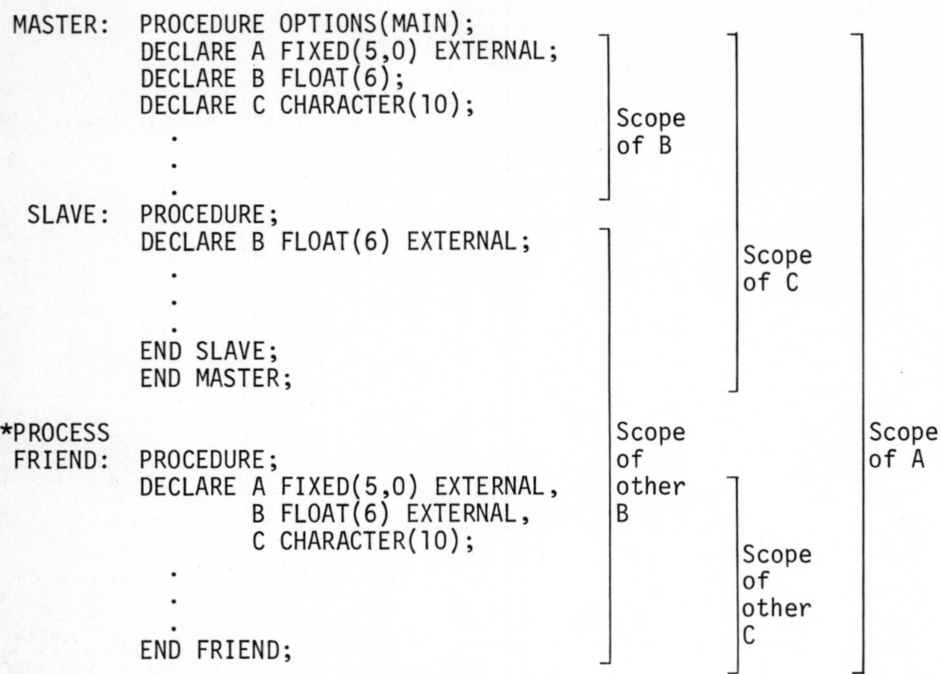

```
 MASTER:  PROCEDURE OPTIONS(MAIN);
          DECLARE A FIXED(5,0) EXTERNAL;
          DECLARE B FLOAT(6);
          DECLARE C CHARACTER(10);
             .
             .
             .
  SLAVE:  PROCEDURE;
          DECLARE B FLOAT(6) EXTERNAL;
             .
             .
             .
          END SLAVE;
          END MASTER;

*PROCESS
 FRIEND:  PROCEDURE;
          DECLARE A FIXED(5,0) EXTERNAL,
                  B FLOAT(6) EXTERNAL,
                  C CHARACTER(10);
             .
             .
             .
          END FRIEND;
```


Fig. 11.6 The Effect of EXTERNAL on Scope of A and B

11.4.2 Library Procedures

Instead of saving your external procedure programs in card-deck form, you can also create a library of these often-used routines inside the computer system on some other medium, such as magnetic tape or disk.[3] One reason for storing procedures in this way is to avoid including cumbersome card decks for the procedures within your program. You need only tell the system the name of the procedure in the library which you intend to use. This information is furnished by means of the *INCLUDE control card, whose general form is:

*INCLUDE <procedure entry-name>

As with the other control cards, *INCLUDE is punched beginning in column 1.

Another reason for storing procedures in a system library is to make them truly public. Such procedures are available for use by any PL/I user, not necessarily their original author. PL/C does not (as of this writing) come with a library of specially written procedures. However, your installation may have prepared its own library of

---

[3]Whether and how you can save your own procedures in this way depends on your local installation and is not properly part of PL/C or PL/I.

```
                                                     /* FIGURE 11.7 */
  1                                SHELL:   PROCEDURE OPTIONS (MAIN);

                                            /* PROGRAM USING A LIBRARY PROCEDURE */

                                            DECLARE
  2      1          1                           ARRAY(50) CHARACTER (10),
                                                UP_DOWN CHARACTER (1),
                                                (K,N) FIXED (5,0);

  3      1          1                       GET LIST (N);
  4      1          1                       GET EDIT ((ARRAY(K) DO K = 1 TO N)) (SKIP,A(10));
  5      1          1                       PUT EDIT ((ARRAY(K) DO K = 1 TO N)) (SKIP,A(10));
  6      1          1                       UP_DOWN = 'A';
  7      1          1                       CALL CISSRTC (ARRAY,N,UP_DOWN);
  8      1          1                       PUT SKIP(2);
  9      1          1                       PUT EDIT ((ARRAY(K) DO K = 1 TO N)) (SKIP,A(10));

 10      1          1                       END SHELL;

*PROCESS

 11                                CISSRTC:
                                            PROCEDURE (ARRAY,SIZE,UPDOWN);
                                            /* A SIMPLIFIED SHELL SORT TO SORT A CHARACTER
                                                ARRAY OF LENGTH "SIZE" INTO ASCENDING OR
                                                DESCENDING ORDER AS INDICATED BY "UPDOWN".
                                                TRANSLATED FROM FORTRAN BY GRAHAM BISHOP AT THE
                                                UNIVERSITY OF GUELPH. */
                                            DECLARE
 12      1          2                           (ARRAY(*),UPDOWN) CHARACTER (*),
                                                SIZE FIXED (5,0);
                                            DECLARE
 13      1          2                           TEMP CHARACTER (50) VARYING,
                                                (GAP,MAX,K,KPLUSGAP,LOWER,HIGHP1) FIXED (5,0),
                                                FLAG BIT (1);
 14      1          2                       IF SIZE > DIM(ARRAY,1) THEN
 15      1          2              TOOLARGE:    DO;
 16      1    1     2                               PUT SKIP(4) EDIT (' ERROR - NO. ELEMENTS',
                                                        ' REQUESTED FOR SORTING IS LARGER THAN',
                                                        ' SIZE OF ARRAY ** PROGRAM TERMINATED**')
                                                        (A);
 17      1    1     2                               STOP;
 18      1    1     2                           END TOOLARGE;
 19      1          2                       GAP = SIZE;
 20      1          2                       LOWER = LBOUND(ARRAY,1);
 21      1          2              LOOP1:   DO WHILE (GAP > 1);
 22      1    1     2                           GAP = GAP/2;
 23      1    1     2                           MAX = LOWER - 1 + SIZE - GAP;
 24      1    1     2                           FLAG = '1'B;
 25      1    1     2              LOOP2:       DO WHILE (FLAG);
 26      1    2     2                               FLAG = '0'B;
 27      1    2     2              LOOP3:           DO K = LOWER TO MAX;
 28      1    3     2                                   KPLUSGAP = K + GAP;
 29      1    3     2                                   IF ARRAY(K) > ARRAY(KPLUSGAP) THEN
 30      1    3     2              SWAP:                    DO;
 31      1    4     2                                           TEMP = ARRAY(K);
 32      1    4     2                                           ARRAY(K) = ARRAY(KPLUSGAP);
 33      1    4     2                                           ARRAY(KPLUSGAP) = TEMP;
 34      1    4     2                                           FLAG = '1'B;
 35      1    4     2                                       END SWAP;
 36      1    3     2                               END LOOP3;
 37      1    2     2                           END LOOP2;
 38      1    1     2                       END LOOP1;
 39      1          2                       IF UPDOWN = 'D' THEN
 40      1          2              DESCEND:     DO;
 41      1    1     2                               HIGHP1 = LOWER + SIZE;
 42      1    1     2              DOWN:            DO K = LOWER TO (LOWER - 1 + SIZE - SIZE/2);
 43      1    2     2                                   HIGHP1 = HIGHP1 - 1;
 44      1    2     2                                   TEMP = ARRAY(K);
 45      1    2     2                                   ARRAY(K) = ARRAY(HIGHP1);
 46      1    2     2                                   ARRAY(HIGHP1) = TEMP;
 47      1    2     2                               END DOWN;
 48      1    1     2                           END DESCEND;
 49      1          2                       END CISSRTC;
```

Fig. 11.7 Shell Sort Executed from a Library

routines which can be accessed by anyone. At our own installation, such a library has been prepared, and Fig. 11.7 is an example of a program executing one of these procedures. It is named CISSRTC and happens to be an array sorting method known as a "Shell sort." We will not explain how the Shell sort works, though, because the point is precisely that we only care what it does and not how it works. The deck organization is shown in Fig. 11.8.

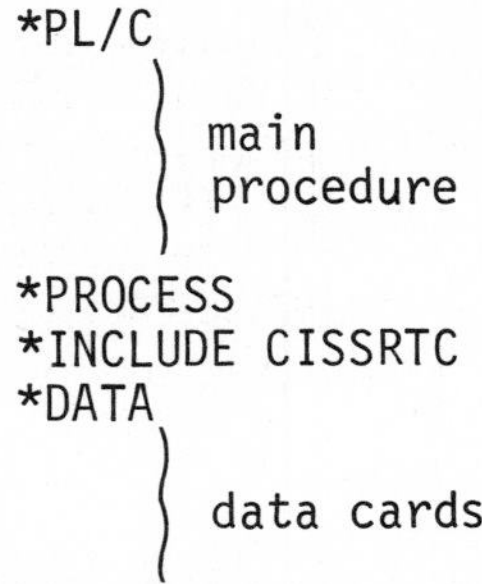

Fig. 11.8 Deck Organization Using a Library Procedure

Note that *PROCESS is needed as well as *INCLUDE since CISSRTC is an external procedure. Incidentally, the *INCLUDE card is not printed even though it was used in the deck.

11.5 RECURSIVE PROCEDURES

11.5.1 Recursion in English

In English it is sometimes appropriate to define something in terms of itself. For example, once a digit has been defined as one of the symbols 0,1,2,...,9, you might try to define an integer as a digit, possibly followed by another digit, possibly followed by another digit, etc. But this attempt to define an integer solely in terms of a simpler concept (digit) led to an unfortunate use of "etc." Of course, to us humans this suggests some indefinite amount of "looping" on the phrase "possibly followed by another digit," but is probably acceptable. However, this definition would not be sufficiently precise for implementation on a computer.

A much neater and more precise definition of integer is:
(i) a digit;
or (ii) a digit followed by an integer.
When a definition of a term includes the same term itself, the definition is said to be recursive.

Though the concept of integer is employed in its own definition, in any concrete application of this definition, the actual integer involved in Step (ii) is simpler (by having fewer digits) than the actual integer being defined. For example, let us attempt to verify that '123' is an integer. Since 123 is not a digit (i), we must see whether it conforms to alternative (ii). The first character '1' is a digit and '23' may be an integer. Now we are faced with the problem of testing whether '23' is actually an integer, which means reapplying the definition to this shorter string of symbols. Since '23' is not a digit (i), we try alternative (ii) and discover that '2' is a digit followed by a possible integer, '3'. Once again we apply the definition to test the even simpler candidate, 3. This time we find that 3 is a digit (i) and therefore an integer. Working backwards, we now know that '23' is a digit followed by an integer and therefore is itself an integer. One more step confirms that 123 is a digit followed by an integer, and therefore 123 is itself an integer.

Though this appears unduly tedious, it is obviously more precise. This sort of precision is needed in a program.

The important point about this example, though, is that each successive application of the definition was for successively shorter candidates. This guarantees that the process will stop. Eventually you will either encounter a character which is not a digit or else work down to only a single digit which can be confirmed as an integer by part (i) of the definition. This part (i) very significantly did not involve the concept of integer; it therefore provides a way to break the cycle.

Such recursive definitions are subtle. If they do not keep reducing the complexity of the problem, or if they fail to provide an alternative stopping criterion like (i), which does not involve the same concept over again, then you may have to keep testing forever. In English such definitions are called "circular." For example, if you define a cow as a female animal whose mother was a cow, you really get nowhere. Someone who has never seen a cow could spend a lifetime cycling through this definition without ever discovering what a cow really is.

11.5.2 Recursion in PL/I

The motive for all the discussion on recursive definitions in English was to pave the way for recursive definitions in PL/I. In an analogous way, it is possible to define a PL/I procedure in terms of itself, i.e., to have within the code which constitutes the procedure definition, a call which (ultimately) invokes the same procedure. Most of the observations about recursive definitions in English also apply to these so-called "recursive procedures" in PL/I.

A recursive procedure is one which can call itself -- either directly or indirectly. So far we have prohibited calls of the kind shown below:

```
M:  PROCEDURE;                    P:  PROCEDURE;
        }                                 }
    CALL M;                           CALL Q;
        }                                 }
    END M;                        Q:  PROCEDURE;
                                          }
                                      CALL P;
                                          }
                                      END Q;
                                      END P;
```

However, these are the specialized sorts of CALL we are now about to permit. Of course, function procedures and external procedures may also be used recursively.

Returning to our recursive definition of an integer, for example, we could write a corresponding algorithm to test whether a string of characters represents an integer:

```
1.      if the string consists of a single character then
1.1        if that character is a digit then
              answer 'yes';
1.2        otherwise
              answer 'no';
2.      otherwise do the following;
2.1        isolate the first character from the balance;
2.2        if the first character is a digit and the
              balance is an integer, then
              answer 'yes';
2.3        otherwise
              answer 'no';
3.      end.
```

Now assume that we have a function procedure named DIGIT, which examines a single character and returns the value 'YES' if that character is a digit and 'NO' otherwise. We could then convert our algorithm into a function procedure named INTGR. INTGR returns the value 'YES' if it was given a string of digits (i.e., an "integer") as its parameter and returns 'NO' otherwise.

This procedure is a straightforward transcription of the algorithm. Notice that the procedure INTGR contains a <u>call</u> to INTGR, just as the recursive definition of integer included the word "integer." The only new language feature is the keyword RECURSIVE on the same line as the PROCEDURE statement to denote this very special feature. (See Fig. 11.9.) Note that the code for DIGIT has not been shown yet.

```
INTGR:   PROCEDURE (STRING)
            RETURNS (CHARACTER(3) VARYING) RECURSIVE;
         DECLARE STRING CHARACTER(*) VARYING;
         DECLARE (FIRST_CHAR,BALANCE) CHARACTER(80) VARYING;
         IF LENGTH(STRING) = 1 THEN
            IF DIGIT(STRING) = 'YES' THEN
               RETURN('YES');
            ELSE
               RETURN ('NO');
         ELSE

BREAKUP:    DO;
               FIRST_CHAR = SUBSTR(STRING,1,1);
               BALANCE = SUBSTR(STRING,2);
               IF DIGIT(FIRST_CHAR) = 'YES' &
                  INTGR(BALANCE) = 'YES' THEN
                  RETURN ('YES');
               ELSE
                  RETURN ('NO');
            END BREAKUP;

         END INTGR;
```

Figure 11.9

Any procedure which is intended to be used recursively must have the keyword RECURSIVE following the parameter list (if any). Thus the general form of a recursive procedure is:

```
<entry-name>:  PROCEDURE (<parameter-list>)  RECURSIVE;
                   .
                   .
                   .
               END <entry-name>;
```

Since recursive procedures are prone to the same potential difficulties as recursive definitions in English (i.e., eternal looping), it is most important to clearly define the stopping criteria. There must be some path for flow of control through the procedure which does not encounter a recursive call, and you must be certain that such a path will ultimately be followed. Consequently, the stopping conditions in a recursive procedure should be contained in the first lines of code. One other tip is to be doubly sure that <u>every</u> variable is either a parameter or declared locally. Global variables can be especially troublesome with recursion and should be avoided.

Figure 11.10 shows the procedure INTGR in the context of a main procedure and the function DIGIT. Note that DIGIT is <u>not</u> recursive since it never calls itself or INTGR. The data item used was '123,' and we suggest comparing the output generated by the program with the English analysis of '123' in Section 11.5.1.

11.5.3 A Recursive Procedure for the Binary Search

As explained in Chapter 7, the motive for sorting collections of data is to facilitate later searches for specific items in the collection. The "binary search" is a search algorithm which exploits the ordering of the data even more effectively than did the "quadratic search" (Section 7.5.3).

The basic idea is simple: when looking for a specific item in an <u>ordered</u> array, the most useful place to begin is in the <u>middle</u>. If the middle element is not the one you are seeking, at least you know which half of the array might contain the desired item. If the middle element was too large, then you must continue looking in the first half of the array. If the middle element was too small, then you can concentrate on the second half of the array. Whatever the outcome, this single comparison enables you to eliminate half of the array from consideration. This general strategy can be written:

```
1.     find the middle element of array;
2.1       if middle element = desired item then
             the search ends;
2.2       otherwise
2.2.1        if middle value > desired item then
                search first half of array;
2.2.2        otherwise search second half of array;
3.     end.
```

This outline needs certain refinements. First of all, the algorithm should "report" the result of the search. The "result"

```
STMT LEVEL NEST BLOCK MLVL  SOURCE TEXT

                                        /* FIGURE 11.10 */
  1                        RECUR:  PROCEDURE OPTIONS (MAIN);
  2    1         1                 DECLARE SAMPLE CHARACTER(80) VARYING;
  3    1         1                 GET LIST (SAMPLE);
  4    1         1                 PUT DATA (SAMPLE);
  5    1         1                 IF INTGR(SAMPLE) = 'YES' THEN
  6    1         1                    PUT SKIP LIST ('VALID INTEGER');
  7    1         1                 ELSE
                                      PUT LIST ('INVALID INTEGER');

  8    1         1         INTGR:  PROCEDURE (STRING)
                                      RETURNS (CHARACTER(3) VARYING) RECURSIVE;
  9    2         2                 DECLARE STRING CHARACTER(*) VARYING;
 10    2         2                 DECLARE (FIRST_CHAR,BALANCE) CHARACTER(80) VARYING;
 11    2         2                 PUT SKIP EDIT ('IN INTGR TESTING ',STRING) (A);
 12    2         2                 IF LENGTH(STRING) = 1 THEN
 13    2         2                    IF DIGIT(STRING) = 'YES' THEN
 14    2         2                       RETURN('YES');
 15    2         2                    ELSE
                                         RETURN ('NO');
 16    2         2                 ELSE

                           BREAKUP:   DO;
 17    2    1    2                       FIRST_CHAR = SUBSTR(STRING,1,1);
 18    2    1    2                       BALANCE = SUBSTR(STRING,2);
 19    2    1    2                       IF DIGIT(FIRST_CHAR) = 'YES' &
                                            INTGR(BALANCE) = 'YES' THEN
 20    2    1    2                          RETURN ('YES');
 21    2    1    2                       ELSE
                                            RETURN ('NO');
 22    2    1    2                    END BREAKUP;

 23    2         2                 END INTGR;

 24    1         1         DIGIT:  PROCEDURE (ONE_CHAR) RETURNS(CHARACTER(3) VARYING);
 25    2         3                 DECLARE ONE_CHAR CHARACTER(*) VARYING;
 26    2         3                 PUT SKIP EDIT ('IN DIGIT TESTING ',ONE_CHAR) (A);
 27    2         3                 IF INDEX('0123456789',ONE_CHAR) ¬= 0 THEN
 28    2         3                    RETURN ('YES');
 29    2         3                 ELSE
                                      RETURN ('NO');
 30    2         3                 END DIGIT;

 31    1         1                 END RECUR;

SAMPLE='123';
IN INTGR TESTING 123
IN DIGIT TESTING 1
IN INTGR TESTING 23
IN DIGIT TESTING 2
IN INTGR TESTING 3
IN DIGIT TESTING 3
VALID INTEGER


IN STMT   31  PROGRAM RETURNS FROM MAIN PROCEDURE.

IN STMT   31  DYNAMIC FLOW TRACE:
                0019->0008    0012->0016    0019->0024    0027->0028    0028->0019    0019->0008    0012->0013
                0013->0024    0027->0028    0028->0013    0013->0014    0014->0019    0019->0020    0020->0019
                0019->0020    0020->0005    0005->0006    0031->0000

IN STMT   31  SCALARS AND BLOCK-TRACE:

***** MAIN PROCEDURE RECUR

SAMPLE='123'
```

Figure 11.10

will be either the *location* of the item within the array of items or else a 0 to denote failure to find the item. Secondly, if the array contains an even number of items, there is no "middle item." In this case we shall adopt the convention of choosing the smaller (earlier) of the two elements which straddle the middle. Finally, there is no point searching an array which contains no elements. A vacuous array is indicated when the lower bound is greater than the upper bound. This condition should be tested first. Only if the lower bound is not greater than the upper bound should the subdivision and further searching be performed. These refinements are incorporated in the version of the algorithm shown in Fig. 11.11.

```
1.      if low bound > high bound then report failure (0);
2.      otherwise
2.1        find middle element;
2.2        if middle element is desired value then
              report middle position;
2.3        otherwise
2.3.1         if middle element > desired value then
                 search first half of array;
2.3.2         otherwise
                 search second half of array;
3.      end.
```

Fig. 11.11 Binary Search Algorithm

Having narrowed the field of candidates by half, we must proceed to search the remaining half of the array (either in Step 2.3.1 or 2.3.2). However, since "half" of an ordered array is still an ordered array, we may apply *exactly* the same algorithm to this smaller array! In other words, inspect *its* middle element, and if it is not the desired item, then search one half of *this* array (again in the same way). Thus the algorithm of Fig. 11.11 is recursive, in that it is reapplied to successively smaller (by half) portions of the original array. It zeros in on the correct region until either the desired item has been found or the search fails because the item is not in the array. Thus the algorithm is guaranteed to stop. Fig. 11.12 shows this algorithm applied to an original array whose size is conveniently chosen as 15.[4] You should use this algorithm in an attempt to find a value which is *not* stored in the array, such as 75.

The algorithm of Fig. 11.11 can be converted directly into the recursive procedure BINARY shown in Fig. 11.13. The array name is passed as the first parameter, so the procedure can work on any one-dimensional array. The first and last locations of interest within the array are the second and third parameters. On successive calls, these numbers will be approaching one another to narrow the extent of the search. The fourth parameter is the desired item, and the fifth is the result, which will be returned to the procedure which called

---

[4]If the array contains $2^n -1$ elements, then *every* application of the algorithm finds a true "middle element" and two equal-sized "halves."

BINARY (this often being an "earlier" version of BINARY itself). Once again, note the word RECURSIVE on the first line, and the absence of any global variables.

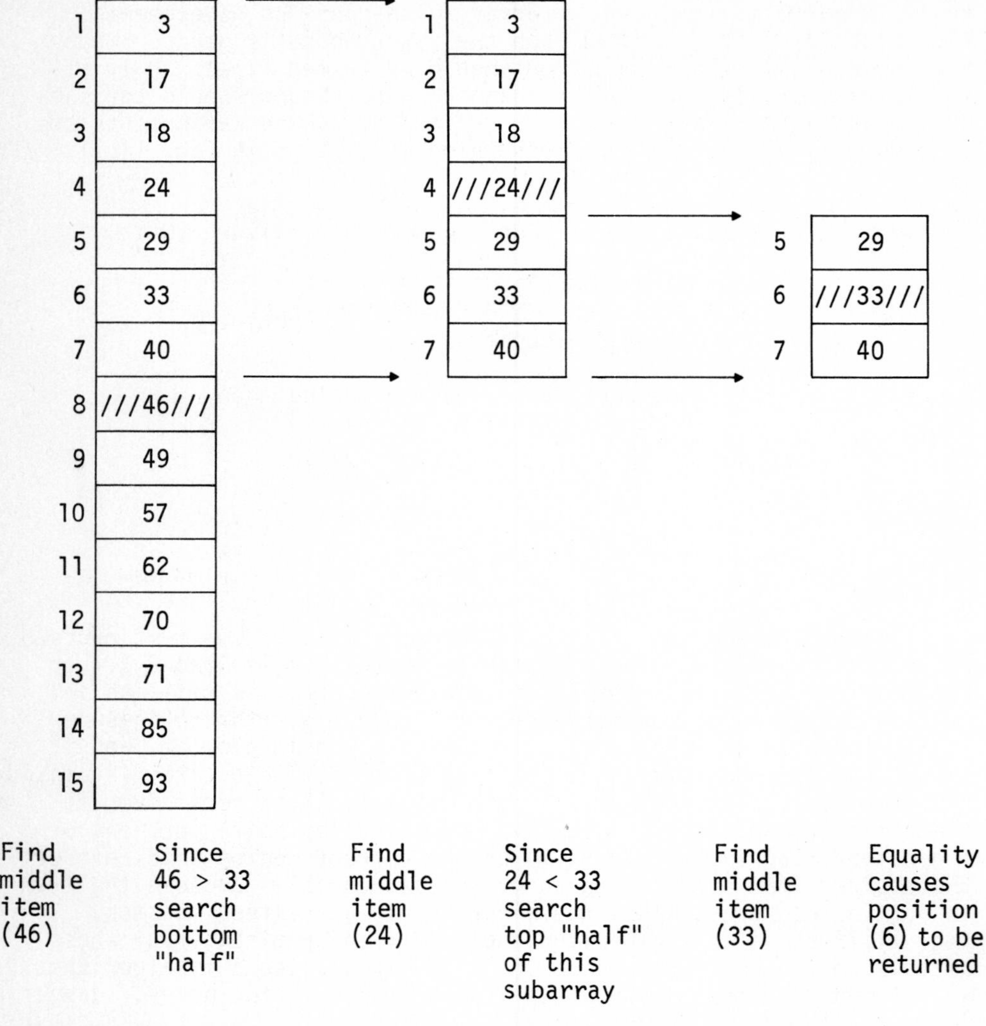

Fig. 11.12 Successive Steps in the Binary Search for Value 33

```
        /* FIGURE 11.13 */
SEARCH: PROCEDURE OPTIONS (MAIN);

        /* AN IMPLEMENTATION OF THE BINARY SEARCH USING
           A RECURSIVE PROCEDURE */

        DECLARE
           A(15) FLOAT (6), /* NOS. TO BE SEARCHED */
           VALUE FLOAT (6), /* NO. SOUGHT */
           PLACE FIXED (5,0); /* POSITION OF NO SOUGHT */
        GET LIST (A);
        GET LIST (VALUE);
        CALL BINARY (A,1,15,VALUE,PLACE);
        PUT SKIP DATA (VALUE,PLACE);

BINARY: PROCEDURE (ARY,FIRST,LAST,ITEM,RESULT) RECURSIVE;
        DECLARE (ARY(*), /* ARRAY TO BE SEARCHED */
                 ITEM) FLOAT(6), /* VALUE SOUGHT */
                 (FIRST, /* LOW BOUND OF ARRAY */
                 LAST, /* HIGH BOUND OF ARRAY */
                 RESULT) FIXED (5,0);  /* 0 = NOT FOUND */
        DECLARE MIDDLE FIXED (5,0);
        PUT SKIP EDIT ('SEARCHING POSITIONS',FIRST,' TO',LAST)
           (A,F(3));

        IF FIRST > LAST THEN
           RESULT = 0; /* UNSUCCESSFUL SEARCH */
        ELSE

AGAIN:     DO; /* TRY AGAIN */
              MIDDLE = (FIRST + LAST) / 2;
              IF ARY(MIDDLE) = ITEM THEN
                 RESULT = MIDDLE; /* FOUND IT */
              ELSE

SPLIT:           DO; /* SPLIT ARRAY IN HALF & SEARCH ONE HALF */
                    IF ARY(MIDDLE) < ITEM THEN
                       CALL BINARY (ARY,MIDDLE + 1,LAST,ITEM,RESULT);
                    ELSE
                       CALL BINARY (ARY,FIRST,MIDDLE - 1,ITEM,RESULT);
                 END SPLIT;

           END AGAIN;
           PUT SKIP EDIT (ITEM,' IS AT POSITION',RESULT)
              (F(3),A);

        END BINARY;


SEARCHING POSITIONS  1 TO 15
SEARCHING POSITIONS  1 TO  7
SEARCHING POSITIONS  5 TO  7
 33 IS AT POSITION  6
 33 IS AT POSITION  6
 33 IS AT POSITION  6
VALUE= 3.30000E+01       PLACE=        6;
```

Fig. 11.13 Binary Search Procedure

11.6 REVIEW OF RULES

1. Functions are invoked (called) by using their names with an argument list in an appropriate context. Recalling that a function returns a value, the statement containing the call must be able to utilize this value in place of the function call.

2. Built-in functions are supplied as part of PL/I and are listed in Appendix D. Most may be given either a single value or an array as an argument. If given an array, they return an array of the same size. This flexibility is not available in user-defined functions.

3. You may define your own function procedures as follows:

```
<entry-name>:  PROCEDURE(<parameter list>) RETURNS(<attributes
                                                   of results>);

                  code for function, including
                  RETURN(<value to be returned>);

               END <entry-name>;
```

4. An external procedure may be placed on the same level as (i.e., not within) the single MAIN procedure. Each external procedure must be preceded by a *PROCESS control card. Any procedure may call an external procedure.

5. If the external procedure is from a system library, rather than on cards within your job, you must also use the control card:

```
*INCLUDE <external procedure name>
```

   which in effect places the procedure within your job.

6. Any procedure which may call itself either directly or indirectly must be specified as RECURSIVE as part of the PROCEDURE statement.

7. The normal scope rules may be extended to allow procedures to communicate via special public variables called external variables. Each procedure using such a variable should contain:

```
DECLARE <variable> <attributes> EXTERNAL;
```

11.7 EXERCISES

11.1 The median of a set of numbers is defined as that number such that there are as many numbers greater than it as there are numbers less than it. If the number of values in the set is even, then the median is the average of the two middle numbers.

```
e.g., median (1,4,11,12,50) = 11
      median (1,4,11,12) = 7.5
```

Write a function procedure to determine the median of an arbitrary set of numbers.

11.2 The mode of a set of values is that value which appears most frequently. It may or may not be unique.

e.g., mode (2,4,13,7,13) = 13
mode (13,4,13,4) = (13,4)

Write a function procedure to find the mode of an arbitrary set of numbers. If the mode is unique the procedure should return the mode and the message UNIQUE. Otherwise it should return the first mode found and the message NOT UNIQUE.

11.3 Portions of the code for MEAN and STD_DEV, given in the eighth chapter can be used to compute the sample correlation coefficient

$$r = \frac{\sum_{i=1}^{n} (x_i-\bar{x})(y_i-\bar{y})}{\sqrt{\sum_{i=1}^{n} (x_i-\bar{x})^2 \sum_{i=1}^{n} (y_i-\bar{y})^2}}$$

Write a function procedure to compute the sample correlation coefficient for two one-dimensional arrays. All computation should be done in FLOAT(16) arithmetic.

11.4 The factorial of n (written n!) is defined as

$$0! = 1$$
$$1! = 1$$
$$n! = 1\times2\times3\times\ldots\times n$$

This can be rewritten as

$$0! = 1$$
$$n! = n\times(n-1)!;\ n=1,2,\ldots$$

Write a recursive function to compute n!.

11.5 One method for calculating the square root of a positive number x is given by the formula

$$r = 0.5\times(a+x/a)$$

where a is any approximation to $\sqrt{x}$. We can get a better approximation to the root by setting a to the value of r and repeating the calculation.

Write a function procedure which will return the square root of X as a FLOAT(16) number. Your procedure should stop when the difference between two successive values of r is less than 10^{-10}. How do your function's answers compare with the built-in function SQRT?

11.6 Simpson's Rule for approximating

$$\int_a^b f(x)dx$$

is given by

$$\int_a^b f(x)dx \approx h/3[f(a)+4f(a+h)+2f(a+2h) +4f(a+3h)+...+2f(a+(n-2)h)+4f(a+(n-1)h)+f(b)]$$

where n is the <u>even</u> number of partitions chosen and

$$h = \frac{b-a}{n}$$

Write a function procedure to evaluate an integral using Simpson's Rule. Your procedure is given values for a, b, and n as parameters and should return the value of the integral as its value. The main procedure should repeatedly evaluate an integral using Simpson's rule with increasing values for n (n=10,20,30,etc.) until one value of the integral differs from the previous value by less than 10^{-10}.

11.7 The Tower of Hanoi is said to be practiced by Brahman priests to predict the end of the world. The story goes that at the dawn of creation, three diamond needles appeared and stacked on one of them were 64 golden discs of decreasing size (largest one on the bottom). The Brahman priests decided that their task was to move the discs, one at a time, from their present needle to any other, always maintaining the order of decreasing size. Clearly the third needle was to be used to help in this task.

Write a recursive procedure to move 5 discs from the original needle to any other. Do <u>not</u> move all 64 lest the world end at completion of your program. If your needles are denoted by A, B, and C then your program should print results like:

MOVE DISC N FROM A TO C

The general solution for moving N discs is:

move N-1 discs from A to B
move disc N from A to C
move N-1 discs from B to C.

Chapter 12
Other Topics

In this chapter we cover some specialized features of PL/I which often prove useful in serious programming applications. The first four sections deal with the representation of data and allocation of storage. The following three sections explain some special mechanisms for recognizing extraordinary conditions and altering the flow of control.

12.1 STATIC AND AUTOMATIC STORAGE

The amount of main memory in a computer is limited, and for large programs memory can become a precious commodity. For this reason, PL/I normally allocates memory for variables only when those variables could possibly contain accessible information. It does this by deferring assignments of memory locations for variables until the procedure declaring those variables is called and by releasing (deallocating) the storage as soon as the procedure returns. This type of storage allocation is called AUTOMATIC. This may be listed among the attributes of a variable but need not be, since it is the default of PL/I.

This is one reason why local variables in internal procedures cannot be accessed outside the procedure -- they do not even correspond to real memory locations when the procedure is not in use. This also explains why local variables do not contain their former values from one call of an internal procedure to the next. In the meantime some other procedure may have been allowed to use the same memory for *its* local variables. In fact, in a RECURSIVE procedure, each call causes brand new locations to be assigned to the local variables, so that they don't interfere with values associated with previous and later calls.

However, in order to get external procedures to communicate via global variables, the special declaration EXTERNAL was required for these global variable names. This declaration (among other things) causes memory to be permanently assigned to the variable names, so that their values will remain intact from one external procedure to another.

When memory is assigned to a variable for the duration of a program, never to be released, this is called STATIC allocation. You may declare any variable STATIC which you wish to be "preserved," even during portions of a program which are outside its scope, i.e., which cannot access it. For example, if you want a local variable in an internal procedure to "remember" information from a previous call to that procedure, it may be declared STATIC. Note that this attribute does not extend the scope of a variable, only its longevity.

There are actually four classes of storage in PL/I, called AUTOMATIC, STATIC, CONTROLLED, AND BASED. PL/C, however, does not have CONTROLLED or BASED storage, which enable the programmer to allocate and release storage in more flexible and refined ways.

12.2 BEGIN BLOCKS

One important property of a PROCEDURE is its ability to declare local variables. Such a variable is for the procedure's own internal use and cannot affect the surrounding program, even if other parts of the program contain the same name (for a different variable).

This ability to declare local variables (without all the other properties of procedures, such as calls and parameters) can be had via a language feature called the BEGIN block. Its general form is:

```
<label>:  BEGIN;
                 } declaration of local variables

                 } statements to be executed

          END <label>;
```

As a control structure, the BEGIN block works much like a DO group. It serves to group several statements and make them appear as one (possibly complex) statement to the surrounding program. It may appear wherever a single statement may appear, just like a DO group. Control flows into a BEGIN block. It is not "called" or otherwise invoked from different places in a program. It has no parameters.

However, unlike a DO group, it does permit the declaration of local variables. Such local variables are not strictly required within a BEGIN block, but if they are not used, an ordinary DO group could and should be used instead.[1]

---

[1]The DO group is sufficient unless the group is needed as the object of an ON statement (Section 12.6) or with a prefix condition (Section 12.7).

The BEGIN-END grouping is called a "block" rather than "group", because a block is some region of code over which a local variable can be declared. Thus a PROCEDURE is also a type of block. Unless otherwise specified, variables declared in either type of block are AUTOMATIC and occupy memory locations only for the duration of the block.

Besides its general ability to define the scope of certain variables, a BEGIN block has one very special ability, which can also be used with PROCEDURE. A BEGIN block can declare arrays whose sizes are determined during execution. In all the array problems so far, it has been necessary to declare arrays with a constant size, large enough to accommodate the maximum number of data items which might ever arise. Such conservative, space-wasting allocations are no longer necessary. In a BEGIN block, an array can be declared with a size given by a global variable. Fig. 12.1 illustrates this dynamic array allocation.

```
DYNAMIC:  PROCEDURE OPTIONS(MAIN);
          DECLARE N FIXED(5,0);
          GET LIST (N);
SOME:     BEGIN;
             DECLARE NAMES(N) CHARACTER(20);
                )
                )
          END SOME;
          END DYNAMIC;
```

Fig. 12.1 Dynamic Array Allocation with BEGIN

Here the array NAMES will be allocated N storage locations. The value for N must be provided as a global variable outside the BEGIN block. It should be apparent from the structure of Fig. 12.1 that the first value on the data cards tells how many values are to be read into the array. This use of BEGIN blocks can not only save storage but also provide full arrays to work on. This, in turn, may permit the use of entire arrays by mentioning just their names as well as use of LBOUND and HBOUND.

BEGIN blocks are useful in limiting the amount of storage consumed by a program in another way. Consider Fig. 12.2 where two arrays are needed at two different times. In this case the program requires 2,000 locations as a two-dimensional array in another quite separate BEGIN block. Because local variables exist only for the time the block is executing, the same 2,000 locations could be reused by the second BEGIN block. Without the BEGIN we would have required 4,000 locations, at least 2,000 of which would be unused at any one time.

If the ENDFILE condition is to cause more than one statement to be executed, a group of such statements can be designated by a BEGIN block. Fig. 12.3 shows a program which reads and counts an arbitrary number of values. When it runs out of data it prints the count and then stops.

```
TWO:    PROCEDURE OPTIONS(MAIN);
             )
             (
             )
VECT:   BEGIN;
            DECLARE X(2000) FLOAT(6);     ]
             )                            | Duration of
             (                            | allocation of X
             )                            |
        END VECT;                         ]
MAT:    BEGIN;
            DECLARE Y(40,50) FLOAT(6);    ]
             )                            | Duration of
             (                            | allocation of Y
             )                            |
        END MAT;                          ]
             )
             (
             )
        END TWO;
```

Fig. 12.2 Storage Conservation with BEGIN

```
NOFLAG:  PROCEDURE OPTIONS(MAIN);
         DECLARE (N,COUNT) FIXED(5,0);
         ON ENDFILE (SYSIN)
            BEGIN;
               PUT SKIP LIST (COUNT);  )   Execute only
               STOP;                   )   when ENDFILE
            END;                           condition occurs
         COUNT = 0;
LOOP:    DO WHILE ('1'B);
            GET LIST (N);
            COUNT = COUNT + 1;
         END LOOP;
         END NOFLAG;
```

Fig. 12.3 The BEGIN Block as an ON-unit

There are several points of interest about Fig. 12.3. Note that there is no label on the BEGIN block. When BEGIN is used as an ON-unit the label must be omitted. The condition on the DO WHILE, '1'B, is the BIT string '1' (see Section 12.3). This is the way of denoting the value "TRUE" in PL/I. Each time the program comes to the DO WHILE, the condition is always true, causing the loop to be repeated indefinitely -- until data runs out and the ENDFILE condition is invoked. When ENDFILE occurs, control transfers to the BEGIN block where the value of COUNT is printed and the program is terminated by the STOP statement. This instruction does not cause the computer to come to a grinding halt but merely causes it to cease execution of this program. (Nasty things would happen if the STOP statement were not there.)

12.3 OTHER DATA ATTRIBUTES

The fundamental storage in a computer is all binary, i.e., sequences of 0's and 1's. Hence the more familiar decimal or "character" symbols must be encoded into binary so that they can be stored. Various types of encoding are possible, depending on how the symbols are to be used, i.e., certain encodings are more efficient for certain processes within the computer. When the declaration of a variable specifies it as FIXED or FLOAT or CHARACTER, or as BINARY or DECIMAL, then, in fact, the kind of encoding for its contents is being prescribed.

Although not all PL/I attributes (encodings) are available in PL/C, there is a sufficient variety to enable you to solve any problem which can be defined for computer solution. In this section we examine the differences among such attributes as they affect the user and introduce one more data type, the BIT string. (Internally, PL/I and PL/C handle some of these attributes differently, but such differences should not significantly affect the user.)

Whenever data is to be manipulated arithmetically, it must have a numeric encoding, i.e., a FIXED or FLOAT attribute. Of these two basic types, FIXED is probably more familiar and straightforward. However, even a FIXED variable can come in two flavors: DECIMAL and BINARY.

<u>FIXED DECIMAL</u> In this representation (which is the default if only FIXED is specified), the individual decimal digits still retain their separate identities, though each is encoded as a binary number. One result is that the conversion between fixed decimal representation and the encoding of separate characters required by the card reader and printer is simple and efficient. Another result is that decimal arithmetic operations are slow, since for most computers, doing arithmetic on separate decimal digits is "unnatural." Hence FIXED DECIMAL is recommended primarily for business applications where the amount of numeric manipulation is modest compared to the amount of input-output. It is not recommended in applications in which the relative amount of arithmetic processing is high.

<u>FIXED BINARY</u> We can considerably speed up computation by having the computer store its numbers in BINARY, rather than DECIMAL form. For integers, the attribute should be FIXED BINARY(15) or FIXED BINARY(31), the default and maximum values, respectively. The maximum values which can be stored are 32,767 (2^{15}-1) for FIXED BINARY(15) and 2,147,483,647 (2^{31}-1) for FIXED BINARY(31). The smallest numbers which can be stored under these attributes are the negative values of the maxima.

The reason for two "precisions" of 15 and 31 is this: some numbers are larger in magnitude than 32,767 and therefore <u>cannot</u> be encoded to fit into a FIXED BINARY(15) location. If it is possible that you will be dealing with numbers which exceed this size, you must provide a "larger" space for them, e.g., a FIXED BINARY(31) location. However, you pay a price. These "larger" BINARY(31) locations actually consume twice as much computer memory as the "smaller" BINARY(15) locations. In fact, if you are processing large arrays or structures, the "space" consumed may be a limiting factor.

Incidentally, even if your original values are of only moderate magnitude (e.g., under 32,000), multiplications and divisions can produce surprisingly large or small results. For example, 5,000 times 5,000 is 25 million, which is too large to be stored in a BINARY(15) location. Additions and subtractions are not so likely to produce extreme values, unless a great many additions or subtractions occur. Consequently when doing moderate amounts of arithmetic, use BINARY(31).

However, when doing a great deal of arithmetic, when numbers are extremely small or unusually large, or when doing operations on numbers of widely differing magnitudes, the results can be too large or small even for a FIXED BINARY(31) location. If there is any possibility of this, e.g., whenever much arithmetic is done, be even more flexible by using floating-point numbers.

A floating-point number corresponds to scientific notation (Section 6.1) and consists of a fraction (f), a base (b), an exponent (e), and a sign. The fraction is usually specified to have a maximum number of digits (t). Using this notation, any number (x) can be represented approximately as

$$x = \pm f \times b^{e}$$

For example, if the maximum number of digits is 6 (t = 6) and the base is 10 (decimal number system), then we could represent 129.48 as

$$+0.129480 \times 10^{3}$$

Similarly, -0.000012948 could be represented as -0.129480×10^{-4}. Usually there is a maximum and minimum value for the exponent. In the IBM 360 and 370 series of computers, these values are 75 and -78 (approximately). Hence we can represent magnitudes as big as 10^{75} and as small as 10^{-78}. Zero can also be represented as a special case: $+0.000000 \times 10^{0}$, i.e., both e = 0 and f = 0.

However due to the limited number of digits allowed in the fraction, unexpected results can occur. Consider how we would represent 1234567.89 using t = 6 and b = 10. Since we can only store 6 digits of the fraction, we must take the six most significant digits and so we get an approximation:

$$1234567.89 \simeq +0.123456 \times 10^{7}$$

which converts back as 1234560.00 and we do not end up with the same number as the one with which we started. A further complication is that some perfectly legitimate rational numbers in the decimal system (such as 0.2) cannot be represented exactly in the binary system (they are nonterminating in base 2). A complete discussion of floating-point number systems is beyond the scope of this book. We mention the topic merely to point out that floating-point numbers are usually only approximations to the real numbers. The approximations tend to be poorer for numbers with extreme exponents.

Nevertheless, because of the enormous range of magnitudes which can be stored in FLOATing-point variables, we recommend their use in most mathematical computations. Fortunately, many computers are designed to manipulate floating-point information directly, almost as rapidly as fixed binary information.

PL/C gives the impression that you can specify the actual number of digits to be carried for the fraction. In actual fact, all floating-point numbers in PL/C are carried inside the computer to 16 decimal digits of precision. The precision attribute which you specify is only invoked on input and output to trim values to the number of significant digits you wish to see. On the other hand, a FLOAT(16) variable in PL/I actually requires twice as much storage space as a FLOAT(6) variable.

BIT(n) This attribute permits a variable to store a string of binary digits (0's or 1's), for instance, '0'B or '1101'B. The minimum length is 1 and the maximum is 256. BIT strings can also be made to vary in length by adding the VARYING attributes as with CHARACTER variables. Note how BIT string constants must be followed by the letter B to distinguish them from CHARACTER strings.

BIT strings are otherwise analogous to CHARACTER strings. They may be concatenated, given to the LENGTH and SUBSTR functions, and passed as arguments to procedures which declare them as BIT(*).

This particular attribute is useful in saving space if you are dealing with variables which only take on the values zero or one, such as a "flag." The arrays of Section 9.5, which used only 0 or 1 entries to depict necessary orderings, could have been declared as arrays of BIT(1) elements.

A BIT string (of length 1) may also be used as a variable in "Boolean algebra," i.e., in logical manipulations involving &, |, ¬. Here a value of '1'B is "true," and '0'B is "false." In fact, the condition tested by an IF or DO WHILE statement is this type of true-false value. It would be possible to store the outcome of a condition in a BIT(1) variable and simply refer to this variable in a subsequent IF or DO WHILE statement:

```
      .
      .
      .
      DECLARE BVAR BIT(1);
      .
      .
      .
      BVAR = X > Y;
      IF BVAR THEN ...
      .
      .
      .
```

12.4 THE INITIAL ATTRIBUTE

When storage is first allocated for a variable then there is no value in that location. Values normally appear as the result of assignment and GET statements. However, the INITIAL attribute permits us to store values in locations as soon as the storage is allocated. The attribute is used in the DECLARE statement as:

```
DECLARE <variable> <attributes> INITIAL (<value>);
```

For example, the following line of code creates the variable SUM and puts the value zero in it:

```
DECLARE SUM FIXED(5,0) INITIAL(0);
```

Due to idiosyncrasies in the operation of this attribute, it is advisable to give a separate initial attribute for each simple variable. For example, to initialize X and Y to 3 and 4, respectively, one uses:

```
DECLARE X FIXED(5,0) INITIAL(3),
        Y FIXED(5,0) INITIAL(4);
```

When many simple variables with identical attributes are to be initialized to the <u>same</u> value, the form to be used is:

```
DECLARE (<list of variables>) <attributes> INITIAL (<value>);
```

Both X and Y can be initialized to the <u>same</u> value by:

```
DECLARE (X,Y) FIXED(5,0) INITIAL(3);
```

The power of the INITIAL attribute is best illustrated in the initialization of arrays. The general rule for initializing arrays is that there should be as many values in the list of initial values as there are elements in the array to be initialized. For example.

```
DECLARE A(4) FIXED(5,0) INITIAL(10,20,30,40);
```

will give A the following initial values:

A(1)	10
A(2)	20
A(3)	30
A(4)	40

If there are fewer values than array elements, then only those elements for which values are given will be initialized. The statement:

```
DECLARE A(4) FIXED(5,0) INITIAL(0);
```

will initialize only A(1) to zero and leave the other elements of A undefined.

To initialize several consecutive array elements to the same value, repetition factors may be introduced into the list of initial values:

```
DECLARE A(4) FIXED(5,0) INITIAL((4)0);
```

which is equivalent to:

```
DECLARE A(4) FIXED(5,0) INITIAL(0,0,0,0);
```

If you must use INITIAL, we strongly recommend using a different INITIAL attribute for each array.

The initialization of character variables in PL/C differs from PL/I. Simple variables can be initialized by:

```
DECLARE WORD CHARACTER(5) INITIAL ('START');
```

However, in PL/C when repetition factors are introduced, the initial value must be enclosed in parentheses:

```
DECLARE NAMES(20) CHARACTER(15) INITIAL((20) ('b̸'));
```

In conclusion, let us suggest that when the INITIAL attribute is being used, only one simple variable or array be initialized at a time unless every variable is being initialized to the same value.

12.5 THE GO TO STATEMENT

We have emphasized throughout that in clear, well written programs, control should flow from top to bottom, using the control mechanisms of (i) normal sequential flows, (ii) IF_THEN_ELSE for alternatives, (iii) DO WHILE for repetition, and (iv) CALL to execute another procedure before continuing the current one. We have tried to conceal the existence of another statement which can be used to control the flow of control in an arbitrary manner -- the GO TO statement. We admit that it exists. But we have delayed mentioning it until now because beginning programmers tend to look on it as a panacea for all ills and use it to write unreadable, hopelessly complicated programs to do quite simple things. Now that you have gone beyond the beginner stage and have learned the appropriate statements for the major types of flow control, we venture to show the legitimate use of GOTO.

The general form is:

GO TO <label>;

or

GOTO <label>;

On encountering the instruction, control will immediately transfer to the statement bearing the similar label . A label, followed by a colon (:), may be appended to any statement. Thus the GOTO can send control virtually anywhere. This is its power as well as its great source of danger.

The GOTO can be helpful when your program reaches a point where some process is definitely complete, such as input or searching. Rather than setting a flag which must then be tested and possibly retested, control can immediately move on to the place where the flag would eventually have sent it.

For example, Fig. 12.4 contrasts two methods of adding the numbers from data cards. Fig. 12.4(a) uses a conventional flag to signal end of input, while Fig. 12.4(b) immediately branches out of the loop when data runs out.

```
      SUM = 0;
      ON ENDFILE (SYSIN) FLAG = 1;
      FLAG = 0;
      GET LIST (AMT);
 INPT:DO WHILE (FLAG = 0);
         SUM = SUM + AMT;
         GET LIST (AMT);
      END INPT;
      PUT DATA (SUM);
```

(a)

```
      SUM = 0;
      ON ENDFILE (SYSIN) GO TO OUT;
 INPT:DO WHILE ('1'B);
         GET LIST (AMT);
         SUM = SUM + AMT;
      END INPT;
 OUT: PUT DATA (SUM);
```

(b)

Fig. 12.4 Two Methods of Terminating an Input Loop. (a) Use of Flag; (b) Use of GOTO.

Note that in Fig. 12.4(b), the unsuccessful attempt to GET data causes control to bypass the following assignment statement, so the last AMT is not added to SUM a second time.

If GOTO is to be used at all, then it should be reserved for such instances as these. It should never be used in place of simple, straightforward DO WHILE or IF_THEN_ELSE constructions and, at all costs, should never be used to transfer control to a statement which precedes it anywhere in the program.

12.6 OTHER ON CONDITIONS

In Chapter 3 we introduced the ENDFILE condition to handle the exceptional case of the SYSIN file running out of data during the execution of a GET statement. Whenever the computer cannot execute a statement normally because of some unpredictable, extraordinary or erroneous event, the normal execution is said to be interrupted. There are many other causes for interrupts besides running out of data.

Interrupts often result in abnormal termination of your program or, worse still, allow execution to continue with incorrect values. The result of these interrupts usually depends upon the operating system under which your program is executing. However, PL/I permits you to detect such interrupts and specify the action which you desire to be taken in the event the interrupt-causing event should occur.

This action is specified by the ON statement whose general form is:

```
ON <condition> <ON-unit>;
```

The "condition" indicates the event whose occurrence will trigger the action, and the ON-unit specifies the action. An <ON-unit> must be a simple unlabeled statement or an unlabeled BEGIN block.

For instance, without an ON statement your program will be terminated with an error message should you run out of data during the execution of a GET. This is the standard system response to this interrupt. However, if you specify, say,

```
ON ENDFILE (SYSIN) FLAG = 1;
```

then, should the interrupt occur, your ON-unit (FLAG = 1;) will be executed and the program permitted to continue.

The conditions which may be invoked in PL/C are grouped into several types. These groups are:

1. Computational

    CONVERSION
    FIXEDOVERFLOW
    OVERFLOW
    SIZE
    UNDERFLOW
    ZERODIVIDE

2. I/O

ENDFILE
ENDPAGE
NAME
RECORD[2]
TRANSMIT[2]
UNDEFINEDFILE[2]

3. Program Debugging

CHECK
STRINGRANGE
SUBSCRIPTRANGE

4. System Action

ERROR
FINISH[2]

For a thorough discussion of all PL/I conditions, the reader should refer to IBM SRL publication GC28-8201. The following discussion outlines the meaning of each condition.

CHECK This special debugging condition is described in Section 12.7.

CONVERSION This condition is raised whenever an illegal conversion is attempted on character data; for example when a character other than 0 or 1 occurs in a character string being converted to a bit string. Standard PL/C response is to generate an error and stop.

ENDFILE This condition is raised when an input file contains insufficient data to complete a GET statement. The standard PL/C response is to generate an error and stop. This condition is specified by

```
ON ENDFILE (<file-name>) <ON-unit>;
```

If the file name is omitted (and the parentheses as well), SYSIN is assumed. See Section 3.6 for discussion of this condition.

ENDPAGE The general form for this condition is:

```
ON ENDPAGE (<file-name>) <ON-unit>;
```

This condition can only occur with an output file which happens to be a printer. The normal name for this file in PL/C is SYSPRINT (which is assumed if the file name is omitted). The condition occurs when an attempt is made to write more than the maximum specified number of lines (usually 60) on one page of printer paper. Standard PL/C response is to begin a new page and continue. The user can print continuously from one page to another by specifying a null ON-unit:

```
ON ENDPAGE (SYSPRINT);
```

[2]Not discussed in this book.

This tells PL/C to do nothing special if the condition occurs, i.e., keep printing on the next line. This technique is useful when doing computer art programs.

<u>ERROR</u> This condition occurs whenever an error is encountered for which there is no corresponding ON statement. Standard PL/C response is to print an error message and, if possible, take corrective action and continue. If an ON statement is specified, the ON-unit will be executed and <u>then</u> the standard system action will be taken. For example, the use of ON ERROR allows you to print crucial values before letting the system take over, and

```
ON ERROR STOP;
```

will cause the program to terminate upon the first occurrence of the ERROR condition. This is one good way of avoiding PL/C's "help" in correcting run-time errors.

<u>FIXEDOVERFLOW</u> This condition is raised whenever a fixed-point-arithmetic operation produces a result with more digits than the maximum length allowed in the system implementation. Standard PL/C response is to print an error message and continue with the program, retaining the maximum number of digits allowed by the system implementation.

<u>NAME</u> This condition occurs when a GET DATA statement references a variable which does not appear in the input stream. Standard PL/C response is to print an error message and continue.

<u>OVERFLOW</u> This condition occurs whenever the value of a floating-point number or intermediate result exceeds 10^{75} or 2^{252} (approximately). Standard PL/C response is to print an error message, set the value which overflowed to 1, and continue.

<u>STRINGRANGE</u> and <u>SUBSCRIPTRANGE</u> These conditions are (or should be) automatically enabled by the standard PL/C compiler, and so do not require corresponding ON statements in PL/C. They are <u>not</u> enabled automatically in PL/I.

STRINGRANGE occurs whenever the second or third arguments of SUBSTR violate the rules. Standard PL/C response is to print an error message and adjust the value(s) of the offending argument(s) to conform to the rules.

SUBSCRIPTRANGE occurs whenever an attempt is made to reference an element outside the bounds of the array. Standard PL/C response is to print an error message and take corrective action as follows. If the reference is to the nth dimension of the array X and the reference is less than the lower bound of that dimension, then PL/C will reference LBOUND(X,n). Otherwise it will reference HBOUND(X,n).

<u>UNDERFLOW</u> This condition occurs whenever the value of a floating-point number or intermediate result is less than 10^{-78} or 2^{-260} (approximately). Standard PL/C response is to print an error message, set the value to zero and continue.

<u>ZERODIVIDE</u> This condition occurs whenever an attempt is made to divide by zero. Standard PL/C response is to print an error message and set the quotient to 1.

12.7 PREFIX CONDITIONS

Many of the conditions which can cause interrupts also have opposites. For example the "opposite" of ZERODIVIDE is called NOZERODIVIDE. The reason for opposites, when they exist, is to enable you to turn-off, suppress, ignore, and otherwise inhibit the interrupt which would normally be caused.[3] However, since interrupts provide the way in which your program or the system can respond to unpredictable errors and anomalies, you must be very careful about suppressing them. In fact, you are only allowed to suppress certain interrupts over a limited range of a program -- one statement, one BEGIN block, or one procedure. This is done by appending a "prefix condition" to the statement or block being affected.

The conditions in PL/C and their defaults are given below; the default implementation is underlined. Abbreviations for some conditions are given in brackets

CHECK (NOCHECK)

CONVERSION (CONV) NOCONVERSION (NOCONV)

ENDFILE

ENDPAGE

ERROR

FINISH

FIXEDOVERFLOW (FOFL) NOFIXEDOVERFLOW (NOFOFL)

NAME

OVERFLOW (OFL) NOOVERFLOW (NOOFL)

RECORD

SIZE (NOSIZE)

STRINGRANGE (STRG) NOSTRINGRANGE (NOSTRG)

SUBSCRIPTRANGE (SUBRG) NOSUBSCRIPTRANGE (NOSUBRG)

TRANSMIT

UNDEFINEDFILE (UNDF)

UNDERFLOW (UFL) NOUNDERFLOW (NOUFL)

ZERODIVIDE (ZDIV) NOZERODIVIDE (NOZDIV)

To change the default conditions for any statement, BEGIN block, or procedure, append the desired prefix condition as follows:

(<condition>): <label>: PROCEDURE;

or

(<condition>): <label>: BEGIN;

or

(<condition>): <label>: <statement>;

---

[3]The one exception is CHECK which allows you to "turn-on" a normally ignored condition (NOCHECK). See Section 12.7.1.

When used for procedures or BEGIN blocks the condition will be in effect for the entire procedure or BEGIN block which it prefixes. Thus for example

```
(NOFOFL): RANDOM: BEGIN;
                    }
                  END RANDOM;
```

would permit the execution of the BEGIN block, RANDOM, such that no special action would be taken if the fixed-point overflow condition occurs inside the block.

12.7.1 The CHECK Prefix

One of the most powerful uses of a prefix condition lies in the use of CHECK.

CHECK is used primarily as a debugging tool to monitor changes to variable names specified in a "check-list." If the CHECK condition is raised, say by assigning a value to a variable in the list, the standard system response is to print the designated name(s) appearing in the "check-list" together with the corresponding value(s) if any. In this way the programmer can examine both the flow of control and changes in selected variables, while the program executes.

Unfortunately CHECK does not operate in the same way in PL/C as it does in PL/I, and so our discussion is limited to PL/C.[4]

The general form of the CHECK prefix is:

(CHECK (<check-list>)):

where the <check-list> is a list of names separated by commas. CHECK can <u>only</u> be used as a prefix for procedures or BEGIN blocks and <u>not</u> for single statements. Each name to be monitored must be a simple variable name, an entire array name (but not an individual subscripted variable), a structure name, a statement label, a procedure entry-name, or some other entry-name. The names in the check-list refer only to names known within the block or procedure to which the prefix is attached.

The CHECK condition is raised whenever a variable name in the check-list has its value changed, or when part of it has a value changed (as with an array or structure), or after return from a user-defined procedure in which the name was used as an argument. If the name in the check-list is a label of any kind (procedure entry-name) the condition is raised just prior to passing control to the statement with the entry name or label. An example of the use of CHECK and its corresponding output is given in Fig. 12.5.

The CHECK condition is not raised if the value of a name is changed through the INITIAL attribute or if the value is changed through a parameter. Unlike PL/I, if the name in a check-list is an array or structure, then only the element which has its value changed will be displayed in PL/C.

---

[4]For PL/I rules, the reader is again referred to the IBM SRL publication GC28-8201, Section 4.

```
                /* FIGURE 12.5 */
(CHECK(VALU,SUM,LOOP)):
DEBUG:   PROCEDURE OPTIONS (MAIN);

         DECLARE (VALU,SUM,K) FIXED (5,0);
         SUM = 0;

LOOP:    DO K = 1 TO 10;
            GET LIST (VALU);
            SUM = SUM + VALU;
         END LOOP;
         PUT SKIP LIST (SUM);

         END DEBUG;


CHECK IN STMT 0003:      SUM=         0;
CHECK IN STMT 0004:      LOOP;
CHECK IN STMT 0005:      VALU=        10;
CHECK IN STMT 0006:      SUM=        10;
CHECK IN STMT 0005:      VALU=        20;
CHECK IN STMT 0006:      SUM=        30;
CHECK IN STMT 0005:      VALU=        30;
CHECK IN STMT 0006:      SUM=        60;
CHECK IN STMT 0005:      VALU=        40;
CHECK IN STMT 0006:      SUM=       100;
CHECK IN STMT 0005:      VALU=        50;
CHECK IN STMT 0006:      SUM=       150;
CHECK IN STMT 0005:      VALU=        60;
CHECK IN STMT 0006:      SUM=       210;
CHECK IN STMT 0005:      VALU=        70;
CHECK IN STMT 0006:      SUM=       280;
CHECK IN STMT 0005:      VALU=        80;
CHECK IN STMT 0006:      SUM=       360;
CHECK IN STMT 0005:      VALU=        90;
CHECK IN STMT 0006:      SUM=       450;
CHECK IN STMT 0005:      VALU=       100;
CHECK IN STMT 0006:      SUM=       550;
      550


IN STMT     9   PROGRAM RETURNS FROM MAIN PROCEDURE.
```

Fig. 12.5 Use of CHECK with Sample Output

12.8 THE GET DATA STATEMENT

Data may be read in by means of the GET DATA statement whose general form is:

GET DATA (<list of variables>);

The names in the list of variables may be simple variables, subscripted variables, or fully qualified variables in the case of structures. The data cards which are referenced by this statement must have the form:

<name> = <constant>, <name> = <constant>, ...

For example if the statement:

```
GET DATA (A,B,C);
```

references the data card:

```
A = 9, C = 12, B = 17
```

then the result will be to assign values as:

A	9	B	17	C	12

Note that the ordering of the values on the data card need not correspond to the ordering in the input list. The drawback is that the data cards must use the same variable names as the program.

Chapter 13
Disk File Fundamentals and Stream I/O

13.1 INTRODUCTION

In addition to the main memory, most computer systems also contain fairly large amounts of secondary memory, consisting mostly of magnetic tapes and disks.[1] Rather than reading programs and data into a system from cards, the programs and data may be kept within the system on tape or disk and be read into the main memory when required. Collections of related data items are known as "files". This chapter and the next deal primarily with how to create them, retrieve items from them and update them. The discussion of disk files will include the principles of processing files stored on tape as well.

There are two ways to view a file from the perspective of a PL/I program. One is to see the file as a STREAM of character data, i.e. as one long sequence of consecutive characters. The other is to see it as a collection of distinct, clearly delineated RECORDs, which may contain other kinds of data besides characters. This chapter discusses only STREAM files, since they are simpler to deal with.

Either STREAM or RECORD files may be processed sequentially, i.e. by proceeding from one data item to the next according to the order in which items are stored. SEQUENTIAL processing is the only way to

---

[1] Many other devices may also be used, such as drums, fixed head disks, data cells and others. However, magnetic tape and disk are the most common and certainly typical.

handle STREAM files or any files which are stored on magnetic tape. The algorithms discussed in this chapter are therefore for sequential processing in general.

However, if a file consists of distinct RECORDs, resides on a disk-type (direct access) device, and has other structural properties, it is possible to access any specific record DIRECTly, without examining all preceeding records. Chapter 14 will deal with DIRECT access and other properties of RECORD files.

13.2 SECONDARY MEMORY

13.2.1 Why it is Needed

If you have done any cooking you must realize the need for keeping the kitchen counter clear of unnecessary clutter. Cookbooks which are not in use are stored on a shelf, and ingredients which you are no longer using are returned to the cupboard. The counter is where the action takes place, but its space is limited. The shelf and the cupboard provide much more space which is close at hand -- but not in the way.

For similar reasons the programs (recipes) and data (ingredients) which inhabit a computer system are not all kept in the main memory, where the processor has access to them. Main memory space is limited. At any one time most of the programs and most of the data are not needed. Consequently, a computer system contains a relatively large amount of secondary memory to keep these items "nearby" -- but outside of the rather precious main memory itself until they are actually needed for processing.

At first this extra storage may not seem necessary. After all, your experience has suggested that programs as well as data are entered through a card reader whenever needed and reside in main memory only until the results have been displayed by the printer. Actually this experience is academic and rather atypical of most industrial computing. Many programs are either too large or used too often or needed by too many people to be entered into the system through a card reader every time anyone wishes to run them. The cards are simply too cumbersome a recording medium and the card reader too slow a device. A good example of both a large and frequently used program is the PL/I compiler which translates your PL/I programs and everyone else's into executable form. The compiler is surely not read in from cards every time it is executed. Rather it remains "within the system" on a secondary memory device.[2]

You have made use of other programs which are kept on secondary memory devices. For example, any built-in functions, such as INDEX and SUBSTR, are actually separate programs which are copied from some secondary storage area for incorporation into your program.

Despite the foregoing, your own PL/I programs will probably continue to appear on cards for a while, since they are neither large nor intended for numerous executions. However, the data on which they operate and the results they produce will soon be coming from

---

2 On some systems the compiler may be used so heavily that it is actually kept in main memory, but this is exceptional.

and going to secondary memory. For one thing, card readers and printers are too slow. For another, the results of one program may be passed on as the input to another. Just as some cooking process may yield a sauce which is only one ingredient in a later concoction, so may one program validate, modify, sort, or compute data to be processed by another. Secondary memory is the ideal place to keep such data until one gets around to processing it further. (Results should only be directed to the printer if they are finally ready for human consumption.)

Many collections of data are truly enormous. Even the student records (of, say, 400 characters each) for a medium-sized university of 10,000 students would require 4 million characters of storage. This is by no means an unusually large amount of data. Yet, this is larger than the total capacities of most main memories. On the other hand, this data would require 50,000 cards to record. Eliminating cards and main memory as feasible storage media, the only plausible place to keep such a collection of data is on secondary memory.

Many collections of data are of such importance or interest that they are kept for long periods or are accessed by many different programs for different purposes. Regardless of the quantity, data which must remain readily available should also reside in the secondary memory so that they are still "within the system."

Hopefully, you are beginning to see that secondary memory is a major part of almost every computer system. As a result, the movement of data between the main memory and secondary memory is a vital function of most commercial data processing programs.

13.2.2 Storage and I/O Devices

The most common storage media in secondary memories are tapes and disks. Computer tape is similar to ordinary magnetic recording tape. The tape drives on which the tapes are mounted come in either reel-to-reel or casette form and often appear in science fiction movies. Rather than record music or voice, however, they are designed to record binary data on the tapes and can later play them back. Disk memories are also magnetic recording devices but in appearance resemble phonograph albums, often stacked on spindles like records in a juke box. They are "played" by moving what looks like a tone arm to the appropriate place over the rapidly rotating platter. Of course, this tone arm, or "head", can also record data on this disk.

The physical details do not concern us here, but a few properties are of real importance. These devices are much faster than card readers, printers, and terminals. Programs and data stored there can be moved into the main memory very rapidly when required. These devices have fairly large storage capacities compared to the size of main memory. They are usually less expensive than an equivalent amount of main memory. Consequently, most computer systems have several tape devices and disk drives, giving a secondary memory with a storage capacity hundreds or thousands of times larger than that of the main memory.

There is one crucial difference between tapes and disks. The only way to move from one place to another on a tape is to traverse all of the tape in between. This means the data on a tape can only be retrieved in the same order in which it was placed on the tape, i.e. in the order of its physical position. When data are processed in order by consecutive physical position, this is called sequential processing. We will say more about sequential processing in Section 13.5. Devices like tape drives, which allow only this type of processing, are called sequential devices. Card readers and printers are also sequential devices, since the cards are always read in order and the printer paper never backs up.

Disk, on the other hand, does not have this sequential limitation. The read/write heads can be positioned anywhere over the disk surface, without the need to process the data at every intervening position. Such devices are called direct access devices because it is possible to directly access any desired position in a small amount of time. Of course, these devices do not preclude sequential processing; they simply provide a more flexible alternative. You have seen this in the case of an array in main memory -- it may either be processed

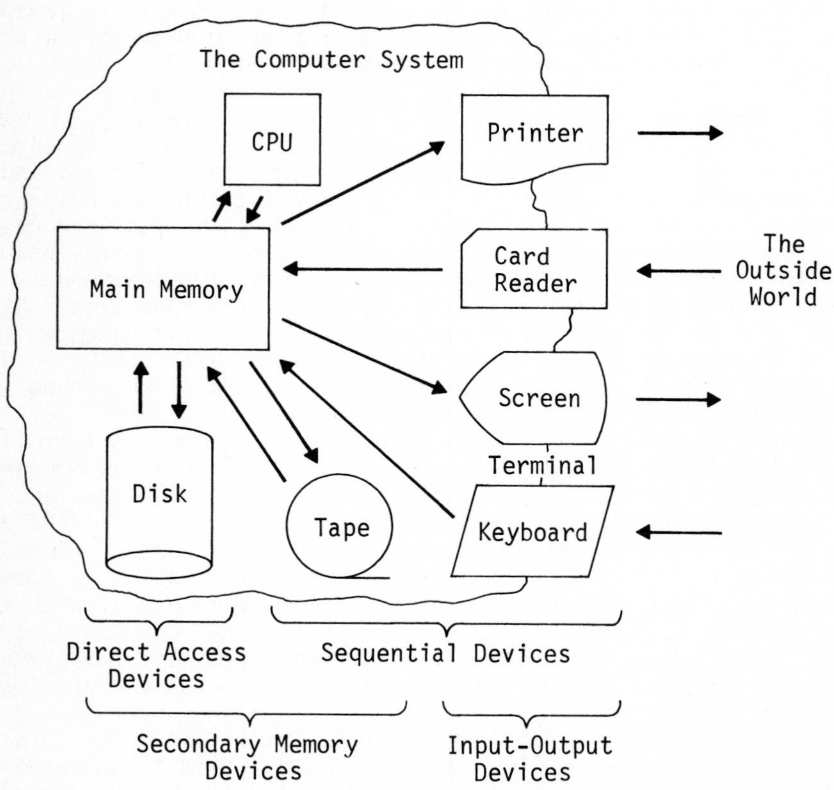

Fig. 13.1 Classification of Devices

sequentially or else have selected locations referenced.

Fig. 13.1 summarizes this classification of devices. Notice that the figure includes terminals, which appear to the system like a pair of separate devices: a keyboard for input and a screen or hard copy device for output. The designation "input-output devices" refers to devices which are one-directional gateways into or out of the "system". This is in contrast to secondary memory devices which are within the "system" and provide two directions of data flow (only one would not be very useful!). On the other hand, the terms "input" and "output" always refer to the direction of flow with respect to the main memory, which remains at the heart of the system. Note also that the processor may only examine and change data in main memory. This suggests that the processing programs will have to explicitly move all appropriate data to and from main memory. The techniques for doing this are the subject of the remainder of this chapter and the next.

13.3 FILES

13.3.1 Basic Definitions

A data item is a unit of data which can be manipulated by a processor. This usually corresponds to a character string or a single numeric quantity. Related data items are often treated as a group and given a collective name. An array is a familiar example of a linearly organized group of similar data items. A more pertinent example is a PL/I structure, which can group data items of different types and sizes under a common structure name. When such a group of items is recorded on secondary memory or moved to or from an I/O device, it is called a record. A record is, therefore, the unit of data moved in and out of main memory as a result of executing an input or output statement. Of course, a record may consist of only a single data item, but it is usually a composite. Thus, the target area in main memory for an incoming record is frequently a structure, as is the source for many outgoing records. The individual data items within a record are normally called fields.

A collection of related records is called a file. There may be thousands of files stored in a computer system. Every file must have a name so that the system can distinguish one file from another. For example, STUDENT might refer to the set of records describing each student registered at the university. PAYROLL may be a file consisting of records pertaining to each employee, SYSIN refers to the file of records which happen to be on consecutive cards at the card reader. You have used SYSIN and the printer file, SYSPRINT, many times, even if you did not realize it. These concepts are depicted in Fig. 13.2.

A file is not simply a haphazard heap of records. There are many different ways in which the operating system may place these records on storage devices and later present the data to the program for processing. The simplest form of file organization is the STREAM file, which means that the processing program views the file as a continuous STREAM of characters. STREAM files, therefore, resemble giant character strings whose underlying records are invisible to the program. SYSIN and SYSPRINT are both STREAM files, as

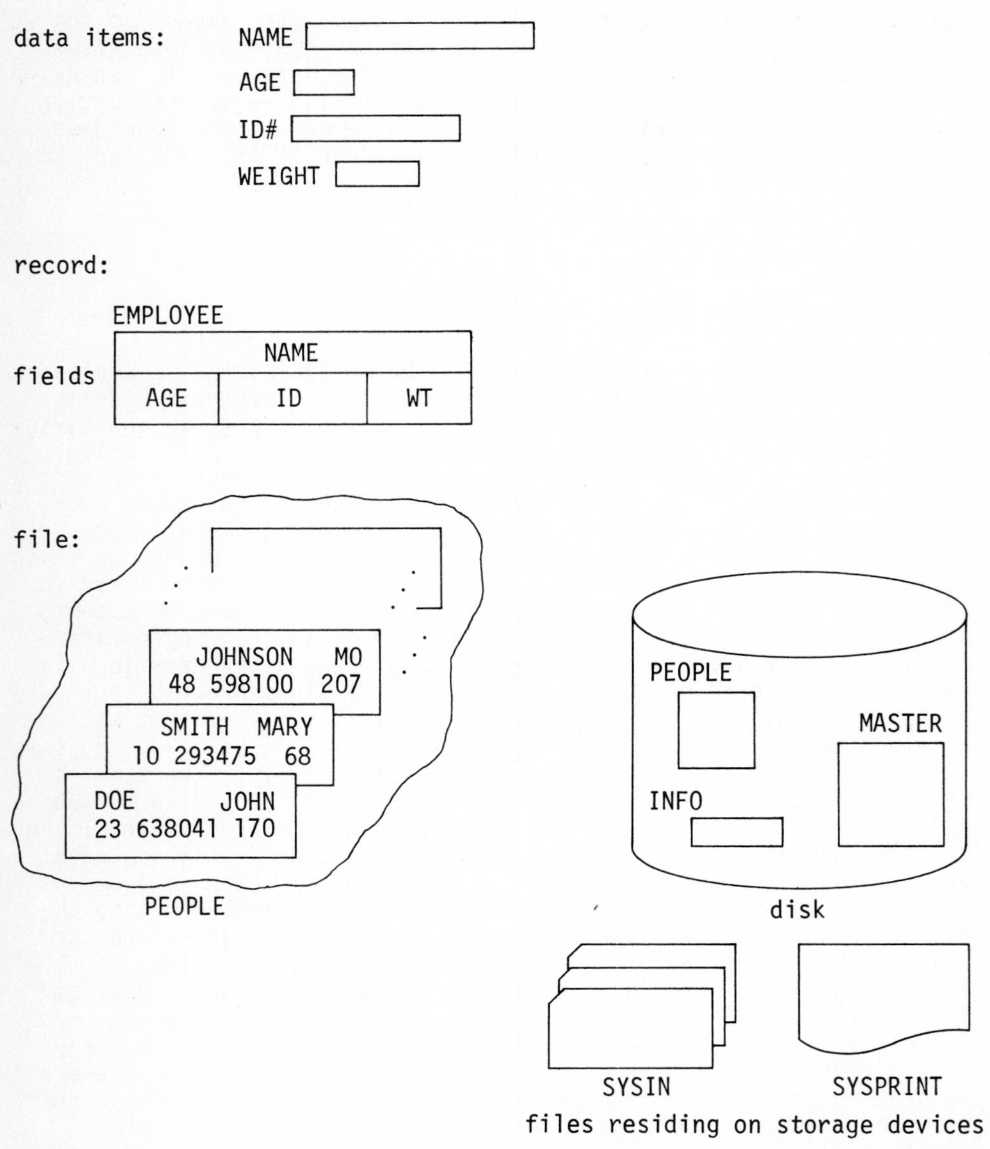

Fig. 13.2 Data Items, Records and Files

are all the other files discussed in this chapter.

13.3.3 SYSIN and SYSPRINT

Just about every program you have run so far has probably had a warning message like:

```
NO FILE SPECIFIED.  SYSIN/SYSPRINT ASSUMED.
```

This message is the result of using I/O statements (GET or PUT) without specifying exactly which file is involved. In these cases the compiler assumes, quite correctly, that every GET refers to SYSIN and every PUT refers to SYSPRINT. It is possible to specify these files directly in the PUT or GET statements. For example, the equivalent form of GET LIST is

```
GET FILE (SYSIN) LIST
```

and the equivalent form of PUT EDIT is

```
PUT FILE (SYSPRINT) EDIT
```

While there is no need to use these complete forms, their use will eliminate the warning message.

On the other hand, the programmer can direct I/O to certain other files by statements[3] of the form:

```
                            ( LIST )
( GET )                     (  or  )
{  or }   FILE (<filename>) { EDIT }
( PUT )                     (  or  )
                            ( DATA )
```

Notice that the only addition is the keyword FILE together with the name of the file, in parentheses, after the GET or PUT. The rest of the statement does not change.

This ability to point GET and PUT at different files is illustrated in Fig. 13.3 However, a few additional statements are actually required to establish the basic routes for the data. These statements (DECLARE and OPEN) will be described in the next section (13.4).

There is really little difference between doing I/O through the reader and printer files and doing I/O through the disk system. In fact, all I/O on modern batch systems actually goes through the disk system. When your program and data cards are placed in the card reader your data cards are copied to a file somewhere on a disk, and that collection of data values becomes known to your program as the file SYSIN. Each GET which is executed in your program causes one or more values to be read from the disk file called SYSIN rather than

---

[3]These statements apply only to STREAM files. This redirection of files is done outside the PL/I program by commands to the operating system. The basic technique will appear in Section 14.6.

from the card reader.[4] A similar situation exists for PUT statements which actually move records to a disk for later transfer to the printer itself. Of course, this mechanism has no noticeable effect on your program; we only mention it to show that you have, in fact, used disk files.

13.4 BASIC STREAM FILE PROCESSING

There are three types of statements which a PL/I program uses to describe and manipulate files:

(1) DECLARE
In order to distinguish the various files needed by a program, unique names are used. These names must be identified in a DECLARE

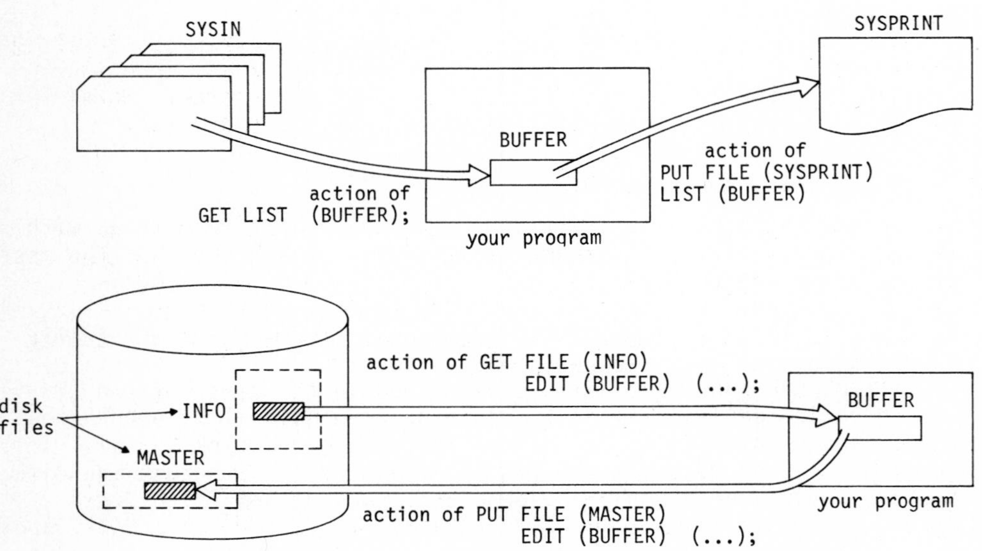

Fig. 13.3 Data Flow to and From Files

---

[4]This explanation is meant to be conceptual rather than technically exact.

statement and designated as FILE names. (The names used by the program do not have to be the actual file names known to the system, but we will assume for now that they are.[5])

(2) OPEN and CLOSE
These statements "connect" (or disconnect) the program to the real files in preparation for actual processing. OPEN also specifies how the file is to be used, e.g. for INPUT or for OUTPUT.

(3) GET and PUT
These statements cause the actual flow of data between the files and main memory. These particular statements are used only in STREAM files; other file types have their own file manipulation statements. Fig. 13.4 illustrates the effect of each of these statements.

Fig. 13.5 is a simple program to copy a list of names from data cards to the disk file INFO, assuming a maximum of 20 characters per name. We will examine each new statement in the program.

13.4.1 File Declaration

In statement 2, we have declared INFO to be a STREAM FILE. The STREAM attribute causes the file INFO to be seen as a continuous stream of data items. This is the default attribute for files because it specifies the simplest data organization.

We should also note that file names must not exceed eight characters and must never contain the underscore character. These restrictions are imposed because of operating system constraints. The file declaration is not strictly necessary for STREAM files since the compiler can deduce the file attributes from the program. However, we still recommend that everything in a program be declared.

13.4.2 Opening and Closing Files

In a manual filing system, there is one thing a person must do before consulting a file and one thing he should do when he is finished. Prior to consulting a file the person must first open the drawer or folder containing the information. After the file has served its purpose, the drawer should be closed. Corresponding actions should also be specified for computer files.

Statement 6 of Fig. 13.5 specifies that INFO should be OPENed for OUTPUT. Because disk files may be either written on or read from, it is desirable to state the purpose for which you wish to use the file. STREAM files may only be opened for INPUT or OUTPUT. These keywords indicate the direction of the flow of data with respect to main memory, e.g. a file which is going to have data written on it must be opened for OUTPUT.

The general forms of the OPEN statement are:

```
OPEN FILE (<filename>) INPUT;
OPEN FILE (<filename>) OUTPUT;
```

---

[5]The program names are associated with actual file names by JCL statements; of course, the program name and file name may be identical. See Section 14.6.

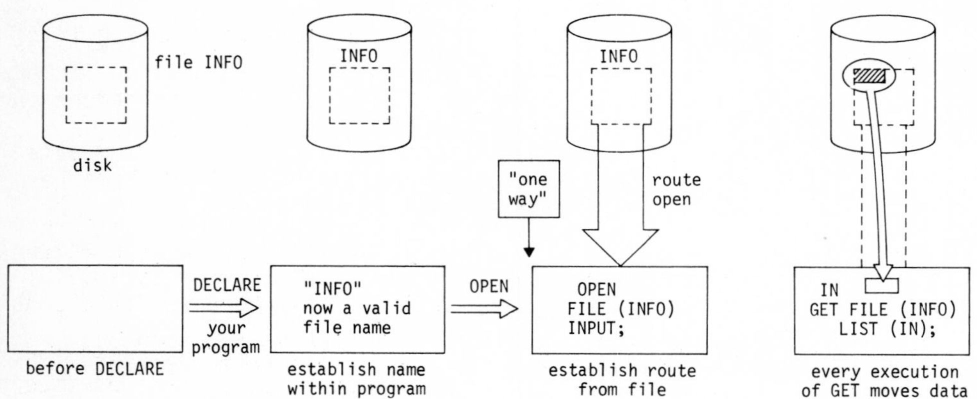

Fig. 13.4 Effect of the DECLARE, OPEN and GET/PUT Statements

```
                 /* FIGURE 13.5 */
 1  DISK1:    PROCEDURE OPTIONS (MAIN);
              DECLARE
 2               NAME CHARACTER(20),
                 MORE BIT(1),
                 INFO FILE STREAM;
 3            MORE = '1'B;
 4            ON ENDFILE (SYSIN) MORE = '0'B;
 6            OPEN FILE (INFO) OUTPUT;
 7            GET FILE (SYSIN) LIST (NAME);
 8  LOOP:     DO WHILE (MORE);
 9               PUT FILE (INFO) LIST (NAME);
10               GET FILE (SYSIN) LIST (NAME);
11            END LOOP;
12            CLOSE FILE (INFO);
13            END DISK1;
```

Fig. 13.5 Writing to a Disk File

These statements must appear before any processing of the associated file is attempted.

One effect of the OPEN statement is to cause the read/write head of the disk to be positioned at the start of the file. Once a STREAM file has been opened for a specific operation, only that operation may be performed on it.

When a file has been opened for INPUT, for example, you may only read from that file. The programmer cannot write on it until it has been closed and opened again for OUTPUT. In this way STREAM files are quite different from manual files.

Statement 12 of Fig. 13.5 shows the CLOSE statement for the file INFO. The general form is:

CLOSE FILE (<filename>);

The effect of CLOSE on this file depends on the purpose for which the file was opened. In our example the file was opened for OUTPUT. In this case, the CLOSE statement will cause a special "end-of-file marker" to be written on the file.[6] This is a special pattern which can cause the ENDFILE condition if it is ever encountered by a GET statement at a later time. If the file had been opened for INPUT, no such marker would be written by CLOSE.

Notice that the OPEN statement in Figure 13.5 was only executed one time! Once a file is OPENed, an arbitrary number of appropriate data transmission statements (GET or PUT) may be executed. It is not only wasteful, but usually wrong to keep OPENing the same file before every I/O operation!

The only reasons a file should be CLOSEd and then reOPENed are either (1) to reposition the file at the beginning; or (2) to change its mode of use. In STREAM files changing modes usually makes sense only when changing from OUTPUT mode to INPUT. To go the other way would imply overwriting (in OUTPUT mode) everything that was there before. Even if no PUT statements were executed, closing the OUTPUT file would write an end-of-file mark (at the beginning). Remember: OPEN always causes the access mechanism to be positioned at the beginning of the file.

Note also that if the program in Fig. 13.5 is run, there will be no printed output from it. All output is directed to the disk file INFO by statement 9. The output exists only in magnetic form on the disk system.

13.4.3 Copying Files

Just as the program of Figure 13.5 copied a file from cards (SYSIN) to disk (INFO), one may also copy one disk file onto another. Assuming that the operating system kept the data which was placed on INFO in the previous section[7], we will show a program which copies

---

[6]The action of OPEN and CLOSE also depends on other file characteristics. What is described here pertains only to STREAM files.

[7]A request to keep files is made to the operating system via JCL. A PL/C system may keep the data by default, at least until the next job is executed.

this disk file onto another. In fact, it will make two copies: one on disk (MASTER) and another on the printer (SYSPRINT), so that a human can see exactly what data was copied. The route of the data is shown in Fig. 13.6 and the program is shown in Fig. 13.7.

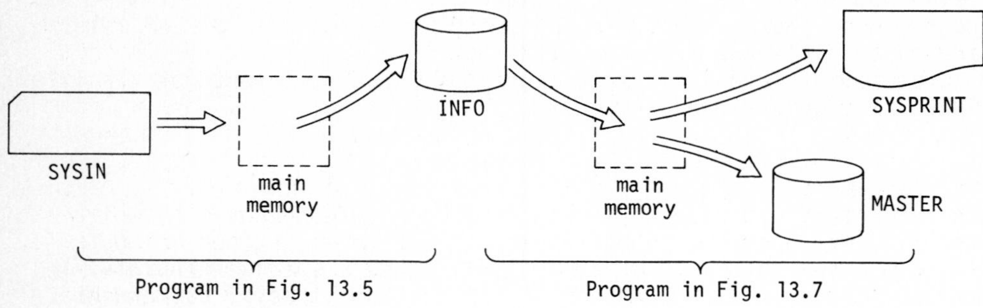

Fig. 13.6 The Route of the Data

When all this is finished, there will be four copies of the original file: the original still on cards outside the system; two copies on disk within the system (INFO is <u>not</u> destroyed by copying); and one on paper, readable to a human but irretrievable to a computer. Whatever may have been on MASTER prior to this copy is now gone forever.

```
                /* FIGURE 13.7 */
DISK2:  PROCEDURE OPTIONS (MAIN);
        DECLARE
           NAME CHAR(20),
           MORE BIT(1),
           INFO FILE STREAM,
           MASTER FILE STREAM;
        /* COPY DATA FROM INFO TO MASTER
           AND THE PRINTER */
        MORE = '1'B;
        ON ENDFILE (INFO) MORE = '0'B;
        OPEN FILE (INFO) INPUT;
        OPEN FILE (MASTER) OUTPUT;
        GET FILE (INFO) LIST (NAME);
LOOP2:  DO WHILE (MORE);
           PUT FILE (MASTER) LIST (NAME);
           PUT FILE (SYSPRINT) LIST (NAME);
           GET FILE (INFO) LIST (NAME);
        END LOOP2;
        CLOSE FILE (INFO);
        CLOSE FILE (MASTER);
        END DISK2;
```

Fig. 13.7 Copying a Disk File

There are some important things to observe. First, provided INFO was kept after the first program created it, it may remain in the system for a long period of time, possibly years. The second program could have made the copy at any time during this period.

Second, the copy program in Fig. 13.7 looks very similar to that in Fig. 13.5. The copy algorithm is the same; only the source and destination change. STREAM files also behave similarly whether they reside on disk or on cards or the printer.

Finally, notice that the copy program in Fig. 13.7 retrieved the data from INFO in a way which corresponds to the way it was originally placed on INFO. In other words, GET LIST was used because the file was generated by PUT LIST statements. If the file has been produced by PUT EDIT, it would have been read by GET EDIT statements, using identical format lists! Though the variable names may differ, the form of the variable NAME in Fig. 13.7 must be equivalent to the variable used in Fig. 13.5. The need for this correspondence between the original OUTPUT statements and all subsequent INPUT statements is a new concept with disk files. However, if this correspondence is not maintained, you may not be able to later retrieve exactly what was originally placed on the file.

Incidentally, the SYSIN and SYSPRINT files were never explicitly DECLAREd, OPENed, or CLOSEd. Although it would be legal to do so, the system automatically defines and correctly opens these two special files for you.

13.4.4 Merging Two Disk Files

In Chapter 10 we discussed the problem of merging two sorted arrays into one. The most common instance of merging is that of merging two ordered files into one. To demonstrate, we shall merge the two sets of sorted data used in the review problem of Chapter 10. This problem involved student records, separated into males and females, both ordered by increasing grade average. The male student records are on INFO, the female students are on TEMP1, and we wish to merge all students (still sorted by average) onto MASTER. We will further assume that the data on INFO and TEMP1 have been placed there by the statement:

```
PUT FILE (<filename>) EDIT
  (A(20), F(10), F(9,2));
```

Each collection of data on the files will then have the following format:

POSITION	DATA
1-20	name
21-23	blank
24-30	ID number
31-34	blank
35-39	average

Again, it is necessary that we know the exact format of data on a disk file so that we can properly read and interpret the data, using the corresponding type of GET statement and identical format. Unlike a datacard, we cannot examine the data physically. The program to perform the merge is shown in Fig. 13.8. You will notice that the logic of this program is basically the same as that in the procedure MERGE of Fig. 10.8. We have, however, introduced some new PL/I features.

We have declared the structure FEMALES to be LIKE the structure MALES. The effect of this is to give FEMALES exactly the same structuring as was given to MALES without having to write all the details a second time. It is particularly useful when the programmer needs several identical structures with different names. The structure, names, and attributes of everything below the name following LIKE is copied. The dimensionality of the specified name is not copied. Thus, if MALES had been an array of 100 constituent structures, then our declaration for FEMALES would have given only one copy of the structure. To get a similar 100-element array for FEMALES we would have had to say:

```
DECLARE 1 FEMALES (100) LIKE MALES;
```

The LIKE attribute can also be applied to minor structures. We can declare major structures LIKE a minor or major structure and declare minor structures LIKE major or minor structures.

Note the multiple files in the OPEN and CLOSE statements. The only important point here is that the keyword FILE must precede each filename. We have also used a filename as a parameter in the procedure READ_ONE. This enables us to use a single procedure to read from various files by merely passing the appropriate filename in the CALL statement.

13.4.5 Updating Stream Files

In Chapter 7 we discussed elementary techniques for updating arrays. While the problem carries over to auxiliary files, there are certain constraints in manipulating data on files which do not apply to data in main memory. These limitations are particularly severe in the case of STREAM files which must be processed sequentially.

Consider changing the address for one person in a file which contains a collection of names and addresses. The straightforward solution is:

1. find the name and address required;
2. change the address;
3. put the amended version back on file.

It is the last step which causes problems in STREAM files. Recall that these files can only be opened for either INPUT or OUTPUT. Further, each OPEN statement brings us to the start of the file. Now the problem becomes obvious. While searching for the required name and address, the file must be open for INPUT; to replace the updated record the file must be open for OUTPUT, which implies being repositioned at the beginning. The only solution to this dilemma for

```
MERGER: PROCEDURE OPTIONS (MAIN);
        DECLARE
           1 MALES,
              2 IDENT,
                 3 NAME CHARACTER(20),
                 3 ID_NO FIXED BINARY(31),
              2 AVERAGE FLOAT(6),
           1 FEMALES LIKE MALES,
           (INFO,MASTER,TEMP1) FILE STREAM,
           (MOREINFO,MORETEMP) BIT(1);
        MOREINFO = '1'B;
        MORETEMP = '1'B;
        ON ENDFILE (INFO) MOREINFO = '0'B;
        ON ENDFILE (TEMP1) MORETEMP = '0'B;
        OPEN FILE (INFO), FILE (TEMP1) INPUT;
        OPEN FILE (MASTER) OUTPUT;
        GET FILE (INFO) EDIT (MALES)
           (A(20),X(3),F(7),X(4),F(5,2));
        GET FILE (TEMP1) EDIT (FEMALES)
           (A(20),X(3),F(7),X(4),F(5,2));
BOTH:   DO WHILE (MOREINFO & MORETEMP);
           IF MALES.AVERAGE <= FEMALES.AVERAGE THEN
              CALL READ_ONE (MALES,INFO);
           ELSE
              CALL READ_ONE (FEMALES,TEMP1);
        END BOTH;
MORE_MALES:
        DO WHILE (MOREINFO);
           CALL READ_ONE (MALES,INFO);
        END MORE_MALES;
MORE_FEMALES:
        DO WHILE (MORETEMP);
           CALL READ_ONE (FEMALES,TEMP1);
        END MORE_FEMALES;
        CLOSE FILE (INFO), FILE (TEMP1), FILE (MASTER);
        OPEN FILE (MASTER) INPUT;
        ON ENDFILE (MASTER) STOP;
        DO WHILE ('1');
        GET FILE (MASTER) EDIT (MALES)
           (A(20),F(10),F(9,2));
        PUT SKIP EDIT (MALES) (A(20),F(10),F(9,2));
        END;
READ_ONE:
        PROCEDURE (RECORD,FILEX);
        DECLARE
           1 RECORD,
              2 ID,
                 3 NA CHARACTER(*),
                 3 I FIXED BINARY(31),
              2 AV FLOAT(6),
           FILEX FILE STREAM;
        PUT FILE (MASTER) EDIT (RECORD)
           (A(20),F(10),F(9,2));
        GET FILE (FILEX) EDIT (RECORD)
           (A(20),X(3),F(7),X(4),F(5,2));
        END READ_ONE;
        END MERGER;
```

Figure 13.8

STREAM files is to create a new version of the file, most likely using the general update algorithm given in Fig. 13.9

```
1.   repeat until end of (old) file;
1.1       read a record from old file;
1.2       if record requires updating then
1.2.1         update the record;
1.3       write the record to new file;
2.   end
```

Fig. 13.9 General Update Algorithm for STREAM Files.

This algorithm ensures that all records stay in their original order and allows the programmer to both read and write, although to different files! It has the disadvantage of placing the updated records on a different file from the original one. Of course, if necessary the new file can always be copied back to the old file. However, the overwhelming disadvantage is that nearly the entire file must be copied even if only one record is being updated!

Updating an ordered STREAM file involves a merge-type algorithm. One set of records is the original ordered file; the other is the set of changes, ordered the same way as the file records themselves. As the original file is read, records which are not slated for update are copied to the new file. But records which match those in the list of changes have an updated version placed in the new file. The update request, from the top of the list of changes, and the original version of the record can then be discarded.

Deleting a record from a file is similar. An ordered list of records to be deleted is kept, so that only the top element on this deletion list need be consulted as file records are inspected. When a record that is slated for deletion is encountered, it is simply not copied onto the new file, and the top element on the list of deletions is discarded.

Obviously, adding new records may be done by a conventional merge.

Thus, adding, deleting, or modifying records in a STREAM file involves some variation of the basic merge algorithm. This, unfortunately, is the case even if only a single record is to be altered! The "list" of changes would only contain one entry, but practically the entire original file would still have to be copied. For large files this is a very expensive proposition. STREAM files are clearly not suitable for applications requiring frequent, small changes. RECORD files should be used in these cases. Incidentally, even RECORD files which are stored on tape, or have "sequential organization" on disk, suffer the same limitations as STREAM files in this regard.

13.5 SEQUENTIAL PROCESSING IN GENERAL

Sequential processing refers, of course, to the movement through successive data items in the same order as their respective locations on the storage device. All of the algorithms in this chapter have been sequential. For example, whether a file was being copied or whether two files were being merged, the records in the old files were obtained in their order of occurrence, and the new file was built record-by-record from beginning to end. Such algorithms are certainly straightforward and relatively simple to implement.

Of course the files described in this chapter had to be processed sequentially because STREAM files are inherently sequential. If a file has been created with the STREAM attribute, it behaves as thought it resides on a sequential device, even if it happens to be on disk.

However, the copy and merge algorithms were encountered in an earlier chapter (7.5.1.2 and 7.5.4, respectively) dealing with arrays. Even though an array may have arbitrary elements referenced and is, therefore, not necessarily sequential, the algorithms to copy and merge arrays were essentially the same as those for files. The only real difference in these algorithms for array and file applications is the source and destination of the data. The algorithms themselves are sequential and are typical of the large class of sequential processing algorithms.

Other examples of sequential processing are the algorithms to find a minimum value in an array (sections 3.5.1 and 7.5.1.1) and to locate a specific array item by a linear search (section 7.3.2). Of course these algorithms could also be adapted to file processing.

Sequential processing is the only alternative when the data is on a sequential device or has an inherently sequential structure. (e.g. STREAM files). Even when a more flexible alternative may exist, say with data in an array or a RECORD oriented file on disk, sequential processing is the desirable choice in some applications. These tend to be situations in which almost the entire file or a substantial subsection must be processed anyway. (This may be the case if desired items are scattered throughout the file or array.)

This condition is obviously met in the problems of copying, merging, or finding a minimum value in a set, whether of array elements or of file records. Since every item in the collection must be inspected anyway, they might as well be inspected in order, so that the simplicity of sequential processing may be enjoyed.

Some typical sequential applications are, therefore:

(1) to copy or move an entire set of items, e.g. to append one file onto another;

(2) to find extremal or summary values over an entire set, such as the maximum, average, total, or number of items satisfying some selection criterion; and

(3) to extract or select all the items from a set which meet certain criteria, assuming that either (i) many such items exist or (ii) that there is no special structuring or ordering of the data which can facilitate the selection.

Since sequential file processing is usually the simplest method for both the programmer and the operating system, it is the default processing mode. If you wish to make it explicit that you are processing files sequentially, you may say:

```
                                { INPUT  }
        OPEN FILE (<filename>)  {   or   }  SEQUENTIAL;
                                { OUTPUT }
```

Despite its attractiveness in some situations, sequential processing is not appropriate in many cases. We have seen the difficulty in making a simple modification to a STREAM file in Section 13.4.5. Any change or set of changes required almost the entire file to be copied in the course of "merging in" the changes. There has to be a faster way! The same difficulty arises with tape files, as anyone knows who has tried to record in the middle of a home recording tape.

Given the right circumstances (arrays or the right type of RECORD files on disk), one can sometimes update an item in the middle of the file without recopying the rest. Even then, a sequential algorithm is not practical for making isolated changes. A single update may be too expensive, simply due to the effort in sequentially locating the record to be changed. Deletions are also feasible but only by marking (i.e. updating) the doomed record in such a way that it will be recognizable as invalid and treated as missing. Insertion into the middle of a sequential file is out of the question unless a previously "deleted" record can be reused. In an ordered file this is extremely unlikely. In summary, though sequential files can be updated, they do not easily lend themselves to change and should not be used if many isolated alterations are expected.

Another problem is that sequential algorithms are not efficient enough in many situations. Sequential algorithms tend to be "exhaustive", plowing through an entire collection of data. They take little or no advantage of special structuring within the data, such as ordering. Searching for a specific value in a set of ordered data is a good example, since much better non-sequential algorithms exist. For example, the quadratic (Section 7.5.3) and binary (Section 11.5.2) search algorithms both tend to locate the desired value much faster than the sequential search. However these algorithms depend on the ability to "jump around" in the data non-sequentially. For many such applications, sequential processing is simply too slow.

Chapter 14 will first describe the so called RECORD alternative to STREAM files. Then it will describe one way to free RECORD files on disk from the limitations of sequential processing. Until that time you are limited to sequential file processing and are warned to be wary that sequential processing is really appropriate for your application.

13.6 REVIEW OF RULES

1. Stream files may be declared by:

```
DECLARE <filename> FILE STREAM;
```

2. Stream files are opened for reading by:

```
OPEN FILE (<filename>) INPUT;
```

   They are opened for writing by:

```
OPEN FILE (<filename>) OUTPUT;
```

   OPEN always repositions you at the beginning of the file.

3. All files are closed by:

CLOSE FILE (<filename>);

CLOSE writes an end of file mark on OUTPUT files.

4. Stream files may only be read from or written to at any one time.

5. PL/I structures may be declared to be LIKE another major or minor structure:

DECLARE 1 <structure2> LIKE <structure1>;

The effect is to copy the structure, names and attributes of all levels below the name <structure1>.

13.7 REVIEW PROBLEM

In this section we will take a more practical approach to the problem of Section 7.8. In a commercial environment, the accounts receivable records for a firm are usually stored in order on an auxiliary file. The transaction records to update the master accounts receivable file are also usually maintained in the same order. The sorting may be done by an electro-mechanical device called a card sorter if the transactions are on cards or by computer program if they are on another auxiliary file.

In this version we shall assume the accounts receivable records are on the disk file MASTER, in alphabetical order by customer name, and that each record has the form:

position 1 - 40 - last name, first name

46 - 52 - balance owing (decimal in pos. 50)

Transaction records are on data cards, also sorted in alphabetical order and in the format:

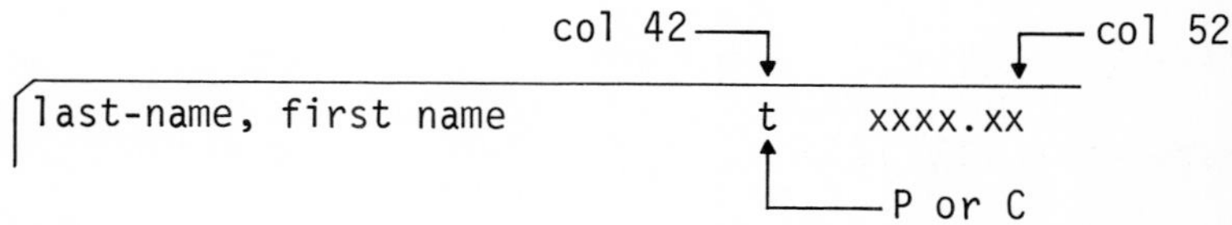

If the transaction represents a payment, column 42 will contain a 'P'; otherwise it will contain a 'C'. We will allow transactions for customers who did not previously appear on the master file, i.e. new accounts. It is also reasonable to delete from the new master file those customers whose balances have been reduced to zero. The output from our program should be the new updated accounts receivable records on the same file, MASTER, as the old records.

The solution to this problem boils down to the basic logic of a two-way merge with minor modifications. As long as the records from each file (SYSIN and MASTER) have different customer names, the merge proceeds as usual. It is only when the names are the same that we

```
        /* FIGURE 13.10 */
ACCREC: PROCEDURE OPTIONS (MAIN);
    /* A PROGRAM TO UPDATE AN ACCOUNTS
       RECEIVABLE FILE. */
    DECLARE
       1 ACCOUNT, /* MASTER RECORD */
          2 NAME CHARACTER(40),
          2 DUMMY CHARACTER(1),
          2 BALANCE FIXED(7,2),
       1 XACT, /* TRANSACTION RECORD */
          2 NAME CHARACTER(40),
          2 TYPE CHARACTER(1),
          2 AMOUNT FIXED(7,2),
       (MASTER,INFO) FILE STREAM,
       (MOREX,MOREM) BIT(1);
    MOREX = '1'B; /* EOF FOR SYSIN */
    MOREM = '1'B; /* EOF FOR MASTER */
    OPEN FILE (INFO) OUTPUT;
    OPEN FILE (MASTER) INPUT;
    ON ENDFILE (SYSIN) MOREX = '0'B;
    ON ENDFILE (MASTER) MOREM = '0'B;
    GET FILE (SYSIN) EDIT (XACT)
       (A(40),X(1),A(1),X(3),F(7,2));
    GET FILE (MASTER) EDIT (ACCOUNT)
       (A(40),X(1),A(1),X(3),F(7,2));
    CALL MERGE; /* UPDATE MASTER FILE */
    CALL MORE_MASTER; /* RESIDUAL MASTER RECORDS */
    CALL MORE_XACT; /* RESIDUAL TRANSACTIONS */
    CLOSE FILE (INFO), FILE (MASTER);
    CALL COPY; /* PUT UPDATED FILE BACK ON MASTER */
    CLOSE FILE (INFO), FILE (MASTER);
    END ACCREC;
```

Figure 13.10

```
            /* FIGURE 13.11 */
MERGE:   PROCEDURE;
         DO WHILE (MOREX & MOREM);
            IF ACCOUNT.NAME < XACT.NAME THEN
               CALL COPYM (MASTER,INFO); /* NO UPDATE */
            ELSE IF ACCOUNT.NAME = XACT.NAME THEN
               CALL UPDATE; /* UPDATE ACCOUNT */
               ELSE CALL NEW_ACCT; /* NEW ACCOUNT */
         END;
         END MERGE;
UPDATE:  PROCEDURE;
         DO WHILE ( (ACCOUNT.NAME = XACT.NAME) & MOREX );
            IF TYPE = 'P' THEN
               AMOUNT = -AMOUNT;
            BALANCE = BALANCE + AMOUNT;
            GET FILE (SYSIN) SKIP EDIT (XACT)
               (A(40),X(1),A(1),X(3),F(7,));
         END;
         IF BALANCE = 0.00 THEN /* DELETE ZERO BALANCES */
            GET FILE (MASTER) EDIT (ACCOUNT)
               (A(40),X(1),A(1),X(3),F(7,2));
         ELSE
            CALL COPYM (MASTER,INFO);
         END UPDATE;
```

Figure 13.11

insert additional code to take care of the update. With this in mind, we shall merge SYSIN and MASTER into the file INFO and then copy the updated accounts receivable from INFO back into MASTER. The outline program to accomplish this is shown in Fig. 13.10.

The procedure MERGE, will update the master file as long as we have records in both the master file and transaction file. MORE_MASTER will copy any remaining master file records to the updated file while MORE_XACT will handle any remaining transactions. It is important that MORE_XACT be capable of handling more than one transaction for a new account since it is feasible that a charge and a payment to a new account happen in the same period. COPYM will have two files as parameters; it will write one copy of ACCOUNT to the second file and then read a new record into ACCOUNT from the first file. Fig. 13.11 fills in the detail of MERGE and its associated procedure UPDATE. The details of COPY, COPYM, MORE_MASTER and MORE_XACT are left to the reader as an exercise.

The procedure MERGE is the basic procedure for matching transactions against master file records. If the master record has no corresponding transaction, we simply write the master record from ACCOUNT to the intermediate file INFO and read a new record from file master. This is done by the procedure COPYM which we have not shown.

MERGE handles the updating of existing accounts in the same way as was done in Fig. 7.20. The only additional code we have added is to delete zero balance accounts. This is accomplished by simply overwriting such records - they are not written out to the disk file.

If the program finds a transaction card for which there is no existing account records, it sets up a new account on the output file by calling NEW_ACCT. The logic for this procedure must be carefully designed to handle several transactions for such accounts and to avoid destroying the data in ACCOUNT. We take care of the second problem by setting up a local variable to mirror ACCOUNT. Provided we remember that XACT will have valid data in it when NEW_ACCT is called, the logic proceeds much like the basic updating shown in MERGE. The new account procedure is shown in Fig. 13.12.

```
                  /* FIGURE 13.12 */
NEW_ACCT:
        PROCEDURE;
        DECLARE
           1 AC,
              2 NAME CHARACTER(40),
              2 DUMMY CHARACTER(1) INITIAL (' '),
              2 BALANCE FIXED(7,2) INITIAL (0.00);
        AC.NAME = XACT.NAME; /* NEW NAME */
        DO WHILE ( (AC.NAME = XACT.NAME) & MOREX );
           IF TYPE = 'P' THEN
              AMOUNT = -AMOUNT;
           BALANCE = BALANCE + AMOUNT;
           GET FILE (SYSIN) SKIP EDIT (XACT)
              (A(40),X(1),A(1),X(3),F(7,2));
        END;
        PUT FILE (INFO) EDIT (AC)
           (A(40),X(1),A(1),X(3),F(7,2));
        END NEW_ACCT;
```

Figure 13.12

To complete the program, the procedures MORE_XACT and COPY have to be added. MORE_XACT will repeatedly call NEW_ACCT until end of file is encountered on SYSIN. COPY will simply read from INFO and write onto MASTER. We should point out that it is often helpful to print a copy of everything being written on an auxiliary file. That way you can actually see what data are being written on the file. This is a particilarly useful procedure during the early program development stages. The statements to do the printing can always be removed in the final version.

13.8 EXERCISES

13.1 Complete the missing procedures in the review problem (Section 13.7): MORE_MASTER, MORE_XACT, COPY and COPYM. Then generate the master (MASTER) and transaction (INFO) files and complete the update process. Your update program should print out the new version of MASTER as suggested in the review problem.

13.2 A certain disk file contains 10,000 data items in random order. Suppose you are only able to store 2,500 of these items in main memory at one time, but have an unlimited number of disk files at your disposal. Explain how you would go about sorting the 10,000 items into, say, ascending order.

13.3 Suppose a sequential disk file contains the records for 5,000 students in ascending order by student number. Each semester the grades for these records are recorded on data cards, in random order. Would there by any advantage to sorting the grades before updating the student master file? Justify your answer.

13.4 One of the most common data processing applications in business is the preparation of name and address labels from a mailing list file. Labels are often prepared in "three-up" fashion, i.e. three labels are printed across the printer sheet.

Consider a mailing list file on disk where each record is 140 bytes long with the format:

```
Byte   1 - 30 - name
      31 - 80 - blank
      81 -115 - street
     116 -135 - city/state
     136 -140 - zip code
```

(a) Write a procedure to create this mailing list file on disk from data supplied on cards. Notice that the pertinent information will just fit on one data card.

(b) Write a program to prepare "three-up" labels where each label has four lines of print and there are three blank lines between each set of three labels. The printer format for the labels is:

```
line1     col 1 - 30     name1
              41 - 70    name2
              81 -110    name3
line2     col 1 - 35     street1
              41 - 75    street2
              81 -115    street3
line3     col 1 - 20     city/state1
              41 - 60    city/state2
              81 -100    city/state3
line4     col 1 -  5     zip1
              41 - 45    zip2
              81 - 85    zip3
```

Note that the last line of labels may not have exactly three names and addresses.

13.5 A useful procedure to have at hand is one which will copy cards onto a disk file and sequence number them in byte positions 73 through 80. Write a procedure with parameters DISKFILE, START, and INCR to perform this function. The procedure should copy 80-byte records from SYSIN, number the nth record as START + (n-1)*INCR and write the record out to file DISKFILE. You will also require a procedure to copy an arbitrary DISKFILE to SYSPRINT so that you can see the results of the sequence numbering procedure.

13.6 Modify problem 10.5 so that the team records are maintained on disk in order. You may assume a maximum of ten teams so that sorting can be done in main memory.

13.7 Suppose you have two collections or "sets" of objects named X and Y, defined as follows:

X = (a,b,c) and Y = (a,c,e)

This notation means that X contains the three objects a, b, and c, for example. Some basic binary set operations are:

(i) union, denoted by ∪, which yields the set of objects in either or both of the original sets;

e.g. X ∪ Y = (a,b,c,e)

(ii) intersection, denoted by ∩, which yields the set of objects common to both original sets;

e.g. X ∩ Y = (a,c)

(iii) set difference, denoted by -, which yields the set of objects appearing only in the first set;

e.g. X - Y = (b)

If the original sets are ordered, these set operations can be implemented by variations of the basic merge algorithm, which of course preserves the ordering.

(a) Assuming the "sets" are ordered disk files of last names, implement the three indicated set operations as three procedures.

(b) Write a procedure to implement "exclusive-OR", which is the set of items appearing in exactly one of the original sets (either but not both).

(c) Though not as "efficient" as the direct merge implementation, it is possible to write an "exclusive-OR" procedure which merely calls the other procedures from part (a). Write this procedure. Explain why it is less efficient than a merge implementation.

Chapter 14
Processing Record Files

14.1 INTRODUCTION

STREAM files are a very useful illusion conjured up by the operating system. In reality the stream of characters imagined by the programmer is stored as a collection of distinct records. One hint of this underlying reality is the use of the keyword SKIP on GET statements, applied to the card reader. To what point is one supposed to SKIP in a pure stream file? Only when you understand that distinct data cards (records) comprise the "stream" does SKIP acquire a meaning.

All files are in reality stored as records. The STREAM attribute is a point of view which your program is allowed to have and which the operating system sustains. The alternative "point of view" is to see the file as it really is[1] - as a collection of separate RECORDs. Files which are to be treated this way are declared by the statement:

DECLARE <filename> FILE RECORD;

RECORD files are not merely concessions to reality. They are more commonly used in commercial applications than STREAM files for three

---

1 This does not mean that a file which was created as a STREAM file may be accessible as a RECORD file. A file should always be retrieved in a manner corresponding to its creation.

very good reasons.

One reason is efficiency. RECORD files tend to consume less secondary storage than their STREAM counterparts and require less work by the operating system to transmit. (The STREAM illusion is had at the expense of extra processing by the operating system.) The reasons and consequences will be discussed in Sections 14.2 - 14.4.

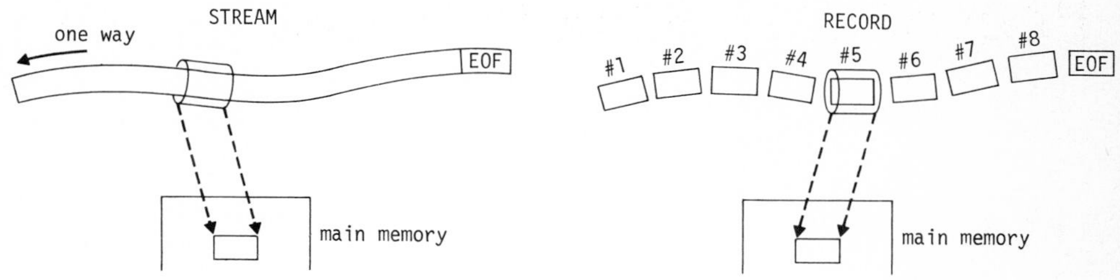

Figure 14.1 Two Views of Files as Seen by a PL/I Program

The second reason is flexibility. A STREAM file is by its nature sequential. The only method of processing it is to move through consecutive locations. Only when the processing program and operating system agree that the file is comprised of individual records, is it even conceivable to jump to any particular record without having to traverse a "stream" of intervening characters. Under the right conditions, RECORD files allow the user direct access to the record of his choice, much as arrays permit immediate access to any element. RECORD files are therefore needed in order to exploit the direct capabilities of disks. This will be the subject of Sections 14.7 - 14.9.

On the other hand, RECORD files do not have to be used in this way. RECORD-oriented sequential files may also offer the benefits of efficiency, and so it is with these that we begin the next section.

A third reason for RECORD files is universality. Other languages, such as COBOL and FORTRAN, can produce and process RECORD files but have no built in capability for handling STREAM files. Thus RECORD files must be used to transport data from one program to another if the programs were written in different source languages. Though this is an important commercial motive for RECORD files, we will not discuss it further.

14.2 A SIMPLE EXAMPLE OF SEQUENTIAL RECORD I/O

In this section we present two simple programs. The first program (Fig. 14.2) creates a RECORD file on disk. The input is from cards, each containing the age (cols. 1-2) and weight (cols. 4-6) of a subject. This program generates a record for each subject consisting of these two numbers. The second program (Fig. 14.3) will later inspect the file sequentially to determine the average weight of subjects in their 30's.

The three types of PL/I statements for RECORD I/O are similar to the statements used in STREAM I/O:

(1) The filename is DECLARED as a FILE with the attribute RECORD;

(2) OPEN and CLOSE are used as before to designate the mode of operation as INPUT or OUTPUT (other options will be available eventually); and

(3) Data is transmitted by executing the statements READ or WRITE. These are the RECORD-oriented counterparts of GET and PUT (which are used only with STREAM files).

Their general forms are:

```
READ FILE (<filename>) INTO (<variable>);
                   and
WRITE FILE (<filename>) FROM (<variable>);
```

The <variable> is the source or destination of the data in main memory, and must not be a subscripted variable nor any structure name which is not a level 1 name. In addition, the amount of main storage reserved for <variable> must be exactly the same as the length of the records in <filename>, assuming all records are of uniform length.

The change from STREAM to RECORD files for the examples in this section did not require new and different algorithms. Basic sequential processing algorithms are independent of whether the file is STREAM or RECORD. The only changes appear to be linguistic: the declaration of MYFILE as RECORD and the use of READ instead of GET and WRITE instead of PUT. There are, however, many subtle differences between these file organizations which will be discussed in later sections.

14.3 A RECORD I/O EXAMPLE INVOLVING THE PRINTER AND CARD READER

Since the printer and card reader are fundamentally record oriented devices, it is possible for a program to communicate with them using RECORD I/O. Consider the simple problem of reading data cards and writing card images on the printer. The card file is SYSIN and the printer file is SYSPRINT, as usual. However, SYSIN records are 80 bytes long (the number of columns on a data card) and SYSPRINT records vary according to printer; we assume the printer record length is 121 as shown in the preface. A record to the printer is usually one line of output. However, the first character in each record is to be used for carriage control, i.e. controlling the vertical spacing on the printer. This character is never printed but instead instructs the printer how many lines to skip before printing the remaining characters in the record. The printer we are using can display at most

```
        /* FIGURE 14.2 */
CREATE: PROCEDURE OPTIONS (MAIN);
        DECLARE
           BUFFER(2) FIXED BINARY(15),
           MORE BIT(1) INITIAL ('1'B),
           MYFILE FILE RECORD;
        ON ENDFILE (SYSIN) MORE = '0'B;
        OPEN FILE (MYFILE) OUTPUT;
        GET FILE (SYSIN) EDIT (BUFFER) (F(2),X(1),F(3));
        DO WHILE (MORE);
           WRITE FILE (MYFILE) FROM (BUFFER);
           GET FILE (SYSIN) SKIP EDIT (BUFFER)
              (F(2),X(1),F(3));
        END;
        CLOSE FILE (MYFILE);
        END CREATE;
```

Fig. 14.2 Program to Copy Cards to RECORD File on Disk

```
             /* FIGURE 14.3 */
AVERAGE:
        PROCEDURE OPTIONS (MAIN);
        DECLARE
           1 RECD,
              2 AGE FIXED BIN(15),
              2 WEIGHT FIXED BIN(15),
           (TOTAL, NUMB) FLOAT(6) INITIAL (0,0),
           NOTDUN BIT(1) INITIAL ('1'B),
           MYFILE FILE RECORD;
        ON ENDFILE (MYFILE) NOTDUN = '0'B;
        OPEN FILE (MYFILE) INPUT;
        READ FILE (MYFILE) INTO (RECD);
        DO WHILE (NOTDUN);
           IF ( AGE >= 30 & AGE <= 39 ) THEN
              DO;
                 TOTAL = TOTAL + WEIGHT;
                 NUMB = NUMB + 1;
              END;
           READ FILE (MYFILE) INTO (RECD);
        END;
        PUT LIST ('AVERAGE IS:', TOTAL/NUMB);
        CLOSE FILE (MYFILE);
        END AVERAGE;
```

Fig. 14.3 Program to Determine Average Weight of Subjects in their 30's from File Created in Fig. 14.2

120 characters per line. The common carriage control characters and their stream equivalents are shown in Fig. 14.4.

Control Character	Stream I/O Equivalent
ƀ blank	PUT SKIP
0	PUT SKIP (2)
-	PUT SKIP (3)
+	PUT SKIP (0)
1	PUT PAGE

Fig. 14.4 Common Carriage Control Characters

Every record from the card reader contains exactly the same number of characters or "bytes"(80). When the records of a file have a uniform size, they are called "fixed-length records". In our example, SYSPRINT also has fixed-length records (121 bytes). Although the operating system allows records of varying lengths to be intermixed on the same file, varying length records are of more limited usefulness and greater complexity and do not illuminate the issues of RECORD I/O. Consequently, we will confine all our discussion to files with fixed-length records.

An important point about fixed-length records is that the main memory locations used for input and output must be exactly the same size as the respective record lengths. In our example we will require two variables of lengths 80 and 121, respectively, as shown in Fig. 14.5.

```
                /* FIGURE 14.5 */
COPY:     PROCEDURE OPTIONS (MAIN);
          DECLARE
             CARDIN CHAR(80),
             CARDOUT CHAR(121),
             (SYSIN,SYSPRINT) FILE RECORD;
          OPEN FILE (SYSIN) INPUT;
          OPEN FILE (SYSPRINT) OUTPUT;
          ON ENDFILE (SYSIN) BEGIN;
             CLOSE FILE (SYSIN), FILE (SYSPRINT);
             STOP;
          END;
          DO WHILE ('1'B);
             READ FILE (SYSIN) INTO (CARDIN);
             CARDOUT = ' ' || CARDIN;
             WRITE FILE (SYSPRINT) FROM (CARDOUT);
          END;
          END COPY;
```

Fig. 14.5 Program to Copy Cards to Printer Using RECORD Files

The statement

```
CARDOUT = ' ' || CARDIN;
```

includes the addition of a blank carriage control character to the card image before storing it in CARDOUT. Had we not supplied it explicitly, the first character from the card image would have been used for carriage control and not be printed. This statement also pads CARDOUT on the right with blanks, so that the output record really does contain 121 characters.

14.4 DIFFERENCES BETWEEN STREAM AND RECORD I/O

14.4.1 Conversion of Data

STREAM files consist of character data only. When a value such as 123 is displayed by the printer, it is actually printing the character 1, followed by the character 2, followed by the character 3. Characters are the only data type which can be seen by human beings. In main memory, the character string '123' is stored in a sequence of three separate bytes, each encoded to depict its respective character. If the 123 is intended for communication with humans, this is appropriate.

However, if 123 is viewed as a particular numeric quantity for use in arithmetic operations, it is encoded as one single numeric value[2] - not as three distinct digits. This numeric version is entirely different from the encoding for a sequence of three characters because it is specifically designed for manipulation by the processor's arithmetic unit, rather than for viewing by human beings.

Consequently, whenever a numeric variable is PUT on the printer or on any STREAM file, its encoding must be deciphered and translated into the corresponding character string by the operating system. This conversion is implied by the format lists of PUT EDIT statements. Consider the statement:

```
PUT EDIT (NUMBER,STRING) (F(6),A(10));
```

The F(6) in the format list directs the system to (i) convert the presumably numeric value in variable NUMBER into an equivalent character string; and (ii) make sure the number of characters is six, by either truncating extra characters or appending blank characters on the left, if necessary. These six bytes of character data followed by the first 10 characters for variable STRING are transmitted to the file. Of course, a reverse conversion takes place on input. GET statements cause some character strings to be interpreted as numbers and re-encoded to reflect that interpretation.

The first observation is that this conversion of arithmetic values

---

2 Or at least in a form which is different from character data, as in the case of FIXED DECIMAL numbers.

is unnecessary if the data is being placed on disk only to be read back into memory later for use as arithmetic data. Since no one can "see" what is on disk anyway, why bother to temporarily store numeric data in character format? It is clearly faster and cheaper to store the numeric version and avoid a useless conversion on each direction of transmission. The programs of Figs. 14.2 and 14.3, therefore, keep the internal encodings of ages and weights on the file MYFILE.

One essential difference between STREAM and RECORD files is that conversion to/from character format always occurs with STREAM files and never occurs with RECORD files. The data are transmitted to and from RECORD files in their undisturbed internal form.

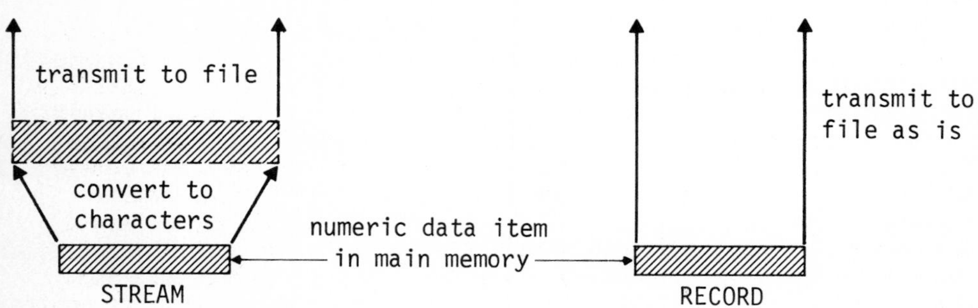

Fig. 14.6 STREAM vs. RECORD Transmission of Data in Terms of Conversion

As a result, RECORD files can contain arbitrary binary encoded patterns or any data type whatsoever. They are not limited to characters or to data types (such as numeric) which are capable of being expressed as character strings.

Another advantage of RECORD files is that unconverted numeric (and other) data is often more compact than its character string equivalent. For example, the string '123' requires three bytes of storage (one per digit), whereas the numeric value of 123 might be stored in a two-byte variable, although its binary representation will actually fit in one byte.

A simplified comparison of STREAM and RECORD transmission is shown in Fig. 14.6, and the storage requirements for common types of PL/I variables are shown in Fig. 14.7.

A complete listing of the storage requirements is given in Section K of IBM Publication GC28-8201. The reader should note that GC28-8201 does not apply to the PL/C compiler; storage requirements for this compiler are given in Appendix A.

14.4.2 The Indivisibility of Records

As the name implies, RECORD files are completely oriented towards entire records. This means that a record is the smallest, seemingly

Attribute	Number of bytes
CHARACTER(n)	n
FLOAT (n)	4 if n <7 8 if 6 <n <17
FIXED BINARY (n)	2 if n <16 4 if 15 <n <32
FIXED (p,q)	CEIL ((p+1)/2)

Fig. 14.7 OS/370 Storage Requirements

indivisible unit of data which can be transmitted by a READ or WRITE statement.

In order to appreciate what this means, let us contrast RECORD files with STREAM files. STREAM I/O could be called "field-oriented" rather than "record-oriented". Every GET and PUT statement specifies a list of variables which correspond to individual fields, (each with its own format specified in an EDIT-type statement). If these data items are logically related, the group of items is sometimes loosely called a "record". However, such "records" are defined by the conglomeration of variables given in a particular GET or PUT statement - not by any physical reality. The same fields could have been transmitted one at a time by separate GET or PUT statements. Even when several fields are transmitted by one GET or PUT, they are moved and converted one at a time. In fact, the conversion provided by STREAM I/O is possible only because the fields are individually indentified and independently handled.

The only requirement is that the "fields" (as prescribed explicitly by the format list in a GET EDIT or PUT EDIT statement) be stored consecutively on the file. However, because each field is transmitted independently, the corresponding variables in memory need not be consecutive parts of a structure or related in any way whatsoever.

This contrasts sharply with RECORD I/O, as shown in Fig. 14.8. Here the records are physically separate packages of data. They are defined by the storage medium and operating system rather than be some group of fields appearing in an I/O statement. The record is moved intact, as a single string of bits, with no breakdown into component fields.

While "fields" may be of no consequence to the RECORD I/O process, they make all the difference to the processing program. As a record is input into a memory area (usually a structure), its field are being placed into variables (usually elementary items of the structure). As we have already seen, these variables must be of exactly the same type as the data in the corresponding fields of the records, since no conversion is done on the fields. Now we see that these variables must also be of precisely the same size and at exactly the same position within the structure as the corresponding field within the record. Since the record is moved as a contiguous unit, the variables in the structure must be aligned perfectly with the fields of the

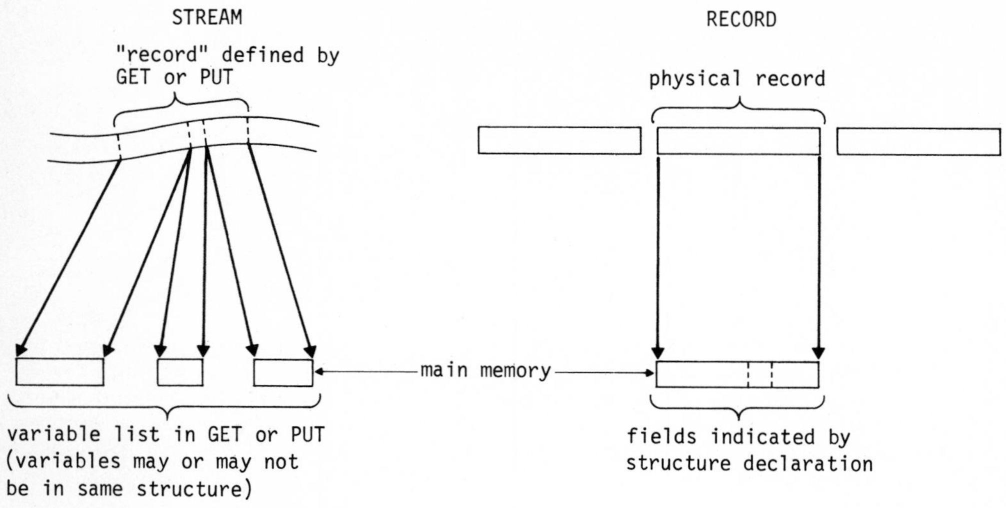

Fig. 14.8 The Field Orientation of STREAM I/O vs. The Indivisibility of Records in RECORD I/O

record in order to receive the correct values. Any mistakes in this alignment can lead to errors, as shown in Fig. 14.9.

14.4.3 Data Transfer in RECORD I/O

This need for alignment forces the programmer to do either of two things in order to isolate and process an individual field of a record. One alternative is to read the record into a structure which is identical to the structure from which the record was originally written onto the file. The other alternative is to design another suitable structure containing the fields of interest, which will require precise knowledge of the physical record layout: in particular the size of every field in the physical record.

If all the fields contain character data, this alignment of fields is not too difficult. However, problems begin as soon as other data types are involved. As a glance back at Fig. 14.7 should indicate, the number of bytes consumed by a numeric field depends critically on how it was originally declared. The rules for determining this space allotment are more numerous than those shown in Fig. 14.7 and, in any case, tend to be complicated and hard to remember. Not only that, they may differ from the PL/I-F complier to the PL/C compiler, not to mention COBOL, RPG, and other languages which may be used to produce or process RECORD oriented files.

What is needed is some mechanism to specify the layout of fields within a record, which specifies clearly the size of each field, is

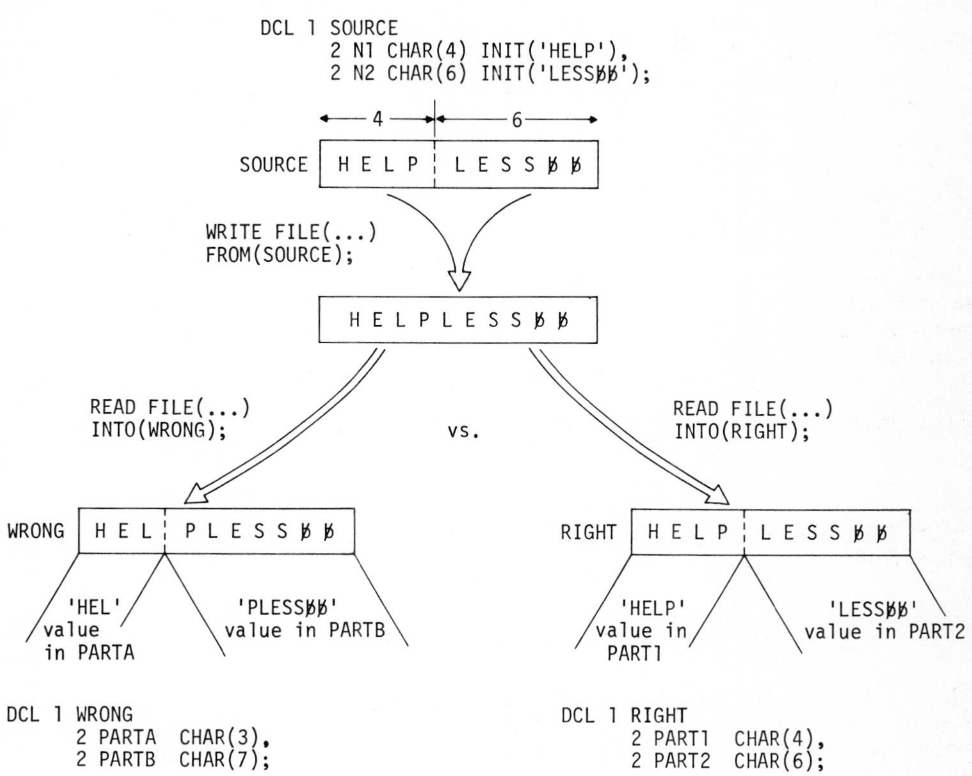

Fig. 14.9 The Need for Aligning Structure Items with Record Fields

simple to use, and is uniform from one compiler to another[3]. This need is satisfied by a facility called the PICTURE attribute to be described in Section 14.5. In effect, PICTURE permits the user to define each field in terms of how its data might "look" character by character - even if it is not "character" data.

---

[3] The ability to pass RECORD files between programs in different languages is also facilitated by using PICTURE data, but requires more discussion which is beyond the scope of this book.

If the elementary items of a structure to be used in RECORD I/O are declared using the PICTURE attribute, there will be no doubt about the number of bytes in each field or the number of bytes from the beginning of the record at which the field is located. Of course, use of PICTURE will not remove the need to have the structure for input correspond to the originating structure from which the record was written; it will merely make the correspondence easier to achieve.

We must emphasize that the PICTURE attribute does not imply any conversion of data during RECORD I/O. If any conversion takes place at all, it occurs when data is being moved in or out of the structure by some other statements of the processing program. READ and WRITE simply move whatever is already in the source to the appropriate destination without alteration. PICTURE merely facilitates the original structure layout. This is summarized in Fig. 14.10.

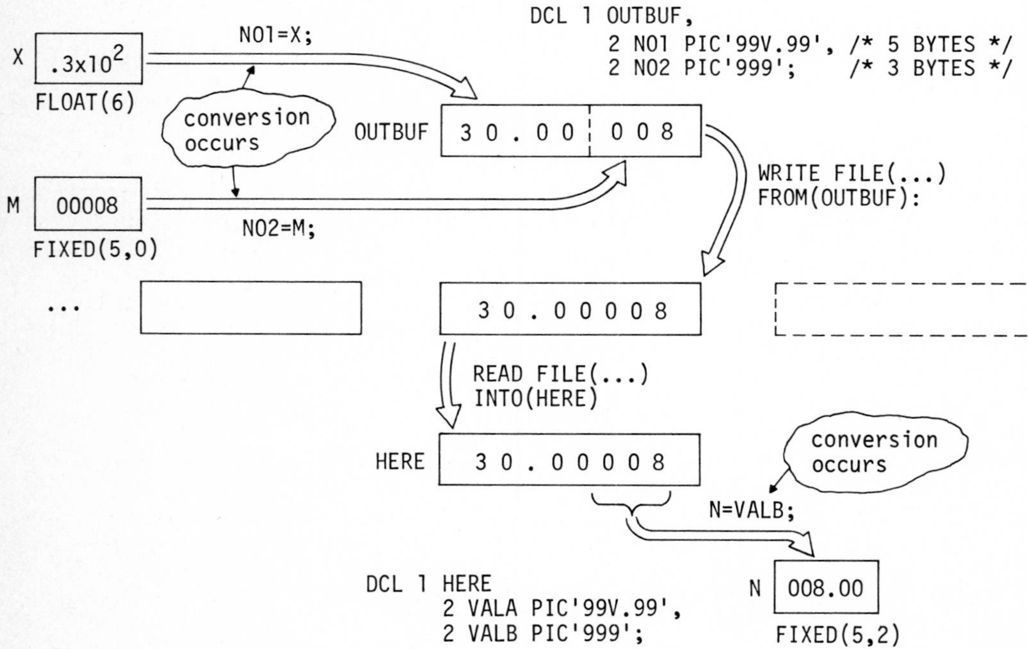

Fig. 14.10 Conversion to/from PICTURE Occurs Before Input or After Output

14.5 THE USE OF PICTURE DATA IN RECORD I/O

14.5.1 Decimal Pictures

A number, such as 123.45, can be stored in a variable X declared as FIXED(5,2). However, it is not clear, without knowing the rules, just how many bytes of storage X consumes. If 123.45 is typical of the values to be stored in X, X could have been defined as follows:

```
DECLARE X PICTURE'999V99';
```

The '999V99' is a pattern which "pictorially" describes how stored values might look. It means "three digits to the left of an implied decimal point and two digits to the right". The space allocated to X will be exactly five bytes. To see this, count the 9's. Do not count the V, since this is an implicit or assumed decimal point, which is not actually stored as such. There are several other symbols which may be used to describe these patterns, depending on what type of thing should be stored in the corresponding byte. Each of these symbols except the V contributes precisely one byte to the length of the field being declared. In general, the number of digits to be retained in a decimal picture is indicated by a series of 9's and the position of an assumed decimal point is indicated by a "V". If no "V" is present, the decimal is assumed to be to the right of the number.

A few examples will illustrate the basics of the PICTURE attribute. Consider first:

```
DECLARE A PIC'99999';
```

Note that PIC is the abbreviation for PICTURE. This declaration allows us to store positive integers with up to five digits. All five digits, including leading zeroes (if any), will be stored. Thus A=123; will cause 00123 to be stored. These leading zeroes will also be printed by a subsequent PUT statement! Notice in the DECLARE statement that the series of 9's must be enclosed in quotes.

Let us reconsider:

```
DECLARE A PIC'999V99';
```

This statement allows up to 5 digits with an assumed decimal point between the third and fourth. If we later say A=23.45; then the value stored will be 023‸45, where "‸" denotes an assumed decimal point. On the other hand, A=12345; will result in A taking on the value 34500. Truncation takes place on the left and two zeroes are padded to the right of the decimal. For long pictures we can factor the number of 9's as:

```
PIC '(n)9V(m)9'
```

This form is equivalent to "n" explicit 9's before the "V" and "m" explicit 9's after it. Thus PIC '(5)9V(3)9' is the same as PIC '99999V999'. Note that the repetition factors must be in parentheses and inside the quotes.

In the examples above, no provision was made for the sign for the number. If we assign -123.45 to variable A, where A has been declared PIC'999V99', then the value stored will be 123‸45. The sign will be lost because we made no explicit provision for it. There are three straightforward ways of specifying a sign in decimal pictures: you may use one of the three additional picture characters: 'S', '+', or '-'. The use of these characters is illustrated in Fig. 14.11.

PICTURE SPECIFICATION	ASSIGNED VALUE	STORED VALUE
PIC'S999V99'	+123.45	+123‸45
PIC'S99V99'	-7.8	-07‸80
PIC '+999'	123	+123‸
PIC'+999'	-45	b̸045‸
PIC'+999'	0	+000‸
PIC'-9V9'	-12.34	-2‸3
PIC'-99V99'	45.67	b̸45‸67
PIC'-99'	-0	b̸00‸

Fig. 14.11 Sign Specification in Decimal Pictures

When the 'S' picture character is used, the sign of the value to be stored must be given. Further, the sign character must be the leftmost or rightmost character in the picture specification. When '+' or '-' is specified in the picture, a value with the opposite sign causes a blank to be stored instead of the sign. In all cases, an assigned value of -0 behaves as if it were +0.

Two more aspects of decimal pictures are the explicit decimal point and the problem of leading zeros. Consider the example:

```
DECLARE A PIC'999V99'; /* 5 BYTES */
A=123.45;
PUT LIST (A);
```

The value 12345 will be printed. Although an implicit decimal point is carried internally and the stored value is correct, no explicit decimal point is provided for printing. This may be provided for by adding a decimal point in the picture specification, immediately after the 'V'. Although there are other placements for the decimal point, it should normally be placed immediately to the right of the 'V'. Now if we say

```
DECLARE A PIC'999V.99'; /* 6 BYTES */
A=1.23;
PUT LIST (A);
```

then the value of 001.23 will be printed. Note that the "." is counted in the number of bytes, for it is really stored, as is the sign if S, + or - is specified.

Unfortunately there are two leading zeros which may not be desirable. These may be suppressed by replacing the '9' with a 'Z' in the picture specification. For example,

```
DECLARE (A,B) PIC'ZZ9V.99';
A=1.23;
B=456.78;
PUT LIST (A,B);
```

will cause the values b̸b̸1.23 and 456.78 to be printed. The use of the 'Z' picture character to the left of the decimal point causes all leading zeros to be replaced with blanks. Hence, all 'Z' characters must appear before any '9' characters. When used to the right of the decimal point, all trailing zeros are replaced with blanks. In this case the Z's must appear after any '9' characters.

14.5.2 Character Pictures

Character strings may be defined by use of the 'A', 'X', or '9' picture characters. The 'X' picture character specifies that the associated position in the string may contain any character. Thus PIC '(15)X' is equivalent to CHAR(15). The 'A' picture character restricts the character in the associated position to being either a letter of the Roman alphabet or a blank. The '9' picture character specifies that the character in the associated position may only be one of the decimal digits. As we find little advantage in these picture characters, we will continue to DECLARE character variables in the usual way, i.e. CHAR(n).

14.5.3 An Example of RECORD I/O with PICTURE Data

Suppose sales orders for the products of a company are recorded on data cards in the format:

```
Col. 1-5  product number
     6-55 client name and address
    56-57 quantity ordered
```

To help detect key-punching errors, each product code conforms to the rule that the fifth digit is equal to the sum of the first four digits, modulo 10. That is, if we add the first four digits of the code, the last digit of this sum should be the same as the last digit of the product code; if this is not the case, then the code does not represent a product of the company.

We will design a program to process these sales orders by copying all valid orders to disk and making a listing of those with erroneous code numbers. The algorithm for processing one card is straightforward:

1. read a sales record;
2. if a code number is valid then
2.1 write record to disk;
3. otherwise write record to printer;
4. end.

Determining whether or not the code number is valid is most easily done by use of the MOD built-in function. In mathematical terms a MOD b = c if and only if a-c is evenly divisible by b. In everyday terms, if a is a positive integer, then a MOD b is the remainder after dividing a by b. Thus 125 MOD 10 is 5 and 16 MOD 7 is 2. When any positive integer is operated on modulo 10, the result is always the right-most digit of the number.

The program to separate valid orders from invalid ones is shown in Fig. 14.12. The sum of the first four digits in the code number is computed in the loop DIGITS; this is accomplished by adding the right-most digit into SUM, using the MOD function, and then chopping this digit off by dividing by 10.

Writing on the lineprinter with RECORD I/O presents one new problem; lines will be printed continuously, even across the perforation from one page to the next. It is necessary for the programmer to include his own page control when using RECORD I/O. The program in Fig. 14.12 will print at most 25 invalid orders per page. Each new page begins by writing the header whose first (carriage control) character is 1, causing the printer to begin a new page.

Each invalid order printed requires two lines (notice the carriage control character in BAD_CODES) and the header requires one line. Hence, after printing 51 lines, we should begin a new page with the header. Assume we have added a variable LINE_COUNT, initialized to one. We must then replace:

```
WRITE FILE (SYSPRINT) FROM (BAD_CODES);
```

with:

```
IF LINE_COUNT>50 THEN
    DO; /* NEW PAGE */
        LINE_COUNT=1;
        WRITE FILE (SYSPRINT) FROM (HEADER);
    END;
WRITE FILE (SYSPRINT) FROM (BAD_CODES);
LINE_COUNT = LINE_COUNT + 2;
```

This ensures that each new page begins with a header and that the line count is properly reset to 1.

14.6 A TASTE OF JOB CONTROL LANGUAGE

Your PL/I program does not run alone. It shares the main memory, if not with other users, at least with the operating system. The operating system is, roughly speaking, the set of programs which

```
              /* FIGURE 14.12 */
EDITOR: PROCEDURE OPTIONS (MAIN);
        DECLARE
           1 CARD, /* SALES ORDERS */
              2 CODE PIC '(5)9',
              2 CUSTOMER CHAR(50),
              2 QUANTITY PIC '99',
              2 FILLER CHAR(23),
           1 BAD_CODES, /* INVALID ORDERS */
              2 CC CHAR(1) INITIAL ('0'),
              2 FILLER1 CHAR(20) INITIAL (' '),
              2 COPY LIKE CARD,
              2 FILLER2 CHAR(20) INITIAL (' '),
           1 HEADER, /* TITLE FOR INVALID CODE NUMBERS */
              2 CC CHAR(1) INITIAL ('1'),
              2 FILLER1 CHAR(20) INITIAL (' '),
              2 TITLE CHAR(80) INITIAL
                 ('SALES ORDERS WITH INVALID CODE NUMBERS'),
              2 FILLER2 CHAR(20) INITIAL (' '),
           FLAG BIT(1) INITIAL ('1'B),
           (SUM,CODE1,K) FIXED BINARY (15),
           (MASTER,SYSIN,SYSPRINT) FILE RECORD;
        WRITE FILE (SYSPRINT) FROM (HEADER);
        ON ENDFILE (SYSIN) FLAG = '0'B;
        OPEN FILE (MASTER) OUTPUT;
        READ FILE (SYSIN) INTO (CARD);
ALL:    DO WHILE ( FLAG );
           /* CHECK FOR VALIDITY OF CODE */
           CODE1 = CARD.CODE / 10; /* 1ST FOUR DIGITS */
           SUM = 0;
DIGITS:    DO K = 1 TO 4; /* ADD DIGITS IN CODE1 */
              SUM = SUM + MOD(CODE1,10);
              CODE1 = CODE1 / 10;
           END DIGITS;
           IF MOD(SUM,10) = MOD(CARD.CODE,10) THEN /* VALID */
              WRITE FILE (MASTER) FROM (CARD);
           ELSE DO; /* INVALID */
              BAD_CODES.COPY = CARD;
              WRITE FILE (SYSPRINT) FROM (BAD_CODES);
           END;
           READ FILE (SYSIN) INTO (CARD);
        END ALL;
        CLOSE FILE (MASTER);
        END EDITOR;
```

Figure 14.12

control the flow of activities in the computer system. As far as file processing is concerned, the user sees two different aspects of the operating system which we might call the master and the slave. This dual role is indicated in Fig. 14.13.

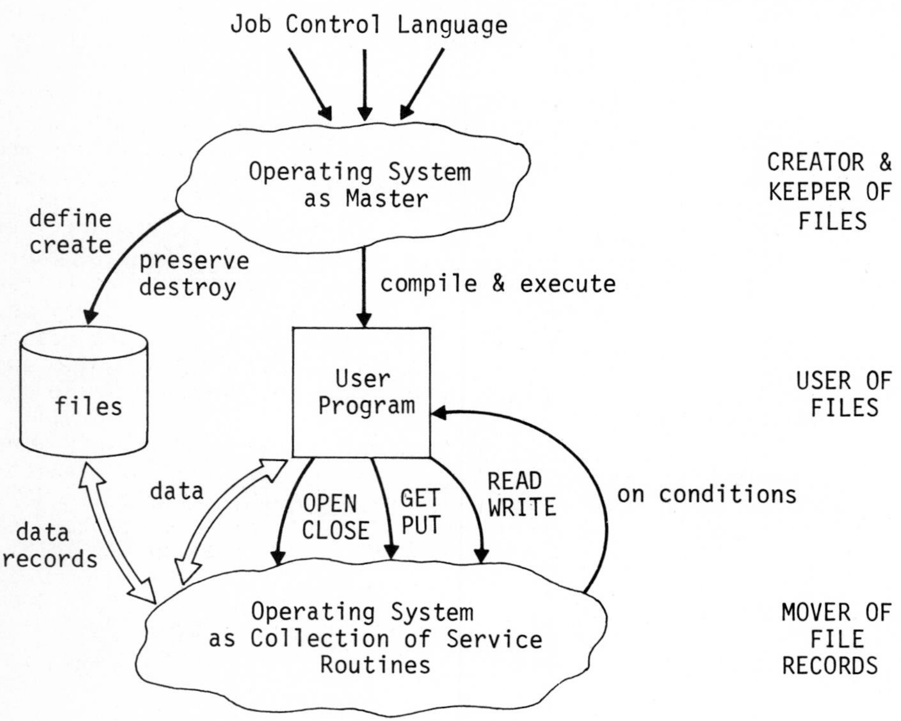

Fig. 14.13 Relationship Between Operating System and User

It is the operating system as slave with which you are probably more familiar. By this we mean the set of service routines which are available to perform special functions for any user. Some of these routines control the input-output and secondary memory devices. When you execute any I/O command, such as OPEN, READ, WRITE or CLOSE, within your program, it is ultimately an operating system program which carries out the requested function. Thus all records are transmitted through these routines. Without having to know how they actually work, the I/O statements in PL/I are essentially requests to this lower level of the operating system. If a request cannot be fulfilled, the system may reply by raising an ON condition.

At the same time, your program is under the control and "watchful eye" of the operating system as master, which is responsible for compiling, executing and eventually terminating your program.

Another very important function of this higher level is the creation of new files, their preservation from one use to the next and their eventual deletion.

This high level part of the operating system must also be told what to do - but not from within a user's PL/I program, since you must be able to at least request compilation and execution before your program can even begin executing. Thus a special system-oriented language, external to any programming language like PL/I, is required for conveying high level requests to the operating system. This system language will be called the job control language or JCL for short.

A very simple example of JCL is the language required to compile and run PL/C jobs. In a typical job, one has the JCL statements *PL/C and *DATA. The * in column 1 identifies these statements as special system commands, outside the PL/C program. The *PL/C requests (i) the PL/C compiler to prepare a program for execution and (ii) execution of that program. The *DATA card delimits two separate files on the card reader (SYSIN). The first file contains input to the compiler (i.e. your PL/I program itself); the second file contains input to your program (i.e. your data cards). Simple as it may be, this language suggests the basic functions of any job control language: to specify the steps required to complete the job (e.g. compile and then execute) and to specify the files (e.g. source program and data cards) needed by these job steps.

The job control language for more sophisticated systems is more complex in order to request more varied services. Yet its requests are somewhat similar. For example, Fig. 14.14 shows the basic JCL needed by the OS/MVT system to compile and run the program from Fig. 14.5.[4] This example shows the three basic types of JCL statement:

(1) JOB to identify the job and give accounting information;
(2) EXEC to identify the program(s) to be executed during the course of this job; and
(3) DD (data definition) to describe the files required by this job.

These cards are identified as special system commands by the // in columns 1 and 2. Any string which begins in column 3 is considered the name of the corresponding command. For example, MYNAME is the name of the job. PL1L.SYSIN is called a ddname since it names a DD card.

In Fig. 14.14 we ask to EXECute a sequence of programs, collectively called PL1LFCG. The sequence begins with the F compiler for the PL/I language (PL1L). The last two letters, CG, indicate how far to continue the progression toward execution, in this case compile (C) followed by execution (G, meaning "go"). In order to run these two programs, the compiler and your own, we requested 100K (100 x 1024 = 102,400) bytes of main memory.

---

4 The JCL conventions in each installation differ somewhat. All we can present is the basic idea. Check with your computer center before trying to run a job using JCL.

```
//MYNAME    JOB   (accounting info)
//          EXEC  PL1LFCG,REGION=100K
//PL1L.SYSIN  DD  *

              PL/I program
              from Fig. 14.5

//GO.SYSPRINT DD  SYSOUT=A,DCB=(RECFM=FA,LRECL=121)
//GO.SYSIN    DD  *

              your
              data

//
```

Fig. 14.14 JCL for Program of Figure 14.5

Since the PL/I program could have been on any input or secondary memory device, we must specify where the compiler PL1L should obtain its input (SYSIN). Thus the ddname PL1L.SYSIN was not an arbitrary choice. Since your PL/I program is on cards in this case, the * specifies that this SYSIN file consists of the cards which follow immediately.

If the program compiles successfully it will start to GO (execute). Notice from Fig. 14.5 that this program requires two files. SYSPRINT and SYSIN. These files must be defined with data definition (DD) statements whose respective ddnames are GO.SYSPRINT and GO.SYSIN. In this case the file called SYSPRINT within the program was defined as the standard system output device (SYSOUT=A), in other words the printer. The file known to the program as SYSIN was defined as the immediately following cards (*).

The names SYSIN and SYSPRINT are not sacred within programs which you write. You could have declared your input file as:

```
DECLARE FRED FILE RECORD;
```

and then defined it in JCL to be the card reader by:

```
//GO.FRED  DD *
```

On the other hand, the DD statement could have pointed your input and output file names to other places besides the card card reader and printer. In particular, either or both could have been disk files instead.

For example, Fig. 14.2 shows a program to copy cards onto a disk file named MYFILE. Fig. 14.15 shows the JCL to run this program and create this new file whose name in the system will be MYJUNK.

program and create this new file.

```
//JOBID   JOB  (accounting)
//         EXEC   PL1LFCG,REGION=100K
//PL1L.SYSIN DD  *

               PL/I program
               from Fig. 14.2


//GO.MYFILE   DD DSN=MYJUNK,DISP=(NEW,CATLG,DELETE),
//          SPACE=(TRK,1),UNIT=3330,DCB=(LRECL=4,RECFM=F),
//          LABEL=RETPD=30
//GO.SYSIN     DD  *


               your
               data


//
```

Fig. 14.15 JCL to Create New File

The only real difference here is the DD statement named GO.MYFILE. The MYFILE shows which file name is used by your program, whereas MYJUNK is the name by which the operating system knows the file. In JCL, a file is referred to as a "data set"; hence the data set name for this file is specified by DSN=MYJUNK. The DISPosition parameter tells the system what to do with this file: it is a NEW file which should be cataloged (CATLG) in the system directory if successfully initialized but DELETEd if not. SPACE requests 1 track (TRK) of secondary storage, and UNIT says that it should be stored on a 3330 disk. The parameter called DCB (for "data control block") describes the physical structure of the file. In this case the record format is fixed length records (RECFM=F) and the length of each record is 4 bytes (LRECL=4). It is essential that this record size be exactly the same as the corresponding memory area in the program! In the BUFFER of Fig. 14.2 there are two items, each FIXED BINARY(15), which total 4 bytes. Hence LRECL=4 was used in the appropriate DD statement. (This would have been much clearer if BUFFER had been declared with PICTURE!) MYFILE will be kept for 30 days from the date of creation because we specified a retention period of 30 days (LABEL=RETPD=30).

The request to catalog this file caused the operating system to save all the pertinent position and structural information about it. Thus when a program, such as that of Fig. 14.3, wishes to use the data on MYJUNK, the appropriate DD statement is:

```
//GO.MYFILE  DD DSN=MYJUNK,DISP=OLD
```

This statement merely points the name MYFILE used in the program to a data set named MYJUNK which has already been created (DISP=OLD) by another program.

This sketch of JCL has only scratched the surface. Yet it should convey an idea of what the operating system must or can be told. The DD statements, in particular, direct the system to create, keep or delete files and convey information about their placement on devices and internal structure. DD statements can also link any file name in a program to a particular file in the system, which provides the mechanism for one program passing data to another through a file. Of course, the structure of the real file, expressed in the JCL, must agree with the declarations and uses of that file within every program which accesses it.

14.7 INDEXED SEQUENTIAL FILES

For many applications, sequential processing is too inefficient. If we are processing customer records in a bank, then to set the balance of account 48911 it would be nice if we could go to it directly without passing over the 48910 accounts which precede it. For updating purposes it becomes even more crucial to be able to update one record without reading and writing the entire file.

This method of accessing, in which arbitrary records can be located without traversing intervening records, is called DIRECT access. DIRECT is the alternative to SEQUENTIAL.

As we have already seen, the ability to access records "directly" presupposes (i) a RECORD oriented file which is (ii) stored on a direct access (disk-type) device and (iii) contains some special organization or structure. This is indicated in Fig. 14.16. The "indexed sequential" organization is one of several ways in which files can be set up to facilitate direct accessing. Since it is probably the simplest to understand and the most widely used method, it is the only one discussed in this book.

Consider how we might organize 100,000 bank accounts in a manual system. We need 100,000 cards, one for each account in the bank arranged in such a way that we can quickly obtain any account. Since account numbers are primarily used to identify accounts, we will maintain the records in ascending account number order. We can speed up the search for an account by dividing the records up into ten trays, each containing 10,000 accounts. These trays can be labelled 1-10000, 10001-20000, etc. The process can be further enhanced by putting ten dividers in each tray for every 1000 records. By organizing the records in this manner, we can go quickly to the group of 1000 containing the desired record. An even faster search could be accomplished using 100 trays, each with dividers at 100 record intervals. One must be careful not to carry this process too far; the ultimate refinement is 100,000 trays of one record each and we are back to the initial problem. The important points to notice in this organization are that the records must initially be in order and that we can find a given record (by account number) without having to search the entire file.

Many operating systems can organize disk files in a comparable manner, called indexed sequential files. When an indexed sequential file is being created, the user must write an ordered set of records onto disk. The operating system augments this file with some tables,

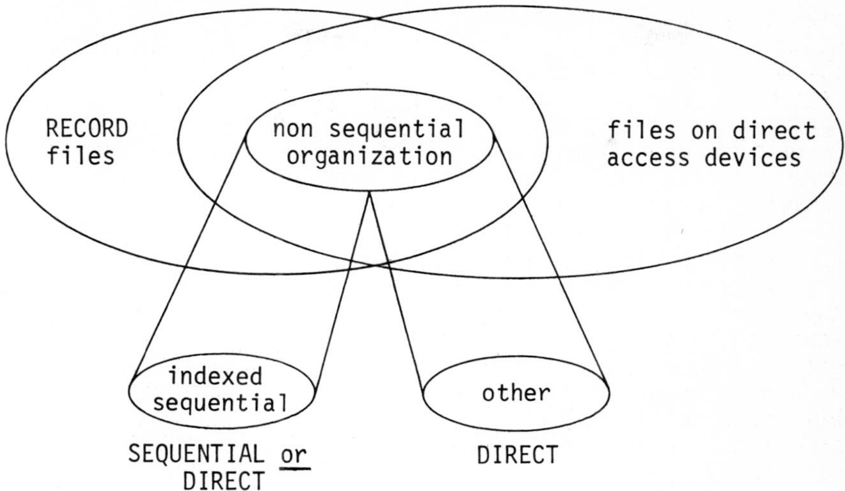

Fig. 14.16 Where DIRECT Mode of Processing Applies

which logically subdivide the file just as the drawers and separators subdivide a manual file. Since the records are stored sequentially, it is still possible to access them sequentially. However, it is also possible to request any specific record. This will cause the system to scan the tables in order to zero in on the desired record.

We are not going to discuss how the file is maintained physically; it is sufficient to know that the computer system provides the indices and does all the housekeeping associated with the records. The main constraint on the programmer is that the records must be presented in ascending order of some value (e.g. account number) when the file is to be created. Thereafter, the individual records may be accessed either sequentially or else directly by specifying the corresponding, identifying value. Records can be added, deleted or updated directly.

The primary key to a record is any data item which uniquely identifies the record. The key is often a field within the record, such as the account number in a banking file. For an inventory file it might be a part number; for a personnel file, the Social Security number; for a library file, the call number. At any rate, the key is the value by which the records are originally ordered and by which particular records can be located.

We are going to illustrate the creation and use of an indexed sequential file under the following constraints:

(i) each record is 80 bytes long,
(ii) the key to each record is part of the record,
(iii) the file is stored on a disk,
(iv) the records are unblocked,

(v) all examples use OS PL/I-F,
(vi) the first byte of each record is for use by the operating system and is to be left blank by the programmer.

14.8 CREATING AN INDEXED SEQUENTIAL FILE

14.8.1 What the System Must Know

We begin by considering what the operating system needs to know about our file in order to maintain it. This information will, of course, be conveyed by JCL statements. Since each record on the file is identified by a key, we must tell the system how many characters are contained in each key (all keys in any one file are the same length). We must also tell how many characters are in a record and that the file is to be organized as an indexed sequential file. There are other factors to be considered at file creation time, but a discussion of these is beyond the scope of this book.

The JCL statement to create an indexed sequential file named MASTER within the program is:

```
//GO.MASTER DD DSN=TELCO,DISP=(NEW,CATLG,DELETE),
//  UNIT=3330,SPACE=(CYL,(1,1)),LABEL=RETPD=365,
//  DCB=(BLKSIZE=80,DSORG=IS,KEYLEN=7,OPTCD=LY,RECFM=F),
//   CYFOFL=1
```

This is clearly more complex than the definition of a sequential file; however most of it should seem reasonable. The specific parameters are:

MASTER - name by which program refers to file;
DD - JCL operand meaning data definition
DSN=TELCO - Data Set Name for the file is TELCO;
DISP - disposition of file;
NEW - the file is being created;
CATLG - if the file is successfully initialized, catalog it;
DELETE - otherwise delete the file from the system;
UNIT - put the file on a 3330 disk drive;
SPACE - use one cylinder of the disk for this file;
LABEL - keep the file on the system for 365 days;
DCB - Data Control Block (file structure);
BLKSIZE - each record contains 80 bytes and each record is recorded in a separate physical block;
DSORG - the data set organization is indexed sequential;
KEYLEN - each key is 7 bytes long;
OPTCD - the option code L indicates that the space formerly occupied by deleted records may be used for new records; Y indicates there is a provision for overflow of records from the main file space;
CYLOFL - use one track on each cylinder for overflow space in case records are added;
RECFM=F - records are of fixed length but not blocked.

Note that once this description has been cataloged, it is "remembered" and another program may use the file by supplying the DD statement:

```
//GO.MINE  DD  DSN=TELCO,DISP=OLD
```

Note that the system identifies this file as TELCO.

14.8.2 What the Program Must Do

We now turn our attention to what the program must know about the file. An indexed sequential file is declared as follows:

```
DECLARE <filename> FILE RECORD KEYED ENV(INDEXED);
```

Of course the file must be of RECORD type, since STREAM files are limited to sequential processing. The attribute KEYED means that there will be an identifying key accompanying each record. ENV is an abbreviation for ENVIRONMENT. This attribute is used to describe the structural organization of the file, in this case INDEXED. We must emphasize that this is the simplest, most concise form of the DECLARE statement. In fact, much of the information contained in the JCL can be placed in the environment (ENV) option. We have chosen to keep the DECLARE statement simple because we do not believe in making the program any more complex or any more limited to specific types of files than necessary.

When an indexed sequential file is being created, the records must be written in ascending order according to the key value. They must be placed on the file in a SEQUENTIAL manner, DIRECT being saved for any later processing of selected records. Consequently the mode of use during file creation is expressed by:

```
OPEN FILE <filename> SEQUENTIAL OUTPUT;
```

The file itself will be composed of a collection of records and their associated keys. The records are said to be unblocked, i.e. there is a gap on the disk surface between each record and its neighbors. In this kind of organization, each key is recorded immediately before the corresponding record, whether or not the key is also part of the record. Physically, the records look like:

key 1   record 1   key 2   record 2   ...

The WRITE statement which transmits a record to the file must also specify the key value associated with the record. This is done by the following general WRITE statement:

```
WRITE FILE(<filename>) FROM (<structure>)
          KEYFROM (<value>);
```

where <value> contains a fixed length character string for the current key value. This statement identifies the file in question, the contents of the record and the value of the key.

We are now in a position to show a program to create an indexed sequential file. Our source records represent a simple accounts receivable system for a small telephone company. The source records are on data cards in the format:

```
col 1     blank
col 2-21  last name
col 22-23 initials
col 24-30 phone number
col 34-35 amount, assumed decimal point between cols 33
          and 34
col 36-80 blank
```

The cards are assumed to be sorted into ascending order by phone numbers. The program is shown in Fig. 14.17, and we shall now consider some of its features.

```
             /* FIGURE 14.17 */
PREPIS: PROCEDURE OPTIONS (MAIN);
        DECLARE
           1 CARD,
              2 DELETE_CHAR CHAR(1),
              2 LAST_NAME CHAR(20),
              2 INITIALS CHAR(2),
              2 PHONE PIC '(7)9',
              2 AMOUNT PIC 'ZZ9V99',
              2 FILLER CHAR(45),
           SYSIN FILE RECORD,
           MASTER FILE RECORD KEYED ENV(INDEXED);

        OPEN FILE (MASTER) SEQUENTIAL OUTPUT;
        ON ENDFILE (SYSIN) BEGIN;
           CLOSE FILE (MASTER);
           STOP;
           END;

        ON KEY (MASTER) BEGIN; /* INPUT KEY ERROR */
           PUT FILE (SYSPRINT) SKIP LIST ('KEY ERROR',ONCODE);
           PUT FILE (SYSPRINT) SKIP LIST (CARD);
           END;

CREATE: DO WHILE ('1'B);
           READ FILE (SYSIN) INTO (CARD);
           WRITE FILE (MASTER) FROM (CARD) KEYFROM (PHONE);
        END CREATE;
        END PREPIS;
```

Fig. 14.17 Program to Create an Indexed Sequential File

The statements pertaining to the indexed sequential file MASTER were:

(1) DECLARE MASTER FILE RECORD KEYED ENV(ENDEXED);

(2) OPEN FILE(MASTER) SEQUENTIAL OUTPUT;

(3) WRITE FILE(MASTER) FROM(CARD) KEYFROM(PHONE);

PHONE, of course, was a fixed length (of 7) character string which happened to be described by the PICTURE attribute.

This would be a good time to glance back at the JCL in Section 14.6 which was written to accompany this program. Note the agreement between: the ddname on the DD card (MASTER) and the file name used by the program (MASTER); the size of the structure (CARD) and the size of the records on the file (BLKSIZE=80); and the length of the key value (PHONE) used in the program and that promised the system (KEYLEN=7).

The key values must be character (or PICTURE) strings. The records must also be presented in ascending order of key value with no duplicates. All of these key requirements (and others) are checked by the system before each record is placed in the file. Should anything be wrong with the key or key sequence, this fact is reported to the program, by raising the KEY condition. If the programmer does not provide an ON-unit to intercept this error signal, the program will terminate. In Fig. 14.17 we have included an ON KEY statement and chosen to write the offending record onto the printer and then allow the program to continue processing the balance of the records. Within this ON-unit we have made use of the built-in function ONCODE. This function returns a numeric value which may be used to determine the specific problem encountered, i.e. the cause of entry to the ON-unit. The most common values associated with the creation of an indexed sequential file are:

ONCODE	Meaning
52	attempt to add duplicate key
53	key sequence error
57	no more space to add record

A complete list of ONCODE values and their meanings may be found in IBM publication GC28-8201.

Another curious point is the blank character at the beginning of every record. The reason for this "extra" blank is that the first byte of each record should be reserved for system use in the following manner. When a record is deleted from an indexed sequential file, it is not physically removed. Instead the system marks it as "not active" by writing eight 1's in the first byte of the record. Hence, the first byte should not contain any character of the record's information. Therefore, if we have N bytes of information, we must use N+1 bytes of storage and do no computation on the first byte.

14.9 PROCESSING INDEXED SEQUENTIAL FILES

The records in an indexed sequential file may be retrieved or updated either sequentially or directly. In addition, one may add or delete arbitrary records to or from the file. We shall examine each of these in turn.

14.9.1 Sequential Processing of an IS File

While permitting DIRECT access to records, the indexed sequential organization still allows sequential processing as well. It is important to note that sequential retrieval will deliver the records in ascending order by key number, even if other records have been added to the file since its creation. Because the file is indexed sequential, it must be declared with the attributes FILE RECORD KEYED ENV(INDEXED). To perform sequential retrieval, the programmer simply uses the OPEN and READ statements as before:

```
OPEN FILE (<filename>) INPUT SEQUENTIAL;
READ FILE (<filename>) INTO (<structure>);
```

The key is obviously not required to do sequential processing of any type. However, if the key value does not happen to be a data item within a field of the record, the programmer may have the key transmitted to memory along with the record by saying:

```
READ FILE (<filename>) INTO (<structure>) KEYTO (<charvariable>);
```

If most of the records in a file are to be altered in some way, they can be updated sequentially. This involves a mode of processing which is neither INPUT or OUTPUT, but rather UPDATE. The OPEN statement in this case would be:

```
OPEN FILE (<filename>) UPDATE SEQUENTIAL;
```

The statement to actually change an existing record is not WRITE, which implies a new record, but rather REWRITE. It must be used in combination with a READ as follows:

```
READ FILE (<filename>) INTO (<structure>);
Code to modify some field(s) of the structure
REWRITE FILE (<filename>) FROM (<structure>);
```

14.9.2 DIRECT Retrieval of Records

DIRECT retrieval is the input of the particular record which has some specified key value. This facility is what motivates indexed sequential files and utilizes the auxiliary tables which the system built while the file was being created.

If a file is to be used in a non-sequential way, the OPEN statement should indicate this by

```
                                  INPUT
                                   or
OPEN FILE (<filename>)          { OUTPUT }        DIRECT;
                                   or
                                  UPDATE
```

The UPDATE mode implies that both input and output are permitted on the file. Therefore, during any retrieval operation, the file should be OPENed with either INPUT or UPDATE, preferably INPUT.

The data transmission statement, of course, is READ. However, to identify which record is to be read, the READ statement must supply the desired key value to the operating system so that it can locate the record. The general form of the READ statement is then:

```
READ FILE (<filename>) INTO (<variable>) KEY (<value>);
```

which causes the system to copy the contents of the record having a key of the given value into the main storage area specified.

Since KEY is often confused with KEYFROM and KEYTO, we summarize their meanings below:

(1) KEY specifies a key value to be conveyed to the system for use in locating a record; it is not to be written onto the file;

(2) KEYFROM specifies a key value which is to be written on the file together with a record;

(3) KEYTO requests that a key value be copied from the file into the specified variable.

Of course the key value used in the direct location of a record must be a character string which is hopefully identical to a key in the existing file. Again the supplied key value is checked by the system. Any irregularity or failure to locate a matching value in the file is reported to the program by an ON condition. Thus it is good practice to use an ON KEY unit when doing direct retrieval, especially to cover the possibility that the requested key may not exist. This is not necessarily an error. The READ may only have been attempting to discover whether some key value exists.

ONCODE can, of course, be used to determine the exact cause of the ON condition. During retrieval operations, the most common values are:

ONCODE	MEANING
51	no matching key found in file
54	invalid key (not a character string)

An interesting use of the indexed sequential (IS) organization can be demonstrated by combining both sequential and direct retrieval. Suppose we wish to print all the records in the IS file created in

Fig. 14.17 provided they have key values from 3631928 to 8244120, inclusive. One way would be to sequentially process the file as in Fig. 14.18.

```
              OPEN FILE (MASTER) SEQUENTIAL INPUT:
              READ FILE (MASTER) INTO (RECORD);
SKIP:         DO WHILE (PHONE  <'3631928');
                   READ FILE (MASTER) INTO (RECORD);
              END SKIP;
PROCESS:      DO WHILE (PHONE <= '8244120');
                   PUT SKIP LIST (RECORD);
                   READ FILE (MASTER) INTO (RECORD);
              END PROCESS;
```

Figure 14.18

The loop, SKIP, in Fig. 14.18 is wasteful of computer resources. It is possible, with the IS organization, to reposition the file to a particular record by using the direct access form of the READ. In this way we avoid directly examining potentially many records just to get to the one we want. This method is shown in Fig. 14.19.

```
              OPEN FILE (MASTER) SEQUENTIAL INPUT;
              READ FILE (MASTER) INTO (RECORD)  KEY  ('3631928');
PROCESS:      DO WHILE (PHONE <= '8244120');
                   PUT SKIP LIST (RECORD);
                   READ FILE (MASTER) INTO (RECORD);
              END PROCESS;
```

Fig. 14.19 Printing Part of an IS File

Notice that even though we have one direct READ statement in Fig. 14.19, the file must be opened for SEQUENTIAL processing. Note also that the key values are given as character strings, thus conforming to the PICture attribute of the phone number. (See Fig. 14.17)

14.9 SELECTIVE MODIFICATIONS TO AN EXISTING IS FILE

Records may be added, deleted or altered in an existing IS file by OPENing the file for DIRECT UPDATE.

To add a new record (with a new key value) anywhere in the file, use the WRITE statement with the KEYFROM option:

```
         OPEN FILE (<filename>) DIRECT UPDATE;
    WRITE FILE (<filename>) FROM (<structure>) KEYFROM (<value>);
```

The new record will appear to be inserted at the right place in the ordering.

The modification of an existing record is usually accomplished by reading the appropriate record, changing some part and then writing the modified version back to the file, using the REWRITE statement:

REWRITE FILE (<filename>) FROM (<structure>) KEYFROM (<value>);

When the programmer wishes to delete a record from an IS file, the system marks the appropriate record as inactive by placing (8)'1'B in the first byte. The deletion is activated by the statement

DELETE FILE (<filename>) KEY (<value>);

(The DELETE statement should never be used with blocked records whose keys begin in the first position of the record.)

An example of all these statements in action is given in the review problem of section 14.11.

14.10 REVIEW OF RULES

In all the following rules, <structure> refers to any unsubscripted variable or level 1 structure; <value> refers to a fixed length character (or PICTURE variable).

1. The general form of declaration for a RECORD file is:

   DECLARE <file> FILE RECORD;

2. The general forms of the RECORD I/O statements are:

   READ FILE (<file>) INTO (<structure>);
   WRITE FILE (<file>) FROM (<structure>);

3. In any RECORD I/O transfer the area of main storage to (or from) which the transfer is made must be exactly the same size as the record length of the associated file.

4. The simplest form of the declaration for an indexed sequential (IS) file is:

   DECLARE <file> FILE RECORD KEYED ENV(INDEXED);

5. To create an IS file, use the following general forms:

   <u>Open</u>: OPEN FILE (<file>) SEQUENTIAL OUTPUT:

   I/O: WRITE FILE (<file>) FROM (<structure>) KEYFROM (<value>);

   The records must be written in increasing order of key values.

6. To retrieve all records in an IS file, use the following general

forms:

Open: OPEN FILE (<file>) SEQUENTIAL INPUT;

I/O: READ FILE (<file>) INTO (<structure>);
or
READ FILE (<file>) INTO (<structure>) KEYTO (<variable>);

7. To modify all records in an IS file, use the following general forms:

Open: OPEN FILE (<file>) SEQUENTIAL UPDATE;

I/O: READ FILE (<file>) INTO (<structure>);
followed by:
REWRITE FILE (<file>) FROM (<structure>);

8. To retrieve selected records in an IS file, use the following general forms:

Open: OPEN FILE (<file>) DIRECT INPUT:

I/O: READ FILE (<file>) INTO (<structure>) KEY (<value>);

9. To modify selected records in an IS file, use the following general forms:

Open: OPEN FILE (<file>) DIRECT UPDATE:

I/O: REWRITE FILE (<file>) FROM (<structure>) KEY (<value>);

10. To add new records to an existing IS file, use the following general forms:

Open: OPEN FILE (<file>) DIRECT UPDATE:

I/O: WRITE FILE (<file>) FROM (<structure>) KEYFROM (<value>);

11. To delete records from an unblocked IS file, use the following general forms:

Open: OPEN FILE (<file>) DIRECT UPDATE:

I/O: DELETE FILE (<file>) KEY (<value>);

12. ON KEY FILE (<file>) may be used to intercept errors of mismatches when using a keyed file. The exact cause of the ON condition can be found by inspecting the number returned by ONCODE. (See Sections 14.8.2 and 14.9.2.)

14.11 REVIEW PROBLEM

We consider updating the IS file created in Fig. 14.17. The standard transactions one might encounter in a telephone accounting system are the recording of charges and payments, the termination of service and the addition of new accounts. We assume the transactions (abbreviated xact) are recorded on cards in the format:

```
col 1      blank
col 2-21   last name
col 22-23  initials
col 24-30  phone number
col 31     blank if xact is a charge
           minus if xact is a payment
col 32-36  exact amount, assumed decimal
           point between cols 34 and 35
col 37     'N' if a new account
           'D' if service to be disconnected
col 38-80  blank
```

The transaction cards are assumed to be in random order, thus requiring direct access to the master file. While processing the transactions we will attempt to detect errors such as different names for the same phone number and payments or charges to non-existent accounts. Transactions in these categories will be rejected and printed for further action. For pedagogical reasons, we will print the updated file in a report format showing the use of a floating "$" sign and the insertion of decimal points.

Our approach to the update problem for one transaction is as follows:

```
1.      read a transaction;
2.      if this is a new account then
2.1          add it to the master file;
3.      otherwise do;
3.1          find the corresponding master record;
3.2          if no master record exists then
3.2.1             write transaction to error journal;
3.3          otherwise if master and transaction names
                  do not match then
3.3.1             write transaction to error journal;
3.4          otherwise if account is to be disconnected then
3.4.1             delete master record from file;
3.5          otherwise do;
3.5.1             add transaction amount to master amount;
3.5.2             rewrite master record to file;
4.      end
```

Notice that in step 3.5.1, we do not have to worry about whether the transaction amount is a payment or a charge. The sign in col. 31 of the transaction card automatically takes care of this decision. The basic program is shown in Fig. 14.20(a) and the report writer is shown in Fig. 14.20(b).

```
              /* FIGURE 14.20(A) */
UPDATE: PROCEDURE OPTIONS (MAIN);
        DECLARE
           1 XACT, /* TRANSACTION RECORD */
              2 FILL1 CHAR(1),
              2 LAST_NAME CHAR(20),
              2 INITIALS CHAR(2),
              2 PHONE PIC '(7)9',
              2 AMOUNT PIC'S999V99',
              2 TYPE CHAR(1),
              2 FILL2 CHAR(43),
           1 MAST, /* MASTER RECORD */
              2 DELETE_CHAR CHAR(1),
              2 LAST_NAME CHAR(20),
              2 INITIALS CHAR(2),
              2 PHONE PIC '(7)9',
              2 AMOUNT PIC'999V99',
              2 FILLER CHAR(45),
           SYSIN FILE RECORD,
           MASTER FILE RECORD KEYED ENV(INDEXED),
           FLAG BIT(1) INITIAL ('1'B);

        OPEN FILE (MASTER) DIRECT UPDATE;
        ON ENDFILE (SYSIN) FLAG = '0'B;
        ON KEY (MASTER) BEGIN;
           PUT SKIP FILE (SYSPRINT) EDIT ('KEY ERROR',ONCODE,XACT)
              (A,X(5),F(5),X(12),7 A);
           GO TO NEXT; /* READ NEXT TRANSACTION RECORD */
           END;

        READ FILE (SYSIN) INTO (XACT);
ALL:    DO WHILE ( FLAG );
           IF TYPE = 'N' THEN /* NEW ACCOUNT */
NEW:          DO;
                 MAST = XACT, BY NAME;
                 DELETE_CHAR = ' ';
                 FILLER = ' ';
                 WRITE FILE (MASTER) FROM (MAST) KEYFROM(MAST.PHONE);
              END NEW;
           ELSE /* EXISTING RECORD */
OLD:          DO;
                 READ FILE (MASTER) INTO (MAST) KEY (XACT.PHONE);
                 IF MAST.LAST_NAME ¬= XACT.LAST_NAME THEN
MISMATCH:           DO;
                       PUT SKIP FILE (SYSPRINT) EDIT
                          ('NAME MISMATCH - XACT',XACT)
                          (A,X(10),7 A);
                       PUT SKIP FILE (SYSPRINT) EDIT
                          (' - MASTER',MAST) (X(13),A,X(8),6 A);
                    END MISMATCH;
                 ELSE IF TYPE = 'D' THEN /* DISCONNECT SERVICE */
                    DELETE FILE (MASTER) KEY (XACT.PHONE);
                    ELSE /* UPDATE ACCOUNT */
ADJUST:                DO;
                          MAST.AMOUNT = MAST.AMOUNT + XACT.AMOUNT;
                          REWRITE FILE (MASTER) FROM (MAST)
                             KEY (MAST.PHONE);
                       END ADJUST;
              END OLD;
NEXT:      READ FILE (SYSIN) INTO (XACT);
        END ALL;
        CLOSE FILE (MASTER);
        CALL REPORT;
```

Figure 14.20(A)

```
/* FIGURE 14.20(B) */

REPORT: PROCEDURE;
        DECLARE
           1 HEADER,
              2 CC CHAR(1) INITIAL ('1'),
              2 F1 CHAR(10) INITIAL (' '),
              2 T1 CHAR(19) INITIAL ('LAST NAME'),
              2 T2 CHAR(4) INITIAL (' INIT'),
              2 F2 CHAR(7) INITIAL (' '),
              2 T3 CHAR(7) INITIAL (' PHONE'),
              2 F3 CHAR(10) INITIAL (' '),
              2 T4 CHAR(6) INITIAL ('AMOUNT'),
              2 F4 CHAR(57) INITIAL (' '),
           1 LINEOUT,
              2 CC CHAR(1) INITIAL (' '),
              2 F1 CHAR(1 ) INITIAL (' '),
              2 LAST_NAME CHAR(20),
              2 INITIALS CHAR(2),
              2 F2 CHAR(8) INITIAL (' '),
              2 PHONE PIC '(7)9',
              2 F3 CHAR(9) INITIAL (' '),
              2 AMOUNT PIC '$ZZ9.V99',
              2 F4 CHAR(57) INITIAL (' '),
           LINECOUNT FIXED BINARY INITIAL (1),
           PRINTER FILE RECORD;

        OPEN FILE (PRINTER) OUTPUT;
        OPEN FILE (MASTER) SEQUENTIAL INPUT;
        ON ENDFILE (MASTER) BEGIN;
           CLOSE FILE (MASTER);
           STOP;
           END;
        WRITE FILE (PRINTER) FROM (HEADER);

        DO WHILE ('1'B);
           READ FILE (MASTER) INTO (MAST);
           LINEOUT = MAST, BY NAME;
           IF LINECOUNT > 50 THEN
              DO; /* START NEW PAGE */
                 WRITE FILE (PRINTER) FROM (HEADER);
                 LINECOUNT = 1;
              END;
           LINECOUNT = LINECOUNT + 2;
           WRITE FILE (PRINTER) FROM (LINEOUT);
        END;
        END REPORT;

        END UPDATE;
```

Figure 14.20(B)

Note the use of the GO TO statement in the first ON-unit associated with MASTER. This is an example of the judicious use of GO TO. The KEY condition could be raised by several errors, e.g. recording a payment or charge to a non-existent account, deleting a non-existent account or adding an account which already exists. In any event, the condition will have been raised somewhere within the loop, ALL. Having printed out the offending transaction, we must proceed to process the next transaction. The simplest way to do this is to direct control to the statement which reads the next transaction.

14.12 EXERCISES

14.1 (a) Write the basic file merging procedure from Section 13.4.4 using RECORD files instead of STREAM files. This will require a procedure to create the two source files and another to display the merged result.

(b) In the procedures of part (a), treat the card reader and printer as RECORD devices.

(c) By using procedures IN and OUT to move the next input record from a specified file to a structure and copy a structure to an output file, respectively, the merge algorithm can easily be generalized to use any source and destination files. Write IN and OUT so that various files can be merged. Try merging a STREAM and a RECORD file onto a RECORD file.

14.2 Modify the programs of either

(a) exercise 13.5; or

(b) exercise 13.6; or

(c) exercise 13.7

to deal with RECORD files.

14.3 Try using the PICTURE attribute in the program(s) of exercise 14.2.

14.4 Write the ordered sequential update program suggested in exercise 13.3, using READ and REWRITE statements, plus the PICTURE attribute. Assume the grades are numeric (between 0 and 100) and keep a current average in each student record.

14.5 (a) Write a procedure to create an indexed-sequential file of student records, where the primary key is 6-character student ID number.

(b) Write a procedure to print all the student records from this file.

(c) Write a procedure to read ID numbers from data cards and selectively print the records for the corresponding students.

(d) Write a file editor, which can add a new student, delete an old student, and display or modify the record of an existing student, based on commands from data cards. Design a command format which should include the desired operation, the student ID, and any new information to be placed in the file. Allow for the possibility of an attempted update or deletion of a student ID which is not on file.

14.6 (a) Write a procedure to place "family records" for a strictly patriarchal society on an indexed sequential file. The records should contain the person's name, his father's name and the names of up to four children. The primary key is the person's own name.

(b) Display all the members of this "family".

(c) For any given family member, display his entire paternal ancestry, i.e. his father, grandfather, etc., until some ancestor name is encountered which is not on the file.

(d) For any given family member, display his children and grandchildren (if any). Present the output with grandchildren listed and indented beneath their respective parents.

(e) Write a procedure extending part (d) to display the entire "tree" of descendents to whatever generation is recorded on the file.

Appendix A Differences Between PL/I and PL/C

DIFFERENCES BETWEEN PL/I and PL/C

The following pages describe the differences between PL/I and PL/C and are taken from the User's Guide to PL/C.

SECTION D. SUMMARY OF DIFFERENCES BETWEEN PL/C AND PL/I

PL/C IS A SUBSET OF PL/I. IT IS INTENDED TO BE "UPWARD COMPATIBLE" WITH PL/I. A PROGRAM THAT RUNS WITHOUT ERROR UNDER THE PL/C COMPILER SHOULD RUN UNDER PL/I(F) AND PRODUCE THE SAME RESULTS.

HOWEVER, CERTAIN INCOMPATIBLE DIAGNOSTIC FEATURES HAVE BEEN ADDED TO PL/C. IF THE PROGRAMMER WISHES TO USE THESE FEATURES FOR DIAGNOSTIC RUNS UNDER PL/C AND STILL BE ABLE TO RUN THE SAME PROGRAM UNDER PL/I HE MUST ENCLOSE SUCH FEATURES IN "PSEUDO-COMMENTS". IF THE PROGRAMMER ELECTS TO USE THE INCOMPATIBLE PL/C MACRO FEATURE IT IS IMPOSSIBLE TO PRESERVE COMPATIBILITY WITH PL/I.

PL/I(F) FEATURES NOT INCLUDED IN PL/C

1. REGIONAL AUXILIARY FILES.
2. CONTROLLED AND BASED STORAGE, AND LIST PROCESSING.
3. MULTI-TASKING.
4. COMPILE-TIME FACILITIES, EXCEPT FOR INCLUDE AND AN INCOMPATIBLE MACRO FACILITY (SEE SECTIONS I AND J).
5. 48 CHARACTER SET OPTION.
6. MESSAGE DISPLAY TO THE OPERATOR.
7. DEFINED AND LIKE ATTRIBUTES.
8. A FEW BUILT-IN FUNCTIONS AND PSEUDO-VARIABLES (SEE SECTION G).

ADDITIONAL RESTRICTIONS IMPOSED BY PL/C

1. 33 STATEMENT KEYWORDS AND 6 AUXILIARY KEYWORDS ARE RESERVED AND CANNOT BE USED AS IDENTIFIERS.
2. THE NAMES OF BUILT-IN FUNCTIONS AND PSEUDO-VARIABLES ARE NOT RESERVED AND MAY BE USED AS IDENTIFIERS, BUT IF THEY ARE TO BE USED IN THIS WAY THEY SHOULD BE EXPLICITLY DECLARED--CONTEXTUAL DECLARATION OF THESE PARTICULAR IDENTIFIERS MAY SUCCEED (DEPENDING UPON CONTEXT) BUT WILL PRODUCE A WARNING MESSAGE.
3. PARAMETERS CANNOT BE PASSED TO THE MAIN PROCEDURE OF A PL/C PROGRAM FROM THE OS EXEC CARD.
4. STRING CONSTANTS AND COMMENTS MUST BE CONTAINED IN A SINGLE SOURCE CARD UNLESS THE PL/C NOMONITOR=(BNDRY) OPTION IS SPECIFIED.
5. STRING CONSTANTS CANNOT HAVE REPETITION FACTORS.
6. THERE ARE RESTRICTIONS ON THE END, ENTRY, FORMAT, PROCEDURE, READ AND WRITE STATEMENTS.
7. THERE ARE RESTRICTIONS ON DIMENSION, ENTRY, ENVIRONMENT, INITIAL, LABEL AND LENGTH ATTRIBUTES.
8. NOT ALL OF THE PL/I(F) CONDITION CODES ARE USED BY PL/C AND THE DEFAULT CONDITION STATES UNDER PL/C ARE NOT EXACTLY THE SAME AS UNDER PL/I(F).

INCOMPATIBLE FEATURES ADDED TO PL/C

1. CHECK, NOCHECK, FLOW AND NOFLOW STATEMENTS; A FLOW CONDITION; ONORIG, ONDEST, STMTNO BUILT-IN FUNCTIONS.
2. DIAGNOSTIC OPTIONS ON THE PUT STATEMENT.
3. A BUILT-IN FUNCTION TO GENERATE PSEUDO-RANDOM NUMBERS.
4. COMMENTS THAT ARE CONVERTIBLE TO SOURCE TEXT DEPENDING UPON THE FIRST LETTER OF THEIR CONTENTS.
5. A TEXT-REPLACEMENT MACRO PROCESSOR.

DIFFERENCES IN INTERNAL REPRESENTATION OF DATA

INTERNALLY PL/C CARRIES OUT ALL FLOATING-POINT ARITHMETIC OPERATIONS IN DOUBLE-PRECISION FORM, ADOPTING USER-SPECIFIED PRECISION ONLY ON OUTPUT. THIS MEANS THAT COMPUTATION IS OFTEN SOMEWHAT MORE PRECISE THAN WOULD BE THE CASE UNDER PL/I(F). THE RESULT IS USUALLY A SLIGHT DIFFERENCE IN THE LEAST-SIGNIFICANT FIGURES OF RESULTS, BUT OF COURSE IT IS POSSIBLE FOR THE DIFFERENCES TO BECOME HIGHLY SIGNIFICANT.

PL/C ASSIGNS A FULL WORD OF STORAGE TO EACH FIXED BINARY VARIABLE AND A DOUBLE WORD OF STORAGE TO EACH FIXED DECIMAL VARIABLE, REGARDLESS OF THE DECLARED PRECISION. THIS MEANS THAT PL/C VARIABLES MAY HOLD VALUES LARGER THAN THEIR PL/I(F) COUNTERPART. HOWEVER, THE DEFAULT STATE FOR THE SIZE CONDITION IN PL/C IS "ENABLED" SO THAT SITUATIONS IN WHICH PL/C WOULD GIVE DIFFERENT RESULTS FROM PL/I(F) ARE DETECTED.

EACH BIT IN A PL/C BIT-STRING IS ACTUALLY ASSIGNED AN ENTIRE BYTE IN STORAGE. (EACH PL/C STRING VARIABLE ALSO HAS AN EIGHT BYTE CONTROL BLOCK CALLED A DOPE VECTOR SO THAT AN ARRAY OF SHORT STRINGS TAKES A SURPRISING AMOUNT OF CORE.)

DECIMAL-BASE VARIABLES IN PL/C ARE MAINTAINED INTERNALLY IN FLOATING-BINARY FORM AND CONVERTED ON OUTPUT.

THIS INTERNAL REPRESENTATION DOES NOT APPLY TO RECORD FILES, WHICH ARE WRITTEN IN STANDARD PL/I(F) REPRESENTATION, AND ASSUMED TO BE IN THAT REPRESENTATION WHEN READ. THIS MEANS THAT PL/C AND PL/I(F) ARE COMPATIBLE WITH RESPECT TO RECORD FILES--FILES WRITTEN BY EITHER COMPILER CAN BE READ BY EITHER.

ORDER OF EVALUATION IN DECLARE STATEMENTS

PL/I(F) WILL REORDER THE EVALUATION OF BOUNDS AND LENGTHS AND THE INITIALIZATION OF VARIABLES SO THAT, IN THE ABSENCE OF CIRCULAR DEPENDENCIES, VARIABLES WILL BE ALLOCATED AND INITIALIZED BEFORE THEY ARE USED TO ALLOCATE OR INITIALIZE OTHER VARIABLES. PL/C USES A SIMPLER STRATEGY WHICH DEPENDS UPON THE ORDER IN WHICH DECLARE STATEMENTS APPEAR IN THE BLOCK, AND THE ORDER IN WHICH VARIABLES ARE LISTED IN A DECLARE STATEMENT:

1. FIRST, ALL SCALAR ARITHMETIC AND LABEL VARIABLES ARE GIVEN THEIR INITIAL VALUE.

2. THEN, PROCEEDING IN THE ORDER IN WHICH THEY ARE DECLARED, STRINGS, ARRAYS AND STRUCTURES ARE ALLOCATED SPACE AND INITIALIZED. ANY EXPRESSIONS IN THE BOUNDS OR LENGTH FIELDS ARE EVALUATED BEFORE SPACE IS ALLOCATED. AFTER SPACE HAS BEEN ALLOCATED, THE VARIABLE IS INITIALIZED BEFORE PROCESSING THE NEXT VARIABLE IN THE ORDER OF DECLARATION.

THIS STRATEGY DOES NOT ELIMINATE ANY ALLOCATION SCHEME AVAILABLE IN PL/I(F) BUT DOES REQUIRE THE PROGRAMMER TO ORDER HIS DECLARATION OF VARIABLES TO AVOID THE USE OF UNALLOCATED OR UNINITIALIZED VARIABLES DECLARED IN THE SAME BLOCK.

DIMENSIONAL LIMITS IN THE COMPILER

THE INTERNAL STRUCTURE OF THE PL/C COMPILER IS VERY DIFFERENT FROM THAT OF THE PL/I(F) COMPILER AND IT WAS NOT FEASIBLE TO LIMIT CERTAIN CRITICAL DIMENSIONS OF THE SOURCE PROGRAM IN EXACTLY THE SAME WAY. THIS MEANS THAT THERE ARE PROBABLY SOME UNUSUALLY LARGE AND COMPLEX PROGRAMS THAT WOULD BE ACCEPTED BY PL/C BUT WOULD EXCEED SOME DIMENSIONAL LIMIT IN PL/I(F). (THE OPPOSITE IS CERTAINLY TRUE.) THE COMPILATION LIMITS IN PL/C ARE THE FOLLOWING:

1. MAXIMUM NESTING OF IF STATEMENTS IS 12.
2. MAXIMUM STATIC (SYNTACTIC) NESTING OF PROCEDURE, BEGIN AND DO STATEMENTS IS 11.
3. MAXIMUM NESTING OF FACTORS IN DECLARE IS 6.
4. MAXIMUM NUMBER OF LABEL PREFIXES ON A SINGLE STATEMENT IS 87.
5. MAXIMUM DEPTH OF PARENTHESIS NESTING IN EXPRESSIONS IS 14.
6. MAXIMUM NUMBER OF IDENTIFIERS IN A FACTOR OR STRUCTURE IN DECLARE IS 88.
7. NO SINGLE EXPRESSION CAN CONTAIN MORE THAN 256 SYMBOLS.

THESE LIMITS ARE FIXED BY THE STRUCTURE OF THE COMPILER AND CANNOT BE RELIEVED BY INCREASING THE CORE MADE AVAILABLE TO THE COMPILER. IN MOST OTHER RESPECTS THE COMPILER'S LIMITS ARE RELATED TO THE AMOUNT OF CORE AVAILABLE--FOR EXAMPLE, LENGTH OF PROGRAM AND SIZE OF ARRAYS. IN THESE CASES WHEN THE COMPILER INDICATES THAT A LIMIT HAS BEEN EXCEEDED THE USER CAN RESUBMIT THE PROGRAM WITH A LARGER REGION. THE ERROR MESSAGES IN SECTION C INDICATE WHICH ERRORS INVOLVE FIXED LIMITS, AND WHICH CAN BE ALLEVIATED WITH ADDITIONAL CORE. FOR ADDITIONAL INFORMATION ON CORE USAGE IN PL/C, SEE SECTION K.

Appendix B Reserved Words in PL/C

RESERVED KEYWORDS

The following keywords are reserved and may not be used as variable names in any PL/C program. Note that there are no reserved words in PL/I.

ALLOCATE	EXIT	PROCEDURE
BEGIN	FLOW	PROC
BY	FORMAT	PUT
CALL	FREE	READ
CHECK	GET	RETURN
CLOSE	GO	REVERT
DECLARE	GOTO	REWRITE
DCL	IF	SIGNAL
DELETE	NO	STOP
DO	NOCHECK	THEN
ELSE	NOFLOW	TO
END	ON	WHILE
ENTRY	OPEN	WRITE

Appendix C Error Messages in PL/C

ERROR MESSAGES IN PL/C

The following pages list all error messages which may occur in PL/C Release 7.6. The list is taken from the User's Guide to PL/C.

SECTION C. ERROR MESSAGES

IN THE TEXT OF THE FOLLOWING MESSAGES, THE UPPER-CASE LETTERS ARE SHOWN AS THEY APPEAR ON THE PL/C PROGRAM LISTING, BUT THE LOWER-CASE WORDS ARE REPLACED BY VARIABLE INFORMATION AS FOLLOWS:

```
IDEN      -A VARIABLE OR LABEL NAME WILL BE PRINTED
STRING    -A CHARACTER STRING WILL BE PRINTED
NUMBER    -A FIXED OR FLOATING POINT NUMBER WILL BE PRINTED
RTN       -THE NAME OF A SUBROUTINE WILL BE PRINTED
LINE      -A STATEMENT NUMBER WILL BE PRINTED
ATTRIBUTE -AN ATTRIBUTE WILL BE PRINTED
```

THE ERROR MESSAGE NUMBERS IN PL/C ARE PREFIXED WITH A TWO LETTER CODE INDICATING THE PHASE IN WHICH THE ERROR OCCURRED. THE CODES AND THEIR MEANINGS ARE:

```
SY OR MD SYNTACTIC ANALYSIS PHASE
              (MD FOR ERRORS DURING MACRO DEFINITIONS)
SM   SEMANTIC ANALYSIS PHASE
XR   CROSS REFERENCE PHASE
CG   CODE GENERATION PHASE
EX   EXECUTION PHASE
PM   POST-MORTEM DUMP PHASE
```

ONE GROUP OF MESSAGES, NUMBERED E2-EA, CAN APPEAR IN ANY PHASE OF THE COMPILER. THE PREFIX GIVEN WILL BE THAT FOR THE PHASE IN WHICH THE ERROR OCCURS. ALL OF THE OTHER MESSAGES APPEAR IN ONLY ONE PHASE, AS LISTED BELOW.

A LINE REFERRING TO A PROGRAM CHECK OR A COMPILER ERROR INDICATES A PROBLEM IN THE PL/C COMPILER AND NOT A USER ERROR (ALTHOUGH IT MOST OFTEN OCCURS IN RESPONSE TO SOME USER ERROR.) PLEASE BRING SUCH PROGRAMS TO THE ATTENTION OF YOUR SYSTEMS PROGRAMMING STAFF SO THAT THE PL/C PROJECT WILL BE NOTIFIED.

VARIABLE PREFIX ERRORS THAT CAN OCCUR IN ANY PHASE

```
NUMBER   MESSAGE

E2       ERROR LIMIT EXCEEDED
E3       LINE LIMIT EXCEEDED
E4       PAGE LIMIT EXCEEDED
E5       TIME LIMIT EXCEEDED
E6       TIME LIMIT EXCEEDED - PROBABLE COMPILER LOOP
            (THE SPECIFIED TIME LIMIT HAS EXPIRED AND AN
            ADDITIONAL SECOND HAS PASSED WITHOUT THE COMPLETION
            OF A SOURCE STATEMENT. THIS IS PROBABLY A COMPILER
            ERROR. SEE BEGINNING OF SECTION C.)
E7       I/O ERROR: STRING
            (THE OPERATING SYSTEM REPORTED A "SYNAD"-TYPE
            I/O ERROR. THE STRING GIVEN IS THE SYNADAF
            MESSAGE. SEE APPROPRIATE IBM SYSTEM MANUALS.)
E8       UNABLE TO PROCESS INCLUDE COMMAND
            (SEE SECTION J)
```

E9 SYMBOL-TABLE OVERFLOW. USE LARGER REGION OR INCREASE TABSIZE.
(SEE TABSIZE OPTION IN SECTION B)

EA COMPILER ERROR IN ERROR-MESSAGE WRITER.
(A COMPILER ERROR, SEE BEGINNING OF SECTION C)

<u>SY OR MD PREFIX</u> ERRORS DURING THE SYNTACTIC ANALYSIS PHASE

IN SOME CASES, PARTICULARLY IN DECLARATIONS, ERRORS ARE DISCOVERED TOO LATE IN THE ANALYSIS OF THE STATEMENT FOR PL/C TO CONVENIENTLY CORRECT THE TEXT OF THE STATEMENT. THE INTERNAL FORM OF THE PROGRAM HAS BEEN ALTERED TO A CORRECT CONSTRUCTION (OFTEN JUST A NULL STATEMENT) BUT THE USUAL DISPLAY OF CORRECTED SOURCE TEXT IS OMITTED. MESSAGES THAT FREQUENTLY ARE ISSUED IN SUCH CIRCUMSTANCES ARE MARKED WITH A * IN THE FOLLOWING LIST.

NUMBER MESSAGE

00 MISSPELLED KEYWORD
(APPARENT MISSPELLING OF ONE OF THE RESERVED KEYWORDS. SEE LIST UNDER DECLARE IN SECTION E.)

01 EXTRA (
(DELETED)

02 MISSING (
(SUPPLIED)

03 EXTRA)
(DELETED)

04 MISSING)
(POSSIBLY MISSING OPERATOR, RIGHT PAREN IS SUPPLIED)

05 EXTRA COMMA
(DELETED)

06 MISSING COMMA
(SUPPLIED)

07 EXTRA SEMI-COLON
(DELETED)

08 MISSING SEMI-COLON (OR MISUSE OF RESERVED WORD)
(A SEMI-COLON IS SUPPLIED. A FREQUENT CAUSE OF THIS ERROR IS THE USE OF A RESERVED KEYWORD AS AN IDENTIFIER. THIS FORCES THE START OF A NEW STATEMENT SO THE STATEMENT PREMATURELY ENDED APPARENTLY LACKS A SEMI-COLON. THE USER MAY NEED TO CHOOSE A NON-RESERVED IDENTIFIER RATHER THAN SUPPLY A SEMI-COLON)

09 MISSING :
(SUPPLIED)

0A MISSING =
(SUPPLIED)

0B * IMPROPER ATTRIBUTE ON PARAMETER

0C INEFFECTIVE IF
(WARNING; A POINTLESS IF STATEMENT HAS BEEN GIVEN. THE THEN UNIT IS NULL AND THERE IS NO ELSE UNIT.)

0D * IMPROPER ENTRY/RETURNS ATTRIBUTE

0E MISSING END
(*PROCESS, *DATA, OR END OF PROGRAM ENCOUNTERED WITH A BLOCK STILL OPEN; END SUPPLIED)

0F MISSING KEYWORD
(THE REQUIRED KEYWORD IS SUPPLIED)
10 INCOMPLETE EXPRESSION
11 MISSING EXPRESSION
12 MISSING VARIABLE
13 MISSING ARGUMENT, 1 SUPPLIED
14 EMPTY LIST
15 IMPROPER NOT
(¬ CANNOT BE USED AS A BINARY OPERATOR. ¬= SUBSTITUTED)
16 IMPROPER ELEMENT
(AN ELEMENT THAT WON'T FIT HAS BEEN DISCARDED)
17 IMPROPER SYNTAX, TRANSLATION SUSPENDED
(THE STATEMENT HAS BEEN ABANDONED AND REPLACED BY A NULL STATEMENT. PL/C SCANS AHEAD FOR A SEMI-COLON OR RESERVED WORD TO START THE NEXT STATEMENT.)
18 INCONSISTENT OPTION, STATEMENT DELETED
(AFTER THE STATEMENT WAS COMPLETED, IT WAS FOUND TO CONTAIN INCONSISTENT OPTIONS. IT IS DELETED AND REPLACED BY A NULL STATEMENT.)
19 NOT ENOUGH CORE, TRY LARGER REGION.
(PROGRAM WILL NOT BE EXECUTED AS IS)
1A NESTING TOO DEEP
(NESTING DEPTH EXCEEDS CAPACITY OF PL/C. SEE RESTRICTIONS IN SECTION D.)
1B INACCESSIBLE STATEMENT
(WARNING; THIS STATEMENT CANNOT BE REACHED IN EXECUTION)
1C MISSING MAIN PROC
(WARNING; NO PROCEDURE HAS OPTIONS(MAIN) PHRASE; THE FIRST PROCEDURE IS ASSUMED TO BE MAIN)
1D MISSING PROCEDURE STATEMENT
(A STATEMENT IS NOT CONTAINED IN AN EXTERNAL PROC, OR AN IDENTIFIER DECLARED ENTRY APPEARS AS A NON-ENTRY LABEL. A PROC STATEMENT IS SUPPLIED BY PL/C. THIS CONDITION IS SOMETIMES A BY-PRODUCT OF ANOTHER ERROR; FOR EXAMPLE, AN EXTRA END IN THE INTERIOR OF A PROCEDURE ENDS IT PREMATURELY AND CAUSES SUBSEQUENT STATEMENTS TO BE APPARENTLY OUTSIDE OF ANY PROCEDURE.)
1E MISSING *PROCESS (OR EXTRA END)
(EITHER THE REQUIRED *PROCESS BETWEEN EXTERNAL PROCEDURES HAS BEEN OMITTED, OR AN EXTRA END HAS PREMATURELY ENDED A PROCEDURE. PL/C SUPPLIES A *PROCESS)
1F MISPLACED ENTRY STATEMENT
(ENTRY CANNOT BE IN A BEGIN BLOCK OR IN AN ITERATIVE DO LOOP)
20 IMPROPER OPTION(S)
(IMPROPER OPTION ON STATEMENT, OR INVALID OPTION ON *PL/C, *PROCESS OR *OPTIONS CARD. SEE SECTION B.)
21 IMPROPER FORMAT ITEM
22 IMPROPER I/O PHRASE
23 IMPROPER TO PHRASE
24 IMPROPER BY PHRASE

```
25        IMPROPER WHILE PHRASE
26        IMPROPER SPECIFICATION
            (ERROR IN ITERATION SPECIFICATION OF DO STATEMENT)
27        MULTIPLE DECLARATION
            (THIS IDENTIFIER HAS ALREADY BEEN USED IN A WAY THAT
            PRECLUDES ITS APPEARANCE HERE. IN MOST CONTEXTS THE
            IDENTIFIER IS REPLACED BY A NEW IDENTIFIER GENERATED
            BY PL/C.)
28 *      IMPROPER ATTRIBUTE ATTRIBUTE FOR IDEN
            (THE ATTRIBUTE INDICATED CANNOT BE APPLIED TO THIS
            IDENTIFIER, USUALLY BECAUSE OF PREVIOUS ATTRIBUTES)
29        IMPROPER FACTORING
2A *      IMPROPER DIMENSION
2B *      IMPROPER PRECISION
2C *      IMPROPER SCALE
2D *      IMPROPER VARYING ATTRIBUTE
            (STRING TYPE NOT SPECIFIED; VARYING DELETED)
2E        IMPROPER FILE-NAME
            (THE IDENTIFIER IN A FILE PHRASE IS NOT A VALID
            FILE-NAME)
2F        EXTERNAL NAME TOO LONG
            (WARNING, PL/I ALLOWS A MAXIMUM OF 7 CHARACTERS
            FOR AN IDENTIFIER IN THIS CONTEXT)
30 *      IMPROPER INIT ATTRIBUTE
            (INITIAL IS INCOMPATIBLE WITH PREVIOUS ATTRIBUTES)
31 *      IMPROPER STRUCTURE LEVEL
            (THIS MAY BE IMPROPER CONSTRUCTION OF A STRUCTURE
            DECLARATION.  IT ALSO ARISES FROM ANY STRAY
            INTEGER IN A FAULTY DECLARATION.)
32 *      IMPROPER ATTRIBUTE IN STRUCTURE
            (MAJOR AND MINOR STRUCTURE NAMES CANNOT HAVE TYPE
            ATTRIBUTES, LEAVES CANNOT HAVE STORAGE CLASS ATTR)
33        TOO MANY IDENTIFIERS
            (THERE IS A PL/C LIMIT OF 88 IDENTIFIERS IN A
            SINGLE FACTOR OR STRUCTURE; PROGRAM IS NOT EXECUTED)
34        IMPROPER THEN OR ELSE
            (THEN OR ELSE GIVEN ON A STATEMENT NOT FOLLOWING
            AN IF)
35        IMPROPER THEN OR ELSE UNIT
            (THIS STATEMENT IS NOT ALLOWED AS A THEN|ELSE
            UNIT. ELSE IS DELETED; NULL STATEMENT INSERTED
            AFTER THEN.)
36        MISSING THEN
            (THEN SUPPLIED)
37        IMPROPER CHECK OR NOCHECK
            (PREFIX APPLIED TO A STATEMENT OTHER THAN
            BEGIN OR PROCEDURE; PREFIX DELETED)
38        IMPROPER PREFIX ORDER
            (WARNING- EXECUTES CORRECTLY UNDER PL/C
            BUT INCOMPATIBLE WITH PL/I(F))
39        EXTRA LABEL
3A        IMPROPER LABEL
3B        MISSING LABEL OR ENTRY NAME
            (A NEW IDENTIFIER IS GENERATED BY PL/C)
```

3C IMPROPER ON-CONDITION
(OFTEN TRIGGERED BY AN EXTRA LEFT PAREN, AS FOR EXAMPLE AROUND THE LEFT SIDE OF AN ASSIGNMENT, WHICH IS TAKEN TO BE THE BEGINNING OF A CONDITION PREFIX)

3D IMPROPER ON-UNIT
(THIS STATEMENT IS NOT ALLOWED AS A SIMPLE ON-UNIT. BEGIN AND END ARE SUPPLIED.)

3E IMPROPER SPACE
('NO' IS IMPROPERLY SEPARATED FROM REST OF KEYWORD. SPACE IS REMOVED. EXAMPLE: NO CHECK BECOMES NOCHECK)

3F PL/I FEATURE NOT IN PL/C
(THE FEATURE USED IS NOT INCLUDED IN CURRENT PL/C)

40 FEATURES INCOMPATIBLE WITH PL/I(F) HAVE BEEN USED
(WARNING: AN INCOMPATIBLE PL/C FEATURE HAS BEEN USED AND IS NOT ENCLOSED IN A PSEUDO-COMMENT. THE PROGRAM WILL NOT BE ACCEPTED BY PL/I(F).)

41 INCOMPATIBLE OPTION

42 MISSING OPTION

43 IMPROPER LOGICAL UNIT
(DOS ONLY: IMPROPER LOGICAL UNIT IN MEDIUM OPTION OF ENVIRONMENT ATTRIBUTE)

44 MISSING DECIMAL INTEGER

45 NON-* BOUND/LENGTH FIELD
(* AND NOT AN EXPRESSION MUST BE GIVEN FOR SUBSCRIPT BOUND OR STRING LENGTH IN THIS CONTEXT)

46 DECLARATION FOR ENTRY IDEN DOES NOT AGREE WITH CORRESPONDING PROC OR ENTRY POINT. DCL IGNORED.

47 PROCEDURE IDEN IS NOT PRESENT
(IDEN HAS BEEN DECLARED AS AN ENTRY-NAME, BUT NO CORRESPONDING PROCEDURE DEFINITION APPEARS)

48 *-LENGTH NOT ALLOWED. 256 USED

49 TOO MANY DIGITS IN EXPONENT

4A ILLEGAL EXPONENT
(ILLEGAL CHARACTER APPEARED AFTER E. A SPACE IS INSERTED BEFORE THE E.)

4B ILLEGAL BINARY NUMBER
(IT IS TREATED AS DECIMAL)

4C ILLEGAL USE OF COLUMN 1 ON CARD
(IF SM=(2,X,1) THE VALUE IN COLUMN 1 IS CONCATENATED WITH THE STRING BEGINNING IN COLUMN 2)

4D */ NOT IN COMMENT
(IT IS IGNORED)

4E NAME > 31 CHARACTERS
(FULL NAME IS USED BY PL/C, BUT PL/I WOULD USE THE FIRST 16 AND LAST 15 CHARACTERS)

4F ILLEGAL CHARACTER
(IT IS IGNORED)

50 STRING CONSTANT RUNS ACROSS CARD BOUNDARY
(A ' IS SUPPLIED)

51 IMBEDDED BLANK(S) IN OPERATOR
(THE BLANKS ARE IGNORED. EXAMPLE: * * BECOMES **)

52 COMMENT RUNS ACROSS CARD BOUNDARY
(THE COMMENT IS TERMINATED AT THE END OF THE CARD)

53 2 DECIMAL POINTS IN NUMBER
(NUMBER IS ENDED BEFORE THE 2ND DECIMAL POINT)
54 EXPONENT RUNS ACROSS CARD BOUNDARY
(IT IS IGNORED)
55 SPACE MISSING BETWEEN NUMBER AND LETTER
(REQUIRED SPACE IS SUPPLIED)
56 MISSING */ BEFORE END OF FILE OR CONTROL CARD
57 INVALID BIT STRING
58 MISSING QUOTE BEFORE END OF FILE OR CONTROL CARD
59 STRING LENGTH > 255
5A MISPLACED *MEND CARD
5B ERROR STACK OVERFLOW - MESSAGE(S) LOST
5C TABSIZE TOO LARGE. NUMBER IS USED
5D OPTION(S) NOT ALLOWED AT THIS INSTALLATION
(OPTION SPECIFIED ON *PL/C, *PROCESS OR *OPTIONS
CARD IS PROHIBITED BY THIS INSTALLATION)
5E TOO MANY SIGNIFICANT DIGITS, 16 USED
5F TOO MANY SIGNIFICANT DIGITS, 53 USED
60 MACROS NOT ALLOWED. COMPILATION TERMINATED.
(MACROS PROHIBITED BY THIS INSTALLATION)
61 TOO MANY OPERANDS IN CHECK OR FLOW STATEMENT.
62 NUMBER TOO LARGE/SMALL, NUMBER USED
(0 OR 10**75 IS SUPPLIED, AS APPROPRIATE)
63 MISSING *MEND BEFORE END OF FILE OR CONTROL CARD
64 MISSING MACRO NAME
65 MISSING %; BEFORE END OF FILE OR CONTROL CARD
66 MACRO NAME ILLEGAL OR ALREADY IN USE
67 MISSING PARAMETER NAME IN MACRO DEFINITION
68 MACRO PARAMETER NAME > 31 CHARACTERS. FIRST 31 USED.
69 TOO MANY MACRO PARAMETERS. LIST TRUNCATED.
6A MACRO PARAMETER NAME APPEARS TWICE IN LIST.
6B SYMBOL TABLE AREA OVERFLOW. INCREASE CORE AVAILABLE.
6C ILLEGAL CHARACTER(S) ON CARD. BLANK(S) USED.
6D MACRO EXPANSION CAUSES REPRINTING OF ABOVE LINE
6E DYNAMIC CORE OVERFLOW DURING MACRO EXPANSION.
INCREASE REGION.
70 COMPILER ERROR--ILLEGAL INTERNAL MACRO PARM ID.
(COMPILER ERROR, SEE BEGINNING OF SECTION C)
71 MISSING (IN MACRO CALL
72 MACRO ARGUMENT > 256 CHARACTERS. FIRST 256 USED.
73 TOO FEW ARGUMENTS IN MACRO CALL.
NULL STRING(S) SUPPLIED.
74 MISSING COMMA IN MACRO CALL
75 MISSING) IN MACRO CALL
76 END OF FILE OR CONTROL CARD WITHIN MACRO CALL
77 PICTURE SPECIFICATION FOR IDEN TOO LONG;
COMPLEX ATTRIBUTE DELETED
78 NUMERIC SPECIFICATION FOLLOWING SIGN
IN PICTURE SPECIFICATION
79 IMPROPER NUMERIC SPECIFICATION FOLLOWING V
IN PICTURE SPECIFICATION
7A IMPROPER CHARACTER IN CHARACTER PICTURE SPECIFICATION
7B MORE THAN ONE SIGN OR CR/CB IN PICTURE SPECIFICATION
7C MORE THAN ONE V IN PICTURE SPECIFICATION
7D V IN EXPONENT IN PICTURE SPECIFICATION

7E MORE THAN ONE E OR K IN PICTURE SPECIFICATION

7F MISSING EXPONENT FIELD IN PICTURE SPECIFICATION

80 INCOMPLETE CR/DB IN PICTURE SPECIFICATION

81 CR/DB USED IN FLOATING PICTURE SPECIFICATION

82 MIXED Z AND * IN PICTURE SPECIFICATION

83 Z OR * FOLLOWS 9,I,R OR T IN PICTURE SPECIFICATION

84 Z OR * FOLLOWS DRIFTING FIELD IN PICTURE SPECIFICATION

85 INVALID Z OR * FOLLOWING V IN PICTURE SPECIFICATION

86 A OR X USED IN NUMERIC PICTURE SPECIFICATION

87 F USED IN FLOATING PICTURE SPECIFICATION

88 CHARACTER(S) FOLLOWING SCALE FACTOR
IN PICTURE SPECIFICATION

89 VALUE OF REPETITION FACTOR TOO LARGE
IN PICTURE SPECIFICATION

8A CR/DB OR MISPLACED SIGN IN FLOATING PICTURE
SPECIFICATION. EXPONENT DELETED

8B MORE THAN ONE DRIFTING FIELD IN PICTURE SPECIFICATION

8C PL/I RESTRICTS THE USE OF S + - $
IN FLOATING PICTURE SPECIFICATION

8D TOO MANY $'S IN PICTURE SPECIFICATION

8E ILLEGAL PICTURE SPECIFICATION. SEE STMT LINE

8F SCALE FACTOR IS < -128 OR > 127
IN PICTURE SPECIFICATION

90 NO DIGITS SPECIFIED IN NUMERIC PICTURE SPECIFICATION

91 MORE THAN 15 DIGITS SPECIFIED IN FIXED NUMERIC
PICTURE SPECIFICATION

92 MORE THAN 16 DIGITS SPECIFIED IN FLOAT NUMERIC
PICTURE SPECIFICATION

93 EXPONENT MORE THAN 2 DIGITS LONG
IN PICTURE SPECIFICATION

94 TOO MANY DIGITS IN SCALE OR REPETITION FACTOR
IN PICTURE SPECIFICATION

95 NON-NUMERIC CHARACTER IN SCALE OR REPETITION FACTOR
IN PICTURE SPECIFICATION

96 INVALID CHARACTER IN PICTURE SPECIFICATION

97 PICTURE SPECIFICATION IS TOO LONG

<u>SM PREFIX</u> ERRORS DURING THE SEMANTIC ANALYSIS PHASE

WHEN STATEMENTS IN ERROR ARE RECONSTRUCTED DURING THE SEMANTIC ANALYSIS PHASE, AN ADDITIONAL LINE IS PRINTED, LABELED DECLARED IN BLOCK. THIS LINE SPECIFIES THE BLOCK IN WHICH EACH VARIABLE HAS BEEN DECLARED.

NUMBER MESSAGE

40 VARIABLE NOT PERMITTED
(MUST HAVE CONSTANT IN THIS CONTEXT)

41 WRONG TYPE FOR EXPRESSION
(EXPRESSION TYPES ARE ARITHMETIC, STRING, LABEL,
OR FILE, AND THE WRONG ONE HAS BEEN USED HERE.)

42 WRONG STRUCTURE OR DIMENSIONALITY FOR EXPRESSION
(SCALAR NEEDED WHERE AN ARRAY OR MATCHING STRUCTURE
HAS BEEN USED)

43 ILLEGAL SUBSCRIPTING
(SUBSCRIPTS ARE NOT ALLOWED IN CERTAIN CONTEXTS, E.G., GET DATA)

44 ILLEGAL USE OF PSEUDO-VARIABLES
(E.G., CHECK PREFIXES, GET/PUT DATA)

45 NAME NEEDED
(IN THIS CONTEXT, E.G., INITIALIZING LABEL CONSTANTS

46 ENTRY-NAME NEEDED
(CALL MUST HAVE ENTRY NAME)

47 NO STRUCTURE APPEARED
(IN BY NAME ASSIGNMENT)

48 STRUCTURES DO NOT MATCH
(IN BY NAME ASSIGNMENT)

49 FUNCTION ARGUMENTS MISSING

4A OPERAND OF BINARY OPERATOR STRING HAS IMPROPER TYPE

4B OPERANDS OF BINARY OPERATOR STRING DISAGREE IN TYPE, STRUCTURE OR DIMENSIONALITY

4C OPERAND OF UNARY OPERATOR STRING HAS IMPROPER TYPE

4D SUBSCRIPT NUMBER OF IDEN NOT NUMERIC

4E IDEN HAS TOO MANY SUBSCRIPTS. SUBSCRIPT LIST DELETED

4F IDEN HAS TOO FEW SUBSCRIPTS. SUBSCRIPT LIST DELETED

50 NAME NEVER DECLARED, OR AMBIGUOUSLY QUALIFIED
(EXPRESSION REPLACED OR CALL DELETED)

51 SUBSCRIPT NUMBER OF IDEN NOT SCALAR

52 IDEN HAS TOO MANY ARGUMENTS. FUNCTION REFERENCE DELETED

53 ARGUMENT NUMBER OF FUNCTION IDEN DISAGREES WITH CORRESPONDING PARAMETER

54 IDEN HAS TOO FEW ARGUMENTS. FUNCTION REFERENCE DELETED

55 ARGUMENT NUMBER OF FUNCTION IDEN WAS *. ILLEGAL ARGUMENT.

56 TABLE OVERFLOW. EXPRESSION DELETED
(PROCESSING EXPRESSION. TRY LARGER REGION.)

57 TABLE OVERFLOW. EXPRESSION DELETED
(PROCESSING EXPRESSION SKELETON. TRY LARGER REGION.)

58 TABLE OVERFLOW. EXPRESSION DELETED
(PROCESSING EXPRESSION TREE. TRY LARGER REGION.)

59 TABLE OVERFLOW. EXPRESSION DELETED
(PROCESSING ENTRY PARAMETER. TRY LARGER REGION.)

5A IDEN HAS WRONG # OF SUBSCRIPTS
(BY NAME ASSIGNMENT. STRUCTURES DON'T MATCH)

5B MISMATCHED DIMENSIONALITY
(BY NAME ASSIGNMENT. STRUCTURES DON'T MATCH)

5C ILLEGAL LABEL VARIABLE IDEN
(SUBSCRIPTED LABEL NOT DECLARED IN BLOCK)

5D ILLEGAL ASSIGNMENT TARGET

5E ASSIGNMENT SOURCE INCOMPATIBLE WITH TARGET

5F MAJOR STRUCTURE NAME NEEDED

60 DEFAULT ATTRIBUTES FOR ENTRY NAME IDEN CONFLICT WITH RETURNS OPTION IN STMT LINE

61 IDEN IS ASSUMED A USER-DEFINED NAME, NOT A BUILT-IN FUNCTION
(WARNING)

XR PREFIX ERRORS DURING THE CROSS-REFERENCE PHASE

```
NUMBER   MESSAGE

62       NOT ENOUGH CORE FOR CROSS-REFERENCE.
            (USE LARGER REGION)
63       CROSS REFERENCE ABBREVIATED DUE TO LACK OF SPACE.
            (USE LARGER REGION)
64       COMPILER ERROR IN XREF PHASE--INVALID STATEMENT CODE.
            (A COMPILER ERROR. SEE BEGINNING OF SECTION C)
```

CG PREFIX ERRORS DURING THE CODE GENERATION PHASE

```
NUMBER   MESSAGE

00       FORMAT WILL BE EXECUTED ONLY ONCE
            (THE FORMAT SPECIFICATION OF THE EDIT STATEMENT
            DOES NOT CONTAIN ANY FORMAT ITEMS WHICH WOULD CAUSE
            DATA TO BE TRANSFERRED BETWEEN THE I/O LIST AND THE
            I/O BUFFER --I.E. NO A,B,C,E,F OR R FORMAT
            ITEM. IF RUN UNDER PL/I(F) THE PROGRAM WOULD LOOP)
01       CONSTANT BOUND, LENGTH, SUBSCRIPT OR ITERATION FACTOR
               EXCEEDS 32767 IN MAGNITUDE. 10 IS USED.
            (PL/I LANGUAGE RESTRICTION)
02       WORKSPACE OVERFLOW IN STATEMENT PROCESSING
            (THE COMBINED NESTING OF BEGIN AND PROCEDURE
            BLOCKS, ITERATIVE DO GROUPS, AND IF STATEMENTS IS
            TOO DEEP FOR THE CODE GENERATION PHASE. THE REST OF
            THE PROGRAM IS NOT SCANNED FOR CODE GENERATION
            ERRORS. INCREASING THE REGION SIZE WILL NOT HELP.
            THE NESTING DEPTH MUST BE REDUCED)
03       IDEN REQUIRES TOO MUCH SPACE. UPPER BOUND OF
               SUBSCRIPT NUMBER IS SET TO LOWER BOUND
            (MORE THAN 2**31 BYTES WOULD BE REQUIRED FOR THE
             ARRAY AS DECLARED)
04       PRIMARY DATA STORAGE AREA FOR BLOCK # NUMBER
               EXCEEDS SIZE LIMIT BY NUMBER BYTES.
            (PRIMARY DATA STORAGE DOES NOT INCLUDE SPACE FOR
            ARRAYS OR STRINGS. TRY ADDING SOME MORE BEGIN
            BLOCKS)
05       LENGTH OF  IDEN (  NUMBER ) IS NOT IN PROPER
               RANGE. 80 IS USED.
            (LENGTH IS <0 OR > 256)
06       IDEN REQUIRES TOO MUCH SPACE. LOWER BOUND OF
               SUBSCRIPT NUMBER IS SET TO ZERO.
            (THE ARRAY ELEMENT WITH ALL SUBSCRIPTS ZERO MUST
            BE WITHIN 2**31 BYTES OF THE ARRAY ELEMENT WITH ALL
            SUBSCRIPTS AT THEIR LOWER BOUND.  MOVE THE LOWER
            BOUNDS CLOSER TO ZERO AND RESUBMIT)
07       ARITHMETIC FIRST ARGUMENT TO SUBSTR PSEUDO-VARIABLE.
               A STRING TEMPORARY IS USED.
            (ARITHMETIC ARGUMENT REMAINS UNCHANGED)
08       SEVERE ERRORS. EXECUTION SUPPRESSED.
            (A PREVIOUS CODE GENERATION ERROR HAS MADE IT
            IMPOSSIBLE TO CONTINUE INTO EXECUTION. ALL CODE
            GENERATION ERRORS HAVE BEEN REPORTED)
```

09 CONVERSION REQUIRED TO MATCH ARGUMENT IDEN OF IDEN
(WARNING. PL/C HAS GENERATED CODE TO CONVERT THE ARGUMENT OF A PROCEDURE CALL SO THAT THE ATTRIBUTES OF THE VALUE PASSED WILL MATCH THE ATTRIBUTES OF THE CORRESPONDING PARAMETER. PL/I(F) WOULD NOT DO THIS CONVERSION BECAUSE THE ATTRIBUTES OF THE PARAMETER HAVE NOT BEEN SPECIFIED IN AN ENTRY DECLARATION)

0A SCALAR ARGUMENT SUPPLIED TO AGGREGATE PARAMETER IDEN OF IDEN . ((1:10) USED FOR ALL BOUNDS.)
(THIS IS A PL/C RESTRICTION, SEE SECTION E. ASSIGN THE CONSTANT TO AN ARRAY WITH THE PROPER BOUNDS AND PASS THAT ARRAY TO THE PROCEDURE.)

0B WORKSPACE OVERFLOW IN EXPRESSION PROCESSING
(EITHER THE SITUATION WHICH WOULD GENERATE ERROR CG02 EXISTS OR THE NESTING OF ARRAY EXPRESSIONS, ARRAY SUBSCRIPTING, FUNCTION REFERENCES, OR PARENTHESIZED EXPRESSIONS IS TOO DEEP. SIMPLIFY THE EXPRESSION. INCREASING REGION SIZE WILL NOT HELP)

0C NO FILE SPECIFIED. SYSIN/SYSPRINT ASSUMED.
(WARNING)

0D IDEN IS A PARAMETER IN I/O LIST OR CHECK PREFIX
(WARNING. PL/I(F) DOES NOT ALLOW PARAMETERS IN DATA- DIRECTED I/O LISTS NOR IN CHECK PREFIXES. PL/C WILL ACCEPT THE PARAMETER)

0E BOTH FORMS OF INITIALIZATION USED FOR LABEL VARIABLE IDEN
(PL/I(F) DOES NOT PERMIT A LABEL VARIABLE TO BE INITIALIZED VIA BOTH THE INITIAL ATTRIBUTE AND SUBSCRIPTED STATEMENT LABEL CONSTANTS. BOTH FORMS ARE ACCEPTED BY PL/C. WHERE THERE IS CONFLICT THE INITIAL ATTRIBUTE TAKES PRECEDENCE)

0F STORAGE CAPACITY IS EXCEEDED
(OBJECT CODE EXCEEDS AVAILABLE SPACE, SPECIFY LARGER REGION)

10 ILLEGAL COMPLEX COMPARE. REAL PARTS WILL BE COMPARED

11 IDEN IS ILLEGAL OPERAND IN INITIAL, LENGTH OR DIMENSION ATTRIBUTE OF STATIC VARIABLE. CONSTANT IS USED.
(THE BOUNDS, LENGTHS, AND ITERATION FACTORS USED WITH A STATIC OR EXTERNAL VARIABLE MUST BE OPTIONALLY SIGNED DECIMAL CONSTANTS. A NON-CONSTANT HAS APPEARED IN THIS CONTEXT AND HAS BEEN REPLACED BY A CONSTANT OF APPROPRIATE TYPE)

12 NON-CONSTANT OPERAND(IDEN) IN INITIAL, LENGTH OR DIMENSION ATTRIBUTE OF STATIC VARIABLE.
(WARNING: A STATIC OR EXTERNAL VARIABLE, BUILT-IN FUNCTION, EXTERNAL USER-DEFINED FUNCTION HAS BEEN USED IN THE BOUNDS, LENGTH, OR ITERATION FACTOR FOR A STATIC/EXTERNAL VARIABLE. THIS IS NOT ALLOWED IN PL/I. PL/C USES THE VALUE OF THE OPERAND IN ERROR)

13 PL/C BUILT-IN FUNCTION USED.
(WARNING. A BUILTIN FUNCTION THAT IS NOT INCLUDED IN PL/I(F) HAS BEEN USED)

14 ARGUMENT TO MAX OR MIN IS COMPLEX. REAL PART IS USED.

15 NO SCALE FACTOR ARGUMENT APPEARED. RESULT IS SET FLOAT.
(SEE EXPLANATION OF ERROR CG16)

16 UNNECESSARY SCALE FACTOR ARGUMENT APPEARED. RESULT IS SET FIXED.
(FOR ADD, DIVIDE OR MULTIPLY, BOTH A PRECISION ARGUMENT (P) AND A SCALE FACTOR ARGUMENT (Q) MUST BE PRESENT IF THE RESULT IS TO HAVE FIXED SCALE. ONLY ARGUMENT P MAY APPEAR IF THE RESULT IS TO HAVE FLOAT SCALE. IF EITHER REQUIREMENT IS VIOLATED, PL/C CONVERTS THE ARGUMENT TO THE SCALE IMPLIED BY THE NUMBER OF ARGUMENTS GIVEN)

17 ARGUMENT SHOULD BE AN ARITHMETIC CONSTANT. 10 IS USED.
(CERTAIN ARGUMENTS TO THE BUILTIN FUNCTIONS ADD, BINARY, DECIMAL, DIVIDE, FIXED, FLOAT, MULTIPLY, PRECISION AND ROUND MUST BE DECIMAL CONSTANTS IN PL/I(F))

18 ABS(ARGUMENT) > 32767. 10 IS USED.
(CONSTANT ARGUMENTS TO BUILTIN FUNCTIONS MENTIONED IN EXPLANATION OF ERROR CG17 MUST BE LESS THAN 32768 IN MAGNITUDE)

19 ARGUMENT SHOULD BE REAL. IMAGINARY PART IS USED.
(CONSTANT OF THE FORM "NI" APPEARED WHERE REAL CONSTANT WAS REQUIRED. THE "I" IS IGNORED)

1A ILLEGAL COMPLEX ARGUMENT. REAL PART IS USED.

1B ILLEGAL ARGUMENT TO BUILT-IN FUNCTION. SHOULD BE REAL, FIXED DECIMAL CONSTANT.
(WARNING: PL/I(F) REQUIRES THAT CERTAIN ARGUMENTS OF THE BUILT-IN FUNCTIONS BIT, CHAR, HIGH, LOW, AND REPEAT BE UNSIGNED DECIMAL CONSTANTS. PL/C WILL TAKE THE ARGUMENT AS WRITTEN)

1C RESULT SCALE FACTOR = NUMBER >127 IN MAGNITUDE. RESULT SCALED INCORRECTLY TO 127*SIGN(NUMBER)
(FOLLOWING THE RULES FOR PL/I EXPRESSION EVALUATION, THE SCALE FACTOR ,Q, OF THE RESULT WOULD BE OUTSIDE THE PERMITTED RANGE -127 TO 127. SO THAT EXECUTION MAY BE ATTEMPTED, THE RESULT IS SCALED TO THE CLOSEST BOUND OF THE LEGAL RANGE. THE VALUE OF THE RESULT WILL BE INCORRECT)

1D PROGRAM MAY LOOP IF THIS FORMAT IS EXECUTED
(THE FORMAT STATEMENT DOES NOT SPECIFY A DATA TRANSMISSION FORMAT ITEM. SEE EXPLANATION OF ERROR CG00)

1E VARIABLE IDEN HAS A * BOUND OR LENGTH FIELD. 10 IS USED.
(ONLY PARAMETERS IN PL/C MAY HAVE * BOUND OR LENGTH)

1F PARAMETER IDEN HAS A NON-* BOUND OR LENGTH FIELD
(PARAMETERS MUST HAVE A * IN THIS FIELD IN PL/C)

20 LOWER BOUND OF SUBSCRIPT NUMBER OF IDEN EXCEEDS UPPER BOUND. (0:10) IS USED.

21 SPECIFIED P(NUMBER) TOO LARGE. MAX PRECISION IS USED.
(INSTALLATION MAXIMUM PRECISION, E.G. 31 FOR FIXED BINARY, 15 FOR FLOAT DECIMAL)

22 STRING ARGUMENT TO COMPLEX PSEUDO-VARIABLE.
(THE ASSIGNMENT IS PERFORMED ANYWAY.)

```
23        TOO MANY ERRORS DURING COMPILATION. EXECUTION
                SUPPRESSED.
24        COMPILER ERROR DURING CODE GENERATION. PROGRAM ABORTED.
             (A COMPILER ERROR, SEE BEGINNING OF SECTION C)
25        ILLEGAL ARGUMENT TO REAL OR IMAG PSEUDO-VARIABLE.
                (THE ASSIGNMENT IS PERFORMED ANYWAY.)
             (ARGUMENT MUST BE COMPLEX ARITHMETIC)
26        IMPLIED ARITHMETIC/STRING CONVERSION INVOKED.
             (MONITOR MESSAGE.  CONVERSION IS PERFORMED)
27        STRING CONSTANT IN INITIAL, LENGTH OR DIMENSION
                ATTRIBUTE OF STATIC VARIABLE.
             (CONVERSION IS PERFORMED)
28        BIT STRING IN GET OR PUT STRING. STATEMENT DELETED.
```

EX_PREFIX ERRORS DURING THE EXECUTION PHASE

```
NO   ON   MESSAGE
     CODE

00   0004 PROGRAM RETURNS FROM MAIN PROCEDURE.
01   0004 PROGRAM IS STOPPED.
          (NORMAL TERMINATION-- A STOP OR EXIT HAS
          BEEN EXECUTED)
02   0070 END OF FILE REACHED.
          (THE ENDFILE CONDITION IS RAISED. SYSTEM ACTION
          TERMINATES THE PROGRAM.)
03   0300 EXPONENT OVERFLOW. RESULT IS SET TO 1.
04   0300 EXPONENT OVERFLOW. RESULT IS LEFT UNCHANGED.
05   0310 FIXED-POINT OVERFLOW.
          (LOW ORDER DIGIT SET TO 1)
06   0310 FIXED-DECIMAL OVERFLOW.
07   0310 NUMBER TOO LARGE TO CONVERT TO FIXED BINARY. 1 IS USED.
08   0320 FIXED-POINT QUOTIENT TOO LARGE. PROBABLE DIVISION BY 0.
             RESULT IS SET TO 0.
09   0320 FIXED-POINT QUOTIENT TOO LARGE. PROBABLE DIVISION BY 0.
             RESULT IS LEFT UNCHANGED.
0A   0320 FLOATING-POINT DIVISION BY 0. RESULT IS SET TO 1.
0B   0320 FLOATING-POINT DIVISION BY 0. RESULT IS LEFT UNCHANGED.
0C   0330 EXPONENT UNDERFLOW. RESULT IS SET TO 0.
0D   0330 EXPONENT UNDERFLOW. RESULT IS LEFT UNCHANGED.
0E   0340 SIZE RAISED. RESULT IS LEFT UNCHANGED.
          (OCCURS WHEN THE VALUE OF AN EXPRESSION IS ASSIGNED
          TO A VARIABLE WHOSE PRECISION IS TOO SMALL TO HOLD
          THE VALUE. IN PL/C, NO LEFT-TRUNCATION OCCURS.
          INSTEAD THE COMPUTED VALUE IS ASSIGNED TO THE
          VARIABLE, REGARDLESS OF ITS DECLARED PRECISION.)
0F   0340 SIZE RAISED DURING CONVERSION. RESULT IS SET TO 0.
10   0340 SIZE RAISED DURING STRING-TO-ARITHMETIC CONVERSION.
             VALUE USED IS NUMBER
11   0340 NUMBER TOO LARGE TO CONVERT TO SPECIFIED BIT STRING.
             (SIZE CONDITION)  NUMBER IS NUMBER
             STRING USED IS STRING
12   0340 RESULT OF BIT-TO-ARITHMETIC CONVERSION GREATER THAN
             2**56-1. (SIZE CONDITION)  STRING IS STRING
             VALUE USED IS NUMBER
```

```
13   0341 NUMBER TOO LARGE FOR FIELD. TRUNCATED ON LEFT.
               FULL FIELD WOULD BE STRING
          (IN A PUT STATEMENT, THE VALUE IS TOO LARGE TO FIT
          IN THE SPECIFIED FIELD (FOR EDIT) OR THE FIELD
          IMPLIED BY THE ATTRIBUTES OF THE ITEM (FOR LIST).
          SIGNS AND DIGITS ARE LOST ON THE LEFT AS IN PL/I.
          THE MESSAGE INDICATES THE FULL FIELD BEFORE
          TRUNCATION.)
14   0350 INDEX OF SUBSTRING < 1 (NUMBER)
          (SECOND ARGUMENT OF SUBSTR IS LESS THAN ONE)
15   0350 INDEX OF SUBSTRING (NUMBER) > STRING LENGTH (NUMBER)
          (SECOND ARGUMENT OF SUBSTR IS GREATER THAN
          THE LENGTH OF THE FIRST ARGUMENT)
16   0350 LENGTH OF SUBSTRING < 0 (NUMBER)
          (VALUE OF THIRD ARGUMENT OF SUBSTR IS NEGATIVE.
          IT IS REPLACED BY 0.)
17   0350 SUBSTRING REQUESTED RUNS OVER END OF STRING
19   0520 SUBSCRIPT NUMBER OF IDEN IS OUT OF BOUNDS (NUMBER).
               NUMBER IS USED.
1A   0602 TOO MANY CHARACTERS FOLLOWING CLOSING QUOTE. ALL ARE
               IGNORED. FIELD IS STRING
1B   0603 TOO MANY DIGITS IN NUMBER, PRECISION LOST.
               STRING IS STRING
1C   0604 TOO MANY EXPONENT DIGITS, EXTRA DIGITS IGNORED.
               STRING IS STRING
1D   0605 INVALID CHARACTER(S) IN FIELD. 0 USED FOR EACH.
               ORIGINAL STRING IS STRING
               FIRST BAD CHARACTER IS STRING
          (THE CONVERSION CONDITION HAS BEEN RAISED)
1E   0615 ILLEGAL CHARACTER(S) IN CHARACTER-TO-BIT CONVERSION.
               0'S USED.
1F   0900 ATTEMPT TO USE MATH BUILTIN FUNCTION IN "CALL"
               STATEMENT. STATEMENT IGNORED.
20   0901 IDEN REFERENCED RECURSIVELY. "RECURSIVE" ATTRIBUTE
               HAS NOW BEEN APPLIED.
          (INDICATED PROCEDURE IS BEING USED RECURSIVELY
          BUT DID NOT HAVE RECURSIVE OPTION)
21   0902 IDEN HAS IMPROPER LENGTH (NUMBER). 80 IS USED.
          (LENGTH IS LESS THAN ZERO OR GREATER THAN 256 AND
          VIOLATES A PL/C RESTRICTION)
22   0903 LOWER BOUND ON SUBSCRIPT NUMBER OF IDEN
               EXCEEDS UPPER BOUND. (1:10) IS USED.
          (EXPRESSIONS FOR ARRAY BOUNDS ARE EVALUATED BEFORE
          ANY STATEMENTS IN THE BLOCK IN WHICH THE ARRAY IS
          DECLARED ARE EXECUTED.  VARIABLES USED IN THESE
          EXPRESSIONS MUST BE INITIALIZED IN AN OUTER BLOCK)
23   0904 RETURN FROM IDEN VIA STMT LINE DOESN'T RETURN
               A VALUE AS EXPECTED IN STMT LINE .
               BLANKS OR 0 USED.
24   0905 RETURN FROM IDEN VIA STMT LINE REQUIRES
               ILLEGAL CONVERSION. 0 IS USED.
          (PL/C RESTRICTION, PL/I(F) WOULD CONVERT)
25   0906 RETURN FROM IDEN VIA STMT LINE RETURNS A VALUE
               TO "CALL" IN STMT LINE. VALUE IGNORED.
          (RESULTS WOULD BE UNPREDICTABLE IN PL/I(F))
```

26 0907 CALL TO IDEN FROM STMT LINE RETURNS VIA
STMT LINE WITH STRING LONGER THAN DECLARED
LENGTH. RETURNED LENGTH IS USED.

27 0908 CALL TO IDEN FROM STMT LINE RETURNS VIA
STMT LINE WITH STRING SHORTER THAN DECLARED
LENGTH. IT IS PADDED.

28 0909 BOUNDS OF IDEN DO NOT MATCH BOUNDS IN THE REST
OF THE EXPRESSION.
(EXECUTION IS TERMINATED)

29 0910 IDEN HAS NOT BEEN ALLOCATED.
(IN A PROCEDURE INVOKED TO INITIALIZE A VARIABLE A
REFERENCE HAS BEEN MADE TO AN ARRAY OR STRUCTURE OR
STRING WHICH HAS NOT BEEN ALLOCATED SPACE. VARIABLES
ARE ALLOCATED AND INITIALIZED IN THE ORDER IN WHICH
THEY ARE DECLARED. SEE SECTION D.)

2A 0911 FORMAT LABEL IN GOTO
(EXECUTION IS TERMINATED)

2B 0912 VALUE OF LABEL VARIABLE (IDEN IN STMT LINE) IS
IN A CURRENTLY-INACTIVE BLOCK.
(EXECUTION IS TERMINATED)

2C 0913 IDEN INVOKED FOR INITIALIZATION IN STMT LINE
TERMINATES VIA GOTO.
(EXECUTION IS TERMINATED)

2D 0914 IDEN IN STMT LINE IS IN A CURRENTLY-
INACTIVE ITERATIVE DO GROUP
(EXECUTION IS TERMINATED)

2E 0915 SECOND ARGUMENT OF BIT/CHAR IS NOT POSITIVE. IMPLIED
LENGTH IS USED.

2F 0916 STRING > 256 CHARACTERS LONG.
(PL/C LIMITATION. ONLY THE 256 LEFT-MOST CHARACTERS
ARE RETAINED)

30 0917 ATTEMPT TO ASSIGN INVALID BIT STRING TO FIXED-DECIMAL
DATA ITEM. 0 IS USED.
(MAY OCCUR IN UNSPEC PSEUDO-VARIABLE, OR DURING
A READ STATEMENT. SEE SECTION G, PSEUDO-VARIABLES.)

31 0918 UNDEFINED ENTRY. STATEMENT IGNORED.
(THE PROCEDURE $UENTRY, SUPPLIED BY PL/C
TO REPAIR SOME SEMANTIC ERROR, HAS BEEN REFERENCED)

32 0919 DELETED STATEMENT ENCOUNTERED
(THIS MESSAGE IS PRODUCED DURING EXECUTION OF A
PROGRAM WHEN A STATEMENT DELETED BY AN EARLIER
PHASE OF THE COMPILER IS ENCOUNTERED)

33 0920 UNDEFINED LABEL IN GOTO
(EXECUTION IS TERMINATED)

34 0921 UPPER BOUND ON SUBSCRIPT FOR IDEN > 32767
IN MAGNITUDE. 10 IS USED.

35 0922 LOWER BOUND ON SUBSCRIPT FOR IDEN > 32767
IN MAGNITUDE. 1 IS USED.

36 0923 LABEL COUNTER OVERFLOW. IT IS RESET TO 0.
(WARNING: A LABELED STATEMENT HAS BEEN EXECUTED
MORE THAN 10 MILLION TIMES CAUSING AN INTERNAL PL/C
COUNTER TO OVERFLOW. THIS MAY INDICATE A LOOP IN
THE PROGRAM.)

37 0924 MULTIPLE INTERRUPTS, 2ND AND SUBSEQUENT ONES IGNORED.
(OCCURS ON 360/91 AND 370 ONLY)

```
38   0925 RECORD I/O STRUCTURE VARIABLE IDEN CONTAINS VARYING
               STRINGS. MAXIMUM LENGTHS ARE USED.
          (ONLY FIXED LENGTH STRINGS MAY BE MEMBERS OF
          STRUCTURES USED BY RECORD I/O)
39   0926 INVALID PARAMETER REFERENCE (OR COMPILER ERROR)
          (A PARAMETER HAS BEEN REFERENCED WHICH WAS NOT IN
          A PARAMETER LIST OF THE ENTRY POINT USED TO CALL
          A PROCEDURE)
3A   0927 ATTEMPT TO USE AUTOMATIC ARITHMETIC-STRING CONVERSION
          (AN ARITHMETIC VARIABLE OR EXPRESSION IN AN I/O
          LIST HAS BEEN ASSOCIATED WITH A STRING FORMAT ITEM
          OR STRING DATA -- OR VICE-VERSA. MONITOR MESSAGE.
          CONVERSION IS PERFORMED.)
3B   0928 OUTPUT STRING TOO LONG. FIRST 32767 CHARACTERS USED.
3C   0929 INVALID BLANK FIELD IN GET EDIT. 0 IS USED.
3D   0930 DIMENSION SPECIFIED IN HBOUND, LBOUND OR DIM < 1.
               1 IS USED.
3E   0931 DIMENSION SPECIFIED IN HBOUND, LBOUND OR DIM > MAXIMUM.
               MAXIMUM IS USED.
3F   1002 ATTEMPT TO WRITE OVER END OF STRING. STATEMENT
               TERMINATED.
40   1002 ATTEMPT TO READ OVER END OF STRING. STATEMENT
               TERMINATED.
41   1018 CLOSING QUOTE MISSING IN INPUT FIELD: STRING
               QUOTE SUPPLIED.
42   3798 ONSOURCE/ONCHAR PSEUDO-VARIABLE USED OUT OF CONTEXT
          (ONCHAR OR ONSOURCE MAY BE CHANGED BY THE
          PROGRAM ONLY WHEN THEY HAVE BEEN SET TO POINT TO A
          STRING IN ERROR, WHEN THE CONVERSION CONDITION
          ARISES. AT OTHER TIMES AN ATTEMPT TO CHANGE (ASSIGN
          TO) EITHER IS AN ERROR)
43   3799 IMPROPER RETURN FROM CONVERSION ON-UNIT. SOURCE IS
               STRING
          (THE CONVERSION ON- UNIT DID NOT CHANGE THE
          CHARACTER WHICH WAS IN ERROR)
44   0936 FEATURE NOT AVAILABLE IN THIS RELEASE
          (PL/I(F) FEATURE USED THAT IS NOT IMPLEMENTED IN
          THE CURRENT RELEASE OF PL/C)
45   0937 IDEN IS AN ILLEGAL FORMAT LABEL
          (THE LABEL REFERENCED BY THE R( LABEL ) FORMAT
          ITEM IS ILLEGAL. THIS MAY BE:
             A) BECAUSE IT IS NOT THE LABEL OF A FORMAT
                STATEMENT, OR
             B) BECAUSE IT LABELS A STATEMENT INTERNAL TO SOME
                BLOCK OTHER THAN THE BLOCK CONTAINING THE
                R( LABEL )
          THE REMOTE FORMAT ITEM IS IGNORED)
46   0010 STRING IS AN ILLEGAL NAME
          (SOMETHING OTHER THAN AN IDENTIFIER WAS READ DURING
          A GET DATA STATEMENT, WHERE AN IDENTIFIER SHOULD
          HAVE APPEARED. THE NAME CONDITION IS RAISED.)
```

```
47   0938 INVALID FORMAT OPTION
          (AN OPTION IN THE FORMAT USED WITH A GET OR
          PUT EDIT STATEMENT APPEARED IN AN ILLEGAL CONTEXT:
             A OR B FORMAT: APPEARED WITHOUT A FIELD-WIDTH
                 PARAMETER ON INPUT
             COLUMN FORMAT: APPEARED WITHOUT A TARGET COLUMN
                 PARAMETER, OR WAS USED IN GET/PUT
                 STRING STATEMENT
             F FORMAT: APPEARED WITHOUT A FIELD-WIDTH
                 PARAMETER
             LINE FORMAT: APPEARED WITHOUT A TARGET LINE
                 PARAMETER
             LINE OR PAGE: WAS USED IN A GET
                 STATEMENT, IN A PUT STRING, OR A PUT
                 FILE(X) WHERE X WAS NOT A PRINT FILE
             P FORMAT: APPEARED WITHOUT A VALID PICTURE
                             SPECIFICATION.
             SKIP FORMAT: WAS USED IN A GET/PUT STRING
                 STATEMENT
             X FORMAT: APPEARED WITHOUT A FIELD-WIDTH
                 PARAMETER
          THE FORMAT ITEM AND CORRESPONDING LIST ITEM
          ARE DROPPED)
48   0939 INVALID FORMAT ITEM OPERAND
          (IN FORMATS E(W,Q), F(W,Q) OR F(W,Q,P) EITHER:
             A) A NEGATIVE Q APPEARED ON INPUT; OR
             B) ON OUTPUT, EITHER 0>W, W>255, 0>Q, OR Q>W
          THE FORMAT ITEM AND CORRESPONDING LIST ITEM
          ARE SKIPPED)
49   0010 STRING IS NOT KNOWN TO PROGRAM
          (IN A GET DATA STATEMENT, THE NAME ON THE DATA
          CARD HAS NOT BEEN USED IN THE PROGRAM. THE NAME
          CONDITION IS RAISED. THE DATA-CARD ASSIGNMENT IS
          SKIPPED)
4A   0010 INCOMPATIBLE STRUCTURE FOR IDEN
          (IN A GET DATA STATEMENT A NAME IN THE INPUT
          WAS QUALIFIED, ALTHOUGH IT WAS DECLARED WITHOUT SUB-
          STRUCTURES. OR, AN UNQUALIFIED NAME APPEARED IN THE
          DATA, ALTHOUGH IT WAS DECLARED AS A STRUCTURE IN THE
          PROGRAM. THE NAME CONDITION IS RAISED. THE
          DATA-CARD ASSIGNMENT IS SKIPPED)
4B   0010 IDEN IS NOT IN GET LIST
          (IN A GET DATA STATEMENT, A NAME APPEARED IN
          THE INPUT WHICH WAS NOT IN THE DATA LIST. THIS ERROR
          CAN ARISE FOR A QUALIFIED NAME IF ITS FIRST
          IDENTIFIER (MAJOR STRUCTURE IDENTIFIER) IS NOT IN
          THE DATA LIST. THE NAME CONDITION IS RAISED.
          THE DATA-CARD ASSIGNMENT IS SKIPPED)
4C   0010 ARRAY ERROR FOR IDEN
          (IN A GET DATA STATEMENT, SUBSCRIPTS APPEARED
          ON A NAME IN THE INPUT, BUT THE NAME WAS NOT
          DECLARED AS AN ARRAY AND MAY NOT BE SUBSCRIPTED. THE
          DATA-CARD ASSIGNMENT IS IGNORED)
```

```
4D  0520 STRING BOUND ERROR. NUMBER IS USED.
         (IN A GET DATA STATEMENT, A SUBSCRIPT ON A NAME
         IN THE INPUT IS OUT-OF-BOUNDS. THE UPPER OR LOWER
         BOUND IS USED, AS INDICATED)
4E  0010 NO BOUNDS SPECIFIED FOR IDEN
         (IN A GET DATA STATEMENT, NO SUBSCRIPT APPEARED
         IN THE INPUT FOLLOWING AN ARRAY NAME. THE
         DATA-CARD ASSIGNMENT IS IGNORED)
4F  0081 CONFLICTING FILE ATTRIBUTES SPECIFIED OR IMPLIED.
            CODE= NUMBER
         THE CODES ARE
            0: PUT TO RECORD FILE (SYSPRINT WILL BE USED
                                           IF POSSIBLE)
            1: GET FROM OUTPUT OR RECORD FILE
            2: MORE THAN ONE OF INPUT, OUTPUT, UPDATE
                                           SPECIFIED
            3: STREAM FILE SPECIFYING NON-CONSECUTIVE
                                           ORGANIZATION
            4: BOTH RECORD AND STREAM SPECIFIED
            5: BOTH DIRECT AND SEQUENTIAL SPECIFIED
            6: BOTH DIRECT AND CONSECUTIVE SPECIFIED
            7: SEQUENTIAL CONSECUTIVE AND KEYED SPECIFIED
            8: DIRECT OUTPUT AND INDEXED SPECIFIED
50  0084 FILE CANNOT BE OPENED. CODE= NUMBER
         THE OPERATING SYSTEM REFUSES TO OPEN A FILE.
         THE CODES ARE
            1: BLKSIZE NOT MULTIPLE OF LRECL (RECFM=F OR FB)
            3: MISSING DD CARD (OR UNKNOWN REASON) (OS ONLY)
            6: RECFM,LRECL,BLKSIZE NOT SPECIFIED FOR
                                       NON-PRINT FILE
            7: SPANNED RECORDS NOT SUPPORTED (OS ONLY)
            8: BLKSIZE NOT LARGE ENOUGH (RECFM=V OR VB)
           10: INPUT FILE ASSIGNED TO PUNCH (DOS ONLY)
           11: INVALID LOGICAL DEVICE NAME (DOS ONLY)
           12: INVALID PHYSICAL DEVICE TYPE (DOS ONLY)
           13: AUXILIARY I/O NOT PERMITTED BY INSTALLATION
           15: FILE NOT RECFM F OR V (ISAM ONLY)
           16: KEYLENGTH NOT SPECIFIED (ISAM ONLY)
           17: ONLY ONE BUFFER IS ALLOWED FOR A DIRECT FILE
                                       (ISAM ONLY)
           18: RKP OUT OF RANGE (TOO HIGH OR LESS THAN 4 FOR
                                       V FORMAT FILE) (ISAM ONLY)
           19: DELETE OPTION CANNOT BE SPECIFIED WITH THE KEY
                                       OCCUPYING FIRST BYTE OF THE
                                       RECORD (ISAM ONLY)
51  0932 SYSTEM DATA SET CANNOT BE RE-ALLOCATED WHILE OPEN
            UNDER ANOTHER FILE
         (AN ATTEMPT HAS BEEN MADE TO OPEN SYSIN OR
         SYSPRINT WHILE IT IS OPEN UNDER ANOTHER FILENAME)
52  0933 FILE NOT OPENED IN UNDEFINEDFILE ON-UNIT
53  0934 INVALID ARGUMENT TO LINENO. IDEN NOT A PRINT FILE.
54  0935 INVALID ARGUMENT TO COUNT. IDEN NOT A STREAM FILE.
```

```
55   1004 STRING OPTION INVALID. FILE DOES NOT HAVE "PRINT"
              ATTRIBUTE.
          (THE LINE AND PAGE OPTIONS ARE INVALID IN
          A PUT FILE(X), UNLESS X HAS THE PRINT
          ATTRIBUTE. THE OPTION IS IGNORED)
56   1009 FILE CANNOT BE USED FOR STREAM INPUT.
          (FILE IS OPEN AS A RECORD OR OUTPUT FILE)
57   1009 FILE CANNOT BE USED FOR STREAM OUTPUT.
          (FILE IS OPEN AS A RECORD OR INPUT FILE.
          SYSPRINT WILL BE USED IF POSSIBLE.)
58   1009 FILE CANNOT BE USED FOR RECORD I/O.
          (FILE IS OPEN FOR STREAM I/O)
59   1009 FILE CANNOT BE USED FOR INPUT.
          (FILE IS OPEN FOR OUTPUT)
5A   1009 FILE CANNOT BE USED FOR OUTPUT.
          (FILE IS OPEN FOR INPUT)
5B   1009 I/O STATEMENT AND/OR OPTIONS INCOMPATIBLE WITH FILE.
              CODE= NUMBER
          (GIVEN FOR SPECIAL RECORD I/O OPTIONS. CODES ARE
              0: KEY/KEYTO/KEYFROM SPECIFIED FOR NON-KEYED FILE
              1: "KEY" NOT VALID FOR THIS TYPE OF FILE
              2: "KEY" OR "KEYFROM" REQUIRED
              3: OTHER INCOMPATIBILITY)
5C   0940 COMPILER ERROR - NO NAME FOR UNINITIALIZED VARIABLE AT
              OFFSET NUMBER
          (MAY OCCUR IF SUBSCRIPTRANGE IS DISABLED AND AN
          UNINITIALIZED VALUE IS REFERENCED. OTHERWISE,
          THIS IS A COMPILER ERROR.)
5D   0941 IDEN HAS NOT BEEN INITIALIZED. IT IS SET TO STRING
5E   0942 FORMAT IDEN HAS INVALID CONDITION PREFIXES.
          (THE CONDITIONS IN EFFECT FOR A FORMAT STATEMENT
          MUST BE THE SAME AS THOSE IN EFFECT FOR THE EDIT
          STATEMENT WHICH REFERENCES THE FORMAT STATEMENT.
          THE CONDITIONS ON THE FORMAT STATEMENT ARE IGNORED
          AND EXECUTION CONTINUES)

NOTE: FOR ERRORS EX5F THROUGH EX6D
        SEE  IBM DOCUMENT C28-6590 FOR EXACT FORMULAE USED.

5F   1509 RTN ABS(X) >= (2**50)*K; FOR TAN(X), K=PI.
              FOR TAND(X), K=180. RESULT IS SET TO 1.
          (ISSUED BY TAN OR TAND. TAN(X) IS CALLED
          DIRECTLY BY TANH(A+BI) AND TAN(A+BI).
          THE ARGUMENT IS TOO LARGE IN ABSOLUTE VALUE.)
60   1513 RTN ABSOLUTE VALUE OF REAL ARGUMENT ( NUMBER ) IS
              > 175.366. RESULT IS SET TO 1.
          (ISSUED BY SINH OR COSH)
61   1507 RTN ARGUMENT( NUMBER ) IS GREATER THAN PI*2**50 =
              .3537E+16. RESULT IS SET TO 1.
          (ISSUED BY COS OR SIN.  COS(X) AND/OR SIN(X)
          ARE CALLED BY COSD, SIND, SIN(A+BI), COS(A+BI),
          SINH(A+BI), COSH(A+BI), AND EXP(A+BI))
```

```
62   1501 RTN ARGUMENT (NUMBER) IS NEGATIVE. RESULT IS
              SET TO SQRT(ABS(ARG)).
          (ISSUED BY SQRT(X). SQRT(A**2+B**2) IS USED TO
          CALCULATE ABS(A+BI), AND VARIOUS REAL SQRT CALLS
          ARE MADE IN CALCULATING SQRT(A+BI). IN THESE
          INDIRECT CASES, MESSAGE EX8D SHOULD NOT OCCUR,
          BUT CALCULATIONAL ERRORS MIGHT PRODUCE IT)
63   1511 RTN BOTH ARGUMENTS ARE 0. RESULT IS SET TO 1.
          (ISSUED BY ATAN(Y,X) OR ATAND(Y,X). ATAN(Y,X) IS
          USED IN LOG(A+BI), ATAN(A+BI), AND (A+BI)**(C+DI))
64   1505 RTN ARGUMENT( NUMBER ) <= 0. RESULT IS SET TO 1.
          (ISSUED BY LOG(X). LOG(X) IS CALLED TO COMPUTE
          LOG2(X), LOG10(X), (A+BI)**(C+DI), LOG(A+BI), AND
          ATANH(Y). ATANH(Y) IS IN TURN USED IN ATAN(A+BI)
          AND ATANH(A+BI))
65   1559 RTN Z=+I OR -I IN ATAN(Z) OR  Z=+I OR -I IN ATANH(Z).
             RESULT IS SET TO 1+0I.
          (ISSUED BY ATAN(A+BI) OR ATANH(A+BI))
66   1515 RTN ABSOLUTE VALUE OF ARGUMENT IS >=1. RESULT IS SET
              TO 1.
          (ISSUED BY ATANH(X). ATANH(X) IS USED IN
          CALCULATING ATANH(A+BI) AND ATAN(A+BI))
67   1557 RTN Z1=0 AND IMAG(Z2) ¬= 0 OR REAL(Z2) <= 0. RESULT IS
              SET TO 1.
          (ISSUED BY (A+BI)**(C+DI))
68   1556 RTN IN COMPLEX EXPONENTIAL FUNCTION REAL ARGUMENT IS
              > 174.673. RESULT IS SET TO 1+0I.
          (ISSUED BY EXP(A+BI). EXP(A+BI) IS USED IN
          CALCULATING Z**W, WHEN W OR Z IS COMPLEX)
69   1556 RTN IN COMPLEX EXPONENTIAL FUNCTION IMAGINARY ARGUMENT
              IS > PI*2**50 =.3537E+16. RESULT IS SET TO 1+0I.
          (ISSUED BY EXP(A+BI). SEE MESSAGE EX61)
6A   1555 RTN Z=0 AND N <= 0 IN Z**N. RESULT IS SET TO 1+0I.
          (ISSUED BY X**Y)
6B   1505 RTN BOTH REAL AND IMAG ARGUMENTS ARE 0. RESULT IS SET
              TO 1+0I.
          (ISSUED BY LOG(A+BI). LOG(A+BI) IS USED IN
          CALCULATING Z**W, WHEN W OR Z IS COMPLEX)
6C   1553 RTN ARGUMENT (NUMBER) IS > 174.673. RESULT IS SET TO 1.
          (ISSUED BY EXP(X). EXP(X) IS CALLED IN
          CALCULATING ERF, ERFC, TANH, SIN(A+BI), COS(A+BI),
          SINH(A+BI), COSH(A+BI), AND EXP(A+BI). EXP(A+BI)
          IS IN TURN USED IN CALCULATING Z**W, WHEN W
          OR Z IS COMPLEX)
6D   1551 RTN X=0 AND Y <= 0 IN X**Y. RESULT IS SET TO 1.
71   1009 FILE CANNOT BE USED FOR UPDATE.
             (FILE IS OPENED FOR INPUT OR OUTPUT)
75   0943 FILE BEING CLOSED IS IN USE IN INTERRUPTED I/O
              STATEMENT. IT IS NOT CLOSED.
76   0944 INVALID ATTRIBUTES FOR SYSTEM FILE.
77   0023 FILE NAME - ATTEMPT TO READ/WRITE RECORD OF
     0024         ZERO LENGTH.
```

```
78  0021 FILE NAME - LENGTH OF VARIABLE( NUMBER ) ¬= LENGTH
    0022         OF RECORD( NUMBER ).
              (THE NUMBER OF BYTES OF STORAGE OCCUPIED BY THE
              VARIABLE MUST EQUAL THE NUMBER OF BYTES IN THE
              RECORD)
79       CONDITION (IDEN) SIGNALLED. NO ON-UNIT PENDING.
7A       IDEN SIGNALLED. "ERROR" RAISED AS STANDARD SYSTEM
              ACTION.
7B       KEY CONDITION RAISED. ONCODE= NUMBER.
7C       NORMAL RETURN FROM "ERROR" ON-UNIT. PROGRAM IS STOPPED.
7D       NORMAL RETURN FROM "FINISH" ON-UNIT. PROGRAM IS
              STOPPED.
7E       ABOVE ERROR IS FATAL. PROGRAM IS STOPPED.
7F       NOT ENOUGH CORE. TRY LARGER REGION.
80       AUXILIARY I/O LIMIT EXCEEDED.
            (SEE  AUXIO OPTION IN SECTION B)
81       ATTEMPT TO SWITCH FILE TO SYSPRINT HAS FAILED.
```

Appendix D
Built-in Functions

BUILT-IN FUNCTIONS

This appendix contains a brief description of the more common built-in functions available in PL/I. It should be noted that RAND is only available in PL/C and a complete description of it may be found in the PL/C User's Guide. A complete discussion of all the PL/I built-in functions may be found in IBM SRL Publication GC28-8201-X.

In general, these functions accept arrays as arguments as well as individual values. When an array is supplied as an argument the function will return an array of the same bounds whose elements are obtained by applying the function to the individual elements of the argument array(s).

Functions Not Included

The following functions are not included in this appendix because they are beyond the scope of this book.

ADD	EMPTY	NULLO
ADDR	HIGH	POLY[1]
ALLOCATION	LINENO	PRECISION
BOOL	LOW	PRIORITY
COMPLETION	MULTIPLY	ROUND
COUNT	NULL	STATUS

---

[1]POLY is not available in PL/C

Mathematical Functions

All mathematical functions accept floating point arguments, and will convert other attributes to floating point. The result is always a floating point number. Except as noted, all arguments may be real or complex, and all may be arrays. Unless noted otherwise, arguments to trigonometric functions are in radians.

Function Name	Argument Restrictions	Result
ATAN(x)	$x \neq \pm i$	$\mathrm{Tan}^{-1}(x)$
ATAN(x,y)	x and y real not both equal to zero	$\mathrm{Tan}^{-1}(x/y)$
ATAND(x,y)	same as ATAN	$\mathrm{Tan}^{-1}(x/y)$ in degrees
ATANH(x)	$\lvert x \rvert \geq 1$	$\mathrm{Tanh}^{-1}(x)$
COS(x)		$\cos(x)$
COSD(x)	x in degrees	$\cos(x)$
COSH(x)		$\cosh(x)$
ERF(x)	x must be real	$\frac{2}{\sqrt{\pi}} \int_0^x e^{-t^2}\, dt$
ERFC(x)	x must be real	$1 - \mathrm{ERF}(x)$
EXP(x)		e^x
LOG(x)	$x > 0$, x is real $x \neq 0+0i$, x is complex	$\log_e x$
LOG10(x)	$x > 0$, x is real	$\log_{10} x$
LOG2(x)	$x > 0$, x is real	$\log_2 x$
RAND(x)	not available in PL/I	See Sec 11.1.2
SIN(x)		$\sin(x)$
SIND(x)	x in degrees	$\sin(x)$
SINH(x)		$\sinh(x)$
SQRT(x)	if x is real, $x \geq 0$	$\sqrt{x}$
TAN(x)		$\tan(x)$

Function Name	Argument Restrictions	Result
TAND(x)	x in degrees	tan(x)
TANH(x)		tanh(x)

Arithmetic Functions

All arithmetic functions return an arithmetic value. The result attributes are the same as the argument attributes except as noted. All arguments may be arrays except as noted.

Function Name	Argument Restrictions	Result
ABS(x)		$\lvert x \rvert$
BINARY(x)		x expressed as a base 2 number
CEIL(x)	x must be real	$\lceil x \rceil$ e.g.CEIL(3.2) = 4
COMPLEX(x,y)	x,y must be real	x+iy
CONJG(x)	x must be complex	a+ib if x = a-ib a-ib if x = a+ib
DECIMAL(x)		x expressed as a base 10 number
DIVIDE(x,y,m,n)	x,y must be real	x÷y expressed as a fixed point number with m digits, n of which are to the right of the decimal point
FIXED(x)		x converted to fixed point
FLOAT(x)		x converted to floating point
FLOOR(x)	x must be real	$\lfloor x \rfloor$ e.g.FLOOR(3.9) = 3
IMAG(x)	x must be complex	b if x = a+ib
MAX($x_1,x_2,\ldots,x_n$)	x_i must be real	maximum value of the x_i
MIN($x_1,x_2,\ldots,x_n$)	x_i must be real	minimum value of the x_i

Function Name	Argument Restrictions	Result
MOD(x,y)	x,y must be real	x mod y
REAL(x)	x must be complex	a if x = a+ib
SIGN(x)	x must be real	1 if x > 0 0 if x = 0 -1 if x < 0
TRUNC(x)	x must be real	CEIL(x) if x < 0 FLOOR(x) if x > 0

Character and String Handling Functions

In PL/C all arguments for these functions must be BIT or CHARACTER. This is not the case in PL/I. Arguments may be arrays unless otherwise noted.

Function Name	Argument Restriction	Result
BIT(x,k)	x must be CHARACTER in PL/C	the bit representation of x; the bit string will have length k.
CHAR(x,k)	x must be BIT	the character representation of x; the character string will have length k.
INDEX(x,y)		See Section 5.6.2
LENGTH(x)		See Section 5.5
REPEAT(x,k)		x concatenated with itself k times; e.g. REPEAT('JOE',1) = 'JOEJOE'
STRING(x)	x may be a scalar, array or structure	a string formed by concatenating all the elements of x
SUBSTR(x,k,j)		See Section 5.7
TRANSLATE(x,y,z)		See Section 11.1.2
UNSPEC(x)	x may have any attributes	a bit string with the internal representation of x
VERIFY(x,y)		See Section 11.1.2

Array Generic Functions

All arguments must be arrays. All functions return a scalar value.

Function Name	Argument Restrictions	Result
ALL(x)	x must be BIT	a string obtained by AND-ing all the bit strings in x
ANY(x)	x must be BIT	a string obtained by OR-ing all the bit strings in x
DIM(x,k)		HBOUND(x,k) - LBOUND(x,k) + 1
HBOUND(x,k)		the upper bound of the kth dimension of x.
LBOUND(x,k)		the lower bound of the kth dimension of x
PROD(x)	x must have arithmetic attributes in PL/C	product of all elements of x
SUM(x)	x must have arithmetic attributes in PL/C	sum of all elements of x

Miscellaneous Functions

Function Name	Result
DATE	a character string of length 6 of the form yymmdd
TIME	a character string of length 9 of the form hhmmssttt where ttt is milliseconds

Index

Index